Tell Dafana Reconsidered:
The Archaeology of an Egyptian Frontier Town

François Leclère and
Jeffrey Spencer

with contributions by
Alan Johnston, Sabine Weber,
Mohamed Abd el-Maksoud, Aiman
Ashmawy Ali, Al-Sayed Abd el-Aleem,
Hisham Hussein, Mustafa Nur el-Din,
Michela Spataro, Rebecca Stacey,
Satoko Tanimoto and Paul Craddock

The British Museum

Publishers
The British Museum
Great Russell Street
London WC1B 3DG

Series editor
Sarah Faulks

Distributors
The British Museum Press
38 Russell Square
London WC1B 3QQ

Tell Dafana Reconsidered:
The Archaeology of an Egyptian Frontier Town

François Leclère and Jeffrey Spencer

ISBN 978 086159 199 2
ISSN 1747 3640

© Trustees of the British Museum 2014

Front cover: The mounds of the casemate building at Tell
Dafana in Petrie's 1886 photograph (above) and in 1999 (below)
(Egypt Exploration Society Lucy Gura archive/P. Spencer)

Printed and bound in the UK by 4edge Ltd, Hockley

Papers used in this book by The British Museum Press are of
FSC Mixed Credit, elemental chlorine free (ECF) fibre sourced
from well-managed forests

All British Museum images illustrated in this book are
© The Trustees of the British Museum

Further information about the Museum and its collection can
be found at britishmuseum.org

Contents

Preface

This volume arises from the British Museum research project 'Egyptian–Greek Relations at Daphnae (Nile Delta) in the Seventh Century BC', funded by the Leverhulme Trust for three years from 2008. The main aim of this project was to re-assess the objects discovered in the excavations carried out by Flinders Petrie for the Egypt Exploration Fund at the site of ancient Daphnae in 1886. This site, on the eastern edge of the Nile Delta in Egypt, was already known at that time by the name Tell Defenneh, which survives today with the modern transliteration of Tell Dafana. Study of the finds has been combined with a reconsideration of the site and the architecture of its monuments to determine the extent of Archaic Greek influence and whether Petrie's interpretation of the ancient town as a camp for Greek troops has any validity. Arising from his discovery of some fine Greek ceramics at the site, it seemed that Petrie's assessment, made soon after his discovery of the great Archaic Greek centre at Naukratis on the other side of the Nile Delta, and heavily influenced by the writings of Herodotus, may have overestimated the impact of the Greeks at Tell Dafana.

Since the majority of objects from the 1886 excavations are in the British Museum, these were the natural focus for primary investigation and cataloguing, followed by a comparison with material which had been distributed to other museums and collections. Information on the latter was collected by arranged study visits where possible, or through written enquiries. The project complemented a parallel one on the site of Naukratis, directed by Alexandra Villing of the Department of Greece and Rome in the British Museum. Together, it is hoped that the projects will help to reveal similarities or differences between the nature of Egyptian and Archaic Greek contact at the two sites.

The authors would like to thank the Leverhulme Trust for funding the project and the British Museum for adopting it into the research programme and providing the means to prepare this publication. The original funding application owed much to the kind assistance of J.D. Hill, British Museum Research Manager. Thanks are also due to Vivian Davies, during whose Keepership of the Department of Ancient Egypt and Sudan the project was conducted, and all the other staff of the Department, especially Senior Museum Assistant Evan York and the Museum Assistant team of Emily Taylor, Mark Haswell, Simon Prentice and Robert Dominey. The cooperation of David Saunders, Keeper of the Department of Conservation and Scientific Research, and his staff, is also gratefully acknowledged. Assistance was also provided by Tanya Szrajber and Jonathan Whitson Cloud of Collections Services, and by British Museum photographers John Williams and Dudley Hubbard. To all we are most grateful.

We also wish to express our thanks to the staff of the various institutions in the UK and abroad which have provided access to their collections or shared information: The Egyptian Museum, Cairo; The Boston Museum of Fine Arts; Penn Museum, Philadelphia; The Oriental Institute Museum, Chicago; The Royal Ontario Museum, Toronto; The McGill Museum, Montreal; The Musées royaux d'Art et d'Histoire, Brussels; The Ägyptisches Museum, Berlin; The Nicholson Museum, Sydney; The

Ashmolean Museum, Oxford; The Fitzwilliam Museum, Cambridge; The Petrie Museum of Egyptian Archaeology at University College London; Bolton City Museum; The World Museum, Liverpool; Sheffield Weston Park Museum; St Helens World of Glass Museum; Warrington Museum and Art Gallery; Brighton Royal Pavilion and Museums; Bristol Museum and Art Gallery; The National Museum of Scotland, Edinburgh; The McLean Museum and Art Gallery in Greenock; The McManus Art Gallery and Museum, Dundee; Birmingham City Museum and Kelvingrove Museum, Glasgow. Additional thanks are due to Vincent Razanajao at the Griffith Institute, Oxford; Stephen Quirke of the Petrie Museum; and Chris Naunton at the Egypt Exploration Society for permission to use archive material in their care. The kind cooperation of Dr Mohamed Abd el-Maksoud is acknowledged for agreeing to the inclusion of the results of the 2009 season of excavation at Tell Dafana in this volume.

Grateful acknowledgements are also due to those individuals who have assisted with particular aspects of the research by offering the benefit of their expertise: Neal Spencer, Keeper of the Department of Ancient Egypt and Sudan in the British Museum, for reading the text and offering several suggestions; Brian Muhs and Rob Demarée for insights on demotic ostraca; Alexandra Villing for many helpful points and assistance with copy-editing; the staff of the Naukratis Project: Marianne Bergeron, Aurelia Masson-Berghoff and Ross Thomas; and Patricia Spencer for checking the entire text. Thanks are also due to the editor of the British Museum Research Publications series, Sarah Faulks, for much assistance and for seeing the book through to production.

For those unfamiliar with British Museum object numbers, a little explanation may be helpful. This publication includes objects from both the Department of Ancient Egypt and Sudan (AES) and the Department of Greece and Rome (GR). Objects in either department have a Registration Number, originally made up of the calendar date of acquisition followed by an individual item number (more recently, the year when registration took place, a departmental code and a lot number and item number). However, the Registration Number is not used as the primary reference for items in AES; instead, another series of simple running numbers is used (known as the 'Big Number'). This regularly appears prefixed by 'EA' in publications, derived from the former name of the Department (Egyptian Antiquities). In the catalogues in Chapters 3 and 5 both numbers are given, but the Big Number takes precedence. Registration Numbers from the Department of Greece and Rome have been distinguished by the prefix 'GR' in this volume.

A note on spellings: much of Petrie's work was concentrated on a building he described by the Arabic term *Kasr*, 'palace, citadel'. In his notes and publications he used the spelling with an initial *K*, so this has been retained for the discussion of his work and finds in Chapters 1 and 2, and in all direct quotes from Petrie. Modern transliteration, however, prefers the more accurate rendering Qasr, using 'Q' for the Arabic *qaf* (as this is certainly not equivalent to 'K') so this version has been adopted elsewhere in the volume, particularly for the catalogues in Chapters 3 and 5. This should also be more helpful to researchers because it is the spelling used in the British Museum collection database, available online (www.britishmuseum.org/collection).

Chapter 1
Tell Dafana
Identity, Exploration and Monuments

François Leclère

Geographical situation

The site of Tell Dafana is situated in the north-western part of El-Ismailiya governorate, region of El-Qantara West, on the eastern fringe of the Delta plain, about 13km to the west of the Suez canal at the latitude of the town of El-Qantara.[1] The ancient town lay beside the most easterly diffluent of the Pelusiac branch of the Nile or, during the Late Period, a narrow canal stemming from it a few kilometres upstream and running eastwards towards the lagoons watering ancient Sile/Mesen (Tell Abu Seifa, Tell Hebua), some 18km to the east. Tell Farama, the ruins of ancient Pelusium, is a further 40km to the north-east, Tell Belim/Tell esh-Sherig (ancient Herakleopolis mikra/Sethrum) 13km to the north, and Tell Fara'on/Petrie's Tell Nebesha (ancient Imet/Buto of Arabia) 24km to the west (**Pl. 1a**).

At the end of the 19th century – and in fact until almost the end of the 1980s when the agricultural development of the region took place[2] – the site was very isolated in a semi-desert, semi-marshy landscape far from the populated places of Salhiya, in the cultivated region to the west, and El-Qantara to the east (**Pls 1b, 2a**). It lay on the south-western part of a series of flat sandy 'islands' (Geziret el-Ghizlan, Geziret Umm 'Ileita, as well as Geziret el-Zarzariya) forming a protrusion at the very northern tip of the eastern desert, into the low-lying, marshy and seasonally inundated plain bordering the southern side of Lake Manzala.[3] Brackish, shallow offshoots of Lake Manzala framed the ruins: Birket Kom/Tell Dafana[4] to the west and Sayiah el-Sibeita to the east (**Pl. 2b**). In antiquity, the locality occupied a strategic position near the end of the ancient caravan land route from Syria-Palestine. Upon reaching the Nile Delta on the desert route across north Sinai, travellers arriving from the east could have taken alternative routes after passing the oasis of Qatiya: they could either turn towards the north-west, in order make a stop at Pelusium near the seashore, or to skirt directly around the swamps by carrying on in a straight line, on the El-Qantara landbridge between the paleo-lagoons and Lake Ballah near ancient Sile, all the way to Daphnae (Tell Dafana) and, only a few kilometres further, to a bend in the Pelusiac branch – although during the Late Period the river was not as navigable as before.[5]

From the Late Period to Late Antiquity, Daphnae was thus the first large town, properly situated in Egyptian territory (although still at the fringe of the plain), to be reached from the east.[6] It must also have been an ideal and easily provisioned starting point for expeditions towards Asia. In this regard, it was a true gateway of the country.[7] The surrounding landscape is now quite different. All the depressions in the area have been drained and all the farmable land is now cultivated, including most of the old sandy *geziras* to the north of the site, and encircled by roads along canals, while fish farms are developing step-by-step in the sandy land to the south. Cuts in the archaeological ground itself leave no doubt as to the very real threat of the total disappearance of the site within a short time if left unprotected.

Names and identification (Fig. 1)

Modern name

Until now, the site has been most commonly known to scholars by the name '(Tell) Defenneh', spelled with a double 'n', popularized by Petrie's publications of his excavations at the site, but which seems to originate from some maps of the *Description de l'Égypte* (**Pl. 3a**), followed by a few authors such as J.G. Wilkinson in the 1840s, and marked on several other 19th-century maps.[8] From the beginning of the 19th century however, the toponym also appears in the literature and on some maps with various other spellings with only one 'n', such as Deféïnéh or Defeyneh – in some other parts of the *Description* itself – as well as Déffenieh, Tefeneh,[9] and sometimes in two syllables instead of three, such as Dèfné, (Tel-) Dephneh, (Tell) Defneh, Tell el-Deffné, (Tell) el-Daphné, Tel-el-Dafneh, Taphne, Tephne, etc.[10] Petrie himself reckoned that 'Defeneh' or 'Defn'eh' was a local pronunciation, somehow closer to the ancient one(s), a fact already stressed by G.J. Chester in 1880, and later by F.L. Griffith and N. Aimé-Giron.[11]

The site is called كوم/ تل دفنة Kom/ Tell Dafana, on the Arabic/English maps of the Survey of Egypt (**Pl. 2b**).[12] This is the transcription that we have chosen to favour, though Tell Dafna would also be perfectly correct.[13] As the root *d-f-n* in Arabic, related to 'what is buried/concealed/hidden',[14] appears rarely in Egyptian modern toponyms, for instance 'El-Araba el-Madfuna', Tell Dafana/Dafna almost certainly derives directly, as so often is the case, from the ancient designation of the locality.

Ancient names and problems of identification

Since the Napoleonic expedition[15] the site has been identified with Δάφναι αἱ πηλούσιαι, mentioned twice by Herodotus (2.30, 2.107) – *Daphnae Pelusiae* in the Latin translation – a garrison town founded by Psamtik I to guard the north-eastern frontier. This toponym has long been identified with *Dafno*, that the *Antonine Itinerary* incorrectly places at a distance of only 16 Roman miles (23.6km) from Pelusium on the way to Memphis,[16] as well as with [Δάφνη] πλησίον Πηλουσίου, '[Daphne] near Pelusium', recorded by Stephanus of Byzantion, beside several other homonyms outside of Egypt.[17] These names had already long been linked[18] with biblical 'Tahpanhes' – תַחְפַּנְחֵם / תַחְפְּנְחֵם (ketiv תחפנם) – transcribed Τάφνας (invariable) and Τάφναι (declinable) in the LXX, ⲧⲁⲫⲛⲁⲥ in the Coptic version, *Tafnae* in the Vulgate[19] – a place in Egypt where Judeans from Jerusalem, including the prophet Jeremiah, are said to have taken refuge when they fled the Neo-Babylonian repression during the reign of Apries. Tahpanhes also appears in a few fragments of para-biblical compositions among the Qumran scrolls, some of them possible apocrypha of Jeremiah.[20] It is also mentioned in a Phoenician letter on papyrus, written in Aramaic, of the 6th or 5th century BC, found in Saqqara, as a locality where the god Baal-Saphon was worshipped, among other deities.[21] A 'region of [...]hpanes' appears in one or (probably) two Aramaic grain delivery contracts found in Elephantine and dating to year 3 of Xerxes, but it might not necessarily concern north-eastern Tahpanhes.[22] During the first half of

the 5th century BC, a Greek individual called Timarchos also left a graffito in the second court of the temple of Seti I at Abydos, where he designates himself a 'Daphnaite'.[23] A Nabatean dedication dating from the reign of Cleopatra VII, year 18 (34 BC), on a limestone block from Tell el-Shuqafiya, at the western entrance of the Wadi Tumilat, also mentions *Bdpn'mṣryt*, possibly corresponding to 'Egyptian Daphnae'.[24]

The biblical toponym is also mentioned by exegetic commentators of the 3rd–5th century AD, such as Hippolytus (Τάφναι, decl.), Eusebius of Cesarea (Ταφνάς, invar.), Jerome (*Tafnae*),[25] as well as, possibly, in Egeria's pilgrimage travel account (*Tat[h]nis*).[26] ⲧⲁⲫⲛⲁⲥ is also mentioned in a mid-4th century AD episcopal list as the hometown of a bishop called Eulogios,[27] and in the Coptic Romance of 'Cambyses' (Nebukadnezzar)'s invasion of Egypt (6th–7th century AD).[28] The latter document must certainly have been one of the sources of John of Nikiu's *Chronicle* – probably written at the end of the 7th century AD, but only known by a much later translation in Ethiopian Ge'ez – where Taphnas should be recognized, from the context, in the metathesis 'Tenfas'.[29] According to S. Timm, the name of the locality might also be recognizable in Arabic *Dafnās* – variant *Daqnās* – hometown of Isidore, weaver and companion of the soldier Sina, who are both recorded in the Copto-Arabic *Synaxarion* as martyrs in Pelusium.[30] Tahpanhes also appears in late Hebrew texts, such as the compilation of homilies *Pesiḳta Rabbati* (17.4; 9th century AD),[31] and in the *Chronicles* of Jerahmeel Ben Solomon (42.1; see also 56.3–4; 13th century AD).[32]

Definitive evidence confirming the identifications of all these ancient toponyms with the site of Tell Dafana is still lacking, although, as J.-Y. Carrez-Maratray noted, it might be over-cautious not to consider them more than plausible.[33] Besides, Daphnae can no longer be equated, as has sometimes been suggested,[34] with Aphnaion in George of Cyprus, Hierocles, on the Madaba map and possibly in an itinerary on a 5th century AD papyrus, in addition to a few other sources. This Byzantine diocese must in fact have been situated in north Sinai, far to the east of Pelusium.[35] We shall return below to Petrie's incorrect identification of Daphnae with the *Stratopeda* mentioned by Herodotus (2.154).[36]

Ancient classical and biblical names of the locality, as well as the modern one, must originate from an ancient Egyptian toponym.[37] W. Spiegelberg recognized in 1904 that the second part of Hebrew Tahpanhes must correspond to Egyptian *Pȝ-nḥsy*, a common anthroponym[38] as well as a designation for 'The Nubian/Southerner/Dark-skinned', or, as recently suggested, also interpreted as 'The Blessed'.[39] The first part of the toponym is less obviously restorable. Spiegelberg first attempted a **Tȝ Ḥwt-(n-)Pȝ-nḥsy*, 'The Castle of Panehesy', which remains unattested,[40] but a toponym of a similar construction appears in several demotic documents of the Ptolemaic Period, a geographical *onomasticon* on papyrus (Cairo 31169) and four literary texts, three written on papyrus (Paris BN 215; Berlin 13588; London BM EA 10508) and one on an ostracon (Karnak LS 462.4),[41] with a content highly suggestive of a 26th dynasty context. Reading, translation and etymology of the toponym in question remain delicate and debated, but it might

دفنه کوم / تل‎   TELL (/KÔM) DAFANA / DAFNA (maps of the *Survey of Egypt*)
Other earlier transcriptions from Arabic : Defeïneh, Defeyneh (*Descr. de l'Ég.*), Dèfné (L. de Bellefonds),
                    Defenneh (Wilkinson, Petrie), Defn'eh, Defeneh (Petrie, Griffith), etc.

Δάφναι αἱ Πηλούσιαι (Lat. = *Daphnae Pelusiae*)	Herodotus	(mid 5th c. BC)
Dafno (Lat.)	*Antonine Itinerary*	(end of 3rd c. AD)
[Δάφνη] πλήσιον Πηλουσίου	Stephanus of Byzantium	(mid 6th c. AD)
(Τίμαρχος) Δαφναίτες	graffito in Abydos (temple of Seti I, 2nd courtyard)	(5th c. BC)
Δάφναι	Eustathius of Thessalonica	(12th c. AD)
Bdpn' msryt ? (Nabatean)	Inscription from Tell el-Shuqafiya, Wadi Tumilat	(36 BC)
دفناس *Dafnās* ? [var. دقناس *Daqnās*]	Copto-Arabic *Synaxarion*	(14th c. AD?)

תחפנחס *Thpnḥs* (Aramaic)	Phoenician Pap. from Saqqara (Cairo Mus.)	(6th-5th c. BC)

O.T. :

תַחְפְּנְחֵס *Taḥpanḥēs*	Jeremiah (2.16; 43.7-9; 44.1; 46.14)	(6th c. BC)
[ketiv: תַחְפְּנֵס *Taḥpənēs*	Jeremiah (2.16)]	
תְחַפְּנְחֵס *Təhapnəḥēs*	Ezekiel (30.18)	(6rd c. BC)
Τάφνας (invar.) / Τάφναι (décl.)	LXX (Jer. 2.16; 50.7-9; 51.1; Ez., 30.18 + Judith 1,9)	(3rd c. BC)
Taphnae / *Taphnes* (Lat.)	Vulgate	(4th c. AD)
·ⲦⲀⳐⲚⲀⲤ	Coptic Version	(3rd-4th c. AD)

See also :

Greek	Latin	Hebrew
Hippolytus of Rome (3rd c. AD)	Jerome (4th-5th c. AD)	*Pesikta Rabbati* (mid 9th c. AD)
Eusebius of Caesarea (3rd-4th c. AD)	Etheria/ Egeria (end of 4th c. AD)	Jerahmeel Ben Solomon (mid 12th c. AD)
Vitae prophetarum (3rd-4th c. AD?)	Gregorius I (end of 6th c. AD)	
Pseudo-Athanasius (4th-5th c. AD)	Isidore of Seville (end of 6th c. AD)	
Pseudo-John Chrysostom (end of 4th/10th c. AD?)	Rabanus Maurus (9th c. AD)	
Theodoret of Cyrus (5th c. AD)	Walafrid Strabo (9th c. AD),	
Olympiodorus (Diaconus) of Alexandria (6th c. AD)	Usuardus of Saint-Germain-des-Prés (9th c. AD)	
	Peter the Deacon (12th c. AD)	
	Petrus Comestor (12th c. AD)	
	Thomas Aquinas (13th c. AD)	
	Gregory XIII (end of 16th c. AD)	
	Cesare Baronio (end of 16th c. AD)	

·ⲦⲀⳐⲚⲀⲤ	*Vita Athanasii* (Pap. Turin 7119 [63000, cod. 9])	(4th c. AD)
·ⲦⲀⳐⲚⲀⲤ	*Coptic Romance of Cambyses* (Pap. Berlin 9009)	(6th-7th c. AD)
ⲦⲚⳘⲤ: *Tenfas* (Ge'ez)	*Chronicle of John of Nikiou*	(beg. 17th c. AD; original in Greek and Coptic, 7th c. AD, later translated into Arabic and then into Ge'ez)

[metathesis of ⲦⳑⳘⲤ: *Tefnas;* see O.T. in Ethiopian version, for ex.: Jeremiah 43.7-9; other writings in Jeremiah 2.16; 44.1;
                    Ezekiel 30.18; *Legends about Jeremiah*]

**T3-wḥyt P3-nḥs* ? (demotic)	(reconstruction J. Quack)	
[**T3-ᶜhy-(n)-P3-nḥs* ?	(reconstruction K.Th. Zauzich)]	
T3-jḥt-P3-nḥs	*Geographical Onomasticon (*Pap. Cairo 31169)	(4th-2nd c. BC)
T3y=w-ᶜ3m-P3-nḥs	*Teaching of Chascheschonqi* (Pap. BM EA 10508)	(1st c. BC)
T3y=w-ᶜ3m-n-nḥs	Pap. Berlin 13588	(2nd-1st c. BC)
T3y=w-ᶜ3m-nḥs	Ostracon Karnak (Ostr. Dem. K-LS)	(mid 3rd c. BC)
T3y=w-ᶜ3m-P3-nḥs	*Tale of Amasis and the skipper* (Pap. BN 215, v.)	(mid 3rd c. BC)

Figure 1 The names of Tell Dafana

actually correspond indirectly to Tahpanhes/Daphnae. In the Cairo *onomasticon*, J. Yoyotte and F. de Cenival, on the one hand, and K. Zauzich on the other, independently identified *T3-jḥt-(n-)p3-(nḥsy?)*, 'The-Cow-of-Panehesy'. In the papyri of Berlin, Paris and London, as well as the Karnak ostracon, the toponym previously read as *N3ꜥ3m-(n-)p3-nḥs* has been subsequently re-read *T3-ꜥ3m[.t]-p3-nḥs* (Paris BN 215)/*T3y=w-ꜥ3m n-nḥs* (Berlin 13588)/*T3y=w-ꜥ3m-P3-nḥs* (London 10508)/*T3y=w-ꜥ3m-nḥs* (Karnak LS 462.4).

A	B
The-Shepherdess of [?]	Panehesy/Pinehas [?]
(Those-of-)the-herdsman [?]	the-Nubian/Southerner/Dark One?
(Those-of-the)Asiatic (and)[?]	The Blessed [?]

Difficult to understand and to translate,[42] all these variants are now explained as non-etymological writings of an older and unattested toponym, whose original meaning was eventually lost, possibly *T3-ꜥhy(.t)-n-p3-nḥs*,[43] or more simply and logically, as J. Quack recently suggested, *T3-wḫyt-(n-)p3-nḥs*, 'The Settlement-of-Panehesy', *T3-wḫyt* often designating a military place.[44]

Daphnae/Tahpanhes has also sometimes been identified with an Egyptian toponym Tjebn(et), attested as early as in a letter of the Ramesside Period (Pap. Anastasi VI), as well as in two Ptolemaic demotic papyri already mentioned, Cairo 31169 and Berlin 13588,[45] but this identification must certainly be rejected.[46] As mentioned above, in the two latter documents, Tahpanhes/Daphnae has already been recognized in another toponym which better matches the possible etymology of the Hebrew and Aramaic names of the locality; moreover, the position of Tjebn(et) in the geographical *onomasticon* seems to imply a more central location in the Delta. It has been suggested that it could be an abbreviation of the demotic version of the toponym Sebennytos (*Ṯbnw nṯr*).[47]

The absence of any attestation of a toponym matching the locality in the Assyrian Annals[48] argues against its existence before the 26th dynasty. This also fits in well with the absence, so far, of archaeological material at Tell Dafana pre-dating the Saite Period – with the exception of a single New Kingdom sherd[49] – as well as with the clearly anachronistic character of the Herodotean mention of the presence of a King 'Sesostris' at Daphnae (2.107).[50]

Tell Dafana: history of archaeological exploration

The site in the 19th century

In the modern era, a visitor would have found the site spread over an extensive and flat sandy surface, 1600m east–west and at least 1000m north–south, covered in some areas with remains of mudbrick constructions levelled by natural erosion, and strewn with pottery and stone chips. Among the main visible features are two extensive low mounds to the north-west, visible from afar, on either side of a long, narrow and sinuous furrow running from west to east across the northern part of the site, the bed of a watercourse which might have been a relic of a narrow dead diffluent or derivation from the Pelusiac Nile river itself (**Pls 3a–b,**

9–10).[51] According to Petrie, the south-eastern mound was apparently the actual site called 'Tell Defenneh', while the north-western one would have been 'Tell Debowan', a toponym formerly placed a few kilometres to the west by the cartographers of the Napoleonic expedition.[52] The 'many large hewn blocks of granite, sandstone and limestone [...] lying about in different parts of the ruins, and especially around the central mound', which Chester saw in 1880,[53] were apparently no longer visible when Petrie's arrived.

In the middle of the extensive plain to the south-east of these flat mounds, the main visible feature was a group of relatively small hillocks, in which Petrie immediately recognized the eroded ruins of massive mudbrick constructions, partly burnt, apparently called 'Kasr el-Bint el-Yahudi',[54] as the local Bedawin told him (**Figs 2–3**). This must have been the point that Chester said was called 'Tell Farmah',[55] and possibly that marked as 'El-Qala'ah' on the map of the Napoleonic expedition.[56] The good state of preservation of these mudbrick constructions, at a relatively high level compared to the rest of the site, must have resulted from the cover of burnt bricks left on the top from the burning of the superstructure.[57]

Visits and supposed 'excavations' before Petrie

No one seems to have undertaken any major excavations before Petrie started his work in 1886. Due probably to the difficulties of access, the site had been rarely visited with the exception of F. de Lesseps in June 1861,[58] the orientalist painter N. Berchère in December 1861[59] and by Chester in 1880, who left a more substantial description of it.[60] A certain Dr. Bourbouraki (?), about whom we know almost nothing except that he was a Greek medical officer residing with his British wife in the newly founded canal-town of El-Qantara in the 1860s, was apparently digging at the site in his spare time, as well as collecting stray finds from the whole region.[61]

Petrie mentions the short stay of up to three days by an Egyptian *reis* from the Bulak Museum in Cairo.[62] At first, it appears tempting to link this mention with two groups of objects registered in the Cairo Museum *Journal d'entrée* in November 1882 and May 1883,[63] described as 'Purchased and excavated in Tell-Daphne'. The second lot at least may correspond to the objects that a certain Mr 'Allemand (*sic*)' – certainly the French dealer Eugène Allemant – showed to C.E. Wilbour in April 1883 and claimed to have found at the site.[64] Both lots included terracotta antefixes and figures, Neo-Babylonian clay cylinders, bronze objects (patera, figure, vase handles) and fragments of stone statues.

In fact, there are many reasons to discount these items as actual finds from Tell Dafana:[65] stylistically, some of them are clearly Etruscan and South Italian, while others seem to be from the Near East. Among the antefixes (JE 25207, 25413–14, 25420),[66] of Campanian-Etruscan type, the first one at least has exact parallels from Capua.[67] A pair of rectangular bronze handles with horse-head protomes (JE 25434), from a large vessel, possibly a *podanipter*, also seem to be Etruscan.[68] Twenty-two of the terracotta figures (JE 25208, 25410–12, 25415–19, 25421–3, 25426–9, 25435–40) are closely similar to figures found in the tens of thousands at Tarentum, particularly in the 'Fondo Giovinazzi', where

Figure 2 Petrie's photograph across the site to the mounds of the *Kasr* before excavation in 1886 (EES, Lucy Gura archive)

Figure 3 Petrie's photograph showing the mounds of the *Kasr* in 1886 (EES, Lucy Gura archive)

excavations were undertaken not long before these objects arrived in the Cairo Museum.[69] The three cylinders of Nebukadnezzar (JE 25431–3) were soon recognized as modern forgeries,[70] casts from antiquities found in excavations near Baghdad.[71] A bronze patera (JE 25212) shows a mixture of different influences (e.g. Egyptian pattern, with lotus and birds, in the centre of the underside, and handles in the shape of Bes-headed winged sphinxes, with Achaemenid style bull-heads at the ends of the wings) which might suggest a Phoenician or Cypriot origin.[72] An oriental (perhaps Babylonian?) influence also seems possible for a bronze female statuette (JE 25209).[73] The fragments of marble and limestone statue heads (JE 25424 and 25425) were also later recognized as not coming from the site.[74] Consequently, though we do not know why and how these objects originally arrived in Egypt, the dealer who sold them to the Bulak Museum – most probably E. Allemant – was obviously unscrupulous enough, as G. Maspero soon suspected, to conceal their true provenance.

A stela that entered the Cairo Museum (JE 25147) as early as July 1881 has also often been linked with Tell Dafana and even said to come from the site, as it bears a representation of a Near-Eastern deity, sometimes identified with Baal-Saphon. However, according to the *Journal d'entrée* of the Cairo Museum, the stela was actually purchased in Alexandria, so a Tell Dafana provenance, based only on a suggestion of G. Daressy relayed by M. Müller in 1906,[75] remains very dubious. The identity of the deity, represented standing on a lion, remains unclear, although it certainly belongs to a Phoenico-Palestinian context; other features are Egyptian, such as the top *cavetto*-cornice with winged sun-disc, the symbolic ears for 'hearing-the-prayers' and the *was*-sceptre of the deity.

Petrie's season at the site in 1886

Close reading of Petrie's publications,[76] alongside his handwritten unpublished documents such as letters forming part of his excavation Journal,[77] as well as his Notebooks and Pocket Diary,[78] make it possible to reconstruct the sequence of his excavations in different parts of the site and to gain a better understanding of the progression of his work and the methodology he applied (**Figs 5–6**).

Petrie's season at the site lasted exactly eight weeks, from Friday 26 March to Saturday 22 May 1886. Having arrived at the site at sunset on 25 March, after a seven-hour hike from the neighbouring site of Tell Nebesha where he was previously excavating, he installed his tent along the series of sandy hillocks, covered with bushes of tamarisks (**Fig. 4**), bordering the southern bank of the dried riverbed crossing the northern part of the site, somewhere to the north-east of the 'Ptolemaic' mound'.[79] Excavations initially started with the help of 40 workers who had come with him from Tell Nebesha, a team which quickly increased to 85 and then fluctuated between 55 and 70.[80] Some Bedawin living in the area, mainly old women, brought and sold to him small stray finds (weights, scraps of gold, arrowheads, etc.) from the surface of the site that they were scouring, and possibly also from other places in the area.[81]

Petrie immediately concentrated his work on the hills of the *Kasr*, i.e. the massive mudbrick structures in the centre of the plain, where he worked until 12–14 May. After clearing the outlines of the greater of these two cellular constructions, he soon extended the work to the esplanade on its north side (7 April)[82] and to the north-east and eastern annexes (from 8 April), to the south of which he eventually (from mid-April, and especially from 19–20 April) started to find rooms containing great quantities of Greek pottery.[83] During the

Figure 4 Petrie's camp at Tell Dafana. The workers slept under the bushes (EES, Lucy Gura archive)

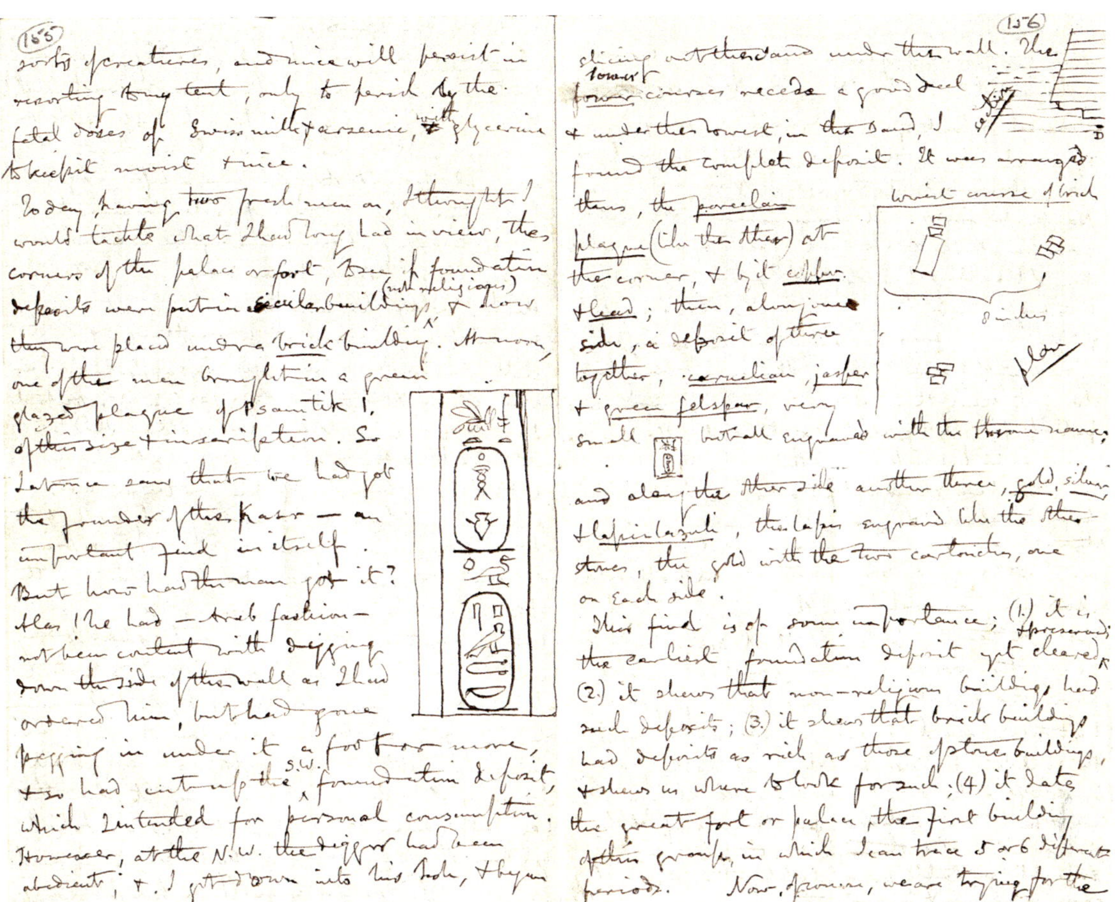

Figure 5 Pages 155–6 from Petrie's Journal 1885–6, with details of the foundation deposits of the *Kasr* (© Griffith Institute, University of Oxford)

Figure 6 Page 56 from Petrie's Notebook 74.f (left); Pocket Diary 1886, 25–7 March (right) (courtesy of the Petrie Museum of Egyptian Archaeology, UCL)

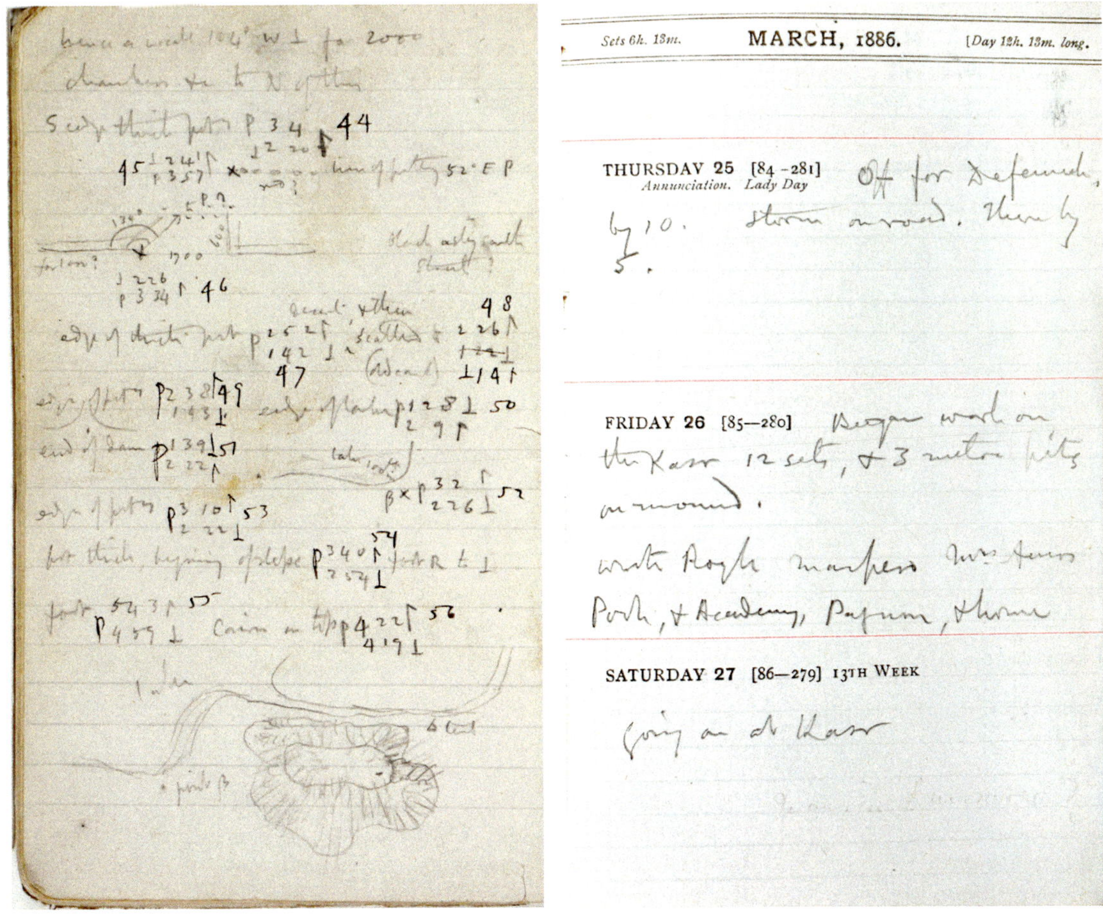

first week of May, after having finished emptying most of the cells of the larger casemate building (**Fig. 7**), he excavated the foundation deposits of Psamtik I located under its corners.[84] Before 4 April, he had also started to dig in the area of a complex of walls in the eastern part of the site,[85] a quarter to which he apparently returned later.[86] As for the *Kasr*, the plan of this quarter was already completed by 8 May.[87]

From the first few days Petrie also put a team to work on the large mound to the north-west of the *Kasr*, close to his dig camp to the south of the watercourse, but stopped as early as 17 April, after having pitted it all over without finding any major features.[88] He then moved the workers from there to an area a few hundred metres to the south-east of the *Kasr*, strewn with metal items suggestive of a quarter of bronze and iron workshops. From 10 May, most of the workmen working on the *Kasr* had joined the work in this area.[89] The aim was to turn over systematically the top 15cm layer of the soil, but without actually clearing structures, merely looking for objects across the extensive surface area.[90] As this method did not need particular watching, Petrie was then free to complete a general survey and to map the main features of the site – including ones he had only just discovered, such as the levelled remains of a massive enclosure wall around the *Kasr*, with a limestone gate at the south and traces of walls and a 'dromos' in the northern part.[91] From 12 May, he began to pack his numerous finds in preparation for departure.[92]

At an indeterminate moment in the season, Petrie also rapidly excavated a small mound covered with pottery at the southern edge of the site, 600m or so from the enclosure.[93] There he found some brick walls and parts of an *in situ* limestone pavement, placed near the intersection of the axis of the enclosure and the caravan road. He had no time or even intention to excavate the mound to the north-west of the waterway but only noted, when going for a walk in the area with A.H. Sayce, who visited in mid-April, that it was strewn with Late Roman glass sherds and that there must have been tombs there, some of them built with limestone.[94]

To summarize, the main areas excavated were:
1. The large levelled enclosure wall with its southern entrance.
2. The complex of two large casemate buildings close to the centre of the enclosure, with an esplanade to the north and a series of annexes to the east.
3. The south-eastern quarter of the enclosure.
4. A group of constructions in the eastern part of the site.
5. Some architectural remains near the southern edge of the site.
6. The southernmost of the two north-west mounds.

In order to record the provenance of the finds in the different areas excavated and facilitate the description of the structures in the publication, Petrie attributed Findspot numbers to specific places or areas excavated, rooms in the structures (cells in the casemate buildings, chambers in the annexes), groups of walls and distinctive groups of finds.[95]

After Petrie

Petrie did not return for further seasons at the site and no major excavations were undertaken there again until recently.[96] A.L. Fontaine visited the site sometime before 1947, collected Late Roman glass sherds on the north-western mound and gave a report of his visit.[97] P. and J. Spencer visited the site in December 1999.[98] In 2009 and 2010, from mid-April to the end of June, the Supreme Council of Antiquities in Egypt conducted two excavation seasons, under the supervision of Dr M. Abd el-Maksoud.[99] During the first season, the Egyptian team worked in the southern part of the main enclosure detected by Petrie, to the south of the complex of casemate buildings. They followed the edges of the levelled enclosure wall on both sides and, in the central part of this area, cleared the remains of the massive mudbrick structures that had already been detected in 2006 by the present author, on the basis of the analysis of new satellite images of the site,[100] which clearly belonged to a large temple opening to the south with three successive courts flanked by storerooms on its eastern and south-western sides. In 2010, the excavations

Figure 7 Petrie's photograph of the *Kasr* after excavation (EES, Lucy Gura archive)

concentrated on the area in the north-eastern corner of the enclosure. Results of the first season are given in Chapter 8.

What was Tell Dafana? Re-assessing the written sources

Problems with Petrie's interpretation

Prior to the recent re-examination and the new fieldwork, our understanding of Tell Dafana had largely depended on Petrie's finds and his own interpretation of their context in connection with classical and biblical sources. From the end of the 18th century,[101] Tell Dafana had been identified with the garrison town of Daphnae, founded by Psamtik I and mentioned by Herodotus (2.30), and with the locality of Tahpanhes, at which Jeremiah (43.9) describes a royal Egyptian palace. Petrie found this identification confirmed by his finds of quantities of Archaic Greek painted pottery as well as iron and bronze tools and weapons within the context of a Saite casemate mudbrick structure located inside a rectangular mudbrick enclosure. However, he went one step further by adding yet another identification, namely the *Stratopeda*. According to Herodotus (2.154), the *Stratopeda* were camps that had been given by Psamtik I to his Greek mercenaries which were to be found at an imprecise location on either side of the lower course of the Pelusiac Nile branch. For Petrie, the remains he had discovered could hardly be anything other than a military camp occupied by Greek soldiers, with a fortified keep in the middle, interpreted by Petrie as a 'palace-fort, where a ruler would have lived with his troops'.[102] Petrie saw additional confirmation for such an interpretation in the similarity of the larger of the two casemate buildings at Tell Dafana to a structure he had discovered in his excavations a year earlier at Naukratis. The Naukratite building too was located inside a large walled enclosure, which Petrie believed to be a fortified Greek camp, identical with the Hellenion mentioned by Herodotus.[103]

Although a few authors questioned the identification of Daphnae with the *Stratopeda* and/or with the site of Tell Dafana soon after Petrie's publication,[104] most scholars were convinced at first. Still today – in spite of the more or less general rejection of an association with the *Stratopeda* – Petrie's overall interpretation of the remains has a firm hold on scholarship and the enclosure of Tell Dafana is still considered essentially as a Greek military compound.[105] Our re-assessment of the archaeological data and the finds, as well as the textual sources, leads to quite a different view. Of course, a possible presence in the area of Daphnae of a Greek population among other foreign communities, at least for some time during the Saite Period, cannot be ruled out and indeed seems to be implied by the nature and size of the Greek pottery assemblage from the site. However, the architectural remains revealed by Petrie are first and foremost Egyptian in nature. Their features correspond to those of a classical temple town functioning as a frontier-post, and it is in this specific context that the presence of imports must be understood.

Daphnae and Stratopeda *in Herodotus and Diodorus*

In the Second Book of Herodotus' *Histories*, Daphnae is mentioned twice (2.30, 2.107) and *Stratopeda* once (2.154). The context of the appearance of both toponyms is different in each passage. The first excerpt (2.30) follows a geographical description of the Nile and of different parts of Egypt, particularly Elephantine and the Nubian and Ethiopian regions upstream to Meroe and beyond:

> From this city you make a journey by water equal in distance to that by which you came from Elephantine to the capital city of Ethiopia, and you come to the land of the Deserters. These Deserters are called Asmakh, which translates, in Greek, as 'those who stand on the left hand of the king'.[106] These once revolted and joined themselves to the Ethiopians, two hundred and forty thousand Egyptians of fighting age. The reason was as follows. In the reign of Psammetichus, there were watchposts [φυλακαί] at Elephantine facing Ethiopia, at Daphnae of Pelusium[107] facing Arabia and Assyria, and at Marea facing Libya. And still in my time the Persians hold these posts as they were held in the days of Psammetichus; there are Persian guards at Elephantine and at Daphnae. Now the Egyptians had been on guard[108] for three years, and no one came to relieve them; so, organizing and making common cause, they revolted from Psammetichus and went to Ethiopia. Psammetichus heard of it and pursued them; and when he overtook them, he asked them in a long speech not to desert their children and wives and the gods of their fathers. Then one of them, the story goes, pointed to his genitals and said that wherever that was, they would have wives and children. So they came to Ethiopia, and gave themselves up to the king of the country who, to make them a gift in return, told them to dispossess certain Ethiopians with whom he was feuding, and occupy their land. These Ethiopians then learned Egyptian customs and have become milder-mannered by intermixture with the Egyptians.[109]

From this quote, we can see that Daphnae was not far from Pelusium, in the north-eastern region of the country, and that it was, with Marea in the north-west and Elephantine in the south, one of the three Egyptian garrison posts guarding the frontiers of Egypt from the reign of Psamtik I onwards. The soldiers living in these garrisons are clearly described as Egyptians and there is no mention here of any foreign contingents with them. Apart from Marea, these garrison-posts were still in use during the Persian Period. The second passage (2.107) concerns an episode of the reign of King Sesostris:

> Now when this Egyptian Sesostris (so the priests said) reached Daphnae of Pelusium on his way home, leading many captives from the peoples whose lands he had subjugated, his brother, whom he had left in charge in Egypt, invited him and his sons to a banquet and then piled wood around the house and set it on fire. When Sesostris was aware of this, he at once consulted his wife, whom (it was said) he had with him; and she advised him to lay two of his six sons on the fire and make a bridge over the flames so that they could walk over the bodies of the two and escape. This Sesostris did; two of his sons were thus burnt but the rest escaped alive with their father.[110]

Although this Sesostris appears to be more of an anachronistic legendary figure than one of the sovereigns of the Middle Kingdom,[111] Daphnae is here presented logically as near Pelusium and as the first Egyptian town that royal military expeditions reached on their return from Asia. The context of the passage where the *Stratopeda* are mentioned (2.154) concerns specifically the employment of the Greek mercenaries in the army of Psamtik I:

To the Ionians and Carians who had helped him, Psammetichus gave places to live in called The Camps, opposite each other on either side of the Nile; and besides this, he paid them all that he had promised. Moreover, he put Egyptian boys in their hands to be taught Greek, and from these, who learned the language, are descended the present-day Egyptian interpreters. The Ionians and Carians lived for a long time in these places, which are near the sea, on the arm of the Nile called the Pelusian, a little way below the town of Bubastis. Long afterwards, king Amasis removed them and settled them at Memphis to be his guard against the Egyptians. It is a result of our communication with these settlers in Egypt (the first of foreign speech to settle in that country) that we Greeks have exact knowledge of the history of Egypt from the reign of Psammetichus onwards. There still remained in my day, in the places out of which the Ionians and Carians were turned, the slipways for their ships and the ruins of their houses.[112]

This passage makes it clear that the *Stratopeda* were two plots of land that had been given to Greek soldiers and were situated on either side of the Pelusiac branch of the Nile in its lower course. A minor contradiction lies in the fact that they are said to be at the same time at the mouth of the branch, close to Pelusium, and only 'a little' downstream from Bubastis, the two cities actually being some 110km apart as the crow flies. The *Stratopeda* were evacuated during the reign of Amasis and were in ruins during the Persian Period.

From Herodotus' testimony alone there does not seem to be any reason to identify the two toponyms with each other: Egyptian Daphnae was still occupied during the Persian Period while the Ionian and Carian *Stratopeda* were already abandoned. The *Stratopeda* are also mentioned in Diodorus Siculus' *Bibliotheca historica* (1.67):

[1]. [...]; and among the mercenaries he [Psamtik] distributed notable gifts over and above their promised pay, gave them the region called The Camps [Στρατόπεδα] to dwell in, and apportioned to them much land in the region lying a little up the river from the Pelusiac mouth; they being subsequently removed thence by Amasis, who reigned many years later, and settled by him in Memphis. [2]. And since Psammetichus had established his rule with the aid of the mercenaries, he henceforth entrusted these before others with the administration of his empire and regularly maintained large mercenary forces. [3]. Once in connection with a campaign in Syria, when he was giving the mercenaries a more honourable place in his order of battle by putting them on the right wing and showing the native troops less honour by assigning them the position on the left wing of the phalanx, the Egyptians, angered by this slight and being over two hundred thousand strong, revolted and set out for Ethiopia, having determined to win for themselves a country of their own. [4]. The king at first sent some of his generals to make excuse for the dishonour done to them, but since no heed was paid to these he set out in person after them by boat, accompanied by his friends. [5]. And when they still continued their march along the Nile and were about to cross the boundary of Egypt, he besought them to change their purpose and reminded them of their temples, their homeland, and of their wives and children. [6]. But they, all crying aloud and striking their spears against their shields, declared that so long as they had weapons in their hands they would easily find homelands; and lifting their garments and pointing to their genitals they said that so long as they had those they would never be in want either of wives or of children. [7]. After such a display of high courage and of utter disdain for what among other men is regarded as of the greatest

consequence, they seized the best part of Ethiopia, and after apportioning much land among themselves they made their home there.[113]

Diodorus 1.67.1 clearly derives from Herodotus 2.154, whereas the episode of the Egyptians defecting to Ethiopia (1.67.3–7), with Psamtik in pursuit, is connected with the account in Herodotus 2.30, although Daphnae is not specifically mentioned here. The *Stratopeda* are said to be a little upstream from Pelusium. Nevertheless, the fact that Diodorus' account seems to combine the two different passages from Herodotus in no way implies that Daphnae and the *Stratopeda* were identical or located at the same place.[114]

As Daphnae and the *Stratopeda* are unlikely to have been the same, there is no reason to continue believing that the enclosure that Petrie uncovered was a military camp occupied by Greek mercenaries. Freed from this preconception, we shall see below that a fresh look at the archaeological data actually lends little support to the hypothesis of military facilities; instead, the excavated structures reveal themselves as typical elements of classical Egyptian Late Period settlements. This hypothesis is supported by other, non-classical sources.

Tell Dafana in other sources

If one accepts the identification of Tell Dafana and Daphnae with Tahpanhes (discussed above, pp. 2–4), the main information given by the biblical and exegetic texts[115] about the locality, apart from the presence of Judean refugees in the town during the reign of Apries (after 586 BC), is that the town must have been of some importance. First, it is mentioned alongside other key places such as Migdol, Memphis (Noph), Thebes and the land of Pathros (Upper Egypt), where Judeans also supposedly settled (Jeremiah, 2.16, 44.1, 46.14). Second, it is said to possess a 'house/palace of Pharaoh', with a 'brick-paved courtyard' at the entrance (Jeremiah, 43.9). Petrie wanted to identify this with the complex of casemate buildings he discovered, with a terrace in front – he completely turned over this area in the hope of finding the 'stones' that the Eternal had ordered Jeremiah to bury there openly under the eyes of his compatriots, in order to mark the place where, according to Jeremiah's prophecy, Nebukadnezzar's throne and his royal tent would be installed at the time of his victory on Egypt. These biblical sources suggest at least an important royal Egyptian foundation at Tahpanhes, but they neither mention the presence of Greeks in the locality, nor the existence of military contingents.

A strong Egyptian royal presence also shows through in much later literary documents. According to the Coptic Cambyses Romance,[116] Taphnas was a royal residence of Apries, a cult-place of Amun and the main place where the Egyptian resistance against the invader was being organized. For John of Nikiu,[117] if one accepts the identification of *Ṭānbās* with Daphnae, King Apries was residing in the locality, and it is here that 'Cambyses' (Nebukadnezzar) captured and killed him. Demotic literary texts that mention an Egyptian toponym which one may link with Daphnae[118] further confirm the close connections the Saite Pharaohs had with the place: the ostracon from

Karnak refers to an expedition lead by a King Psamtik (probably Psamtik I) from here towards Syria; according to Pap. Berlin 13588, Psamtik I died and was embalmed in the neighbourhood; in the *Instructions of Chaschechonqi* (Pap. London BM EA 10508), the narrator recounts that he was imprisoned there and tells of how he received his daily pittance from the nearby royal palace.

The archaeology of the site: topography and architecture

The great enclosure wall

The walled enclosure occupying the central part of the site, in which Petrie excavated the complex of casemate buildings and cleared an area of what may have been a quarter of coppersmiths and ironsmiths workshops, occupied a large area, almost perfectly rectangular, of 605–10m north–south x 350–5m east–west (**Pls 3, 10**, area A).[119] The surrounding wall was around 15m thick[120] near its base – bringing the total size of the precinct, wall included, to a maximum of 640 x 385m – and almost completely levelled to the ground (**Fig. 8**). Petrie was able to trace its outlines because its eroded surface was clear of sherds. He did not clear it entirely, but excavated the north-east and south-west corners in a vain search for foundation deposits. Other pits in the area of the north-west corner proved insufficient to fix its exact position – Petrie argued that it was impossible to distinguish the wall from the surrounding mud, but the wall might also have been swept away below its foundations in this area – and it was only reconstructed from the orientation of the north and west sections of the wall. According to the results of the Egyptian excavations of 2009 (see Chapter 8), the foundations in the southern part of the wall are preserved only to a few courses of bricks. The size of the mud bricks with which the wall was built remains uncertain, as does the type of brickwork and the bond.[121] The recent satellite images (**Pl. 8**) seem to indicate in some parts a construction with shallow recesses in plan view, a feature which has been confirmed by the recent Egyptian excavations only for the outer face of the wall.

In the middle of the southern section of the wall, Petrie excavated the foundations of a limestone gateway, of which only three heaps of chips remained (**Fig. 9**).[122] This gateway proved to be the main axial entrance to the enclosure, giving access from the south (and from the main caravan desert road 650m further to the south) to a very large building, probably the main construction inside the precinct. Petrie's plan also indicates a 15–20m gap in the northern wall of the enclosure, approximately in the axis of the road leading southwards to the complex of casemate buildings.[123] Therefore, it is possible that there was also a northern gate there. The large Saite quartzite stela found by Petrie 100m to the west of this gap (see below, **Figs 22–3**)[124] outside the enclosure might originally have stood in front of this entrance, if not elsewhere in the enclosure.

As most of the material found inside as well as outside the walls seems to date from the Saite Period, one can only assume that the enclosure was very likely built during this period, possibly as early as sometime during the reign of Psamtik I, as the foundation deposits of the main casemate building would seem to indicate. Nevertheless, one must admit that there is no actual evidence for a precise dating of the enclosure wall. Another thick east–west wall revealed by the recent Egytian excavations to the south-west of the *Kasr* might correspond to another enclosure. Whether this massive structure was a partition wall inside the main enclosure or an earlier phase of development will need to be clarified in the future. If the walls are from different periods, it is possible that the main enclosure may have been a later enlargement of an original, smaller complex, including the casemate building of Psamtik I.

In size, shape, extent and technique of construction, the wall clearly differs from Egyptian military fortresses, such as those of the Middle and New Kingdoms in Nubia,[125] as well as the few known Late Period examples, such as the Saite fort of Dorginarti in Nubia,[126] the successive Persian fortresses of Tell el-Herr in North Sinai[127] or even the successive Saite enclosures of Tell Kedwa,[128] between Tell el-Herr and Pelusium (**Pl. 4**). The mud brick enclosures of these fortifications are much smaller in extent[129] and show clear military features such as strong bastions or towers on the outer edge, features which do not appear at Tell Dafana. On the contrary, the Dafana enclosure compares better with the monumental walls surrounding sacred areas of classical Egyptian temples in the Nile Delta and the Nile Valley, particularly from the Late Period. With a surface area of around 22ha or so (24ha with the wall included), it would fit into the range of the largest of these monuments.[130] Among numerous examples, the two Late Period enclosures of Memphis – the southern one around the temple of Ptah (Middle Birka) and the northern one (Kom Tuman) with the 'palace' of Apries in the north-western corner – would be the closest parallels.[131] Late Period temple enclosure walls were constructed, from the 26th dynasty onwards, with a wavy masonry and slightly recessed sections at regular intervals on both sides – both architectural features being interlocked.[132] From the results of the recent Egyptian excavations at Tell Dafana, this does not seem to be exactly paralleled by the outer enclosure wall.[133] At any rate, given its large extent and lack of bastions, the enclosure wall of Tell Dafana would have been indefensible from a military point of view.

Figure 8 The eroded enclosure wall in 1998 (photo: F. Leclère)

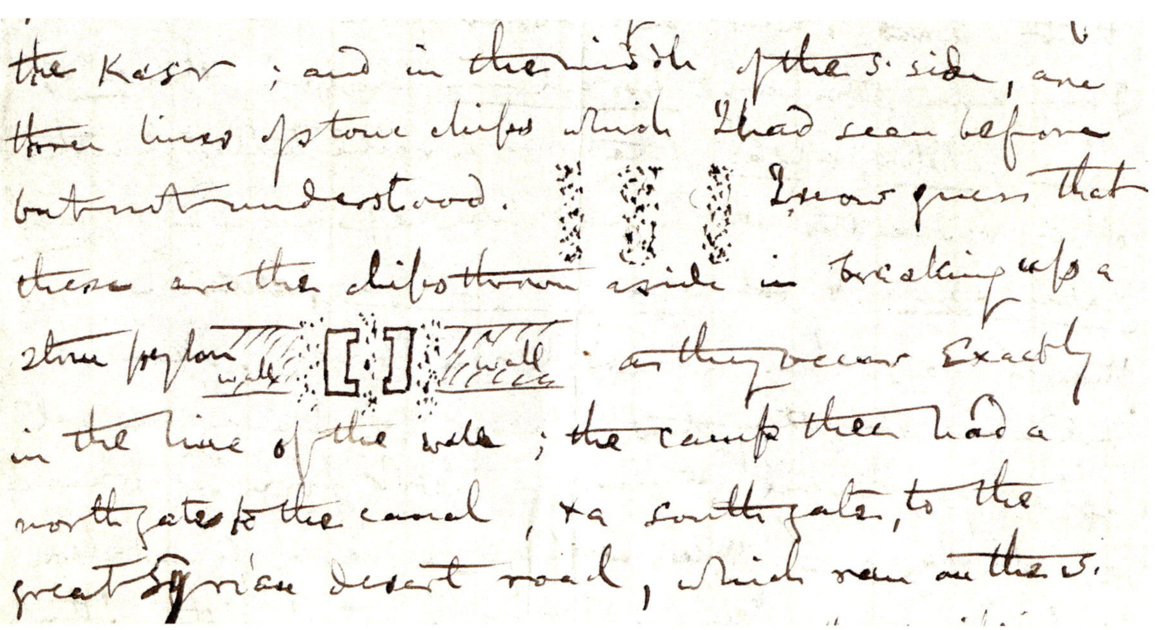

Figure 9 Sketch and description of the south gate in the enclosure, page 163 from Petrie's *Journal 1885–6* (© Griffith Institute, University of Oxford)

The casemate buildings and their annexes (Pls 5, 6, and area B on Pl. 10)

The complex of buildings that Petrie excavated to the east of the centre of the enclosure, which he termed the *Kasr*, was for the most part composed of two mudbrick square constructions, a smaller one (designated 'B' by Petrie) placed just north of the north-east corner of a larger one ('A').

Casemate Building A[134]

The larger casemate building measures slightly over 43m on each side and was preserved to a height of over 8m above the lowest level of the foundations.[135] The south-eastern corner was preserved to a higher level and the preserved rounded top generally sloped (3 to 4%) towards the north-west.[136] The size of the bricks used in the construction varies from 41.1 x 20 x 10.7cm to 41.6 x 20.5 x 12.4cm, with some longer bricks (up to 44.2cm) in the central part.[137]

As usual for such buildings, the structure was composed of a thick outer wall and an internal net of smaller walls dividing up the space into small square or rectangular cells, with no communication between them. The outer wall was between 4.25 and 4.5m thick,[138] that is, about twice the thickness of most of the internal partition walls (2–2.5m),[139] with foundations at a deeper level, at least 1.2m, while the partition walls seem to have been built directly on the sandy ground. Although Petrie does not explicitly mention it, the shallow concavity of the slightly battered outer faces of the building, evident from the plan, suggests that the structure was built with concave courses of bricks, probably reinforced with wooden beams.[143] This conclusion is supported by the evidence of the sections of the foundation deposits,[140] photographs preserved in the Egypt Exploration Society (EES) archives (**Figs 10–12**)[141] and a sketch-plan in Petrie's Notebook (**Fig. 13**).[142] The masonry was carefully done and the outer face covered by two or three coats of plaster (**Fig. 11**).[144]

The remaining part of the construction corresponded only to the cellular foundation of a high platform, of which the upper floor was not preserved. This floor was certainly not much higher than the upper preserved level of the structure: Petrie observed that some of the foundation cells must have been roofed by domes or vaults, of which part of the springing was still visible in the corners;[145] the floor level must have been set just above the top of this covering.[146]

Apart from two large rectangular north–south spaces of 9.5 x 5m lined up in the central part of the building – 21m long with the partition wall between both spaces – the other cells, square or rectangular in plan, were of much smaller size, most of them with a side width of 2 to 3.5m and a length that rarely reached 4 or 5m. In the south-eastern quarter, some cells were even smaller (1.5 to 2m square), but one might wonder if they were not initially larger and if their small size was not due to a brick fill too difficult to distinguish from the partition walls, or to their domed covering, better preserved in this higher part of the ruins. Some of the cells were filled with brick rubble[147] or with brickwork, some others with sand, such as the southern large central room. According to Petrie, the sand filling in this large space might have served as a foundation for a stone structure built above the floor of the platform.[148] Large quantities of limestone chips, found in the structures abutted to the southern face of Building A (Findspot 12, see below), might have come from the destruction of this upper stone room, or from other stone parts of the superstructure.[149] However, the large fallen blocks found at the bottom of the northern large central room, or the numerous limestone chips found in some cells nearby[150] might also have belonged to a dismantled building of an earlier phase, of which Petrie detected several mud brick walls at the bottom of the cells (see below).

The similar and better preserved example of a casemate building excavated by Petrie at Naukratis in the 'Great Temenos'[151] shows that the plan of the rooms above the platform corresponded to the plan of the cells in the foundations. At Tell Dafana, the cells appear less regularly and symmetrically distributed than those in the building of

Figure 10 Casemate Building A after excavation (EES, Lucy Gura archive)

Naukratis – or in the further close parallel excavated more recently at Tell el-Balamun (**Fig. 14**)[152] – although some features, such as the long central 'gallery', are present in several other casemate buildings.[153] At Tell Dafana, this central 'gallery' is composed of two large consecutive cells – and possibly a smaller one to the south, unless this latter feature was in fact a southern passage from west to east, behind the 'gallery', along the southern side of the building – but does not extend across the entire length of the building from south to north, occupying only the southern two-thirds of it. If one accepts Petrie's hypothesis of a stone structure in the southern part, this structure could have been a sort of chapel, with a forecourt in front. Although there is no actual evidence for the way the building was roofed, it is possible that the whole or part of the central 'gallery' was open air. This would have helped to bring light into the roofed rooms flanking it.

To the north of this main central feature, a series of 14 roughly square cells separated by thinner walls than in the rest of the construction and distributed in two parallel east–west rows along the northern side of the building – actually occupying just the eastern two-thirds of this side – might be interpreted as the foundations of another large 'gallery', 24m long and at least 6.5m wide, possibly with a roof supported by a range of six columns resting on the intersections of the partition walls in the foundations.[154] The

Figure 11 Plaster face of Building A (EES, Lucy Gura archive)

Figure 12 Pan-bedded bricks in Building A (EES, Lucy Gura archive)

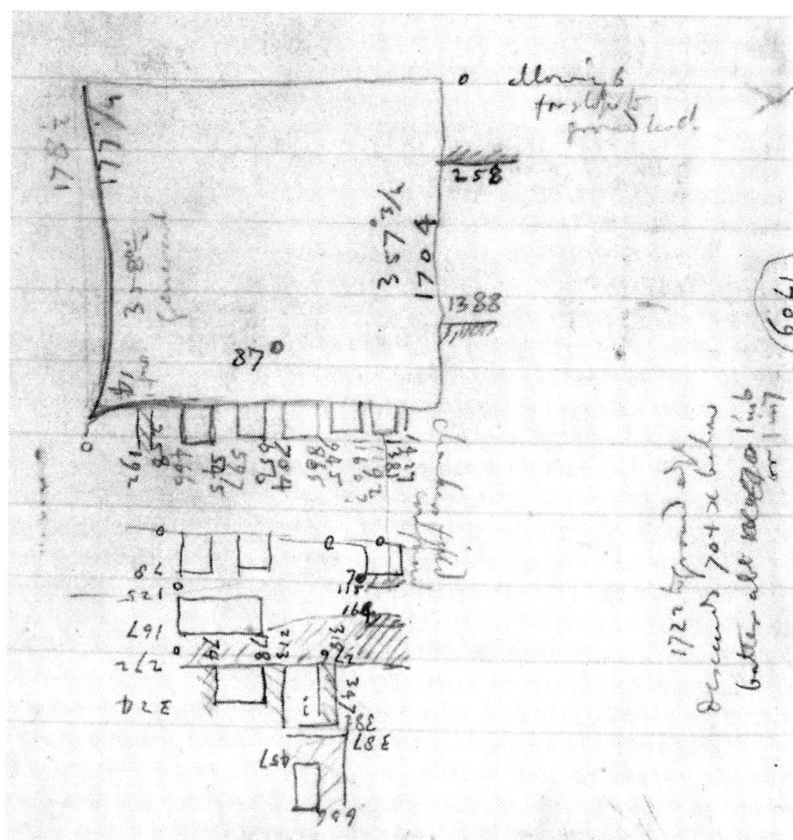

Figure 13 Sketch plan of Casemate Building A in Petrie's Notebook 74.f, 24 (courtesy of the Petrie Museum of Egyptian Archaeology, UCL)

cells of the northern row were slightly smaller than those of the southern row, while the northern perimeter wall of the building was thicker in this area, as if it had been widened, at least in the foundations, for an unknown reason. If the outer wall had the same size as in the rest of the perimeter above the platform, then this gallery would have been 1m wider, and the supposed colonnade would have been exactly in the middle.

To the west of this possible columned 'gallery', another group of at least five (or perhaps six) squarish cells organized in two north–south rows occupies the north-western corner of the building. This particular group might have something to do with the main entrance to the building – a space with two columns, or a chicane-shaped corridor (see further below), or possibly a stairwell leading to the roof terrace or an upper floor.

The organization of the rest of the building, east and west of the central gallery, to the south, is more difficult to reconstruct. Comparison with the similar buildings of Naukratis and Tell el-Balamun invites a reconstruction of narrow corridors giving access to small rooms, but does not permit an understanding of their precise dispositions. The western and eastern sides seem to be asymmetrical: the west side is occupied by three long parallel series of cells orientated north–south, the two eastern ones being identical to each other but different from the western one; the east side is even less clear, all the more so since some of the cells in this area were filled with brick, and some large square cells lay next to very small ones. They may have been distributed in two groups, to the north and south of an east–west narrow corridor, accessible from the central 'gallery'. Nevertheless, one must admit that our overall understanding of these areas remains limited.

The dating of the construction is well assured by the inscribed foundation deposits of Psamtik I under the four corners,[155] although it is unfortunately impossible to determine precisely when these were placed during the long reign of the king (664–610 BC). The earliest Archaic Greek sherds found in the area seem to indicate a date of the end of the 7th or early 6th century BC for the beginning of occupation.[156]

Earlier constructions below Casemate Building A

At the bottom of several cells that Petrie completely emptied, particularly in the north-western part of the building, he observed segments of mudbrick walls belonging no doubt to an earlier phase of construction or occupation, with the same orientation as the later building,[157] and built with bricks of similar size (42.1 x 20.8 x 10.9cm).[158] Apart from a few lines in the cells of Building A on Petrie's plan of the *Kasr*, these remains were insufficient to be planned.[159] At the bottom of the southern central cell, a room of 3.5 x 3.65m was founded at a deeper level than the walls of the cell, approximately at the level of the outer wall of the casemate building. The eastern wall of the cell partly covered the eastern wall of the lower earlier room.[160] It is unfortunately impossible to determine if all these older walls belonged to an earlier casemate building, to an initial construction phase of Casemate Building A, or to several structures of other types. The pottery found at this level, according to Petrie, was also from the 26th dynasty, although one sherd might date from the Ramesside Period.[161]

Under the northern part of the vast mudbrick terrace to the north of Building A (see below), Petrie also found the south-western corner of an earlier structure about 5m square, built of fired bricks (size: 31.7 x 15.7 x 8.1cm), levelled

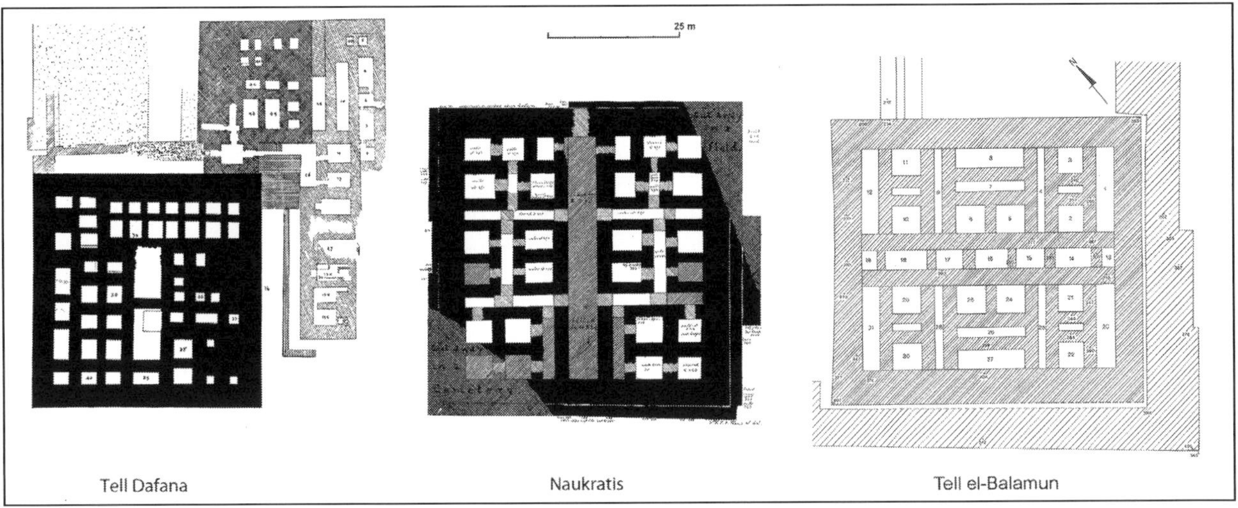

Figure 14 Plans of the Casemate buildings of Tell Dafana, Naukratis and Tell el-Balamun

to two or three courses, with a slightly different orientation from the other constructions.[162] On the basis of the similar size of the red bricks used in 'Ramesside' tombs at the neighbouring site of Tell Nebesha, he suggested that this structure might also have been of Ramesside date. Although the evidence of comparing brick sizes on different sites cannot be valid in itself, this could explain the presence of a New Kingdom sherd in the foundations of Building A. Nevertheless, the evidence is too slim to suppose an extensive occupation in the area before the Saite Period. If this had been the case, sherds of earlier periods might have been found more frequently in later levels.

Casemate Building B

According to Petrie, the smaller casemate building to the north-east of the main Building A was constructed in a subsequent phase.[163] It measured approximately 21.75m east–west and 22.75m north–south.[164] Mud bricks used in the construction vary in size from 40.9 x 20.3 x 12.7cm to 43.7 x 22 x 12.9cm.[165] Building B was linked to Building A by an extension block of masonry, 10m east–west and 5.75m north–south, connecting the western part of the southern face of B and the eastern end of the northern face of A. This block was actually a mid-level vestibule, giving access to Building B at its south-western corner (see below).

As for the main building, the outer wall was thicker (2.5m at the east to 3m at the north) than the internal partition walls (1–2.25m). It is less clear, though probable, that the outer wall's foundations were at a deeper level than those of the internal partition walls. From the description of the eastern face ('room' 22) and possibly from a photograph in the EES archives (**Fig. 15**),[166] it seems clear that the faces of the outer wall were battered and that its masonry was made of slightly concave courses of mud bricks, reinforced at several levels with a series of wooden beams at regular intervals.[167]

The preserved height from the foundation level up to highest spot of the mound, on the eastern side, seems to reach 6.25m. The preserved top surface was more irregular, as shown in the east–west section on Petrie's plate xliv, and sloped down to the north-west. The upper level of the platform was not preserved, and the plan of the

superstructure is difficult to understand from the dozen cells that Petrie recognized in the foundations. These cells are restricted to the eastern two-thirds of the building, and were possibly distributed in two groups north and south of a narrow east–west corridor. Apart from two large cells in the middle of the southern part (2.75–3m x 5m), most were of small size (1.25 to 2.75m square). Some were still partly filled with sand.[168]

The western third of the building presents different features: most of the northern part of this side seems to be plain masonry, but it is also possible that there were cells filled with bricks. The south-west corner shows a group of small rooms and corridors with a floor-level preserved at a mid level, and connected, at the south, with the vestibule linking Buildings A and B. This ensemble formed the entrance to the building, certainly giving access a little further to the north to an internal ramp or staircase leading to the upper level of the platform, 5 or 6m above, according to Petrie. This staircase was not preserved because of the denudation of the surface below the floor level.

The vestibule itself[169] was a rectangular room 4.5 x 3.7m in size, open to the east and west with corridors of approximately 3m length and 1.5m width, with door-jambs in some places. The western end of the western corridor was equipped with a threshold made of two superimposed

Figure 15 Room 22 from the south (EES, Lucy Gura archive)

limestone blocks, the lower one sculpted with a protruding gutter, probably the only remains of an entrance built entirely of stone.

On the northern side of the vestibule was the entrance to Building B[170]: a corridor, 2.5m long and slightly more than 1.5m wide, with door-jambs at both ends, giving access to a small rectangular space, opening to the west and to the north onto two perpendicular corridors. Equipped with door-jambs at the entrance, the western corridor was only 1m wide and around 5m long, ending close to the western face of the building.[171] Slightly wider (1.5m), the northern corridor was preserved to a length of only 4m, the denuded surface of the ruins sloping down under the floor-level further to the north. According to Petrie, the ramp or staircase giving access to the upper platform was certainly to the north of this corridor. If there was a spiral staircase, the western corridor might have been a kind of storage space under the upper flight of steps. The walls and floor of the vestibule and the corridors were covered with a coat of white plaster (**Fig. 16**).[172] According to Petrie, the vestibule was decorated with a limestone cornice and moulding.[173] He also found fragments of a cavetto cornice on the west side of Building B, suggesting that they came from decoration running around the top of the edifice,[174] but they might alternatively have come from the top of the vestibule entrance.

The open-air northern terrace and access to the platforms
Both buildings were accessible from a large terrace (that Petrie called a 'mastaba') to the north of Building A and to the west of Building B.[175] Measuring 42.5m long from north to south and up to 33m wide from west to east, the terrace was composed of brickwork 0.5 to 1m thick laid directly on top of the sandy plain. Its shape was irregular, with some straight edges, unaligned, in different places. Buried in the debris, the southern part was well preserved whereas the northern part was much eroded. The edges were set 0.3m deeper into the ground and part of the northern edge was apparently bordered by a kind of retaining wall, founded 0.9m deeper.[176] On the east side, 3m to the west of Building B, the terrace was interrupted by a straight gap running north–south, 6.5m wide at its southern end. Although Petrie apparently did not recognize it (he assumed the access route to the vestibule to have been the ledge along Building B), one can suggest that this gap originally contained a limestone pavement, forming a road running straight from the north, which was looted later. Some blocks that Petrie mentions as 'laying loose on the terrace', might have come from this pavement.[177] Lines of chips indicated the presence of this roadway further to the north, up to the break in the northern segment of the enclosure wall.[178]

To the south of the terrace, at a distance of 2.5 to 3.75m along the northern face of Building A, several mudbrick

Figure 16 Petrie's photograph of the corridors of Building B (EES, Lucy Gura archive)

structures are more difficult to interpret. As for the walls to the west, Petrie considered them as the corner of a structure covered by an awning – with two recesses that Petrie interpreted as places for guards' sentry-boxes, while, to the east, broader masonry – 3.5m thick and about 3m high from its foundations on the sand – would have been an east–west causeway with a parapet on both sides, leading to the entrance of the vestibule between Buildings A and B, 2m above the terrace.[179] The gap between these structures and Building A would have functioned as a sort of ditch. As, according to Petrie, Building B was built during a later phase, he supposed that Building A was originally accessible through removable flights of wooden stairs spanning this ditch.[180]

This interpretation may, however, have to be revised, due to the following observations:

1. The broader wall to the east (Petrie's 'causeway', dotted on his plan) is exactly at the southern end of the reconstructed stone roadway. Its length of 14m exceeds the width of the roadway equally on both sides, and must be seen in connection with it.

2. The thinner walls (1.25–2m) to the west form a right-angle. The northern face of the southern wall has two narrow and shallow recesses to the west and a thicker part in the middle. Its orientation is not exactly parallel to the northern face of Building A, but slightly closer at its western end.

3. A thick, rectangular block of masonry (4.25 x 3.5m) was joined to the corner of these walls and the western end of the northern face of Building A. The western end of the 'ditch', i.e. the eastern face of this block, was aligned with the western side of the group of cells of the north-western corner of Building A that may be interpreted as an upper vestibule entrance.

4. Although the vestibule extension of Building B is clearly abutted onto Building A and must certainly have been built after it, there is no tangible evidence regarding the timespan between the two phases of construction. The construction of Building B might have followed immediately after that of Building A as part of the same project.

5. As most of the limestone parts of the buildings and the roadway seem to have been removed later by looting, much more stone may originally have been used in the construction, particularly in the masonry of the staircases.

These observations allow us to propose a new hypothesis for the manner in which both buildings would have been accessed in ancient times (**Fig. 17**)[181] through a monumental limestone plain staircase, with a first flight of stairs at the southern end of the paved roadway leading to an intermediate landing at the level of the vestibule between Buildings A and B. Another flight of steps would have led from the western end of this landing, along the northern face of Building A leading to its north-west corner, where an upper vestibule has been suggested. According to this hypothesis, the square block of masonry at the western end

of Building A would have been the abutment of this second flight of stairs, and the south wall of the terrace its spandrel; the fact that this wall was not parallel to the casemate building is explained by the batter of the outer faces of the casemate. In this arrangement, the stairs would have had a consistent width from bottom to top. The function of the double recess on the spandrel remains unexplained. It recalls the niche found in the spandrel of the ramp of much earlier mudbrick casemate constructions, such as the 18th dynasty palace G in Tell el-Dab'a/'Ezbet Helmi (**Fig. 18**).[182] A corner entrance to the casemate building is not as surprising as it might at first appear: other examples of the same period exist, such as the casemate building of Tell el-Balamun, with a long double wall, interpreted as the foundation of a ramp leading to an entrance in the corner of the building; for the similar edifice in Naukratis, Petrie supposed an axial access to the central gallery, but one could also imagine a corner entrance, possibly with a ramp along the face of one of the outer walls.[183]

A further hypothesis as regards to access to the upper platforms can be proposed: a thick and high block of mudbrick masonry, 8 x 10m, was also built to the east of Building A's north-east corner, turning around this corner to join the southern part of the vestibule between Buildings A and B. Built with bricks measuring 40.9 x 20.3 x 10.6cm,[184] it was still preserved to a height of 6m from its foundations.[185] To the south of this block was a narrow (1m thick) L-shaped wall running to the south, parallel to the eastern face of Building A, at a distance of 4m from it, 27.5m long before turning to the east around the south-east corner of Annexe C for at least 6.5m.[186] This wall was built with bricks of 33.5 x 17.2cm.[187] Petrie attributed these additions to two successive subsequent phases of construction (Periods E and F respectively), later than the 'Period C' annexes.[188] The combination of these structures recalls the side access ramps of much earlier buildings, such as the palaces on casemate platform foundations built during the 18th dynasty (**Fig. 18**).[189] If this suggestion is correct, Building A would also have been accessible via a ramp along its eastern side (Findspot 16), leading to an upper gateway near the north-east corner, opening into the long east–west 'gallery' where a

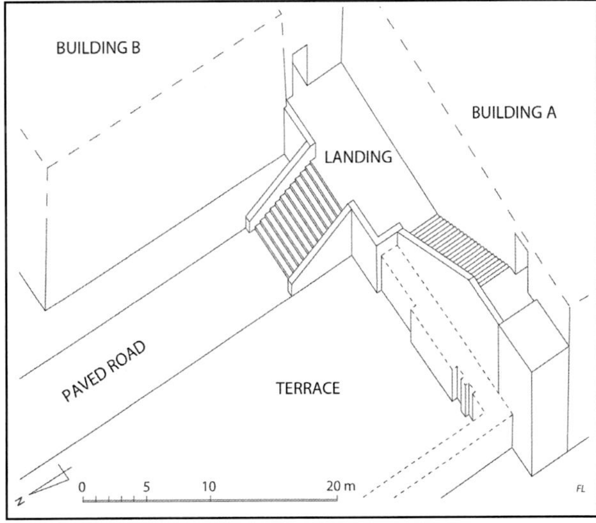

Figure 17 Suggested reconstruction of access to the casemate buildings from the north (drawing: F. Leclère)

central colonnade has been suggested. These assumptions, of course, are just working hypotheses that would need to be confirmed by new fieldwork.

The Eastern Annexes ('Period C')

To the east of Buildings A and B, Petrie excavated a long series of rooms running north–south, probably belonging to different structures and possibly varying construction phases,[190] even if Petrie grouped them all in his 'Period C'. They can possibly be interpreted as annexes to the casemate buildings.[191] It is difficult to describe and understand them in detail, as their edges are not always clearly defined and they are not all on similar alignments. Some rooms or groups of rooms had their access from the outside preserved at ground level; others seem isolated, and might have been, as Petrie suggested, accessible from an upper level. The whole ensemble was 59m long north–south with a maximum width of 16.5m. Most of the main walls were 2–2.5m thick. The size of the bricks used in the masonry ranges from 40.6 x 19.8 to 41.9 x 20.3cm.[192] Three possible main groups of rooms can be identified:

1. A northern cluster, which was 11.5m wide and at least 28m long (eastern face), with an unclear southern edge. Two small square cells (5 and 45) occupied the northern end, and a long narrow room or cell (10) the western side (12.75 x 2.5m). The eastern side contained a series of four rooms (4, 2, 3, 9), alternately rectangular and square – in fact a long narrow space of 19 x 3m subdivided by three smaller walls with doorways on one side or the other. The wall south of Room 10 extended further to the west in order to abut against the south-east corner of Building B. The eastern series of rooms was accessible from outside by a doorway at ground level to the east of Room 2, with a limestone threshold still *in situ*.[193] The preserved floors were approximately at the same level as the surface of the large terrace to the west and north of the casemate buildings. Both northern cells 5 and 45 and the western Room 10 were apparently isolated and must have been accessible from above. Part of a pavement was found in cell 45, 20cm above the floor in Room 4, while a mortared floor in Room 10 was nearly 13cm higher.[194] According to Petrie, the 2m wide space left between the annexe and Building B was later turned into an isolated 'room' (22)[195] by the addition of a 10.5m long 'blocking' in the northern part (Petrie's 'Period D').[196] Petrie suggested that the 10m long room thus defined was covered by a light sloping roof made of wood and mud. A clay floor was preserved at the bottom. On a photograph that must have been taken in this area (see **Fig. 15**),[197] the section visible at the back of the image indicates that the fill in the northern part was probably more complicated than a simple plain 'blocking'. In this area a limestone block was found, finely decorated with a *kheker*-frieze carved in low relief and painted red and blue (**Fig. 19**),[198] but there is no evidence, contrary to Petrie's

Figure 18 Comparison of Tell Dafana Building A with the palace foundations of Tell el-Dab'a with outer staircases (after Bietak 2010, 58–9, figs 29–30, 32)

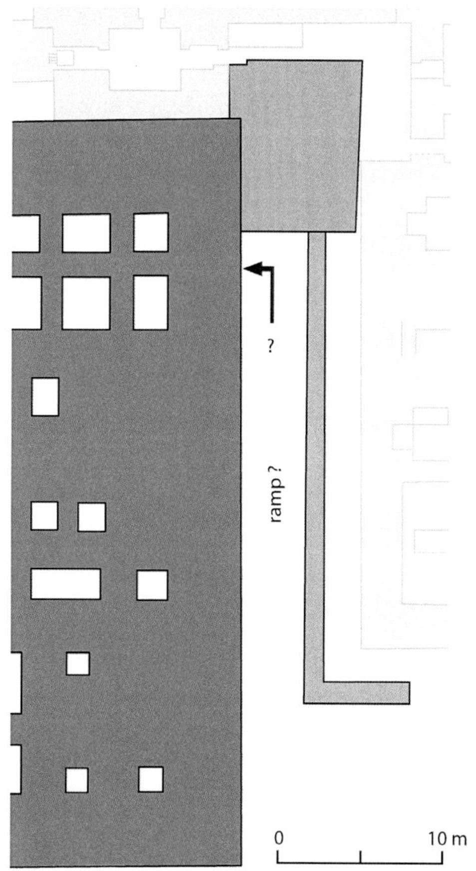

Tell Dafana, Eastern side of Casemate Building A

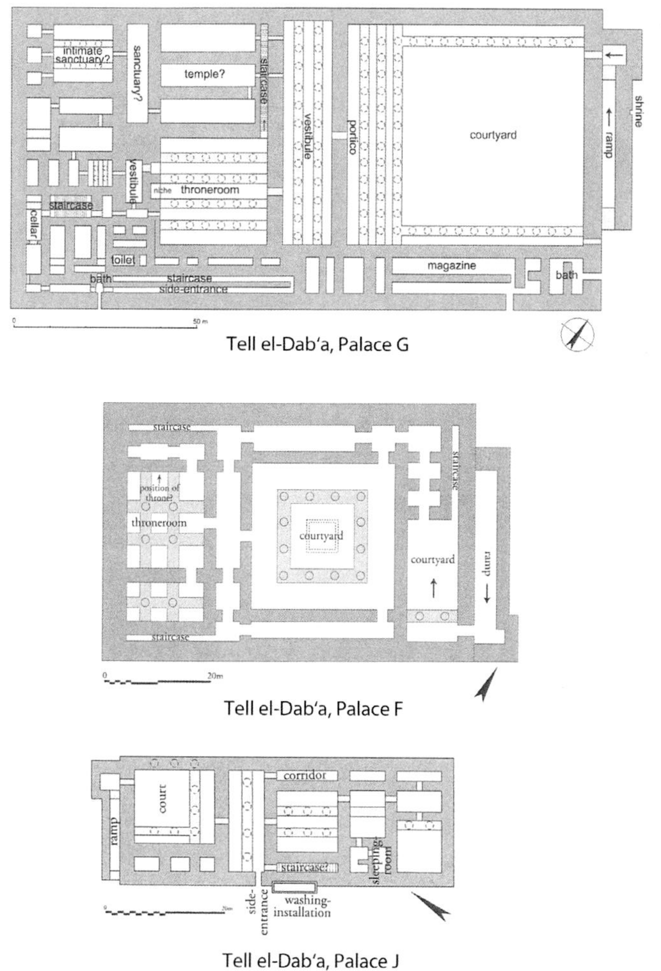

suggestion, that this block belonged to the decoration of this particular room. It might have come from the destruction of the superstructures above the platforms. The median wall between Room 10 and the eastern series of rooms might have extended further to the south for up to a dozen metres, but the plan seems to indicate in fact that, from Room 9 onwards, the southern continuation of the eastern face of this wall was not precisely aligned with the northern part, but had a slightly different orientation. This extension might be better interpreted as the eastern wall of the following group of rooms, in the central part of the annexe.

2. To this second group belonged at least the rectangular rooms 11 and 17 (4 x 3–3.5m),[199] both accessible by a non-axial doorway on the western side from a probable open-air area numbered 26, which the later construction of the massive 'Period E' block of masonry at the north-eastern corner of Building A (possibly the abutment of a ramp to the east of Building A, see above) turned into an L-shaped corridor. The western end of this corridor was narrowed again by another small rectangular addition of brickwork against the southern face of Building B and the northern part of the vestibule between A and B, adapting the passage to the width of the eastern doorway of this vestibule. Although Petrie attributed this addition to 'Period F', possibly on the basis of relative stratigraphy, it was built with bricks of a size (40.9 x 19.8 x 10.4cm)[200] similar to that of examples used the brickwork of 'Period E' on the other side of the corridor.

The reason why these architectural arrangements were made remains unknown. From the plan alone, one might conclude that rooms 11 and 17 were accessible directly from the vestibule, but the levels given by Petrie show that their floors were initially more than 2m lower than that of the vestibule.[201] Later, these rooms were partly filled in order to raise the floors, a doorsill was set at the entrance to Room 11 and the walls were re-coated.[202] This doorsill was 1.2m above the initial floor,[203] but still almost 1m below the vestibule's floor and 0.6m below the floor of the corridor between the vestibule and the rooms.[204] Though the communication between the different parts of the annexes remains unclear, it is interesting to note that the initial floor of Room 11 (and probably Room 17) was approximately at the same level as the floor in Room 10, and the later floor 1.5m higher than the floors of rooms 2, 3, 4 and 9. To the south of Room 17, a third room of similar size (unnumbered on Petrie's plan) might have belonged to the same group, at least to the eastern part of it – the western part possibly belonged to the third group of rooms, to the south.[205] This central part was then 8.5m wide and might have been up to 17.5m long.

3. The third group of rooms of the annexe, to the south, is rather more difficult to interpret. Judging from its better preserved western and southern sides, the group seems to have occupied a space about 28m long north–south by 10.5m wide, and was aligned more to the west than the previous group of rooms. The eastern face is only preserved to 15m from the south-eastern corner, with another possible short segment preserved a few metres further to the north. Apparently, the north-eastern corner was not preserved and

Figure 19 Limestone block with a *kheker*-frieze from Room 22, Museum of Fine Arts, Boston, MFA 87.714 (courtesy Museum of Fine Arts)

the connection with the previous series of rooms is unclear. It is possible that both groups belong to different phases partly superimposed on each other. Outer walls were built with a slight batter and covered with a coat of white plaster.[206] A small oval pit dug in the sand (0.1m wide at most, and 0.3m deep) under the south-western corner certainly corresponded to a foundation deposit, with burnt charcoal and bones of a bird.[207]

Three rooms are distinguishable in the southern part (19A, B, C) and another space immediately to the north (27) might have been an additional room, though its outlines are uncertain. Another area between 27 and the unnumbered room south of 17 is also unclear and too narrow to correspond to a room. As for the unnumbered room, its western part was aligned with the western edge of the rooms of the southern group and there was an axial niche in the western wall, similar to the one in Room 19A. No doorway has been recognized for rooms 19A, B and C and, as Petrie suggested, they were probably cellars accessible from an upper level.[208] The narrower and unclear area 27, to the north, might have been used for access to the upper level. Each of the rooms 19A, B and C had a specific arrangement: 19A was 6 x 3m in size and had an axial recess in the western wall, a sort of rectangular bench in the north-west corner[209] and a partitioned space in the south-east corner, with a rectangular niche in its south-east angle. The space left in the north-east corner might have been used for a wooden staircase or ladder. Petrie mentions a sink-jar somewhere in the room, partly buried in the floor and the underlying sand, possibly to be identified with the 'dry well' (32) mentioned in Petrie's Notebook and Journal, and containing a quantity of sherds.[210] Rooms 19B and 19C were slightly smaller (4.5 x 2.75–3m) and connected by a doorway at the western end of the partition wall separating them. Room 19B had a deep recess in the north-eastern corner, possibly the place of another wooden staircase. To the east of a recess near the south-eastern corner of 19C another sink-jar was built into the masonry, with a small recess north and south of it.[211] This jar was full of pottery, fish bones and organic material. As for that in Room 19A and others across the site, these 'dry wells' filled with sherds,[212] generally placed into or near walls, were certainly part of a drainage system for rain and waste water, possibly latrines. The one in 19C might have been connected to an installation at the level of the upper floor.

Unfortunately, no information was given about the floor levels in this part of the annexe. Three additional short segments of walls are noted on Petrie's plan to the east of 'room' 27, up to 9m from the eastern façade of the annexe, but their interpretation is impossible.

'Period G' constructions

Many other structures around the casemate buildings and their annexes are grouped by Petrie under his 'Period G', though they may not all be from the same period and their relation to the structures of the other phases is, as Petrie says, 'uncertain; but of Psamtik I, mostly'. Petrie also ascribed to this phase the walls between the northern terrace and the northern façade of Building A, which we have proposed to link with a possible staircase along this façade. Apart from these walls, four main groups of structures can be identified:

1. Almost nothing can be said about the rectangular Room 6 immediately to the north of Annexe C, apart from noting its dimensions: 2.5 x 3m. No finds were recorded from it.[213]

2. A second series of wall segments are found grouped to the north-west of Building A, including a long thin north–south wall (1.25m wide, preserved for a distance of more than 25m, but only to a height of a few centimetres) with a slightly oblique orientation.[214] To this group belong several other walls, of which only one face was detected, surrounding spaces of different shapes and sizes, but which are not interpretable. These structures were built directly on the sandy surface of the ground. Among the spaces recognized, Petrie particularly noted the chamber 8 (7.5 x 3m orientated north–south), where he found many fragments of jar sealings stamped with the nomen of King Psamtik I[215] and a number of small pottery domed lids.[216] The walls around this space were built of bricks measuring 36 x 17.7 x 8.9cm. Bricks in the walls between Room 8 and Building A were slightly larger (38.6 x 18.5 x 9.4cm).[217] Immediately beside the north-west corner of Building A was a curious rectangular room with small square recesses in the corners. To the north-east of this room was a narrow L-shaped space (numbered 1) where Petrie found, directly on the sand, a Greek painted sherd[218] and a block of iron measuring 10 x 10 x 2.5cm.[219]

3. Several other structures were abutted to the southern face of Building A and linked to a thicker wall (2.75m) running parallel to it, at a distance of 4.25m, for at least 25m. These constructions, built with bricks measuring 41.6 x 20.5 x 11.4cm,[220] were preserved to a great height, particularly in the eastern part, where they reached the top surface of Building A. They possessed cells or rooms of various sizes, and corridors, but their interpretation remains difficult. They were filled with quantities of limestone chips, possibly coming from part of the superstructure of Building A. The area numbered 12, near the middle of the southern face of the platform, was filled with a great mass of sherds.[221]

4. Apart from a small segment of a wall perpendicular to the eastern face of Building A, to the south of area 16, another important group of structures attributed to 'Period G' was preserved to the south-east of the complex, a few metres to the south of Annexe C. Two ensembles were defined, 18 to the west and 29 to the south-east.[222] Only the internal faces of the outer walls of these spaces were recognized and their exact shape is not precisely understandable. For instance, 18 apparently forms roughly a large rectangle (24 x 9.5m orientated north–south) subdivided by internal partition walls at the north and south, but its 'eastern side' seems in fact to belong to the structures linked to 29. Petrie does not provide any information about levels, apart from the top of a stone 'threshold' preserved in the middle of the northern side of 18, corresponding approximately to the surface of the north-western terrace and the lower floors in the northern part of Annexe C. Room 29 was 4m square, with a small recess in the north-eastern corner and a narrow doorway at the southern end of its eastern wall, leading to another small, rectangular room of 3.5 x 2.25m.

The importance of these two findspots derives from the fact that 90% of the painted Archaic Greek pottery from Tell Dafana was found here,[223] in a 20–5cm thick layer of dust immediately beneath the surface, on a clay floor corresponding to a later phase of occupation. The Greek sherds were mixed with Egyptian material, including a jar handle stamped with the cartouche of Nekau II, plaster jar sealings of Psamtik II and Amasis, fragments of demotic pottery ostraca, fragments of iron scale armour, some tools and weights and various other Egyptian objects.[224] Under a 0.6 to 0.9m fill beneath the floor, Petrie found exclusively Egyptian Saite pottery (Findspot 28), corresponding to an earlier occupation.[225] A few metres to the south of 18, Petrie isolated a Findspot 25, where he found Egyptian pottery and three weights, without giving any details on the context of these finds.[226]

Analysis: the function of the complex of casemate buildings

As already mentioned above, Petrie's interpretation of the casemate buildings of Tell Dafana was much influenced by the similar construction he had excavated a year earlier in the southern enclosure of Naukratis. He first interpreted this Naukratite precinct as a Greek military camp, then as the Hellenion of Amasis that Herodotus counted among the sanctuaries founded by the Greeks in the town, but at least as a Greek temenos, while he considered the casemate building itself as a citadel or fort for the Greek garrison with storage spaces in the foundations.[227] In 1889, D.G. Hogarth excavated another area in the northern part of the site, where he thought he had found Herodotus' Hellenion, and so suggested that Petrie's southern enclosure was an Egyptian military camp – with a fort inside – before finally even denying the very existence of such an enclosure.[228] It was only much later that this area was recognized definitely as the Egyptian temenos of the Egyptian god Amun-Ra Baded,[229] while the casemate building was interpreted in turn as a military redoubt, temple treasury, fortified residence, ritual royal palace, or highly secured official administrative centre.[230]

Indeed, the complex of casemate buildings at Tell Dafana shares a number of common features with the Naukratis platform, as well as with many other structures of the same, similar or different types from the Late Period onwards[231] that have been discovered in the Nile Delta, in Upper Egypt and in the Oases[232] since Petrie's excavations at Tell Dafana and Naukratis. Their interpretation remains debated.[233] Apart from the example at Naukratis, the closest parallel to the Tell Dafana structures is the casemate building excavated in 1992–3 by J. Spencer at Tell el-Balamun, also Saite in date, and in fact almost identical in plan to the Naukratis edifice (see **Fig. 14**).[234] This close resemblance constitutes one of the arguments to suggest that the Naukratis platform should also date from the 26th dynasty,[235] even though a dating to the Ptolemaic Period is often supposed.[236]

Many other buildings with casemate foundations, more or less similar, though usually of smaller size, have been found inside Late Period and Hellenistic enclosures, whose function as Egyptian temple precincts has never been in doubt. Examples in the Delta region are recorded from Tanis, Tell el-Maskhuta, Tell Belim, Tukh el-Qaramus, Kom Firin and Abu Rawash. Late temple enclosures in Upper Egypt, particularly in the Theban region, also accommodated such buildings on platforms.[237] The latter at least are interpreted, with the help of a few preserved inscriptions, as 'pure storehouses' dedicated to the preparation and consecration of divine offerings.[238] Some others, such as the so-called 'sanatorium' of Dendara, the *Wabet* of Apis in the south-western corner of the temple of Ptah at Memphis, the *Wabet* of the Falcon in Athribis (described in the biographical inscriptions of Djed-Hor the Saviour),[239] as well as the particular case of a Ptolemaic sanctuary in the fortress of Tell el-Herr,[240] should also be mentioned as they share at least some features (platform shape, cellular structure and construction techniques) with the casemate buildings. The much larger and more sophisticated 'Palace of Apries' in the northern enclosure of Memphis, which Petrie excavated later, and to which the central complex of buildings in the temenos of Sais – unfortunately destroyed before any serious investigation had been undertaken – can be compared, shows the same technique of construction with casemate foundations, but on a larger scale.[241]

Casemate buildings also existed outside Late Period religious enclosures at many sites, such as Mendes, Buto, Memphis, Karnak and East Karnak, as well as in North Saqqara.[242] Apart from the last example, the larger buildings are usually considered as having an economic function. At any rate, from the Saite Period onwards the technique began to be used extensively for building multi-storey domestic square blocks, also described as 'tower-houses', on a more or less stereotyped model.[243] Large square constructions as well as smaller houses of this type also exist in many areas of the civil quarters of Tell Dafana, as shown by the satellite imagery (see below).

All these examples show that the interpretation of the casemate buildings of Tell Dafana, Naukratis and Tell el-Balamun must be considered in a wider context, and that similar techniques of construction could be used for structures with different purposes. Their common architectural features can be summarized as follows:

All the buildings had the form of an elevated structure on a podium made of a high casemate foundation, with a thick outer wall built in concave courses of bricks, sometimes reinforced with wooden beams, and a grid of thinner partition walls dividing the internal space into cells. These cells were filled with sand, earth or rubble, but not always completely. At least some were covered by a vault or dome, above which lay the internal occupation level. This elevated floor was only accessible from the lower surroundings through an external ramp or flight of stairs leading in several cases to the corner of the building. Elevation and limited access certainly addressed the need to safeguard the building's contents, while partly filled cells covered with vaults and domes created crawlspaces or voids that helped ensure floor insulation. Some key elements, such as stairs (or parts of stairs), passages, columns, pavements, plinths and specific internal features may have been stone built.

Although most of the edifices are destroyed below the platform level, better preserved examples such as that of Naukratis show with some certainty that the arrangement of the rooms in the superstructure corresponded to the distribution of the cells in the foundation – with the possible exception, in some cases, of specific groups of cells supporting the floor of a larger space above with rows of columns placed at the intersection of the partition walls.

For the larger buildings there remains the question of interior lighting. The substantial thickness of the outer wall, though reduced in the upper parts by the batter of the outer faces, does not seem to have allowed for openings to the exterior in the perimeter rooms. Corridors, galleries and rooms must have been illuminated through narrow ceiling skylights. This reinforces the idea that there cannot have been any second floor above the roofing, unless some specific arrangement is present to suggest the presence of an internal stairwell. In several examples, such as in Tell Dafana, Naukratis, Tell el-Balamun, as well as in one of the Tanis casemate buildings, a long and wide gallery divided the edifice into two symmetrical – or almost symmetrical – parts. If this gallery was not covered, or not entirely covered, it would have functioned as a kind of lightwell to illuminate the surrounding rooms in the central part of the building.[244]

Careful consideration of all the casemate buildings indicates that any military interpretation has to be discarded. In this regard, the comparison, still made by some,[245] with the fortified enclosure wall of Tell Kedwa (see **Pl. 4**), which is also built in a casemate construction technique, is irrelevant: just because a fortress wall was built with this technique, it does not mean that every casemate building, whatever its size or shape, had to have the same function. Likewise, the fact that some of the buildings on platforms can be identified positively by means of inscriptions as 'pure storehouses' does not imply that all of them must necessarily be interpreted as such. Nevertheless, the sizes and distribution of the cells in Building A of Tell Dafana, as well as in the platforms of Naukratis and Tell el-Balamun, with galleries and corridors leading to a series of rooms of relatively small and standardized size, points towards a storage function rather than a residential or palatial purpose, for which one would expect spaces of more differentiated dimensions with a clearer specialization, as in

New Kingdom palaces and the Memphite 'palace' of Apries. The genesis of casemate-type construction is obscure, though an origin from the Levant, where such edifices also existed during the Iron Age,[246] might be an option.

In the case of the buildings of Tell Dafana, we can only speculate about what might originally have been kept inside this storehouse: perishable goods, precious commodities, cultic equipment or implements. In all likelihood they were goods or objects connected in some way with the functioning of the cult and/or the economy of the sanctuaries in the immediate surroundings, and with the position of the city on the major traffic artery to and from the Levant.

The remainder of the enclosure

Petrie concentrated his work mainly in the area of the *Kasr*, and on some parts of the enclosure wall. In the remainder of the enclosure he only excavated, relatively superficially, a large area in the south-eastern quarter, but he also mentions several other architectural features in different places.

The northern part of the enclosure

To the north of the complex of casemate buildings, the former track of the north–south roadway leading to the entrance of the *Kasr* was partly visible, delimited on both sides by lines of stone chips and extending apparently up to the gap in the northern wall of the enclosure (see **Pl. 3b**). At a distance of approximately 80m to the north of Building A, this roadway crossed an east–west mudbrick wall, a few metres thick,[247] extending west by at least 20 or 30m and east by 50 to 60m. The wall was almost entirely levelled and only detectable by the lines of stone chips and pottery along its edges. The road passed through a stone gate in this wall, of which Petrie gives no further details. The function of this inner enclosure wall is not clear. It is only slightly visible on the recent satellite images (**Pl. 8**). To the east, it seems to continue as far as the eastern side of the great enclosure wall; to the west, it might connect with a north–south segment to the west of the supposed location of the road. If this is correct, this inner wall might have surrounded a rectangular area of about 150 x 130m in the north-eastern part of the enclosure (**Pl. 10**, area C). The function of this area as yet remains unknown. But in the north-eastern corner of the enclosure, Petrie noted a high concentration of chips of

Figure 20 Concentration of stone chips and blocks in the north-eastern area of the enclosure, looking north-east (photo: F. Leclère 1998)

different kinds of hard stones (basalt, granite, quartzite/sandstone, limestone) scattered on the ground[248] and this is still the case today (**Fig. 20**). Fragments of blocks of quartzite are also visible in the vicinity. They possibly bear witness to a substantial stone building, and/or to activities related to stone exploitation.

The north-western and central part of the enclosure

The north-western part of the enclosure did not reveal any particular features and Petrie even had some difficulties in tracing the enclosure wall in this area. The satellite image seems to indicate that this part of the site is much denuded, perhaps having been eroded to below the level of any constructions which may once have stood there (see **Pls 8 and 10**).

Immediately to the west of the *Kasr*, Petrie succinctly describes several structures filled with limestone chips.[249] The narrow east–west oriented dotted area on his plan (**Pl. 3b**) suggests that these structures extended between 25 to 50m from the western side of Building A. From the eastern end of this line of dots, Petrie's plan shows another series of dotted patches, perpendicular to the previous one and extending towards the south by some 100m. They seem to be exactly on – or very close to – the north–south central axis of the main enclosure, and must correspond to traces of one or several limestone structures, perhaps a thick wall or several gates, of which we unfortunately know nothing more. Taken together, all these remains give the impression of a large limestone structure of which only the north-eastern corner was preserved.

About 20m south of the *Kasr*, Petrie's plan indicates another straight east–west line to the east side of these limestone constructions, with a corner at the western end, certainly the north face of a wall perpendicular to it and 30m long at least. All these remains are uninterpretable, but might have been more or less coherent parts of the large temple recently detected and excavated in the middle of the southern part of the enclosure (see Chapter 8).

The south-eastern part of the enclosure: metal 'workshops'

In the second part of his season and particularly during the final days, Petrie put most of his workmen in the south-eastern part of the enclosure, in order to clear an area of about 2.4 hectares ('6 acres'), only turning over the top 15cm of surface dust without removing it (see **Pls 3b and 10**, area D).[250] This technique did not permit any clear identification or description of the 'quantity of buildings' apparently visible in the area, including a few chambers excavated more deeply here and there. Nevertheless, the work provided many objects and scraps of metallic material, notably bronze and iron tools and weapons,[251] including many arrowheads – found in great quantities along the south side of the enclosure – iron swords, iron and bronze chisels and/or wedges, fragments interpreted as horse-bits, as well as iron and copper slag,[252] which Petrie considered as remains from the workshops of an 'armoury'. This area must correspond to Petrie's Findspots 52 and 53.[253]

Along the northern face of the eastern part of the southern enclosure wall a small cache was found, or perhaps part of the leftovers of a precious metal workshop,[254] including a silver bowl and a dipper with a twisted handle ending in a duck's head,[255] This area, alongside the enclosure wall, might correspond to Findspot number 55. Some 0.60kg of silver lumps[256] were also found together with a gold tray handle at another location in the enclosure, some distance to the east or south-east of the *Kasr*, on the very last day of the excavations.[257]

Two small identical faience plaques of Apries were apparently also found in this area, at a deeper level.[258] They must originally have been parts of foundation deposits of an important building here and one can only regret that the context of these finds remains unclear in Petrie's documentation. Many objects in the British Museum's collection are recorded in the registers as coming from the 'Camp', with no further details. Although we do not know where exactly in the main enclosure they were found, there is a good chance that they came from this south-eastern quarter of the enclosure.

The southern part of the enclosure: an Egyptian 'temple' with magazines

In the middle of the southern part of the enclosure, Petrie did not detect any particular structures (**Pl. 3b**). During short visits to the site in 1998 and 2000,[259] many traces of thick and long mudbrick walls were observed on the surface, made visible from the surrounding ground by their colour and humidity differences, resulting from their different material density and porosity. These structures were so massive that it was not possible for someone walking on the ground to gain a good understanding of them (**Fig. 21**). From 2005, Google Earth[260] began to publish online new satellite images with a relatively high resolution,[261] from which it was possible to recognize, in this specific area of the site, the outlines of what must have been a large Egyptian-type mudbrick-built temple, surrounded by magazines, as well as the enclosure wall and many other architectural features (**Pl. 10**, areas D and E).[262] Orientated to the south, the temple was accessible through the axial limestone gate of which Petrie excavated the foundations in the middle of the south wall of the enclosure. The existence of this temple was confirmed by the Egyptian excavations undertaken in 2009 (see Chapter 8).[263]

The temple was 76m wide and at least 170m long, or possibly up to 210m. It was composed of a succession of three rectangular courtyards, separated by two thick walls – possibly pylon-shaped – and bordered on both east and west by walls about 6m thick. The first courtyard, larger than the two others, measured 64 x 64m. In its southern part, immediately behind the axial gate, a north–south aligned rectangular feature measuring 30 x 15m must correspond to the foundation of a specific structure, presumably a portico. The second and third courtyards are narrower and shorter than the southern one, at 54m wide and 44m long. The northern end of the temple, where one would expect the sanctuary to lie, is less clear. The northern side of the third courtyard actually consists of the foundations of a very thick mudbrick wall built with undulating courses of bricks and recesses, at least on the southern side, much resembling an enclosure wall. The Egyptian excavators were able to trace it further east and west over a total length of at least 140m,

temple width included. Whether this wall continued on both sides and turned somewhere to the north is not yet known. To the north of this wall is a long rectangular area measuring about 140m east–west and 34m north–south, which is divided into three sectors. In the central sector, the foundations of a structure some 20m square are set in the axis of the temple, apparently abutted to the northern face of the east–west 'enclosure wall', and containing rectangular cells. This axial structure actually occupies the position where a sanctuary might be expected. It is possible that the thick wall between it and the third courtyard was an earlier enclosure wall pre-dating the temple, which was levelled when this temple was built – if not integrated into its structure. As the architectural remains are reduced to only a few courses of brick, erosion may have removed the architectural link between the courtyards to the south of this wall and the 'sanctuary' to the north. The remains of Petrie's *Kasr* are some 80–90m to the north–north-east of this area.

Further structures visible on the satellite image on either side of the temple were excavated in 2009 by our Egyptian colleagues (see Chapter 8). To the east of the two northern courtyards is a north–south oriented rectangular area of 36 x 90m, separated from the temple by a straight, narrow lane, and divided up into a series of long east–west oriented galleries about 3m wide; the galleries themselves are each irregularly subdivided by partition walls into two or three parts. This structure must have been a series of storerooms, although one could also see them as stables.[264] Whether these storage spaces extended further to the south, alongside the first temple courtyard, is not yet known. Immediately to the east and south-east lies the 'south-eastern' area of 'metal workshops' cleared by Petrie, where the satellite image does not reveal anything clear.

Similar structures also appear – and were partly excavated in 2009 – immediately to the west of the first courtyard, alongside the internal face of the main enclosure wall. A rectangular area measuring 54m north–south and at least 45m – possibly up to 70m – east–west, is delimited and divided by 2.5m thick walls into long, parallel north–south oriented galleries of some 4.5m width. Six of them were excavated in 2009, but there must be several more to the west. Further to the west, as far as the south-western corner of the main enclosure, several other constructions are detectable, including further

Figure 21 Traces of levelled walls on the ground surface in the southern part of the enclosure, looking north (photo: F. Leclère 1998)

long galleries and two squarish constructions, possibly on casemate foundations, measuring 14 to 17m in length. More structures appear to the north of this area and to the west of the two northernmost temple courtyards, but they are not clear enough to permit interpretation.

If the main axial structure really was a temple and the rectangular enclosure a temenos, the question arises of the identity of the divinity to whom the temple was dedicated. Inscriptions from the site are very scarce, and local cults appear not to have been mentioned in Egyptian inscriptions found anywhere else, as far as we know. A possible candidate could be Min, as the last line of the fragmentary Saite stela that Petrie found to the north of the enclosure[265] states that the monument was erected in a temple (*ḥt*) of that deity.[266] The name of the locality of which Min is said to be the Lord has unfortunately disappeared in a break, except for small parts of a few illegible signs; most authors, however, have followed Griffith's original reading and interpretation that this must have been *Gbtyw*/Koptos, suggesting that the stela was a local copy of an original Coptite monument. Alternatively, P. Montet suggested – less convincingly – an identification as 'Imet', the neighbouring town to the west of Daphnae, where Min, identified with Horus Chief-of-the-Deserts, was worshipped.[267] A photograph of the stela is kept in the EES archives (**Fig. 22**)[268] and a copy of the text, made by Petrie, appears in his Notebook (**Fig. 23**),[269] but unfortunately they do not provide any further information to improve the reading. Whichever way the toponym is read,[270] the cult of a deity such as Min, possibly imported, would be quite appropriate for a town located on the fringes of the Eastern Desert. Min was also worshipped in neighbouring Tjaru/Sile as a defender of the Egyptian border against enemies.[271] At Tell Dafana, Min is mentioned in one of the rare inscriptions on stone found at the site, a limestone chip with the vertical cartouche of Amasis on top of the standard of Min.[272] It is however impossible to say if this fragment comes from wall decoration or another kind of monument and where exactly it was found on the site.

Other Egyptian deities also appear at Tell Dafana, such as Amun and Neith, in the titles of priests on some objects found at the site, such as the bezels of rings[273] or fragments of New Year flasks.[274] Whether they too had temples at Tell Dafana is impossible to say. A new Saite quartzite stela, recently found to the south of the site, unfortunately does not add any further information about the pantheon of Tell Dafana.[275] In addition, finally, there is a reference to Baal-Saphon together 'with all the gods of Tahpanhes' in a Phoenician letter written on papyrus found in Saqqara,[276] but this was probably a secondary cult, or an *interpretatio phoenicia* of a local Egyptian cult.

Outside the enclosure wall

Outside the enclosure, Petrie excavated in several places, but apart from the eastern quarter, he gives very little information on his findings: remains of structures near the caravan road, in the axis of the temple, and the 'Ptolemaic' and 'Roman' mounds to the north-west, on both sides of the 'river'. Surveying the site, he was able to trace the limits of the archaeological area around the enclosure, covered with traces of walls, potsherds and stone chips. Recent satellite images provide much more information about these areas. They also reveal other regions densely covered with constructions belonging to the civic quarters (**Pls 9, 11–14**).

The eastern quarter

Some 270m to the east of the main enclosure wall, and east–north-east of the area of the *Kasr*, Petrie excavated an area measuring 100m east–west by 90m north–south, where walls from different mudbrick structures, levelled to the ground, were still visible (see **Pls 3b and 10**, area F).[277] This is the area that he called the 'Eastern Temple' in his Notebook, an interpretation that he finally discarded in his publications.[278]

The northern part was delimited by a long straight wall, 2.75m thick and extending further to the west of the area, its whole preserved length attaining about 160m, with an orientation at right-angles to the main enclosure wall. Just under 4m to the south of it, Petrie discovered a small chamber with a similar orientation, measuring 9.5 x 4.5m and opening to the south, with remains of two 1m thick partition walls in the eastern part.[279] Twelve and a half

Figure 23 Saite quartzite stela found to the north of the enclosure, sketch in Petrie's Notebook 74.f, pp. 14–15 (courtesy of the Petrie Museum of Egyptian Archaeology, UCL)

Figure 22 Petrie's photograph of the stela (EES, Lucy Gura archive)

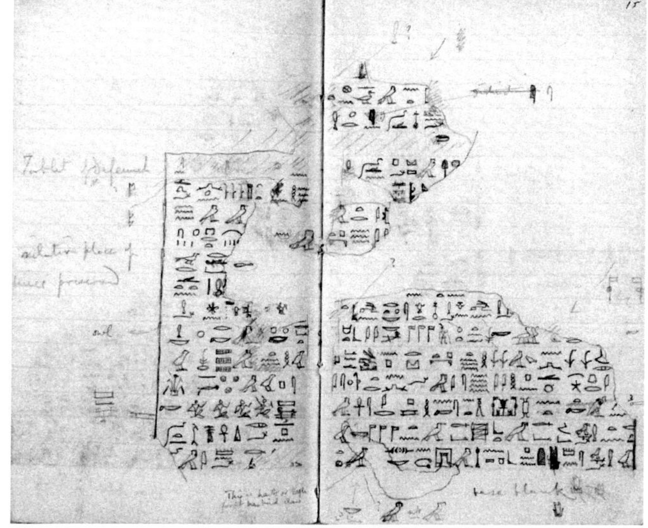

metres to the south-west lay the north-eastern corner of another construction with a slightly different orientation, and of much larger dimensions – at least 33m long north–south and 16m wide east–west – of which Petrie detected only the internal faces of the north and east walls. Further to the south, 40 to 50m from the northern long wall, is the main group of walls he discovered, covering a rectangular area measuring 34m north–south and 55m east–west, with a different orientation from those described previously (10° to the south-west, compared with the northern long wall) and such an intricate arrangement that it is actually not possible to understand whether the walls belonged to one or several different buildings. To the west of this a polygonal addition was found, with walls measuring up to 20m in length, and 15m to the east lay another isolated north–south wall with a different orientation. The wall thickness varies from 0.75 to 2.25m. From the overall plan, it remains difficult to understand the exact function of these structures but they probably belonged to civic, domestic or administrative buildings.

This area corresponds to Findspot 51, as well as 50, a 'dry well' filled with pottery that was partly set into the long northern wall on the west side.[280]

On the satellite image (**Pl. 11b**), these structures are recognizable in some detail. Petrie's northern wall, for instance, must be the southern side of a long structure, at least 200m long east–west and 16m wide, made up of three parallel and equidistant walls, with the spaces in between possibly divided up by cross-walls at regular intervals. Whether this was part of a casemate-type enclosure wall or barracks along a street is not clear. The other structures with different orientations on Petrie's plan were clearly part of two town quarters, some 30m wide and separated by a 4m wide street running east–west and preserved to a length of 80–90m. The location of the polygonal structure to the west, too, seems to be discernible.

South-eastern and south-western domestic quarters
The satellite images show at least two further areas with a great density of domestic constructions, one to the south-east, some 250m from the south-eastern corner of the enclosure, covering an irregular area which extends approximately 350m east–west and more than 400m north–south (**Pls 10**, area G, **12a**), the other immediately to the west of the south-western corner of the enclosure, extending over 400m to the west and 400m to the south (**Pls 10**, area H, **12b**). The south-eastern quarter might originally have been connected to the eastern one; the ground in between is today very low, judging from the recent contour map (0.8m ASL) so that the connection, if it ever existed, may have been lost. Some of the features noted on Petrie's map (corners of two structures at the south-west, 'chambers' a little further to the south, a small hillock with 'much pottery' at the south-east) are more or less recognizable.

In these areas, the occupation is characterized by many rectangular or square buildings of relatively small dimensions – usually 10 to 20m in length, including the foundations of casemate tower-houses typical of the Late Period, as well as larger and more irregular structures with thinner walls, which might correspond to boundaries around the courtyards of properties. Straight walls can be followed for distances of up to 60m in some cases, on both sides of narrow lanes. One of the main features of these settlement quarters is the irregularity in plan and the different orientations of the buildings from one 'block' or small quarter to another – or sometimes within one and the same quarter. Apart from indicating an organically grown settlement rather than an officially and centrally planned urban development, these features might also result from a long occupation with several phases of reconstruction. The modern satellite image gives the impression that urban areas are separated from each other by large zones of wasteland, covered with 'scattered pottery'.[281] Nevertheless, there is a strong probability that these quarters were more extensive in antiquity, and that most of the surface of the sandy plain was once occupied.

Immediately to the south-east of the south-eastern corner of the enclosure, and south-west of the south-eastern domestic quarter, there is another feature, apparently different in nature and more difficult to interpret (**Pl. 10**, area I): what is visible on the satellite image (**Pl. 13a**) is a roughly rectangular shape measuring 240m x 140m, orientated to the south, but not aligned with the enclosure. At the south-western corner of this rectangle, a structure some 44–5m square might well be the ruins of a casemate building, as such constructions are also sometimes found outside precincts.[282] The precise nature of these particular structures, however, remains enigmatic.

Near the caravan road at the southern edge of the site, right in the axis of the enclosure (**Pl. 10**, area J), Petrie rapidly excavated the remains of a structure that he interpreted as a temple or as a guard house (see **Pl. 3b** and **Fig. 24**).[283] A few walls were revealed, built with mudbricks measuring 39–41 x 22 x 12.5cm and joining at right angles to create a rough T-shape, set within a space measuring approximately 30m square. The orientation differs slightly from that of the main enclosure. The buildings that once stood here must have been built (at least in part) of stone, as shown by the discovery of remains of a limestone pavement and numerous limestone chips, as well as some granite and basalt fragments. On the satellite image (**Pl. 13b**), an irregular grey patch on the sandy area to the south of the site, measuring 70 x 70m and located 40m north of the modern road, must be the location of these structures, but no traces of walls or pavement are now visible.

Nearby, or slightly further to the south-east, in the sandy plots to the south of the modern road, several fragments of a large quartzite stela of Apries, dating to year seven of his reign, were discovered by accident in 2011. Written in columns, the text mentions military expeditions towards the East.[284] The monument might have been erected along the ancient caravan track in order to be seen by any arriving or departing traveller. Although different in content, it complements the fragmentary quartzite stela of the Saite Period that Petrie discovered immediately to the north of the main enclosure.[285]

The 'North-West Ptolemaic Mound'
To the north-west of the main enclosure is an extensive flat hill, immediately to the south of the dried riverbed, standing

7 to 8.5m above the plain (**Pls 3b, 10**, area K). There Petrie dug some large and deep sondages ('metre pits') without great success,[286] apart from finding layers of burnt material with broken pottery, a few mudbrick walls and chambers that he did not draw, and a few objects, such as three bronze cylindrical vases[287] and a group of crude faience amulets, apparently wrapped in cloth.[288] The hill is irregular in shape, roughly polygonal with rounded corners, and wider at the north (620m) – along the dry river channel – where it also reaches its highest altitude. Its north–south dimension is 430m. The top is now covered by an artificial sandy hillock, created to support a chevron-shaped modern concrete ramp, now disused and ruined, presumably a remnant of a military installation of the 1960s or 1970s.[289]

While Petrie says little about what he found there, the satellite image (**Pl. 13c**), as in the other urban quarters, shows a strong concentration of domestic buildings particularly in the northernmost and highest area, among which are many casemate foundations of tower-house type buildings, 10–15m square, as well as other smaller structures. The orientation of the buildings is overall north–south/east–west, but with much minor variation and no regular street layout emerging.

Near the western edge of the hill, the satellite image (**Pl. 10**, area K') shows the north, south and east sides of a quadrangular structure which certainly corresponds to an enclosure wall, *c.* 5m thick, 85m wide north–south and at least 100m long east–west, with a general orientation to the west-south-west (**Pl. 14a**). The western side is missing. This peribolos seems to surround a rectangular building measuring 25 x 45m, with a different – more east–west – orientation. To the south-east of this building is another rectangular shape (18 x 30m) with yet another orientation, and it appears that its north-western corner was partly overlaid by the south-eastern corner of the other building. Whether these were two successive buildings and whether they must be interpreted, together with the enclosure wall,

as religious structures, Egyptian or not in nature, is up for debate until the situation is clarified by excavations.[290]

According to Petrie, the material found on this mound dates from a later period ('Ptolemaic') than that from the rest of the central plain. However, one may wonder on what his dating is based, as no pottery seems to have been collected there – or at least none has been recorded as coming from this area. One or two Ptolemaic jar-stoppers were found here, but none of the other finds (bronze containers and amulets) can be dated with any precision.[291]

The river and the north-western Roman and Byzantine mound

Immediately to the north of the 'Ptolemaic' mound ran the 'river', meandering slightly towards the north-east from a large lake at the west (see **Pls 3b, 9–10**, area L). The depression of the river-bed is bordered on both sides by a string of small sandy hills, probably created by wind-blown sand becoming trapped by the tamarisks that grew along the water's edge, rather than by dredging. The river-bed itself does not seem to be wider than 20 to 30m. In the north-eastern part of the site, relatively large flat depressions covered with clay silt (called 'swamp' on Petrie's map) must correspond to natural overflow basins during the inundation. These overflows might have been partly responsible for the progressive destruction of the north-western area of the central enclosure.

North of the western part of this riverbed, i.e. to the north/north-west of the 'Ptolemaic mound,' is another flat mound, almost of the same height, and of oval shape, measuring some 350m north–south and 300m east–west (**Pl. 10**, area M). Petrie only walked across this area without doing any digging at all, but spotted numerous fragments of 'Roman glass' strewn across the surface, picked up a glass seal[292] and noted some remains of rifled tombs, which might belong to earlier periods, and from which some of the gold earrings that the locals brought to him might have come.[293]

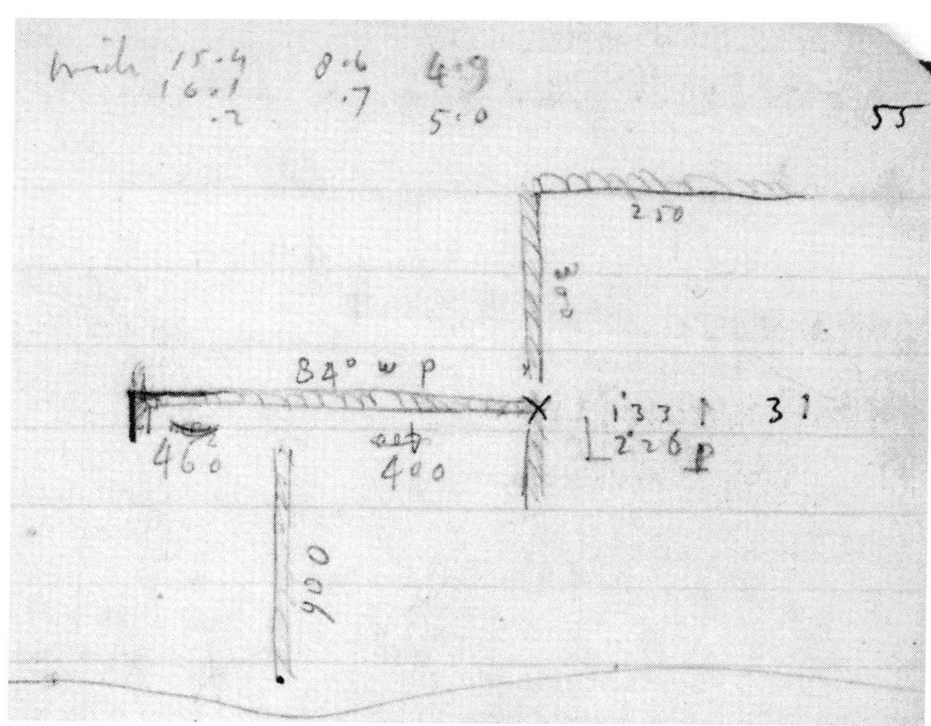

Figure 24 Sketch plan of a structure at the southern edge of the site, from Petrie's Notebook 74.f, p.55 (courtesy of the Petrie Museum of Egyptian Archaeology, UCL)

When visiting the site in 1998, some glass fragments of the
4th to 6th centuries AD were noticed on the ground, as well
as some sherds of Late Roman pottery (**Fig. 25**).[294]

As in other parts of the site, the satellite image shows
dense domestic occupation here (**Pl. 14b**). At least one
tower-house measuring 20m square can be made out in the
central part, and possibly, some 40m to the east, a massive
straight feature, perhaps a mudbrick wall, 13m thick and
more than 100m long, with the same north–south
orientation. Thinner walls of many other structures are also
visible, with a similar orientation, in the eastern part of the
settlement, but with a different one – north-west to south-
east – in the western part. Some long and irregular traces
give the impression that the central part of this settlement
possessed a quadrangular border, possibly a wall, about 150
to 200m long east–west and 120 to 130m north–south. Unless
these traces result from a modern occupation, such as a
military encampment, they might be suggestive of a fortified
village, dating from Late Antiquity.

The rest of the northern part of the site, to the north-east
of the 'Roman' mound (**Pl. 10**, area N), is an extensive
elevated sandy area (950 x 850m), as high as the other
mounds in its central part – the 'Sandy hills' on Petrie's
map.[295] This part of the site does not seem to have been
occupied – at least it does not show any visible remains.

The material culture of Tell Dafana: finds and contexts

Re-contextualization of the finds: the findspots
The original context of the finds made during Petrie's work
at Tell Dafana is not always exactly known. The precision of
the provenance information varies greatly from one object
or category of objects to another. This variation, which is
reflected in the following catalogue (Chapter 3), results from
a number of different factors.

First, a large proportion of the objects are stray finds
picked up from the surface of the site by local people –
including scraps of gold, bronze and iron arrowheads and
most of the numerous metal and stone weights[296] – or

brought by them from other places in the neighbourhood,
particularly to the north of the site as far as Tell Sherig/Tell
Belim, and sold to Petrie on a daily basis.[297] In such cases,
Petrie was not able to gain much information from the sellers
about the precise origin of the finds.

Second, as regards to objects from his own excavations, it
is clear from the extant documentation that Petrie tried his
best to record findspot information, using a standard set of
terminology for the different areas he explored on the site:
'Camp', for the central rectangular enclosure; '*Kasr*',
'palace', 'fort', for the complex of casemate buildings and
their annexes, 'East of *Kasr*', for the civic quarters to the east
of the enclosure; 'Ptolemaic' and 'Roman mounds', for the
hills to the north-west, etc. Whenever possible, moreover, he
made use of numbered Findspots that corresponded to
particular spaces in the excavated structures (such as cells
and rooms), or to specific features or groups of finds outside
buildings; these reference numbers he created as he went
along. Although never properly listed in the publication,
these numbers are frequently mentioned throughout the text
and the plates, and some of them are indicated on the plan of
the *Kasr*. Petrie's Notebook and an isolated handwritten
two-page document in the EES archives contain simplified
and incomplete lists of the same findspots.[298] Some of the
finds themselves also have a findspot number scored, marked
or pencilled directly on the object. This applies particularly
to the pottery, both Egyptian and Greek, which Petrie
apparently considered both not too precious to mark and
easy enough to scratch into, but very few objects are also
thus marked. The combination of information from all the
various sources available – publications, archival
documents, museum registers and the items themselves –
proved invaluable, not only for identifying with a greater
degree of certainty objects from Tell Dafana in the
documentation and in the various museum collections to
which they had been dispersed, but also for reconstructing
archaeological assemblages, at least for a substantial part of
the finds.[299] Unfortunately there still remains a large number
of objects for which only very little information – or no

Figure 25 Late Roman sherds and glass
fragments scattered on the surface of the
'Roman' mound (photo: F. Leclère 1998)

information at all – exists about their provenance. This is particularly true for the many objects that Petrie describes as coming from the 'Camp' (i.e. the main enclosure); one can assume that most of them were found during the extensive clearing (with no recording) that Petrie undertook at the end of his season in the south-eastern part of the enclosure, but some may simply have been picked up here or there from the surface.

The list of findspots for Petrie's entire work at the site ranges from number 1 to 61 (**Table 1**) but not all the contexts are as important or precise as others and some gaps exist in the sequence. This is due to several factors:

Numbers 46 to 49 seem never to have been assigned, and one may suppose that Petrie deliberately chose to give number 50 and following to features in the Eastern quarter, which he started to excavate early in the season, while excavations in the *Kasr* (Findspot number 1 onwards) were still ongoing, in order to avoid any possible confusion and to distinguish between the two series of numbers being used in different areas. Perhaps for the same reason, number 60 was assigned to the excavation of the north-west 'Ptolemaic' mound, also excavated early in the season. The gaps in the sequence were then filled progressively with numbers allocated to new Findspots in the various areas, although the system was not always entirely consistent: numbers up to 45 were assigned to findspots in the *Kasr*, while numbers in the eastern quarter ultimately remained limited to 50 and 51, with the following numbers, up to 58, used mainly for other excavations in the south-eastern part of the enclosure. Nevertheless, 59 was ascribed to a set of weights on the Ptolemaic mound, and 61 to a 'dry well' in the south-eastern part of the enclosure.

The attribution of some other numbers is far from clear: for instance Findspot 7 corresponds to an area covering several rooms already numbered 2, 3, 4, 5 and 6 in the northern part of Annexe C of the *Kasr*. The reason for this additional number remains unknown; it might have resulted from the imprecise provenance information available for some objects brought to Petrie by his workmen.[300]

The location of some findspots is difficult to identify precisely, as they are not clearly marked on the published plans: Findspot 13, for example, is only described in Petrie's Notebook 74.e as 'low chambers on south of Great chamber', which one might understand to mean the square chamber at the bottom of the southern part of the central gallery of Building A.[301]

Several numbers were attributed to more or less precise locations, but no finds ever seem to have been linked with them. The most probable reason for this is that these areas did not yield any material at all, though it is also possible that finds were not recorded properly. This situation applies, for instance, to Findspots 5, 6 and 45 in the northern part of the annexe of the *Kasr*, cells 36 to 39 of casemate Building A, the cells 41 to 44 of casemate Building B, and passage 26 between the vestibule and rooms 11 and 17. Other 'finds-free' findspots are more difficult to identify or to locate: Findspot 15 – possibly a cell in the eastern part of Building A; Findspot 23 – described in the Notebook as 'close to the entrance'; Findspot 20 – only described as '*Kasr*, general' and most probably abandoned later; Findspots 33 and 34, which are

not described at all; and Findspot 56 – an area of burnt ground to the south-west of the *Kasr*.

Findspot 53, an area of coppersmiths in the south-eastern quarter of the enclosure, curiously has no finds directly attached. One might suppose that a substantial part of the copper alloy items with no precise provenance in the collections – apart from the arrowheads which were found everywhere and objects from other known findspots – were found in this area, unless they came from other sites in the neighbourhood. In the same way, Findspot 52 – also located in this part of the enclosure, south of 53 – was supposed to be an area of iron workshops, but most of the finds directly recorded as coming from there are actually pottery. One may suppose that most of the iron items, apart from those definitely coming from specific rooms in the *Kasr*, were also found in this area. Area 55, along the inner face of the south-eastern section of the enclosure wall, also has only pottery explicitly assigned to it, but finds of silver and gold described elsewhere might also have come from there.

Although several groups of weights discovered here or there on the surface were given a number, other groups, such as a set of 30 or 40 limestone statuettes of captive prisoners found 'beyond Findspot 29', have no precise findspot number of their own. Similarly, some isolated finds with a more or less precise context were nevertheless not allocated a findspot number (the quartzite stela to the north of the enclosure wall, a silver ring found on the terrace to the north of the *Kasr*[302]), and some excavated areas did not receive a findspot number either (the structures cleared at the southern end of the site, near the caravan road, and the cells of the central gallery of casemate Building A).

Reorganizing Petrie's Findspots by excavation areas is an important step towards understanding the different assemblages of material (**Table 2**). It is most revealing in the area of the *Kasr*, particularly for the material from the rooms of Annexe C and 'Phase G' surrounding the casemate buildings, the latter having yielded very little material from the fill of the cells. They include the assemblages of Greek painted pottery and transport amphorae imported from Greece, Cyprus and the Levant that have been recently re-studied in detail by S. Weber,[303] who also provides an overview of the Greek painted wares in Chapter 6 of this volume. The assemblages of Egyptian pottery and transport amphorae are described by J. Spencer in Chapters 4 and 5.[304]

Ideally, the reconstruction of the assemblages should include complete lists of objects for each findspot with their identification in the collections. However, as long as the study of the complete extant sets of finds is not yet completed this would be premature.[305] The present catalogue therefore only includes the finds kept in the British Museum. Our study of the rest of the material, dispersed in many other collections worldwide, is still ongoing and will certainly result in greater precision regarding find contexts.

The dispersal of the finds to collections

Apart from the objects that Petrie left at the site in the bushes near his tent at the last moment because he had no more time or material to pack them, or was not able to

Findspot no.	Area / phase concerned	Notes
1	Kasr, Phase G, N.W. of Building A, room 1.	
2	Kasr, Eastern annexe C, N. part, room 2.	
3	Kasr, Eastern annexe C, N. part, room 3.	
4	Kasr, Eastern annexe C, N. part, room 4.	
5	*Kasr, Eastern annexe C, N. part, room (or cell) 5.*	
6	*Kasr, Phase G, N. of Eastern annexe C, room 6.*	
7	Kasr, Eastern annexe C, N. part; unclear: = Findpots 2 to 6?	'Kasr, 2 to 6' in Notebook 74e; 'Chamber 2 to 6 in general' - Griffith list.
8	Kasr, Phase G, W. of Building A, room 8.	
9	Kasr, Eastern annexe C, N. part, room 9.	
10	Kasr, Eastern annexe C, N. part, room 10.	
11	Kasr, Eastern annexe C, mid part, room 11.	
12	Kasr, Phase G, along S. side of Building A, rectangular room, filled with sherds.	
13	Kasr, Building A; unclear: possibly the earlier square room at the bottom of the S. part of the central gallery?	'Low chambers on S[outh] of G[rea]t chamber' - Notebook 74e; not on the plan pl. xliv; if identification is right, some Saite pottery and a New Kingdom sherd from here (BM EA 23777).
14	Kasr, Building A; unclear: cell(s) beside the central large one?	'Chambers by G[rea]t chamber' in Notebook 74e; not marked on plan pl. xliv; only one bronze situla found (unidentified yet).
15	*Kasr, Building A; unclear: cell (?) in the eastern part (?)*	*'Passage E[ast] of G[rea]t chamber' in Notebook 74e; not marked on plan pl. xliv.*
16	Kasr, Building A, long corridor along E. side.	
17	Kasr, Eastern annexe C, mid part, room 17.	
18	Kasr, Phase G, S.E. of annexe C, room 18.	
19	Kasr, Eastern annexe C, S. part, rooms 19A, 19B and 19C.	
20	*Kasr; unclear, number probably abandoned.*	*'Kasr general' in Notebook 74e, but crossed out; not marked on the plan pl. xliv.*
21	Kasr, short distance to the S.W., pottery 'dry well'.	Not marked on plan pl. xliv.
22	Kasr, between Building B and Eastern annexe C, 'room' 22.	
23	*Kasr; unclear: possibly near the gate between Buildings A and B (?)*	*'Close to the entrance' of Kasr (Notebook 74e+Griffith list); not marked on plan pl. xliv.*
24	Kasr, Phase G, rooms full of chips of limestone S. of Building A.	
25	Kasr, area S. of Findspot 18 (no information).	
26	*Kasr, bent passage to the N.E. of Building A and S. of Building B, access to central part of Eastern annexe C (rooms 11 and 17).*	
27	Kasr, Eastern annexe C, southern part, room 27.	
28	Kasr, Phase G, S.E. of annexe C, lower level of room 18.	
29	Kasr, Phase G, S.E. of annexe C, room 29.	
30	Kasr, Building A, cell.	Some pottery found (BM EA 22331).
31	Kasr, Eastern annexe C, S. part, pottery 'dry well' E. of room 19A.	
32	Kasr, Eastern annexe C, S. part, pottery 'dry well' below room 19A	
33	*?*	
34	*?*	
35	Kasr, Building A, cell.	Also 'chamber γ' in Notebook 74f; chips of decorated limestone blocks.
36	*Kasr, Building A, cell.*	*Also 'chamber β' in Notebook 74f.*
37	*Kasr, Building A, cell.*	*Also 'chamber α' in Notebook 74f.*
38	*Kasr, Building A, cell.*	*Also 'chamber λ' in Notebook 74f.*
39	*Kasr, Building A, cell.*	*Also 'chamber ζ' in Notebook 74f.*
40	Kasr, Building A, cell.	Also 'chamber δ' in Notebook 74f; captive figure (Cairo, EM, JE 27393).
41	*Kasr, Building B, cell.*	*Also 'chamber η' in Notebook 74f.*
42	*Kasr, Building B, cell.*	*Also 'chamber θ' in Notebook 74f.*
43	*Kasr, Building B, cell.*	*Also 'chamber ν' in Notebook 74f.*
44	*Kasr, Building B, cell.*	*Also 'chamber ξ' in Notebook 74f.*
45	*Kasr, Eastern annexe C, northern part, room 45.*	*Also 'chamber A' in Notebook 74f.*
46 to 49	*? Probably never attributed.*	
50	E. quarter, pottery 'dry well' partly cut into the long north wall.	
51	E. quarter, buildings.	
52	Enclosure, S.E. part, quarter of iron workshops, S. of Findspot 53.	Only noted on plates in Petrie 1888; some objects marked 52 W (West?).
53	*Enclosure, S.E. part, quarter of copper workshops, N. of Findspot 52.*	*Mentioned only in Notebook 74e and Griffith's list.*
54	Enclosure, S.E. part, pottery 'dry well' N. of Findspot 52 (in Findspot 53?).	
55	Enclosure, S.E. part, along inner face of the enclosure wall (N. face of S. section).	
56	*Enclosure, short distance S.W. of the Kasr, burnt ground.*	
57	Enclosure, S.E. part, set of 4 weights in Findspot 52.	Possibly the set of 4 weights from 'another chamber' in Petrie 1888, 94?
58	Enclosure, S.E. part, set of 19 weights in Findspot 52.	See detail in Petrie, 1888, 92, 93 (who describes only 17 weights) and Notebook 74f, 46 (19 weights, with some discrepancies in the figures compared to the published list).
59	N.W. 'Ptolemaic' mound, set of 2 weights.	Petrie 1888, 94 (though not specifically mentioned as Findspot 59).
60	N.W. 'Ptolemaic' mound.	
61	Enclosure, S.E. part, pottery 'dry well' in Findspot 53.	

Table 1 List of Petrie's findspots (those in italics contained no finds)

Location			Findspot	Type / description	Main categories of finds
Enclosure : Kasr	Earlier building (?)		13	Cell (?) at bottom of S. central gallery of Building A	Eg. pottery
	Building A		14	Cell(s)	Bronze situla
			30	Cell	Eg. pottery
			35	Cell	Chips of limestone decorated blocks; Eg. pottery
			40	Cell	Fragment of limestone statuette of captive
			16	Corridor (ramp ?) on E. side	Eg. pottery
			15	*Cell (?)*	
			36	*Cell*	
			37	*Cell*	
			38	*Cell*	
			39	*Cell*	
	Building B		*41*	*Cell*	
			42	*Cell*	
			43	*Cell*	
			44	*Cell*	
	Eastern Annexe : N. part		22	Room (?) between Building B and Annexe C	Eg. pottery, various objects (plaster jar-sealing of Nekau II, limestone block with a kheker-frieze, fragments of wooden beams)
			2	Room	Imported transport amphorae, Eg. pottery, various objects (faience: amulets, seal, draughtmen, button, vessel rim; stone weights; bronze: staple, weight, arrowhead, knife, sistrum head, situla)
			3	Room	
			4	Room	Eg. pottery, faience amulet, weights (?).
			9	Room	Transport amphorae, Eg. pottery, game-board and pieces, weights (?)
			7	Rooms (= 2 to 6)	Eg. pottery
			10	Cell or room	Eg. pottery, limestone fragment
			5	*Cell ?*	
			45	*Cell ?*	
		Mid part	11	Room	Greek sherds, imported transport amphora, Eg. pottery, iron chisel
			17	Room	Greek sherds and vases, Eg. pottery, various objects (plaster jar-sealing of Psam. II (?); block of sulphur; fragment of incense (?); iron rasps; stone: whetstone, weights; faience: amulets, shabti [?], draughtman)
			26	*Corridor/courtyard, access to 11 and 17 from vestibule between Buildings A and B*	
		S. part	27	Room or access to 19 (?)	Greek sherds, imported transport amphorae, Eg. pottery, various objects (ivory: dice; stone: cake-mould [?], weights)
			19A	Room	Greek sherds, imported transport amphorae, Eg. pottery, various objects (iron: trident, dagger, knifes, pokers, chisels and wedges, fastener; bronze: chisel, stamp of Amasis, stem of a dipper, cup, arrowheads; faience: New Year flask; stone: whetstone, pumice, fragment of syenite bowl, weights)
			19B	Room	
			19C	Room	
			32	Pottery "drywell" at bottom of 19A	Eg. pottery
			31	Pottery "drywell", E. of 19A	Eg. pottery
	"Phase G" constructions around Casemate buildings and Annexe		1	Room N.W. of Building A	Greek sherd, block of iron (?)
			8	Room W. of Building A	Greek sherd (?), Eg. pottery, plaster jar-sealings of Psam. I
			12	Rooms S. of Building A	filled with sherds; imported transport amphorae
			24	Rooms S. of Building A	filled with chips of limestone
			6	*Room N. of Annexe C*	
			18	Room S.E. of Building A, S. of Annexe C	Large amount of Greek sherds, imported transport amphorae, Eg. pottery (including a pottery handle stamped Nekau II), and various objects (plaster jar-sealings of Psam. II and Amasis; demotic ostraca; faience: shabti [?], amulets; iron: fragments of scale-armour, knife, blade; bronze: statuette of Osiris and kohl stick; stone: weights)
			28	Room S. of Annexe C, lower level under 18	Eg. pottery
			29	Room S. of Annexe C, E. of 18	Large amount of Greek sherds, Eg. pottery (?), various objects (plaster jar-sealing of Psam. II and Amasis; faience amulet)
	Miscellaneous		*23*	*Close to the entrance (?)*	
			25	Area (?) S. of 18	Eg. pottery, stone weights
			21	Pottery "drywell", S.W. of Kasr	Imported transport amphorae, Eg. pottery
			56	*Burnt ground S.W of Kasr*	
			Beyond 29	?	30 or forty small limestone statuettes of captives
	S.E. part of enclosure		52	Iron workshops	Greek sherd, imported amphorae, Eg. pottery, bellows, whetstones and fragments of limestone plaques with scored grid; iron finds (?)
			57	Set of 4 weights in 52	Weights
			58	Set of 19 weights in 52	Weights
			54	Pottery "drywell" N. of 52 (in 53 ?)	Eg. pottery
			53	*Copper workshops, N. of 52*	Copper finds (?)
			61	Pottery "drywell" in 53	Eg. pottery (little cups and lids)
			55	Along inner side of S.E. section of enclosure wall	Imported transport amphorae, Eg. pottery, and possibly metal objects (silver lumps, silver bowl and dipper and gold handle?)
E. quarter			51	Buildings in E. quarter	Greek sherds, imported transport amphorae, Eg. pottery, various objects (stone and terracotta figures)
			50	Pit dug in long N. wall in 51	Imported transport amphorae, Eg. pottery
N.W. Ptol. mound			60	N.W. Ptol. mound	Bronze vessels, iron key (?), set of faience amulets; stone amulets (?)
			59	Set of 2 weights in 60	Weights

N.B.: 20, 33-34, 46-49 excluded from this table; italic = no find or record of find.

Objects for which Petrie gives only a general provenance (e.g. 'Camp'= the main enclosure) must be added: Imported transport amphorae, Eg. pottery, terracotta figure, faience objects (New Year flasks, amulets and beads, bezel, feather fly-flaps, plaque of Apries), ivory objects, fragments of white coral branch, iron objects (fragments of implements, knife, arrowheads), bronze objects (fragments of implements, mirror, lid, bowl, dipper, chisels or wedges, knife, arrowheads, statuette of Apis bull), silver objects (pair of uraci, ram-head) stone objects (steatite amulet, model grinder, weights).

Table 2 List of findspots arranged by excavation areas, with associated categories of finds

carry them,[306] and apart from the selection of objects that went to the Bulak Museum in Cairo,[307] most of the finds made by Petrie at Tell Dafana were shipped to England at the end of the season. After their arrival in London, a choice of objects was put on display in the Egypt Exploration Fund's annual exhibition, organized by Petrie in the three first weeks of September 1886 at the Archaeological Institute, Oxford Mansions, near Regent Street.[308] Soon after, the division of finds was agreed at the next annual meeting of the subscribers of the Egypt Exploration Fund: the largest part went to the British Museum (as the national collection, it was traditionally the largest recipient of finds in the early days of the Egypt Exploration Fund), while the rest was distributed to a number of other institutions subscribing to the Egypt Exploration Fund, partly in the UK, but also in many other places in the world. The largest batches of items after the British Museum went to the Museum of Fine Arts in Boston and the Royal Ontario Museum of Toronto. A few other museums also received substantial groups of objects.

In the EES archives are several distribution lists, more or less precise,[309] which show that while much of the dispersal happened immediately, some objects were also still being sent out much later, up until the early decades of the 20th century and possibly even later. Combining the information in these lists from a perusal of studies of some categories of material as well as from contact with and research in museums, we now know that there are at least 50 institutions that received material from Tell Dafana. Most of these still exist to this day and the majority, though not all, still possess all or some of the objects they received. A few institutions have since disappeared and their collections are not traceable, such as, for instance, the Chautauqua Archaeological Museum, torn down in 1930, while others actually deaccessioned some of the material. Moreover, several museums in the UK as well as the Museum of Berlin suffered heavy losses in the Second World War, and some objects from Tell Dafana were destroyed. In many cases, however, objects were catalogued long after they were received, when not all relevant documentation was still available, meaning that doubts linger over the provenance of certain objects, notably as regards to their potential provenance from one of the other sites that Petrie excavated during the same year of 1886 (including Naukratis, Tell Nebesha and Tell Gemaiyemi) and from which finds were often dispatched to museums as part of the same consignment as objects from Tell Dafana. While complete certainty cannot be achieved in every single case, the extensive research conducted in museums and archives worldwide for the present project has, however, done much to clear up the situation. As noted above, it is not the aim of the present publication to present the finds from Tell Dafana in their totality, which lies well beyond its scope, but relevant pieces in other collections are frequently cited and occasionally illustrated throughout the discussion. A list of collections holding Tell Dafana material is given in Appendix 2 in the hope that it might be useful for scholars in the meantime.

Notes

1 Coordinates: 30°50'55" – 52'26" N, 32°09'55"–11'30" E. For details of access to the site, see Spencer 2001, 10.

2 The analysis of the series of Landsat satellite imaging (available online at http://earthexplorer.usgs.gov/) shows that the agricultural development of the region started after 1985 to the east and north-east of the site, first with the digging of long rectilinear canals dividing the area into large plane-parallel plots, soon subdivided into numerous smaller plots. By the end of the 1980s, this operation was already almost completed. Black and white satellite images taken from the mid-1960s (CORONA program, declassified in 1996 and available from the United States Geological Survey) also give a good idea of the landscape in the region prior to development (e.g. images of 25 January 1965, 19 June 1967); see here **Pl. 2a**.

3 The limit between the actual plain and the swampy zone, running north-west, parallel to the edge of the Manzala lagoon, is clearly indicated on most 19th-century maps of the area (see for example Jacotin 1826a, sh. 2; Jacotin 1826b, sh. 31). It was flanked by a dyke or a levée when G.J. Chester visited the region (Chester 1880, 145; see also possibly the 'Gisr' mentioned in [Anon.] 1886a, 13). Although the formation of the Manzala lagoon, as we know it today, apparently did not take place before the mid-1st millennium AD, due to subsidence and intrusion of the sea inland, the landscape of the north-eastern Delta was already marked by large areas of wetland and brackish water lagoons, while the seashore progressively prograded towards the north. On the geomorphological evolution of the region in antiquity, see Daressy 1915, 202; Audebeau 1919, 117; Clédat 1923, 66; Daressy 1933, 169–78; Carrez-Maratray 2005–6, 195; also, with further literature: Coutellier and Stanley 1987, 257–75, esp. 268–9, 271, fig. 7D; Said 1992, 264; Said 1993, 76–7; Embabi 2004, 79–80; Gascoigne 2007, 161–3; Stanley and Toscano 2009, 158–70, esp. 165–9; Tronchère 2010, 32–7.

4 Birket Abu Deif on the *SoE* (*Survey of Egypt*) map 1/100,000 (kilom. series), no. 88/72 (El-Qanṭara), 1925; see also Daressy 1929, 329, fig; Daressy 1930, map; Fontaine 1948, 45, pl. 2. A short description of the water landscape near the site was also given by N. Berchère in 1861 (Wright 2010, 13); see also Chester 1880, 145; Petrie 1888, 47; Griffith Institute, Petrie Mss, Journal 1885–6, 109, 112 (hereinafter cited as 'Journal').

5 See the map of the Napoleonic expedition (Jacotin 1826a, sh. 2), our **Pl. 3a**; also Daressy 1933, 198–9, 201–2; Figueras 2000, 7–15. The *Antonine Itinerary* (ref. below, n. 16) seems to suggest that travellers were stopping first at Pelusium, before passing by Daphnae and then Tacasarta etc., all the way to Heliopolis and Memphis; without coming back to the Oasis of Qatiya, they were probably joining the desert road again immediately to the south of Pelusium, probably in the area of Tell Kedwa and Tell el-Herr.

6 However, recent Egyptian excavations at Tell Hebua I and II have revealed some traces of re-occupation of the New Kingdom fortresses during the Late Period.

7 On the geographical and hydraulic context of the region, as well as the strategic character of the position of the ancient locality, see Bietak 1975, 27–30, 47, n. 146, pp. 82–4, 131–2, fig. 10, pl. 4; Marcolongo 1992, 23–31; Figueras 2000, 5–118; also the earlier sources Griffith 1886, 11–12; Petrie 1888, 47, pl. xliii; Mallet 1893, 55. For a satellite view (Landsat 7, 2001) of the region, see Amin 2005, 49 (south-western corner).

8 Jacotin and Jomard 1818a and 1818b (2nd edn: Jacotin and Jomard 1830a and 1830b); Wilkinson 1842, 5; Wilkinson 1843, 447–8; Wilkinson 1847, 222; Wilkinson 1880, 328; Parthey and Pinder, 1848, 331; Prisse d'Avennes and Hamon 1848, 175; Heath and Corbaux 1855, 43, n.*; Schleiden 1858, 52, 163; Kiepert 1860, pl. 34 ('Tell Defenne' in later editions); Haigh 1868, 83; Millie, 1869, 7; Brugsch 1879, 644, 932; Maspero 1883, 400; Baedeker 1885, v (map), 424 (map), 48; see also the 1/200,000 British intelligence map: [Anon.] 1882a, sh. 2. For other variants deriving from this 'Defenneh', see for instance Johnston 1861, pl. 39 ('Tel Definneh'); Foucart 1901, 73, 74, 79 ('Dafanneh'); Spiegelberg 1904, 38; Spiegelberg 1930, 59 ('Defenne'); Baedeker 1928, 190 ('Tell Defenne', 'Tell ad-Daffâna').

9 'Deféïnéh': Jacotin and le Père 1809, pl. 10 (see also Jacotin and le

Père 1822, 2nd ed.); Jomard 1822, 822; Jacotin 1826a, sh. 2; Jacotin 1826b, sh. 31; Jomard 1830, 173; Hamilton and Lizars 1831, pl. 57; see also Griffith in Petrie 1888, 101; Griffith 1931, 75; 'Defeyneh': Jomard, loc. cit.; 'Tel Deffeïneh' and 'Tell Daffiné': Linant de Bellefonds 1855; ibid., 1882; 'Dapheineh': Badger 1862, 35 ('Dafeineh' on the front map); 'Tell Défenieh': Desplaces 1861c, 398; 'Tell-Deffenéh': Berchère 1863, 50, 53, 55, 108 (see Wright 2010, 20, 21); 'Tephene': Spratt 1860a, 454 [16]; 'Tefeneh': Desplaces 1866, 184.

10 'Tell el-Defné': Miles 1866a, 171; 'Tel Dephneh': Fortia d'Urban 1845, 44 ; Chester 1880, 144–6; 'Tel Defneh': ibid., map between 144 and 145; de Vaujany 1885, 226; 'Tell el-Deffné': Desplaces 1861b, 211, 212; 'Daphné', 'Tel-Daphné': Linant de Bellefonds 1872–3, 144–5, 169, 177, 180; '(Tel) el-Daphné': Desplaces 1861a, 190; Desplaces 1861c, 398; Miles 1866b, 367; Paponot 1884, 199, 206; 'Tel-el-Dafneh': Berchère (Wright 2010, xviii); 'Tel-Daphneh', 'Tell Daphneh': Socin 1881, 155; Badger 1862, 35; 'Tel Dafnieh', Larcher 1844, 336; 'Taphne' on the detail inset 'Das Nil Delta' of the map Die Nilländer oder Aegypten, Nubien und Habesch, 1853, in Weiland and Kiepert 1855, pl. 53; see also Spratt 1860a, 454–5 [16–17]; Brooks 1860, 199 ('Daphne', 'Tephne'); Spratt 1860b, 455 [17], 458–9 [20–21] ('Dephne', 'Tephanes', 'Defneh').

11 Chester 1880, 146; admitted by Petrie 1886a, 458; Petrie 1888, 47, 52; Griffith in Petrie 1888, 15, n. 1, pp. 100, 101, 102 107; Griffith 1888, 331; see also [Anon.] 1886dd, 565; Tomkins 1886, 172; Tomkins 1888, 207; Petrie 1892, 50; Petrie 1910, 41; Griffith 1931, 75; Aimé-Giron 1941, 445, n. 5. According to T.A.B. Spratt (1860a, 454 [16]; see also Brooks 1860, 199), people from the area were even using the pronounciation 'Tephne'. For other toponyms mentioned as parts of the site (Tell Farmah, El-Kalaah, Kasr el-Bint el-Yahudi, Tell Debowan), see below, nn. 52–5.

12 'Tell Dafana' on the SoE map 1/100,000, no. 88/72 (El-Qantara), 1945; see also Mahmud bey 1872; [Anon.] 1882b ('Tell el Dafaneh'); Bouteron and Chekib Pasha 1888; ibid., 1/400,000 ('Tell Dafanah'); Audebeau et al. 1897 ('Tells Dafanah'); 'Kom Dafana' on the following SoE maps: 1/25,000, no. 90/720 (Gezîret el Ghizlan), 1949 (here **Pl. 2b**); 1/50,000, no. 57 (El-Managât, V-V. NE), 1912; 1/100,000 ('quadrant' series) no. C12 (Ismailia), 1914; 1/100,000 ('kilom.' series), no. 88/72 (El-Qantara), 1925; 1/100,000 (Ismaileya), 1950; 1/100,000 (Al-Ismailiya), 1953; see also [Anon.] 1951; Engelbach 1931, 17, 18, 42; [Ministry of Finance, Egypt] 1928, 12; Ramzī 1953–4, 246 (wrongly transcribed 'Kom Dafanna' by Timm 1984, 554, n. 3); Bernand 2000, 1119. But see also [Ministry of Finance, Egypt] 1914, 33 ('Tell Defna'). The spelling and vocalization 'Dafanu' proposed by Budge (1920, 1059, 1062) is inaccurate. On the final '–a' (transcription of a tā' marbūṭa, here mostly written without the diacritic dots) instead of '–eh', see Arnaudiès 2005, 250–1.

13 'Kawm Dafnah' on the most recent SoE map 1/50 000, no. NH36-J5c (Maṣraf Baḥr al-Baqar), 1997.

14 See Erman 1890, 959, n. †; Griffith 1931, 77; Aimé-Giron 1941, 445. D-f-n gives for instance dafn, 'burial'; madfan/madafin, 'cemetery (/-ies)'; dafina/dafna, 'buried treasure(s)', etc.: de Biberstein Kazimirski, 1860, 714; Wehr 1979, 331; Müller 2000, 28; Steingass 2005, 367; El-Kadi and Bonnamy 2007, 123, n. 1, p. 295.

15 Jacotin 1826b, pl. 31; Jomard, 1830, 173.

16 Itinerarium provinciarum Antonini Augusti, 162, 6; Parthey and Pinder 1848, 73; Ball 1942, 141; Fontaine 1955, 53; Timm 1984, 552; Timm 1992, 2510, n. 9; Worp 1991, 292–3; Carrez-Maratray 1999, 32, 69, no. 77.

17 Von Lemm 1900, 82; Daressy 1933, 200–1, 202; Ball 1942, 167, 171; Timm 1984, 554, n. 2; Carrez-Maratray 1999, 32, 71, no. 83. Billerbeck and Zubler 2011, 18–19, no. 35; cf. Eustathius of Thessalonica, Commentarii in Dionysium Periegetem, 916, who also refers to Daphnae – with the Herodotean plural form – near Pelusium, beside several other Daphne (Müller 1861, 379; Carrez-Maratray 1999, 71, no. 84, with wrong reference to Müller). On the multiple Daphne in the ancient Mediterranean world, see, for instance, de la Martinière 1768, 606–7; de la Martinière 1776, 42–4; Bischoff and Möller 1829, 404; Ruge et al. 1901, 2136–8; Bürchner 1903, 338; about another Daphne in the Fayum: Calderini 1973, 93; Daris 1996, 42; Daris 2007, 51; Verreth 2008, 125, 636.

18 Cf. Carrez-Maratray 1999, 24–7, 32. The equations between the classical and biblical toponyms were already long supposed and accepted in the 18th century (see for instance Polus 1685, 670; Calmet 1714, 452; Calmet 1715, 314; Calmet 1722, 404; de la Martinière 1738, 286; Pococke 1743, 20; see also R. Pococke's map Tabulam Aegypti, London [Overton ed.], 1743; Zedler 1744, 1504, 1779; Diderot 1765, 895), when J.-B. Bourguignon d'Anville (1766, 44–5, 96) tried to link these toponyms with a town Safnas mentioned by M. Al-Edrisi, an Arab geographer of the mid-12th century (Sionita and Hesronita 1619, 102; Dozy and de Goeje 1886, 184, § 154; see also Toussoun 1922, 97, pl. II; Daressy 1931, 194–5, 197, 200). This identification was soon justifiably questioned by E. Quatremère (1811, 296–8), but was still echoed in many publications and maps during the 19th century. C. Weigel's map, Aegyptus inferior sive Delta, Nürnberg, 1720, for J.D. Koehler's Descriptio Orbis Antiqui in XLIV Tabulis exhibita, already mentioned 'Tahpanhes/Daphnae Pelusiae', situated approximately in the right area. Daphnae appears on one of Bourguignon d'Anville's maps (Aegyptus Antiqua Mandato Serenissimi Delphini publici juris facta, 1765), as well as on earlier maps since the 16th–17th centuries: T. Stella, Itinera Israelitarum ex Aegypto loca et insignia miracula diversorum locorum et patefactionum divinarum, Antwerp, 1559 (where 'Taphnis' is identified with 'Sylae' and 'Sethrois'); [Anon.], Patriarchatus Alexandrini Geographica descriptio, Paris, 1640 ('Daphnis'); Duval, L'Egipte dressée sur le second livre d'Hérodote, undated (probably 3rd quarter of the 17th century; 'Daphene de Peluse'); G. Robert de Vaugondy, Veteris Aegypti tabula, Paris, 1743 ('Daphnae Pelusiae'); R. Pococke, Tabulam Aegypti, London [Jefferys ed.], 1743 ('Daphnae Pelusiae').

19 MT (Hebrew) and Vulgate (Latin): Jeremiah 2.16; 43.7–9; 44.1; 46.14; Ezekiel 30.18; LXX (Greek) and Coptic version: Jeremiah 2.16; 24.16 (only in Sahidic Coptic); 50.7–9; 51.1; Ezekiel 30.18; Judith 1.9; attestations are gathered in von Lemm 1900, 81–4; Koehler and Baumgartner 1990, 1584; Görg 1999, 24; Carrez-Maratray 1999, 77–8, nos 105–10; Verreth 2006, 726, 841–6; Contardi 2009, § 1.1; see also Petrie 1888, 52; Müller 1903, 4887–8; Spiegelberg 1904, 39–40; Spiegelberg 1930, 59; Vigouroux 1912b, 1991–4; Aimé-Giron 1941, 443–4; Alt 1943, 66–8; Lambdin 1962, 510; Golb 1965, 269, no. 30; Zimmerli 1983, 134; Timm 1984, 552; Timm 1992, 2510–11; Jones and Fiema 1992, 308–9; Winnicki 1998, 44, n. 70; Schipper 1999, 281–2; Maier 2002, 37–8, 49, 196–8, 205, 208, 210–11, 264–6, 271–3, 276; Verreth 2003, 52–5; Devauchelle 2005, 875, 878–9.
In Greek, beside the most common invariable form 'Taphnas' (LXX, Eusebius of Caesarea) on which the invariable Coptic equivalent is based, a declinable 'Taphnai' also appears occasionally (Ezekiel [LXX] 30.18; Hippolytus; [Anon.], Vitae Prophetarum; Pseudo-Athanasius; Olympiodorus; Theodoret – ref. below, n. 25); Lemm 1900, 84, n. 275; Alt 1943, 66; Albright 1950, 14, n. 4; Timm 1992, 2510–11; Schwemer 1995, 165, n. 14; Schwemer 1997, 570–1, n. b; Winnicki 1998, 44, n. 70; Carrez-Maratray 1999, 32.
On the equivalence between 'Taphnas/Taphnai', probably closer to the reality of the ancient Egyptian toponym (below, nn. 37–44) and Herototus' 'Daphnai', see Albright, op. cit.; Quaegebeur 1995, 252; Müller 2000, 28–9. Daphnai ('The-Laurels') might well have been only a paronym, more meaningful for Greeks, of the local Egyptian/Hebraic designation.
The mention of Taphnis in Ezekiel (Vulgate) 30.14 must be put aside because it actually corresponds to Tanis in the Hebraic version and Greek LXX, see Verreth 2003, 54–5; Verreth 2006, 842–4, 846. A similar confusion appears in Egeria and Peter the Deacon (ref. below, n. 26), as well in other texts (von Lemm 1900, 86; see also Rabanus Maurus, paraphrasing Jerome [ref. below, n. 25]). For the various forms ('Tefnas', 'Tafnas', 'Tafnes', 'Tafches'), in the Ethiopian Ge'ez version of the Bible (and 'Tefeni', in the Legends about Jeremiah), see von Lemm 1900, 82, 85.

20 4Q384.7.2; 4Q385.16.ii.1; 4Q385a.18.ii, 1 & 6: Dimant 1994, 14, 17, see also 12, 22; Smith 1995, 137, 142, 143; Dimant 2001, 95, 98, 105, 108, 163–4, 166; Brady 2005, 100, n. c, p. 108; Jassen 2007, 225, n. 41. The Qumran manuscripts also include a mention of Tahpanhes in a fragment of Jeremiah 43.7–9 (4Q72a.2.7–8; Tov 1992, 538, 540; Tov 1997, 203, 205).

21 Aimé-Giron 1941, 439, 442–3, pl. 40; Donner and Röllig 1966, 12,
   no. 50; Donner and Röllig 1968, 67–8, no. 50; Magnanini 1973, 81,
   no. 4; Pardee 1982, 165–8; Oren 1984, 36; Chuvin and Yoyotte
   1986, 42, n. 4; Bonnet 1987, 121–2; Lipiński 1995, 247, n. 177, 183;
   Winnicki 1998, 44, n. 70; Carrez-Maratray 2000, 165, n. 25;
   Lindenberger 2003, 138–9, no. 70; Vittmann 2003, 66, n. 94;
   Verreth 2006, 427–8 (with further lit.); Contardi 2009, § 1.2. The
   papyrus is kept at the Egyptian Museum in Cairo.
22 Pap. Cairo JE 43485 and Pap. Berlin 13493, see Porten and
   Yardeni 1989, 106–11, nos B4.3–4, p. xliv.
23 Perdrizet and Lefebvre 1919, 109, no. 614; Austin 1970, 21, n. 4;
   Jeffery 1990, 355, 358, no. 51, pl. 70; Carrez-Maratray 1999, 246,
   no. 407; Carrez-Maratray 2000, 165, 170.
24 Jones *et al.* 1988, 47–57; Fiema and Jones 1990, 239–48; Zayadine
   1990, 156–7, 171, fig. 10; Lacerenza 1996, 112, no. N4; Vittmann
   2003, 189, n. 43. The fact that 'Daphnae' was here precisely
   designated as 'Egyptian' probably has nothing to do with the
   necessity to differentiate it from its homonym in the Antiochia
   suburbs, but might simply imply that the locality was, for the
   Nabateans, on Egyptian territory, beyond the Pelusian frontier
   (pers. comm. Laurent Tholbecq, ULB, Brussels); see also Bowers
   Peterson 2006, 40 ('Daphnae [which is known] in Egyptian
   language').
25 – Hippolytus of Rome, *Commentarii in Danielem*, 1.13.19 (Carrez-
   Maratray 1999, 78, no. 111; Bonwetsch and Richard 2000, 28–31);
   about the tradition of Jeremiah's stoning and burial in Taphnas,
   see also [Anon.], *Vitae Prophetarum*, 5.1–2 (*PG* 43, 421): von Lemm
   1900, 86; Schwartz 1949, 78, n. 2; Timm 1992, 2513, n. 3;
   Schwemer 1995, 159, 165–72; Schwemer 1997, 570–1, n. b (see also
   pp. 546, 550); Carrez-Maratray, 1999, 79, no. 112; Yeung 2002, 110;
   Kopeliovich 2009, 9–10; see also Usuardus, Isidorus of Sevilla and
   Baronius Caesar (ref. below);
   – Eusebius of Cesarea, *Onomastikon*, 164.24; cf. the Latin version in
   Jerome, *Liber de situ et nominibus locorum hebraicorum*, 166 (*PL* 23, 971;
   Klostermann 1966, 164, l. 24, p. 165; Carrez-Maratray 1999, 79,
   no. 113, 80, no. 116; Freeman-Granville *et al.* 2003, 91, 159; Notley
   and Safrai 2005, 154–5, § 911, p. 192); see also Eusebius of Cesarea,
   De vitis prophetarum, *Ieremias* (*PG* 22, 1269), paraphrasing Jeremiah
   44.1, repeated by (Pseudo-) Athanasius, *Synopsis scripturae sacrae*,
   20.39 (*PG* 28, 364; see Verreth 2006, 726, n. 3152);
   – St Jerome (Eusebius Sophronius Hieronymus), *Commentariorum in
   Esaiam*, 9.15 (Is 30.1–5; Adriaen 1963, 382, 383; Gryson and Somers
   1996, 1073, 1075); id., *Commentariorum in Hiezechielem*, 9.30.1–19
   (Glorie 1964, 418–22, 427, 429); id., *Commentariorum in Hieremiam*,
   1.1.1–3.4; 1.2.16–17, .18; V, 24, 1–10.14; Reiter 1960, 3, 19, 20, 236);
   id., *Liber interpretationis hebraicorum nominum*, 55.23, 58.29 (de
   Lagarde 1959, 128, 132; Carrez-Maratray 1999, 79–80, nos 114–15);
   see also id., *Epistulae*, 142 (most recently Fürst 2002, 452–3; Fry
   2010, 439, 442).
   Later authors (4th–16th centuries AD) also mention Taphnas/
   Taphnes, more or less quoting and/or paraphrasing the biblical
   text:
   – (Pseudo-)Joannes Chrysostomus, *Fragmenta in Jeremiam* (in
   catenis), 2.16 and 43.13 (*PG* 64, 764, 1012); id., *Synopsis scripturae
   sacrae*, in Jeremia, 386 (*PG* 56, 380);
   – Theodoret of Cyrus, *Interpretatio in Jeremiam*, 1.2.16, 8.43.8–9 (*PG*
   81, 508, 700), 9.46.14 (*PG* 81, 712; see Verreth 2006, 726, n. 3153);
   id., *Interpretatio in Ezechielem*, 12.30.18 (*PG* 81, 1116);
   – Olympiodorus (Diaconus) of Alexandria, *Commentarii in Jeremiam*
   (in catenis), 43.8 (*PG* 93, 701), 46.14 (*PG* 93, 704);
   – Gregorius I Magnus, *Moralia in Iob*, 25.10.27 (*PL* 76, 338; Adriaen
   1985, 1252; simply quoting Jeremiah 2.16);
   – Isidore of Seville, *De ortu et obitu Patrum*, 38.1–2 (*PL* 83, 142;
   Chaparro Gomez 1985, 166–7);
   – Rabanus Maurus, *Commentarii in Ezechielem*, 11.30 (*PL* 110, 805,
   806, 809, 810; paraphrasing Jerome, *Commentarii in Hiezechielem*,
   9.30; Verreth 2006, 844, n. 3173); Rabanus Maurus, *Expositio super
   Ieremiam prophetam*, 14.43, .44 (*PL* 111, 1091, 1092; paraphrasing
   Jerome, *Commentariorum in Esaiam*, 9.15). In both cases, Rabanus
   Maurus (as well as Jerome) confused Tanis and Taphnis;
   – Walafrid Strabo, *Prophetia Jeremiae*, 50.8 (*PL* 114, 58);
   – Usuardus of Saint-Germain-des-Prés, *Martyrologium per anni
   circulum*, Die 1 Maji (*PL* 124, 10; Dubois 1965, 221);

   – Petrus Comestor, *Historia Scholastica*, 13 (*PL* 198, 1440);
   – Thomas Aquinas, *Biblica. Super epistulam ad Timotheum Primam*,
   6.4 (simply quoting Jeremiah 2.16); see Baer 2007, 92, par. 280;
   – Gregorius XIII, *Martyrologium Romanum...*, Venice, 1583, 73 (and
   the revision by Baronius Caesar, *Martyrologium Romanum ad novam
   Kalendarij rationem & ecclesiasticae historiae veritatem restitutum*,
   Antwerp 1589, Die 1 Maji).
26 Aetheria/Egeria, *Itinerarium*, 9.5–6 (see also Peter the Deacon, *De
   Locis Sanctis*, 5.9; Gingras 1970, 63–4, 186–8; Donner 1979, 102–3,
   n. 80; Wilkinson 1981, 103, 203, 217; Maraval 1982, 82–3, 164, n. 1;
   Schwemer 1997, 571; Carrez-Maratray 1999, 67, no. 73, p. 80, no.
   117; Wilkinson 2002, 93, 118). At first glance, the text would appear
   to concern Tanis, if the location of the place visited by the pilgrim,
   between Arabia (= Phakoussa, modern Fakus) and Pelusium on
   her travels towards Palestine at the end of the 4th century AD, did
   not fit better with the position of *Dafno* in the *Antonine Itinerary*
   (Timm 1984, 552–3, nn. 11–13; Jones and Fiema 1992, 309;
   Schwemer 1995, 166, n. 19; Carrez-Maratray, loc. cit., n. 38): it is
   thus plausible that Egeria passed by Daphnae/*Dafno* under an
   incorrect impression that it was Tanis.
27 Pap. Turin 7119 (63000, cod. 9); von Lemm 1900, 82; Orlandi 1968,
   95, l. 7, p. 125 (who incorrectly read 'Afnas', because of an
   inaccurate interpretation of the toponym as 'Aphnaion' [below,
   nn. 34–5]); Timm 1984, 553; Timm 1992, 2511–2; Verreth 2006,
   525, n. 2184.
28 Pap. Berlin 9009, 5.23, 12.13; Möller 1904, 37, 44, nos 31.5.23,
   31.12.13; Jansen 1950, 64, 69, see also pp. 22, 31, 40, 48. See also von
   Lemm 1900, 81; Schwartz 1949, 74, 77–8; Spalinger 1977, 238–9;
   Timm 1984, 555, n. 12; Timm 1992, 2512, n. 8; Döpp 2003, 2–4, 5;
   Ladynin 2004, 4–5; Dillery 2005, 397; Demaria 2006, 66; Ladynin
   2007, 1075; Contardi 2009, § 3.
29 *Chronicle* 51.18, .25, .28, 72.17; Zotenberg 1883, 49, 50, 67 (text in
   Ge'ez), 271–2, 293; Charles 1916, 37–8, 55 (both wrongly
   translating 'Thebes'); Crum 1917, 208. Colin (1995, 50, 51) reads
   Ṭānbās, but translates 'Daphnae'; see also von Lemm 1900, 84–5;
   Schwartz 1949, 77; Timm 1992, 2512; Ladynin 2004, 4–5; Ladynin
   2007, 1075; Contardi 2009, § 3.
30 Timm 1984, 553; MacCoull 1986, 52, nn. 3–4; Timm 1992, 2511,
   2512, Jones and Fiema 1992, 309; Verreth 2006, 562.
31 Neubauer 1868, 408–9; Braude 1968, 367.
32 Gaster 1899, 102, 165.
33 Carrez-Maratray 1999, 25, contra Austin 1970, 20; see also Timm
   1992, 2512. For Alt (1943, 64, 68), Daphnae/*Dafno* has nothing to
   do with biblical Tahpanhes/Taphnas, which he locates further to
   the east (see also Simons 1959, 443; Timm 1984, 552).
34 Still in Di Berardino 1988, 92, 96; Jones and Fiema 1992, 309;
   Schwemer 1997, 571.
35 Most recently Figueras 2000, 162–3; Verreth 2006, 67, n. 158, pp.
   522–9, 1003–5, esp. 524–5, 1003; see also Calderini 1966, 284;
   Timm 1984, 137–9, 552, 554; Timm 1992, 2512–3, nn. 10–11;
   Carrez-Maratray 1999, 25–6, 33, nos 79–80, p. 49, no. 25, pp.
   69–70, nos 78–9; Donner 1983, 86; Donner 1992, 78; Piccirilo and
   Alliata 1999, 94, fig. p. 87.
36 See pp. 9–10.
37 Already suspected by Champollion 1814, 78–9, 200; von Lemm
   1900, 83.
38 Attested from the end of the Middle Kingdom (Nehesy), frequent
   in the New Kingdom, and also attested during the Late Period
   (Panehesy), cf. Ranke 1935, 113.13, 209.4, see also 304.20; Ranke
   1952, 354; Albright 1950, 13; 22; Loprieno 1998, 212–13; Winnicki
   1998, 35; Muchiki 1999, 86–7.
   On the Semitic anthroponym Phinehas considered as deriving
   from it, see Vigouroux 1912a, 319–20; Albright 1950, 13, n. 2;
   Lambdin 1962, 510; Mauch 1962, 799–800; Spencer (J.R.) 1992,
   346–7; Loprieno 1998, 216–17; Görg 1999, 25, nn. 7–9; Görg 2001,
   151; Thon 2007; Angerstorfer 2007; Muchiki, loc. cit.
39 Spiegelberg 1904, 39–40; Spiegelberg 1930, 59–60; Wilson 1997,
   536; Loprieno 1998, 214–17; Winnicki 1998, 45; Görg 1999, 26–7;
   Schipper 1999, 282; Devauchelle 2005, 879; Contardi 2009, § 3.
   Nḥs, *Nḥsy*, *Pȝ-nḥsy* appear in several other Egyptian toponyms,
   see Spiegelberg 1914, 142, n. 1; Gauthier 1925b, 30; Gauthier 1926,
   97, 98; Spiegelberg 1930, 60; Tresson 1935–8, 824, 828; Gardiner
   1937, 52; Gardiner 1948, 121; Albright 1950, 14, n. 2; Caminos 1954,

200, 211; Vernus 1978, 108, n. a, pp. 121, 123, 126, n. k, pp. 362, 364, 457–8; Chappaz 1982, 73, 75–6, n. i-k, p. 77; Winnicki 1991a, 418; Winnicki 1998, 43–4, 45; Leitz 2002a, 290; Ritner 2009, 433; see also Tod I, 60.5, II, 280.7, 282.6.

40 Followed by Aimé-Giron 1941, 444; Albright 1950, 13–14; Montet 1957, 192; Lambdin 1962, 510 ; Görg 1999, 25; Muchiki 1999, 236.

41 Winnicki 1991a, 418–19; Winnicki 1998, 45–6; Winnicki 2000, 169 n. 18; Devauchelle 2005, 878–9; Verreth 2006, 34; Verreth 2011, 222–3.
– Pap. dem. Cairo 31169, r° III, 10 [x+ 69] (4th–2nd centuries BC): most recently de Cenival and Yoyotte 2012, 259–60; see also Spiegelberg 1906–8, 272; Daressy 1910–11, 166, no. 10; Müller 1911, 196; Gauthier 1925a, 103; Chuvin and Yoyotte 1986, 48, n. 33; Zauzich 1987, 87, 90; Den Brinker 2005, 135; Verreth 2006, 50, 51; Johnson 2012, 3–4;
– Pap. dem. Paris BN 215, v° a, l. 16, 18 (2nd quarter 3rd century BC): Spiegelberg 1914, 26–8, 142, no. 608; Spiegelberg 1930, 59; Aimé-Giron 1941, 445; Smith and Hughes, 1980, 154, n. 11; Hoffmann 1992–3, 20–1; Johnson 2004, 11; Devauchelle 2005, 878; Hoffmann and Quack 2007, 161; Contardi 2009, § 4.2; Verreth 2011, 222;
– Pap. dem. Berlin 13588, 3, l. 3 (2nd–1st centuries BC): Spiegelberg 1930, 59, 60; De Meulenaere 1951, 35, n. 114; Erichsen 1956, 60, 70; Smith and Hughes 1980, 154–5, n. 12; Quaegebeur 1990, 261; Smith 1991, 101–4; Winnicki 1998, 46; Johnson 2004, 11; Devauchelle 2005, 878; Guermeur 2005, 307–8; Gilmore, Ray 2006, 192; Contardi 2009, § 4.2; Verreth 2011, 223;
– Pap. dem. London, BM EA 10508, 4, l. x+6, 9, 18 (1st century BC): Glanville 1955, 12–15, pl. 4; Thissen 1984, 18, 142; Stricker 1958, 59, 60; Lichtheim 1980, 163, n. 14; Quaegebeur 1990, 251, n. 48, pp. 260–1, 263; Thissen 1991, 254–5; Johnson 2004, 11; Devauchelle 2005, 878; Hoffmann and Quack 2007, 279; Contardi 2009, § 4.4; Smith 1968, 211, 212, n. 1; Smith and Hughes, 1980, 146, n. aq, pp. 152, 154–5; Verreth 2011, 223; Agut 2011, 45–6, 51–2;
– Ostr. dem. Karnak LS 462.4, l. 3 (3rd century BC): most recently Chauveau 2011, 39–45, esp. 41–2, n. 3.b, p. 44; see also Zauzich 1984, 193; Winnicki 1991b, 89–91; Guermeur and Thiers 2001, 214, n. 37; Johnson 2004, 11; Devauchelle 2005, 878; Contardi 2009, § 4.1; Verreth 2011, 222.

42 See, for example, Stricker 1958, 59, 60; Winnicki 1991a, 418–9; Winnicki 2000, 169, n. 18; Johnson 2004, 11; Devauchelle 2005, 879–80; Winnicki 1998, 45–7; Verreth 2006, 34. For J.K. Winnicki, the toponym may have originated from the presence of Asiatic and Nubian populations in the region.

43 Zauzich 1985, 115–16; Zauzich 1987, 87; see also Verreth 2003, 52; den Brinker *et al.* 2005, 135. On the meaning of *ꜥḥy* as 'aviary' and its use in toponyms, see Vandorpe 1991, 115–22.

44 Quack 2000, 4; Contardi 2009, § 3.

45 Spiegelberg 1930, 59, 60; De Meulenaere 1975, 990; Timm 1984, 551; Quaegebeur 1995, 252, n. 51; Winnicki 1998, 45, 46; Schipper 1999, 282; Jansen-Winkeln 2004, 80.
– Pap. Anastasi VI, 2, 2–3: Brugsch 1879, 931–2; Chester 1880, 146, n.*; Wilkinson, in Baedeker 1885, 482, n. †; von Lemm 1900, 83; Gauthier 1929, 73, 74; Spiegelberg 1930, 59; Gardiner 1937, 73, 2, 2–3; Aimé-Giron 1941, 460, n. 1; Gardiner 1941, 58, n. 2; Caminos 1954, 280, 283, n. 10; Montet 1957, 191–2; Vandier 1964, 67; De Meulenaere 1975, 990; Devauchelle 2005, 876, 879;
– Pap. dem. Cairo 31169, II, 8: Spiegelberg 1906–8, 271, n. 6; Daressy 1910–11, 160, no. 8; Gauthier 1929, 41, 104; Spiegelberg 1930, 59; Johnson 2012, 152; de Cenival and Yoyotte 2012, 249;
– Pap. dem. Berlin 13588, 2.6, 2.8, 2.10, 3.1: Spiegelberg 1930, 59; Erichsen 1956, 53, 54, 55, 59, 60, 65–6, 67, 69–70; Hornung 1965, 39, n. 1; Smith and Hughes 1980, 155; Quaegebeur 1990, 261; Smith 1991, 101; Winnicki 1998, 46–7; Guermeur 2005, 307–8; Lull 2007, 255; Verreth 2011, 222–3; Quack 2009, 72; Johnson 2012, 152, 153;
The *tbny* supposed to be mentioned several times in the Archive of Hor (reign of Ptolemy VI), and usually associated with this Tjeben(et) (Ray 1976, no. 7, l. 6–7, pp. 35–6, n. h, pp. 36–7, n. f, no. 26 r°, l.1, pp. 93–5, no. 60, l. 1–2, pp. 169, 170 n. a; Winnicki 1998, 45, n. 71; Carrez-Maratray 1999, 33, n. 75; Devauchelle 2005, 878), first re-read as a possible abbreviation of Sebennytos (Betro *et al.* 1982, 36, 38–9, n. 6; see also below, n. 47), was in fact a misreading

of a military title (Smith 1989, 53, n. 17; Den Brinker *et al.* 2005, 839, 840, n. 16; Verreth 2011, 222; Johnson 2012, 152–3, 174). For another uncertain attestation of 'Tjeben' in a Ptolemaic graffito in Medinet Habu, cf. Thissen 1989, 146–7, no. 236, l. 17; Edgerton 1937, pl. 60; Verreth 2011, 222.

46 Albright 1950, 14, n. 4; Loprieno 1998, 216, n. 46; Görg 1999, 25; Leclère 2008, 510, n. 12; Contardi 2009, § 3; Weber 2012b, 220, 221, n. 212; see already Gauthier 1929, 74.

47 Daressy 1910–11, 160; Budge 1920, 1063 (but see ibid., 1059, 1062); Gauthier 1929, 74, 104; Spiegelberg 1930, 59; Gardiner 1941, 58, n. 2; Albright 1950, 14, n. 4; Caminos 1954, 283, n. 10; Albright 1950, 14, n. 4; Betro *et al.*, loc. cit. A third Egyptian toponym in the Cairo *onomasticon*, *Tpḥnw*, had been linked unconvincingly with Daphnae/Tahpanhes, cf. Daressy, 1910–11, 162, no. 18; Gauthier 1929, 41, 155.
One evidently has to disregard the attempts of Daressy (1929, 316–18, 320) and Brugsch (1879, 644) to identify the site respectively with Piramesse and with the fort of Tjarou mentioned in Pap. Anastasi V, as well as the hypothesis of Griffith (in Petrie 1888, 108; still followed by Clédat 1924, 40–3; see also Mallet 1893, 56, n. 1, much less convinced) to introduce the toponym *Bnw(t)* into the debate (Gauthier 1925b, 21–2; Gauthier 1927, 67; see Daressy 1931, 219–20; Loprieno, 1998, 216, n. 46), along with other etymological attempts by von Lemm 1900, 83–4.

48 Already noted by Spiegelberg 1904, 38, n. 3, see also p. 40, n. 1. On the eastern border of Egypt from these texts, see Verreth 1999.

49 Sherd found at the bottom of a cell of the larger casemate building (A), see below, n. 161. The New Kingdom dating of the brick construction noted by Petrie under the pavement to the north of the casemate building complex (Petrie 1888, 47; still admitted by Bietak 1975, 83, 103, n. 386, p. 170, n. 712, p. 179; Weber, in Schlotzhauer and Weber 2005, 82, n. 40), as well as the same dating, by L. Borchardt, of a limestone statuette fragment of captive found in the foundations of the larger casemate building and now kept in the Cairo Museum (JE 27393 = CG 749; Petrie 1888, 53, 54; Journal, 132, 135; Borchardt 1930, 73, pl. 139; Porter and Moss 1934, 7; Devauchelle 2005, 877) are based on no valid arguments. Incidentally, G. Maspero (1902, 185, no. 711; id. 1903, 264) had already dated the statuette to the 26th dynasty.

50 Below, n. 111.

51 Clédat 1924, 56–7; Bietak 1975, 27–8, 30, 82, 84, fig. 10, p. 105, fig. 16, pp. 131–2, pl. 4; Carrez-Maratray 2005–6, 196; Carrez-Maratray, Defernez forthcoming. This canal might correspond to the one mentioned by Strabo – quoting Artemidorus (*Geography*, 17.24; see Jones 1932, 75–6; Charvet and Yoyotte 1997, 120–1, n. 261) – as filling the 'Marsh Lakes', probably Lake Ballah and the paleo-lagoons of El-Qantara. The watercourse was called 'Bahr Mansoura' on the map of the Napoleonic Expedition (Jacotin 1826b, pl. 31; see also Daressy 1929, 321, 329, fig.) and was still partly watered in the 19th century (Journal, 112–13, 134, 135; Petrie 1888, 2; see also Berchère 1863, 54; Chester 1880, 145).

52 Journal, 109; Jacotin 1826b, pl. 31; elsewhere spelled 'Debouân' (Jomard 1822, 822; Jomard 1830, 173). This tell to the west would in fact fit with 'Tell Abou Ekeim' (or Akim) of the *SoE* maps; see also Clédat 1924, 72, 78; Daressy 1929, 308, 316; Bietak 1975, 30–31. On the recent *SoE* map 1/50,000 NH36-J5c (see above, n. 13) the northern mound is called 'Tell Kafri' ('Ruin mound'), the southern one 'Kawm Dafnah'. According to the *SoE* map 1/100,000 (kilom. series), no. 88/72 (El-Qantara), 1925, some hills at the southern edge of the site, both sides of the track, were called Tulul Ghannam and Tell el-Ragam.

53 Chester 1880, 146; see also Berchère 1863, 54–5.

54 'The Castle of the Jew's daughter', only attested for Tell Dafana by Petrie (Journal, 108; Petrie 1886b, 17; Petrie 1887, 31–2; Petrie 1888, 47, 50, 52, 53; Petrie 1892, 51; Petrie 1911a, 89–90; Petrie 1931, 68). According to Petrie, this would refer to the princesses who were among the Judeans who fled from Jerusalem to find refuge in Tahpanhes (Jeremiah, 43.3). However, one should not place too much emphasis on the allusive nature of this designation, in the context of the possible identification of the site with biblical Tahpanhes (see already Erman, 1890, 959; Müller 1903, 4888, n. 1): the giant granite naos of Amasis in Mendes bore the same name (Daressy 1890, 185); it also evokes the *Kasr al-bint al-Faraʿun*, 'Castle

of Pharaoh's daughter' given by the Bedawin to the Nabatean temple of Dushares in Petra, Jordan, as well as the *Kasr al-Banat* – ancient Euhemeria, in the Fayyum.

55 According to Chester (1880, 146), this toponym included the flat part of the site to the south of the hillocks. 'Tell Farmah' recalls the modern name of ancient Pelusium, Tell el-Farama, last avatar of an old pharaonic name (Carrez-Maratray 1999, 471; index, s.v. Péluse), although one cannot rule out that it might have been an incorrect transcription of a Tell *Fahma, 'The-mound-of-Charcoal', which would fit better with the burnt aspect of the hills.

56 'The citadel'; Jacotin 1826b, pl. 31. For Daressy (1929, 321), 'El-Qalaah' would have corresponded to the area south of the canal, while 'Defeineh' was on the northern side.

57 Petrie letter EES Mss XVI f 122; Journal, 108, 116; Petrie 1888, 53.

58 Desplaces 1861b, 211, 212; Daressy 1929, 326.

59 Berchère 1863, 50–6; Wright 2010, xviii, 20–2.

60 Chester 1880, 144–6.

61 Miles 1866a, 171 ('Bourboubaki'); Miles 1866b, 366–7 ('Bourbokaki'); Daressy 1929, 327, n. 2 ('Bourbouraki'); certainly the Dr B., mentioned by Clédat (1909, 117, n. 1), who reported in February 1862 the find of a few scarabs and bronze statuettes in a freshwater canal at the site; see also Berchère 1863, 42–3; Servin 1948, 67; Wright 2010, 18. This canal was an artificial channel dug to the east of Tell Dafana in 1862, from the river crossing the northern part of the site, to supply the 'camp' of El-Qantara, built at the beginning of the digging of the Suez canal, with freshwater (Badger 1862, 35; Daressy 1928, 326; Fontaine 1948, pl. 2; Servin 1948, 64).

62 Petrie 1888, 47. According to Petrie (Letter EES Mss Petrie XVI.f 117, 3), G. Maspero, director of the Antiquities service and the Bulak Museum, himself considered excavating at the site.

63 November 1882: JE 25207–25209, 25212; May 1883: JE 25409–25435.

64 Wilbour 1936, 253 (Thursday 12 April 1883); the objects seen by him include 'some small terracotta heads (...) almost as fine Greek art as the Tanagra statues', matching the objects registered in May 1883 in the Cairo (Bulak) Museum. On E. Allemant, see Wilbour 1936, 7, n. 1; Bierbrier 2012, 14. In a letter to R.S. Poole, 7 November 1883 (EES Mss XVI f 5), Petrie reports having been told by G. Maspero that 'he had found at Tell Defenneh Assyrian, Carian, & Roman remains and supposed it to be a site of early Greek settlers'; see also Sayce 1884, 51.

65 Already suspected by Maspero 1883, 401; see also Edgar 1904b, 73: 'most of the objects registered as 'Achat et fouilles de Daphnae' come from dealers and have no connection with Daphnae'.

66 Maspero 1883, 400, nos 5827, 5835, p. 401, nos 5900–1; Maspero 1894, 108, nos 362, 376; Maspero 1902, 274, nos 362, 376; Maspero 1903, 361, nos 362, 376; Maspero 1915, 545, nos 5570–1; Mallet 1893, 69, n. 6; Carrez-Maratray 1999, 289, n. 473.

67 Knoop 1987, 89–118, figs 29–37 (Cairo piece: p. 103, n. 281, fig. 37); still published as from Tell Dafana by Empereur 2002, 31–3, fig. 11.a, c (in which 'b' is a piece from Mendes [=JE 60607], not 'a'). For JE 25413, see a good parallel from Satricum, today in the Villa Giulia Museum in Rome (Knoop 1987, 178, n. 264, fig. 85 – I am grateful to Alexandra Villing for bringing this reference to my attention); Weber 2006, 145, n. 10.

68 = CG 27963–27964; Maspero 1883, 405, no. 5876; Edgar 1904a, 81–2, nos 27963–4, pl. 10; see Naso 2006, 194, no. 26, p. 198, n. 58.

69 See Maspero 1883, 400–1, who already suspected a Tarentine provenance. In the same lot however, JE 25409 is an Egyptian terracotta figurine from the Hellenistic Period. The other fragments are particularly close to a series of statuettes called the *Groupe du Banquet* coming from the 'Fondo Giovinazzi', where some excavations were conducted by François Lenormant, son of Charles Lenormant, a travel companion of J.-F. Champollion (see Bierbrier 2012, 323–4); see Wuillemier 1939, 399–410, 502, pls 28–30; Besques 1986, ix. For Tarentine terracottas of the same type, from the early 6th century BC onwards, see for instance Winter 1903, cv, 198–210; Herdejürgen 1978, 13–68; Besques 1986, 25–6, pls 21, pp. 78–80, pls 70–2, pp. 111–13, pls 110–11, pp. 122–7, pls 119–24; Higgins 1954, 336–70, pls 170–7, 180–1, 186–9. I am grateful to Céline Boutantin for her suggestions.

70 Maspero 1883, 402–3, nos 5830–2; Erman 1890, 959, n. ††; Mallet

1893, 57, n. 3; Maspero 1894, 133, no. 443; Maspero 1902, 260, no. 443; Maspero 1903, 345, no. 443; Maspero 1915, 253, no. 1191; Wiseman 1966, 155, n. 11. Petrie (1888, 51, 57) apparently considered these cylinders, which 'a native sold to the Bulak Museum', as authentic, and believed they had been found on the site. Sayce (1884, 51; 1886b, 144–5; 1890, 14) too, first took them for antiques that 'Maspero has exhumed at Tell Defenneh' (see also Brown 1887, 171), but recognized two of them as duplicates, and gave a translation of the third one; he later admitted that the items had been brought from Baghdad and not from Tell Dafana (Sayce 1889b, 345); see also Beecher 1889, 34, n. */3.

71 The cylinders mention the construction of an enclosure wall at Babylon. They are similar to other cylinder casts – with no provenance – acquired by the Cairo Museum in January 1883 (JE 25249 and 25250), in January 1888 (JE 28177.a-d, four items, purchased from 'Philip'), and in February (?) 1888 (JE 28208.a-b, two items purchased from 'Mohamed'). The texts of JE 28177.a-d and 28208.b also mention the construction of an enclosure wall in Babylon under Nebukadnezzar II, while the others evoke the foundation of the temple of the goddess Ninmaḥ in Babylon, under the same ruler, a sanctuary that H. Rassam excavated from 1879 to 1882 (mound of the 'Kasr'), and from where he had purchased a cylinder in 1878 (BM ME 91133 = Rm 676; see Ball 1889, 248–53). I am grateful to Michael Seymour (British Museum) for his comments and suggestions on this topic.

72 Re-registered JE 31665 = CG 3554; Maspero 1902, 167, no. 1407; id., 1903, 246, no. 1407; [Anon.] 1898, 283; von Bissing 1901, 62–3; von Bissing 1923–4, 193–4, fig. 4; Gubel and Cauet 1987, 196, n. 8.

73 =CG 27920; initially identified with the goddess Mylitta or Aphrodite; Maspero 1883, 399, no. 5821; Mallet 1893, 69, n. 2; von Bissing 1903, 150, 151 fig. 5b; Edgar 1904a, 72, no. 27920, pl. 2; possibly Maspero 1915, 252, no. 1189.

74 Edgar 1904b, 21, 73, nos CG 27498, 27499, pl. 11.

75 =TR 30/12/20/11; Müller 1906, 30–1, pl. 41; see also Vigouroux 1912b, 1991, 1992, fig. 445; Gressmann 1927, 101, pl. 144, fig. 354; Schäfer 1937, 54–6, pl. 7.b; Seyrig 1944, 73, n. 1; Albright 1950, 11, n. 1; Segall 1956, 78, fig. 5; Aimé-Giron 1941, 447–53, pl. 42; Bonnet 1987, 122; Jones *et al.* 1988, 52; Jones and Fiema 1992, 308 (wrongly called a statue); Carrez-Maratray 1999, 289, n. 474; Vittmann 2003, 66, n. 95, p. 67, fig. 28; Verreth 2006, 428, n. 1774; Devauchelle 2005, 877; Leclère 2008, 527, n. 94; Wasmuth and Ögüt 2010, 567–78; Weber 2012b, 216, n. 172, pp. 220–1, n. 211. Before 1906, the monument was only attributed a more general 'Lower Egypt' provenance (Maspero 1883, 358, no. 5492; Maspero 1894, 132, no. 438; Maspero 1902, 259–60; Maspero 1903, 345; and also Maspero 1915, 252, no. 1188).

76 Mainly Petrie 1888; see also Petrie 1886a, 458–9; Petrie 1886b, 17–19; Petrie 1887, 30–42; Petrie 1892, 50–63; Petrie 1911a, 85–93; Petrie 1931, 65–72. The discoveries were mentioned in several periodicals, newspapers and local gazettes in England and worldwide very soon after Petrie's return to England (for instance: [Anon.] 1886a, 13; [Anon.] 1886b; [Anon.] 1886c, 3; [Anon.] 1886d, 22–3; [Anon.] 1886e, 81–3; [Anon.] 1886f, 189–90; [Anon.] 1886g, 4; [Anon.] 1886h, 3; [Anon.] 1886i, 4; [Anon.] 1886j, 6; [Anon.] 1886k, 4–5, 6; [Anon.] 1886l, 3; [Anon.] 1886m, 3; [Anon.] 1886p, 3; [Anon.] 1886r, 11; [Anon.] 1886s, 564–7; [Anon.] 1886u, 3–4; [Anon.] 1886v, 3; [Anon.] 1886w, 602–6; [Anon.] 1886x, 3; [Anon.] 1886y, 3; [Anon.] 1886z, 3; [Anon.] 1886aa, 16; [Anon.] 1886bb, 5; [Anon.] 1886ee, 460–1; [Anon.] 1886ff, 350; [Anon.] 1886gg, 7; [Anon.] 1886hh, 433; [Anon.] 1887b, 3; [Anon.] 1887c, 3; B.[?] 1892, 832–3; [Anon.] 1894, 3) and when he organized, during the three first weeks of September 1886, an exhibition in London at the Archaeological Institute, Oxford Mansions, near Regent Circus, now Oxford Circus ([Anon.] 1886n, 142; [Anon.] 1886o, 13; [Anon.] 1886q, 159; [Anon.] 1886t, 329; [Anon.] 1886cc, 703–4; Frothingam Jr. 1886, 503. See also Brown 1886, 430–1; Miller 1886, 636–7; Sayce 1886a, 311; Sayce 1886b, 144–5; Smith 1886, 293–6; [Anon.] 1887a, 36; Brown 1887, 169–72; [Anon.] 1888, 590–1; Frothingam Jr. 1886, 461, 463–4; Frothingam Jr. 1889, 53–54; Ely 1889, 346–8; Dickerman 1890, 279–81. This list is not exhaustive.

77 The aforementioned Petrie Journal for 1885–6, in the Grifffith Institute, Oxford, particularly 106–78. A photocopy of this journal

is kept at the Petrie Museum, London. Some extracts are published in Petrie 1931, 65–72; Drower 1995, 98–9; Drower 2004, 61–6; see also Sayce 1923, 240–1. Thirteen photographs of the site before and during the 1886 excavations are preserved in the archives of the Egypt Exploration Society. Some were used as models for engravings in newspapers (Smith 1886, 293–5; see also [Anon.] 1886w, 605–6; Görg 1999, 27, 30 fig. 2), with the addition of small human figures which are misleading about the true scale of the photographed ruins. Some of the photographs are published in Spencer 2000, 27; Spencer 2007, 62–3; Leclère 2007a, 15.

78 Two Notebooks (Mss 74.e-f) and one Pocket Diary (Mss 9/5), kept in the archives of the Petrie Museum, London. Notebook 74.e includes for the most part a daily attendance record of the workmen for payment and accounting calculations, as well as a list of the findspot numbers at Tell Dafana. Notebook 74.f gives more archaeological information (lists of finds, sketches of complete pots, a copy of the text of the stela found in the northern part of the central enclosure, levels, sketches with measurements for the plan of the constructions and the site map, measurements of bricks, etc.). Some unpublished correspondence is kept in the archives of the Egypt Exploration Society: Mss Petrie XVI.f.117, .119, .122, .123, .125, .126, .127, .128, and .130, all written at the site, except for the first one.

79 Journal, 106–7, 111, 113, 116; Petrie 1886b, 17; Petrie 1888, 2–3, with a description of the rough nature of the shelters made by his workmen; see also EES archives, photo no. 485, here **Fig. 4**, showing Petrie's encampment (see also the illustration in Smith 1886, 293); the exact position is indicated on a sketch in his Notebook (Mss 74.f), 56 (here **Fig. 6**, left).

80 Journal, 116; Petrie 1886b, 17; Petrie 1888, 2; Petrie 1892, 50.

81 Journal, 117, 119, 122, 123–4, and also 126, 127, 129, 137, 140, 144, 145, 149, 152, 169.

82 Journal, 125–6; Diary, 7 April; area recleared later, before mid-May, see Journal, 166.

83 Journal, 135, 137–40, 159–60; Diary, 8, 19–22, 29 April.

84 Journal, 155–9, 160, 161–2; Diary, 3, 4 and 7 May.

85 Journal, 109–10, 117, mentioning a couple of bowls (BM GR 1888,0208.62-3, see Chapter 5, pp. 44, 93, 98, 100) and a Greek sherd with an inscription 'PET' (BM GR 1888,0208.60; Weber 2012b, 373–4, no. TD 291) from this area (see below, pp. 128–9).

86 Journal, 144, with mention of stone and terracotta statuettes (BM GR 1906,0301.3-4, see below, pp. 44, 56, 58).

87 Journal, 129, 162.

88 Journal, 118, 127; Diary, 26 March, 17 April; Petrie 1888, 60–1; Notebook 74.f, 56.

89 Journal, 136; Diary, 17 April, 10, 16–22 May; Petrie 1888, 59, pl. xliii.

90 Journal, 166–7; Petrie 1886a, 458; over an area of 1.2 (Journal, 167) to 2.4 ha (Petrie 1888, 59, pl. xliii).

91 Journal, 162–3; Diary, 8 May; Notebook 74.f, 52–7. The fragments of the large quartzite stela with hieroglyphic inscriptions of the Saite Period discovered to the north of the enclosure wall (below, nn. 124, 265) were discovered as early as the first week of work (Journal, 118–19).

92 On the packing, Journal, 170–2; Diary, 16–22 May; Notebook 74.f, 48–9, 58–9.

93 Petrie 1888, 60, pl. xliii (marked 'Pottery' and 'Temple'?); Notebook 74.f, 55; the excavation is not mentioned in Petrie's Journal.

94 Journal, 134; Notebook 74.f, 57; Petrie 1888, 52, 61, pl. xliii. Petrie supposed that the gold earrings brought to him by the Bedawin might have originated from these graves.

95 See below, pp. 27–31 and **Tables 1–2**.

96 A.H. Sayce (1889a, 314; 1889c, 227; see also Wenzel 1889, 1132–3) mentions excavations at the site in 1888 by a native 'allowed by the authorities of Bulaq', from which he supposed came a seal with an Aramaic inscription mentioning Jeremiah, purchased in Cairo by Wl. Golenischeff.

97 Fontaine 1948, 45, with n.*. A.L. Fontaine noted some remains of domestic houses in the north-eastern part of the site (ibid., 46, pl. II, 'traces d'habitations'), immediately to the south-east of the 'swamp' on Petrie' plan, along the left bank of the canal, and some large sandstone weights, corn-rubbers and fragments of basalt grindstones on Petrie's north-west 'Ptolemaic Mound' (ibid.). He also mentions (ibid., 41, n.**) a 10cm high head of a small black granite statuette of Osiris in the Museum of Ismaïliya (no. 456), with a label indicating 'Tell Daphnae'. Some photos published by Aimé-Giron (1941, 446, pl. 41) give an idea of the state of preservation of the site, particularly of the *Kasr*, in 1940.

98 Spencer, 2000, 26–7; Spencer 2001, 10; see also www.deltasurvey. ees.ac.uk/dafana212.html.

99 Fieldwork originally planned by the Department of Ancient Egypt and Sudan of the British Museum unfortunately proved impossible. A similar project on behalf of the *Institut français d'archéologie orientale* in 2000 had previously failed (Grimal 1999, 535; Mathieu 2000, 541; Mathieu 2001, 573).

100 Leclère 2007a; Leclère 2008, 528–9, pl. 11.5.b–6.

101 Above, nn. 15–19.

102 Petrie 1888, 53; see also Petrie 1887, 30–2; Petrie 1890, 272; Petrie 1892, 51, 52; Petrie 1905, 329–30; Petrie 1911a, 87, 89, 92, 93; Journal, 116, 128 (king's 'shooting-box'); Petrie 1886a, 458 ('palace or hunting-box of the kings'). According to Petrie, the 'camp' would have been occupied by the Greek troops while the surrounding quarters would have been the settlement of Greek merchants and sailors (Petrie 1888, 49; Petrie 1887, 31, 32).

103 Below, nn. 227–8.

104 A. Furtwängler (1890, 917–8) believed that Daphnae and the *Stratopeda* mentioned by Herodotus could not be the same place, but that Tell Dafana would have corresponded better to the *Stratopedon* given to the Ionians than to Daphnae itself, which would have to be searched for somewhere else in the neighbourhood. For A. Erman (1890, 959–60), the identification of Tell Dafana with Daphnae is uncertain; see also Murray 1892, 82; Mallet 1893, 54, nn. 3–4, p. 55, n. 1, p. 70; Dümmler 1895, 36, n. 2.

105 For the rejection of the identification, see mainly Rumpf 1925, 330; Rumpf 1927, 139; Rumpf 1925, 330; Rumpf 1933, 60; Cook 1933–4, 87, n. 3; Cook 1937, 227, 232–6; Roebuck 1951, 214, 217, n. 9; Cook 1954, 59–69; Austin 1970, 15, 16, 19, 20; Lloyd 1975, 17 (but see Lloyd 1988a, 137); Amborn 1976, 109–11; Boardman 1999, 117, 133; Haider 1988, 199–200; Kammerzell 1993, 174–5; Carrez-Maratray 2000, 160–3; Niemeier 2001, 21–2; Weber, in Schlotzhauer and Weber 2005, 83; Verreth 2006, 865–70, 1139; Weber 2007, 299–300, n. 3; Weber 2012b, 219–20; see also Lammert 1931, 329; Ball 1942, 8, 17; De Meulenaere 1951, 35–6 (but see p. 137); De Meulenaere 1975, 990; Braun 1982, 44; Perreault 1986, 163, 164; Haider 1996, 97–8; Baurain 1997, 302, n. 2; Bernand 2000, 1122; Weber 2001, 131, n. 33; Vittman 2003, 199; James 2003, 245, n. 50; Devauchelle 2005, 877; Weber 2006, 145; Carrez-Maratray 2010, 174; Pasek 2011, 242. Other authors have a less definite opinion (*Stratopeda* at, or possibly at, or adjacent to, or near Daphnae, more or less explicitly): Sourdille 1910, 87–8; How and Wells 1912, 175; Clédat 1923, 158–9; Parke 1933, 5; Aimé-Giron 1941, 445–6; Otto 1958, 239, 244; Lloyd 1988b, 44; Ray 1976, 36; Salmon 1981, 16, 20; Pernigotti 1985, 83; Quaegebeur 1990, 262, 264; Bettalli 1995, 63–4; Mumford 1998, 881; Schipper 1999, 282, n. 563; Möller 2000, 34–5; Haider 2001, 199, n. 16; Höckmann 2001, 226; Smoláriková 2002, 96–101; Ladynin 2004, 3, 7–9, 11; Jansen-Winkeln 2004, 80; Smoláriková 2006, 245, 246; Snodgrass 2006, 11–12; Ladynin 2007, 1076: Moyer 2011, 54.
The hypothesis of an identification of Tell Dafana with at least one of Herodotus' *Stratopeda* seems to have regained some popularity since the mid-1970s, after E.D. Oren's excavations of the site of Tell Kedwa (= Oren's 'T21'), south of Pelusium, that he identified with biblical Migdol and Herodotus' *Magdolos* (Oren 1979; Oren 1984) – though for the excavator himself (Oren 1979, 191; Oren 1984, 36–8), the *Stratopeda* were located at Tell Kedwa and not at Tell Dafana (see also below, n. 128).

106 This expression, as well as the story of a rebellion in the Egyptian army under Psamtik I, appears in a much later Ptolemaic demotic papyrus: Quack 2010–11, 79–80; Ryholt 2012, 346–9.

107 Literally Daphnae-'the-Peatlands'/'the-Marshes' (Carrez-Maratray 1999, 4, 21–32).

108 Verb φρουρέω, 'to guard'.

109 Godley 1920, 308–11; see also other translations: Grene 1987, 142–3; de Selincourt 1954, 113; Macaulay 1890, 128–9.

110 Godley 1920, 394–397; see also Obsomer 1989, 20–1; Grene 1987, 174–5; de Selincourt 1954, 141; Macaulay 1890, 162.

111 Spalinger 1978, 50–3; Lloyd 1988a, 16–18; Obsomer 1989, 28, 140, 141–6, 161, 168, 173; Malaise 1991, 200–1; Carrez-Maratray 1999, 282; Devauchelle 2005, 878. On Sesostris as a legendary king in the demotic literature and the possible parallel of this particular story in a demotic ostracon of the Late Ptolemaic/Early Roman Period (O. Leipzig UB 2217), see Ryholt 2010, 429–34, esp. 433–4; see also Quack 2013, 63–6. D. Wildung (1984, 186–8, no. 164) mentions a 12th dynasty bronze statuette (kept in a private collection in Switzerland) possibly representing a seated prince from Byblos, and supposedly coming from Tell Dafana; yet dating, provenance and identification are highly speculative, as shown by Wastlhuber (2011, 95, no. 83, pp. 153–4).

112 Godley 1920, 464–7; see also Grene 1987, 199–200; de Selincourt 1954, 164; Macaulay 1890, 189.

113 Translation Oldfather 1933, 231–5.

114 The episode described in Herodotus 2.107 appears in Diodorus, 1.57.6–8, but Pelusium is mentioned instead of Daphnae.

115 Above, nn. 19–20, 25. According to the *Vitae prophetarum* and the *Martyrologium Romanum* (see also John of Nikiu's *Chronicle*, 72.17; Zotenberg 1883, 293; Charles 1916, 56), Jeremiah was stoned and buried in Taphnas, in 'Pharaoh's house' (Timm 1984, 552; Timm 1992, 2511, n. 3; 2512, n. 8; Schwemer 1995, 167–71; Schwemer 1997, 546, 550, 570–2).

116 Above, n. 28.

117 Above, n. 29.

118 Above, n. 41.

119 Petrie gives the dimensions as 3 x 2 furlongs – roughly 600 x 400m – or 1000 x 2000 feet – approx. 300 x 600m (Journal, 162, 167; Petrie 1886a, 458; Petrie 1888, 60); Mallet 1893, 57–8; Petrie 1911a, 92; Petrie 1931, 69; Fontaine, 1948, 48; Leclère 2008, 512.

120 '50 feet' (Journal, 163; Petrie 1886a, 458); '40 feet' (Petrie 1892, 53; Petrie 1911a, 87; Petrie 1931, 69).

121 Petrie (1888, 60) cut into the wall somewhere, but was not able to trace joints between the bricks.

122 Journal, 163; Notebook 74.f, 54; Petrie 1888, 59–60.

123 Journal, 163; Petrie 1888, 58.

124 Journal, 118–9; Notebook 74.f, 14–15; Petrie 1886a, 458; Petrie 1888, 59, pl. xlii, xliii; Griffith, in ibid., 107–8; below, n. 265.

125 Most recently Vogel 2004; Vogel 2010; Monnier 2010, *passim*.

126 Most recently Heidorn 1999, 307–10; Heidorn 2013, 293–307 (with further literature).

127 Most recently Valbelle *et al.* 2011, 627–8, 634–5, pl. 1–2; Valbelle 2011, 647, pl. 1.

128 Oren 1984, 10, fig. 3; Redford 1998, 45–60; Hussein and Abd el-Aleem 2013, 5–7, fig. 9. One could also add the example of the 5th century BC fort of Meẓad Ḥashavyahu, on the Levantine coast (Fantalkin 2001), although the wall there was less bastioned.

129 Dorginarti: approx. 165 x 70m, with irregular shape; Tell el-Herr: 120 x 120m for the earlier fortress (5th century BC), 135 x 150m maximum for the later one (4th century BC); Tell Kedwa: 195 x 205m; Meẓad Ḥashavyahu: less than 100 x 80m, L-shaped. Older Nubian fortresses are in the same range, only a few being larger, such as Aniba, Buhen and Mirgissa (above, n. 125), although still smaller than the enclosure of Tell Dafana. One could also mention the large New Kingdom enclosures of Tjaru at Tell Hebua I in North Sinai (Abd el-Maksoud 1998, 45–6, 111–13, 128, fig. 1, p. 135, fig. 10), although they belonged to a fortified town rather than to a fortress, as at Tell el-Retaba in the Wadi Tumilat (most recently Rzepka *et al.* 2009, 244, fig. 2, p. 276, fig. 33; Rzepka *et al.* 2011, 139–48; see also Górka and Rzepka 2011; Rzepka *et al.* 2012, 108, fig. 1, pp. 114–17) and possibly at Tell el-Dabʿa (most recently Bietak and Forstner-Müller 2007, 34–7, fig. 2, pp. 53–4, fig. 30; Forstner-Müller 2010, 117, fig. 12, see also p. 109, fig. 4).

130 For a comparison, see Leclère 2008, 595–8, table 2 and also pp. 583–5, figs 2–4. In Upper Egypt, the sacred areas are of a similar size range: Karnak and Hermopolis Magna are, for instance, about 30 ha.

131 Ibid., 65–6, 73–7, pl. 1.1–2, 1.5–6, 1.8. The northern enclosure of Memphis is usually considered – again on the basis of Petrie's excavations – as a military and administrative fortified precinct, linked to the Saite 'palace'. In fact, one cannot exclude the possibility that this area was also a temenos, possibly dedicated to Neith (ibid., 66). Perhaps the current excavations undertaken

there since 2000 by the University of Lisbon will help to clarify this dilemna (most recently http://home.utad.pt/~apries/index_port.html; Trindade Lopes 2012).

132 Not from the 30th dynasty as previously supposed: Leclère, op. cit., 606. For the technique, see Spencer 1979, 114–16.

133 Nevertheless, it seems to have been the case for a thick east–west cross-wall, of which a segment was discovered by the Egyptian team in 2009 to the south of the *Kasr*, in the northern part of the 'Great Temple' (see Chapter 8).

134 Petrie 1888, 53–4, pl. xliv; sketch-plan in Notebook 74.f, 25.

135 Petrie 1888, 53. Some discrepancies appear between the figures given in the text (ibid., 53, 54) and the calculation that one can deduce from the precise levels given elsewhere in the publication (ibid., 94–5).

136 Petrie (1888, 95; see also Notebook 74.f, 19) gives a curiously low figure (349 inches) for a 'general level' in the middle of the building, when compared with the much higher levels in the corners. This might be an error, or the figure actually may not correspond to the surface of the platform, but rather to the top of the fill in one of the central rooms.

137 Petrie 1888, 95; Notebook 74.f, 50.

138 Up to 5m for the eastern part of the northern section, but this might be due to a thickening on its southern internal face along a particular group of cells.

139 From Petrie's plan, the thicknesses of the internal walls seem irregular, some were a little bit thicker (over 3m), some narrower (1–1.5m).

140 Petrie 1888, pl. xxiii.

141 EES archives, photos nos 476, 477, 480 and 486; see also Smith 1886, 293–5.

142 Notebook, 74.f, 24. On the same page, a note indicates the batter of the wall faces.

143 This also applied to Casemate building B (p. 15).

144 Petrie 1888, 54; see EES archives, photo no. 477; Smith 1886, 294.

145 Journal, 129; Petrie 1888, 53; Petrie 1892, 52; Petrie 1931, 69. Domed cells have been observed or supposed in other similar structures (Kemp 1977b, 103–6, fig. 3).

146 Petrie (1888, 53) estimated this floor level at about 9m above the surrounding ground.

147 Petrie thought that this rubble originated from the erosion and the collapse of the upper part of the structure, falling into empty cells. This might only partly be true. The rubble might also have been deposited inside the cells during or close to the end of the construction phase. It was almost clear of pottery or any other finds, and Petrie does not state clearly, in his description, whether it contained burnt material or not. As the upper part of the building suffered from fire, traces of burning would be expected if its remains collapsed into empty cells.

148 Journal, 129; Petrie 1888, 53. Petrie thought that this room was too large to have been covered by a vault but, contradicting himself, did not rule out vaulting for the northern large central space, in spite of the almost identical proportions.

149 Petrie 1888, 58. Many fragments are chips from a finely sculptured block (Journal, 132, 135; Letter EES Mss Petrie XVI.f 123, 4; Petrie 1886a, 458; Petrie 1888, 53); Petrie gathered them in order to set them into a slab of plaster, but no such item appears to be recorded among the Tell Dafana finds in museum collections; perhaps it was one of the objects he was forced to abandon at the site – in the bushes near the riverbed, probably near his encampment – on the day of his departure (Journal, 172). However, some 'fragments of sculptured and painted stone decoration' were mentioned among the items displayed in the exhibition held in the Archaeological Institute in London (Oxford Mansions) in September 1886 ([Anon.] 1886o, 13).

150 Cell 35; Petrie, 1888, 53, 54; see also Journal, 110, 132, 135.

151 See Leclère 2008, 134–7, 150, pl. 2.3.a–b.

152 Leclère 2008, 290–2, 311, pl. 6.5 (with further literature).

153 Also visible in the rectangular casemate building north of the Amun temple at Tanis (Leclère 2008, 447–9, 484, pl. 9.10).

154 Cf. the features observed by Kemp (1977b, 103–6, fig. 3) for the palace of Apries in Memphis (see also Leclère 2008, 66–9).

155 Journal, 155–9, 160, 161–2; Notebook 74.f, 42–3, 45; Diary, 3, 4, 7 May; Petrie 1886a, 458; Petrie 1886b, 18; Petrie 1887, 36; Petrie

1888, 48, 54–5, pls xxii–xxiii; see also Smith 1886, 293, lower fig. 2, p. 296; the deposits were shared between several museums: British Museum (EA 23556, 23557), Egyptian Museum in Cairo (JE 27385), Boston, MFA (nos 87.528–9, 87.653, 87.719–20; RES.87.14-15 [?]); and Berlin, ÄM 10080, a large faience plaque of Psamtik I, unfortunately lost or destroyed during WWII; see Porter and Moss 1934, 7). Some of the items belonging to the deposits are still missing, such as the pair of quartzite corn rubbers, the libation cup and the half-crescent calcite item from the south-western deposit, as well as one small plaque of green felspar from the north-eastern deposit, one fragment of copper ore from the south-eastern deposit, one plaque of lapis lazuli. The heavy corn rubbers might have been left on the site, among the items that Petrie finally abandoned there when he departed (Journal, 172) (see **Pl. 86**).

156 Most recently Weber 2012b, 349, no. TD 190; for other possible early sherds, see nos TD 1, 2, 91, 189, 230, 318, 320, 329, 333, 344.

157 Petrie 1888, 53–4; Notebook 74.f, 25.

158 Petrie 1888, 95, for the squarish room with deeper foundations at the bottom of the southern central cell; see Notebook 74.f, 50.

159 Petrie 1888, 53–4, pl. xliv.

160 Petrie's description is not entirely clear in this respect: one could take from it that the walls of the earlier room were preserved up to a height of '8 to 10 feet' – 2.4 to 3m – above which rested the walls of the central southern cell. If this height is accurate, the description would be correct for someone standing inside the lower room and looking at its eastern wall. Outside this lower room there is no reason to suppose that the base of the walls of the central southern room was not approximately at the same level as the other partition walls of the casemate building, i.e. the general sandy ground level.

161 EA 23777 (see below, p. 116).

162 Petrie 1888, 47, 58, 96; Notebook 74.f, 32.

163 Petrie 1888, 55–6, pl. xliv; sketch-plan in Notebook 74.f, 27, with eastern face p. 21 curiously including Chamber 22. Petrie explored the foundation of one corner but did not find any foundation deposit (Journal, 159).

164 From Petrie's plan, the western and the northern faces are slightly shorter, 22.50m and 21.25m respectively.

165 Petrie 1888, 95; Notebook 74.f, 50.

166 EES archives, photo no. 478; also the engraving in Smith 1886, 294.

167 From the EES photo, at about every twelve courses of bricks.

168 Petrie 1888, 95; cell 43 had a fill of sand with a surface sloping down from north to south.

169 Petrie 1888, 56.

170 Ibid.

171 The wall between the end of the western corridor and the outer western face of the building was narrower than any other wall in the building: less than 1m.

172 EES archives, photo no. 479; see also the engraving in Smith 1886, 294.

173 Petrie 1888, 56; fragments BM EA 23818 and 23820 might be parts of it. In a letter (EES Mss Petrie XVI.f 122, 1), Petrie mentions 'many pieces of limestone cornice', 'scaled off by the fire'.

174 Ibid.

175 Journal, 125–6; Notebook 74.f, 28, 32 (sketch-plan); Petrie 1886a, 458; Petrie 1888, 50–1, 57, pl. xliv; Petrie 1892, 54. Petrie proposed some 3D reconstructions of this side of the complex, seen from the north-west: ibid., 52, fig. 38; Petrie 1905, 330, fig. 138; Petrie 1911a, 88, fig. 43; Petrie 1931, 68.

176 According to the levels given by Petrie 1888, 57, 95.

177 Petrie 1888, 51, although he points out that they were covered with burnt earth and therefore probably fell from the top of the burnt platforms. Petrie's Notebook (74.f, 22) includes a section of the eastern edge of the western part of the terrace.

178 Journal, 163; Petrie 1888, 58.

179 Two metres from the 'mastaba' to the doorsill of the vestibule gate (Petrie 1888, 51, 56, 57, 95) and less than 0.5m more to reach the centre of the vestibule (ibid., 56, 95).

180 Petrie 1888, 51, 54, 57–8.

181 Hypothesis previously suggested in Leclère 2007a, 16, fig. p. 15; Leclère 2008, 514–5, 537, pl. 11.3.

182 Bietak and Forstner-Müller 2003, 45, 48, fig. 12.

183 The south-western and north-eastern corners of the buildings were missing, but masonry abutting to its eastern side – of which only part remained – was perhaps a ramp leading to the north-eastern corner (Leclère 2008, 135–6).

184 Petrie 1888, 95; Notebook 74.f, 50.

185 Journal, 161; Petrie 1888, 57.

186 Petrie 1888, 57, pl. xliv; sketch-plan in Notebook 74.f, 29.

187 Petrie 1888, 95; Notebook 74.f, 50.

188 Although it is impossible to verify in detail the relative stratigraphy on the basis of Petrie's records, it seems clear that this brickwork and L-shaped wall were built later than the southern part of the 'Period C' annexe: the L-shaped wall is later than the 'Period E' massive brickwork – certainly abutting it – and delimited a 2m wide corridor around the south-western corner and along the western side of the 'Period C' annexe. Yet this corridor had no function as it ended in a *cul-de-sac* at the brickwork of Period E, which already occupied the entire width of the space between Building A and Annexe C and completely blocked any circulation towards rooms 11 and 17, 'court' 26 and the access to the vestibule between Buildings A and B.

189 Tell el-Dab'a ('Ezbet Helmi): most recently Szafranski 2003, 213–17, figs 3–4; Bietak and Forstner-Müller 2003, 40, 43–5, figs 3–6, p. 49, fig. 13; Bietak 2005, 146–8, figs 10–11, pp. 152–4, figs 13–14, p. 155, fig. 15, p. 159; Bietak and Forstner-Müller 2005, 68, 72–3, fig. 7; Bietak 2007, 757, 759, fig. 7, pp. 760–2, fig. 8, p. 766, fig. 12; Bietak 2010, 22, 57–9, figs 28–30, 32; Kom el-'Abd: Kemp 1977, 72, figs 2–3, pl. 11.2; Bietak 2005, 163–4, fig. 21; see also, at Deir el-Ballas: Smith 1998, 159–60, figs 275, 277; Lacovara 1990, 5, 40, fig. 1.14, pl. vii.b; Lacovara 2006, 189, 191, fig. 4; see also Pagliari 2010, 335–6.

190 Petrie 1888, 56–7, pl. xliv.

191 For Petrie: 'kitchens or store-rooms'.

192 Petrie 1888, 95; Notebook 74.f, 50.

193 Petrie 1888, 56.

194 Ibid., 95.

195 Ibid., 54, 56. A clay floor was preserved in this 'room', at a level of a few centimetres under that of the floors in the north-eastern part of Annexe C and the surface of the 'mastaba'. A jar sealing of Nekau II was found on it (ibid., 54, 56, 58, 72, 109, pl. xxxvi, 2; EA 23793, see below p. 68).

196 The size of the bricks used in this part may have been 40.8 x 20.3 x 12.7cm, if one correctly understands the 'additions' that Petrie mentioned in his list of brick sizes (Petrie 1888, 95; Notebook 74.f, 50 [B2]) as the masonry of 'Period D'.

197 Photograph no. 478, EES archives. The architectural features visible on the image (sloping groove, beam holes and coating on the wall to the left; mudbrick 'blocking' at the back) seem to fit well with Petrie's description (Petrie 1888, 56).

198 Petrie 1888, 56; shown as an engraving in Smith 1886, 293, fig. 1; this block is Boston, MFA 87.714.

199 Petrie 1888, 56, pl. xliv; sketch-plan in Notebook 74.f, 29 (cf. p. 21).

200 Petrie 1888, 95; Notebook 74.f, 50.

201 Petrie 1888, 95.

202 Ibid., 56.

203 Ibid., 95.

204 Ibid., 56.

205 The axial recess in the western wall of this unnumbered room recalls the shape of Room 19A further to the south.

206 Ibid., 57.

207 The bird was a duck and not a pigeon, as Petrie suggested (Journal, 161; Petrie 1887, 36; Petrie 1888, 55; Notebook 74.f, 44); see EA 23641 (below, p. 55).

208 Petrie 1888, 56, pl. xliv; sketch-plan in Notebook 74.f, 31 (cf. p. 29).

209 Both the recess and the bench were covered with many pieces of pottery (ibid.).

210 Notebook 74.e, 60; Journal 152; Petrie 1888, 57, 66; see below, n. 212.

211 Journal, 141–2, 143; Petrie 1888, 57.

212 Journal, 141–2, 143; Petrie 1886a, 458–9; Petrie 1888, 60; Petrie 1931, 70; see the list of findspots in Notebook 74.e, 59–61 and the EES 'Griffith's list' (above, pp. 27–8, **Tables 1–2** and n. 298): nos 21 (south-west of the *Kasr*; also mentioned in Petrie 1888, 66, and possibly 60), 31 (east of 19, outside; ibid.), 32 (in 19A at a lower level;

ibid.), 50 (eastern quarter 51, outside the enclosure; ibid., 61, 66), 54 (ibid., 67) and 61 (both south-east of the *Kasr*, in the quarter of metal workshops in the south-eastern area of the enclosure [Findspot 53]). Some of them were preserved to a height of 1.2 to 1.5m (Journal, 142), one up to 3m to the south-west of the *Kasr* (Petrie 1888, 60; probably Findspot 21). Others were excavated by the SCA Egyptian team in 2009 (see below, Chapter 8).

213 Petrie 1888, pl. xliv; sketch-plan in Notebook 74.f, 21. One fragmentary pot (Petrie 1888, pl. xxxv, 59: EA 22281, p. 104) was found in a Findspot numbered 7, an indistinct area, neither marked on Petrie's plan nor described in the publication, but mentioned in his Notebook (74.e, 61) as comprising rooms '2 to 6'and in in EES 'Griffith's list' (below, n. 298) 'chamber 2 to 6 in general'. In Petrie 1888, 66, this pottery is said to come from the group of rooms 2, 3, 4, 9.

214 Petrie 1888, 58, pl. xliv; sketch-plan in Notebook 74.f, 30.

215 Petrie 1888, 58, 66, 72, pl.xxxvi, 1, including EA 23791 and 23792 (below, p. 68); see also Journal, 119–20, 129; Petrie 1892, 60.

216 Petrie, 1888, 64, 66, 72, pl. xxxvi, 88, 91–3, including EA 23742 (below, p. 109). From the same findspot come the small pot EA 22338 and the sherd EA 23766 (below, pp. 105, 115).

217 Petrie 1888, 95; Notebook 74.f, 50.

218 Petrie 1888, 58, pl. xxiv, 6; see also Journal, 110; Weber 2012b, 349, no. TD 190.

219 Petrie 1888, 78–9.

220 Petrie 1888, 95; Notebook 74.f, 50.

221 Petrie 1888, 58, 66 (sketch-plan of this area in Notebook 74.f, 24). Of this pottery, Petrie seems to have kept only a little (ibid., 64, 66, pl. xxxiii, 10; including EA 23751, now unfortunately missing (below, p. 116). Many of these sherds certainly belonged to Samian transport amphorae with potter's marks on the shoulder (incorrectly identified as 'Greek letters' by Petrie).

222 Journal, 135, 137–40, 159–60; Petrie 1888, 58–9; sketch-plan in Notebook 74.f, 29, 47.

223 Petrie 1886a, 458; Petrie 1886b, 17; Petrie 1887, 33; Petrie, 1888, 58, 61; Petrie 1892, 56; Petrie 1931, 68. The remaining 10% come from Findspot 1, near the north-western corner of Building A, rooms 11, 17, 27 and 19 in Annexe C, and Findspots 51–2 in the eastern quarter outside the enclosure.

224 Petrie 1888, 51, 58, 59, 71, 74, 77, 78, 94.

225 Journal, 143; Petrie 1888, 58–9.

226 Petrie 1888, 64, 65, 66, 94.

227 Petrie 1885, 205; Petrie 1886c, 23–6; Petrie 1892, 42–3; see also most recently Leclère 2008, 128–38; Spencer (A.J.) 2011, 33, 35.

228 Hogarth *et al.* 1898–9, 42–5; Hogarth *et al.* 1905, 110–16.

229 See Leclère 2008, 128–19, nn. 76–9 (bibl. ref.).

230 Leclère 2008, 136–7 (bibl. ref., add also Smoláriková 2008, 70–7).

231 As already mentioned (above n. 189), some buildings on cellular platforms, interpreted as palaces, already existed at the beginning of the New Kingdom.

232 And in Sudan, if one adds the Meroitic palatial structures into consideration, although with the difference that here some rooms of the lower level were occupied, while others were filled foundations of rooms located at the level above; see esp. Hinkel and Sieverstsen 2002, 65–71 and most recently Baud 2010 (with bibl. ref., p. 243); Baud 2011 (with bibl. ref., pp. 344–5, nn. 4–5); Maillot 2013; Maillot forthcoming 1; Maillot forthcoming 2; see also Pagliari 2010, 337–9; the 'treasury' of Sanam Abu Dom was compared by von Bissing (1951, 58–9) with the casemate buildings of Tell Dafana and Naukratis, a comparison later rejected as irrelevant by J. Spencer (1996, 57).

233 Most recently Muhs 1994; Spencer 1996, 56–62; Spencer 1999; Weber, in Schlotzhauer and Weber 2005, 83; Weber 2006, 145, nn. 7–8; Leclère 2007b; Smoláriková 2008; Leclère 2008, 628–36; Pagliari 2010; Colin 2011, 62–8; Weber 2012b, 217–18.

234 Spencer 1996, 51–62; Spencer 1999; Smoláriková 2008, 65–70; Leclère 2008, 290–2.

235 Spencer 1999, 298–9; Spencer (A.J.) 2011, 36–7, 38, n. 23. Similarly, it is not impossible that the enclosure wall discovered by Petrie also dates from the 26th dynasty, see ibid., 36, fig. 9, p. 38.

236 Muhs 1994, 101–4; relayed by Leclère 2008, 136.

237 For a non-exhaustive list, see Leclère 2007b, 101–2, nn. 28–35, 45–6; Leclère 2008, 630–6; on the casemate building of Qasr 'Allam, in the oasis of Bahariya, which might also have been connected to a temple, now see Colin 2011, 59, 62–8, 76, fig. 12, pp. 80–1, figs 21–3; on those at Kom Firin, see Spencer 2008, 6–10, pls 61, 62, 92; Spencer 2009, 2, figs 4–5; Spencer (N.) 2011, 559–64, figs 50, 82–96; Spencer (N.) 2014, 161–74 and figs 73–112, pls 307–79.

238 Traunecker 1987, 147–62.

239 Leclère 2007b, 102, nn. 36–9 (ref. bibl.); Leclère 2008, 59–60, 63–4, 78–79, 85–6, 87–8, 107, pl. 1.7, pp. 247–54, pl. 5.4.

240 Leclère 2007b.

241 Leclère 2007b, 101, nn. 23–4 (ref. bibl.); Leclère 2008, 65–9, 108–10, pl. 1.8–10, pp. 174–5, 628–30.

242 Leclère 2007b, 102, nn. 40–4 (ref. bibl.); on the casemate buildings at Buto, add Hartung *et al.* 2007, 99–100; Hartung *et al.* 2009, 87–9, fig. 3, pp. 115–19, fig. 10; Hartung and Ballet 2010, 168, 191–2, figs 31–3; Marouard, forthcoming; at Tell el-Dab'a, see Lehmann 2011, 59–63, fig. 7; Lehmann 2012, 29–30.

243 Most recently Marouard 2010, 382–4; id. forthcoming; Lehmann 2013.

244 Cf. the central lightwell of the Meroitic palaces in Sudan.

245 Oren 1984, 10–13; Smoláriková 2008, 13–14, 47–53. Petrie's military interpretation was already rejected as 'phantastisch' by von Bissing 1949, 1–2; von Bissing 1951, 54–64.

246 Sharon and Zarzecki-Peleg 2006, 145–67. These constructions are defined by the authors as 'lateral access podium structures', because of the outside ramp or stairs leading to the upper entrance of the platform, in most cases at a corner, a feature reminiscent of the corner ramp of the casemate building of Tell el-Balamun, and the more hypothetical ramps of the edifices of Naukratis and Tell Dafana; see also Bietak 2005, 164–6.

247 Petrie 1888, 58, 59, pl. xliii. Judging from Petrie's plan, this wall must have had a thickness of about 5m.

248 Notebook 74.f, 54; Petrie 1888, 59, pl. xliii.

249 Ibid.

250 Above, nn. 89–90. Judging from Petrie's plan (1888, pl. xliii), the area called 'Buildings iron and copper smiths' covered a rectangle of at least 2ha, measuring about 200m north–south by 100m east–west.

251 Journal, 136, 166–7; Petrie 1886a, 458; Petrie 1886b, 18; Petrie 1887, 34; Petrie 1888, 59, 75, 76 77–9; Petrie 1892, 58.

252 Including 'a complete crucible bottom of [iron] slag mixed with charcoal' (Petrie 1888, 79), identified with EA 23990, actually a smithing hearth bottom (See Appendix 1, iii); see also the small lump of copper (?) slag EA 23991, in section 15 of the catalogue. A small silver lid of a cup was also found in the same area (Journal, 167; Diary, 11 May; Cairo, EM JE 27384), today apparently lost, unless it corresponds to CG 53269 (Vernier 1927, 420).

253 Findspot 52 is not mentioned in the text of Petrie's publication, only in the plates. In his Notebook (74.e, 59) and in 'Griffith's list', it is clearly described as the area of 'iron workshops' in the south-eastern quarter of the enclosure, 53 being an area of 'coppersmiths' to the north of 52. Two of the 'dry wells', 54 and 61, were also in this area north of 52 (see above, n. 212), and Findspots 57 and 58 were assigned to two groups of weights found in 52.

254 Journal, 148–9, 151, 152–3, 176; Petrie 1886a, 458; Petrie 1887, 35–6; Petrie 1888, 75, 76, location marked 'silver bowl' on pl. xliii; Petrie 1931, 70. On the silver bowl, see also Notebook 74.f, 47.

255 Cairo, EM, JE 27382–27383, apparently lost. They were missing before 1901 as they are not published in Bissing's catalogue of the metal vessels in the Cairo Museum (Bissing 1901).

256 These silver lumps are not those of EA 23851, which fit better with the 'many pounds of silver, melted and roughly cut up' brought to Petrie by local people (Petrie 1888, 76; Petrie 1931, 70).

257 Journal, 176–7; Petrie, 1887, 35; Petrie 1888, 75, 110, pl. xli, 10; see also Petrie 1931, 71: the gold tray handle is Boston, MFA 87.763 (see below, pp. 42, 43, **Fig. 1**). Electrotype copies of this handle were made; one is kept at the Petrie Museum, London (UC 38087A); see Vassilika 1992, 270.

258 Journal, 167; Petrie 1888, 51, 75. One is EA 18562, ibid., pl. xl (see below, pp. 43, 55), the other is Cairo, EM, JE 27386.

259 Grimal 1999, 535; Mathieu 2000, 541.

260 Earth.google.com.

261 Images DigitalGlobe taken 24 August 2004. New images with a higher resolution, dating from 12/2/2010, are now displayed.

262 Leclère 2007a, 14–17; Leclère 2008, 528–9, 539–40, pl. 11.5b–6.
263 See below, Chapter 8.
264 Cf. most recently Rzepka *et al.* 2011, 129–35 (133–4 with reference to parallels in Amarna and Qantir).
265 Above, n. 124; bibliographic references gathered in Leclère 2008, 525, nn. 83–4, to which add Meeks 2003, 70–1; Kahn 2008, 146–7.
266 Petrie himself admitted the possible existence of a temple of Min at Tell Dafana, but never elaborated on it (Journal, 141; Petrie 1888, 48, 59 [temple of 'Khem']).
267 Montet 1957, 192. P. Montet also suggests that Min could have been the -*nḥsy* – 'black-skinned' – that is the ending of the Egyptian name of Daphnae (above, nn. 38–44). Similarly, the '*nḥsy* of Punt' in some texts, designated the priest presiding over the feasts of Min (ref. in Leclère 2008, 527, n. 90).
268 EES archives, photograph no. 481; see Leclère 2007a, 15; Leclère 2008, 538, pl. 11.4.a.
269 Notebook 74.f, 14–15.
270 Among all the epithets starting with *nb* – 'Lord of…' – borne by the god Min (Leitz 2003, 227–230), *nb Gbtyw* (Leitz 2002a, 766) here remains the most probable reading for the few signs, parts of signs and space available in the break. From Petrie's notes on his own copy of the inscription (above, n. 269 and p. 24, **Fig. 23**), the bird-sign of which only the lower part is preserved must be a 'hawk or eagle for it has hind claw', more likely the former than the latter.
271 Efdou I/3, 396, l. 8; Verreth 2006, 742, 751, n. 3264; Leitz 2002b, 875.
272 EA 23646 (see below, p. 55).
273 EA 23852, 23853, 23854; see also the other bezel rings from the site, inscribed with priestly titles and anthroponyms: EA 18302, 23855, 23856, 23892 (see below, pp. 67–8). A cult of Amun of Tjeben is mentioned in Pap. Berlin 13588, but we have seen that Tjeben is certainly not to be identified with Tell Dafana / Daphnae (above, nn. 45–7). The 'Coptic Story of Cambyse' also mentions 'Ammon' at Taphnas, in parallel with Apis at Memphis (above, n. 28).
274 EA 23756 (see below, p. 52); see also Boston, MFA RES.87.146a and RES.87.146.f. A shuttle of Neith is engraved on a sherd from an imported transport amphora, EA 23762.
275 See below, n. 284.
276 See above, n. 21.
277 Journal 109–10, 117, 144; Notebook 74.f, 38–40; Petrie 1886a, 458; Petrie 1888, 60–1, pl. xliv–xlv.
278 Notebook 74.f, 11–12, 16.
279 Notebook 74.f, 38.
280 Notebook 74.e, 59; Notebook 74.f, 12; 'Griffith's list', 1.
281 Petrie 1888, pl. xliii.
282 For instance a large platform at East Karnak (most recently Redford 1994); see above, n. 242.
283 Petrie 1888, 60, pl. xliii; sketch-plan in Notebook 74.f, 55; see also ibid., 50 (size of bricks).
284 Abdel-Maksoud and Valbelle 2013.
285 Above, nn. 124, 265. The stela found by Petrie mentions an expedition to the mountains of Punt, which a miraculous rain saved from certain death by thirst. According to D. Meeks (2003, 71), Punt might designate here a part of the Arabian Peninsula. Tell Dafana would have been a departure point for expeditions towards this region. Another connection between the Arabian peninsula and the desert region neighbouring Bouto of Arabia (Imet) is found in Herodotus' report (2.75–6; cf. also 3.107–9) about 'winged snakes' flying to Egypt from Arabia, of which he saw quantities of bones. About this legend, which appears in many other texts, see most recently Barbara 2012, 17–19, 22–3; Radner 2008; Radner 2007 (confusing Buto of Arabia with Buto of the north-western Delta); Rollinger and Lange 2005; Rollinger 2004; Braun 2004; Carrez-Maratray 1999, 285–6, 361.
286 Journal, 118, 127; Notebook 74.f, 10, 56; Petrie 1886a, 459; Petrie 1888, 52, 60–1, 79, pl. xliii.
287 Two of them are in the British Museum (EA 23644 and GR 1888,0208.146); a third in Boston, MFA 87.496a (see below, pp. 42, 51–2). The fragmentary 'large bronze pan' (Petrie 1888, 79) found in the same context could be Boston, MFA 87.500 (apparently deaccessioned).
288 Most probably comprising the following: EA 18635–18636, 18641–18642, 20531, 20663–20664, 20672–20680, 20683–20692, 20694 (see below, pp. 45, 60–5).
289 Carrez-Maratray 2005–6, 204.
290 One might be tempted to speculate, for example, about this being the location of a sanctuary of a foreign deity, such as Nabatean Dushara, whose cult in Daphnae is attested by an inscription dating from the reign of Cleopatra, found at Tell el-Shuqafiya (above, n. 24).
291 EA 23750, with a similar piece in Bristol, CMAG H 1998. The fragment of an amphora, EA 23788 (see below, p. 117), with demotic inscription and possibly of Ptolemaic date, unfortunately has no precise provenance.
292 Boston, MFA 87.693.
293 Journal, 134; Notebook 74.f, 57; Petrie 1886a, 459; Petrie 1888, 52, 61, pl. xliii.
294 Leclère 2008, 530, n. 111.
295 Petrie 1888, pl. xliii.
296 Above, n. 81.
297 This was the case, for instance, for most of the stone beads and the glass objects (beads and fragments of cups), as well as for certain other items, such as the jasper scarab GR 1888,0208.161 (see below, p. 66) or the bronze bell Boston, MFA 87.499 (Petrie 1888, 80, pl. xxxix, 3).
298 Notebook 74.e, 59–61. The list kept in the EES archives (unnumbered) is headed 'Griffith' at the top; the handwriting seems to be Petrie's, so it must be a document given to or made for Griffith; Findspot numbers 13 to 15, 33 to 49, and 60 and 61 are not described in the document – while in the Notebook 74e, Findspots 33–34 and 36–40 are mentioned but not described, and 41–9 are not even listed.
299 For previous attempts at reconstructing assemblages, see Mumford 1998, 803–88 (only from Petrie's publication, with no identification of finds in museum collections); Weber 2012b, 221, 223–30, fig. 8 (with many identifications, particularly for the Greek pottery, but still incomplete for the rest of the material, and including a small number of mistakes).
300 Some objects were assigned to this number: one pot (EA 22331, see below, p. 105) has the number 7 scratched onto it, confirming the provenance indicated on the plate (Petrie 1888, pl. xxxv, 59); three small objects (EA 18469, 18510, 20657; see below, pp. 59, 63, 67) are said to be from 'Chamber 7' in the caption of plate xli (ibid., p. 111) but are described as coming from chamber 2 or 3 in the text (ibid., 74).
301 Above, nn. 160–1.
302 EA 23857 (see below, p. 67).
303 Weber 2012b, 231–44, 309–88; see also her previous articles: Weber 2001, 131–4; Weber, in Schlotzhauer and Weber 2005, 84–91; Weber 2006; Weber 2007, 305–10.
304 Chapter 5 consists of a full catalogue of this material.
305 In this respect, see S. Weber's comment about her table in her most recent publication (Weber 2012b, 221; see also Weber in Schlotzhauer and Weber, 2005, 85, n. 49).
306 Notebook 74.f, 49, 58–59; Journal, 171–2.
307 Journal, 174–7.
308 See above, n. 76.
309 A list made by Griffith gives a relatively detailed catalogue of the objects or groups of objects sent to each institution by the end of 1886.

Chapter 2
Introduction to the Objects from Tell Dafana

François Leclère

The objects in the British Museum from Tell Dafana, discovered by Petrie in his excavations for the Egypt Exploration Fund in 1886, are described in the catalogue in Chapter 3. This collection is the largest group in any institution and, with the exception of three particular categories, forms a representative selection of all the antiquities discovered at the site. The most important of the absent categories comprises the stone and metal weights which were found in the hundreds at Tell Dafana or in its neighbourhood.[1] Petrie kept these in London for some years together with other weights found at Naukratis, until the Egypt Exploration Fund (EEF) decided to present them to collections, mostly American museums, although a few items are in the Egyptian Museum in Cairo.[2] The other two, much smaller, categories are the coins and the engraved gems. Of the few coins that Petrie mentions among the finds,[3] five silver tetradrachms were sent to Montreal according to the EEF distribution lists and one gold coin is now in Boston.[4] The engraved gems collected in the area around Tell Dafana are also now in Boston.[5] The ceramics from Tell Dafana, both Egyptian and Greek, including the ostraca, are considered separately in Chapters 4 to 7.

This introduction will be limited to brief remarks on the different categories of objects presented in the catalogue. Mention is made whenever possible and a few examples are illustrated of the hundreds of objects from Tell Dafana preserved in other collections, including several parallels for the items in the British Museum. The research undertaken in the preparation of the catalogue has highlighted the overwhelmingly Egyptian nature of the finds assemblage, reinforcing the impression given by the architecture at the site that Tell Dafana was an Egyptian frontier temple town of traditional type, a conclusion which is further supported by the examination of the contents of the other collections.

Methodological note

Within the catalogue, the objects have been grouped in separate categories according to function, and unsurprisingly, these classes are similar to those generally found in other Late Dynastic sites, especially in the Delta. The items are distinguished by their British Museum collection numbers[6] and the entries follow a standard format including description, dimensions, context, bibliography and parallels. Where context is absent this means that no specific findspot is recorded for the piece at the site, although other information shows it to have come from Tell Dafana. The sequence of catalogue entries is, so far as practicable, matched by the order in which the objects are presented in the plates. Whenever possible, objects have been identified with items mentioned in Petrie's publication or in his archival notes – with different levels of certainty, depending on the detail available in the documentation. The good quality of the drawings on the plates of the original publication allows immediate recognition of the objects illustrated there, and, through the references to these illustrations, the objects also can be identified positively in the text. The majority of the objects illustrated in Petrie's publication are now in the British Museum, with relatively few in other collections. Many objects are mentioned only in the text and not illustrated, but if the description is sufficiently specific, these can also be identified; for less distinctive objects, such as amulets, beads or arrowheads, it is more difficult or sometimes impossible to identify them precisely in the various collections. Substantial information can also be found in Petrie's manuscript Journal and Notebooks, in addition to the original EEF distribution lists,[7] although these are not always completely accurate. The Museum registers also provide some information confirming or clarifying the identification and context of the items received. Unfortunately, the finds from Tell Dafana and those from other sites that Petrie excavated during the same season of 1886 (including Tell Nebesha, Tell Gemaiyemi, Zuwelein and El-Qantara) were registered in the Egyptian Department within the same lot (Registration Number 1887,0101). In some rare cases where the provenance is not specified in the Museum register, it remains unclear to which site certain objects should be attributed. Where relevant to the interpretation, this uncertainty is reflected in the present catalogue.

Although we were able to identify the vast majority of the finds published by Petrie in the collection of the British Museum or in other museums, a few objects, including some important or illustrated ones, have yet to be traced. We hope that future investigations, including research on the finds from the other sites that Petrie excavated during the same season, will resolve some of these issues.

Categories of objects

The first division of the catalogue, for non-pottery vessels (stone, metal, faience), contains very few examples of stone. This is hardly surprising given the limited range of stone vases produced in the Late Period. The most common form at that time was the calcite *alabastron*, which increased in popularity from Late Dynastic to Hellenistic times. Only a few examples were found at Tell Dafana[8] and although none seem to be held in the British Museum, except possibly one piece,[9] others are preserved in the museums of Boston, Bolton and Bristol.[10] This type of vessel and its production was much better represented at Memphis.[11] In addition to these *alabastra*, most of the stone vessels of the later dynasties were heavy hardstone mortars. None of the latter were brought back from Tell Dafana, although it is likely that some were present as they are ubiquitous on Late Dynastic Delta sites. They were probably regarded as too common to be of much interest. A miniature model version is the only vessel of this type to have come to the British Museum (EA 18559). Petrie also records a 'piece of finely-polished syenite' found in Chamber 19,[12] but this item has not yet been identified. A 'piece of stone dish' was sent to the Chautauqua Archaeological Museum.[13]

Metal vessels in copper alloy were frequently used in Late and Ptolemaic times and several examples were recovered at Tell Dafana. Of three cylindrical containers found by Petrie in 'Ptolemaic' contexts in the north-west mound,[14] two are in the British Museum (EA 23644, GR 1888,0208.146) and the third in Boston (MFA 87.496a). These vessels belong to a category of standardized measuring vessels for liquids, in use from the Late Period onwards, recently considered by T. Pommerening.[15]

The discovery of these vessels is mentioned in Petrie's unpublished notes:

In the main mound, nearly all the pits I have sunk have cut into nothing but burnt earth and broken pottery, apparently a waste heap; in one such pit two brass pots were found, & I got them on the whole, about 4 ins across & high: with them was a brass dish, which the men broke up, & a quantity of little amulet figures, which seemed to have been wrapped in cloth (Journal, 118).

Another brass pot [here the Journal includes a sketch of a cylindrical vessel], like the two previous ones, was found in the town mound today. I have pretty well done trying in the town mound now; it is seldom we ever hit on a wall, & when we do they are only of Ptolemaic period (ibid., 127).

The broken 'brass dish' that Petrie mentions in association with the cylindrical pots must correspond to the 'parts of a large bronze pan with a handle' described in the publication as having been found in the same context,[16] and which can be identified with Boston, MFA 87.500 (now deaccessioned), similar in type to the smaller utensils presented here in the catalogue, EA 23904. Some of the amulets, at least the rougher ones found nearby 'wrapped in cloth', can be identified with objects in the British Museum (see below).

The more massive bronze lid EA 29305 must have fitted a much larger vessel such as were produced by the substantial metalworking capability of the Late Period, perhaps something like a large bronze bucket from Tell Nebesha.[17] It was found in the main enclosure together with a bronze dipper, and a large bronze bowl,[18] both now in Boston (MFA 87.496b–497). A smaller flat bronze lid from Tell Dafana, with a central handle, is also in Boston (MFA 87.501). In spite of its similar size, it does not appear to correspond to the bronze cover published in Petrie 1888, pl. xxxix, 22, which seems to have a vertical rim at the edge. The fragment of a bronze vessel with handle EA 23806 (1887,0101.611) was almost certainly from a double-handled cooking pot, a metal version of the pottery form represented by EA 23658. To complete this list of bronze vessels from the site, we should also mention two small bronze situlae found in Chambers 3 and 14.[19]

The silver vessel EA 23859, together with a silver bowl and dipper in the Cairo Museum (JE 27383 and 27382)[20] and the unique gold vessel handle, Boston, MFA 87.763,[21] are rare examples of luxury products from the site, but the presence of substantial amounts of silver for processing suggests that objects in this metal were more common than might be inferred from the few surviving pieces (EA 23851, in section 15 of the catalogue). Other small silver items were also found at Tell Dafana,[22] including several priests' signet-rings (detailed here in section 7 of the catalogue), two plaques in the foundation deposits of Psamtik I under the Casemate building A (see below), a small ram-headed amulet (EA 18300), found with two silver uraei,[23] a small box for a gold amulet (EA 38005), a small figure of Horus[24] and five tetradrachms.[25]

The use of unmodified and carved Tridacna-shell for vessels (GR 1906,0301.13-14) in Egypt is mainly paralleled at Naukratis,[26] Memphis, Saqqara and Tell el-Maskhuta; a carved button found at Tell Dafana (GR 1906,0301.12, here in section 12) seems to be made of the same material. These shell items were probably made in southern Syro-Palestine from large clams obtained from the Red Sea and the Persian Gulf and widely distributed in the whole Mediterranean and the Near East between 650–630 and 600–580 BC. They could well have been brought to Egypt by Greeks or other foreigners.[27] Nevertheless, the presence of these items at Tell Dafana does not imply the lasting presence of a foreign community at the site.

The 'New Year flasks' are particularly characteristic of the Saite Period and are well known from many sites within and outside of Egypt,[28] so it is not surprising that they form the bulk of the glazed composition vessels from Tell Dafana, although most are represented only by fragments. These flasks were made of two moulded halves joined around the edges, with a separately made neck inserted in the body. One fragment (EA 23756) bears an inscription which invokes the goddess Neith and is a little unusual. Other fragments from Tell Dafana, including two pieces with parts of inscriptions – one again invoking Neith – are in the museums of Bolton, Boston and Bristol.[29] According to the EEF distribution lists, other fragments were sent to the Biblical Museum in London and to the Chautauqua Archaeological Museum in the United States, both collections now untraceable.

The foundation deposits (section 2) are the most historically useful antiquities from Tell Dafana, providing a date for the establishment of the main casemate building (A) in the great enclosure, during the long reign of Psamtik I. They are among the first such deposits to have been excavated *in situ*, together with those previously excavated by Petrie at Naukratis and Tell Nebesha and by Griffith at Tell Gemaiyemi. At first Petrie was unsure whether deposits would have been placed below a brick building and, on finding them, inferred that they would be common under such structures. In this he was mistaken, as foundation deposits are actually quite rare under mudbrick buildings (ignoring the brick pyramids of the Middle Kingdom which were really economical substitutes for stone monuments); presumably the religious nature of the casemate building at Tell Dafana as an adjunct to the main temple was the motivation for the deposits.

The contents of the deposits of Psamtik I included much of the typical range of items: bones from animal sacrifice, traditional querns or models of querns, plaques of various materials (some inscribed with the royal names), model bricks and samples of materials. These items were found in the sand immediately under the four corners of the Casemate building A, but Petrie was able to excavate only three of them himself,[30] the south-western deposit having been found first by one of his workmen, who only brought to Petrie a large plaque of green-glazed composition and a small copper plaque. Two short notes in Petrie's Notebook (pp. 43–4) indicate that the plaques inscribed on one side were found with the inscription facing down, at least for the south-eastern and north-western deposits.

The contents of the four deposits were shared between the British Museum, the Cairo Museum, Boston Museum of Fine Arts and the Berlin Museum.[31] According to the information gathered – marks scratched on the back of the glazed composition plaques and some museum records – it

Figure 1 Gold handle from a vessel, Museum of Fine Arts, Boston, 87.763 (courtesy of the Museum of Fine Arts)

seems that specific individual deposits did not go to a single collection, but that items were mixed before distribution (see **Pl. 86**).[32] Moreover, some items still remain unlocated in collections, such as the big quartzite corn-rubbers (one 60cm long, the other 20cm), a calcite half-moon plaque (almost 8cm long) and a small faience goblet (5cm high) which, according to Petrie's description in his Journal, was 'unhappily very rotten, & crushed'.[33]

EA 18562 is a glazed composition plaque inscribed with the cartouches of Apries, found in an undetermined findspot in the southern part of the main enclosure. Together with JE 27386 in the Cairo Museum, almost identical and also from the site, it probably came from foundation deposits of another important building in the precinct.[34] EA 23641 is a fragment of a duck leg bone, the only item left from what Petrie considered as a possible foundation deposit at the south-western corner of Annexe C to the east of the *Kasr*.[35]

The other architectural items catalogued in section 3 are all very fragmentary. Petrie mentions the fine carving of hieroglyphs and other features on certain limestone fragments from the *Kasr*, an indication of high quality relief decoration:[36]

> In one room of the Kasr are an immense quantity of chips off the face of a beautifully inscribed stone; I am recovering such scraps of the hieroglyphs as I can, they are so finely worked that I shall set them in [a] slab of plaster (Journal, 136).

Unfortunately the present location of these fragments is not known and it is possible they were left in Egypt. EA 23646 is a fragment of limestone bearing the cartouches of Amasis, although not particularly well carved and not mentioned in the publication nor in the archival documents. The high quality of stone carving of some pieces from Tell Dafana is better shown by the fragment of a block with a sculpted and painted *kheker*-frieze, found in Room 22 of the *Kasr* and now in Boston (MFA 87.714).[37]

The fragments of cornice and mouldings EA 23820 and 23818 are made of a uniform grey limestone and must have belonged to a single architectural decoration, possibly parts of the cornice and fluted *torus* moulding decorating one of the gates of the entrance vestibule between Casemate Buildings A and B of the *Kasr*.[38] They are unfortunately too few to allow a reconstruction.

Figure 2 Captive figure, Egyptian Museum, Cairo, JE 27393

The wooden pieces EA 23992 and 23993, in addition to Boston, MFA RES.87.16, might be fragments of the beams laid horizontally at regular intervals in mudbrick masonry in order to reinforce the structure of walls, as was usual in Late Period massive constructions with concave courses, such as casemate buildings and enclosure walls.[39] These fragments might come from the eastern face of Casemate Building B, in Room 22, where such holes were visible (see above, p. 15, **Fig. 15**).

The small sculpture (section 4) from Tell Dafana includes items in metal, pottery and stone. Copper alloy pieces were apparently found in large numbers, but only a very few were recorded in contexts: the fragment of arms holding a 'tambourine' EA 23866 in a chamber of the *Kasr*,[40] a figure of Osiris in Chamber 18, a sistrum-head in Chamber 3[41] and a bronze figure of Apis found in the main enclosure (possibly Boston, MFA RES.87.36);[42] the rest were collected and brought to Petrie by his workmen as stray finds from the surface of the site or from its neighbourhood. The rough list given by Petrie[43] includes numerous common figures or fragments of figures of deities, which should really be considered as amuletic figures. Fragments of cultic utensils are also listed. Unless it is specifically mentioned, it is impossible to know if any of these items were found at the site or not. The miniature aegis of Bastet (EA 23431) is the only one identified so far from a group of three similar pieces – unless one supposes that Petrie mistakenly included in this category the cat head published on his plate xxxix, 2 (Bristol, CMAG, H1090).[44] The glass eye-shaped inlay EA 18493 may have come from such a statuette. A large number of the small bronze figures and/or amulets were unfortunately sent to collections now dispersed and untraceable, such as the Chautauqua Archaeological Museum, the Manchester Heywood Free Library and the Biblical Museum in London.[45]

The British Museum also holds an unprovenanced bronze statuette of a kneeling king with the arms missing,

EA 23458. An additional document in the archives of the Department of Ancient Egypt and Sudan in the British Museum[46] indicates that this statuette came from Tell Dafana, but its pre-Saite style would rather point towards another provenance, possibly Tell Nebesha,[47] as the position of the item in the British Museum register would suggest. It may perhaps be identified with the bronze 'kneeling king' mentioned by Petrie[48] among the finds from Tell Nebesha – unless this one corresponds to Boston, MFA 87.445[49] – which is why we have chosen not to include this piece in the present catalogue. In his publication, Petrie also mentions some silver figures or fittings for statuettes – a small figure of Horus and uraei – but none of them are in the British Museum.[50]

A few terracotta figures were also found at the site, some of them in the area of Findspot 51, the domestic quarter to the east of the main enclosure (GR 1906,0301.4 and also probably GR 1906,0301.2, found together with the rough limestone figure 1906,0301.3, the 'Persian' bowls GR 1888,0208.62-63 and some Greek sherds, GR 1888,0208.59-61). Although they seem to have been made of local Nile silt, their shape recalls terracotta figures of the Archaic Period from Cyprus and Rhodes.[51] Another fragment of a finely made miniature figure or figured vessel (GR 1906,0301.10), not mentioned by Petrie but recorded in the British Museum registers as coming from the site, is more difficult to interpret as it is reduced to an ovoid torso; it may be of Corinthian origin.

A limestone statuette of rough style, the horse-rider GR 1906,0301.1, which lacks a precise findspot, belongs to a category of small sculpture well represented at Naukratis and at a few other Late Period Delta sites, sometimes by more elaborate pieces. Less common pieces are the six limestone figurines of bound foreign prisoners (EA 23825–23830), which belong to a group of 30 to 40 figures found together to the south-east of the *Kasr*, beyond Room 29.[52] Some of the remainder were distributed to other collections (Boston, Bristol, Dundee, Liverpool, Oxford and Chautauqua).[53] The figures are very roughly carved and represented lying down[54] with their arms and legs bound at the back. The fragment of the upper part of a much better carved example, slightly bigger, and probably of a kneeling type, was found in the fill of cell 40 of Casemate Building A; it is now in the Cairo Museum (JE 27393, **Fig. 2**).[55] Petrie suggested they may have been used as game-pieces, but it is more likely that they had some magical connotation, since amulets in the shape of bound prisoners are also known.[56] Certainly these symbolize the defeat of Egypt's foes, in the same manner as the captives shown beneath the royal throne.[57] Such figures of bound captives were used in magical execration rituals to subdue rebels or enemies.[58] Many have been found at the Nubian fortresses. The practice of such rituals would fit well with the context of a frontier-post such as Tell Dafana.

The limestone 'trial-pieces' included in this section are all fragments of simple drafting boards with a grid of squares, which were probably used for initial sketches to set the proportions of figures. Most come from the western part of Findspot 52, i.e. in the south-eastern quarter of the main enclosure. There are no examples among the Dafana material of the more elaborate test carvings of hieroglyphs or royal heads, which although often described as trial-pieces, seem to have been made as *ex votos* for donation to sanctuaries.[59]

Section 5 groups the amulets according to their shape (symbols – *wedjat*-eyes, *wadj*-columns, crowns, etc.; animal-headed deities, animal hypostases – mammals, amphibians, fishes and insects and also hybrid forms) and materials (metal, stone, glazed composition). Typologically, all the items match well the numerous amulets of the Late Period kept in museums or found everywhere across Egypt and in the neighbouring regions. Although many items were sent to other collections, the large selection in the British Museum mirrors the usual pattern of popularity, with the *wedjat*-eye being most common. Their provenance is not always clear, as Petrie did not always record the findspot of an amulet with the same precision he applied to other categories of objects and the British Museum register does not always indicate clearly whether they actually come from Tell Dafana or from one of the other sites that Petrie excavated during the same season in the region. As is the case with other categories of objects, some amulets must have been brought to him from neighbouring sites or from the surface of the site, such as the gold *wedjat*-eyes (EA 18251 and 18269) or the tiny gold figure of a solar god set in his silver shrine (EA 38005), one of the finest pieces in the assemblage along with the pendant of the silver ram head (EA 18300). A substantial proportion of the amulets mentioned by Petrie among the stone objects have been successfully identified (EA 18484, 18513, 18556, 20654, 20658 and 20662) but none of them, unfortunately, has a precise findspot, apart from EA 20660, found in the main enclosure.[60]

Most of the glazed composition amulets (and beads) probably come from the main enclosure, as Petrie specifically says that 'a selection of these will be kept together in the British Museum to show the style of known work of the twenty-sixth dynasty'.[61] A few were found in several rooms of the eastern annexes of the *Kasr* – Chambers 2 and/or 3, 4, 17, 18, 29 – but except for EA 18510, 20654, 20657, 20661, 20666 and possibly 18512, 18514, most of them are not yet identified.[62] A particular series of roughly made glazed composition amulets probably corresponds in part to a group of items found together with the bronze cylindrical vessels (see above) on the north-west 'Ptolemaic' mound (EA 18635–6, 18641–3, 20531, 20672–5, 20683–4, 20686–9, 20692 [with the missing EA 18637],[63] and – for the 'much smaller and ruder ones' – EA 20676–80, 20685, 20690–1, 20694 and possibly 23885). According to Petrie's Journal, they 'seemed to have been wrapped in cloth'.[64]

The scarabs (section 6) were considered by Petrie to be unimportant.[65] They represent a small number of items, without precise known context, possibly picked up in the general neighbourhood of Tell Dafana. Whilst some of them are clearly Late Period, others are earlier, dating back to the Second Intermediate Period or, more probably, the New Kingdom. Of the scarabs published on plate xli of Petrie's volume, not all are in the collection of the British Museum, with some in Edinburgh.[66] Several of the inscribed examples have not yet been located in any collection: numbers 52, 61–2 and 64–5 on Petrie's plate xli.[67] Others without inscriptions are mainly in the Boston Museum of Fine Arts (notably one of three haematite scarabs,[68] the 'banded agate' scarab,[69] a silver scarab-bezel[70] and a few lapis lazuli scarabs).[71] The green jasper fragment GR 1888,0208.161 is an import which belongs to a well-known series of Classical Phoenician scarabs dating from the later 6th to mid-4th centuries BC;[72] unfortunately it was not actually found at Tell Dafana, but somewhere to the north of the site. Two glazed composition naturalistic beetle amulets with a loop on the underside are catalogued with the amulets in section 5 of the catalogue (EA 18635 and 18636). The item EA 18269, mentioned by H.R. Hall as coming from Tell Dafana,[73] is actually from Tell Nebesha.[74]

Section 7 comprises the seals and finger-rings from the site. The most substantial piece is the bronze stamp-seal of Amasis (EA 23903) from chamber 19 of the eastern annexes of the *Kasr*. This is one of the very few objects in this category to have a secure provenance, with the glazed composition seal EA 18469, found in one of the northern chambers of the eastern annexes of the *Kasr* and the silver ring EA 23857, found on the surface of the pavement to the north of Casemate Building A.[75] Several other silver rings of the same type were picked up on the surface of the site by the Bedawin and passed on to Petrie.[76] According to B. Fay,[77] rings of this type always possess an elongated, oval bezel, cast separately from the shank and soldered together; the bezel underside is curved to follow the finger. The narrow shank is round in section and of uniform diameter throughout its entire length. Inscriptions were cast on the bezel with details added by chasing; they read from right to left and usually contain only names and titles of the owner.[78] The representation of a standing figure holding crocodiles on the discoid bronze seal EA 23864, unfortunately with no precise provenance, is a common pattern on scarabs[79] and also recalls the 'Persian' clay sealings that Petrie found in the area of the palace of Apries in Memphis, on which the central figure holds griffins or lions.[80]

The jar sealings in section 8 provide valuable dating information for some of the contexts around the casemate buildings, although in many cases these contexts were not closed. Most of the seals were stamped with the cartouches of Psamtik I and Amasis, but one also bears the cartouches of Nekau II (EA 23793) and a few other have impressions of the cartouches of Psamtik II, while some have illegible cartouches, which Petrie thought might have been of Apries. The sealings of Psamtik I were all found in Findspot 8, to the west of Casemate Building A, together with large quantities of lids of the same type as EA 23742,[81] whilst those of Psamtik II and Amasis were found with the Egyptian pottery in the lower layers of Chambers 18 and 29, to the south-east of the *Kasr* (Psamtik II mostly in 29).[82] The seal of Nekau II was found in Room 22, between Casemate Building B and the eastern annexes.[83] As such jar sealings were found in substantial quantities, examples were distributed to many different collections, but only a few actually survive today.[84] Together, they form an assemblage that remains unequalled in Egypt for this period.

As Petrie noted,[85] some of the pieces allow us to reconstruct the actual process of sealing: a pottery lid, such as EA 23749 or 23750, was fixed on top of the jar-neck with a string or a linen cloth (of which traces are visible on EA 23797), after which a lump of clay was put in the middle of this lid on top of the string and sealed with small oval seals, of which the negative is visible on EA 23797. These seals were probably of types similar to the metal ones found at the site or in the surroundings (EA 23852–7 catalogued in section 7). The lid thus sealed was covered with a mass of plaster that also enveloped the rim of the vessel, roughly rounded and sealed with a royal cartouche, using a seal probably of the same type as the bronze example EA 23903, found in Chamber 19. The jar sealing EA 22356, stamped with the cartouches of Amasis, is of particular interest as it is still attached to the top of a Chian amphora.[86]

Extensive metalworking at Tell Dafana is indicated by the great quantity of metal objects (weapons, tools, fittings and pieces of equipment) recovered at the site, here catalogued in sections 9 (weapons) and 10 (metal tools), together with pieces made of other materials in section 12 (equipment and fittings). Most interesting is the fairly regular use of iron alongside bronze. In Egypt at the beginning of the Saite Period, the use of iron was no longer the rare and exotic practice it had been previously.[87] Finds at other sites also attest an increasing use of iron at the end of the Third Intermediate Period and into the 26th dynasty.[88] Nevertheless, together with Naukratis,[89] Tell Dafana remains one of the rare pre-Ptolemaic settlements where such quantities of iron items were found.[90]

In addition to the hundreds of iron and bronze arrowheads picked up on the surface of the site by the locals and brought to Petrie on a daily basis, metal items with a provenance were mainly found in two series of findspots, within rooms of the eastern annexes of the *Kasr*, and in two contiguous areas in the south-eastern quarter of the main enclosure – Findspot 52 and, immediately to the north, Findspot 53. Here Petrie suspected workshops of ironsmiths and coppersmiths to have been located, on the basis of the large quantities of metal objects found during his quick clearing of the surface at the end of the excavation season.

Petrie also found numerous arrowheads in the clearing of the south-eastern quarter, but unfortunately it is now impossible to distinguish them from the ones he bought from the local people. Only a few bronze examples are recorded with a precise findspot, in the annexes of the *Kasr* (EA 23917 in Chamber 3, some in Chamber 19C, unidentified).[91] They are not easy to date as certain types remain unchanged for relatively long periods between the 26th dynasty and the Hellenistic era, and, even if the British Museum holds a good selection, an accurate typological study should also include the far larger number of arrowheads from the site that were sent to many other collections;[92] such a study still remains to be undertaken.

Nevertheless, some preliminary observations can be made. The bronze arrowheads – leaf-shaped, with a rhombic, trefoil or triangular section – all seem to date from the Late Period to the Ptolemaic Period (some not earlier than the 5th century BC, others not earlier than the 3rd century BC).[93] The iron arrowheads, by contrast, do not necessarily predate the mid-1st century BC; most are triangular in section and tanged, apart from a few leaf-shaped and lozenge-shaped ones which cannot be dated

precisely.[94] This means that they cannot be considered as evidence for – as long assumed – a strong presence of Greek mercenaries in the area during the 26th dynasty, but might correspond to a much later occupation of the area from the end of the Hellenistic and/or the beginning of the Roman Period. This is also the case for three barbed spikes in the British Museum (EA 23970–2) initially considered as possible spurs or 'helmet-peaks' which actually might be fragments of 'cage fire head' or 'basket fire' arrowheads. A few iron leaf-shaped spearheads (one in the British Museum, EA 23943) were also found at the site, most probably in the enclosure. They, too, are difficult to date precisely.[95]

Therefore, the metal arrowheads and spearheads cannot be taken as an evidence of a large garrison occupied exclusively during the 26th dynasty but might rather attest the continuity in the occupation or a re-occupation of the site after the Saite Period.

The finds in the eastern annexes of the *Kasr* (Chambers 3,[96] 11,[97] 17,[98] 18, 19A and C) include some iron and bronze tools and weapons. Two groups of iron items are particularly interesting: the dagger EA 23946, found in Chamber 19A – together with several other iron items (trident EA 23945, knives EA 23947 and EA 23942, three pokers, one of which is EA 23944, chisels and wedges EA 23953, 23955–7, and an iron staple, possibly GR 1888.0208.167) – and the many fragments of scale armour found in Chamber 18,[99] of which only four were kept at the British Museum (EA 23982–5) and the rest dispersed to many other institutions. Chamber 18 also contained two iron blades EA 23948 and 23949 and a bronze rod, possibly GR 1888.0208.145a.

The dagger is of the type of the *Akinakes* short sword, of Scythian origin and common from the 5th century BC onwards, notably in the military equipment of Achaemenid Persia.[100] Scale armour in general was well known in the Eastern Mediterranean and Near East from the mid-2nd millennium BC, but the fragmentary piece from Tell Dafana is of a type which seems to have developed mainly during the 5th–4th centuries BC.[101] One of the closest parallels was later found by Petrie in the palace of Apries at Memphis, together with other types of iron and bronze scales, bigger and rounded in the lower part.[102]

Both *Akinakes*-daggers and armour are known from later texts and archaeological finds to have been dedicated as *ex votos* in Greek temples[103] and deposited in treasuries. Their presence in the context of the annexes of the casemate buildings at Tell Dafana would fit with the interpretation of this complex as temple magazines or treasuries, even if this temple was an Egyptian one. Their dating remains an issue: if they were contemporary with the rest of the material found in the *Kasr*, they should date from the 6th century BC and would thus be among the earliest known examples of the type. If they date from the 5th century BC as the parallels seem to suggest, they would indicate a later occupation of the enclosure and the buildings of the *Kasr*. As the layers filling the chambers of the complex mostly contain material from the end of the 7th century BC to the end of the third quarter of the 6th century, they would have to belong to a phase of re-use during the 5th century BC, with the reason for the predominance of earlier material being that the rooms were undisturbed magazines or cellars. However, given the uncertainties over the dating of the scale armour, such a conclusion is by no means certain. Moreover, as argued by H. Amborn,[104] there is no reason to think that the iron scale armour belonged to the Greek 'brazen men' of Psamtik I mentioned by Herodotus (2.152): they were more likely to have worn the bronze 'bell'-corslets of the Greek hoplites, which would have impressed the Egyptians far more than scale armour, which had after all been long known in Egypt. Besides, it may be worth remembering that Herodotus mentions on several occasions (2.159, 2.182, 3.47) dedications of a linen breastplate ('linothorax') by Egyptian Saite rulers to Greek sanctuaries. Although this type of equipment does not necessarily have to include metal scales, it is possible that the scale armour in the annexes of the *Kasr* might have resulted from a similar dedication, in this case to an Egyptian temple.

The majority of metal items were apparently found in the south-eastern quarter of the main enclosure, together with some ore slag, and also, in Findspot 52, with significant quantities of Egyptian pottery (see Chapters 4 and 5). Many other objects of different types and materials are also mentioned by Petrie as having been found in the 'Camp' and they, too, probably came from the south-eastern quarter. The conditions under which the clearing took place, with no record of any structures discovered, make it impossible to understand whether the quarter was really just an area of workshops or whether it might also have included a domestic settlement.

Unless it is specifically mentioned or can be reconstructed from other information, it is not always clear in Petrie's paragraph concerning the iron-working[105] whether the iron objects found at Tell Dafana come from this area, but we assume this to be most probable. Petrie describes some specific groups of iron finds:

> A large quantity of iron scraps, apparently a workman's scrap heap, was found in the camp, including the side piece of a horse's bit, arrows, a hook, a cruciform piece of thin sheet-iron, squares of sheet-iron 1½, 1⅛, ¾ inch, &c.; a piece with a square-toothed edge, probably for riveting it on by a row of laps to another piece of sheet, and much slag. In another place was a mass of thin sheet-iron with strips of bronze and iron, apparently part of some armour inlaid with ribs of metal. The amount of slag found all over the S.E. of the camp was astonishing; some was brought away, including a complete crucible bottom of slag mixed with charcoal. Some very fine haematite was also found. It is evident that Defenneh was as important a place for smelting, and iron working, as Naukratis.[106]

Unfortunately, apart from the 'side piece of a horse's bit' which might correspond to EA 23981 and the 'crucible bottom of slag mixed with charcoal', which is EA 23990 (see Appendix 1, iii), none of the objects described in this passage can be identified.

Among the various metal objects probably excavated in this area, the chisels and wedges deserve particular mention. Forty examples were found, most of them made of iron, including some from the eastern annexes of the *Kasr*, and of which several are now in the British Museum (EA 23954, 23958–62).[107] They are too small to have served as tools for quarry workmen, but they might have been used by

sculptors or craftsmen working with metal, unless they were produced for miners. There are also two small mattocks, of which one is EA 23953. The iron adzes EA 23908 and 23951 might have been carpentry tools. Another interesting category of objects is the series of items interpreted as parts of iron horse bridle-bits (EA 23965–8 and possibly EA 23981).[108] This interpretation as horse-bits remains questionable, as the objects have a different shape from the usual style of such bronze bits, but is nevertheless plausible. Even if it is equestrian equipment it would not necessarily be related to the military. These enigmatic objects have been placed in section 12 of the catalogue.

The large quantities of slag mentioned by Petrie (see for instance the fragment GR 1888,0208.170),[109] a large hemispherical iron and charcoal lump from the bottom of a hearth (EA 23990), as well as the pottery bellows (EA 22367)[110] and tuyère (EA 23669), catalogued in Chapter 5, certainly attest metalworking activity in the area. These items are not related to the production of iron from iron ore, but come from a blacksmith's forge where metal tools were produced or simply repaired. Even though our vision of the south-eastern quarter of the enclosure is much hindered by the scarcity or absence of information regarding the contexts in which the objects were found, once we take into consideration the great variety of objects found in this area, we can begin to form a new hypothesis. This area may not have been just a quarter of ironsmiths and coppersmiths as Petrie supposed, but a sector of the enclosure where a more diverse series of workshops were concentrated, dedicated to the production of a greater range of materials, with the metal tools being part of the workshops' equipment, rather than their final products.

Section 11 presents a small miscellaneous collection of stone tools, such as burnishers, grinders and hammers. The presence of a few flint implements shows that the use of flint tools continued to late times (it is known from other sources to have persisted even down to the Late Roman Period). The items catalogued as 'whetstones' are an interesting group, and may have had an entirely different function, as they never show traces of wear as would be expected if they had been used as whetstones. Most of them were also found in the south-eastern quarter of the enclosure and may have been tools used in the crafts practised there, although their function remains to be determined.

Apart from some metal pieces already mentioned above, section 12 of fittings and equipment also includes a variety of small metal items, mostly made of bronze, together with objects in other materials (shell, ivory, glazed composition and sandstone). For the most part, these objects represent miscellaneous pieces from daily life: buckles, pegs, fasteners, buttons, chains, hinges, nails and studs. The diversity of the material held in the British Museum is also mirrored in the other collections.

The jewellery in section 13 is a large group including numerous tiny gold ornaments or fragments, a few bronze pieces and several strings of stone, glazed composition and glass beads, as well as isolated beads and a few metal and stone pendants.

The gold items appear to come mainly from the denuded surface of the site and/or its immediate neighbourhood[111]

where they were picked up by the local Bedawin and sold to
Petrie by weight. Some may have also come from a wider
area including other sites to the north of Tell Dafana.[112] They
comprise finger-rings, crescent-shaped and circular
earrings, beads, settings for stones, pieces of chain and wire,
as well as fragments of foil used in the making of jewels.[113]
Some items are plain work, others show the techniques of
repoussé and granulation. A note in Petrie's Journal (p. 134)
indicates that some of the gold earrings and other pieces may
have come from robbed tombs on the north-west 'Roman
mound', across the river:

> I went across to the N. mound with him [i.e. A.H. Sayce]; it is
> later than this side on the surface, going to Roman; but there
> are some tombs rifled from which many of my gold earrings
> have come. There does not seem to be anything accessible of
> the early Greek time, so I shall not try to work there.

The different provenances might explain the high
proportion of Ptolemaic or even later pieces. The earrings,
in particular, find parallels down to the Roman Period.[114]

The strings of beads and individual beads lack a precise
provenance. Some glazed composition beads were
apparently found in the main enclosure with glazed
composition amulets and 'kept together in the British
Museum to show the style of known work of the twenty-
sixth dynasty',[115] while stone beads seem to come mainly
from the environs of Tell Dafana[116] and the glass beads from
Tell esh-Sherig/Tell Belim, to the north of Tell Dafana.
Their date is more difficult to establish. For some pieces it
also remains unclear, from the Museum register, whether
they were found at Tell Dafana or in its neighbourhood or at
other sites excavated during the same season. According to
a note in Petrie's Journal, large quantities of carnelian
beads might actually have come from a site called Tell
Bahaim, between Tell Dafana and San el-Hagar.[117] Among
the few metal and stone pendants, a silver ram's head found
in the Saite enclosure (EA 18300) stands out as a
particularly fine piece. It is of the same type as many other
items of this form, typical of the end of the 25th and 26th
dynasties.

Among the games in section 14, the most interesting
objects are the three pottery game-boards. They were made
from a common type of pottery platter, adapted by incising a
rough grid after firing. The boards EA 22323 and 23803
certainly appear to be platters or dishes that were reused.
The fragmentary piece EA 23802, found in chamber 9 of the
eastern annexes of the *Kasr*, is rectangular but was also cut
from a round platter similar to EA 22323, although it
remains unclear if the sides were recut before or after firing.
Petrie records 'many other pieces of plates scored up in the
same way' and 'two or three stone slabs similarly divided'[118]
which have not yet been identified in any collection. The
number of squares incised on the preserved pieces, their
disposition in three rows and the few hieroglyphic signs cut
in the middle of the squares on EA 23803 leave no doubt as
to the function of these boards: they were clearly for the
Egyptian senet game. We might even, at a pinch, agree with
Petrie that 'it was probably the idle life of a garrison which
causes these objects to be commoner here than elsewhere',
but the soldiers playing with them would have been
Egyptians and not Greeks.

Finally, section 15 on drill-cores, samples and slag
includes the pieces of slag mentioned above in the discussion
of iron-working and some interesting cylindrical drill-cores
made of different stones, including calcite – probably
remnants of the production of vessels such as the *alabastra* of
which examples have been found at the site.[119] A few other
samples of materials such as pumice, lapis lazuli, sulphur,
blue frit and galena were also collected. EA 23851 is
particularly noteworthy as it comprises 19 chunks of silver,
some of which have a roughly cubical shape as if they had
been melted and cut. Unfortunately, this group has no
findspot, as it was found by the Bedawin.[120]

Notes

1 Petrie 1888, 80–94, esp. 80–1, 85–8, 92–4; in his Journal, Petrie
   very often mentions that weights were brought to him on a daily
   basis by the local Bedawin, in addition to the few weights found in
   excavations (Journal, 119, 120, 122, 126–7, 129, 133, 137, 140, 143–6,
   149, 152–3, 161, 169). He recorded 1,600 metal weights, mostly
   minute bronze weights, which he thought were linked with the
   supposed local activity of jewellers, and 397 stone weights; only 66
   of the latter (plus 3 bronze weights) were actually found with
   certainty at Tell Dafana, with a more or less precise findspot
   (northern chambers of the eastern annexe of the casemate
   buildings, isolated weights scattered in the main enclosure, groups
   found in Findspots 57–58 (within the area numbered 52) and
   Findspot 59 on the north-west Ptolemaic mound); the others were
   stray finds brought to Petrie from the rest of the site and/or from
   other places in the neighbourhood, up to Tell Belim/Tell esh-
   Sherig, to the north.
2 Petrie 1926, 1, 22, 26, 43. Apart from the few stone weights left at the
   Cairo Museum (Weigall 1908, 3–4, 16, 20, 24, 28, 32, 35–6, 39, 50,
   53, 61), the others are mainly in the collections of the Oriental
   Institute, Chicago, and the Royal Ontario Museum, Toronto.
   According to Cour-Marty 1989, one is also in Oxford (AM
   1887.2534) and a dozen are in Musées Royaux d'Art et d'Histoire,
   Brussels. Two further bronze items from Tell Dafana could also be
   considered as weights: Cairo, EM, JE 27374, head-shaped (Edgar
   1904a, 57, pl. xvii, no. CG 27849) and Boston, MFA 87.526,
   heart-shaped (see a parallel in the Cairo Museum: Weigall, op. cit.,
   20, pl. ix, no. CG 1930); EA 23882 and 23885 (this volume,
   catalogue section 5) could also be considered as minute weights.
3 Petrie 1888, 76–7, 80.
4 Boston, MFA 88.339. The 'Cufic dinar' (Petrie 1888, 80) remains
   unlocated.
5 Petrie 1888, 79; Journal, 149–50; Boston MFA 87.692, 87.694-707.
6 For an explanation of British Museum object numbers, see Preface.
7 Kept in the EES archive, with copies of some in the Department of
   Ancient Egypt and Sudan at the British Museum.
8 Petrie 1888, 73.
9 The fragment EA 23806 (1887,0101.841) is presently unlocated.
10 Boston, MFA 87.715-717; Bolton 1886.28.27, 1886.28.118-119; Bristol,
   CMAG H1988.
11 Petrie 1909b, pl. xlv; id., 1909c, pl. xvi, 1–4.
12 Petrie 1888, 73.
13 The calcite vase in Sydney, MAC MU1854, recorded as coming
   from Tell Dafana, may come from Tell Nebesha, according to the
   EEF distribution list of 1886.
14 Petrie 1888, 61, 79.
15 As 'VO-Maß' – a Near-Eastern measure, Pommerening 2005,
   21–2, 31, 32, 49–51, 172–3, 356–7.
16 Petrie 1888, 79.
17 Ibid., 24, pl. xx, 5.
18 Ibid., 77.
19 Ibid., 77. One must be Bristol, CMAG H1991. One should also add
   a bronze ladle/dipper in the Petrie Museum, UC 59871, said to
   come from Tell Dafana, and a small bronze cup in Bristol (H.1992).
20 The silver bowl and dipper in the Cairo Museum were found
   together with lumps of silver in the south-east corner of the main
   enclosure, see Chapter 1, nn. 254–5. For a small silver lid found in

the south-eastern quarter of the enclosure, according to Petrie's Journal – possibly Cairo, EM, JE 27384 – see Chapter 1, n. 252.

21 See Chapter 1, n. 256; on this piece, see Smith 1998, 237, fig. 403; James, in Edwards and James 1984, 146–7, fig. 195b.

22 Petrie 1888, 76–7.

23 See n. 50.

24 See n. 50.

25 See n. 4.

26 Petrie 1886c, 35–6, pl. xx, 10–12, 16: GR 1886,0401.1594-1598; see also GR 1888,0601.86-89.

27 Stucky 1974; Brandl 1984; Reese 1988, 38, 39, 41 (who also mentions uncarved Tridacna shells on other Egyptian sites but of other periods); Brandl and Sease 2004, 29, nn. 2–3; most recently Stucky 2007; Furtwängler 2011.

28 Mainly and most recently (with further literature) Lagarce and Leclant 1976, 242–3, 282–6, esp. nn. 354–72; Hölbl 1979a, 34–41; Homès-Fredericq 1982, 79–91, esp. 80, n. 4; Felder 1988a, 2–4, 92–128, 153–5; Felder 1988b; Blanquet 1992, 49–54; Fazzini 2001, 55–7; Caubet and Pierrat-Bonnefois 2005, 148–51; Guichard and Pierrat-Bonnefois, 2005, 46–51; Abdel-Aziz 2007, 23–6. New Year flasks are also found in Persian contexts (see Felder 1988a, 4; Masson 2007, 614), though it is not clear if they might be residual.

29 Bolton 1886.28.26a-b; Bristol, CMAG H2266; Boston, MFA 76.146.a-h – a and f inscribed, the former with Neith invoked.

30 Petrie 1888, 54–5, pls xxii, xxxiii; Journal, 155–62; Notebook 74.f, 42–3, 45.

31 Cairo, EM JE 27385 – TR 30/1/27/2; Boston, MFA 87.528-529, 87.653, 87.719-720, RES.87.14-15; Berlin, ÄM 100080.

32 Contrary to Weinstein 1973, 327 (NE corner to the BM, NW corner to Boston, MFA, SE corner in Cairo, SW corner in Berlin).

33 Journal, 158; for other foundation deposits of Psamtik I, see Weinstein 1973, 328–9, nos 129–30; Perdu 2002, 110–13, no. 22, pp. 123–4, no. 26, p. 145, no. 33.

34 See Chapter 1, n. 258; for other foundations deposits of Apries, see Weinstein 1973, 331–2, no. 135, p. 333, n. 87, pp. 333–5, nos 137–8.

35 See Chapter 1, n. 207.

36 See Chapter 1, n. 149.

37 See Chapter 1, n. 198 and fig. 19.

38 See Chapter 1, n. 173.

39 See Leclère 2008, 631; Spencer 1979, 131–2.

40 Petrie 1888, 80.

41 Ibid., 77.

42 Ibid., 76, found with the silver ram-headed amulet EA 18300 and a pair of silver uraei, see below n. 50. One bronze Apis bull was also sent to the Chautauqua Archaeological Museum.

43 Ibid., 80.

44 A 'bronze cat' was also sent to Chautauqua.

45 Among the items mentioned by Petrie 1888, 80, apart from the other pieces identifiable in the British Museum (surely: EA 23436, 23868; possibly: EA 23867, 23435, 23885) the 'seated squat' Bes must be Boston, MFA 87.498; one 'Anubis' could be Cairo, EM, JE 27375; another bronze Anubis was sent to Dundee, according to a list published in the *Dundee Courier*, 11 May 1889, but does not seem to be recorded in the McManus Museum collection today.

46 *Folio list no. 35. EES 1883–1931. Collections presented.*

47 Hill 2004, 40, 210, no. 187.

48 Petrie 1888, 27.

49 Similar to the later statuettes EA 24323 and Boston, MFA 87.480, both from Tell Gemaiyemi, possibly corresponding to the gilt bronze figures of a kneeling king mentioned by Petrie, 1888, 39, 40.

50 Petrie 1888, 76–7; the silver uraei are probably Boston, MFA RES.87.10-11 (deaccessioned); Oxford, AM 1887.2530 is a further silver uraeus recorded as coming from Tell Dafana; the silver figure of Horus must be Sydney, MAC MU2125.

51 The terracotta head published by Petrie 1888, 72, pl. xxiv, 7 is Boston, MFA 87.820, previously registered as RES.87.147. The terracotta head GR 1906,0301.5 (ibid., pl. xxiv, 8) seems to be a local Nile silt imitation of a Cypriote figure.

52 Petrie 1888, 53, 54, 73.

53 Boston, MFA 87.810-814 (= RES 87.121-125; 5 items); Bristol, CMAG H1987,1-2 (2 items); Dundee 1975–66; Liverpool 3.2.87.8; Oxford, AM 1887.2496-2497 (2 items). One piece was sent to the Chautauqua Archaeological Museum, now untraceable.

54 According to the typology defined by Haupt 2012, 71–5 (standing, kneeling or lying figures).

55 See Chapter 1, n. 49. For two similar statuettes, see Wiese 2001, 102–3, no. 63.

56 Herrmann and Staubli 2010, 65, 1–4.

57 Herrmann 2003, 373.

58 See Koenig 2007, 223–38, especially 236; Posener 1940; Posener 1987; Ritner 1993, 113–90, esp. 137–8, n. 611, pp. 153–5; Wiese 2001, 102–3.

59 Edgar 1906, viii–x, 52–80; most recently Tomoum 2005, esp. 10–22, 56–73, 150–4; Robins 1994, 177; Liepsner 1980, 170–3.

60 Petrie 1888, 73; the haematite 'Tauret' and 'ape' are in fact two amulets representing Taweret, Boston, MFA 87.688-689; 'snake's head in green felspar' must be Oxford, AM 1887.2539, the steatite crocodile and frog Oxford, AM 1887. 2542-2543. More stone amulets apparently not recorded by Petrie appear in the different collections but it would be premature to give a list of them here.

61 Petrie 1888, 73, pl. xli.

62 Ibid., 74; the blue amulet of Isis and Horus from Room 17 must be Boston, MFA 87.620.

63 The *wedjat*-eyes EA 18455–6, 18511, and 18547 might also have to be considered as belonging to the same group, though this is not certain.

64 Petrie 1888, 79; Journal, 118.

65 Petrie 1888, 73.

66 Edinburgh, NMS 1887.82.1 (Petrie 1888, 73, pl. xli, 54), 1887.82.2 (ibid., 111, pl. xli, 60), 1887.82.3 (ibid., pl. xli, 50), 1887.82.4 (ibid., pl. xli, 44), 1887.82.5 (ibid., pl. xli, 53), 1887.82.7 (ibid., pl. xli, 63), 1887.82.8 (ibid., pl. xli, 67), 1887.82.11 (ibid., pl. xli, 49), 1887.83 (ibid., pl. xli, 48).

67 Three of these five unlocated scarabs might correspond to Edinburgh, NMS 1887.82.6, .9, and .10, destroyed in 1959.

68 Petrie 1888, 73; Boston, MFA 87.690. Another haematite scarab must be Oxford, AM 1887.2544; the third is not yet located.

69 Petrie 1888, 73; Boston, MFA 87.700.

70 Petrie 1888, 76, 111, pl. xli, 37; Journal, 149; Boston, MFA 87.761.

71 Boston, MFA RES.87.95-97; see also RES.87.94. However, Petrie does not seem to mention more than one lapis lazuli scarab from Tell Dafana (Petrie 1888, 73), although two small inscribed ones are in the British Museum, EA 18527 and 18529, possibly three with EA 18461, of less certain provenance. Half a red jasper scarab is also recorded as coming from Tell Dafana in the Bolton Museum, 1886.28.79; see also Bolton 1886.28.30.

72 Boardman 2003, esp. 109–13; see also http://www.beazley.ox.ac.uk/gems/scarab/default.htm.

73 Hall 1913, 252, no. 2522.

74 Petrie 1888, pl. viii, 22.

75 Petrie 1888, 57, 76.

76 Ibid., 76.

77 Fay 1990, 32–3.

78 For other examples of such silver rings, see Fay 1990, 32–3 (Berlin, VAGM 77–84); Canby 1979, 48–9, no. 139 (Baltimore, WAG 57.1487); see also London, PM UC33955, 33960, 33965, 33969–70, 33973, 71803 (silver), 33958–9, 33962–4, 33966, 33980 (bronze); London, BM EA 24777 is more elaborate (Andrews 1990, fig. 148a); Yoyotte 1972, 218, n. 3; Corteggiani 1973, 151–3, pl. 13; De Meulenaere 1964, 25–30; Keel 1995, 140, § 354 (7th–6th century BC); the clay seal impressions that Petrie found in the palace of Apries in Memphis must have been made with rings of similar type (Petrie 1910, 42, 43, pls xxxv–xxxvi, 1–14, pl. xxxvii, 42–5, 47–9).

79 For example Hodjash 1999, 169–70.

80 Petrie 1910, 43, pls xxxv–xxxvi, 22–32.

81 Petrie 1888, 58, 66, 72; Journal, 119–20, 129.

82 Petrie 1888, 58, 59, 72; Journal, 135, 140, 141, 145; one jar sealing of Amasis, Oxford, AM 1887.2506 must also come from Findspot 25, as this number is scratched on the item.

83 Petrie 1888, 54, 72; Journal, 141.

84 According to the EEF distribution lists, apart from the pieces mentioned as parallels for the British Museum objects, fragments of plaster jar sealings from Tell Dafana were also sent to the museums of Birmingham, York, Brighton, St Albans, University College London and Montreal.

85 Petrie 1888, 66, 72.

86 Similar plaster amphora-sealings seem to be represented on an
Attic black-figured amphora in Boston, MFA 1979.618, and a
band-cup in the Louvre, F77 (Brownlee 1989, 8, fig. 5, p. 11, n. 22).

87 Amborn 1976, 47–69.

88 Cf. Spencer 1993, 34, nos 50–7 and pls 28, 31–2.

89 Petrie 1886, 39, pl. xi; Amborn 1976, 69–77.

90 For later periods, see Amborn 1976, 115–31; in Sudan, from the
Napatan Period, ibid., 141–89.

91 Petrie 1888, 77.

92 Between a few and a few dozen were sent to Birmingham, Bolton,
Boston, Brighton, Bristol (and Bath), Cairo, Cambridge,
Chautauqua, Dundee, Edinburgh, Glasgow, Godalming,
Greenock, Liverpool, London (Biblical Museum, Harrow School,
Petrie Museum), Montreal, Oxford, Philadelphia, Sheffield, St
Albans, St Helens, Sydney, and York. The Royal Ontario Museum
of Toronto received the largest selection, of more than 200 pieces.

93 Snodgrass 1964, 144–57; Amborn 1976, 93–5.

94 Amborn 1976, 91. One type (Petrie 1888, pl. xxxvii, 15, not yet
identified) could be Persian (Amborn, op. cit., 91, n. 91).

95 Amborn 1976, 78, 93, n. 98.

96 Knife EA 23912.

97 Iron chisel, as yet unidentified (Petrie 1888, 78).

98 Three iron rasps, EA 23973, 23974 and possibly Boston, MFA
87.519 or Oxford, AM 1887.2503.

99 Petrie 1888, 59, 78; Journal, 132, 135, 143.

100 Amborn 1976, 82–4, 111.

101 Snodgrass 1964, 84–6; Amborn 1976, 85–90.

102 Petrie 1909c, 13, pl. xvi, 5–32.

103 See for instance Miller 1997, esp. 46–9.

104 Amborn 1976, 91, 98.

105 Petrie 1888, 77–9.

106 Ibid., 79; see also p. 59 about the 'armoury of the camp': 'Iron
arrowheads strewed the ground, and were excavated by hundreds;
the same of bronze; iron and copper slag abounded; and many
other small objects were found'; Journal, 132: 'out on the plain, an
iron factory: ore slag, tools and dozens of iron arrow heads'; ibid.,
136: 'some way, say 1/4 of mile, south of the palace is the iron
factory; slag & ore lying about, & quantities of wrought iron
objects. Arrow heads I reject by the dozen or hundred, but keep as
many as I reject; pieces of iron grating occur, & links of a great
iron chain each 4 or 5 inches long, forged one eye in the other. All
these may be dated before 560 BC'; ibid., 167: 'the work has paid
well; good iron and bronze arrow heads by the handful, iron
chisels, horses bits, two bronze chisels, many other tools (...)'; ibid.,
169: 'there is any amount of iron slag in the camp, & some
beautiful haematite, so it is plain that they smelted here, as at

Naukratis, & the quantity of iron work explains this. (...) The camp
is more prolific than ever; about a hundred bronze arrow heads,
iron arrow heads, tools, &c'.

107 Others are Boston MFA 87.507-508 (deaccessioned) and London,
PM UC 59877 (2 pieces).

108 See also Cairo, EM, JE 27378 (missing); Boston, MFA 87.515
(Petrie 1888, 77); Boston, MFA 87.516 and Oxford, AM 1887.2505.x
(ibid., 77, 110, pl. xxxvii, 6); see also the bronze eight-shaped link,
EA 23884.

109 The object EA 23989, initially registered as fragments of slag; it is
actually a fragmentary tool, possibly part of a plough share.

110 See Appendix 1, iii. Also Amborn 1976, 131–40.

111 Petrie 1888, 76; see also Journal, 119: 'a number of Bedawin spend
their time in hunting all the ground, & nearly all day a few figures
are to be seen slowly stalking over the plain, staring on the ground
for weights. They have also brought me in several small gold
ornaments, so I have quite tapped their confidence'; ibid., 123–4:
'it is excellent to get a thorough scouring of the surface done in this
way, which I now have (...), that everything must be seen by the
hunters. Several scraps of gold jewellery & a fine sacred eye in
gold, have been brought up and bought by weight'; ibid., 126–7:
'three gold earrings and several scraps were also brought in, &
bought for weight. (...) two more gold earrings.'; ibid., 129: '(...)
more gold scraps; I have now bought up 11 earrings, 2 sacred eyes
and a lot of scraps'.

112 Petrie 1888, 80.

113 See also two gold *wedjat*-eyes in section 5 (EA 18251, 18556) with
the same provenance.

114 On crescent-shaped earrings cf. Laurent and Desti 1997, 279, no.
502 (dated Roman). This shape was known from as early as the
New Kingdom, see Fay 1990, 41–4, 59–60; Assyrian example:
Tallon 1995, 63–4, no. 61. They also occur in the Roman Period
(represented on Roman portraits of the 1st–3rd century AD), e.g.
BM EA 74710; Dresden Aeg. 778; see Doxiadis 1995, pl. 43, 11;
spherical pendants, ibid., pls 48, 53–4; for granulated gold
pendants, see ibid., 235; Davidson and Andrew 1984, 89–136.

115 Petrie 1888, 75.

116 Ibid., 79.

117 Journal, 169: 'A fresh party of Bedawin have found out that I will
buy, & they come from a district between here & San. There is a
tell there El Bahaim, (or the place of cattle, called so from
pasturage there), which seems to abound in the small brass weights
(...); beside handful of carnelian beads'.

118 Petrie 1888, 74; Journal, 142.

119 See n. 8.

120 Petrie 1888, 76.

Chapter 3
Catalogue of Objects from Tell Dafana in the British Museum

François Leclère

1. Vessels in materials other than pottery

Stone vessels (Pl. 15)

EA 23831   1887,0101.780
Fragment of a dark green greywacke dish with a large, flat rim.
Length: 22.7cm (max.); width: 11.55cm (max.); thickness: 2.51cm;
diameter (reconstructed): 29.5cm.
Bibliography: Petrie 1888, 73 § 70: 'part of large dish of slate'.

EA 18559   1887,0101.697
Greywacke miniature model of a mortar, with a rounded flat base,
concave upper surface and a flat-topped rim fitted with four
rectangular projections around the perimeter.
Height: 0.3cm; diameter: 1.9cm (max.).
Bibliography: Petrie 1888, 73 § 70, pl. xl, 2: 'model of rubber-stone...
found in the camp, cut in slate'.

EA 23806   1887,0101.841
Calcite sherd from a vessel. Unlocated and not illustrated.
Length: 7.7cm; width: 4.8cm (max.).
Bibliography: perhaps a fragment of one of the 'seven alabastra 2½
inches to 4 inches high, from the camp' mentioned in Petrie 1888, 73 §
70; other calcite vases from the site: Boston, MFA, 87.715, 87.716, 87.717,
Bolton M., 1886.28.27, 1886.28.118-119 and Bristol, MAG, H1988.

Metal vessels (Pl. 15)

EA 23644   1887,0101.776
Corroded copper alloy cylindrical measuring-vessel with a flat base
and vertical sides; part of the upper body and rim are broken away.
Height: 12.3cm; diameter: 9.5cm.
Context: north-west Ptolemaic mound.
Bibliography: Petrie 1888, 79 § 79: certainly one of the 'two bronze
vessels,....cylindrical with flat base, 4.0 in. across and 4.8 in. high',
found on the north-west Ptolemaic mound; see also ibid., 61 § 57, 'three
bronze pots of cylindrical form'. Journal, 118: 'in the main mound,
nearly all the pits I have sunk have cut into nothing but burnt earth
and broken pottery, apparently a waste heap; in one such pit two brass
pots were found, & I got them on the whole, about 4 ins across & high';
ibid., 128: 'Another brass pot, like the two previous ones, was found in
the town mound today'; see also Pommerening 2005, 377, no. M35
(wrongly said from Tell Nebesha).
Parallels: the two other vessels are GR 1888,0208.146 and Boston,
MFA 87.496a; cf. Pommerening 2005, 37–82, nos M31–49, pp. 172–3,
356–7.

GR 1888,0208.146
Cylindrical vessel of copper alloy, repaired from eighteen fragments
with some missing areas restored. The shape was originally truly
cylindrical, similar to the preceding entry, but the vessel has been
somewhat crushed. The surface is entirely coated with corrosion
products.
Height: 12.7cm; diameter: 10.4cm.
Context: north-west Ptolemaic mound.
Bibliography: Petrie 1888, 61 § 57.
Parallels: see under EA 23644 above.

EA 23904   1887,0101.1428
Two copper alloy utensils in the shape of small, hollow and round
'frying-pans' or shallow ladles, stuck one above the other by heavy
corrosion. The upper one, smaller, has a short triangular pointed
handle or tang. The lower one had probably the same kind of tang,
now broken and missing.
Height: 2.99cm; diameter: 13cm (larger vessel); length (with tang):
14.6cm; diameter 10.9cm (smaller vessel).
Context: Saite enclosure (so-called 'Camp').
Bibliography: Petrie 1888, 77 § 76, pl. xxxix, 6, 7: 'two small pans,
which from their concavity cannot be mirrors, seem to be most
probably frying-pans'.
Parallels: from Tell Dafana, Boston, MFA 87.500 (deaccessioned),
which possibly corresponds to the 'parts of a large bronze pan with a
handle' mentioned in Petrie 1888, 79 § 79 (and perhaps illustrated on

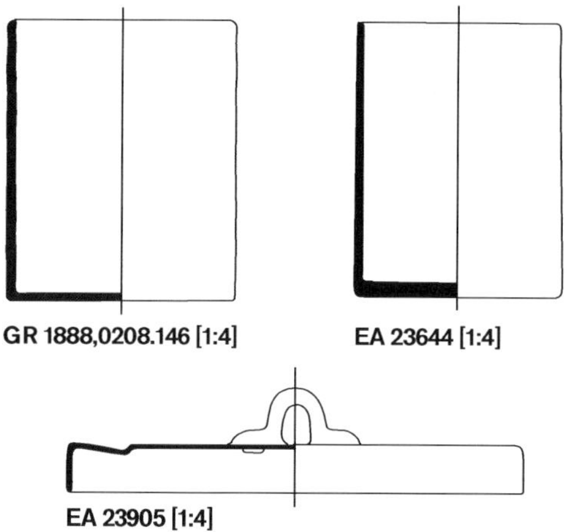

GR 1888,0208.146 [1:4]   **EA 23644 [1:4]**

EA 23905 [1:4]

Figure 1 Examples of metal vessels

pl. xxxix, 7) and to the 'brass dish' mentioned in his Journal (p. 118), found on the north-west Ptolemaic mound with three bronze cylindrical vessels (EA 23644, GR 1888,0208.146 and Boston, MFA 87.496a); cf. Bissing, 1901, 52–3, no. 3534 (Cairo, EM JE 30031, unknown provenance, dating Saite); Petrie 1937, 29, pl. 41, nos 93–4.

EA 23905   1887,0101.1429

Heavily corroded copper alloy circular lid, with a short cylindrical edge, a shallow circular step on the upper surface and a central omega-shaped handle.
Height: 2.2cm; diameter: 21cm.
Context: Saite enclosure (so-called 'Camp').
Bibliography: Petrie 1888, 77 § 76, pl. xxxix, 23: 'large bronze lid, found in the camp' with a 'bronze bowl 7½ inches across and 2 inches deep' (pl. xli [*sic*, read xxxix], 17) and 'a dipper (trua) 17 inches long'. The bowl and dipper are certainly Boston MFA 87.496b and 87.497a.
Parallel: Edgar 1904a, 31, pl. viii, no. CG 27755.

EA 23806   1887,0101.611

Heavily corroded fragment of a copper alloy vessel, comprising a small piece of the side and rim with an attached loop-handle; the curve of the rim indicates that the vessel had a large diameter and a shape similar to that of a casserole.
Height: 5.74cm; width: 5.95cm; depth: 3.32cm (including handle).

EA 23859   1887,0101.779

Small round vessel of silver, broken into several fragments and repaired, with a narrow flat base, cylindrical rim and a spout in the shape of a truncated triangle. There is no evidence of a handle or handles, but it is possible that these might have been fixed onto the missing parts of the rim.
Height: 2.4cm; length: 10.4cm (with spout); diameter: 8.3cm (without spout).
Bibliography: the item is not mentioned in Petrie's publication; however, another silver vessel is mentioned in Petrie 1888, 76 § 75 (see also Journal, 148–50) corresponding to Cairo, EM JE 27383, 'found together with a silver dipper (JE 27382) and lumps of silver'.
Parallel: Bissing 1901, 53, no. CG 3533 (bronze).

Shell vessels (Pl. 15)

GR 1906,0301.13

Uncarved Tridacna shell.
Height: 4.55cm; length: 15cm; width: 8.25cm.
Bibliography: Petrie 1888, 72 § 68, though Petrie does not mention this particular piece.
Parallels: Reese 1988, 40–1.

GR 1906,0301.14

Fragment of Tridacna shell carved on the convex side with rayed semi-circular and linear designs, possibly part of feathers from a wing, probably of a winged sphinx, if not a griffin.
Height: 1cm; length: 4.75cm; width: 2.5cm; thickness: 0.45cm.
Context: surface of the ground.

Bibliography: Petrie 1888, 72 § 68: 'a piece of engraved Tridacna, like those found at Naukratis, was also picked up on the surface'. The fragment is also discussed in Stucky 1974, 32–3, no. 27, pl. xviii, though the identification of the design of the 'upper body of Griffin whose head, which was turned to the right, has been broken off' remains unclear.
Parallels: Petrie 1886c, 35–6, pl. xx, 10–12, 16 (from Naukratis); Hogarth *et al.* 1898–9, 49, fig. 1 (from Naukratis); in general: Stucky 1974, esp. 33, no. 28, pl. xviii (Memphis), p. 33–5 nos 29–35, pls xviii–xxi (Naukratis); Reese 1988, 38.

Glazed composition vessels (Pl. 16)

EA 23755   1887,0101.753

Pale-green glazed composition New Year flask with a round, lentiform body, a short neck terminating in a papyrus capital, and small rough figures of crouching apes at the shoulder, leaning back against each side of the neck. The upper part of the body is decorated on both sides with an incised collar design (two rows of raindrop-shaped beads), while a large band around the edge is lightly cross-hatched. The collars and upper sections of the edge band are covered with a thicker, darker green glaze. The object is reconstructed from many fragments.
Height: 9.06cm; width: 7.06cm; thickness: 4.04cm.
Context: Saite enclosure (so-called 'Camp').
Bibliography: Petrie 1888, 75 § 72: 'one bottle is very peculiar: it is of dark greenish-grey, with a band of bright, thick, green glaze around the wreath and around the edge; it is thin and small, but such thick glaze is rarely, if ever, seen before Roman times'; see also Felder 1988b, 8.

EA 23756   1887,0101.1398

Fragment from the edge and part of both sides of a glazed composition New Year flask, with incised decoration. The raised band around the edge is adorned in the lower part with a design of overlaying rounded scales and inscribed in the upper part with an invocation to the goddess Neith, both parts within a rectangular frame. The inscription in two columns reads from right to left: '(1) May Neith give life, all health (2), "best wishes"(?) to (its) owner'. The sides are decorated with an incised collar design alternating rows of very varied patterns (from bottom to top: raindrop-shaped beads, lotus flowers, vegetal plaits, buttons, vertical lines) separated by double or triple curved lines. The surface is worn.
Height 4.7cm; length: 5.88cm (max.).
Context: Saite enclosure (so-called 'Camp').
Bibliography: Petrie 1888, 75 § 72, pl. xl, 4: among the 'pilgrim bottles' found on the site, many were 'bearing portions of inscriptions, and one a longer wish than usual (pl. xl. 4): 'May Neit give life and health always to the souls of all children' or 'to all beautiful souls'; see also Boston, MFA, RES.87.146.a and f, fragments of other inscribed New Year flasks from Tell Dafana.
Parallels (with similar inscription): see Kischkewitz 1970, 146, n. 42 (with wrong reading); Hölbl, G. 1979b, 22, pl. 10.b, no. 72; Felder 1988b, 37, 125–6, 140–1 (with ref.); on the expression *k3 n nfrw* as 'good luck', 'fortune', 'chance', 'success', see Lipińska 1964, 143–4.

EA 23757   1887,0101.1399

Five rejoined fragments from the side of a glazed composition New Year flask, decorated with a collar design, alternating rows of very varied patterns (from bottom to top: raindrop-shaped beads, lotus flowers, a triangular pattern, rosettes, vertical lines, vegetal plait) separated by double or triple curved lines. The incisions are coloured with brown glaze. A tiny part of the raised band around the edge is preserved at the right end.
Height 3.4cm; length: 8.8cm (max.).
Context: Saite enclosure (so-called 'Camp').
Bibliography: Petrie 1888, 75 § 72.

EA 55345   1887,0101.1400

Fragment from a glazed composition New Year flask, with traces of a floral pattern bounded by a rectangular frame and enclosed in a larger one. The decoration is made of brown glaze filling incisions in the raised band around the edge of the vessel.
Width: 2.2cm; length: 4.2cm; thickness: 0.5cm.

Context: Saite enclosure (so-called 'Camp').
Bibliography: same as for EA 23757 above.

EA 55346   1887,0101.1401
Fragment from a glazed composition New Year flask, with traces of a blue glaze floral pattern filling incisions on the raised band around the edge of the vessel. The glazed composition has suffered decay; it is eroded on the interior and has turned white and chalky.
Width: 2.2cm; length: 2.6cm; thickness: 0.3cm.
Context: Saite enclosure (so-called 'Camp').
Bibliography: same as for EA 23757 above.

EA 21779   1887,0101.751
Cylindrical neck of a green glazed composition New Year flask, terminating in a papyrus capital; there are incised details on the capital and a figure of an ape crouching on the shoulder, leaning back against the bottle neck, holding his snout in his hands (another one, on the opposite side, is broken away).
Height: 5cm; diameter: 3.9cm.
Context: provenance not specified in the Museum register, but certainly from Tell Dafana, according to the context of the item in the list, Saite enclosure (so-called 'Camp').
Bibliography: same as for EA 23757 above.

EA 21780   1887,0101.752
Cylindrical neck of a glazed composition New Year flask, terminating in a papyrus capital; there are incised and modelled details on the capital and a figure of an ape crouching on the shoulder, leaning back against the bottle neck, holding his snout in his hands (another one, on the opposite side, is broken away); chipped and glaze heavily worn.
Height: 4.7cm; width: 5.2cm.
Context: provenance not specified in the Museum register, but certainly from Tell Dafana, according to the context of the item in the list, Saite enclosure (so-called 'Camp').
Bibliography: same as for EA 23757 above.

EA 21781   1887,0101.754
Cylindrical neck of a glazed composition New Year flask, terminating in a wide papyrus capital with incised and modelled details.
Height: 3.4cm; width: 4.9cm.
Context: provenance not specified in the Museum register, but certainly from Tell Dafana, according to the context of the item in the list, Saite enclosure (so-called 'Camp').
Bibliography: same as for EA 23757 above.

EA 21782   1887,0101.755
Cylindrical neck of a glazed composition New Year flask, terminating in a palmiform capital; there are incised and modelled details on the capital and a figure of an ape crouching on the shoulder, leaning back against the bottle neck, holding his snout in his hands (another one, on the opposite side, is broken away); chipped and glaze worn.
Height: 4cm; width: 3.4cm.
Context: provenance not specified in the Museum register, but certainly from Tell Dafana, according to the context of the item in the list, Saite enclosure (so-called 'Camp').
Bibliography: same as for EA 23757 above.

EA 18460   1887,0101.729
Fragment from the wall of a glazed composition vessel, the exterior inscribed with a horizontal line of hieroglyphs of uncertain reading. At the right end is a standing figure with at least one arm upraised; left of this is a possible sign *m* (or perhaps *gs*) above an indeterminate sign and what appear to be *r* and *s*.
Height: 2.56cm (max.); length: 3.36cm (max.); thickness: 0.69cm.
Context: provenance not specified in the Museum register but a number 3 is pencilled on the internal wall of the sherd, possibly indicating a provenance from Tell Dafana, chamber 3 of the east annexe (C) of the 'Qasr'.

EA 18453   1887,0101.710
Description: Green glazed composition fragment of an unidentified artefact, perhaps the neck from a vessel, in the form of a conical shaft tapering out into a quatrefoil, pierced longitudinally.

Height: 3.36cm; diameter: 1.91cm.
Context: provenance not specified in the Museum register, but possibly from Tell Dafana, as suggested by the context of the item in the list, if not from Tell Nebesha or any other eastern Delta site excavated by Petrie in 1886.

EA 18644   1887,0101.881
Fragment from a blue glazed composition vessel, broken on all the edges. The glaze has decayed to leave only patches on the interior and exterior surfaces.
Length: 2.93cm (max.); width 2.2cm; thickness: 0.49cm (max.).
Context: provenance not specified in the Museum register, possibly from Tell Dafana or Tell Nebesha, according to the context of the item in the list.

2. Foundation deposits

Inscribed plaques of King Psamtik I (Pl. 17)

EA 23556   1887,0101.1354
Thick rectangular plaque of glazed composition bearing an incised vertical inscription on one side, read from right to left, with the cartouches of King Psamtik I (prenomen Wahibra and nomen Psamtik), between two vertical lines. All sides, except the back, show traces of a worn brown-green glazed slip.
Length: 7.2cm; width: 3.25cm; thickness: 1.1cm.
Context: 'Qasr', casemate building A, beneath the north-east corner ('NE' scored on the back of the item).
Bibliography: Petrie 1888, 54 § 52, pp. 54–5 § 54, pls xxii, 5, xxiii; Petrie 1889b, pl. 60 no. 1909; see also Porter and Moss 1934, 7; Weinstein 1973, 327; Perdu 2002, 131, no. 28.
Parallels: from Tell Dafana, Cairo, EM JE 27385, Boston, MFA 87.653 and Berlin, ÄM 10080 (destroyed during WW II); cf. Spencer 1996, 85, no. 100b and colour plate 4b for Psamtik plaques from elsewhere.

EA 23556   1887,0101.1355
Thin rectangular gold plaque bearing an engraved vertical inscription on each side, read from right to left, of the cartouches of King Psamtik I (prenomen Wahibra on one side, nomen Psamtik on the other).
Length: 1.3cm; width: 0.6cm; thickness: 0.05cm.
Context: 'Qasr', casemate building A, probably beneath the north-east (or north-west?) corner.
Bibliography: Petrie 1888, 54 § 52, pp. 54–5 § 54, pls xxii, 7, xxiii; Petrie 1889b, pl. 60, no. 1910; see also Porter and Moss 1934, 7; Weinstein 1973, 326; Perdu 2002, 131, no. 28.
Parallels: from Tell Dafana, Cairo, EM JE 27385. For other gold plaques of this king from Tell el-Balamun see Spencer 1996, 85–6, colour plate 4b.

EA 23556   1887,0101.1356
Thin rectangular silver plaque bearing an engraved vertical inscription on one side, read from right to left, of the cartouches (prenomen Wahibra and nomen Psamtik) of King Psamtik I.
Length: 2.3cm; width: 0.85cm; thickness: 0.012cm.
Context: 'Qasr', casemate building A, probably beneath the north-east (or north-west?) corner.
Bibliography: Petrie 1888, 54 § 52, pp. 54–5 § 54, pls xxii, 8, xxiii: Petrie 1889b, pl. 60, no. 1911; see also Porter and Moss 1934, 7; Weinstein 1973, 326; Perdu 2002, 131, no. 28.
Parallels: from Tell Dafana, Cairo, EM JE 27385.

EA 23556   1887,0101.1358
Thin rectangular lead plaque bearing an engraved vertical inscription on one side, read from right to left, of the cartouches of King Psamtik I (prenomen Wahibra and nomen Psamtik). Although the item is heavily corroded the inscription is still visible, except on the lower part, where the object is broken.
Length: 2.8cm; width: 1.4cm; thickness: 0.4cm.
Context: 'Qasr', casemate building A, probably beneath the south-east (or north-west?) corner.
Bibliography: Petrie 1888, 54 § 52, pp. 54–5 § 54, pls xxii, 6, xxiii; see also Porter and Moss 1934, 7; Weinstein 1973, 326; Perdu 2002, 131, no. 28.

Parallels: from Tell Dafana, Cairo, EM JE 27385 and Boston, MFA 87.
529 (from the north-east corner).

EA 23556   1887,0101.1359
Rectangular plaque of red jasper with a vertical inscription engraved
on one side, read from right to left, bearing the cartouche (prenomen
Wahibra) of King Psamtik I.
Length: 0.97cm; width: 0.64cm; thickness: 0.22cm.
Context: 'Qasr', casemate building A, probably beneath the north-east
corner (or north-west).
Bibliography: Petrie 1888, 54 § 52, pp. 54–5 § 54, pls xxii, 4, xxiii; see
also Porter and Moss 1934, 7; Weinstein 1973, 326; Perdu 2002, 131, no.
28.
Parallels: from Tell Dafana, Cairo, EM JE 27385 and Boston, MFA
87.719 (from the south-east corner).

EA 23556   1887,0101.1360
Rectangular carnelian plaque bearing a vertical inscription engraved
on one side, read from right to left, of the cartouche (nomen) of King
Psamtik I.
Length: 0.95cm; width: 0.56cm; thickness: 0.026cm.
Context: 'Qasr', casemate building A, beneath the north-west corner.
Bibliography: Petrie 1888, 54 § 52, pp. 54–5 § 54, pls xxii, 1, xxiii; see also
Porter and Moss 1934, 7; Weinstein 1973, 326; Perdu 2002, 131, no. 28.

Uninscribed plaques (Pl. 17)

EA 23556   1887,0101.1357
Rectangular copper plaque, so heavily corroded that some grains of
sand from where the foundation deposit was found are embedded in
the corrosion. The corrosion prevents a determination whether the
object was originally inscribed or not.
Length: 3cm; width: 1.4cm (up to 1.7cm with corrosion); thickness:
0.5cm (up to 0.9cm with corrosion).
Context: 'Qasr', casemate building A, beneath one of the four corners
(except south-east), probably north-east.
Bibliography: Petrie 1888, 54 § 52, pp. 54–5 § 54, pls xxii, 9, xxiii;
Weinstein 1973, 326.
Parallels: from Tell Dafana, Cairo, EM JE 27385 and Boston, MFA
87.528 (from the south-east corner).

EA 23556   1887,0101.1361
Model of a rectangular mud brick; the surface of the larger sides is
slightly hollow due to hand modelling.
Length: 3.7cm; width: 1.8cm; thickness: 0.9cm.
Context: 'Qasr', casemate building A, beneath the north-east (or
south-east) corner.
Bibliography: Petrie 1888, 54 § 52, pp. 54–5 § 54, pls xxii, 12, xxiii;
Weinstein 1973, 327.
Parallels: see also Cairo, EM JE 27385.

Lead and copper ore samples (Pl. 17)
All these samples come from beneath the south-east corner of the
casemate building A of the 'Qasr'.
Bibliography: Petrie 1888, 54 § 52, pp. 54–5 § 54, p. 74 § 70, pls xxii, 10,
xxiii; Weinstein 1973, 327.

EA 23556   1887,0101.1364
Irregular sample of lead ore.
Length: 4cm; width: 2.7cm; thickness: 0.5cm.

EA 23556   1887,0101.1365
Irregular sample of lead ore.
Length: 3.7cm; width: 2.2cm; thickness: 1.1cm.

EA 23556   1887,0101.1362
Irregular sample of copper ore.
Length: 1.5cm; width: 1.4cm; thickness: 0.6cm.

EA 23556   1887,0101.1363
Irregular sample of copper ore. Comparison with the drawing on
Petrie's plate (pl. xxii, 11, sample immediately above the one at the
lower right corner) shows that a chip is missing.
Length: 1.6cm; width: 1.1cm; thickness: 0.75cm.

EA 23556   1887,0101.1366
Irregular sample of copper ore.
Length: 0.8cm; width: 0.6cm; thickness: 0.35cm.
Bibliography: Petrie 1888, 54 § 52, pp. 54–5 § 54, pls xxii, 11, xxiii;
Weinstein 1973, 327.

EA 23556   1887,0101.1367
Irregular sample of copper ore.
Length: 1.3cm; width: 0.6cm; thickness: 0.5cm.
Bibliography: Petrie 1888, 54 § 52, pp. 54–5 § 54, pls xxii, 11, xxiii;
Weinstein 1973, 327.

EA 23556   1887,0101.1368
Irregular sample of copper ore.
Length: 1.7cm; width: 1.3cm; thickness: 0.8cm.

EA 23556   1887,0101.1369
Irregular sample of copper ore.
Length: 1.6cm; width: 1.1cm; thickness: 0.4cm.

EA 23556   1887,0101.1370
Sample of copper ore.
Length: 2.4cm; width: 1.2cm; thickness: 0.8cm.

EA 23556   1887,0101.1371
Sample of copper ore.
Length: 2.1cm; width: 1.1cm; thickness: 0.7cm.

EA 23556   1887,0101.1372
Sample of copper ore.
Length: 1.8cm; width: 1.7cm; thickness: 0.75cm.

EA 23556   1887,0101.1373
Sample of copper ore.
Length: 1cm; width: 0.8cm; thickness: 0.75cm.

EA 23556   1887,0101.1374
Sample of copper ore.
Length: 1.2cm; width: 0.9cm; thickness: 0.6cm.

Ox bones and teeth (Pl. 18)
All these items come from beneath the south-east corner of the
casemate building A of the 'Qasr' and were possibly once part of a
sacrificial offering.
Bibliography: Petrie 1888, 54 § 52, p. 55 § 54, pls xxii, xxiii, 15;
Weinstein 1973, 327; see also the ox tooth Boston, MFA RES.87.14
and/or RES.87.15. The skull and some bones are supposed to have
been left in the Cairo EM, unregistered.

EA 23557   1887,0101.1375 + 1887,0101.1381
Part of the leg bone of an ox. One long piece of the bone is preserved,
with a few small fragments that join to the broken ends. There is also a
separate small fragment from the joint surface of the long bone.
Length: 18.5cm (max.); width: 5.5cm (max.); thickness 4cm. The
separate fragment measures 3.7 x 3.1cm.

EA 23557   1887,0101.1376
Ox tooth.
Length: 5.9cm; width: 3cm; thickness: 2.3cm.

EA 23557   1887,0101.1377
Ox tooth.
Length: 4.5cm; width: 3cm; thickness: 2.2cm.

EA 23557   1887,0101.1378
Ox tooth.
Length: 4.4cm; width: 3cm; thickness: 2.2cm.

EA 23557   1887,0101.1379
Ox tooth.
Length: 3.9cm; width: 3.1cm; thickness: 1.3cm.

EA 23557   1887,0101.1380
Ox tooth.
Length: 2.4cm; width: 2.5cm; thickness: 2cm.

Plaque of King Apries (Pl. 17)

EA 18562   **1887,0101.728**

Rectangular plaque made of glazed composition, bearing a vertical inscription between two vertical lines incised on both sides, read from right to left, with the cartouches (prenomen on one side, nomen on the other) of King Apries. All sides show traces of a worn light green to beige glaze. Although not discovered *in situ*, this plaque might have been part of a foundation deposit for a building somewhere inside the Saite enclosure.

Length: 4.2cm; width: 2.3cm; thickness: 0.65cm.

Context: a chamber in the southern part of Saite enclosure (so-called 'Camp').

Bibliography: Petrie 1888, 51 § 49, p. 75 § 72, pl. xl, 7, p. 51 § 49: 'of Haa-ab-ra only one plaque with his name'; p. 75 § 72: 'the plaque of Haa-ab-ra (Hophra) (xl, 7), which seems as if made for a foundation plaque, but was found in a chamber in the camp along with other pottery'; Hall 1913, 295, no. 2807; Porter and Moss 1934, 7; Weinstein 1973, 333.

Parallels: another plaque of Apries, Cairo, EM JE 27386, is registered as coming from Tell Dafana, though Petrie only mentions one plaque in his publication. It is so similar in style and dimensions to EA 18562 as to suggest they both came from the same building. The confirmation of the existence of two plaques comes from Petrie's Journal, 167: 'two little plaques of Apries, which complete the series of XXVI dyn. kings' names here. The stuff we turn is all of Amasis, I believe; these two of Apries were in a rather deeper clearance'; see also Matouk 1971, 142, 200, no. 834, p. 221, no. 869.

Miscellaneous (Pl. 18)

See also EA 23900, a model of a tool or arrowhead, strangely considered in the Museum register as part of a Ptolemaic foundation deposit from Tell Dafana.

EA 23641   **1887,0101.1387**

Fragment of tibiotarsus (middle leg bone) of a duck *(Anas sp.*, kindly identified by Dr Wim Van Neer (Royal Belgian Institute of Natural Sciences), part of a foundation deposit.

Length: 3.6cm (max.); width: 0.7cm.

Context: 'Qasr', east annexe (C), beneath the south-west corner of Chamber 19 C.

Bibliography: Petrie 1888, 55 § 54: part of the 'trifling deposit' beneath the south-west corner of Annexe C, to the east of the 'Qasr'; '...a hole had been scooped out of the sand, cylindrical, 4 to 7 inches from W. face, 10 to 14 inches from S. face, and 1 to 12 inches deep below the base of the brickwork. This hole was filled with charcoal, and burnt bones of a small bird, of which I could preserve only one piece'. Journal, 161: 'next day, I cleared under a corner of an additional building, E. of the Kasr; the only deposit was a hole 1 ft deep & 4 ins. wide, filled with charcoal & bones of a small bird; so minor sacrifices were made for minor buildings'; see also Weinstein 1973, 327–8.

EA 18486   **1887,0101.673**

Rhomboidal piece of quartz roughly carved or cut, with an inscription scored on both the large opposite sides; one with an illegible cartouche, the other with two *nfr* signs. The function of the item remains unclear, possibly part of a foundation deposit or a game-piece.

Length: 1.4cm; width: 1.4cm; thickness: 0.9cm.

Bibliography: Petrie 1888, 73 § 70, p. 111, pl. xli, 40: 'calcite' 'natural rhomb .....engraved with the name of the spirit Ket in a cartouche, and two nefers or nefrui on the other side'.

3. Architectural pieces

Wall inscription and relief (Pl. 18)

EA 23646   **1887,0101.1390**

Fragment of limestone with a roughly hewn flat surface bearing parts of two roughly incised vertical cartouches of Amasis, read from right to left, on top of the standard of Min. The left cartouche gives the nomen of the king (Amasis, son of Neith), of which the first sign at the top is lost. The right one is slightly longer and gives the prenomen of the king (Khnemibra), of which only the left half is preserved. The standard of Min is carved under the left cartouche. Part of another

sign or decoration, possibly similar, is visible under the other cartouche. A round sign or part of some decoration (top of a figure?) is also visible further down.

Length: 9.5cm; width: 13.2cm; thickness: 4.57cm.

Context: no specific findspot is recorded.

Bibliography: this fragment does not specifically appear in Petrie's publication, though the author mentions numerous chips with hieroglyphic inscriptions in and around the casemate buildings (see Petrie 1888, 53 § 51); see also the *kheker*-frieze Boston, MFA 87.714 found at Findspot 22 (a room to the east of the north-east casemate building). The finding of large blocks of limestone by Petrie is also noted in his Journal, 110 and ibid., 132: 'the work here has been going on steadily, clearing the Kasr. A quantity of chips of fine hieroglyphs I found there ....'.

Fragments of cornice and mouldings (Pl. 18)

EA 23820   **1887,0101.766**

Grey limestone fragment, probably from the corner of a cavetto cornice, with two perpendicular concave sides and a curved corner edge.

Length: 12cm; width: 8.5cm; thickness: 5cm.

Context: probably from the 'Qasr', in the passage between casemate buildings A and B, or from the west side of casemate building B.

Bibliography: Petrie 1888, 56 § 55: 'open-air court, which had a cornice and fluted moulding around the top of its wall', or possibly one of the 'pieces of cornice with ordinary Egyptian cavetto moulding' found west of casemate building B.

EA 23818   **1887,0101.771**

Grey limestone fragment from the fluted side of a moulding, repaired from two pieces. The exterior surface retains parts of five fluted strips and the reverse side is concave. One original edge of the object is preserved.

Length: 14.6cm (max.); width: 6.4cm; thickness: 1.96cm; diameter: 8.8cm (reconstructed).

Context: very probably from the 'Qasr', passage between casemate buildings A and B.

Bibliography: Petrie 1888, 56 § 55.

Parallels: Martin 1981, 106, pl. 41, no. 1521 (Saqqara; London, PM UC 30625); see also Smith *et al.* 2006, 27, pl. 64.a.

EA 23818   **1887,0101.1413**

Grey limestone fragment from the fluted side of a moulding. Parts of three fluted strips remain on the exterior surface. The reverse side is concave and all the edges are broken.

Length: 7.22cm (max.); width: 6.51cm (max.); thickness: 1.91cm (max.); diameter: 8.8cm (reconstructed).

Context, bibliography and parallels: as EA 23818 (1887,0101.771) above.

EA 23818   **1887,0101.1414**

Grey limestone fragment from the fluted side of a moulding. Parts of four fluted strips remain on the exterior of this small fragment. All the edges are broken.

Length: 5.90 (max.); width: 5.74cm (max.); thickness 1.5cm.

Context, bibliography and parallels: as EA 23818 (1887,0101.771) above.

EA 23818   **1887,0101.1415**

Grey limestone fragment from the angle of a moulding with fluted sides. A small fragment with fluted strips running along two sides at right angles. The central part is slightly raised.

Length: 4.87cm (max.); width: 4cm (max.); thickness: 1.45cm (max.).

Context, bibliography and parallels: as EA 23818 (1887,0101.771) above.

Fragments of beams (Pl. 18)

EA 23992   **1887,0101.936**

Fragment of a wooden beam, roughly rectangular in form, broken at either end. The surface is very split and worn.

Length: 15.3cm; width: 6.3cm; thickness: 3.2cm.

Context: 'Qasr', east-north-east face, according to the Museum register, possibly of the casemate building B.

Bibliography: Petrie 1888, 56 § 55.

Parallels: also from Tell Dafana, EA 23993 (below); Boston, MFA RES.87.16.

EA 23993   **1887,0101.937**

Fragment of a wooden beam, consisting of a lightweight splinter, broken at both ends. One end possibly retains part of a circular drilled hole. The surface is very split and worn.

Length: 11cm; width: 3cm; thickness: 2.2cm.

Context: 'Qasr', east-north-east face, according to the Museum register, possibly of the casemate building B (?).

Bibliography and parallels: as for EA 23992 above.

4. Small sculpture and trial-pieces

Bronze figures (Pl. 19)

EA 23431   **1887, 0101.1055**

Corroded copper alloy aegis with a head of Bastet as a lioness wearing a tripartite headdress, topped by a sun-disc with uraeus, and a semi-circular *wesekh* breastplate, with a stepped upper edge (where falcon-headed terminals of such collars are often depicted in better preserved examples). A vertical suspension ring is welded at the back of the sun-disc, on top of the head. The *menat* counterweight is made of a large vertical strip of metal, bent at the top, hinged to the top of the back of the breastplate, under the headdress, by a pair of small vertical rings interlocked with an oval one, stuck by corrosion. Narrowing slightly downwards and flanked by opposed uraei, the lower part of the counterweight ends with a disc.

Height: 6.4cm; width: 4.53cm; depth: 2.4cm.

Bibliography: Petrie 1888, 80 § 80, pl. xxxix, 4: one of three 'aegis of Bast', the one 'with handle'. For examples of the aegis in gold, see Schulz and Seidel 2009, 112, no. 44; also Canby 1979, 20–51, 22, no. 31; Capel and Markoe 1996, 136, no. 66; Schulz 2003, 123–31. Bronze: Roeder 1956, 471, § 637c, no. 2664, pl. 63p; Droste zu Hülshoff 1991, 349–52, no. 231; Delange 2007, 39–49, figs 20–2; Page-Gasser and Wiese 1997, 256–9, no. 171.

EA 23866   **1887,0101.1059**

Corroded copper alloy object of indeterminate nature, perhaps the arms, including bent elbows, of a figure holding at top and base a vertical disc bearing on both sides a low relief representation of the phoenix *bnw*-bird.

Height: 1.97cm; length: 3.01cm; thickness: 1.06cm.

Context: from a room of one of the casemate buildings of the 'Qasr'.

Bibliography: Petrie 1888, 80 § 80: 'two arms from a figure holding a tambourine, with a bennu on each side of it (...) found in a chamber of the Kasr'.

EA 23868   **1887,0101.1061**

Corroded copper alloy fragment from the headdress of a solid-cast figure of Hathor or Isis, with a sun-disc between high cow horns in front of a pair of tall feathers.

Height: 3.2cm; width: 1.29cm; thickness: 0.78cm.

Bibliography: Petrie 1888, 80 § 80: possibly one of the bronze 'feathers'.

EA 23434   **1887,0101.1062**

Upper part of a corroded copper alloy sceptre in the shape of a gazelle or oryx head.

Height: 3.56cm (max.); width: 0.76cm; depth: 1.45cm.

Bibliography: not specifically mentioned among the bronze finds in Petrie 1888, 80 § 80.

EA 23436   **1887,0101.1068**

Corroded copper alloy fragment of a figure of a demon with spread wings, possibly cat-headed. Alternatively, it may represent a bat. The lower part of the figure seems to be missing.

Height: 0.2cm; width: 2.4cm; depth: 0.9cm.

Bibliography: Petrie 1888, 80 § 80: 'upper part of a winged cat-headed Bast'. For a possible interpretation as a bat, very rarely represented in Egypt, see Vandier d'Abbadie 1937.

Glass inlay (Pl. 19)

EA 18493   **1887,0101.698**

Pupil of an eye in transparent, colourless moulded glass, imitating crystal, in the form of half a drop, the obverse convex and the reverse slightly concave with a bevelled edge; one end is slightly pointed and the other rounded. Presumably made for inlaying into a statue, perhaps of a cat.

Length: 0.85cm; width: 0.73cm; depth 0.35cm.

Bibliography: Petrie 1888, 73 § 70: 'cover of an eye, hemispherical, probably from a cat's head, is brilliantly cut in rock-crystal, with the corners of the eye produced'; see also Cooney 1976, 931.

Context: the Museum register does not specify any precise provenance, but the context of the list may imply a Tell Dafana origin and the item matches Petrie's description (Petrie 1888, 73).

Parallels: London, PM UC39028.

Pottery figures (Pls 19–20)

GR 1906,0301.2

Rough, handmade terracotta figure, of which the lower part is lost. It is made of coarse red-brown Egyptian silt clay and has an oblong oval and flattened shape. In the upper part, the potter just pinched the clay in order to model a long narrow nose and shallow eye-sockets, where eyes, separately made of round clay buttons, have been subsequently inserted before firing (the right now missing). At the very bottom, short legs or feet are roughly indicated by two diverging excrescences, partly broken off. The object seems to represent a figure lying down, possibly a sort of concubine or fecundity figure of local production.

Height: 8.5cm (max.); width: 2.95cm; thickness: 1.72cm.

Context: probably from Findspot 51, domestic buildings in the urban area to the east of the Saite enclosure.

Bibliography: Petrie 1888, 61 § 58, pp. 71, 72 § 68, pl. xxiv, 2; Petrie, ibid., 72 § 68: 'the terra-cotta (fig. 2) is much like some of the idols found by Dr Schliemann in the early Greek sites; here, we, at least, can date it to between 665 and 565 BC but its precise locality on the plain of Defenneh was not known, as it was picked up on the denuded surface'. Nevertheless, at pp. 61 § 58 and 72 § 68, Petrie seems to confirm that the item comes from the buildings in the plain to the east of the 'Qasr' (Findspot 51); see also Higgins 1954, 408, no. 1551, pl. 208.

Parallels: Higgins, ibid., cites a parallel piece from Rhodes, see Winter 1903, pl. 10, no. 7.

GR 1906,0301.4

Handmade terracotta female figure, made from coarse red-brown Egyptian silt ware, partially reconstructed from three fragments (head missing). It represents a woman wearing a garment reaching down to her ankles, with her right arm at her side, her left bent across her body below her breasts. The figure is generally flat, apart from the modelled breasts and arms, with fingers and toes simply incised. The large but short sloping feet show clearly that the figure is not represented standing but lying flat on the back. The item is probably a kind of concubine or fecundity figure of local production.

Height: 10.9cm (max.); width: 5.14cm; depth: 3.16cm.

Context: Findspot 51, domestic buildings in the urban area to the east of the Saite enclosure. The number 51 is scored on the back.

Bibliography: Petrie 1888, 61 § 58, p. 72 § 68, pl. xxiv, 4: 'the terracotta, … is comparatively shapely, but still very rude.' See also Higgins 1954, 408, no. 1552, pl. 208 (dating mid-6th century BC); Journal, 145: 'out in the buildings or rather foundations remaining, some way E. of the Kasr, we have traced out many chambers but never got anything hardly, except pottery – broken; & just the same as, but coarser than, that of the Kasr & elsewhere here. The only exception is a terracotta figure, archaic style, (head lost) draped to ankles, & left arm across below breasts; (…)'.

Parallels: to Higgins, ibid., the figurine recalls certain terracottas from Cyprus and some Attic sculpture but neither of the suggested parallels seems particularly relevant. Some of the Cypro-archaic female terracottas do show arms in the same position (Karageorghis 1999, 146–50, pls xxxvi–xxxix), but they are actually very different; see also Petrie 1909c, pl. xxii, 13, or the Egyptian limestone sculptures representing naked concubines on bed, such as at Naukratis (Petrie 1886c, 40, pl. xix, 8–9; Hogarth *et al.* 1898–99, 82, n. 2, pl. xiv, 1–5).

GR 1906,0301.5

Head of a handmade terracotta male figure, made from coarse red-brown Egyptian siltware. The face is narrow, with the main features roughly indicated: a straight nose, brow ridge, cheekbones

and a protruding or bearded chin. The ears and the eyes are not
represented. The figure wears a high cap with a slightly protruding
axial ridge, a tiara, a crested helmet or a high, flat headress. Other
examples suggest that the head may have belonged to a figure of a
standing soldier, horse-and-rider or charioteer.
Height: 6.3cm (max.); width: 2.72cm; depth: 3.5cm (front to back).
Bibliography: Petrie 1888, 72 § 68, pl. xxiv, 8: 'the terracotta "soldiers"
heads…. are probably of the seventh century also, by the extreme
rudeness of them; they both show the crested helmet'; Higgins 1954,
408, no. 1553, pl. 208 (dating mid-6th century BC); the other head
(Petrie, ibid., pl. xxiv, 7) is Boston, MFA 87.820 (previously RES.87.147,
deaccessioned).
Parallels: the elongated shape of the head with high cap, long straight
nose, protuding chin and the absence of eyes point towards the Cypriote
male figures from the Cypro-Archaic II Period, 600–475 BC (Winter 1903,
12, 15; Higgins 1954, 408; Karageorghis 1995, *passim*), rather than the local
terracottas depicting foreigners, especially the 'Scythian'/'Persian' riders
from Memphis (Petrie 1909b, pl. xl; Petrie 1909c, 17, pl. xxix; Petrie 1910,
46, pl. xlii; Higgins, ibid., 407, pl. 208), and from other Delta sites (Villing
et al. 2013, nos TF.439–445, with further ref.).

GR 1906,0301.6
The torso from a roughly modelled, probably male, terracotta figure,
shown seated on a slightly protruding, thin base. The head, left arm,
right forearm, legs and front part of the base are missing. The back is
not in an upright position but is gently reclining. The spine is indicated
by a smooth vertical groove. Clay buttons are used for the nipples and
a sunken button of clay marks the navel.
Height: 11.7cm(max.); width: 13.2cm; depth: 7.25cm.
Context: Saite enclosure (so-called 'Camp').
Bibliography: Petrie 1888, 74 § 71: 'torso of a seated figure, of rude
work, found in the camp'.
Parallels: Similar to BM, GR 1886.0401.1454 from Naukratis, see
Bailey 2008, 51, pl. 26, no. 3130, considered as a female fecundity
figure.

GR 1906,0301.7
Hand-modelled terracotta whistle, still working, made of greenish-
buff marl clay, with some mica, roughly in the shape of an animal's
head (hound or pig?). On the top is an added spur, not unlike ears.
Height: 3.5cm; length: 4.8cm (max.); width: 2.5cm.
Bibliography: Petrie 1888, 74 § 71: 'whistle in the form of an animal's
head, blown through the mouth'; Bailey 2008, 173, pl. 126, no. 3701.
Parallels: BM EA 22513 (from Tell el-Yahudiya; see Bailey 2008, 173,
pl. 126, no. 3702).

GR 1906,0301.10
Fragment of a small terracotta grotesque figure, or miniature
plastic-vessel in the shape of a monkey or a dwarf (?), the head and legs
missing. The hunchbacked torso is egg-shaped and hollow, with the
navel marked by a small circular hole. The tops of the thighs are
preserved, separated from the torso by a groove, with the right leg
raised, indicating that the figure is meant to be either dancing or
perhaps just sitting. The base of the neck is preserved and shows that
the head originally protruded forward from the humped back. The
arms are represented by thin coils of modelled clay, applied to the
body and outlined by a groove. The right arm extends vertically down
the side of the body, bent upwards at the elbow, so the right hand was
probably holding the head. The left arm encircles the back of the torso,
towards the buttocks. Another thin coil is applied to the left part of the
torso's front, coming up from the groin, curving around the neck and
going down again on the right side, possibly a snake. Production is
possibly Corinthian or Rhodian, early 6th century BC.
Height: 3.25cm (max.); width: 2.46cm (max.); depth: 2.6cm (max.).
Parallels: this item might be reminiscent of a group of some larger
plastic vessels in the shape of a squatting komast (Amyx 1988, 530–2;
Dasen 2000) or an ape, though in these pieces the legs are usually
attached to the body and not freely rendered; one piece has snakes
painted on the body (Boston, MFA 01.8039; see Ducat 1987, 454, no.
13; Dasen 2000, 93, n. 26). Some Proto-corinthian figurines (first half
of 7th century BC) represent crouching, running or standing figures
(Amyx 1988, 530; Wallenstein 1971, 95, pls 1–2, no. I/A.1–3; p. 100, pl.
4, no. II/A.6); see also a crouching monkey in the Louvre, with ovoid

body and detached legs (Pottier 1933, 6, pl. 7.6 and 11, no. H14).
Thanks to A. Villing for bibl. ref.

GR 1906,0301.8
Oblong, thick and flat artefact made of Nile silt clay, with two deep
and almost semi-cylindrical holes in the middle of one side, possibly a
kind of lid with grip holes, if not a figure-stand with mortises for tenons
under a statuette.
Height: 2.9cm; length: 8.85cm; width: 6.5cm; depth of holes: 2.3cm (max.).

Stone figures

Bound Asiatic prisoners (Pl. 20)

Context: all the pieces below are from a group of about 30 to 40 similar
figures, found together to the east of the annexe of the 'Qasr', beyond
Petrie's chamber 29; see Petrie 1888, 73 § 70, pl. xl; Posener 1987, 4;
Ritner 1993, 137, n. 611, p. 154, n. 701.
Parallels: from Tell Dafana, Boston, MFA, 87.810-814 (= RES
87.121-125; 5 items); Bristol, CMAG H1987,1-2 (2 items); Dundee
1975-66. Liverpool, WM 3.2.87.8; Oxford, AM 1887.2496-2497 (2
items); possibly also London, PM UC38725 (no provenance recorded).
The slightly larger and better worked figure in Cairo (EM, JE 27393),
was found in Room 40 of the larger casemate building (Petrie 1888, 53,
§ 51, p. 54 § 53; Borchardt 1930, 73, pl. 139; Vandier 1958, 480, n. 1, pl.
clxiv,3). Petrie mentions this one in his Journal, 132: 'the upper part of
a small figure of a captive of very good work'; and ibid.,135: 'the work
at the Kasr does not produce anything much, except in outlying
chambers. (…) In another room, was the upper part of a figure of
captive, of excellent work'; from other sites or with no provenance:
Petrie 1914, 19, pl. 5, no. 60.c; Posener 1987, esp. p. 6, nn. 1–3 (with bibl.
ref.) – these figurines are so close to the ones from Tell Dafana that
they actually could belong to the group; see also Schoske and Wildung
1985, 83, no. 65; Ritner 1993, 137, n. 611; Wiese 2001, 102–3, no. 63;
Christies 2012, 85, no. 122; Haupt 2012, 71–5.

EA 23825	1887,0101.730

Limestone figure of a bound prisoner, the arms by the sides of the body
but lashed at the elbows behind the back, the legs doubled up from the
knees behind the body to allow the feet to be caught under the same
binding as the arms. The carving is crude with planes of working
showing in the soft limestone, although the face of this example,
especially the eyes, is better done. The figure wears a headdress in the
style of a cap or hood with high axial ridge, falling down at the back to
the base of the neck.
Height: 6.3cm; width: 1.66cm; depth: 1.5cm.
Bibliography: Petrie 1888, 73 § 70, pl. xl, 12, see also p. 53 § 51, p. 54 § 53.

EA 23826	1887,0101.731

Limestone figure of a bound prisoner, similar to EA 23825, but of
larger size. The carving of the front exhibits clear planes of chiselling
and the facial details are extremely rough. The binding of the arms
and legs at the back is more clearly shown. The cap on this figure lacks
the high axial ridge.
Height: 6.3cm; width: 1.8cm; depth: 2.1cm.
Bibliography: Petrie 1888, 73 § 70, pl. xl, 11, see also p. 53 § 51, p. 54 § 53.

EA 23827	1887,0101.732

Limestone figure of a bound prisoner of the same type as EA 23825.
The body of this example has been better modelled, with a rounded
belly and heavy thighs. The bound arms and legs behind the figure are
schematically rendered as a ridge along the edge of the piece, partly
broken on one side. The cap has a high axial ridge.
Height: 6.02cm; width: 1.5cm; depth: 1.6cm.
Bibliography: Petrie 1888, 73 § 70, pl. xl, 10, see also p. 53 § 51, p. 54 § 53.

EA 23828	1887,0101.733

Limestone figure of a bound prisoner of the same type as EA 23825.
This figure wears a high headdress with a central ridge. The face is flat
with slight details of features. The arms at the sides extend forwards,
but are lashed at the elbows across the back of the body. The binding
also holds the doubled-back legs by the feet, which are shown in some
detail, as is the pattern of the cord binding.

Height: 6.1cm; width: 1.72cm; depth: 1.5cm.
Bibliography: Petrie 1888, 73 § 70, pl. xl, 9, see also p. 53 § 51, p. 54 § 53.

EA 23829   **1887,0101.734**

Limestone figure of a bound prisoner of the same type as EA 23825.
This small example is carved in a summary fashion, with working
planes evident and very schematic details. The figure wears a high cap
with a pointed top.
Height: 5.1cm; width: 1.02cm; depth: 1.17cm.
Bibliography: Petrie 1888, 73 § 70, pl. xl, 13, see also p. 53 § 51, p. 54 § 53.

EA 23830   **1887,0101.735**

Limestone figure of a bound prisoner, again of the same type as the
foregoing examples. The figure is carved in a very abbreviated fashion
with few details. The face, arms and legs are quite indistinguishable
although the basic style of a bound captive is still evident.
Height: 5.89cm; width: 1.52cm; depth: 1.2cm.
Bibliography: Petrie 1888, 73 § 70, pl. xl, 8, see also p. 53 § 51, p. 54 § 53.

Other stone figures (Pl. 20)

GR 1906,0301.1

Flat limestone figure rudimentarily carved, certainly representing a
horseman. The animal has a large body and a very small head
separated from the chest just by a vertical groove, while the neck is
characterized only by the curve of its upper contour. Forelegs, thighs
and hind legs are broken and lost. The rider is indicated by a
triangular hump with a rounded top in the middle of the back, with
pairs of short horizontal notches scored on the front part of the sides.
Height: 6.9cm; length: 1cm; thickness: 2.33cm.
Bibliography: Petrie 1888, 71 § 68, pl. xxiv, 1: 'the horseman (fig. 1) was
picked up by chance, and the precise locality is unknown; but its
similarity to the stone idol (fig. 3) [= GR 1906,0301.3] and the complete
absence of Greek objects after the middle of the 6th century BC,
warrants us in dating it to the seventh century'.
Parallels: several Late Period limestone figures of horsemen, some
more elaborate, were found in Naukratis (Petrie 1886c, 40, pl. xix,5;
Hogarth *et al.* 1898–9, 30, 39, 55, nos 58–9, pl. xiv, 10–11; Hogarth *et al.*
1905, 122, 12; see BM EA 68821, 68822, 68855, GR 1886,0401.1493,
1900,0214.27, 1965,0930.952; Bolton 1966.90.A; Brussels, MRAH
A.1850; Cairo, EM JE36257, JE33573.2; Heidelberg ST48; Oxford,
AM AN1896-1908-G.109, .1007, .1013, .1027, .1039, .1040, .1041; see also
Cairo, EM TR14/1/34/8 (from Buto); Martin 1981, 29, pl. 26, no. 303
(from Saqqara).

GR 1906,0301.3

Flat limestone figure rudimentarily carved, with a slightly convex
body in front, roughly squared at the sides, back and underside. The
sloping shoulders are attached to a large, round flat head without any
depiction of the neck. A sloping ledge at the bottom of the front
indicates the feet.
Height: 10.2cm; width: 5.95cm; thickness: 2.75cm.
Context: Findspot 51, domestic buildings in the urban area to the east
of the Saite enclosure (so-called 'Camp'). The number 51 is scored on
the back, under the left shoulder.
Bibliography: Petrie 1888, 61 § 58, pp. 71–2 § 68, pl. xxiv, 3: 'stone idol';
'the stone figure (3) is of the rudest type possible, without limbs or
features; were it not for a ledge representing the feet, it might be also
doubted if it were not a loom weight, with a notch to tie a string in'.
Journal, 144: 'out in the buildings or rather foundations remaining,
some way E. of the Kasr, we have traced out many chambers but never
got anything hardly, except pottery – broken; & just the same as, but
coarser than, that of the Kasr & elsewhere here (…); and an excessively
rough stone figure; this latter is valuable, as showing that the Greeks had
such things in the 6th century BC; & therefore they do not all belong to
the archaistic or decadence age as we had thought might be the case, at
Nauk[rati]s'.

Stone trial-pieces (Pl. 21)

EA 23814   **1887,0101.840**

Part of a limestone slab (four fragments re-joined), probably from a
trial-piece, with regular grids of slightly different scales incised on both

of the flat faces (squares of 2.05 to 2.1cm on one face, 1.77cm on the other
face). The incised lines of the grid of the smaller scale show traces of red
colour. One original edge of the object is preserved, showing a narrow
border between the grid and the chamfered edges. The border is wider
on the side with the grid of larger scale. The findspot reference '52W' is
written on the item with a pencil. EA 23815 (1887,0101.840) is possibly a
fragment of the same item but does not join.
Length: 25cm (max.); width: 16.5cm (max.); thickness: 1.5cm.
Context: western part of Findspot 52 – south-eastern quarter of the
Saite enclosure (so-called 'Camp') – according to the pencilled mark.
Bibliography: Petrie 1888, 74 § 70: one of the 'many pieces of designing
tablets of limestone ruled in squares found in the camp and in a
chamber of the fort'.
Parallels: from Tell Dafana, EA 23815–17 (see below); another
fragment was sent to the collection of the Chautauqua Archaeological
Museum, now dispersed. For comparison, see Edgar 1906, 52–80, pls
xxii–xxxviii, esp. 77, nos CG 33467-8, pl. xxxviii; Spiegelberg 1909,
32–3, pl. xv, no. 64; Petrie 1927, 67, pl. lviii, 94 (Memphis); Hostens-
Deleu 1979, 47, 65, fig. 40, nos E2634, 2213; Martin 1981, 30, pl. 39, no.
309 (Saqqara = London, PM UC30643); Redford 2004, 57–8, 100–1,
figs 53–4, nos 455, 458, 460, 461, 468 (Mendes); Tomoum 2005, 56–73,
esp. 70, n. 104; Delange 2012, 475, pl. 312, no. 1041 (Elephantine, Paris,
ML E12765-12768); see also London, PM UC72525-72529; BM EA
22099 (Tanis, cf. Favard-Meeks 1998, 111), 23593 (El-Qantara), 33859
(Deir el-Bahari), 27449, 48028, 56924; Bristol, CMAG H2025 (Tanis,
cf. Favard-Meeks, op. cit.).

EA 23815   **1887,0101.844**

Part of a limestone slab, probably from a trial-piece, with regular grids
of slightly different scales incised on both of the flat faces (squares of
2.05 to 2.1cm on one face, 1.77cm on the other face). One original edge
of the object is preserved, showing a narrow border between the grid
and the chamfered edges. The border is wider on the face with the grid
of larger scale. On the other face, near a broken edge, one line
perpendicular to the border has been doubled (interval of 1.5 mm
between the two parallel incisions). The findspot reference '52W' is
written on the item with a pencil. EA 23814 (1887,0101.840) is possibly a
fragment of the same item but does not join.
Length: 10.04cm (max.); width: 7.79cm (max.); thickness: 1.71cm.
Context, bibliography and parallels: see under EA 23814 above.

EA 23817   **1887,0101.847**

Part of a thin limestone slab (two fragments re-joined), probably from a
trial-piece, with regular grids of slightly different scales incised on both of
the flat faces (squares of 2.2cm on one face, 1.4cm on the other). One
original edge of the object is preserved, showing a narrow border
between the grid and the chamfered edges. The face with the grid of
larger mostly chipped away and shows only a few lines and a wider
border. The findspot reference '52W' is written with a pencil on the item.
Length: 13.5cm (max.); width: 10.2cm (max.); thickness: 1.13cm.
Context and bibliography: see under EA 23814 above.

EA 23816   **1887,0101.845**

Part of a thin limestone slab probably from a trial-piece, with regular
grids of slightly different scales incised on both of the flat faces (squares
of 2 cm on one face, 1.3/1.4 cm on the other). One original edge of the
object is preserved, showing a rounded profile.
Length: 6.1cm (max.); width: 5.39cm (max.); thickness: 0.88cm (max.).
Context: probably a room or a cell in the Qasr (as the item is not
marked '52W' as EA 23814, 23815, 23817, it is probably the last one of
the 'many pieces of designing tablets of limestone ruled in squares
found in the camp and in a chamber of the fort', mentioned in Petrie
1888, 74 § 70).
Bibliography and parallels: same as for EA 23814 above.

5. Amulets

Symbols

Sacred eyes – gold (Pl. 21)

EA 18251   **1887,0101.542**

Gold amulet in the shape of a hollow double-sided *wedjat*-eye, pierced

lengthwise and made of several sheets of metal embossed and welded, with relief details, including a plait line marking the eyebrows.
Height: 1.05cm; length: 1.5cm; thickness: 0.4cm.
Context: probably from the denuded surface of the site or its neighbourhood.
Bibliography: Petrie 1888, 76 § 73, pl. xli, 26: one of the gold 'symbolic eyes'; ibid., 110: 'hollow, sheet, same both sides, ribs soldered on'; Petrie, Journal, 129: '(...) more gold scraps; I have now bought up 11 earrings, 2 sacred eyes (...)'; Müller-Winkler 1987, 86, § u. The other gold eye must be EA 18556 (see below).
Parallels: from Tell Dafana, Boston, MFA, 87.760; see also Schäfer 1910, 75, pl.17, no. 120; more openwork examples from Sanam, see Griffith 1923, 107, 129, pl. xxxix, no. 8, tomb 694; Müller-Winkler 1987, 152; Dunham 1963, 643, no. 23-M-318.

EA 18269   1887,0101.561

Gold amulet in the shape of a flat *wedjat*-eye, pierced lengthwise, made of two folded metal foils, slightly embossed and welded.
Height: 0.7cm; length: 0.88cm; thickness: 0.18cm.
Context: probably from the denuded surface of the site or its neighbourhood.
Bibliography: Petrie 1888, 76 § 73, p. 110, pl. xli, 30: one of the gold 'symbolic eyes'; Müller-Winkler 1987, 86, § u.

Sacred eyes – diorite (Pl. 21)

EA 18556   1887,0101.703

Black and white diorite amulet in the shape of a *wedjat*-eye without design, pierced lengthwise.
Height: 2.9cm; length: 3.8cm; thickness: 0.7cm.
Context: provenance not specified in the Museum register, but possibly from Tell Dafana, according to the context of the item in the list, if not from Tell Nebesha or any other eastern Delta site excavated by Petrie in 1886.
Bibliography: Petrie 1888, 73 § 70: possibly one of the 'fifteen symbolic eyes (...) of grey syenite'.
Parallels: from Tell Dafana, possibly EA 18513 (see below) and surely Boston, MFA, 87.127, Bristol, CMAG H1165 (2 pieces), Oxford, AM 1887.2541 (2 pieces), Sheffield J87.9, Sydney, MAC, MU1931; some 'syenite' *wedjat*-eyes were sent to Montreal. For comparison, see most recently Herrmann and Staubli 2010, 17, fig. 11, p. 21, fig. 35a, 124, nos 1–2; Herrmann 2006, nos 419–21; Hüttner 1995, nos 1883–5.

EA 18513   1887,0101.704

Black and white diorite amulet in the shape of a *wedjat*-eye without design, pierced lengthwise.
Height: 2.52cm; length: 3.21cm; thickness: 0.94cm.
Context: provenance not specified in the Museum register, but possibly from Tell Dafana, according to the context of the item in the list, if not from Tell Nebesha or any other eastern Delta site excavated by Petrie in 1886.
Bibliography: Petrie 1888, 73 § 70: possibly one of the 'fifteen symbolic eyes (...) of grey syenite'.
Parallels: same as for EA 18556 above.

Sacred eyes – bronze (Pl. 21)

EA 23895   1887,0101.1097

Corroded copper alloy amulet in the form of a *wedjat*-eye, pierced lengthwise.
Height: 0.91cm; length: 1.06cm; thickness: 0.3cm.
Bibliography: Petrie 1888, 80 § 80, among the small bronze finds, though the item is not specified. Journal, 145: 'the next of the days buyings are a good average, (...) bronze sacred eye, (...)'.

Sacred eyes – glazed composition (Pls 21–2)

EA 18510   1887,0101.669

Blue-green glazed composition amulet, pierced lengthwise, in the form of an openwork double-sided *wedjat*-eye within an oval serrated frame, with details incised.
Height: 2.32cm; length: 2.56cm; thickness: 0.62cm.
Context: 'Qasr', east annexe (C), chamber 2 or 3.

Bibliography: Petrie 1888, 74 § 72, p. 111, pl. xli, 71: 'symbolic eye' of 'glazed ware', 'eye plaque'; Müller-Winkler 1987, 90, § E.
Parallels: EA 18515, 18518 (below), possibly from Tell Dafana; see Herrmann and Staubli 2010, 129, nos 44–5; Hermann 1994, no. 1111; Hüttner 1995, no. 4879; Müller-Winkler 1987, 48, 106–7, 144, 147, pls xii–xiii, nos 226–32, particularly no. 227; Rowe 1936, 281–2, pl. xxxi, no. A62. The dating usually accepted for this shape is from the 22nd to the 26th dynasty.

EA 18515   1887,0101.714

White-glazed composition amulet in the form of an openwork one-sided *wedjat*-eye, within a slightly serrated oblong frame, with details incised.
Height: 2.34cm; length: 2.71cm; thickness: 0.59cm.
Context: provenance not specified in the Museum register, but possibly from Tell Dafana, according to the context of the item in the list, if not from Tell Nebesha or any other eastern Delta site excavated by Petrie in 1886.
Parallels: EA 18510 (above) from Tell Dafana, EA 18518 (below) possibly from Tell Dafana.

EA 18518   1887,0101.725

Glazed composition amulet, pierced lengthwise, in the form of an openwork one-sided *wedjat*-eye within a round serrated frame. Coated with faded white glaze.
Diameter: 2.54cm; thickness: 0.54cm.
Context: provenance not specified in the Museum register, but possibly from Tell Dafana, according to the context of the item in the list, if not from Tell Nebesha or any other eastern Delta site excavated by Petrie in 1886.
Parallels: above, EA 18510 from Tell Dafana, and EA 18515, possibly from Tell Dafana.

EA 18455   1887,0101.661

Green-blue glazed composition amulet in the form of a double-sided *wedjat*-eye, with details incised before firing, pierced lengthwise; the eyebrow bears a pattern of parallel oblique lines, while the section below the eye is decorated with vertical lines, three on one side and four on the other.
Height: 2.82cm; length: 3.51cm; thickness: 1.25cm.
Context: provenance not specified in the Museum register, but probably from Tell Dafana or Tell Nebesha, according to the context of the item in the list; if from Tell Dafana, possibly from the north-west Ptolemaic mound.
Bibliography: Petrie 1888, 79 § 79: possibly one of the 4 'eyes' among the 'glazed pottery amulets of late work, probably late Ptolemaic', from the north-west mound.
Parallels: below, EA 18511, 18512, 18547 and 18456 (one-sided), from Tell Dafana; see also Herrmann and Staubli 2010, 127, nos 24–5; Herrmann 2006, nos 344–5, 391, 393; Hermann 1994, nos 1086–7, 1213–15, 1225–6; Müller-Winkler 1987, 44, 157, 159–60, 171, pls viii–ix, nos 168–169a.

EA 18511   1887,0101.664

Whitish (originally green) worn glazed composition amulet in the form of a double-sided *wedjat*-eye, with details incised before firing, pierced lengthwise.
Height: 2.07cm; length: 2.5cm; thickness: 0.92cm.
Context: provenance not specified in the Museum register, but probably from Tell Dafana or Tell Nebesha, according to the context of the item in the list; if from Tell Dafana, possibly from the north-west Ptolemaic mound.
Bibliography: Petrie 1888, 79 § 79: possibly one of the 4 'eyes' among the 'glazed pottery amulets of late work, probably late Ptolemaic', from the north-west mound.
Parallels: above, EA 18455 and below, EA 18512, 18547 and 18456, as well as EA 18514, all possibly from Tell Dafana.

EA 18547   1887,0101.716

Pale green-blue glazed composition amulet in the form of a double-sided *wedjat*-eye, with details incised before firing, pierced lengthwise. The brow is decorated with oblique incised lines and there are vertical lines on the part below the eye.

Height: 3.78cm; length: 4.33cm; thickness: 1.08cm.
Context: provenance not specified in the Museum register, but possibly from Tell Dafana (north-west Ptolemaic mound), according to the context of the item in the list, if not from Tell Nebesha or any other eastern Delta site excavated by Petrie in 1886.
Bibliography: Petrie 1888, 79 § 79: possibly one of the 4 'eyes' among the 'glazed pottery amulets of late work, probably late Ptolemaic', from the north-west mound.
Parallels: above EA 18455, 18511, 18512, and below, 18456, as well as EA 18514, all possibly from Tell Dafana.

EA 18456   1887,0101.662
Green-blue glazed composition amulet in the form of a one-sided right *wedjat*-eye, with details incised before firing, pierced lengthwise.
Height: 2.78cm; length: 3.38cm; thickness: 1.16cm.
Context: provenance not specified in the Museum register, but probably from Tell Dafana or Tell Nebesha, according to the context of the item in the list; if from Tell Dafana, possibly from the north-west Ptolemaic mound.
Bibliography: Petrie 1888, 79 § 79: possibly one of the 4 'eyes' among the 'glazed pottery amulets of late work, probably late Ptolemaic', from the north-west mound.
Parallels: above, EA 18455, 18511, 18547 and below, 18512, as well as EA 18514, all possibly from Tell Dafana.

EA 18512   1887,0101.717
Green-blue glazed composition amulet in the form of a moulded double-sided *wedjat*-eye, pierced lengthwise; the pupil is not in the centre of the eye, but is positioned slightly forwards; the section below the eye is decorated by three parallel vertical lines; on one side at least, the upper edge has a plait design underlining the brow. The front edge is damaged.
Height: 1.42cm; length: 1.81cm; thickness: 0.63cm.
Context: provenance not specified in the Museum register, but possibly from Tell Dafana, according to the context of the item in the list, if not from Tell Nebesha or any other eastern Delta site excavated by Petrie in 1886; if from Tell Dafana, it might be the 'eye in green glaze found (...) in chamber 18' (Petrie 1888, 74).
Parallels: above, EA 18455, 18456, 18511 and 18547, as well as EA 18514 below, all possibly from Tell Dafana; most recently Herrmann and Staubli 2010, 127, no. 25.

EA 18514   1887,0101.720
Egyptian blue amulet in the form of a one-sided right *wedjat*-eye, pierced lengthwise.
Height: 1.2cm; length: 1.46cm; thickness: 0.47cm.
Context: provenance not specified in the Museum register, but possibly from Tell Dafana, according to the context of the item in the list, if not from Tell Nebesha or any other eastern Delta site excavated by Petrie in 1886; if from Tell Dafana, it could be one of the 'finely made symbolic eyes' found in Room 17, described with other 'Egyptian blue' amulets (Petrie 1888, 74 § 72).
Parallels: above, EA 18455, 18456, 18511, 18512, and 18547, all possibly from Tell Dafana; see also Herrmann 2006, no. 386; Wilson, 1982, 31, pl. xxviii, 1.

EA 18643   1887,0101.789
Red glazed composition amulet in the form of a one-sided right *wedjat*-eye with a pierced square suspension ring at the top.
Height: 2.23cm; length: 2.37cm; thickness: 0.83cm.
Context: provenance not specified in the Museum register, but possibly from Tell Dafana, north-west Ptolemaic mound, according to the context of the item in the list, similarity of material with other amulets from the site, and description in Petrie's publication.
Parallels: Herrmann 2006, nos 342–3; Müller-Winkler 1987, 44, 159–60, pls viii–ix, nos 168, 172–3.

EA 18555   1887,0101.663
Green glazed composition amulet in the form of a one sided right *wedjat*-eye, pierced lengthwise, with only the brow and pupil black and represented in low relief.
Height: 2.21cm; length: 3.43cm; thickness: 0.44cm.
Context: provenance not specified in the Museum register, but

probably from Tell Nebesha or Tell Dafana, according to the context of the item in the list.
Parallels: Herrmann and Staubli 2010, 126, nos 20–1; Herrmann 2006, nos 327–31.

Papyrus columns (Pl. 22)

EA 18451   1887,0101.711
Green glazed composition (worn) amulet in the shape of a *wadj*-papyrus column, with a suspension ring at the top (broken away); capital and lower part decorated with incisions before firing.
Height: 5cm (max.); diameter: 1.36cm.
Context: provenance not specified in the Museum register, but possibly from Tell Dafana, according to the context of the item in the list, if not from Tell Nebesha or any other eastern Delta site excavated by Petrie in 1886.
Bibliography: Petrie 1888, 79 § 79; see also ibid., 75 § 72.
Parallels: Herrmann 2006, 228–9, no. 444, pl. c; Müller-Winkler 1987, 55, 258–9, pl. xxiii; Wilson 1982, 32, pl. xxix, 2.

EA 20531   1887,0101.785+799
Glazed composition amulet, rather crudely executed, light brown with reddish patches, in the shape of a *wadj*-papyrus column, topped with a large and roughly square suspension loop. The number 1887,0101.799 applies to the reunited top of the amulet.
Height: 5.5cm; width: 1cm.
Context: provenance not specified in the Museum register, but probably from Tell Dafana, north-west Ptolemaic mound, according to the context of the item in the list, similarity of material with other amulets from the site and description in Petrie's publication.
Bibliography: Petrie 1888, 79 § 79; see also ibid., 75 § 72.
Parallels: Herrmann and Staubli 2010, 135, nos 1–3; Herrmann 2006, 228–9, nos 439–48 (esp. 446), pl. xcix-c; Müller-Winkler 1987, 55–6, 258–9, pl. xxiii, nos 448–52; Wilson, 1982, pl. xxix, 1.

EA 18483   1887,0101.718
Capital of a blue-green glazed composition amulet in the shape of a *wadj*-papyrus column, decorated with incisions, and topped with a suspension ring.
Height: 1.44cm (max.); diameter: 1.17cm.
Context: provenance not specified in the Museum register, but possibly from Tell Dafana, according to the context of the item in the list, if not from Tell Nebesha or any other eastern Delta site excavated by Petrie in 1886.
Bibliography: Petrie 1888, 79 § 79; see also ibid., 75 § 72.
Parallels: from Tell Dafana, Boston, MFA 87.623. Herrmann and Staubli 2010, 135, no. 1; Müller-Winkler 1987, 55–6, 258, pl. xxiii, nos 443–6.

GR 1888,0208.145.c
Part of a pale green glazed composition amulet in the shape of a *wadj*-papyrus column, perhaps the lower part of EA 18483 above.
Length: 2.05cm; diameter: 0.53cm.
Bibliography: Petrie 1888, 79 § 79; see also ibid., 75 § 72.

Offering tables and crowns (Pl. 22)

EA 18509   1887,0101.715
Green glazed composition amulet in the form of a rectangular offering table with raised top edges, an oblong shape in the middle and a projecting axial spout in front.
Length: 2.9cm; width: 2.28cm; thickness: 0.6cm.
Context: provenance not specified in the Museum register, but possibly from Tell Dafana, according to the context of the item in the list, if not from Tell Nebesha or any other eastern Delta site excavated by Petrie in 1886.

EA 18641   1887,0101.784
Glazed composition amulet, light brown with reddish patches, rather crudely executed, in the form of the profile of a royal crown of Lower Egypt, with details in low relief on both sides, and transversely pierced at the top for suspension.
Height: 2.72cm; width: 0.83cm; depth: 1.63cm.

Context: provenance not mentioned in the Museum register, but
probably from Tell Dafana, north-west Ptolemaic mound, according
to the context of the item in the list, similarity of material with other
amulets surely from the site, and description in Petrie's publication.
Bibliography: Petrie 1888, 79 § 79: probably one of the 5 'lower crowns'
described among the 'glazed pottery amulets of late work, probably
late Ptolemaic', coming from the north-west mound.
Parallels: from Tell Dafana, see below the counterpart EA 18642; for
comparison, see also Petrie 1888, 74 § 72 (blue crown of 'delicate work'
from chamber 4, unidentified yet); Herrmann and Staubli 2010, 149,
nos 3–4; Herrmann 2006, 230, pl. c, no. 449, with additional
references cited.

EA 18642 1887,0101.788

Glazed composition amulet, light brown with reddish patches, rather
crudely executed, in the form of the royal crown of Upper Egypt, with
an approximately square suspension ring projecting from the back.
Height: 2.75cm; width: 1.15cm; depth: 1.37cm.
Context and bibliography: same as for EA 18641 above.
Parallels: from Tell Dafana, see above the counterpart EA 18641; for
comparison, see Spencer 1996, 78, no. 36, pl. 74; Herrmann and
Staubli 2010, 149, nos 1–2; Müller-Winkler 1987, 65–6, 362–4, pl.
xxxiii, nos 668–71 (26th dynasty); also the additional references in
ibid., 362.

Deities with human body and animal head

Shu (Pl. 22)

EA 20683 1887,0101.787

Glazed composition amuletic figure, brown with reddish patches,
rather crudely executed in the form of the god Shu, kneeling on the
right knee on a rectangular base, arms upraised by sides of the
sun-disc of his headdress, with a back pillar transversely pierced for
suspension.
Height: 2.5cm; width: 1.56cm; depth: 1.07cm.
Context: north-west Ptolemaic mound?
Bibliography: Petrie 1888, 79 § 79 (?): probably one of the 4 + 2 'Shu'
among the 'glazed pottery amulets of late work, probably late
Ptolemaic', from the north-west mound, and not the 'glazed ware'
'Shu' found in chamber 18 with a smaller green 'Tahuti' (ibid., 74 § 72).
Parallels: below, EA 20684, from Tell Dafana; see also Herrmann and
Staubli 2010, 51–2; Herrmann 2006, nos 72–83 (with additional
references); Rowe 1936, 268, no. A6, pl. xxx; with mention of Petrie
1914, pl. xxx, 37, no. 167; Daressy 1906, pl. viii, nos 38, 110; Hornung
and Staehelin 1976, 99; Wilson 1982, 31, pl. xxviii, 7.

EA 20684 1887,0101.794

Glazed composition amuletic figure, light brown with reddish patches,
rather crudely executed, in the form of the god Shu, kneeling on the
right knee on a rectangular base, arms upraised by sides of the
sun-disc of the headdress, with back pillar transversely pierced for
suspension.
Height: 2.35cm; width: 1.38cm; depth: 0.85cm.
Context: provenance not specified in the Museum register, but very
probably from Tell Dafana, north-west Ptolemaic mound, according
to the context of the item in the list, and similarity with other amulets
surely from the site, particularly EA 20683.
Bibliography: Petrie 1888, 74 § 72, p. 79 § 79 (?): if from Tell Dafana,
possibly one of the 4 + 2 'Shu' among the 'glazed pottery amulets of
late work, probably late Ptolemaic', from the north-west mound, and
not the 'glazed ware' 'Shu' found in chamber 18 with a smaller green
'Tahuti' (ibid., 74 § 72).
Parallels: same as for EA 20683 above.

Ptah (Pl. 22)

EA 20659 1887,0101.713

Green glazed composition fragment of an amuletic figure in the form
of the god Ptah; laterally pierced at the back of the neck for suspension.
Height: 3.2cm; width: 1.47cm; depth: 1.28cm.
Context: provenance not specified in the Museum register, but
possibly from Tell Dafana, according to the context of the item in the
list, if not from Tell Nebesha or any other eastern Delta site excavated
by Petrie in 1886.

Bes (Pl. 22)

EA 18546 1887,0101.727

Dull green glazed composition amuletic plaque in the form of the
flattened face of the bearded god Bes, with a flat back. Hair, brow and
beard are detailed with a series of parallel incised lines; the top of the
head is perforated widthways with a long suspension hole.
Height: 3.3cm; width: 3.5cm; thickness: 0.9cm.
Context: provenance not specified in the Museum register, possibly
from Tell Dafana, according to the context of the item in the list.
Bibliography: Petrie 1888, 79 § 79.

Falcon-headed deities (Pl. 22)

EA 38005

Gold figure of a solar falcon-headed god, standing in a striding
position with the left leg forward, on a rectangular base, wearing a kilt
and a tripartite headdress topped by a large sun-disc with a central
uraeus. Headdress and kilt are decorated with a series of parallel
incisions. The figure was originally housed in a rectangular silver
shrine, with a vertical sliding door in front, and a suspension loop
made of a rounded sheet of metal welded on the back.
Figure: height: 2.6cm; width: 0.5cm; depth: 1.2cm.
Shrine: height: 2.9cm; width: 1.1cm; depth: 1.5cm.
Context: from the plain around the site.
Bibliography: Petrie 1888, 75–6 § 73, p. 110, pl. xli, 8–9: 'another fine
object is the gold statue of Ra (xli. 9), which is highly finished and
burnished, of the finest work of the Saitic period. It was found in the
silver amulet case, or shrine, the sliding lid of which had been left slightly
drawn and forced inwards, showing the toes of the figure. It is the most
satisfactory to find it so, since not only is this little suspensory box a
unique object, but it guarantees the genuineness of the image found
within it, since the lid is stuck tight, and the side of the box had to be
broken open to remove the figure. This was picked up by one of my
workmen on the plain, and brought to me uninjured'. Journal, 136–7:

One man picked up a charming little thing, a little silver amulet box
for suspension, with the sliding lid partly pushed in: and at the bottom
of the lid showed the toes of a gold amulet. I tried to clean the box
with some hopes of withdrawing the lid & taking the amulet out; but
the silver was too brittle (being very thin) & the lid too firmly
corroded in; so I decided the safest thing was to break off one side of
the box as neatly as could be, & then the pieces can be replaced with a
little cement, in no case damaging it for exhibition on the other side.
This I did & took out a statuette of Horus, of the finest work of the
XXVI dynasty, highly burnished, of solid gold. It is a gem, & doubly
valuable as having its case (which I do not remember ever seeing with
an amulet before) & being absolutely above suspicion, having come
from such a case. Forgeries have been made of this class of small gold
figures, so that some warranty for an example is important. I weighed
this, & gave the lucky finder 15 pˢ [pence], rather over its metal value,
because he brought it up without trying to get the gold out of the
case.

Parallels: on this type of amulet, see Brunner and Brunner 1984, 15, 17,
no. 4, p. 41, no. 25, pp. 43–5, nos 26a, 29, 31; Silverman 1997, 53, nos
4–6, p. 58, no. 9 (Memphis, 26th dynasty); Hope 1988, 108–11, nos
55–7; Andrews 1994, fig. 38; Herrmann and Staubli 2010, 61–3; Bakr *et
al.* 2010, 230–3, nos 77–8.

EA 20654 1887,0101.701

Lapis lazuli upper fragment of an amuletic figure in the form of a
hawk-headed god, standing in a striding position with the left leg
forward, wearing the *shendyt* kilt and a tripartite headdress topped by
the royal double crown; the left hand is at the breast holding a sceptre,
the right arm by the side; a suspension ring projects from behind the
head. The lower part of the legs and the base are missing.
Height: 2.1cm; width: 1.7cm; depth: 0.82cm.
Context: provenance not specified in the Museum register, but
certainly from Tell Dafana, according to the context of the item in the
list and information on the old wooden mount.

Bibliography: Petrie 1888, 73 § 70.
Parallels: see Herrmann and Staubli 2010, 61–3.

EA 23867   1887,0101.1060

Corroded copper alloy flat amuletic figure, poorly executed, in the shape of a mummiform falcon-headed (?) figure with the arms folded on the chest, standing on some kind of basket. The head wears a small solar disc with uraeus, behind which is an penannular suspension ring.
Length: 5.01cm; depth: 1.45cm; thickness: 0.69cm.
Bibliography: Petrie 1888, 80 § 80: presumably one of the 10 bronze Horus figures mentioned.

Thoth (Pl. 22)

EA 20673   1887,0101.781

Glazed composition amuletic figure, rather crudely executed, in the form of a tall figure of the god Thoth, ibis-headed, shown standing on a square base. The arms are shown by the sides and the back pillar is pierced by a suspension hole above the level of the elbows. The glaze is light brown with scattered reddish patches, particularly down the front.
Height: 5.2cm; width: 1cm; depth: 1.3cm.
Context: perhaps from the north-west Ptolemaic mound.
Bibliography: Petrie 1888, 79 § 79: probably one of the 4 'Tahuti' among the 'glazed pottery amulets of late work, probably late Ptolemaic', from the north-west mound.
Parallels: Herrmann and Staubli 2010, 34, no. 2; Herrmann 2006, nos 20–6; Hermann 2003, 48–9, nos 111–12, with references.

Khnum (Pl. 22)

EA 20672   1887,0101.783

Glazed composition amuletic figure, rather crudely executed, in the form of a figure of the ram-headed god Khnum, standing with the arms by the sides on a rectangular base. The back pillar is tranversely pierced for suspension behind the arms above elbow level. The glaze is light brown with reddish patches.
Height: 4.7cm; width: 0.9cm; depth: 1.3cm.
Context: perhaps from the north-west Ptolemaic mound.
Bibliography: Petrie 1888, 79 § 79: probably one of the 4 'Khnum' among the 'glazed pottery amulets of late work, probably late Ptolemaic', from the north-west mound.
Parallels: Herrmann and Staubli 2010, 37, no. 2; Herrmann 2006, nos 37–9, with additional references.

EA 23437   1887,0101.1058

Copper alloy amuletic figure, rather crudely executed, of a deity with a human body, wearing the *shendyt*-kilt, standing on a narrow and flat rectangular base, striding with the left leg forward, with the arms alongside the body. The head seems to have an animal face, possibly a ram (?), with an indeterminate headdress, possibly the Atef crown on a tripartite wig. A vertical suspension ring is attached behind the headdress above what might be a uraeus protruding from the back of the figure.
Height: 4.2cm; width: 1cm; depth: 1.8cm.
Bibliography: Petrie 1888, 80 § 80 mentions bronzes collected from the surface of the site.

Hybrid (Pl. 22)

EA 20661   1887,0101.666

Green glazed composition amuletic figure in the hybrid form of a winged dwarf standing on a rectangular base, with a ram head topped by a sun-disc, and a suspension ring (broken away) on the back.
Height: 2.19cm; width: 0.75cm; depth: 1.51cm.
Context: 'Qasr', east annexe (C), chamber 2 or 3. The mount incorrectly indicated the provenance as Tell Nebesha.
Bibliography: Petrie 1888, 74 § 72, p. 111, pl. xli, 70: 'of glazed ware', 'a combination of Ptah-Sokar, Khnum, and hawk'.

Deities in animal form

Lion-headed uraeus (Pl. 22)

EA 20666   1887,0101.700

Lapis lazuli amuletic figure in the form of a lion-headed uraeus on a rectangular base, with a suspension ring projecting from the back of the head.
Height: 0.9cm; width: 0.41cm; depth: 0.84cm.
Context: purchased by Petrie during his excavations.
Bibliography: Petrie 1888, 73 § 70, p. 111, pl. xli, 39: lapis lazuli 'lion-headed uraeus'; Journal, 145: 'I have not mentioned an exquisite lapis lazuli amulet I bought; a cobra serpent, with lion's head, very small, but perfectly worked, lion's ears eyes & mouth in detail'.

Birds (Pl. 22)

EA 20662   1887,0101.668

Lapis lazuli amuletic figure in the form of a vulture, more likely than a hawk, standing on a rectangular base, with a suspension ring projecting on the back.
Height: 1.05cm; width: 0.67cm; depth: 1.12cm.
Bibliography: Petrie 1888, 73 § 70: mention of a lapis lazuli hawk.

EA 20660   1887,0101.696

Pale green feldspar amuletic figure in the form of the god Horus as a falcon standing on a rectangular base and wearing the double crown, with a suspension ring projecting at the back.
Height: 3.47cm; width: 1.09cm; depth: 2.35cm.
Context: Saite enclosure (so-called 'Camp').
Bibliography: Petrie 1888, 73 § 70: 'small hawk in greenish-white translucent steatite…found in the camp'.

EA 20694   1887,0101.801

Reddish brown glazed composition amuletic figure, rather crudely executed, in the form of an animal, possibly a hawk, transversely pierced for suspension.
Height: 1.05cm; width: 0.9cm; depth: 0.56cm.
Context: provenance not specified in the Museum register, but probably from Tell Dafana, north-west Ptolemaic mound, according to the context of the item in the list, similarity of material with other amulets from the site, and description in Petrie's publication.
Bibliography: Petrie 1888, 79 § 79: probably one of the 6 'cats' among the 'much smaller and ruder' 'glazed pottery amulets of late work, probably late Ptolemaic', from the north-west mound.
Parallels: see below the 'cats (?)' EA 20676, 20677, 20678, 20679, 20680, the 'rabbit (?)' 20690 and the 'ape (?)' 20685, all from Tell Dafana.
See also Herrmann 2006, 170, nos 256–7, pl. lxvi, with additional references.

EA 23435   1887,0101.1063

Copper alloy amuletic figure of an ibis on a triangular base, with a vertical suspension loop behind the neck, connected to the rear of the base by a tang.
Height: 2.2cm; width: 0.9cm; length: 2.4cm.
Bibliography: Petrie 1888, 80 § 80 mentions a bronze figure of 'Tahuti', and 'sacred animals'.

EA 20663   1887,0101.1306

Reddish glazed composition amulet, rather crudely executed, in the form of an ibis, with a suspension ring projecting from the back, and the tip of the beak resting on the top of a *maat*-feather.
Height: 1.55cm; width: 0.98cm; length: 2.86cm.
Context: perhaps from the north-west Ptolemaic mound (if one of the amulets mentioned by Petrie, see Bibliography below). Provenance from Tell Dafana is not specified in the Museum register, but is indicated on the object mount. This finds confirmation in the context of the item in the list and in the nature of the material, which is very similar to other amulets from the site.
Bibliography: Petrie 1888, 79 § 79: possibly one of the 4 'Tahuti' among the 'glazed pottery amulets of late work, probably late Ptolemaic', from the north-west mound.

Hippopotami (Pl. 22)

EA 20656   1887,0101.705

Black and white diorite amuletic figure in the form of the goddess Taweret standing on an oblong plinth, with a back pillar transversely pierced for suspension. The surfaces are smooth with only basic

modelling of the features, due probably to the hardness of the material; the arms are so slightly represented as to be almost undetectable.
Height: 4.4cm; width: 1.35cm; depth: 1.7cm.
Context: provenance not specified in the Museum register, but possibly from Tell Dafana, according to the context of the item in the list. However, the 'Taurt of grey syenite ' mentioned in Petrie 1888, 73 § 70 must be EA 20658 (below), clearly from Tell Dafana according to the Museum register.
Bibliography: see Petrie 1888, 73 § 70.
Parallels: surely from Tell Dafana, EA 20658 (below), Boston MFA 87.688-689 (haematite).

EA 20658   1887,0101.706
A small black and white diorite amuletic figure in the form of the goddess Taweret standing on an oblong base, with a suspension ring projecting from the back. The surfaces are smooth with only basic modelling of the features, due probably to the hardness of the material.
Height: 1.6cm; width: 0.55cm; depth: 0.89cm.
Bibliography: Petrie 1888, 73 § 70: probably the 'Taurt of grey syenite'; but see also EA 20656 above.

EA 20657   1887,0101.667
Green glazed composition amuletic figure in the form of the goddess Taweret standing on a narrow rectangular base, with a suspension ring slightly projecting from the back. The figure has been broken and repaired at the foot. The tail at the back is decorated with a chevron design, incised before firing.
Height: 2.32cm; width: 0.76cm; depth: 0.9cm.
Context: 'Qasr', east annexe (C), chamber 2 or 3.
Bibliography: Petrie 1888, 74 § 72, p. 111, pl. xli, 72.
Parallels: from Tell Dafana, EA 20658 (see above); Boston, MFA 87.615; for comparison see also Herrmann 2006, 150–3 nos 204–14, pls lv–lviii, with additional references; Wilson 1982, 30, pl. xxviii, 9–10.

EA 20675   1887,0101.782
Glazed composition amuletic figure, rather crudely executed, in the form of a figure of the goddess Taweret standing on a rectangular base, with arms by the sides, transversely pierced behind the arms above elbow level, for suspension. A back pillar is marked, decorated with incised chevrons, and gently protrudes at the level of the suspension hole, to give the impression of a ring. The glaze is light brown with reddish patches.
Height: 4.9cm; width: 0.95cm; depth: 1.25cm.
Context: north-west Ptolemaic mound?
Bibliography: Petrie 1888, 79 § 79: probably one of the 5 'Taurt' among the 'glazed pottery amulets of late work, probably late Ptolemaic', from the north-west mound.
Parallels: Herrmann 2006, 150–1, 308, nos 206–7; Herrmann and Staubli 2010, 81, n° 6.

Ape (Pl. 22)

EA 20674   1887,0101.795
Glazed composition amuletic figure, rather crudely executed, in the form of a cynocephalus ape standing on a rectangular base, with a roughly square suspension ring projecting at the back, at the level of the chest. The glaze is light brown with reddish patches. Notches incised on the chest indicate the fur.
Height: 4.66cm; width: 1.03cm; depth: 1.43cm.
Context: north-west Ptolemaic mound?
Bibliography: Petrie 1888, 74 § 72, p. 79 § 79: most probably one of the 5 'monkeys' among the 'glazed pottery amulets of late work, probably late Ptolemaic', from the north-west mound and not the 'green glazed monkey from chamber 29' mentioned in ibid., 74 § 72.
Parallels: Herrmann and Staubli 2010, 100, nos 5–6; Herrmann 2006, 169, no. 255, pl. lxvi with additional references. In general Letellier and Ziegler 1978, 83–7.

EA 20685   1887,0101.803
Brownish glazed composition amuletic figure, rather crudely executed, in the form of an animal, possibly a seated cynocephalus ape, pierced transversely for suspension.
Height: 0.92cm; width: 0.64cm; depth: 0.6cm.
Context: provenance not specified in the Museum register, but probably from Tell Dafana, north-west Ptolemaic mound, according to the context of the item in the list, similarity of material with other amulets from the site, and description in Petrie's publication.
Bibliography: Petrie 1888, 79 § 79: if from Tell Dafana, probably one of the 'much smaller and ruder' 'glazed pottery amulets of late work, probably late Ptolemaic', from the north-west mound.
Parallels: see below, the 'cats (?)' EA 20676, 20677, 20678, 20679, 20680, the 'hawk (?)' EA 20694 above, and the 'rabbit (?)' EA 20690, all from Tell Dafana, and of similar manufacture; see also Herrmann and Staubli 2010, 99; Herrmann 2006, 165, nos 247–8, 252–4, pls lxiv–lxvi with additional references.

EA 23885   1887,0101.1082
Corroded copper alloy amuletic figure or weight (?), crudely executed, of a seated ape.
Height: 1.12cm; width: 0.87cm; depth: 0.8cm.
Bibliography: Petrie 1888, 80 § 80: among the small bronze finds, according to the Museum register, though the item is not clearly specified (possibly one of the 'sacred animals'?). Another option would be to consider this item as one of the two 'cynocephalus seated' mentioned among a series of small and rude glazed composition amulets from the north-west Ptolemaic mound (Petrie 1888, 79 § 79).

Bull (Pl. 22)

EA 20686   1887,0101.809
Discoloured glazed composition amuletic figure, rather crudely executed, in the form of the Apis Bull, with a squarish suspension ring projecting from the back. The glaze is light brown with reddish patches.
Height: 1.41cm; width: 0.7cm; length: 1.98cm.
Context: north-west Ptolemaic mound?
Bibliography: Petrie 1888, 79 § 79: most probably one of the 5 'Hapi bull' among the 'glazed pottery amulets of late work, probably late Ptolemaic', from the north-west mound.
Parallels: Herrmann and Staubli 2010, 84; Herrmann 2006, 154, pl. lix, no. 216 with additional references; Rowe 1936, 276, nos A40–41, pl. xxxi; discussion: Hornung and Staehelin 1976, 133–4.

Ram (Pl. 22)

EA 20687   1887,0101.792
Glazed composition amuletic figure, rather crudely executed, in the form of a ram couchant on a rectangular base, with a roughly square suspension ring projecting from the back. The glaze is light brown with reddish patches.
Height: 1.13cm; width: 0.75cm; depth: 2.29cm.
Context: north-west Ptolemaic mound?
Bibliography: Petrie 1888, 79 § 79: most probably one of the two 'ram' among the 'glazed pottery amulets of late work, probably late Ptolemaic', from the north-west mound (the other is EA 20689 below).
Parallels: Herrmann and Staubli 2010, 88, nos 7–8, one from Egypt: Herrmann 2003, 117, no. 577, pl. lxxxiii; one roughly made from Achsib, 720–450 BC: Herrmann 2006, 156–7, pl. lix, no. 221 (see also the references under no. 220); Leospo 1986, 61, no. 23; Rowe 1936, 275, no. A34; Wilson 1982, 32, pl. xxix, 12; Spencer 1996, 78, no. 24, pl. 77.

EA 20689   1887,0101.796
Glazed composition amuletic figure, rather crudely executed, in the form of a ram couchant on a rectangular base, with a suspension ring projecting from the back. The glaze is brown with reddish patches.
Height: 1.3cm; width: 0.76cm; depth: 2.46cm.
Context: north-west Ptolemaic mound?
Bibliography: Petrie 1888, 79 § 79: most probably one of the 2 'ram' among the 'glazed pottery amulets of late work, probably late Ptolemaic', from the north-west mound (the other one is EA 20687).

Hare (Pl. 22)

EA 20692   1887,0101.790
Reddish brown glazed composition amuletic figure, rather crudely executed, in the form of a hare couchant, on a rectangular base, transversely pierced between the ears and the body for suspension.

Height: 1.46cm; width: 0.79cm; depth: 2.47cm.
Context: north-west Ptolemaic mound?
Bibliography: Petrie 1888, 79 § 79: certainly one of the 5 'rabbit' among
the 'glazed pottery amulets of late work, probably late Ptolemaic', from
the north-west mound.
Parallels: Herrmann and Staubli 2010, 96, nos 1–2; Herrmann 2006,
164, no. 245, pl. lxiii (from Dor, Persian), with additional references
there cited. In general Letellier and Ziegler 1978, 53–4.

EA 20690   1887,0101.807

Reddish brown glazed composition amuletic figure, rather crudely
executed, in the form of an unidentified animal couchant (hare, lion?),
with a suspension ring projecting from the back.
Height: 0.67cm; width: 0.47cm; length: 0.91cm.
Context: north-west Ptolemaic mound?
Bibliography: Petrie 1888, 79 § 79: probably one of the 'much smaller
and ruder' 'glazed pottery amulets of late work, probably late
Ptolemaic', from the north-west mound.
Parallels: see below the 'cats (?)' EA 20676, 20677, 20678, 20679,
20680, and above, the 'hawk (?)' EA 20694 and the 'ape (?)' EA 20685,
all of similar manufacture.

Cats (?) (Pl. 23)

EA 20680   1887,0101.800

Brownish glazed composition amuletic figure, rather crudely
executed, in the form of an animal, possibly a seated cat, transversely
pierced for suspension.
Length: 1.15cm; width: 0.89cm; thickness: 0.53cm.
Context: provenance not specified in the Museum register, but
probably from Tell Dafana, north-west Ptolemaic mound, according
to the context of the item in the list, similarity of material with other
amulets from the site, and description in Petrie's publication.
Bibliography: Petrie 1888, 79 § 79: probably one of the 6 'cats' among
the 'much smaller and ruder' 'glazed pottery amulets of late work,
probably late Ptolemaic', from the north-west mound.
Parallels: see below the similar EA 20676, 20677, 20678, 20679 and
possibly above 20685 or 20694, all from Tell Dafana; see also
Herrmann and Staubli 2010, 89, no. 2; Herrmann 2006, 158, pl. lx, nos
224–30, with additional references there cited; Rowe 1936, 276, no.
A39, pl. xxxi; see also Hornung and Staehelin 1976, 120.

EA 20679   1887,0101.802

Glazed composition amuletic figure, rather crudely executed,
probably in the form of a seated cat, transversely pierced for
suspension. The glaze is light brown with reddish patches.
Height: 1.11cm; width: 0.54cm; depth: 0.71cm.
Context: north-west Ptolemaic mound?
Bibliography and parallels: same as for EA 20680 above.

EA 20678   1887,0101.805

Glazed composition amuletic figure, rather crudely executed,
probably in the form of a seated cat, transversely pierced for
suspension. The glaze is brown with reddish patches.
Height: 0.94cm; width: 0.53cm; depth: 0.71cm.
Context: north-west Ptolemaic mound?
Bibliography and parallels: same as for EA 20680 above.

EA 20676   1887,0101.806

Reddish brown glazed composition amuletic figure, rather crudely
executed, probably in the form of a seated cat, transversely pierced for
suspension.
Height: 1.26cm; width: 0.57cm; depth: 0.72cm.
Context: north-west Ptolemaic mound?
Bibliography and parallels: same as for EA 20680 above.

EA 20677   1887,0101.808

Reddish brown glazed composition amuletic figure, rather crudely
executed, probably in the form of a seated cat, transversely pierced for
suspension.
Height: 0.94cm; width: 0.64cm; depth: 0.72cm.
Context: north-west Ptolemaic mound?
Bibliography and parallels: same as for EA 20680 above.

Lion (Pl. 23)

EA 20664   1887,0101.719

Light green glazed composition amuletic figure in the form of a lion
couchant on a rectangular base, with a suspension ring projecting
from the back.
Height: 0.66cm; width: 0.63cm; length: 1.42cm.
Context: north-west Ptolemaic mound?
Bibliography: Petrie 1888, 79 § 79: certainly one of the 5 'lions' among
the 'glazed pottery amulets of late work, probably late Ptolemaic', from
the north-west mound.
Parallels: from Tell Dafana, EA 20688 below; see also Herrmann and
Staubli 2010, 91, nos 1–2; Herrmann 2006, 160–1, nos 234–7, pls lxi–
lxii, with additional references; see also Hornung and Staehelin 1976,
126–7.

EA 20688   1887,0101.791

Light reddish brown glazed composition amuletic figure, rather
crudely executed, in the form of a lion couchant on a rectangular base,
with a suspension ring projecting from the back.
Height: 1.36cm; width: 0.85cm; length: 2.54cm.
Context: north-west Ptolemaic mound?
Bibliography: same as for EA 20664 above.
Parallels: from Tell Dafana, EA 20664 above.

Ichneumon (Pl. 23)

EA 20576   1887,0101.1090

Corroded copper alloy small amuletic figure of a double ichneumon (?)
on a roughly rectangular base, with remains of a suspension ring on
top, in the middle.
Height: 0.8cm; length: 1.3cm; width: 0.8cm.
Bibliography: Petrie 1888, 80 § 80, according to the Museum register,
though the object is no clearly specified among the small bronze finds
(possibly one of the 'sacred animals'?).

Amphibians, fish and insects (Pl. 23)

EA 23882   1887,0101.1078

Corroded copper alloy small figure of a toad or a frog, originally
welded on a base under the rear part. Some kind of small staple is
stuck on the left side by corrosion. The figure could be a frog-shaped
weight or a fragment from a bronze miniature model offering table.
Height: 0.66cm; width: 1cm; length: 1.51cm.
Bibliography: Petrie 1888, 80 § 80, according to the Museum register,
though the object is not clearly specified among the small bronze finds.
Petrie, Journal, 149 mentions bronze 'frog-shaped weights'.
Parallels: Settgast, 1978, no. 218; Herrmann and Staubli 2010, 117, nos
7–8; Herrmann 2003, 153, no. 880, pl. cxiv; Herrmann 2006, 177, no.
274, pl. lxx, with additional references there cited; see also Roeder
1956, 409–10, § 558, pl. 58k. For frogs on top of the spouts of miniature
bronze offering tables, see for instance ibid., § 597–9, 433–5, pls 61b–d,
87b; see also EA 2749, 64027.

EA 23896   1887,0101.1098

Small copper alloy amuletic figure in the form of a Tilapia fish.
Length: 1.21cm; width: 0.63cm; thickness: 0.25cm.
Bibliography: Petrie 1888, 80 § 80, according to the Museum register,
though the object is no clearly specified among the small bronze finds.
Parallels: Herrmann and Staubli 2010, 114, no. 2 (from Achsib,
587–450 BC); also Herrmann 2006, 176, no. 268, pl. lxix, with
additional references; from Tell Dafana, see also Boston, MFA Eg.
Inv.6322-6323 (jasper, glass).

EA 18635   1887,0101.786

Glazed composition scarab with striated elytra, base decorated as the
underside of a beetle, and with a central square protrusion
transversely pierced for suspension or attachment to a mummy cloth.
Height: 1cm; width: 1.5cm; length: 2.4cm.
Context: provenance not specified in the Museum register, but
probably from Tell Dafana, north-west Ptolemaic mound, according
to the context of the item in the list and the nature of the material.
Bibliography: Petrie 1888, 79 § 79: possibly one of the 5 'scarabs'
among the 'glazed pottery amulets of late work, probably late

Ptolemaic', from the north-west mound.
Parallels: from Tell Dafana, EA 18636 below, very similar.

EA 18636   **1887,0101.810**
Glazed composition scarab with striated elytra, base decorated as the underside of a beetle, and with a central square protrusion transversely pierced for suspension or attachment to a mummy cloth.
Height: 0.97cm; width: 1.38cm; length: 2.29cm.
Context, bibliography and parallels: same as for EA 18635 above.

Indeterminate (Pl. 23)

EA 20691   **1887,0101.798**
Reddish glazed composition amulet, rather crudely executed, difficult to identify. A similarity to the upper part of EA 20680 above, suggests the object may be a very poor representation of a cat. Pierced transversely at the top for suspension.
Height: 1.46cm; width: 0.82cm; depth: 0.69cm.
Context: provenance not specified in the Museum register, but probably from Tell Dafana, north-west Ptolemaic mound, according to the context of the item in the list, similarity of material with other amulets from the site and description in Petrie's publication.
Bibliography: Petrie 1888, 79 § 79: probably one of the 'much smaller and ruder' 'glazed pottery amulets of late work, probably late Ptolemaic', from the north-west mound.
Parallels: Müller-Winkler 1987, 63, nos 608–10, pl. xxx; cf. ibid., 311.

EA 23873   **1887,0101.1069**
Corroded copper alloy figure in the form of a naked woman, seated with the legs apart. Part of a suspension ring seems to be preserved behind the head and back.
Height: 1.44cm; width: 2.08cm; depth: 0.71cm.
Bibliography: Petrie 1888, 80 § 80 (?), among the small bronze finds, according to the Museum register, though the item is not clearly specified.
Parallel: Cairo, EM CG 27700 (Edgar 1904a, 18, pl. ii).

6. Scarabs

Inscribed or decorated scarabs (Pl. 23)

EA 18524   **1887,0101.674**
Green glazed composition scarab, pierced lengthwise, with elytra marked and base decorated with an incised hieroglyphic inscription consisting of a sun-disc on top of a lion couchant.
Height: 0.5cm; width: 0.8cm; length: 1.2cm.
Bibliography: Petrie 1888, 111, pl. xli, 59.
Parallels: Keel 2010, 372, no. 815 (19th–20th dynasty).

EA 18564   **1887,0101.675**
Green glazed composition scarab, pierced lengthwise, with elytra and humeral callosities marked, and base decorated with incised decoration consisting of a man riding a horse heading to the right. In front of the horse is a curved feature of uncertain identity. The parallels suggest a date in the 22nd dynasty or later.
Height: 0.6cm; width: 1.05cm; length: 1.5cm.
Bibliography: Petrie 1888, 111, pl. xli, 47.
Parallels: on the representation of horses, rather different from this item, but closer to the still unidentified scarab published by Petrie, op. cit., pl. xli, 49, see Magnarini 2004, 262, no. 09.56 (dated to the 22nd dynasty); also Matouk 1977, 381, nos 424–34, especially nos 425–6; Hornung and Staehelin 1976, 366, nos 904–5; Keel 1997, 45, no. 68 (22nd dynasty); Sotheby's 1993, 511; Hodjash 1999, 166, nos 1268–70. On representations of horses with riders, see Matouk 1977, 91–3, 340.

EA 35420   **1888,0208.162**
Glazed Egyptian blue scarab, badly corroded, pierced lengthwise, with striated legs. The decoration on the underside is now too damaged for interpretation, but Petrie (who viewed it in a better condition), suggested that it showed a winged sphinx.
Height: 0.53cm; width: 0.74cm; length: 1.17cm.
Bibliography: Petrie 1888, 73 § 70, p. 111, pl. xli, 69: one of 'two blue paste scarabs (...) the only representative at Defenneh of the great class of Naukratite scarabs'.
Parallels: the other one is EA 35634 below. Possibly a winged lion passant; see Giveon 1985, 154–5, § 58; cf. Vercoutter 1945, 165.

EA 35634   **1888,0208.163**
Glazed Egyptian blue scarab, badly corroded, pierced lengthwise, with elytra marked and base decorated with an incised hieroglyphic inscription. On the right is the hieroglyph Gardiner M16 ($h3$) followed by a vertical stroke, and then by the sign of the falcon with flail, *bik*.
Height: 0.53cm; width: 0.73cm; length: 1.68cm.
Bibliography: Petrie 1888, 73 § 70, p. 111, pl. xli, 68: one of 'two blue paste scarabs (...) the only representative at Defenneh of the great class of Naukratite scarabs'.
Parallels: the other one is EA 35420 above.

EA 18521   **1887,0101.676**
Green siltstone scarab, pierced lengthwise, with elytra marked and base decorated with an incised representation of a hawk with one wing raised and the other down, standing on a basket. By the tip of the lower wing is a lightly incised *ankh*-sign.
Height: 0.6cm; width: 0.9cm; length: 1.3cm.
Bibliography: Petrie 1888, 111, pl. xli, 51.

EA 18553   **1887,0101.677**
Obsidian scarab, pierced lengthwise, with elytra marked and base engraved with a vertical motto of the three signs R^c, *nfr* and ^cnh, surrounded by meandering border within a second border of a simple incised line. Petrie took the inscription as a royal name, but it is likely that the signs are merely decorative.
Height: 0.6cm; width: 1.1cm; length: 1.4cm.
Bibliography: Petrie 1888, 73 § 70, p. 111, pl. xli, 57; Newberry 1908, 124, no. 30 pl. x. On the spirals, see Keel 1995, 187 § 508.

EA 18531   **1887,0101.678**
White steatite scarab of the 'Anra'-type, pierced lengthwise, with pronotum and elytra divided by a T-shaped trace formed with carved double lines; the wing-cases are bordered by a line and marked by V-shaped humeral callosities; the forelegs are notched and protrude from the body; rings reinforce the threading holes. The base is decorated with engraved inscriptions consisting of two opposed open-ended vertical ovals or pseudo-cartouches surrounding 'an-ra'-type sequences of four and five signs (*nb?, n, r*, and possibly *t*), flanked on each side by addorsed uraei (one missing). Two supplementary *r*-signs are carved above the heads of the cobras.
Height: 0.6cm; width: 1.1cm; length: 1.4cm.
Bibliography: Petrie 1888, 111, pl. xli, 66.
Parallels: on the 'Anra' scarabs in general, see Richards 2001, particularly 72, 79, and fig. 4.19. This type of scarab exists from the Second Intermediate Period onwards, but the presence of humeral callosities could suggest a later dating, probably the beginning of the 18th dynasty. However, the protruding notched legs, the double lines on the back, the marked humeral callosities and the threading holes reinforced by rings could also indicate a Ramesside dating, or even later to the 21st–22nd dynasty, with a remake of the older 'Anra' motif, according to comments about similar items in Magnarini 2004, 154, no. 03.66, p. 162, no. 03.74; see also Hodjash 1999, 92, no. 419. Magnarini 2004, 154, no. 03.66 has the same arrangement of uraei but one long cartouche; cf. Giveon 1985, 179, 6, of the 19th dynasty (with cartouches of Thutmose III).

EA 18520   **1887,0101.679**
Grey glazed steatite scarab, pierced lengthwise, with elytra and humeral callosities marked, and base decorated with a hollow inscription consisting of a *hpr*-scarab topped by a sun-disc and flanked by two opposed *maat* feathers.
Height: 0.6cm; width: 0.9cm; length: 1.1cm.
Bibliography: Petrie 1888, 73 § 70, p. 111, pl. xli, 55: one of the 'rather common scarabs of Sheshonk IV, Rakheper'; see also Hall 1913, 247, no. 2471.
Parallels: for other so-called 'Rakheper' scarabs, see for example Hall 1913, 246–7, nos 2464–70, 2472–3, particularly 2472 (BM GR 1994,1101.348, from a tomb in Amathus, Cyprus); Petrie 1889b, pl. 57,

nos 1802–12, pl. 65, nos 2057–9; Petrie 1917b, 32, pl. 55, nos 46–8 (where Khepermaatra is considered a vassal of Psamtek I); Matouk 1971, 133, 198, nos 810–28, particularly 827–8; Matouk 1977, 157–8, 397, nos 1216, 1231, 1244; Hodjash 1999, 132–4, particularly 133, no. 867; Magnarini 2004, 233. However the inscription has nothing to do with a royal name, even for other examples with the signs enclosed in a cartouche, see Matouk 1971, 133; Hornung and Staehelin 1976, 281, with additional references. But the type is usually still dated to the 22nd dynasty (Magnarini, op.cit.).

EA 18528   1887,0101.685
Green glazed steatite scarab, pierced lengthwise, with elytra marked, and the base decorated with a representation of Taweret holding a knife, in front of the *s3*-sign of protection and a thick and tall vertical sign. Another sign is visible above her, possibly the sign *mr* ('beloved of'); sides and top are damaged.
Height: 0.8cm; width: 1cm; length: 1.5cm.
Bibliography: Petrie 1888, 111, pl. xli, 43.
Parallels: Magnarini 2004, 284 no. 10.22 for bibliography: Hornung and Staehelin 1976, 327, no. 689, 406, no. Va 11; Keel 1997 (Corpus I), 65, no. 128 (7th century BC); Petrie 1925, no. 1075 (18th dynasty?); Hodjash 1999, no. 1468.

EA 18529   1887,0101.680
Lapis lazuli scarab, pierced lengthwise, with elytra marked and base decorated with a design showing a crudely incised figure, seated with one arm raised to the face.
Height: 0.4cm; width: 0.55cm; length: 0.8cm.
Bibliography: Petrie 1888, 73 § 70, p. 111, pl. xli, 45. Petrie mentions only one lapis lazuli scarab from Tell Dafana, but there are at least two in the British Museum (see EA 18527 below), maybe three (see also EA 18461 below, of less certain provenance and uninscribed); see also three others, uninscribed, in Boston, MFA RES.87.95-97.

EA 18527   1887,0101.681
Lapis lazuli scarab, pierced lengthwise, with elytra marked and base decorated with an engraved representation of a seated figure on a basket.
Height: 0.4cm; width: 0.6cm; length: 0.9cm.
Bibliography: Petrie 1888, 73 § 70, p. 111, pl. xli, 46: same comment as for 18529 above.

EA 18565   1887,0101.683
Fragment of a green stone scarab, pierced lengthwise, with elytra marked and base inscribed with the beginning of the personal name Wahibra.
Height: 0.6cm; width: 0.9cm; length: 0.7cm (max.).
Bibliography: Petrie 1888, 73 § 70, p. 111, pl. xli, 56; id., 1889b, pl. 60, no. 1906.
Parallels: the other one, Petrie's pl. xli, 58, is EA 18534 below.

EA 18534   1887,0101.684
Base of a green jasper scarab, pierced lengthwise and inscribed with the hieroglyphs *mn* and *R*ᶜ, perhaps derived from part of the prenomen of Thutmose III. The back is broken away, together with part of the edge of the base.
Height: 0.3cm; width: 0.7cm; length: 1.cm.
Bibliography: Petrie 1888, 73 § 70, p. 111, pl. xli, 58; see also Hall 1913, 151, no. 1547.
Parallels: the other one, Petrie's pl. xli, 56, is EA 18565 above.

GR 1888,0208.161
Fragment of a green jasper scarab of the 'classical Phoenician' type of East Mediterranean origin, engraved on the underside with an idealized, bearded male head, wearing a lion skin headdress (or a lion head helmet?), ending in two volutes at the bottom. The head is framed by a braided pattern along the border. The right part of the scarab (left part of the intaglio) was missing and has been reconstructed. Though the headdress might suggest a representation Herakles or Melqart, it is more probable that the scarab belongs to the traditional series of janiform *grylli*, the other head having been in the missing part.
Height: 1.cm; width: 1.4cm; length: 1.8cm.

Context: north of Tell Dafana.
Bibliography: Petrie 1888, 73 § 70, pl. xli, 42: scarab of 'green paste, imitating jasper, (...) of the regular style of fine Phoenician work'. Walters 1926, 40, no. 321, pl. vi; Zazoff 1983, 91, pl. 22, 6; Boardman 2003, 113, no. 37/28.
Parallels: for Phoenician green jasper scarabs in general, see Boardman 2003, particularly 109–13 (profile heads); Zazoff 1983, 85–98, particularly 91, n. 52, pl. 22, 7 (= Walters 1926, 62, no. 507, pl. ix).

Uninscribed scarabs (Pl. 23)

EA 23865   1887,0101.1057
Copper alloy figure of a dynastid rhinoceros-scarab beetle with an axial horn in front, curving upwards; elytra and prothorax are marked by simple incisions; forelegs and midlegs are barely outlined. The underside is gently concave as if the item was destined to be a decoration stuck or welded to a round object.
Height: 0.86cm; width: 2.21cm; length: 3.63cm.

EA 18530   1887,0101.682
Corroded copper alloy scarab, pierced lengthwise (perforation now filled by corrosion), with elytra marked; no inscription is visible on the base.
Height: 0.6cm; width: 0.7cm; length: 0.9cm.
Context: provenance not specified in the Museum register, but probably from Tell Dafana according to the context of the item in the list.
Bibliography: Petrie 1888, 74 § 70: possibly one of the two 'small bronze scarabs'.

EA 18634   1887,0101.896
Green glazed composition scarab, elytra not marked but humeral callosities present, pierced longitudinally, base plain.
Height: 0.35cm; width: 0.55cm; length: 0.8cm.
Context: provenance not specified in the Museum register, but probably from Tell Nebesha or Tell Dafana, according to the context of the item in the list.

EA 18461   1887,0101.1333
Lapis lazuli scarab, elytra marked, pierced longitudinally, sides and base damaged.
Height: 0.5cm; width: 0.7cm; length: 1cm.
Context: provenance not specified in the Museum register, but possibly from Tell Dafana or Tell Nebesha, according to the context of the item in the list, if not from another eastern Delta site excavated by Petrie in 1886.
Parallels: for inscribed lapis lazuli scarabs from Tell Dafana, see above EA 18529.

7. Seals and rings

Stamp-seals (Pl. 24)

EA 23903   1887,0101.1427
Copper alloy thick rectangular seal, for stamping on jar sealings, with a plumed and disked vertical cartouche deeply incised, containing the nomen of Amasis preceded by the epithet 'Perfect God' and followed by 'Son of Neith'; a large ring-handle is welded on the back in the middle.
Height: 3.24cm; length: 4.93cm; width: 2.55cm; thickness (without ring): 0.67cm; diameter of the ring: 3.05cm.
Context: 'Qasr', east annexe (C), chamber 19.
Bibliography: Petrie 1888, 77 § 76, p. 111, pl. xli, 76: 'bronze stamp of Aahmes'; Hall 1913, 284, no. 2742; see also Journal, 141: 'a massive bronze seal or stamp of Aahmes was found in another of the outside chambers of the Kasr'.
Parallels: a similar but much less fine seal of Psamtik I (Wahibra) from Carchemish (BM ME 116187); see Giveon 1985, 160–1, no. 3; Woolley 1921, 126, pl. xxvi.

EA 23864   1887,0101.1056
Corroded copper alloy stamp, roughly circular, with a small ring

handle in the centre of the back. The surface is engraved with
decoration representing a human figure of a bearded deity with long
hair, standing above a base line, wearing a kilt and a high headdress,
cap or wig. The figure is looking right while walking to the left, and is
holding up two crocodiles by the tails, heads down, jaws opened,
crested on their backs. The image recalls the oriental pattern of the
Master of the Animals, as well as, in an Egyptian context, the young
Harpocrates.
Height: 1.3cm; diameter: 3.2cm; thickness: 0.4cm (without ring).
Context: Tell Dafana or its neighbourhood.
Bibliography: Petrie 1888, 80 § 80, pl. xxxix, 1: 'a curious seal with a
man, bearded, with long hair, holding up two crocodiles by the tails'.
Pattern common on scarabs; see for example Hodjash 1999, 169–70.

EA 18469   1887,0101.665
Glazed composition seal-stone, with the base cut straight, the top
tapered, rounded and perforated horizontally for suspension. The
horizontal cross section would be rectangular if the edges had not been
bevelled off. The base bears a representation of a long-curved-horned
ibex, facing right, with a large lotus flower decorating its chest, and a
longer-stemmed lotus flower behind it.
Height: 1.78cm; length: 1.52cm; width: 1cm.
Context: 'Qasr', east annexe (C), chamber 2 or 3.
Bibliography: Petrie 1888, 74 § 70, 75 § 70, 72, p. 111, pl. xli, 73:
'engraved porcelain' seal-stone 'of Syrian type', 'found in the Kasr', 'in
chamber 2 or 3'.
Parallels: for the shape of the seal, see also EA 18485 below; Bolton,
1886.28.24.c and Boston, MFA 87.710–711, made of stone, unfinished
and unengraved.

EA 18485   1887,0101.686
Pale green quartz unfinished seal-stone, with the base cut straight and
the top rounded. The cross section would be rectangular if the vertical
edges had not been bevelled off, causing them to taper towards the top.
Both small sides were accidentally chipped near the top, as the maker
clearly attempted to drill a horizontal suspension hole. Once broken,
the object was left unfinished, which explains why the base has not
been carved with a design or inscription.
Length: 2.7cm; width: 2.05cm; thickness: 1.2cm.
Context: probably from the north-west Ptolemaic mound.
Bibliography: Petrie 1888, 74 § 70, p. 111, pl. xli, 74: one of the 'four
plain seal-stones unengraved, one broken in drilling (...) three of pale
green translucent calcite (...), of Syrian type'.
Parallels: see also, EA 18469 above (glazed composition), Bolton,
1886.28.24.c and Boston, MFA 87.710–711, unfinished and unengraved.

EA 18482   1887,0101.687
Artefact made of a translucent stone, probably quartz or calcite,
roughly cut in the shape of a narrow rectangular pyramidion
truncated at the top. Numerous parallel scuffs are evident on every
side, particularly on both the opposite larger sides. Possibly an
unfinished seal, if not a weight.
Height: 2cm; width: 1.4cm; thickness: 1.3cm; weight: 8.00g.
Bibliography: Petrie 1888, 74 § 70, p. 111, pl. xli, 75: 'seal-stone' 'of white
crystallized calcite'; 'block for a seal; white calcite'. On this shape of
seal, see Keel 1995, 97–9.

Finger-rings with inscribed or decorated bezel (Pl. 24)

EA 18302   1887,0101.599
Bezel of a silver finger-ring, inscribed with hieroglyphs reading from
right to left, containing a personal name, probably Tadinubhotep.
Length: 0.89cm (max.); width: 0.55cm (max.); thickness: 0.18cm (max.).
Context: from the surface of the site.
Bibliography: Petrie 1888, 76 § 75, p. 110, pl. xli, 33A.

EA 23852   1887,0101.900
Silver bezel of a finger-ring, inscribed with hieroglyphs reading from
right to left, beginning with the title 'Priest of Amun'. Although the
following signs are all fairly clear individually, they are difficult to
interpret as a group, unless they read, 'The servant of Neferibra
(Psamtik II), possessor of the Red Crown'.
Length: 2.03cm (max.); width: 1.35cm (max.); thickness: 0.47cm (max.).

Context: from the surface of the site.
Bibliography: Petrie 1888, 72 § 69, p. 76 § 75, p. 110, pl. xli, 32
(represented unbroken on the plate; EA 23858 (1887,0101.1424–5) might
be fragments of it).

EA 23853   1887,0101.901
Silver bezel of a finger-ring, inscribed with hieroglyphs reading from
right to left: 'The servant of Neith, Psamtiksineith. The figure at the
beginning of the line suits the reading Neith better than Amun, which
was Petrie's first determination in his unpublished notes; in the
published account he changed the reading to Neith.
Length: 1.8cm (max.); width: 1.33cm; thickness: 0.38cm (max.).
Context: from the surface of the site.
Bibliography: Petrie 1888, 72 § 69, p. 76 § 75, p. 110, pl. xli, 34; Hall
1913, 283, no. 2737; Petrie 1889b, pl. 64, no. 2027; Journal, 141: 'the
bezil of a silver ring brought in today is inscribed 'Priest of Amun,
Psamtik si Neit'; I do not see that any Psamtik was called son of Neith,
so which king this man was called after is not clear; I incline to its
being Psamtik III, as Aahmes, just before him, was Si Neit. This is the
second silver ring here of a priest of Amun, so it would seem that there
was a temple of Amun here'.

EA 23854   1887,0101.902
Silver bezel of a finger-ring, inscribed with hieroglyphs reading from
right to left, interpreted by Petrie as: 'The servant of Neith,
Horemheb'. The writing of the personal name could be better
arranged, but no better alternative suggests itself.
Length: 1.59cm (max.); width: 1.12cm (max.); thickness: 0.4cm (max.).
Context: from the surface of the site.
Bibliography: Petrie 1888, 72 § 69, p. 76 § 75, p. 110, pl. xli, 35.

EA 23855   1887,0101.903
Silver bezel of a finger-ring, inscribed with hieroglyphs showing two
seated figures, probably falcon-headed, facing right, followed by a tall
sign of uncertain reading.
Length: 1.34cm (max.); width: 0.96cm (max.); thickness: 0.3cm (max.).
Context: from the surface of the site.
Bibliography: Petrie 1888, 76 § 75.

EA 23856   1887,0101.904
Silver bezel of a finger-ring, with incised representation of a winged
scarab.
Length: 1.77cm (max.); width: 0.77cm (max.); thickness: 0.43cm (max.).
Context: from the surface of the site.
Bibliography: Petrie 1888, 76 § 75, p. 111, pl. xli, 36; Journal, 149.

EA 23857   1887,0101.905
Silver bezel of a finger-ring, inscribed with hieroglyphs reading right
to left, possibly to be interpreted: '(Long) Live the Horus Menkh-Ib
(Psamtik II), beloved of Amun-Ra and Bast'. If so, the sign *mr* has been
reduced to a mere line or elided. Also, the seated divine figure with the
double crown is not a particularly good ideogram for Amun, and may
represent another deity.
Length: 1.6cm (max.); width: 0.88cm (max.); thickness: 0.39cm (max.).
Context: from the surface of the pavement to the north of the casemate
building A of the 'Qasr'.
Bibliography: Petrie 1888, 57 § 56, p. 72 § 69, p. 76 § 75, p. 110, pl. xli,
33; id., 1889b, pl. 64, no. 2029; Hall 1913, 283, no. 2738; Journal, 161.

EA 23858   1887,0101.906
Fragment of a silver finger-ring, comprising about 30 per cent of the
perimeter, circular in section. This piece is unlikely to be part of same
ring as 1887,0101.1424-1425.
Length: 1.8cm; thickness: 0.15cm.
Bibliography: Petrie 1888, 76 § 75.

EA 23858   1887,0101.1424
Fragment of a silver finger-ring, comprising about 20 per cent of the
perimeter, circular in section.
Length: 1.45cm; thickness: 0.2cm.
Bibliography: Petrie 1888, 76 § 75; probably part of the same ring as
1887, 0101.1425, and possibly part of the ring with bezel EA 23852
above, represented unbroken (ibid., pl. xli, 32).

EA 23858   **1887,0101.1425**

Fragment of a silver finger-ring, comprising about 45 percent of the perimeter, circular in section.

Length: 2.1cm; thickness: 0.25cm.

Bibliography: Petrie 1888, 76 § 75; probably part of the same ring as 1887, 0101.1424, and possibly part of the ring with bezel EA 23852 above, represented unbroken (ibid., pl. xli, 32).

EA 23892   **1887,0101.1089**

Oval bezel of an integral corroded copper alloy finger-ring, with a hieroglyphic inscription reading from right to left. The first sign appears to be *wsr*, followed by the hieroglyph for the letter *p* and two other signs of uncertain reading.

Length: 1.14cm (max.); width: 0.93cm; thickness: 0.36cm (max.).

Bibliography: Petrie 1888, 80 § 80: possibly one of the 33 'bronze rings', though the author says that they are 'mainly Roman and Cufic, of no particular interest, with the usual devices'.

EA 23897   **1887,0101.1099**

Bezel and part of the hoop of a corroded copper alloy integral finger-ring, the bezel inscribed with the personal name Ptahhotep.

Length: 1.37cm (max.); width: 0.68cm; thickness: 0.22cm (max.).

Bibliography: Petrie 1888, 80 § 80: a bronze ring, 'Egyptian, minutely inscribed Ptah-hotep'.

EA 18638   **1887,0101.886**

Fragment of the bezel of a green glazed composition finger-ring, with incised decoration, representing the head of Hathor.

Length: 1.42cm (max.); width: 0.96cm; thickness: 0.4cm (max.).

Bibliography: Petrie 1888, 75 § 72, p. 111, pl. xli, 41: 'a ring bezel of grey-blue glaze, almost like that of Tell el-Amarna, bears the head of Hathor'.

EA 23845   **1887,0101.1418**

The oval bezel of a finger-ring, manufactured of layers of glass. The base level is made of red glass, which has actually been cut all around the edge. Above this is a layer of decayed white glass with a final top layer (of smaller size) of polished dark red glass.

Length: 1.7cm; width: 1.1cm (max.); thickness: 0.45cm.

Context: probably from north of the site towards Tell Belim.

8. Jar sealings

Plaster jar sealings (Pls 24–5)

Psamtik I

EA 23791   **1887,0101.757**   **(Pl. 24)**

Fragment of a plaster jar sealing; the right part of the outer convex surface bears a plumed and disked vertical cartouche of a king Psamtik, stamped in low relief and, on the left side and on the top, parts of two other ones. The inner concave part shows the negative impression of the shoulder of the sealed vessel, whilst numerous intersecting horizontal and oblique traces are negative impressions of the fibre string that attached the lid to the neck of the jar.

Length: 12.7cm (max.); width: 10.73cm (max.); thickness: 3.08cm.

Context: Findspot 8, west of the 'Qasr' (number scratched into the object).

Bibliography: Petrie 1888, 58 § 57, p. 66 § 61, p. 72 § 69, p. 109, pl. xxxvi, 1; Hall 1913, 291, no. 2781; see also Petrie, Journal, 119–20: 'to my great delight, in an outside chamber attached to the palace wall, a man turned up half a dozen plaster stoppings of jar mouths, each stamped with the cartouche of Psamtik; this is most valuable, at this stage of work, it proves that the outer and subsequent chambers are not later than the earlier part of the XXVI dynasty, & that jars of oil or wine for, or from, the royal stores were thrown away here: thus confirming exactly my belief that this was a royal residence of the XXVI dynasty'. Ibid., 129: 'the place where the Psamtik jar stoppings are found (on the opposite side of the building) was evidently the chamber for opening wine jars; there are any number of lids & of sealings, but not a single jar; something like a butler's pantry, with nothing but corks & sealing wax in it'.

Parallels: from Tell Dafana, see below, EA 23792, from the same findspot, showing a negative impression of the same stamp; Bolton 1886.28.112 (also from same findspot); Liverpool, WM 3.2.87.6 (destroyed), 47.56.13 (ex-Edinburgh, NMS, 1887–92); Bristol, CMAG H4996 (see Wilson 1891, 14); Sydney, MAC, MU1866, Sydney, NM AML54; Cairo, EM JE27392 (missing); Berlin ÄM 10079 (destroyed during WWII); one fragment was also sent to the collection of the Chautauqua Archaeological Museum, now dispersed.

EA 23792   **1887, 0101.762**   **(Pl. 24)**

Fragment of a plaster jar sealing; the inner concave surface bears part of a hollow impression of a vertical cartouche of a king Psamtik with accompanying plumes and disk. The sealing must correspond to the negative impression, on a second layer of plaster, of a cartouche (see EA 23791, same type) stamped on a first layer of plaster. The outer convex surface bears part of a positive impression of another cartouche, possibly of the same type.

Length: 5.41cm (max.); width: 3.51cm (max.); thickness: 1.57cm.

Context: Findspot 8, west of the 'Qasr' (number scratched into the object).

Bibliography: Petrie 1888, 58 § 57, p. 66 § 61, p. 72 § 69; see also Hall 1913, 291, no. 2782; see also Journal, 119–20, 129.

Parallels: from Tell Dafana, EA 23791 above, from the same findspot, showing the same type of stamp as originally impressed on a first layer of plaster on the neck of the sealed pottery.

Nekau II

EA 23793   **1887,0101.756**   **(Pl. 24)**

Substantial fragment of a plaster outer jar sealing bearing four impressions of a seal engraved with the plumed and disked vertical cartouche of King Nekau II, 'Son of Ra, Ne[kau]'. As the lower part of the edge is broken away, only the upper part of the cartouches are preserved.

Length: 10.24cm; width: 9.41cm; thickness: 3.22cm.

Context: 'Qasr', east annexe (D), 'floor' of chamber 22 (number pencilled on the object).

Bibliography: Petrie 1888, 54 § 52, p. 56 § 55, p. 58 § 57, p. 72 § 69, p. 109, pl. xxxvi, 2; Hall 1913, 291, nos 2783; Journal, 141: 'in another chamber, very low down, a jar plastering was found, which I puzzled at; only just the beginning of the 4 cartouches were left, & all indistinct, but at last I made out an N, & then what may be a bull's back, so it must be Neko'.

Parallels: seals of Nekau from Carchemish in BM ME 116222, 116224, 116225 = Woolley 1921, pl. 26c, 1–4; Giveon 1985, 162–3, § 7 (no. 116222); Porter and Moss 1951, 398; see also EA 23790 below, a jar handle from Tell Dafana stamped with a similar impression.

Psamtik II

EA 23794   **1887,0101.777**   **(Pl. 24)**

Fragment of plaster jar sealing; the outer convex surface bears four impressions of a seal engraved with a vertical cartouche containing the prenomen and epithet of Psamtek II; the inner concave surface is irregular and shows several traces of negative impressions of fibre cords used to attach the lid.

Length: 11.57cm (max.); width: 8.87cm (max.); thickness: 2.63cm.

Context: 'Qasr', east annexe (G), chamber 29.

Bibliography: Petrie 1888, 51 § 49, p. 58, 59 § 57, p. 72 § 69, p. 109, pl. xxxvi, 3; Hall 1913, 291, no. 2785; see also Petrie, Journal, 140: 'in another chamber near there, but low down was a jar sealing of Psamtik'.

Parallels: from Tell Dafana, Boston, MFA RES.87.144 (deaccessioned); according to the EEF distribution list, one piece of jar sealing was sent to the Cairo EM, where it is not recorded.

Amasis

EA 22356   **1887,0101.770**   **(Pl. 64)**

Plaster jar sealing still attached to the mouth of a broken Chian amphora bearing impressions of a seal engraved with a vertical cartouche containing the nomen of Amasis. There are a total of 16 impressions (including partial ones), but they were not all applied in the same sealing operation, as some have been applied above others on a secondary layer of plaster. Parts of three impressions from the first level can be seen.

Seal only: height: 14cm (max.); width: 17.5cm (max.).

Context: 'Qasr', east annexe (G), chamber 18 (The Findspot number

18 has been scratched into the side of the object).
Bibliography: Petrie 1888, 51 § 49, pp. 58, 59 § 57, p. 71 § 67, p. 72 § 69, p. 109, pl. xxxvi, 5; see also Newberry 1908, 14–15, fig. 4; Hall 1913, 292, no. 2788; Johnston 2006, 26, fig. 18; Weber 2012b, 374, TD 296; Villing 2013, 76, fig. 2. Journal, 135: 'in some chambers out on the E. are quantities of broken Greek vases of 550–600 BC, along with jar stoppers stamped by Amasis'; ibid., 141: 'two jar plasterings, stamped by Aahmes, have been found entire, neck handles, stopper plaster, & all, the whole top having broken off the jar, of old'; ibid., 145: 'another very fine Greek amphora was found today, with red scrawly lines over it; one such has the sealing up of Aahmes still on the neck, showing that the Greek ware was used at the royal vine or olive yards for the produce. This is valuable as pointing to its being made in Egypt & not an imported rarity. It has also a star scratched upon it such as I found on a piece of Naukratis pottery, & some people said was Arab!'
Parallels: from Tell Dafana, EA 23795 below, Cairo, EM JE 27391 (which according to Petrie 1888, 72, was attached to the neck of a jar; missing), Dundee 1975.53; London, Harrow School 1887.HE165; Oxford, AM 1887.2506, Philadelphia, PM E172; Sheffield J87.5; Boston, MFA (also attached to the jar-neck of an amphora; according to a manuscript list but the item apparently was not recorded).

EA 23795   **1887,0101.763**   **(Pl. 25)**
Fragment of a beige plaster jar sealing. The outer convex surface bears a vertical cartouche of Amasis stamped in low relief, surmounted by a solar disc between two ostrich feathers. The inner concave surface shows a negative impression of the rim of the jar and traces of another layer of a white plaster.
Length: 8.57cm; width: 5.09cm; thickness: 3.19cm.
Context: 'Qasr', east annexe (G), chamber 18 (The Findspot number 18 has been scratched into the inner surface).
Bibliography: Petrie 1888, 72 § 69; Hall 1913, 292, no. 2787.
Parallels: same as for EA 22356 above.

Illegible
For illegible stamps on plaster jar sealings of Psamtik II or Apries, see Petrie 1888, 72 § 69.

EA 23796   **1887,0101.758**   **(Pl. 24)**
Plaster jar sealing showing the impression of five illegible vertical cartouches stamped on the domed upper surface, one on the top and four regularly distributed on the edge. The lower concave surface shows two layers of plaster and several traces of the twisted string attaching the lid to the jar. In the middle, a round deep cavity shows a negative impression of an illegible cartouche stamped in a material which crumbled and vanished afterwards, used originally to seal the attachment cord.
Diameter: 17cm; thickness: 4.6cm.
Context: 'Qasr', east annexe (C), chamber 17 (The Findspot number 17 has been scratched into the lower part of the object).
Bibliography: Petrie 1888, 72 § 69.
Parallels: Bristol, CMAG H2191 (attached to a fragment of jar-neck).

EA 23797   **1887,0101.761**   **(Pl. 25)**
A plaster jar sealing showing the impression of nine indistinct vertical cartouches surmounted by a plumed disc, stamped on the outer domed surface, two on the top, seven on the edge. A small round hole runs across the object on one side. The lower surface is irregular but almost flat, slightly concave, and shows several negative impressions of a twisted string attaching the lid to the jar. In the centre, a round cavity shows at least six negative impressions of several small oval bezels of finger-rings (similar to EA 23852, 23858 and 18302 from Tell Dafana), originally stamped on a lump of material, which crumbled and vanished afterwards, sealing the attaching string.
Length: 14.7cm (max.); width: 13.53cm (max.); thickness: 4.16cm.
Context: 'Qasr', east annexe (G), chamber 18.
Bibliography: Petrie 1888, 72 § 69, p. 109, pl. xxxvi, 4

EA 23798   **1887,0101.764**   **(Pl. 25)**
Fragment of a plaster jar sealing bearing an indistinct stamped cartouche.
Length: 4.85cm (max.); width: 4.55cm (max.); thickness: 2.02cm.
Bibliography: Petrie 1888, 72 § 69.

9. Weapons

Iron arrowheads

Leaf-shaped (Pl. 25)

EA 23940   **1887,0101.1460**
Corroded iron leaf-shaped and tanged arrowhead, with flat rhomboid cross section and longitudinal mid-rib on both sides.
Length: 5.4cm; width: 1.6cm; thickness: 0.95cm.
Bibliography: Petrie 1888, 78 § 77, p. 110, pl. xxxvii, 14; Amborn 1976, 78, 91, fig. 32, 14.

EA 23941   **1887,0101.1461**
Corroded iron leaf-shaped and tanged arrowhead, with longitudinal mid-rib on both sides. The tip and the tang are broken and missing.
Length: 5.21cm (max.); width: 1.57cm; thickness: 0.95cm.
Context: Saite enclosure (so-called 'Camp').

Lozenge-shaped (Pl. 25)

EA 23939   **1887,0101.1459**
Corroded iron lozenge-shaped and tanged arrowhead, with a flat rhomboid cross section and longitudinal mid-rib on both sides.
Length: 5.4cm; width: 1.6cm; thickness: 0.85cm.
Bibliography: Petrie 1888, 78 § 77, p. 110, pl. xxxvii, 16; Petrie 1917a, pl. xli, R34; Amborn 1976, 78, 91, fig. 32, 16.

GR 1935,0823.111
Corroded iron bifacial lozenge-shaped and tanged arrowhead. The tang is missing.
Length: 3.2cm; width: 1.38cm; thickness: 0.5cm.

Triangular section (Pl. 25)

EA 23930   **1887,0101.878**
Corroded iron tanged arrowhead of triangular section with a cylindro-conical portion between the head and the tang.
Length: 4.6cm (max.); width: 1.03cm.
Bibliography: Petrie 1888, 78 § 77, p. 110, pl. xxxvii, 13.
Parallels: from Tell Dafana, see below GR 1935,0823.90, 1935,0823.96, EA 23931, 23932, 23933, 23934, 23935, 23936, 23937, same or similar type; Petrie 1917a, pl. xlii, R248–251 (also from Tell Dafana), 254–5; Amborn 1976, 92–3, nn. 92–5, fig. 43.

EA 23929   **1887,0101.877**
Corroded iron tanged arrowhead of triangular section with a cylindro-conical portion between the head and the tang; recorded in the Museum register, the item remains unlocated.
Length: 5.08cm (2 ins).
Context: Saite enclosure (so-called 'Camp').
Bibliography: Petrie 1888, 78 § 77, p. 110, pl. xxxvii, 12; Amborn 1976, 91–2, fig. 32, 12.
Parallels: same as for EA 23930 above.

EA 23931   **1887,0101.1451**
Fragment of the tip of a corroded iron arrowhead of rhombic to oval cross section.
Length: 2.78cm (max.); width: 0.73cm; thickness: 0.61cm.

Figure 2 Iron arrowhead types: leaf-shaped, lozenge-shaped and triangular. British Museum, EA 23940, 23939 and 23930 (drawing: Claire Thorne)

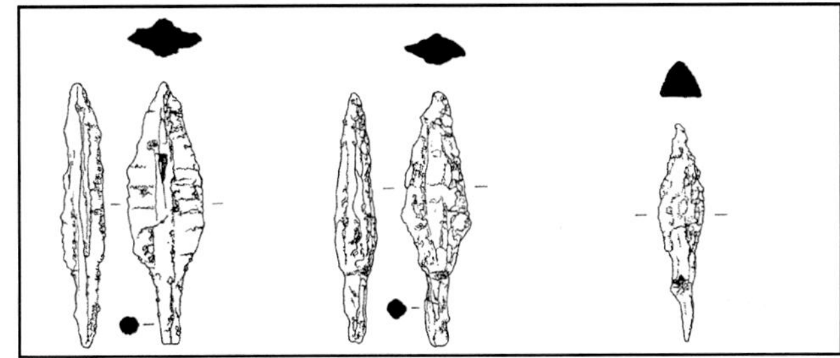

Context: Saite enclosure (so-called 'Camp').
Bibliography: Petrie 1888, 78 § 77.
Parallels: same as for EA 23930 above.

EA 23932   **1887,0101.1452**
Corroded iron tanged arrowhead of triangular section with a
cylindro-conical portion between the head and the tang, most of
which is probably missing.
Length: 4.54cm (max.); width: 0.85cm.
Context: Saite enclosure (so-called 'Camp').
Bibliography: Petrie 1888, 78 § 77, p. 110, pl. xxxvii, 12; Amborn 1976,
78, fig. 32, 17.
Parallels: same as for EA 23930 above.

EA 23933   **1887,0101.1453**
Corroded iron tanged arrowhead of triangular section with a
cylindro-conical portion between the head and the tang. The item is
slightly bent.
Length: 4.45cm (max.); width: 0.96cm.
Context: Saite enclosure (so-called 'Camp').
Bibliography: Petrie 1888, 78 § 77, p. 110, pl. xxxvii, 12.
Parallels: same as for EA 23930 above.

EA 23934   **1887,0101.1454**
Corroded iron tanged arrowhead of triangular section with a
cylindro-conical portion between the head and the tang. Two of the
three corners of the triangular tip are slightly barbed.
Length: 4.75cm (max.); width: 0.79cm.
Context: Saite enclosure (so-called 'Camp').
Bibliography: Petrie 1888, 78 § 77, p. 110, pl. xxxvii, 12.
Parallels: same as for EA 23930 above.

EA 23935   **1887,0101.1455**
Corroded iron tanged arrowhead of triangular section with a
cylindrical portion between the head and the tang.
Length: 4.64cm (max.); width: 0.91cm.
Context: Saite enclosure (so-called 'Camp').
Bibliography: Petrie 1888, 78 § 77.
Parallels: same as for EA 23930 above.

EA 23936   **1887,0101.1456**
Corroded iron arrowhead of triangular section, probably tanged, with
a cylindrical portion between the head and the tang, which is entirely
missing.
Length: 3.19cm (max.); width: 0.77cm.
Context: Saite enclosure (so-called 'Camp').
Bibliography: Petrie 1888, 78 § 77, p. 110, pl. xxxvii, 13; Amborn 1976,
78, fig. 32, 13.
Parallels: same as for EA 23930 above.

EA 23937   **1887,0101.1457**
Corroded iron tanged arrowhead of triangular section with a
cylindro-conical portion between the head and the tang, which is
almost entriely missing.
Length: 3.86cm (max.); width: 1.07cm.
Context: Saite enclosure (so-called 'Camp').
Bibliography: Petrie 1888, 78 § 77.
Parallels: same as for EA 23930 above.

GR 1935,0823.90
Corroded iron tanged arrowhead of triangular section with a
cylindro-conical portion between the head and the tang.
Length: 4.98cm; width: 1.15cm.
Parallels: same as for EA 23930 above.

GR 1935,0823.96
Corroded iron tanged arrowhead of triangular section with a
cylindro-conical portion between the head and the tang.
Length: 4.42cm; width: 0.75cm.
Parallels: same as for EA 23930 above.

EA 23938   **1887,0101.1458**
Corroded iron tanged arrowhead, with square to round cross section,
slightly thicker close to the central part. The tang is short and most of it
is probably missing, as well as the tip.
Length: 5.64cm (max.); width: 1.28cm.
Context: Saite enclosure (so-called 'Camp').
Bibliography: Petrie 1888, 78 § 77.

Barbed spikes (Pl. 25)

The items EA 23970, 23971 and 23972 are interpreted in the Museum
register as possible spurs or helmet-ornaments, and as potential
'helmet-peaks' by Petrie (1888, 110, and ibid., 77–8 § 77): 'the objects 8
to 11 are difficult to explain; possibly they may be ornaments for the
peaks of helmets: the thin strips bent out splay at the base of 9, 10, 11,
seem as if to fasten the spike into some leather object, and yet it would
not be suited for a spur, owing to the barbed form: these barbs could
hardly be for use, as the attachment of the spike by the splay branches
would scarcely be strong enough to bear the wrench of dragging the
barbed spike out from anything. On the whole then they were more
probably ornamental'. This identification is by no means certain. They
could also belong to a special type of 'fire cage' arrowheads.

EA 23970   **1887,0101.1492**
Fragment of a corroded iron artefact in the shape of a spike barbed on
two opposite sides, with a pointed extremity opposite a thicker one
ending in three thin splayed branches, slightly curved and broken at
their ends (one missing). The actual function of the item is uncertain; it
might be the tip of a broken 'cage fire head' or 'basket fire' type
arrowhead.
Length: 4.53cm; width: 1.72cm.
Context: Saite enclosure (so-called 'Camp').
Bibliography: Petrie 1888, 77–8 § 77, p. 110, pl. xxxvii, 11; Petrie 1917a,
pl. xliii, R58; Amborn 1976, 78, 101, fig. 32, 11.

EA 23971   **1887,0101.1493**
Fragment of a corroded iron artefact in the shape of a short spike
barbed on one side, with a pointed extremity and another ending in
three splay branches, slightly curved and broken at their end. The
actual function of the item is uncertain; it might be the tip of a broken
'cage fire head' or 'basket fire' type arrowhead.
Length: 3.48cm (max.); width: 2.09cm.
Context: Saite enclosure (so-called 'Camp').
Bibliography: Petrie 1888, 77–8 § 77, p. 110, pl. xxxvii, 9; Petrie 1917a,
pl. xliii, R58; Amborn 1976, 78, 101, fig. 32, 9.

EA 23972   **1887,0101.1494**
Fragment of a corroded iron artefact in the shape of a short spike with
a pointed extremity and another one ending in at least two splayed
branches, slightly curved and broken at their ends (one missing). The
actual function of the item remains uncertain; it might be the tip of a
broken 'cage fire head' or 'basket fire' type arrowhead.
Length: 3.95cm; width: 1.75cm.
Context: Saite enclosure (so-called 'Camp').
Bibliography: Petrie 1888, 77–8 § 77, p. 110, pl. xxxvii, 10; Petrie 1917a,
pl. xliii, R58; Amborn 1976, 78, 101, fig. 32, 10.

Bronze arrowheads

Leaf-shaped (Pl. 25)

EA 23921   **1887,0101.1444**
Corroded copper alloy large leaf-shaped arrowhead, with a mid-rib on
both sides ending with a conical socket.
Length: 5.32cm (max.); width: 2.07cm; thickness: 0.6cm.
Context: Saite enclosure (so-called 'Camp').
Bibliography: Petrie 1888, 77 § 76, pl. xxxix, 14; Petrie 1917a, 34, pl. xli,
R42; Snodgrass 1964, 151, n. 40, p. 152, fig. 10 (type 3A1); Amborn 1976,
93, fig. 44, 14.
Parallels: from Tell Dafana, see below, GR 1935,0823.117; see also
below, GR 1935,0823.115, 1935,0823.106 and 1935,0823.113; in addition
to EA 23922, 23923 and 23924.

GR 1935,0823.117
Corroded copper alloy leaf-shaped arrowhead with a mid-rib on both
sides ending with a conical socket.

Length: 4.71cm; width: 1.62cm; thickness: 0.55cm.
Parallels: same as for EA 23921 above.

EA 23923   1887,0101.1446
Corroded copper alloy large leaf-shaped arrowhead, with a mid-rib on both sides ending with a conical socket.
Length: 4.37cm (max.); width: 1.43cm; thickness: 0.58cm.
Context: Saite enclosure (so-called 'Camp').
Parallels: same as for EA 23921 above.

EA 23924   1887,0101.1447
Corroded copper alloy short leaf-shaped arrowhead, with a mid-rib on both sides ending with a conical socket.
Length: 2.88cm (max.); width: 1.05cm; thickness: 0.51cm.
Context: Saite enclosure (so-called 'Camp').
Bibliography: Petrie 1888, 77 § 76, pl. xxxix, 16; Petrie 1917a, pl. xli, R44; Snodgrass 1964, 151, n. 40, p. 152, fig. 10 (type 3A1); Amborn 1976, 93, fig. 44, 16.
Parallels: same as for EA 23921 above.

GR 1935,0823.106
Corroded copper alloy short leaf-shaped arrowhead, with a mid-rib on both sides ending with a conical socket.
Length: 3cm; width: 1.03cm; thickness: 0.48cm.
Parallels: same as for EA 23921 above.

EA 23922   1887,0101.1445
Corroded copper alloy narrow leaf-shaped arrowhead, with a central rib on both sides and a conical socket.
Length: 6cm (max.); width: 0.67cm; thickness: 0.67cm.
Context: Saite enclosure (so-called 'Camp').
Bibliography: Petrie 1888, 77 § 76, pl. xxxix, 13.
Parallels: same as for EA 23921 above.

GR 1935,0823.115
Corroded copper alloy leaf-shaped arrowhead with a mid-rib on both sides ending with a conical socket.
Length: 3.55cm; width: 1.15cm; thickness: 0.6cm.
Parallels: same as for EA 23921 above.

GR 1935,0823.113
Corroded copper alloy leaf-shaped arrowhead with a mid-rib on both sides ending with a conical socket.
Length: 3.71cm; width: 1.05mm; thickness: 0.57cm.
Parallels: same as for EA 23921 above.

GR 1935,0823.112
Corroded copper alloy leaf-shaped arrowhead, with a mid-rib on both sides ending in a conical socket. Barbed on one edge.
Length: 2.93cm; width: 1.1cm; thickness: 0.65cm.
Parallels: Snodgrass 1964, 151, 152, fig. 10 (type 3A2).

GR 1935,0823.116
Corroded copper alloy leaf-shaped and barbed arrowhead with a mid-rib on both sides ending with a conical socket.
Length: 2.79cm; width: 1.18cm; thickness: 0.55cm.
Parallels: Snodgrass 1964, 151, 152, fig. 10 (type 3A3).

EA 23920   1887,0101.1443
Corroded copper alloy large leaf-shaped arrowhead, with rounded tip and a mid-rib on both sides ending with a conical socket.
Length: 4.8cm; width: 2.17cm; thickness: 0.82cm.
Bibliography: Petrie 1888, 77 § 76, pl. xxxix, 10; id., 1917a, 34, pl. xli, R25.

EA 23915   1887,0101.1439
Corroded copper alloy leaf-shaped arrowhead, with a central rib on both sides. The edges are rounded near the tip, and converge in a straight line towards the other end to form the tang.
Length: 7.41cm (max.); width: 1.54cm; thickness: 0.79cm.
Context: Saite enclosure (so-called 'Camp').
Bibliography: Petrie 1888, 77 § 76, pl. xxxix, 11.
Parallels: from Tell Dafana, see below, EA 23916 and GR

1935.0823.114; see also Petrie 1917a, 35, pl. xlii, R236; Amborn 1976, 95, n. 105.

EA 23916   1887,0101.1440
Corroded copper alloy leaf-shaped arrowhead, with a central rib on both sides. The edges are slightly rounded near the tip and converge in a straight line towards the other end to form the tang.
Length: 5.58cm (max.); width: 1.22cm; thickness: 0.39cm.
Context: Saite enclosure (so-called 'Camp').
Bibliography: Petrie 1888, 77 § 76, pl. xxxix, 11; id., 1917a, 35, pl. xli, R122; Amborn 1976, 95, fig. 44, 11.
Parallels: same as for EA 23915 above.

GR1935,0823.114
Corroded copper alloy leaf-shaped arrowhead, with a central rib on both sides. The edges are slightly rounded near the tip and converge in a straight line towards the other end to form the tang.
Length: 7.11cm; width: 1.36cm; thickness: 0.57cm.
Parallels: same as for EA 23915 above.

Rhombic section (Pl. 25)

EA 23919   1887,0101.1307
Corroded copper alloy arrowhead of rhombic cross section with a long and thick tang of round cross section.
Length: 5.96cm (max.); width: 0.87cm; thickness: 0.63cm.
Context: Saite enclosure (so-called 'Camp').
Bibliography: Petrie 1888, 78 § 77.

Rhombic section and barbed (Pl. 25)

EA 23917   1887,0101.1441
Corroded copper alloy barbed arrowhead of rhombic cross section, with a blunt tip, nicked edges and a thick tang (broken and incomplete) of round cross section.
Length: 6.53cm (max.); width: 1.68cm; thickness: 0.93cm.
Context: 'Qasr', east annexe (C), chamber 3.
Bibliography: Petrie 1888, pl. xxxix, 20; Petrie 1917a, 35, pl. xli, R131; Snodgrass 1964, 145, fig. 9, pp. 146–7 (type 1C2); Amborn 1976, 95, fig. 44, 20.
Parallels: Amborn 1976, 95, n. 104.

Trefoil section with short, integral socket (Pl. 25)

EA 23925   1887,0101.1448
Corroded copper alloy arrowhead of trefoil cross section and rhombic profile, with an integral conical socket.
Length: 3cm (max.); width: 1.04cm.
Context: Saite enclosure (so-called 'Camp').
Bibliography: Petrie 1888, 77 § 76, p. 78 § 77, pl. xxxix, 9; Petrie 1917a, 34, pl. xli, R61; Amborn 1976, 94, fig. 44, 9.
Parallels: from Tell Dafana, see below EA 23925, GR 1925,0823.94, 1925,0823.95, 1925,0823.107, and 1925,0823.108, same or similar type; Petrie 1917a, 35, pl. xlii, R245; Snodgrass 1964, 151, n. 43, p. 152, fig. 10 (type 3B3); Amborn 1976, 94, n. 102.

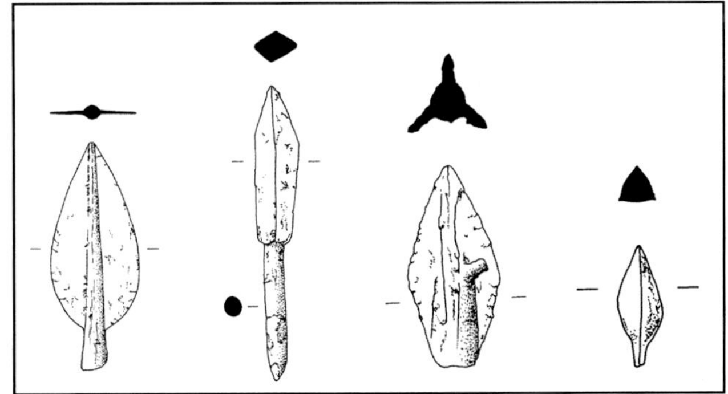

Figure 3 Bronze arrowhead types: leaf-shaped, rhombic, trefoil with socket and triangular. British Museum, EA 23921, 23917, 23927 and 23918 (drawing: Claire Thorne)

EA 23927   **1887,0101.879**
Corroded copper alloy arrowhead of trefoil cross section and large
rhombic profile, with an integral conical socket. The description in the
Museum register mentions traces of a wooden haft in the socket, but
nothing of this is now visible.
Length: 3.25cm (max.); width: 1.3cm.
Context: Saite enclosure (so-called 'Camp').
Parallels: same as for EA 23925 above.

GR 1935,0823.95
Corroded copper alloy arrowhead of trefoil cross section, rhombic
profile, with an integral conical socket.
Length: 3.3cm; width: 1.2cm.
Parallels: same as for EA 23925 above.

GR 1935,0823.107
Corroded copper alloy arrowhead of trefoil cross section and rhombic
profile, with an integral conical socket.
Length: 3.02cm; width: 1.04cm.
Parallels: same as for EA 23925 above.

GR 1935,0823.108
Corroded copper alloy arrowhead of trefoil cross section and rhombic
profile, with an integral conical socket.
Length: 2.58cm; width: 1.11cm.
Parallels: same as for EA 23925 above.

GR 1935,0823.94
Corroded copper alloy arrowhead of trefoil cross section and rhombic
profile, with a conical socket.
Length: 3.04cm; width: 1.02cm.
Parallels: same as for EA 23925 above.

GR 1935,0823.92
Corroded copper alloy arrowhead of trefoil cross section and narrow
rhombic profile, with a conical socket.
Length: 3.43cm; width: 0.9cm.

GR 1935,0823.104
Corroded copper alloy arrowhead of trefoil cross section and
asymmetric profile (one angular foil, the two others leaf-shaped), with
a conical socket.
Length: 2.14cm; width: 0.75cm.
Parallels: from Tell Dafana, see below GR 1935,0823.109,
1935,0823.98, 1935,0823.91 GR 1935,0823.102; Snodgrass 1964, 151–2,
fig. 10 (type 3B1).

GR 1935,0823.109
Corroded copper alloy arrowhead of trefoil cross section and
leaf-shaped profile, with a conical socket.
Length: 2.68cm; width: 0.92cm.
Parallels: same as for GR 1935,0823.104 above.

GR 1935,0823.98
Corroded copper alloy arrowhead of trefoil cross section, leaf-shaped
to rhombic profile, with a conical socket.
Length: 4.35cm; width: 1.13cm.
Parallels: same as for GR 1935,0823.104 above.

GR 1935,0823.91
Corroded copper alloy arrowhead of trefoil cross section and leaf
profile, with a conical socket.
Length: 3.68cm; width: 1.15cm.
Parallels: same as for GR 1935,0823.104 above.

GR 1935,0823.102
Corroded copper alloy arrowhead of trefoil cross section and narrow
leaf-shaped profile, with a conical socket.
Length: 4.44cm; width: 1.2cm.
Parallels: same as for GR 1935,0823.104 above.

EA 23926   **1887,0101.1449**
Corroded copper alloy arrowhead of trefoil cross section and narrow
rhombic profile, with a conical socket.

Length: 5.1cm; width: 0.9cm.
Context: Saite enclosure (so-called 'Camp').
Bibliography: Petrie 1888, 77 § 76, p. 78 § 77, pl. xxxix, 12; Snodgrass
1964, 151, n. 43, p. 152, fig. 10 (type 3B3 long); Petrie 1917a, pl. xli, R58;
Amborn 1976, 93, fig. 44, 12.
Parallels: from Tell Dafana, see below GR 1935,0823.97, 1935,0823.99,
1935,0823.100 and 1935,0823.101.

GR 1935,0823.97
Corroded copper alloy arrowhead of trefoil cross section, leaf shaped
to rhombic profile, with a conical socket.
Length: 3.78cm; width: 0.98cm.
Parallels: same as for EA 23926 above.

GR 1935,0823.99
Corroded copper alloy arrowhead of trefoil cross section and narrow
rhombic profile, with an integral conical socket.
Length: 4.73cm; width: 0.95cm.
Parallels: same as for EA 23926 above.

GR 1935,0823.100
Corroded copper alloy arrowhead of trefoil cross section and narrow
rhombic profile, with a conical socket.
Length: 6cm; width: 1.1cm.
Parallels: same as for EA 23926 above.

GR 1935,0823.101
Corroded copper alloy arrowhead of trefoil cross section and narrow
rhombic profile, with a conical socket.
Length: 4.31cm; width: 0.85cm.
Parallels: same as for EA 23926 above.

Trefoil and barbed (Pl. 25)

GR 1935,0823.103
Corroded copper alloy arrowhead of narrow trefoil cross section, with
a conical socket and barbed on one side.
Length: 4.33cm; width: 0.95cm.

Trefoil and tip with triangular section (Pl. 25)

GR 1935,0823.85
Corroded copper alloy arrowhead of trefoil cross section ending
triangular at the tip, with a conical socket.
Length: 2.95cm; width: 0.82cm.

GR 1935,0823.84
Corroded copper alloy arrowhead of trefoil cross section ending with a
triangular tip. The profile is almond-shaped, with an integral socket.
Length: 3.06cm; width: 0.88cm.

GR 1935,0823.88
Corroded copper alloy arrowhead of trefoil cross section ending
triangular at the tip, narrow almond profile, with an integral socket.
Length: 3.4cm; width: 1cm.
Parallels: close to Snodgrass 1964, 152–3, fig. 10, (type 3C3).

GR 1935,0823.93
Corroded copper alloy arrowhead of trefoil cross section ending
triangular at the tip, almond profile, with a conical socket.
Length: 3.2cm; width: 1.06cm.
Parallels: same as for GR 1935,0823.88 above.

GR 1935,0823.110
Corroded copper alloy arrowhead, with triangular top and trefoil
lower part around an integral conical socket.
Length: 1.81cm; width: 0.8cm.
Parallels: same as for GR 1935,0823.88 above.

Triangular section   (Pl. 25)

EA 23918   **1887,0101.1442**
Corroded copper alloy arrowhead of triangular cross section, almond
profile, with a short tang, also of triangular cross section.

Length: 1.37cm (max.); width: 0.49cm.
Context: Saite enclosure (so-called 'Camp').
Bibliography: Petrie 1888, 77 § 76, pl. xxxix, 15; id., 1917a, 34, pl. xli, R42.

GR 1935,0823.82

Corroded copper alloy long arrowhead of triangular cross section, with a conical socket.
Length: 3.2cm; width: 1.07cm.
Parallels: close to Snodgrass 1964, 152, fig. 10, p. 153 (type 3C1).

EA 23928   1887,0101.1450

Corroded copper alloy short arrowhead of triangular section, with a conical socket; a small round hole is visible on one side.
Length: 1.81cm; width: 1cm.
Context: Saite enclosure (so-called 'Camp').
Bibliography: Petrie 1888, 77 § 76, pl. xxxix, 8; id., 1917a, 34, pl. xli, R75; Amborn 1976, 94, fig. 44, 8.
Parallels: from Tell Dafana, see below GR 1935, 0823.86 and 1935, 0823.83, similar type; Snodgrass 1964, 15–3, fig. 10 (type 3C1); Petrie 1917a, 35, pl. xlii, R247; Amborn 1976, 94, n. 103.

GR 1935,0823.86

Corroded copper alloy arrowhead, of triangular cross section and trefoil at the base around an integral conical socket.
Length: 2.27cm; width: 0.99cm.
Parallels: same as for EA 23928 above.

GR 1935,0823.83

Corroded copper alloy arrowhead with triangular cross section at the top and trefoil at the base, around a conical socket.
Length: 2.16cm; width: 1cm.
Parallels: same as for EA 23928 above.

GR 1935,0823.87

Corroded copper alloy barbed arrowhead of triangular cross section, probably with a tang (missing).
Length: 2.66cm; width: 1.25cm; thickness: 1cm.

GR 1935,0823.89

Corroded copper alloy arrowhead of quadrifoil cross section with an integral socket.
Length: 2.4cm; width: 0.79cm.
Parallels: close to Snodgrass 1964, 154 (type 4).

Spearhead (Pl. 26)

EA 23943   1887,0101.1463

Iron leaf-shaped spearhead with a long, narrow blade, at the base of which is a hollow socket for the haft, formed by wrapping around a sheet of metal.
Length: 17.2cm (max.); width: 3.8cm.
Context: Saite enclosure (so-called 'Camp').
Bibliography: Petrie 1888, 77 § 77, p. 110, pl. xxxvii, 4: one of 'several lance-heads'; Amborn 1976, 79, 93, n. 98, fig. 32, 4.
Parallels: from Tell Dafana, Bolton 1886.28.22.i-j; Boston, MFA 87.523-524 (deaccessioned); London, PM UC59877 (?); Oxford, AM 1887.2502, 1887.2505.x (?); cf. Spencer 1993, 34, nos 50–4, pls 28, 31, 32.

Dagger (Pl. 26)

EA 23946   1887,0101.1466-1467

Two corroded sections from the haft and blade of an iron dagger (not joining). The blade has a narrow, tapering shape, with a rounded tip, slightly convex faces, and a longitudinal mid-rib on both sides close to the guard. The haft is made entirely of iron, with convex edges and a complex cross section creating a longitudinal groove on either side, filled by a series of five oval buttons. The guard is chevron shaped, the branches of the V splaying on the side of the blade. Symmetrically, the pommel has a semi-circular shape. The ends of the guard and pommel are broken and missing. Typologically, the particular shape of the handle would place the dagger in the range of the Scythian/Persian Iranian *Akinakes*-type short swords from the 5th–3rd century BC.
Haft piece (includes 4.6cm of the blade) length: 15.4cm (max.); width: 5.84cm; thickness: 2.5cm (max.).

Blade piece, length: 13.62cm (max.); width: 2.9cm; thickness: 1.35cm.
Context: 'Qasr', east annexe (C), chamber 19 A.
Bibliography: Petrie 1888, 77 § 77, p. 110, pl. xxxvii, 7: 'the sword (fig. 7) shows the guard well developed (though now much broken away), and an equal stay at the end of the handle to prevent its slipping out of the grasp. The blade has a rib on each side for some little way from the hilt. The handle is curiously shaped, with a groove on either side; partly to lighten it, and partly to hold the rivets by which a leather cover was probably fastened on, without a chance of their galling the hand; such a hollow also would help the grip'. Petrie (ibid.) also mentions 'a rather different sword-handle (...) kept in Bulak', 'with a knob or pommel at the end of the handle to balance the blade'. It should correspond to Cairo, EM JE 27377, unfortunately missing. 'Another form, more like an ordinary knife, is fig. 17; the thickness of the middle of blade (the section being rhombic) seems to show that this was for warfare, but, if so, a guard was probably fastened to the handle'. This item might be Cairo, EM JE 27376, also missing; see Journal, 135: 'but in some chambers out on the E. are quantities of broken Greek vases of 550–600 BC, along with jar stoppers stamped by Amasis (…). With these are pieces of iron scale armour (…). Beside that, parts of an iron sword handle, this form, with a wide curved guard, & a large ring at the end'; see also Amborn 1976, 78, 81–4, fig. 32, 7 (who suggests a date from the 5th and/or 4th century BC).
Parallels: from Tell Dafana, Cairo, EM JE 27326 (iron dagger, missing; see Petrie 1888, 77, § 77), JE 27377 (hilt of a sword, missing); Boston, MFA 87.521 (deaccessioned); Petrie, 1888, 77 § 77, pl. xxxvii, 17; Amborn, op. cit., 97, fig. 32, 17); a long sword in the Petrie Museum (UC34339) is also considered as coming from Tell Dafana, but the information remains dubious as it comes from a dealer who sold it to Petrie (Petrie 1917a, 27, pl. 51, E41; Amborn, op. cit., 84; see also a similar piece from Petrie's excavations at Memphis, Petrie 1919, 40, pl. xxxviii, 2; both must be of much later date); for comparison, see Amborn, op. cit., 78, 81–3, n. 57, figs 34–6; Mille 1997, 46–8, esp. 47, n. 79 (iron).

Armour plates and scales

Iron (Pl. 26)

EA 23982   1887,0101.1504

Fragment of corroded iron scale-armour made of thin square scales, each with two superposed lines of three stitching holes in the upper part, through which the scales were sewn together, probably on a textile or leather garment; each scale horizontally overlaps one-third of the next one, each row of scales overlaps two-thirds of the underlying one.
Length: 9.01cm (max.); width: 6.8cm (max.); thickness: 0.62cm.
Context: 'Qasr', east annexe (G), chamber 18.
Bibliography: Petrie 1888, 59 § 57, p. 78 § 77, pl. xxxvii, 19–19a; id., 1917a, pl. xliii, V131–132; Amborn 1976, 78, 84–5, 91, fig. 32, 19–19a. Also Journal, 132: 'also a great amount of broken Greek vases of 550–600 BC, & several pieces of iron scale armour with them'; ibid.,135: 'with these are pieces of iron scale armour [sketch] thin scales, & 8 deep all over, so that the outside looks thus [sketch] 4 laps vertically, & 2 horizontally on each scale'; ibid., 139: 'many more scraps of the iron scale armour have also turned up'; ibid., 143: 'many more pieces of scale armour have been found, & one in better state shows the [sketch] scales to be of this form, with six stitching holes in each. The pieces are much improved by a long soaking & brushing, & that will take the salt out'.
Parallels: many other fragments belonging to the same object were distributed to other collections: Bolton 1886.28.25; Boston, MFA RES.87.82, 87.83; Bristol, CMAG H1990 (4 fragments); Cairo, EM JE 27380 (2 fragments); Edinburgh, NMS A1887.91 (destroyed during WWII); Glasgow 1895.1.m.a (2 fragments); Liverpool, WM 3.2.87.5 (2 fragments according to the EEF distribution list, one missing); London, PM UC 59870 (4 fragments); Oxford, AM 1952.198, 1887.2504; Sheffield J87.4 (2 fragments); Toronto, ROM 885.6.111. According to the EEF distribution list, fragments were also sent to Cambridge, London Harrow School, Montreal and to the collection of the Chautauqua Archaeological Museum, now dispersed, while some iron 'mail armour' went to Birmingham and St Helens. Similar fragments of scale armour were later found in Memphis (Petrie 1909c, 11, 13, pl. xvi, 5; Petrie 1917a, 38, pl. xlii, V127–128; London, PM,

UC63413-63414); for comparison see Amborn 1976, 84–91, esp. 82–6, n. 82, figs 39–41.

EA 23983   1887,0101.1505
Fragment of corroded iron scale-armour made of thin square scales, each with two superposed lines of three stitching holes in the upper part, through which the scales were sewn together, probably on a textile or leather garment; each scale horizontally overlaps one-third of the next one, each row of scales overlaps two-thirds of the underlying one.
Length: 7.9cm (max.); width: 5.57cm (max.); thickness: 0.56cm.
Context: 'Qasr', east annexe (G), chamber 18.
Bibliography: Petrie 1888, 59 § 57, p. 78 § 77, p. 110, pl. xxxvii, 19; Petrie 1917a, pl. xliii, V131; Amborn 1976, 78, fig. 32, 19.
Parallels: see EA 23982 above and EA 23984–5 below.

EA 23984   1887,0101.1506
Fragment of corroded iron scale-armour made of thin square scales, each with two superposed lines of three stitching holes in the upper part, through which the scales were sewn together, probably on a textile or leather garment; each scale horizontally overlaps one-third of the next one, each row of scales overlaps two-thirds of the underlying one.
Length: 6.45cm (max.); width: 5.06cm (max.); thickness: 0.78cm.
Context: 'Qasr', east annexe (G), chamber 18.
Bibliography: Petrie 1888, 59 § 57, p. 78 § 77.
Parallels: see EA 23982–3 above and EA 23985 below.

EA 23985   1887,0101.1507
Fragment of corroded iron scale-armour made of thin square scales, each with two superposed lines of three stitching holes in the upper part, through which the scales were sewn together, probably on a textile or leather garment; each scale horizontally overlaps one-third of the next one, each row of scales overlaps two-thirds of the underlying one.
Length: 7.6cm (max.); width: 0.74cm (max.); thickness: 0.67cm.
Context: 'Qasr', east annexe (G), chamber 18.
Bibliography: Petrie 1888, 59 § 57, p. 78 § 77, pl. xxxvii, 19a; Petrie 1917a, pl. xliii, V132; Amborn 1976, 78, fig. 32, 19a.
Parallels: see EA 23982–5 above.

Bronze (Pl. 26)

EA 23913   1887,0101.1437
Heavily corroded copper alloy rectangular plate, slightly convex, possibly from armour, with a longitudinal double mid-ridge on top, made of two angle plates welded side to side. Five small round fixing holes were perforated along the edge of both short sides.
Length: 5.67cm; width: 1.92cm; thickness: 0.5cm.
Context: Saite enclosure (so-called 'Camp').
Parallels: see Petrie 1909c, 11 § 31, p. 13 § 38, pl. xvi, 24–32; id., 1917a, 38, pl. xlii, V115–7; London, PM UC63401, 63420 (bronze), 63402–3, 63421–2 (iron).

EA 23901   1887,0101.927
Heavily corroded copper alloy fragment of a rectangular plate, pierced by a round hole near the middle, and gently bent on one side. The edge on this side, where the plate seems to have been welded to another element, is irregularly broken.
Length: 3.35cm; width: 2.99cm; thickness: 0.52cm.
Bibiography: Journal, 144: 'the next of the days buyings are a good average, (…) iron knife, 2 chisels,(…)'.

10. Metal tools

Knives (Pl. 26)

Bronze

EA 23912   1887,0101.1436
Heavily corroded copper alloy knife, slightly curved, in the shape of a modern table knife with a long, thin, round-ended blade and a short thickened and also round-ended tang or handle. The item is also somewhat bent and curved on one side. The cutting edge has not been sharpened.
Length: 21.2cm; width: 1.56cm; thickness: 0.65cm.
Context: 'Qasr', east annexe (C), chamber 3.
Bibliography: Petrie 1888, 77 § 76, pl. xxxix, 21: 'the knives found (xxxix, 19, 21) are a puzzle, as they do not seem to have any sort of edge; perhaps they were manufactured here, and not yet sharpened for use; fig. 21, however, is from chamber 3'; Petrie 1917a, 24, pl. xxv, K86.

Iron

EA 23942   1887,0101.1462
Corroded iron knife of large size, with a wide leaf-shaped blade and a narrow tang with rectangular cross section, ending with a flattened circular or semi-circular pommel. Traces of the wooden haft are visible on the rusted surface of the tang and on the base of the blade. The head of the haft was rounded and partly covered the base of the blade on both sides, where three non-aligned rivets fastened the wood to the metal. Two other rivets fixed the wood of the handle to the tang, one of which still protrudes from one side. The haft must have been splayed out close to the blade.
Length: 36cm; width: 7.35cm (max.); thickness: 1.92cm (of the handle, including the rivet), 1.31cm (excluding the rivet).
Context: 'Qasr', east annexe (C), chamber 19 A.
Bibliography: Petrie 1888, 56 § 55, p. 110, pl. xxxviii, 6; ibid., 78 § 78: 'the large double-edged knife (fig. 6) is a splendid specimen in perfect condition, found in chamber 19A; the grain of the wood on the handle is very plain, both the cross-piece on the haft of the blade fastened with 3 rivets, and the handle itself fastened by 2 rivets'; see Journal, 152: 'a large iron knife'; found with 3 pokers, one of which is EA 23944 below; Petrie 1917a, 27, pl. xxx, U31; Amborn 1976, 78, 97, fig. 33, 6.
Parallels: Petrie 1917a, 27, pl. xix, K254; Amborn 1976, 97–8, n. 117, fig. 49.

EA 23947   1887,0101.1468-1469
Two sections of a corroded iron knife (not joined), comprising a large cracked blade, flat with a rounded end and a full tang widening near the blade, with a line of five rivets for attachment of the wooden elements of the handle. The grain of the vanished wood is preserved by many traces in the corrosion.
Length: 31.90; width: 3.45cm; thickness: 0.9cm.
Context: 'Qasr', east annexe (C), chamber 19 A.
Bibliography: Petrie 1888, 77 § 77, p. 110, pl. xxxvii, 20: 'the knife (fig. 20) may be perhaps for civil uses; the handle shows well the grain of the wood, which was fastened on by five rivets of iron'; Petrie 1917a, 27, pl. xxx, U32; Amborn 1976, 78, 97, fig. 32, 20.

EA 23949   1887,0101.1471
Corroded iron plaque of curved shape, possibly the blade of a knife, razor or small sickle, with a concave cutting edge and convex back, no haft preserved.
Length: 14.2cm (max.); width: 3cm; thickness: 0.8cm.
Context: 'Qasr', east annexe (G), chamber 18.
Bibliography: Petrie 1888, 59 § 57, p. 78 § 78, p. 110, pl. xxxviii, 8: 'knife or razor without a handle' 'found in Chamber 18'; Amborn 1976, 79, 101, fig. 33, 8.

EA 23948   1887,0101.1470
Fragment of a corroded iron knife-blade, with a narrow tang in line with the back.
Length: 8.1cm (max.); width: 2.12cm; thickness: 0.68cm.
Context: 'Qasr', east annexe (G), chamber 18.
Bibliography: Petrie 1888, 59 § 57, p. 78 § 78, p. 110, pl. xxxviii, 23: possibly the 'small knife found in Chamber 18'; Petrie 1917a, 24, pl. xxv, K88; Amborn 1976, 79, 101, fig. 33, 23. Another one 'found in the camp' might be GR 1888,0208.145b (below); see also Boston, MFA, 87.512.

GR 1888,0208.145b
Central fragment of an iron blade, probably from a knife with a short tang to be inserted into the handle
Length: 4.5cm (max.); width: 1.92cm; thickness: 0.5cm.
Context: Saite enclosure (so-called 'Camp')?
Bibliography: Petrie 1888, 78 § 78: 'a small knife was found in chamber

18, and another in the camp'. The first one is EA 23948 above, the other one, of similar shape, might be GR 1888,0208.145b or possibly Boston, MFA, 87.512.

EA 23980   1887,0101.1502
Two corroded fragments, not joined, from an iron object, or possibly from two separate objects. The first item consists of a curved sheet of metal in the shape of a kind of carving gouge, larger on the side of the cutting edge and narrower at the other end (the tang?), which is broken. The second item is made of a flat piece of metal, rounded at its narrower end and broken at the other, the larger end surrounded by an oval ferrule made of a large strip of metal. The two parts are stuck together by corrosion mixed with what might be organic material, perhaps wood. This item might be interpreted as the central part of a tool or knife with a handle fixed by a ferrule.
First piece: length: 4.15cm; width: 3.22cm; thickness: 2.7cm.
Second piece: length: 4.46cm; width: 1.6cm; thickness: 1cm.
Context: probably from the Saite enclosure (so-called 'Camp').
Bibliography: Petrie 1888, 79 § 78 mentions only 'a large quantity of iron scraps, apparently a workman's scrap heap was found in the camp'.

Chisels and adzes

Iron chisels (Pl. 26)

EA 23954   1887,0101.1476
Corroded pointed chisel of iron with a tapering and pointed head of circular cross section, and a thicker flat-tipped haft of quadrangular cross section.
Length: 21.1cm; width: 3.45cm; thickness: 2.7cm.
Bibliography: Petrie 1888, 78 § 78, p. 110, pl. xxxviii, 2: 'large long metal chisel (...) with a square shank and pointed end'; Amborn 1976, 79, 99, fig. 33, 2.

EA 23955   1887,0101.1477
Corroded iron chisel, of circular cross section, with a slightly flattened cutting edge at one side end and a tapering, flat-tipped tang at the other. Heavily corroded.
Length: 11.2cm; width: 1.88cm; thickness: 1.7cm.
Context: 'Qasr', east annexe (C), chamber 19.
Bibliography: Petrie 1888, 78 § 78, p. 110, pl. xxxviii, 18; Amborn 1976, 79, 98, fig. 33, 18.

EA 23956   1887,0101.1478
Corroded iron wedge or short chisel, with a rectangular cross section and convex sides tapering to a cutting edge at one end. There is a rounded head at the other end.
Length: 11.2cm; width: 4.2cm; thickness: 3.5cm.
Context: 'Qasr', east annexe (C), chamber 19.
Bibliography: Petrie 1888, 78 § 78, p. 110, pl. xxxviii, 17: 'of civil iron work the most common objects are chisels, of which about forty were kept, beside many rejected'; Amborn 1976, 79, 98, fig. 33, 17.
Parallels: from Tell Dafana, EA 23957–62 (below), Boston, MFA 87.507-508 (deaccessioned), PM UC59877 (2 pieces).

EA 23957   1887,0101.1479
Corroded iron wedge or short chisel, with a rectangular cross section and convex sides tapering to a cutting edge at one end. There is a rounded head at the other end.
Length: 7.7cm; width: 3.43cm; thickness: 2.7cm.
Context: 'Qasr', east annexe (C), chamber 19.
Bibliography: Petrie 1888, 78 § 78, p. 110, pl. xxxviii, 19; Amborn 1976, 79, 98, fig. 33, 19.
Parallels: same as for EA 23956 above.

EA 23958   1887,0101.1480
Corroded iron wedge or short chisel, with a rectangular cross section and convex sides tapering to a cutting edge at one end. There is a rounded head at the other end.
Length: 5.45cm; width: 2.14cm; thickness: 1.99cm.
Bibliography: Petrie 1888, 78 § 78, p. 110, pl. xxxviii, 16; Amborn 1976, 79, 98, fig. 33, 16.
Parallels: same as for EA 23956 above.

EA 23959   1887,0101.1481
Corroded iron wedge or short chisel, with a rectangular cross section and convex sides tapering to the tip, with a flattened head at the opposite end.
Length: 4.94cm (max.); width: 1.66cm; thickness: 1.32cm.
Bibliography: Petrie 1888, 78 § 78, p. 110, pl. xxxviii, 15; Amborn 1976, 79, 98, fig. 33, 15.
Parallels: same as for EA 23956 above.

EA 23960   1887,0101.1482
Corroded iron small, thin chisel or wedge, with a rectangular cross section and slightly convex sides tapering to a cutting edge at one end. There is a flattened head at the opposite end.
Length: 6.15cm; width: 1.17cm; thickness: 0.88cm.
Bibliography: Petrie 1888, 78 § 78, p. 110, pl. xxxviii, 20; Amborn 1976, 79, 98, fig. 33, 20.
Parallels: same as for EA 23956 above.

EA 23961   1887,0101.1483
Corroded iron thin chisel or wedge, with a rectangular cross section and slightly convex sides that taper towards either end, although only one end has a cutting edge.
Length: 10.6cm; width: 1.53cm; thickness: 1.18cm.
Bibliography: Petrie 1888, 78 § 78.
Parallels: same as for EA 23956 above.

EA 23962   1887,0101.1484
Small corroded iron chisel or wedge, with a rectangular cross section and slightly convex large sides tapering to a cutting edge at one end; the other end is barely larger and has a small central boss.
Length: 8.13cm; width: 2.05cm; thickness: 1.26cm.
Bibliography: Petrie 1888, 78 § 78.
Parallels: same as for EA 23956 above.

Bronze chisels (Pl. 26)

EA 23914   1887,0101.1438
Heavily corroded copper alloy chisel, thick in the middle and narrowing to the cutting edge, with a thick tang of circular cross section at the other end. The metal has been split by corrosion.
Length: 11.4cm; width: 2.2cm; thickness: 1.7cm.
Context: Saite enclosure (so-called 'Camp').
Bibliography: Petrie 1888, 77 § 76, pl. xxxix, 28: one of the bronze 'chisels' of 'various shapes'.

EA 23907   1887,0101.1431
Corroded copper alloy blade of quadrangular, long and flat shape, with a narrow straight head at one end, but larger, thicker and bevelled on both sides at the other end to form a cutting edge, now broken and irregular; possibly a chisel or an axe blade.
Length: 11.32cm; width: 3.02cm; thickness: 1.08cm.
Context: 'Qasr', east annexe (C), chamber 19 A.
Bibliography: Petrie 1888, 77 § 76, pl. xxxix, 25: bronze chisel 'found in chamber 19A', with a 'duplicate...kept at Bulak'; Petrie 1917a, 16, pl. xv, Z6.
Parallels: 'Bulak' duplicate is Cairo, EM JE 27368.

EA 23909   1887,0101.1433
Corroded fragment of a copper alloy bar of narrow, rectangular cross section, with one end flattened and flared into a triangular cutting edge. Possibly from the end of a small chisel.
Length: 2.87cm; width: 0.89cm; thickness: 0.28cm.
Context: Saite enclosure (so-called 'Camp').
Bibliography: Petrie 1888, 77 § 76, pl. xxxix, 26.

EA 23910   1887,0101.1434
Corroded copper alloy blade of a chisel made of a thin plate of metal of narrow parabolic shape at one end and with a slightly convex cutting edge at the other.
Length: 6.92cm (max.); width: 2.36cm; thickness: 0.39cm.
Context: Saite enclosure (so-called 'Camp').
Bibliography: Petrie 1888, 77 § 76, pl. xxxix, 24; id., 1917a, 17, pl. xv, Z57.

EA 23900   **1887,0101.880**
Fragment of a corroded copper alloy flat blade with a long tang of
circular cross section. Repaired from three fragments.
Length: 5cm; width: 1.13cm; thickness: 0.19cm.
Context: according to the Museum register, the item, considered as a
blade or a chisel, comes from Tell Dafana but is strangely described as
a possible Ptolemaic foundation deposit.

EA 23908   **1887,0101.1432**
Corroded copper alloy wedge or short chisel, with a flattened and
rounded cutting edge, and a round top irregularly flared by
hammering.
Length: 3.57cm; width: 1.39cm; thickness: 1.68cm.
Context: Saite enclosure (so-called 'Camp').
Bibliography: Petrie 1888, 77 § 76, pl. xxxix, 27: one of the bronze
'chisels' of 'various shapes'; id., 1917a, 41, pl. xlvii, B15.

Adze (Pl. 26)

EA 23951   **1887,0101.1473**
Heavily corroded iron adze-head or pitching chisel with a thick blade
of rectangular cross section, with slightly convex lateral edges, and a
thick axial tang of square cross section. The latter was clearly fastened
in a mortise at one end of a perpendicular wooden haft. The cutting
edge and part of one side are broken and missing.
Length: 16.9cm (max.); width: 7.48cm; thickness: 4.23cm.
Bibliography: Petrie 1888, 78 § 78, p. 110, pl. xxxviii, 24: 'axe (fig. 24)
(...) of a different type to that of Naukratis, which had a socket'; Petrie
1917a, 9, pl. ii, A98; Amborn 1976, 79, 99, fig. 33, 24.

EA 23952   **1887,0101.1474**
Corroded iron small adze-head or chisel blade used for carpentry,
with a rectangular blade of rectangular cross section and a narrow
tang of square cross section, which was clearly fastened in a mortise at
one end of a wooden haft.
Length: 6.27cm; width: 3.65cm; thickness: 1.6cm.
Bibliography: Petrie 1888, 78 § 78, p. 110, pl. xxxviii, 22: 'broad form of
wooden chisel [...] shown on fig. 22'; Petrie 1917a, 9, pl. ii, A99;
Amborn 1976, 79, 99, fig. 33, 22.

Miscellaneous tools

Iron poker (Pl. 26)

EA 23944   **1887,0101.1464**
Heavily corroded iron artefact in the shape of a poker, although the
function may have been different, made of a flat, narrow, straight bar,
widening and then tapering again at one end like a spatula, and bent at
the other to form a kind of flattened loop-pommel.
Length: 23.2cm; width: 2.08cm; thickness: 1.06cm.
Context: 'Qasr', east annexe (C), chamber 19 A.
Bibliography: Petrie 1888, 56 § 55, p. 78 § 78, p. 110, pl. xxxviii, 12: one
of the three 'pokers of the type of that from Naukratis', Petrie 1917a, 57,
pl. lxxii, W119; also Journal, 152: one of 'three small pokers of the flat
or hand types, such as from Naukratis, & Etruria'; Amborn 1976, 79,
100, fig. 33, 12; found in Chamber 19A with the knife EA 23942 (above);
the other pokers might be Boston, MFA, 87.520 (deaccessioned) and
Oxford, AM 1887.2505.x (?), see Petrie 1888, pl. xxxviii, 11.
Parallels: Amborn 1976, 100, n. 128.

Forks and tridents (Pl. 27)

EA 23950   **1887,0101.1472**
Part of the end of a corroded iron tool in the shape of a bident with a
hollow haft of circular section and two curved tapering prongs (one
broken away). Perhaps from a small fork or spear-butt.
Length: 8.9cm (max.); width: 4.94cm; thickness: 1.56cm.
Context: Saite enclosure (so-called 'Camp')?
Bibliography: Petrie 1888, 79 § 78, p. 110, pl. xxxviii, 5: 'trident [*sic*], fig.
5, may be intended either for fishing or for a spear-butt'; Petrie 1917a,
55, pl. lxvii, G48; Amborn 1976, 78, 97, fig. 33, 5.

EA 23945   **1887,0101.1465**
Fragment of a heavily corroded iron tool in the shape of a trident

spearhead with a wrapped socket, one lateral prong missing. Traces of
two symmetric barbs, broken and missing, are visible on each side of
the central prong between the lateral branches and the socket.
Length: 16.5cm; width: 4.92cm (max.); thickness: 1.9cm (socket); 1.4cm
(prong).
Context: 'Qasr', east annexe (C), chamber 19 A.
Bibliography: Petrie 1888, 77 § 77, p. 110, pl. xxxvii, 3: 'The bident [*sic*]
(fig. 3) may be perhaps for fishing, or it may be the butt of a spear like
the bronze tridents of Nebesheh'. Petrie 1917a, 57, pl. lxxii, W54;
Amborn 1976, 87, 97, fig. 32, 3; Makkay 1989, 76, n. 445, fig. 16.2.
Parallels: on iron (and bronze) forks of the same type, see Amborn
1976, 97, n. 116; Makkay 1989, 68–94, esp. 74–7, n. 418, 433, 444, 447,
452, fig. 15.1, 16.1, 16.7, 20.6–8.

Mattock (Pl. 27)

EA 23953   **1887,0101.1475**
Corroded iron mattock-head, with a central cylindrical socket for the
haft, a curved hatchet-blade on one side and a hammerhead on the
opposite, made of a curved cylindrical flat-tipped rod.
Length: 20.8cm; width: 4.37cm; thickness: 3.3cm.
Bibliography: Petrie 1888, 78 § 78, p. 110, pl. xxxviii, 1: one of 'two
pick-axes [...] of a form new to us (fig. 1), none like those found at
Naukratis'; Petrie 1917a, 15, pl. xix, T69; Amborn 1976, 79, 100, fig. 33, 1.
Parallels: Amborn 1976, 100–1, n. 130, fig. 50.

Auger or reamer (Pl. 27)

EA 23963   **1887,0101.1485**
Corroded iron part of a tool made of a long straight rod of circular-
cross section, broken at one end, slightly thickening towards the other,
terminated by a T-shaped head, also of circular cross section, with
narrowing and rounded ends (one end missing). The function of the
item remains unclear. It might be part of a reamer or auger.
Length: 25.4cm; width: 5.7cm; thickness: 2.13cm.
Context: Saite enclosure (so-called 'Camp')?
Bibliography: Petrie 1888, 78 § 78, p. 110, pl. xxxviii, 4: 'large auger or
rymer [*sic*], apparently with a cross-head handle [...] shown in fig. 4'. In
Petrie's drawing the item appears more complete than it is now; see
also Petrie 1917a, 39, pl. xliii, M28; Amborn 1976, 79, 101, fig. 33, 4.
Parallels: Amborn 1976, 101, nn. 131–3.

Plough-shares or hoes (Pl. 27)

EA 23964   **1887,0101.1486**
Corroded iron plough-share or hoe-head, with a flat, ogival pointed
blade and an oval wrap-around socket at the top, whose width,
opposite the blade, decreases from the sides to the centre. About half of
the socket is missing on one side.
Length: 14.12cm; width: 6.83cm; depth: 5.57cm.
Context: Saite enclosure (so-called 'Camp')?
Bibliography: Petrie 1888, 78 § 78, p. 110, pl. xxxviii, 21: 'socketed
plough-share of rough form'; Petrie 1917a, 55, pl. lxvii, G37; Amborn
1976, 79, 100, fig. 33, 21.
Parallels: Amborn 1976, 100, n. 129.

EA 23989   **1887,0101.1332**   **Not illustrated**
Approximately 40 pieces of corroded iron, of which several are joined
fragments of what might be the circular socket and part of the blade of
a tool such as a hoe or ploughshare.
Length: 6.8cm; diameter 8.4cm (socket); 9.4cm, 7cm (blade).
Context: Saite enclosure (so-called 'Camp').
Bibliography: possibly among the iron scraps mentioned in Petrie
1888, 79 § 78. The Museum register wrongly records fragments of iron
slag.
Parallels: same as for EA 23964 above.

Rasp (Pl. 27)

EA 23974   **1887,0101.1496**
Corroded iron artefact in the shape of a conical rasp, grater or borer.
Made of a piece of thin sheet of metal punched all over with small round
holes and coiled round into a cone; originally fitted on a wooden handle.
Length: 3.07cm; diameter: 1.12cm.

Context: 'Qasr', east annexe (C), chamber 17 (according to the Museum register).
Bibliography: Petrie 1888, 78 § 78, p. 110, pl. xxxviii, 9: one of some 'very curious rasps or borers', 'made of a piece of thin sheet-iron, punched all over with holes like a modern grater, and coiled round into a cone; they have been found with string at the base, and fitted on to wooden handles, making a sort of rat-tail file or rasp; five were found, three of them in chamber 17'. The Museum register also describes it as a possible strainer.
Parallels: from Tell Dafana, EA 23973 below, Boston, MFA 87.519; Oxford, AM 1887.2503; for comparison see also Bissing 1901, 54, no. 3538, pp. 58–9, no. 3548 (bronze, Late Period); see also Amborn 1976, 99, n. 126; similar items in bronze, Petrie 1917a, 38, pl. xliv, 134–5.

EA 23973   1887,0101.1495
Rasp or grater. Recorded in the Museum register, the item remains unlocated. The size indicated seems to match with the object represented on pl. xxxviii, 10 of Petrie's publication.
Length: 6.03cm.
Context: 'Qasr', east annexe (C), chamber 17 (according to the Museum register).
Bibliography: Petrie 1888, 78 § 78, pl. xxxviii, 10: one of the three iron 'rasps or borers' found in chamber 17; Amborn 1976, 79, 99, fig. 33, 10.
Parallels: same as for EA 23974 above.

Hooks (Pl. 27)

EA 23977   1887,0101.1499
Corroded iron item in the shape of a thick hook with a narrow gap and a curved tapering point, certainly for suspension and not for fishing. The attachment loop or eye at the other end seems to be broken with part missing.
Length: 3.69cm; width: 2.4cm; thickness: 1.14cm.
Context: Saite enclosure (so-called 'Camp')?
Bibliography: Petrie 1888, 79 § 78: 'a large quantity of iron scraps, apparently a workman's scrap heap was found in the camp, including.......a hook'.
Parallels: from Tell Dafana, EA 23978 and 23979 below, Boston, MFA 87.505-506.

EA 23978   1887,0101.1500
Central part of a corroded iron hook of rectangular cross section, with a straight shank; point and eye are broken and missing.
Length: 3.1cm; width: 1.96cm; thickness: 0.45cm.
Context: Saite enclosure (so-called 'Camp')?
Bibliography: Petrie 1888, 79 § 78, p. 110, pl. xxxviii, 14 (with both ends subsequently lost): part of one of the fish-hooks 'exactly like those of Naukratis'; Petrie 1917a, 37, pl. xliii, V95; Amborn 1976, 79, 101, fig. 33, 14.
Parallels: same as for EA 23977 above.

EA 23979   1887,0101.1501   **Not illustrated**
Iron fish-hook; recorded in the Museum register, the item remains unlocated; the sketch seems to show a suspension eye at the top and a lower part bent to form a loop.
Length: 4.45cm (1 ¾ ins).
Context: Saite enclosure (so-called 'Camp')?
Bibliography: Petrie 1888, 79 § 78.
Parallels: same as for EA 23977 above.

Indeterminate items

Iron (Pl. 27)

EA 23981   1887,0101.1503
Semi-circular fragment of a corroded iron artefact made of a thick plaque of metal, almost flat, just slightly convex. On the convex side, the edge is somewhat bevelled and other items are stuck either by corrosion or welded onto the surface: a long narrow and flat bar of metal crossing the object along the broken edge, and another, shorter and thinner, from the centre of the item to the curved edge, pointed and bent at the outer end. Other small fragments of iron are stuck here and there on the surface. The function of the item is undetermined; Petrie's identification as part of a bridle-bit (as a 'cheek-piece of horse's bit' in the Museum register) remains questionable.

Length: 15.8cm (max.); width: 10.5cm; thickness: 1.95cm (with rivet at end); 1.3cm (centre).
Context: Saite enclosure (so-called 'Camp').
Bibliography: Petrie 1888, 79 § 78: 'side piece of horse's bit', part of the 'large quantity of iron scraps, apparently of workman's scrap heap (...) found in the camp'.
Parallels: if it is part of a bridle-bit, see below p. 78.

EA 23986   1887,0101.1508
Fragment of a heavily corroded iron artefact, possibly part of a key with two parallel wards and the beginning of a curved shank. Corrosion makes the item hardly identifiable; the interpretation as part of a key comes from the Museum register ('wards of a key?'). The Ptolemaic dating proposed in the register would suggest a provenance from the north-west Ptolemaic mound, though this dating remains uncertain.
Length: 3.71cm; width: 2.97cm; thickness: 1.95cm.
Context: north-west Ptolemaic mound?

Bronze (Pl. 27)

GR 1888,0208.145a
Thin and long copper alloy rod of circular cross section, heavily corroded and broken into five fragments, maybe a kohl-stick or the stem of a dipper.
Length: 13.4cm; diameter: 0.55cm.
Context: Possibly 'Qasr', east annexe (C), chamber 19.
Bibliography: Petrie 1888, 77 § 76: possibly the 'double-ended kohl-stick' found in Chamber 18.

EA 23911   1887,0101.1435
Heavily corroded fragment of a copper alloy implement in the shape of a flat and slightly curved prong, splayed on each side of a round hole at the broken end. In spite of the shape, the item seems too thick to be the blade of a knife.
Length: 9.11cm; width: 1.1cm; thickness: 0.67cm.
Context: Saite enclosure (so-called 'Camp').

EA 23987   1887,0101.1509
Corroded fragment of a copper alloy unidentified flat artefact bent at one end, possibly a fragment of the wall and base of a cylindrical vessel. Considered as a possible 'clamp (?)' in the Museum register.
Length: 6.35cm; width: 1.35cm; thickness: 2.3cm.
Context: Saite enclosure (so-called 'Camp').

11. Stone tools (Pl. 27)

EA 23834   1887,0101.695
Pebble of red stone with worn surfaces; one end chipped, the opposite showing traces of use as a marker, like a red chalk.
Length: 3.6cm; width: 3cm; thickness: 1.3cm.

EA 18450   1887,0101.707
A burnisher of oval section, ground from brown flint. The surfaces are entirely smooth and the object is pointed at one end, but partly rounded at the other.
Length: 5.8cm; width: 1.3cm; thickness: 1.09cm.
Context: provenance not specified in the Museum register, but possibly from Tell Dafana, as suggested by the context of the item in the list.
Bibliography: Petrie 1888, 74 § 71 (?): possibly the flint 'burnisher 2¼ inches long'.

EA 23824   1887,0101.759
Quartzite cone-shaped artefact, possibly a kind of hammer, if not a weight, with a rounded edge at the base and a tapering top, partly broken away and missing. The surface of the base is rounded and polished, with a shallow roundish depression hollowed in its centre perhaps the result of use as a hammer.
Height: 3.53cm; diameter: 6.05cm.

EA 23823   1887,0101.767
Grey granite cone-shaped pestle, with rounded ends. The wider end has been chipped, perhaps through use.
Length: 25cm; diameter: from 4cm (min.) to 7.5cm (max.).
Context: Saite enclosure (so-called 'Camp').

Bibliography: Petrie 1888, 74 § 70: possibly one of two 'basalt mullers for grinding' 'found in the camp'.

EA 23642   1887,0101.1388

A long thin flake implement of brown flint, the edges retouched to form a scraper.
Length: 6.3cm; width: 1.4cm; thickness: 0.4cm.
Context: from the desert surface around the 'Qasr'; marked in ink 'D'.
Bibliography: Petrie 1888, 74 § 70: one of three flint 'struck flakes'.
Parallels: the two other flints must be EA 23643 (below) and Boston, MFA RES.87.111 (deaccessioned).

EA 23643   1887,0101.1389

A rectangular fragment from a double-sided thin flake implement of pale brown flint. The edges have been retouched to form a scraper. One angle is broken away.
Length: 3.4cm; width: 1.7cm; thickness: 0.4cm.
Context: from the desert surface around the 'Qasr'. Marked in ink 'D'.
Bibliography: Petrie 1888, 74 § 70.
Parallels: same as for EA 23642 above.

EA 18543   1887,0101.672

Long, thin sandstone whetstone (?) of square cross section. One end is flat, the other one tapered to a point; all edges are slightly blunt.
Length: 6.7cm; width: 1cm; thickness: 0.85cm.
Context: western part of Findspot 52 in the south-eastern quarter of the Saite enclosure (so-called 'Camp'), according to the mark '52W' pencilled on the object, although the provenance is not specified in the Museum register.
Bibliography: Petrie 1888, 74 § 70.
Parallels: from Tell Dafana, see below EA 23822, 18542; Bolton 1886.28.28; Boston, MFA RES.87.126; Bristol, CMAG H1986; Oxford, AM 1887.2528; one piece was also sent to the collection of the Chautaqua Museum, now dispersed.

EA 23822   1887,0101.670

Small part of a sandstone whetstone (?) of square cross section, one intact end, the other broken; short illegible texts of two or three signs only are carved on two opposite sides. Comparison with similar objects suggests that the missing part was longer and tapered.
Length: 4.19cm (max.); width: 1.31cm; thickness: 1.28cm.
Context: Saite enclosure (so-called 'Camp').
Bibliography: Petrie 1888, 74 § 70, pl. xl, 1.
Parallels: same as for EA 18543 above.

EA 18542   1887,0101.671

Part of a long thin sandstone whetstone (?) with square cross section and slightly convex sides. Comparison with similar objects suggests that the missing part was tapered off.
Length: 8.12cm; width: 1.03cm.
Context: Saite enclosure (so-called 'Camp').
Bibliography: Petrie 1888, 74 § 70.
Parallels: same as for EA 18543 above.

EA 23821   1887,0101.742

Rectangular sandstone whetstone (?) gently rounded at one end, broken at the other; the upper surface is smoothly carved or worn. It is slightly concave lengthways and convex across; the underside is flat and partly chipped, with retouched edges.
Length: 22cm (max.); width: 6.4cm; thickness: 3.35cm.
Context: 'Qasr', east annexe (C), chamber 19 A (number scratched on the underside).
Bibliography: Petrie 1888, 74 § 70: 'larger and coarser whetstone, 9 inches x 2,5 inches, of a sharp grit, fine grain sandstone, worn rounded by sharpening knives on it', 'found in chamber 19'.
Parallels: a similar piece was found in Chamber 17 (Petrie 1888, 74 § 70) but is not identified yet; see also from other sites, London, PM UC72516, 72530-72536.

EA 23829   1887,0101.742

Piece of a calcareous whetstone (?). Recorded in the Museum register, the item remains unlocated.
Height: 25.4cm.
Context: 'Qasr', east annexe (C), chamber 10.

GR 1911,0210.1

Fragment of a limestone cake stamp, decorated with a floral pattern and rosettes. Petrie mentions only a single piece, while the BM register records 'three stone fragment[s] of mould for cakes'. The object has not been located and is not illustrated.
Length: 8.9cm; width: 7.6cm; thickness: 6.7cm (according to the Museum register).
Context: 'Qasr', east annexe (C), Chamber 27.
Bibliography: Petrie 1888, 73 § 70, pl. xl, 14–14a: 'of limestone also is the piece of cake stamp (pl. xl. 14, 14A, the reverse side) found in chamber 27. This is clearly Greek, and therefore between the middle of the 6th century, yet the style of it is what otherwise would be attributed to a later period'.

12. Equipment and fittings

Iron bridle-bits (Pl. 27)

EA 23965   1887,0101.1487

Corroded iron part of an implement, possibly a horse's snaffle-bit, made of three imbricate pieces; two fragments would correspond to the central part of the mouthpiece, made of two thin cylindrical bars ('cannons') jointed by loops interlocked and swivelling together, and possibly one shank made of a cylindrical bar with a central thickening around a socket threaded and sliding on one of the cannons. Ends of the cannons and shank are broken away. Considered as a possible bit in the Museum register, as fragment of a horse-bit, 'riveted through cheek-pieces', in Petrie, 1888, 77 § 77, p. 110.
Length: 11cm (max.); width: 3.03cm; thickness: 2.29cm.
Context: Saite enclosure (so-called 'Camp').
Bibliography: Petrie 1888, 77 § 77, p. 110, pl. xxxvii, 5; id., 1917a, 56, pl. lxx, W9; Amborn 1976, 78, 96, fig. 32, 5.
Parallels: Amborn 1976, 78, 95–6, n. 114, fig. 48.

EA 23966   1887,0101.1488

Fragment of a corroded iron artefact in the shape of a gently curved threaded rod stuck into a perpendicular item in a shape similar to a wing-nut. The interpretation of the object as part of a bridle-bit, as suggested by Petrie, remains uncertain in spite of the similarity with the slightly larger item EA 23965 above. If so, the rod should be interpreted as part of the cannon of the mouthpiece of the bit and the 'wing-nut' as part of a shank. Considered as a possible bit in the Museum register, as fragment of a horses' bit, 'riveted through cheek-pieces', in Petrie 1888, 77 § 77, p. 110.
Length: 5.87cm (max.); width: 3.7cm.
Context: south-eastern quarter of the Saite enclosure (so-called 'Camp').
Bibliography: Petrie 1888, 77 § 77, p. 110, pl. xxxvii, 5a; also Journal, 136: 'some way, say 1/4 of mile, south of the palace is the iron factory; (...); pieces of iron grating occur'; Petrie 1917a, 56, pl. lxx, W9; Amborn 1976, 78, 96, fig. 32, 5a.
Parallels: Amborn 1976, 96, n. 112, fig. 47.

EA 23967   1887,0101.1489

Corroded straight iron bar of oval to peanut-shaped cross section with a loop at each end, possibly the mouthpiece of a bridle-bit. One of the loops is broken.
Length: 15.8cm; width: 3.63cm; thickness: 2.59cm.
Context: south-eastern quarter of the Saite enclosure (so-called 'Camp').
Bibliography: Petrie 1888, 77 § 77, p. 110, pl. xxxvii, 2: one of the 'horses' bits' 'with holes for the attachment, as in fig. 2'; see Journal, 136: 'some way, say 1/4 of mile, south of the palace is the iron factory; (...) links of a great iron chain each 4 or 5 inches long, forged one eye in the other'; Petrie 1917a, 55, pl. lxx, W11; Amborn 1976, 78, 97, fig. 32, 2 (who questions the interpretation as a horse bit).
Parallels: other items from Tell Dafana considered as bridle-bits: EA 23968 below; Cairo, EM JE 27378 (missing); Boston, MFA 87.515 (Petrie 1888, 77 § 77); Boston, MFA 87.516 + Oxford, AM 1887.2505.x (ibid., 77 § 77, p. 110, pl. xxxvii, 6); see also possibly EA 23981 below; Amborn 1976, 97.

EA 23968   1887,0101.1490

Corroded iron item in the shape of a slightly curved cylindrical bar,

twisted or threaded, tapering towards the extremities and ending in a
large button in the shape of an oblate sphere. It might be interpreted as
the mouthpiece of a bridle-bit, though a little oversized, which might
have allowed room for shanks on both sides. Repaired from fragments.
Length: 20.6cm (max.); width: 2.6cm (centre); 3.4cm (at ends).
Context: Saite enclosure (so-called 'Camp')?
Bibliography: Petrie 1888, 77 § 77, p. 110, pl. xxxvii, 1: one of the
'horses' bits' which 'are sometimes bars which have had loops of cord
or leather at the ends'; id., 1917a, 55, pl. lxx, W10; Amborn 1976, 78,
95–6, fig. 32, 1 (who interprets it as the side shank of a bridle-bit,
according to representations on reliefs in Niniveh and Persepolis, cf.
ibid., 96, nn. 109–10, figs 45–6).

Miscellaneous iron

Swivel ring (Pl. 27)

EA 23969   **1887,0101.1491**
Large corroded iron round swivel ring, of circular cross section, with a
short thickened segment around a circular socket for a missing
pivoting rod or joint.
Diameter: 10.79cm; thickness: 2.9cm.
Context: 'Qasr', east annexe (C).
Bibliography: Petrie 1888, 78 § 77, p. 110, pl. xxxvii, 18: 'the large swivel
ring (xxxvii. 18) [...] is probably a part of chariot fittings'; cf. Journal,
142: '(…) the outside chambers of the Kasr. It is these outlying offices &
kitchens (?) that produce everything there. Three iron chisels, & a
large swivel ring were found here also'; Amborn 1976, 79, 97, 101, fig.
32, 18.
Parallels: Amborn 1976, 101, fig. 51.

Pegs and fasteners (Pl. 27)

EA 23975   **1887,0101.1497**
Corroded iron item in the shape of a short and thick nail or peg with
one end pointed, the other bent by hammering to create a narrow loop
or eye.
Length: 6.37cm; width: 1.89cm.
Context: Saite enclosure (so-called 'Camp')?
Bibliography: Petrie 1888, 77–8 § 77, p. 110, pl. xxxvii, 18: 'the objects 8
to 11 are difficult to explain; possibly they may be ornaments for the
peaks of helmets...'; Amborn 1976, 78, 98, fig. 32, 8 (who interprets the
item as a pointed chisel, with parallels, ibid., 98, n. 120). The item is
interpreted as a tent-peg in the Museum register.

EA 23976   **1887,0101.1498**
Corroded iron fitting, most probably a fastener in the shape of a split
pin, constructed from a flat and narrow strip of metal bent in half with
a loop at the fold. Part of one leg is missing.
Length: 5cm (max.); width: 1.2cm; thickness: 0.85cm.
Context: Saite enclosure (so-called 'Camp')?
Bibliography: Petrie 1888, 110, pl. xxxviii, 13: 'spring?', certainly not
the 'iron staple' found in Chamber 19 together with an iron chisel
(ibid., 78 § 78; see also the similar item GR 1888,0208.167 below);
Amborn 1976, 101, fig. 33, 13.

GR 1888,0208.167
Part of a corroded iron fitting, possibly a fastener, in the shape of a
spring-type cotter pin with legs missing.
Height: 2.42cm; width: 1.2cm; thickness: 0.9cm.
Context: possibly chamber 19, 'Qasr', east annexe (C).
Bibliography: Petrie 1888, 78 § 78 (?): 'iron staple' found in Chamber 19
together with an iron chisel, if it is not the similar item EA 23976 on pl.
xxxviii, 13.

Miscellaneous bronze

Buckles (Pl. 27)

EA 23869   **1887,0101.1064**
Corroded fragment of a copper alloy small buckle, comprising two
broken parts attached by corrosion: the side of a flat frame in the form of
an eight-shaped double loop (one loop of 'pelta' type, with ends curling
inwards, welded on top of an oval or possibly D-shaped one), and a short

central prong, with a pointing and curved tip and a thicker end grasping
one of the loops in the centre of the frame. On the back of the frame
fragment are welded two short rectangular strips of metal, pierced by a
small round hole (one with the top partly broken and missing), which
were certainly used for fastening another part of the fitting.
Length: 3.51cm; width: 1.58cm; thickness: 0.93cm.
Parallels: from Tell Dafana, see below EA 23886, which is very
probably part of the same object; other possible buckles or parts of
buckles: EA 23870, 23871, 23872 below; similar pierced strip of metal,
possibly for a swivel, on 23871; two other copper alloy buckles from
Tell Dafana, of Roman or Byzantine type, are Cairo, EM JE 27370 a &
b. Compare with PM UC 72301 (dated to the Byzantine Period).

EA 23886   **1887,0101.1083**
Corroded side fragment of a copper alloy flat frame of a small buckle,
in the form of an eight-shaped double loop (one loop of 'pelta' type,
with ends curling inwards, welded on top of an oval or possibly
D-shaped one). On the back is welded a short rectangular strip of
metal, of which the top is broken and missing, pierced by a small round
hole for fastening another part of the fitting.
Length: 2.79cm; width: 1.51cm; thickness: 0.73cm.
Parallels: same as for EA 23869 above, probably part of the same object.

EA 23870   **1887,0101.1065**
Part of a corroded copper alloy buckle of a sophisticated shape: an
openwork rectangular part on one side, with a slightly convex edge at
the end and concave side edges, topped by two thinner parallel shanks
joining with a thicker semi-circular indented end (four sinusoidal
indentations). On the reverse side, the base of the central part of this
indented end, between the two shanks, is bevelled.
Length: 3.15cm; width: 1.78cm; thickness: 0.38cm.
Bibliography: Petrie 1888, 80 § 80 mentions finds of bronze objects, but
this item is not specified.
Parallels: from Tell Dafana, see also other possible buckles or parts of
buckles, EA 23886, 23869 (above), 23871, 23872 (below); two copper
alloy buckles, also from Tell Dafana, of Roman or Byzantine type, are
in Cairo, EM JE 27370 a–b.

EA 23871   **1887,0101.1066**
Corroded copper alloy object, possibly part of a buckle clasp, with a
roughly square plate, decorated with a shallow groove near two
opposite edges, with an anchor-shaped double hook on one side. On
the underside of the plate are welded two parallel metal strips, pierced
by a round hole (one broken) for fastening to another part of the fitting.
Length: 2.36cm; width: 1.78cm; thickness: 0.91cm.
Bibliography: Petrie 1888, 80 § 80 mentions finds of bronze objects, but
this item is not specified.
Parallels: from Tell Dafana, see also other possible buckles or parts of
buckles, EA 23869, 23870, 23886 (above), 23872 (below). Similar
pierced strip of metal, possibly for a swivel, on EA 23869 and 23886;
two copper alloy buckles also from Tell Dafana, of Roman or Byzantine
type, are in Cairo, EM JE 27370 a–b.

EA 23872   **1887,0101.1067**
Part of a corroded copper alloy buckle, made of a flat rectangular
plaque with a round hole perforated in the centre, and a semi-circular
hoop, a bit larger than the plaque, welded at its corners on one side. On
the opposite side, the edge is almost completely and irregularly bevelled.
Length: 3.02cm; width: 1.69cm; thickness: 0.49cm.
Bibliography: Petrie 1888, 80 § 80 mentions finds of bronze objects, but
this item is not specified.
Parallels: from Tell Dafana, see also other possible buckles or parts of
buckles: EA 23869, 23870, 23871, 23886 (above); Boston, MFA 87.503;
two copper alloy buckles also from Tell Dafana, of Roman or
Byzantine type, are in Cairo, EM JE 27370 a–b.

Chains (Pl. 27)

EA 23898   **1887,0101.1100**
Corroded fragment of a copper alloy chain made of three twisted
eight-shaped twisted links, one broken.
Length: 3.8cm; width: 0.74cm.
Bibliography: Petrie 1888, 80 § 80: possibly part of the bronze 'chain of
O and of 8 links', but see also EA 23902 below.

Parallels: from Tell Dafana, see also EA 23906 (below); Oxford, AM 1887.2502.1–4; Philadelphia, PM E76.

EA 23902   1887,0101.1426
Corroded fragment of a copper alloy chain, made of parts of two U-shaped interlaced links and a segment of a third one, stuck to the others by corrosion products.
Length: 2.09cm (max.); width: 1.6cm; thickness: 1.62cm.
Parallels: provenance not specified in the Museum register, but probably from Tell Dafana according to the context of the item in the list; see the mention of finding chain in Petrie 1888, 80 § 80.

EA 23906   1887,0101.1430
Links of a copper alloy chain; recorded in the Museum register, the item remains unlocated.
Length: 1.27cm.
Context: Saite enclosure (so-called 'Camp').
Bibliography: Petrie 1888, 80 § 80: possibly part of the bronze 'chain of O and of 8 links'.

EA 23884   1887,0101.1081
Corroded copper alloy eight-shaped link, with two equal-sized circular loops separated by an oval-shaped central element.
Length: 2.75cm; width: 1.25cm; thickness: 0.33cm.
Bibliography: Petrie 1888, 80 § 80: one of the elements of 'chain of O and of 8 links'.

Hinges (Pl. 28)

EA 23863   1887,0101.1054
Corroded copper alloy butt-hinge from a door or chest, made of two thin metal leaves articulated by three barrels, now blocked by corrosion: the leaf with the central barrel is broken across a round fixing hole near the articulation; the other, with the lateral barrels, is made of a long strip ending with a large disc folded at the other end around the axis of the hinge. Two round holes have been punched for fixing to the door, one in the centre of the distal disc, the other near the knuckle, with its counterpart visible on the broken end of the folded part beneath. The visible side of the fitting is decorated with incised or rather hallmarked circles, two concentric ones around the hole in the middle of the disc, two others, on the central strip near the disc, side by side, and another one or possibly a pair, near the hinge; the last three (or four) surround an internal thin and tight spiral groove. The hole near the knuckle has not been perforated in the centre of the last circle, but partly on its perimeter.
Length: 15.8cm; width: 3.02cm; thickness: 1.6cm (max.); thickness: 0.06cm (metal sheet, min.); thickness: 0.25cm (metal sheet, max.).
Bibliography: Petrie 1888, 80 § 80 mentions finds of bronze objects, but this item is not specified.

EA 23893   1887,0101.1091
Corroded copper alloy hinge articulated by three barrels. One leaf is pierced by a round hole for fixing with a nail, the other by a smaller one beside a possible larger one, broken. A small round hole is also perforated into the side of one knuckle.
Length: 1.91cm; width: 0.73cm; thickness: 0.48cm.
Bibliography: Petrie 1888, 80 § 80 mentions finds of bronze objects, but this item is not specified.

Nails and studs (Pl. 28)

EA 23899   1887,0101.1011
Flat and circular small corroded copper alloy disc, possibly the head of a nail; a shallow groove is visible around the edge.
Diameter: 0.8cm; thickness: 0.2cm.
Context: probably from the surrounding area towards Tell Belim.
Bibliography: Petrie 1888, 80 § 80: one of the bronze 'flat, round' 'nail-heads'.

EA 23876   1887,0101.1072
Heavily corroded copper alloy nail-head or shank button, in the form of a small disc decorated on top with three concentric ridges; a rectangular trace in the middle of the underside indicates where the shank or an eyelet was welded.

Diameter: 1.46cm; thickness: 0.39cm.
Bibliography: Petrie 1888, 80 § 80: very probably one of the bronze 'nail-heads', with 'concentric circles'.

EA 23877   1887,0101.1073
Heavily corroded copper alloy round stud in the shape of an hemispherical button, the round part of it being welded to a round disc with grooved edge. In the middle of the underside remains part of a narrow shank, of rectangular cross section.
Height: 1.32mm (max.); diameter: 1.28cm.
Bibliography: Petrie 1888, 80 § 80: one of the 'nail-heads of all forms, flat, round, massive parabolic, pyramidal, rosette and concentric circles'.

EA 23878   1887,0101.1074
Corroded copper alloy stud with a round head of parabolic profile. In the middle of the hollow underside remains part of a narrow shank, of rectangular cross section, broken at the end.
Diameter: 1.62cm; height: 1.87cm (max.).
Bibliography: Petrie 1888, 80 § 80: one of the 'nail-heads' of 'parabolic' form.

EA 23879   1887,0101.1075
Corroded copper alloy fragment of a stud with a haft of circular cross section and a pyramid-shaped head, blunt at the top.
Length: 1.52cm (max.); width: 0.75cm.
Bibliography: Petrie 1888, 80 § 80: one of the 'nail-heads of all forms, flat, round, massive parabolic, pyramidal, rosette and concentric circles'.

Other fittings (Pl. 28)

EA 23881   1887,0101.1077
Corroded copper alloy object in the shape of a thick flat oval grommet or ferrule, with a rectangular slot in the centre. One side is slightly larger than the other.
Length: 2.07cm; width: 0.65cm; thickness: 0.47cm.
Bibliography: Petrie 1888, 80 § 80 mentions finds of bronze objects, but this item is not specified.
Parallels: see also the pair of similar items EA 23881 (1887,0208.1092 and 1093) below.

EA 23881   1887,0101.1092-1093
Two corroded copper alloy objects in the shape of a flat oval grommet or ferrule, with a rectangular slot in the centre. One is made of thin leaf metal, the other one is thicker. Probably parts of an implement such as the ferrule of a knife.
1887,0101.1092: length: 1.49cm; width: 0.85cm; thickness: 0.34cm.
1887,0101.1093: length: 1.7cm; width: 0.97mm; thickness: 0.06cm.
Bibliography: Petrie 1888, 80 § 80 mentions finds of bronze objects, but this item is not specified.
Parallels: same as for EA 23881 (1887,0208.1077) above.

EA 23894   1887,0101.1096
Corroded copper alloy fitting made of a thin almond shaped and curved strip of metal, with a long central slot. One pointed end has been cut longitudinally, and the tips of the two sides overlap; the function of the item remains undetermined, possibly a kind of grommet.
Height: 0.6cm; length: 1.7cm; width: 1.05cm; thickness: 0.1cm.
Bibliography: Petrie 1888, 80 § 80 mentions finds of bronze objects, but this item is not specified.

EA 23874   1887,0101.1070
Corroded copper alloy short rod with two long cones opposed on each side of a narrower central part and ending with a small sphere at each tip; possibly a model of the sceptre of Min.
Diameter: 0.47cm; length: 2.95cm.
Bibliography: Petrie 1888, 80 § 80 mentions finds of bronze objects, but this item is not specified.

EA 23875   1887,0101.1071
Corroded copper alloy short rod of circular cross section, with a small sphere at each end (one just before the end of the rod), and two

opposed flaring parts each side of the middle; possibly a model of the sceptre of Min.
Diameter: 0.69cm; length: 2.48cm.
Bibliography: Petrie 1888, 80 § 80 mentions finds of bronze objects, but this item is not specified.

EA 23887 1887,0101.1084
Corroded copper alloy inlay element of oval shape with a flat base and a convex top decorated with longitudinal parallel striations. Lightly patinated with green corrosion.
Length: 1.4cm; width: 1cm (max.).
Bibliography: Petrie 1888, 80 § 80 mentions finds of bronze objects, but this item is not specified.

EA 23888 1887,0101.1085
Corroded copper alloy small object, maybe a sort of miniature seal, with a flat eight-shaped base and a handle semi-circular handle with a ridge on top.
Length: 1.84cm; width: 0.97cm; thickness: 0.58cm.
Bibliography: Petrie 1888, 80 § 80 mentions finds of bronze objects, but this item is not specified.

EA 23891 1887,0101.1088
Corroded copper alloy model-fitting, in the form of a bolt from the door of a shrine, with flat base and rounded top. The bolt is of the traditional Egyptian style (like the hieroglyph for the letter *s*), formed of a straight rod with a pair of joined hemispheres in the middle, and an additional integral projection at one end to indicate the handle.
Height: 0.5cm; length: 2.9cm; thickness: 0.45cm.
Context: probably from the area north of the site, towards Tell Belim.
Bibliography: Petrie 1888, 80 § 80 mentions finds of bronze objects, but this item is not specified.

Miscellaneous objects in various materials (Pl. 28)

EA 23883 1887,0101.1079 and 1887,0101.1095
Two corroded copper alloy buttons, circular with domed tops and hollow undersides with a central curved bar for attachment. Part of the edge of one has been chipped off.
1887,0101.1079, height: 0.4cm; diameter: 1.05cm (max.).
1887,0101.1095, height: 0.4cm; diameter: 1cm (max.).
Context: probably from the desert north of the site, towards Tell Belim.
Bibliography: Petrie 1888, 80 § 80: one of the bronze 'buttons made concavo-convex, with a bar across the concave back pierced for sewing on'.

GR 1906,0301.12
Tridacna (?) shell convex button perforated in the centre, with an roughly incised decoration on the convex side: between two circles, one smaller around the central hole and one larger near the outer edge, are scored radiant lines creating summarily the impression of three diverging lotus flowers, with curved double lines on each side and an acute triangle in the middle.
Diameter: 2.2cm; thickness: 0.53cm.
Bibliography: Petrie 1888, 72 § 68, pl. xl, 16: 'A button of shell (pl. xl. 16) is a new form in Egyptian remains'; Brandl 1984, 16.
Parallels: Brandl 1984, *passim* (bigger and more elaborate pieces, including one from Memphis, Oxford, AM 1910.526).

EA 23842 1887,0101.709
Three re-joined fragments of a carved ivory object, circular and domed with a flat base.
Height: 1cm; diameter: 1.5cm.
Context: Saite enclosure (so-called 'Camp').
Bibliography: Petrie 1888, 75 § 72: one of the 'three ivory hemispheres, 0.5 to 0.6 inch across [...] from the camp'.
Parallels: the two others must be Boston, MFA 87.724–725.

EA 18481 1887,0101.708
A possible furniture fitting, part of a knob or the end of a stick or rod. Made of ivory and discoloured to brown-grey, probably by burning; circular with a flared edge, the top slightly convex, with a square recess cut in the underside for attachment.
Diameter: 1.5cm; depth: 0.4cm.

Context: Saite enclosure (so-called 'Camp').
Bibliography: Petrie 1888, 75 § 72: 'top of an ivory papyrus-flower'.

EA 23861 1887,0101.898
Net-sinker made of a roughly rectangular thick strip of lead folded over.
Length: 1.6cm; width: 1.2cm; thickness: 1.25cm.
Bibliography: Petrie 1888, 77 § 76: 'lead pieces of a U-shape, which where doubtless net sinkers'.
Parallels: from Tell Dafana, Boston, MFA RES.87.37-41 (deaccessioned).

EA 23862 1887,0101.899
Lead artefact, possibly a net-sinker in the form of a hollow ovoid blob with large irregular perforations on two sides and gnarled surface, similar in shape to a small closed bell.
Length: 1.8cm; width: 1.50; thickness: 1.3cm.
Bibliography: possibly Petrie 1888, 77 § 76: maybe one of the lead 'net sinkers', though the item is not exactly U-shaped as EA 23861.

EA 18640 1887,0101.885
Green-blue glazed composition pendant (with traces of green-blue glaze on surface) in the form of a lotus-flower with incised decoration, perhaps used as a spacer-bead in a necklace or collar. The object has one large central perforation, flanked by six other perforations, three on either side. All the perforations run vertically.
Height: 2.12cm (max.); width: 1.87cm; thickness: 1.11cm.
Bibliography: Petrie 1888, 75 § 72, pl. xl, 5: one of the 'lotus heads of green and blue glaze (pl. xl, 5, 6), pierced, probably for handles of feather fly-flaps'.
Parallels: Boston, MFA 87.613, cf. Petrie, 1888, pl. xl, 6.
See also Hermann and Staubli 2010, 142, nos 5–6; (Hermann 1985, 457 (dated 19–20th dynasty); Müller-Winkler 1987, 60, 288, pl. xxvii, nos 548–50; Blanchard 1909, 23, pl. xlviii, no. 289; Frankfort and Pendlebury 1933, pls xxviii, 6, xxix, 5, xlix, nos iv.C.26–7 and 54; Brunner-Traut 1981, 155, pl. 16, nos 592–9.

EA 18458 1887,0101.748
Green-blue glazed composition hemispherical fitting, the upper surface is elaborated with a raised five-pointed star with a central boss. The object is pierced in two places close to the edge for attachment.
Diameter: 3.01cm (max.); thickness: 0.96cm (max.).
Context: provenance not specified in the Museum register, possibly from Tell Dafana or Tell Nebesha, or, more probably from El-Qantara, according to the context of the item in the list.

GR 1888,0208.166
Oblong piece of sandstone, divided in two parts by a straight longitude groove all around the sides, certainly for attaching a string. The function of the item remains uncertain, possibly a net-sinker, a small loom-weight, a kind of rough plummet for a plumb line, or simply a handle.
Height: 1.54cm; length: 3.7cm; width: 1.45cm.

13. Jewellery

Gold and bronze work

Gold earrings (Pl. 28)

EA 18250 1887,0101.541
Penannular gold earring in the form of a rounded crescent made of solid-cast metal, with both tapering ends now overlapping.
Diameter: 1.29cm (max.); thickness: 0.38cm (max.).
Context: from the denuded surface around the site, or possibly from the north-west 'Roman mound'.
Bibliography: Petrie 1888, 76 § 73, p. 110, pl. xli, 3 (assuming the position of the thin ends has been adjusted since acquisition). Petrie mentions just generally: 'earrings [...], of which about forty were found (including fragments) by the Bedawin who hunt the neighbourhood'; see also Journal, 134: 'I went across to the N. mound with him [i.e. A.H. Sayce]; it is later than this side on the surface, going to Roman; but there are some tombs rifled from which many of my gold earrings have come. There does not seem to be anything accessible of the early Greek time, so I shall not try to work there'.
Parallels: Petrie 1911b, 24, pl. xxxi.

EA 18280   **1887,0101.572**

Penannular gold earring in the form of a thin rounded crescent made of solid-cast metal.

Diameter: 1.01cm; thickness: 0.2cm.

Context: provenance not specified in the Museum register, but probably from the from the denuded surface of the site or its neighbourhood, as suggested by the context of the item in the list, or possibly from the north-west 'Roman mound'.

Bibliography: Petrie 1888, 76 § 73; also Journal, 134 (see EA 18250 above).

Parallels: from Tell Dafana or its neighbourhood, Bolton 1886.28.93 (2 pieces); Cambridge, FM E1886.3a; Oxford, AM 1887.2507-2508; Sheffield, WPM, J87.6; Sydney, MAC, MU2630.

EA 18261   **1887,0101.550**

Penannular gold earring in the form of a thin rounded crescent made of solid-cast metal, with long, tapering, coiled ends.

Diameter: 1.36cm; thickness: 0.2cm.

Context: from the denuded surface of the site or its neighbourhood, possibly from the north-west 'Roman mound'.

Bibliography: Petrie 1888, 76 § 73, p. 110, pl. xli, 4; also Journal, 134 (see EA 18250 above).

EA 18262   **1887,0101.551**

Penannular gold earring in the form of a thin rounded crescent made of solid-cast metal, elaborated with three coils of gold wire wound side by side onto the central part of the loop.

Diameter: 1.25cm; thickness: 0.25cm.

Context: from the denuded surface of the site or its neighbourhood, possibly from the north-west 'Roman mound'.

Bibliography: Petrie 1888, 76 § 73, p. 110, pl. xli, 6; also Journal, 134 (see EA 18250 above).

EA 18273   **1887,0101.552**

Fragment of a pennanular gold earring in the shape of a thin rounded crescent made of solid-cast metal; the central part of the loop is ornamented on the underside by a granulated bunch of lentiform globules welded together, flanked on both sides by a moniliform? wire coiled up around the loop. One broken end is missing.

Diameter: 1.05cm (max.); thickness: 0.43cm (max.).

Context: from the denuded surface of the site or its neighbourhood, possibly from the north-west 'Roman mound'.

Bibliography: Petrie 1888, 76 § 73, p. 110, pl. xli, 7; also Journal, 134 (see EA 18250 above).

EA 18297   **1887,0101.553**

Granulated gold tetrahedral pendant portion of an earring, made entirely of globules welded together, with three bigger globules superimposed under the lower tip. An oval and concave trace on the centre of the top surface indicates where the ring, now missing, was welded. The object is correctly marked 18297 but wrongly 1887,0101.546 (corresponding to EA 18263, described in the Museum register as a gold cone-shaped pendant, yet to be found).

Height: 1.35cm (max.); width: 1.1cm; depth 1cm.

Context: from the denuded surface of the site or its neighbourhood, possibly from the north-west 'Roman mound'.

Bibliography: Petrie 1888, 76 § 73, p. 110, pl. xli, 13: one of the gold 'pieces of globule work, probably of earrings', 'part of gold earring, trihedral pyramid of soldered globules'; Petrie 1927, 4 and Journal, 134 (see EA 18250 above).

Parallels: Müller and Thiem 1998, 46, fig. 78.

EA 18259   **1887,0101.548**

Thin penannular gold earring, with a foliate lace-like decoration in the lower part, consisting of a series of six filiform 'pelta' type loops, with ends curling inwards, welded side by side on the outer contour of the ring and flanked on each side by an S-shaped loop.

Diameter: 2.2cm (max.); thickness: 0.1cm.

Context: from the denuded surface of the site or its neighbourhood, possibly from the north-west 'Roman mound'.

Bibliography: Petrie 1888, 76 § 73, p. 110, pl. xli, 5; also Journal, 134 (see EA 18250 above).

EA 18249   **1887,0101.540**

Penannular gold earring in the form of a thick hollow crescent made of an embossed sheet of metal. The surface is a little dented.

Diameter: 1.64cm (max.); thickness: 0.64cm (max.).

Context: from the denuded surface of the site or its neighbourhood, possibly from the north-west 'Roman mound'.

Bibliography: Petrie 1888, 76 § 73, p. 80 § 80 (with erroneous plate reference), p. 110, pl. xli, 2; also Journal, 134 (see EA 18250 above).

Parallels: from Tell Dafana or its neighbourhood, Boston, MFA 87.754-756; Bristol, CMAG H1117 (2 pieces); Cambridge, FM E1886.3.b.

EA 18252   **1887,0101.543**

Penannular gold earring, consisting of a fusiform sheet metal curved into a loop and embossed with three longitudinal carinated ridges.

Diameter: 1.05cm; length 0.8cm (max.).

Context: from the denuded surface of the site or its neighbourhood, possibly from the north-west 'Roman mound'.

Bibliography: Petrie 1888, 110, pl. xli, 15: 'gold foil, thick ribbed; from an earring(?)'; also Journal, 134 (see EA 18250 above).

Parallels: from Tell Dafana or its neighbourhood, Boston, MFA 87.751-752.

Bronze earrings (Pl. 28)

EA 23890   **1887,0101.1087**

Earring consisting of a corroded copper alloy hoop with wire of the same material twisted around it.

Diameter: 1.52cm; thickness: 0.25cm.

Bibliography: Petrie 1888, 80 § 80: one of the 'earrings... of wire'.

EA 18298   **1887,0101.598**

Copper alloy penannular earring, much corroded.

Diameter: 2.22cm; thickness: 0.35cm.

Context: provenance not specified in the Museum register, but probably from Tell Nebesha or Tell Dafana, according to the context of the item in the list.

Bibliography: if from Tell Dafana, Petrie 1888, 80 § 80: one of the 'earrings... of wire'.

Parallels: from Tell Dafana or its neighbourhood, Bristol, CMAG H1107.1.

EA 23889   **1887,0101.1086 and 1887,0101.1094**

Pair of corroded copper alloy ear-studs. Each has a convex top with a short, cylindrical peg below.

Height: 1cm; diameter: 1.09cm (1887,0101.1086).

Height: 0.95cm; diameter: 1.22cm (1887,0101.1094).

Context: from the desert surface around the site.

Bibliography: Petrie 1888, 80 § 80: two of the 'nail-heads of all forms, flat, round, massive parabolic, pyramidal, rosette and concentric circles'.

Gold pendant beads (Pl. 28)

EA 18254   **1887,0101.545**

Hollow gold bead or pendant of fusiform shape made of sheets of metal, one embossed and welded on a flat underside. The top of the embossed part is decorated by three horizontal grooves, with a transverse round hole pierced for suspension under the mid groove.

Length: 1.45cm; width: 0.57cm; thickness: 0.29cm.

Context: from the denuded surface of the site or its neighbourhood.

Bibliography: Petrie 1888, 76 § 73, p. 110, pl. xli, 27: 'gold pendant, hollow, flat back'.

Parallels: from Tell Dafana or its neighbourhood: Boston, MFA 87.749.

EA 18263   **1887,0101.546**

Gold cone-shaped pendant; recorded in the Museum register, the item remains unlocated.

Length: 1.27cm.

Context: from the denuded surface of the site or its neighbourhood.

Bibliography: Petrie 1888, 76 § 73?

EA 18266   **1887,0101.556**

Circular gold disc-shaped bead or pendant made of an embossed sheet of metal, and surrounded by a thicker annular edge with a protrusion on

top, folded over and welded in order to create a suspension loop. In front, a globule is welded in the centre of the disc and the edge is doubled by a median chased groove. The outer part of the edge is partly incised and folded, while the surface of the disc is a little dented, giving the impression that the item was originally domed and has been flattened.
Diameter: 0.75cm; thickness: 0.15cm.
Context: from the denuded surface of the site or its neighbourhood.
Bibliography: Petrie 1888, 76 § 73, p. 110:, pl. xli, 23: among the gold 'foil ornaments'.

EA 18264   1887,0101.559
Convex leaf-shaped gold bead or pendant made of an embossed sheet of metal, with a tiny protrusion at the top, folded over for suspension. The surface is a little dented.
Length: 1.24cm (max.); width: 0.74cm (max.); thickness: 0.18cm (max.).
Context: provenance not specified in the Museum register, but from the neighbourhood of Tell Dafana, as suggested by the context of the item in the list.

EA 18267   1887,0101.562
Gold quatrefoil leaf-shaped drop-bead or pendant topped by a loop to which is attached a chain of two folded eight-shaped links.
Length: 1.62cm; width: 0.33cm.
Context: from the denuded surface of the site or its neighbourhood.
Bibliography: Petrie 1888, 76 § 73, p. 110, pl. xli, 25: one of gold 'pieces of chain', 'piece of gold chain with pendant'.
Parallels: from Tell Dafana or its neighbourhood: Boston, MFA 87.748.

Composite gold beads (Pl. 28)

EA 18256   1887,0101.563
Gold oval jewellery fitting, probably a bezel setting, made of a worked sheet of metal, with an outer ridge regularly pinched on the upper part in order to create a granulated or corded aspect. The bezel is missing.
Diameter: 0.89cm; thickness: 0.26cm.
Context: from the denuded surface of the site or its neighbourhood.
Bibliography: Petrie 1888, 76 § 73, p. 110, pl. xli, 29: gold 'setting of a stone', 'gold setting of a gem'.

EA 18293   1887,0101.574
Circular, thick and flat green stone bead, probably dioptase, set in a gold mount made of sheet metal and globules welded together; the mount consists of a shallow cylinder on a flat annular base, slightly larger and decorated with a granulated circle of globules. Two holes on opposites sides in the cylinder, surrounded by a round coil of metal, correspond to the suspension hole pierced lengthwise in the stone.
Height: 0.35cm; diameter: 0.67cm.
Context: from the denuded surface of the site or its neighbourhood.
Bibliography: Petrie 1888, 76 § 73, p. 110, pl. xli, 31: 'piece of dioptase set in gold', 'dioptase in gold setting with row of globules'.
Parallels: Bakr *et al.* 2010, 234–5, n. 79.

EA 18289   1887, 0101.583
Globular bead comprising a glazed composition (?) core, covered with a pleated gold foil.
Diameter: 0.74cm (max.); length 0.85cm.
Context: provenance not specified in the Museum register, but perhaps from Tell Nebesha according to the context of the item in the list, if not from Tell Dafana.
Parallels: from Tell Dafana or its neighbourhood: Sheffield, WPM J87.7; Oxford, AM 1887.2509.

Granulated gold beads (Pl. 28)

EA 18257   1887,0101.558
Gold bead made of two superimposed welded and indented flower-shaped circles of five petals around a central circular hole.
Diameter: 0.48cm; thickness: 0.29cm.
Context: from the neighbourhood of the site.
Bibliography: Petrie 1888, 76 § 73, p. 110, pl. xli, 14: one of the gold 'pieces of globule work [...] probably of chains', 'gold bead of two pentagonal discs soldered together'.

EA 18248   1887,0101.567
Gold granulated bead made of two superimposed welded circles of six globules around a central circular hole.
Diameter: 0.53cm; thickness: 0.33cm.
Context: from the denuded surface of the site or its neighbourhood.
Bibliography: Petrie 1888, 76 § 73, p. 110, pl. xli, 17: one of the gold 'pieces of globule work [...] of chains ', 'gold bead, soldered globules'.
Parallels: from Tell Dafana, see EA 18270 below.

EA 18270   1887,0101.568
Granulated circular gold bead made of five small globules welded around a central hole.
Diameter: 0.38cm; thickness: 0.15cm.
Context: provenance not specified in the Museum register, but probably from the denuded surface of Tell Dafana or its neighbourhood according to the context of the item in the list.
Bibliography: Petrie 1888, 76 § 73: one of the gold 'pieces of globule work [...] of chains'.
Parallels: from Tell Dafana, see EA 18248 above.

EA 18268   1887,0101.569
Cylindrical gold bead of granulated openwork made of three superimposed circles of seven paired globules welded together, linked by two intermediate rows of seven single globules regularly distributed.
Diameter: 0.53cm; thickness: 0.39cm.
Context: provenance not specified in the Museum register, but probably from the denuded surface of the site or its neighbourhood, according to the context of the item in the list.
Bibliography: Petrie 1888, 76 § 73: one of the 40 gold earrings and fragments found 'by the Bedawin who hunt the neighbourhood'.
Parallels: see the larger object EA 18294 below.

EA 18294   1887,0101.573
Granulated goldwork fragment of a fitting, possibly an earring, entirely made of globules welded together in form of an openwork cylinder on a disc made of smaller globules, on the edge of which are fixed two circular and slightly curved loops (one partly missing).
Diameter: 0.88cm (max.); length: 1.36cm (max.).
Context: from the denuded surface of the site or its neighbourhood.
Bibliography: Petrie 1888, 76 § 73, p. 110, pl. xli, 12: one of the gold 'pieces of globule work, probably of earrings', 'gold earring, open work of soldered globules'.

Small gold chains (Pl. 28)

EA 18265   1887,0101.564
Two links of a gold chain made of thin wires of square cross section, double twisted eight-shaped with a small gold ring around the central narrowest part of each link.
Length: 1.8cm; thickness: 0.3cm.
Context: from the denuded surface of the site or its neighbourhood.
Bibliography: Petrie 1888, 76 § 73, p. 110, pl. xli, 24: one of the gold 'pieces of chain', 'piece of gold chain with a band round each link'.

EA 18279   1887,0101.571
Five links of a gold chain made of thin wires of square cross section, four of them double twisted eight-shaped and one single at one end, drawn out into rounded wire, with a twist at the end.
Length: 3.4cm; thickness: 0.35cm.
Context: from the denuded surface of the site or its neighbourhood.
Bibliography: Petrie 1888, 76 § 73, p. 110, pl. xli, 18: one of the gold 'pieces of chain', 'piece of gold chain, a pendant; probably a glass bead lost from end'.
Parallels: from Tell Dafana or its neighbourhood, Boston, MFA 87.757.

Repoussé gold work (Pl. 28)

EA 18253   1887,0101.544
Gold round and domed rosette made of a thin embossed sheet of metal, with a large irregular central hole and six U-shaped petals, either a bead or part of a clasp. The outer edge is partly shredded.

Diameter: 1.29cm.
Context: from the denuded surface of the site or its neighbourhood.
Bibliography: Petrie 1888, 110, pl. xli, 16: 'gold foil, floret'; on the gold
material from Tell Dafana in general, see ibid., 76 § 73–4.

EA 18258   1887,0101.547
Part of a gold clasp from a necklace or a bracelet, with a small ring
welded to the top of a hemispherical hollow cover, and a small round
hole pierced on one side to thread and knot the string.
Height: 0.9cm; diameter: 0.8cm.
Context: from the denuded surface of the site or its neighbourhood.
Bibliography: Petrie 1888, 76 § 73, p. 110, pl. xli, 19: among the gold
'foil ornaments'.

EA 18274   1887,0101.555
Round gold fitting, possibly part of a clasp of a necklace or bracelet,
made of a repoussé sheet of metal, with an irregular edge and a
hemispherical centre surrounded by a groove; a tiny loop of metal is
welded to the centre of the underside, to thread and knot the bead wire.
Diameter: 0.85cm (max.); thickness: 0.27cm (max.).
Context: from the denuded surface of the site or its neighbourhood.
Bibliography: Petrie 1888, 76 § 73, p. 110, pl. xli, 20: among the gold
'foil ornaments'.

EA 18275   1887,0101.557
Part of a gold clasp of a necklace or a bracelet, made of a sheet of metal
shaped in the form of a round domed cover ornamented with an
embossed rosette of ten petals, and pierced by a small round hole near
the centre to thread and knot the string.
Diameter: 1cm; thickness: 0.25cm.
Context: from the denuded surface of the site or its neighbourhood.
Bibliography: Petrie 1888, 76 § 73, p. 110, pl. xli, 22: among the gold
'foil ornaments'.
Parallels: from Tell Dafana or its neighbourhood, Boston, MFA 87.758.

EA 18271   1887,0101.560
Tiny gold artefact in the shape of five-pointed star with a round centre,
made of a repoussé sheet of metal, probably a fitting from a piece of
jewellery.
Width: 0.9cm (max.); thickness: 0.11cm (max.).
Context: from the denuded surface of the site or its neighbourhood.
Bibliography: Petrie 1888, 76 § 73, p. 110, pl. xli, 21: among the gold 'foil
ornaments'.

EA 18296   1887,0101.566
Small hemispherical gold artefact made of an embossed sheet of metal,
perhaps a fitting from a piece of jewellery. The internal surface is
covered by a thick layer of dark brown resin; the edge is slightly dented.
Diameter: 0.42cm (max.); thickness: 0.16cm (max.).
Context: provenance not specified in the Museum register, but
probably from the denuded surface of the site or its neigbourhood
according to the context of the item in the list.
Bibliography: on finds of gold from Tell Dafana, see Petrie 1888, 76 §
74: 'multitude of fragments of goldwork picked by the Bedawin who
hunt over the denuded surface of the site'.

Other gold fittings and fragments (Pl. 28)

EA 18255   1887,0101.565
Part of attachment from a piece of jewellery, comprising a fragment of
a slightly sinuous piece of granulated moniliform gold wire, on which a
pennanular ring of semi-circular cross section is welded.
Length: 1.05cm; thickness 0.1cm.
Context and bibliography: same as for EA 18296 above.

EA 18283   1887,0101.584
Curved tubular artefact, comprising copper alloy core overlaid with gold,
perhaps part of a penannular earring or some other piece of jewellery.
Length: 2.02cm (max.); diameter: 0.51cm.
Context: provenance not specified in the Museum register, but
probably from Tell Nebesha according to the context of the item in the
list, or possibly from the denuded surface of the site or its
neighbourhood.

EA 18285   1887,0101.585
Fragment of a piece of jewellery, possibly from a penannular
crescent-shaped earring, comprising gilded copper alloy core,
ornamented on the outer and side contours with horizontal, vertical
and oblique series of chased lines.
Height 1cm; length: 1.4cm (max.).
Context: same as for EA 18283 above.

EA 18272   1887,0101.554
Tiny flat gold disc, perhaps a fitting from an incomplete piece of
jewellery.
Diameter: 1.11cm; thickness: 0.4cm.
Context: From the surface of the site or the neighbourhood.
Bibliography: same as for EA 18296 above.

EA 18276   1887,0101.570
Fragment of gold twisted wire of square cross section, with a tapering
tip bent inwards like a hook; probably a fitting from a piece of
jewellery. The other end, also bent, is broken and missing.
Length: 2.95cm (max.); thickness: 0.08cm.
Context: from the denuded surface of the site or its neighbourhood.
Bibliography: Petrie 1888, 110, pl. xli, 28: 'Gold wire, square, twisted';
see also ibid., 76 § 73–4.

EA 18310   1887,0101.586
Thin gold wire of square cross section irregularly twisted and bent.
Length: 19.2cm.
Context: provenance not specified in the Museum register, but
perhaps from Tell Nebesha according to the context of the item in the
list, or possibly from Tell Dafana. If from Tell Dafana, it resembles the
wire used for making links of a chain, such as in EA 18279 and 18265,
or coiled around an earring, such as EA 18262 (all above); see also the
twisted wire EA 18276 above.

EA 18260   1887,0101.549
A plain gold ring, recorded in the Museum register. This item remains
unlocated.
Diameter: 0.95cm.
Bibliography: possibly Petrie 1888, pl. xli, 1; see Journal, 149: 'a heavy
gold ring (1 ¼ sov. [sovereign]), which most disgustingly is quite plain'.
Parallels: the EEF distribution lists mention a gold ring sent to the
Cairo Egyptian Museum.

EA 18295   1887,0101.587
Three pieces of plain gold foil; the largest has a circular outer edge.
Length: 2.4cm (largest piece).
Context: provenance not specified in the Museum register, but
perhaps from Tell Nebesha according to the context of the item in the
list, or possibly from Tell Dafana or the neigbourhood.

GR 1888,0208.169
Nine fragments of damaged or unfinished goldwork and jewellery
comprising embossed gold foils, a setting for a cabochon and possible
elements from earrings and beads.
Length: 4cm (fragment 1); width: 0.93cm (fragment 1); thickness:
0.25mm (fragment 1).
Context: from the denuded surface of the site or its neighbourhood.
Bibliography: Petrie 1888, 76 § 74. On fragments of goldwork, see
Petrie, 1888, 76 § 74: 'among the multitude of fragments of goldwork
picked up by the Bedawin who hunt over the denuded surface of the
site, were some important scraps bearing on the manufacture of these
articles at the place'.

Glazed composition, glass and stone beads

Glazed composition beads

EA 23807   1887,0101.1410   (Pl. 29)
String of 110 glazed composition tiny beads of different colours (red,
yellow, green and blue) and shapes (discoid or short cylinders and 15
eight-shaped twins).
Length: 22.8cm (string); width: 0.7cm (twin beads); diameter: 0.4cm
(average).
Context: Saite enclosure (so-called 'Camp').

Bibliography: Petrie 1888, 75 § 72: 'a large number of blue-glazed amulets and beads, &c., were found in the camp, and a selection of these will be kept together in the British Museum to show the style of known work of the twenty-sixth dynasty'.

EA 23808   1887,0101.1411   (Pl. 29)

String of 76 green and blue glazed composition tiny beads of different shapes (tubular, moniliform, disc- or cylinder-shaped, lentiform) and one separate tubular bead.
Length: 19.4cm (string); bead marked with museum number, length: 0.99cm; diameter 0.6cm (max.).
Context: Saite enclosure (so-called 'Camp').
Bibliography: same as for EA 23807 above.

EA 23809   1887,0101.1412   (Pl. 29)

String of 137 tiny ring-shaped, tubular, bi-tubular and globular beads of glazed composition, most of them whitish to yellowish, with a few yellow, blue and green ones. Two of the ring-shaped beads are made of red translucent glass.
Length: 26.2cm (string); bead marked with museum number, length: 0.75cm; diameter: 0.19cm.
Context: Saite enclosure (so-called 'Camp').
Bibliography: same as for EA 23807 above.

EA 18471   1887,0101.721   (Pl. 28)

Glazed composition fusiform bead, pierced lengthwise. The original glaze, probably green, has decayed to white.
Length: 1.37cm; diameter: 0.42cm (max.).
Context: provenance not specified in the Museum register, but possibly from Tell Dafana, as suggested by the context of the item in the list, if not from Tell Nebesha or any other eastern Delta site excavated by Petrie in 1886.

EA 18474   1887,0101.722   (Pl. 28)

Green glazed composition fusiform bead, pierced lengthwise.
Length: 1.37cm; diameter: 0.39cm (max.).
Context: see EA 18471 above.

EA 18473   1887,0101.723   (Pl. 28)

Glazed composition long biconical bead, pierced lengthwise.
Length: 1.28cm; diameter: 0.4cm (max.).
Context: see EA 18471 above.

EA 18472   1887,0101.724   (Pl. 28)

Glazed composition long biconical bead, pierced lengthwise and broken at each end. Faded green glaze.
Length: 1.12cm; diameter: 0.41cm (max.).
Context: see EA 18471 above.

EA 15473   1887,0101.897   (Pl. 28)

Blue glazed composition spacer-bead; pierced twice.
Length: 1.83cm; width: 0.92cm; depth: 0.62cm.
Context: see EA 18471 above.

Stone beads

EA 23468   1887,0101.1516   (Pl. 29)

String of 18 stone beads, comprising three large oblate oval ones of rock crystal, nine small carnelian spheroids and six globular to faceted truncated bicones of chalcedony or quartz.
Length: 16.3cm (string); diameters of beads from 1.9cm to 0.6cm.
Bibliography: Petrie 1888, 79 § 79 for general comments on the beads from Tell Dafana.
Parallels: from Tell Dafana or its neighbourhood: Oxford, AM 1887.2494.

EA 18648   1887,0101.644   (Pl. 29)

String of 68 graduated globular carnelian beads ranging from dark yellow to dark red.
Length: 38.4cm (string); diameters of beads from 1.28cm to 0.5cm.
Context: provenance not specified in the Museum register, perhaps from Tell Nebesha if not from Tell Dafana, according to the context of the item in the list, or Tell Gemaiyemi; possibly from Tell Bahaim, between Tell Dafana and San el-Hagar, according to Journal, 169.

Bibliography: same as for EA 23468 above.
Parallels: from the region of Tell Dafana: Bolton J.87.1; Boston, MFA 87.683-685; Brighton AF246; Bristol, CMAG, H1318, H1320; Oxford, AM 1887.2392-2393; Philadelphia, PM E37 (missing); Sheffield J.87.1; Sydney, MAC MU2659; according to the EEF distribution lists, strings of carnelian beads from the same season were also sent to Birmingham, Cambridge, Chautauqua, Dundee (see also *Dundee Courier* 11 May 1899) and Montreal.

EA 18647   1887,0101.643   (Pl. 29)

String of 19 globular, faceted bicone, and irregularly shaped rock crystal beads.
Length: 25.2cm (string).
Context: provenance not specified in the Museum register, but perhaps from Tell Nebesha if not from Tell Dafana, according to the context of the item in the list, or Tell Gemaiyemi.

EA 18649   1887,0101.645   (Pl. 29)

String of 47 beads of many different materials: 26 small carnelian standard and long truncated convex bicone beads, one barrel disc bead of garnet and one long truncated convex bicone of mottled yellow serpentine. One large spherical bead is of mottled green serpentine and a faceted oblong bead, semicircular in section and bored through the shorter side, is of green quartz. There are five lapis lazuli beads: one disc, one standard convex bicone bead and three short barrels. The string is completed by five amethyst beads: two standard convex bicones, two spherical and one large truncated convex bicone and seven green felspar pieces: a lenticular bead (a flattened circle in shape), one circular tabular bead, four short barrels and an irregularly shaped chip.
Length: 26cm (string).
Context: see EA 18648 above.
Bibliography: Andrews 1981, 74, no. 537.

EA 23470   1887,0101.1518   (Pl. 29)

String of 57 beads and pendant-beads of various shapes (globular, lentiform, fusiform, biconical, cylindrical; some pendant beads pebble shaped and in the form of a poppy seed head) and materials (lapis lazuli, agate, amber, diorite, feldspar, garnet, rock crystal, jasper, steatite, chalcedony, glass, amethyst, and carnelian).
Length: 38.1cm (string), diameters of beads from 1.8cm to 0.45cm.
Context: same as for EA 18648 above.
Parallels: see also the broken pendant-bead EA 23502 (1887,0101.1166) below.
Bibliography: Petrie 1888, 79 § 79.
Parallels: from Tell Dafana, see the broken pendant-bead EA 23502 (1887,0101.1166) below.

EA 23471   1887,0101.1519   (Pl. 29)

String of 22 beads of truncated bicone or barrel shape, ten made of carnelian (one incomplete) and twelve (one bigger) of agate or onyx with black and white stratification.
Length: 34.9cm (string); diameter of beads: 1.35cm (max.).
Context: same as for EA 18648 above.
Bibliography: Petrie 1888, 79 § 79.
Parallels: from Tell Dafana or its neighbourhood, Bristol, CMAG H1319.

EA 23502   1887,0101.1166   (Pl. 28)

Red glass or jasper pendant-bead in the shape of a poppy seed head, with a transverse hole for suspension at one end.
Length: 1.22cm; diameter: 0.62cm.
Context: see EA 18648 above.
Bibliography: concerning glass and stone beads, see Petrie, 1888, 79 § 79; see also Herrmann 2006, 231–3, nos 452–65, pl. ci, nos 453–4, 457–64. For complete beads of this shape from Tell Dafana, see EA 23470 above.

EA 18507   1887,0101.702   (Pl. 28)

Malachite plaque or bead, of rectangular shape, pierced.
Length: 1.9cm; width: 1.3cm; thickness: 0.5cm.
Context: see EA 18648 above.

EA 18484   1887,0101.699   (Pl. 28)

Lapis lazuli bead in the shape of a star, with a loop for attachment on the back.

Height: 0.82cm; width: 0.86cm; thickness: 0.34cm.
Context: probably from the north-west Ptolemaic mound.
Bibliography: Petrie 1888, 73 § 70, p. 111, pl. xli, 38.

Glass beads (Pl. 29)

EA 23473   1887,0101.1520
String of 29 decayed glass beads of irregular fusiform shape, some of them having a yellow end. Seven of the beads are partly broken.
Length: 44.6cm (string); diameter of beads: 1.08cm (max.).
Bibliography: for comments on glass beads, see Petrie 1888, 79 § 79.

EA 23469   1887,0101.1517
String of 54 graduated glass beads of different colours (mostly black or dark grey, with a few light yellow, green and dark blue), of various shapes (globular, twisted, fusiform, moniliform, discoid or cylindrical). One loose bead is kept with the string.
Length: 35.2cm (string); diameter of beads from 1.25cm to 0.5cm.
Bibliography: same as for EA 23473 above.

GR 1887,1220.1
String of 36 graduated millefiori glass beads of various colours and sizes, mostly globular and disc- or cylinder-shaped.
Length: 37.5cm (string); diameter of beads from 2.24cm to 0.6cm.
Bibliography: same as for EA 23473 above.

GR 1887,1220.2
String of 27 glass beads, mostly cylinder- or egg-shaped and fusiform, and one globular pendant with a suspension ring.
Length: 47cm (string); diameter of beads from 2cm to 0.36cm.
Bibliography: same as for EA 23473 above.

GR 1887,1220.3
String of 13 glass beads of various sizes and shapes (cylindrical, globular, lentiform, discoid, biconical, fusiform, moniliform and polyhedral), some gilded.
Length: 10cm (string); diameter of beads from 0.9cm to 0.34cm.
Bibliography: same as for EA 23473 above.

EA 18655   1887,0101.648
String of 72 small, broadly biconical, green and white striated glass beads.
Length: 36.7cm (string).
Context: provenance not specified in the Museum register, but probably from Tell Nebesha if not from Tell Dafana, according to the context of the item in the list, or Tell Gemaiyemi.

Composite beads (Pl. 29)

EA 23472   1887,0101.995-998
String of 43 glazed composition and glass beads and pendants of various shapes and dimensions: two glazed composition grooved bicone beads and two grooved spherical beads; red, orange, green, blue and white globular glass beads; string also contains a number of striated glass short cylindrical beads.
Length: 26.8cm (string).
Bibliography: for comments on glazed composition beads, see Petrie 1888, 75 § 72; for glass beads, ibid., 79 § 79.
Parallels: from Tell Dafana or its neighbourhood, Bristol CMAG H1326, H3614, H7570.

EA 18660   1887,0101.646
String of 30 globular glazed composition and glass beads of various colours and dimensions.
Length: 33.9cm (string).
Context: provenance not specified in the Museum register, but probably from Tell Nebesha if not from Tell Dafana, according to the context of the item in the list, or Tell Gemaiyemi.

EA 18653   1887,0101.647
String of beads of various shapes, materials and dimensions. The string includes a centrally strung amber-coloured glass bicone bead, three agate beads (two globular, one long barrel), a number of rock crystal beads (barrel and long convex bicones, some gilded), other globular, barrel, oblate disc and irregularly shaped green, blue and black glass beads, two globular mosaic glass beads and other glazed composition beads of various shapes, some with impressed decoration.
Length: 36.8cm.
Context: same as for EA 18660 above.

EA 18650   1887,0101.649
String of 13 beads of various shapes, dimensions and materials: a big spherical one made of clay possibly fired; an oblate oval one, broken away, made of white stone (limestone?), with concentric traces of dark green and red glaze on the edge; two tiny rings of yellowish glazed composition; one made of an irregular and twisted cylinder of translucent brown-yellow glass; a big oblate spherical bead of a red glazed composition or glass with narrow radial black traces; seven medium ones of tubular to globular shape, made of opaque red glass imitating red jasper, covering, in five cases, a black or dark translucent internal cylinder.
Length: 8.6cm (string; maximum dimensions of the bead marked with the Museum number are, length: 1.43cm; width: 1.02cm; thickness: 0.65cm).
Context: same as for EA 18660 above.

EA 18658   1887,0101.650
String of beads of various shapes and dimensions; beads of glazed composition include globular beads, some with traces of green glaze, short and standard cylinder beads, one moulded, other beads of this material comprise one of irregular shape with impressed decoration, a green *wedjat*-eye bead, a barrel bead with incised decoration, a green *djed*-pillar bead and a blue diamond-shaped bead; the string also contains a number of shells, both complete and sliced.
Length: 27.8cm (string).
Context: same as for EA 18660 above.

Silver, bronze and stone pendants (Pl. 29)

EA 18300   1887,0101.596
Silver pendant in shape of ram's head wearing the uraeus, with incised details.
Height: 2.75cm; width: 2.07cm (max.); depth: 0.85cm.
Context: Saite enclosure (so-called 'Camp').
Bibliography: Petrie 1888, 76 § 75, p. 110, pl. xli, 11: silver 'fine ram's head with the uraeus on it (pl. xli, 11) [...] found in the camp, with two silver uraei, and a bronze Apis'.
Parallels: for comparison, see a similar gold ram-head in New York, MM 1989.281.98, illustrated in Hill and Schorsch 2007, 92, fig. 49; 208, no. 36; see also Settgast, 1978, no. 252); and a lapis lazuli ram-head pendant in Boston, MFA 1973.661; both items are considered as dating from the 25th dynasty.

EA 23880   1887,0101.1076
Corroded copper alloy pendant in the shape of a simple rod of rectangular cross section, with rounded ends, one gently flattened and pierced by a small round hole for suspension.
Length: 2.89cm; width: 0.69cm; thickness: 0.43cm.
Bibliography: Petrie 1888, 80 § 80, mentions finds of bronze objects, but this item is not specified.

GR 1906,0301.11
Rectangular pendant or tag of dark green stone, perforated at the top, with a design, scored on one side, of several illegible signs encircled within a probable imitation of a cartouche.
Height: 5.13cm; width: 3.02cm; thickness: 1cm.
Bibliography: Petrie 1888, 72 § 68, pl. xxiv, 5: 'the piece of a whetstone is noticeable, as it appears to bear an attempt at a cartouche by some one who knew nothing of hieroglyphs, nor indeed of any writing apparently'.

GR 1906,0301.15
Oval pendant of dark green-black stone with a round transversal suspension hole at the top, and flat rounded cross section.
Height: 3.79cm; width: 3.3cm; thickness: 1.15cm.
Bibliography: Petrie 1888, 74 § 71: possibly the 'syenite pebble pendant.....like the dozens which occur at Naukratis'.
Parallels: Boston, MFA 87.784.

14. Games

Senet games (Pl. 30)

EA 23802   1887, 0101.811

Fragments of a rectangular gaming-board made of coarse red siltware pottery. The fragments have been joined to form two large pieces, one consisting of six fragments, the other of three. Parts of the original edges of the object are preserved, showing either a slight curve or a straight cut. The irregular lower surface shows circular traces confirming that the gaming-board was made from a wheel-made platter, cut on two long sides before firing. The upper surface of the board was scored with a grid pattern of originally 10 x 3 squares, a maximum of 21 being now preserved, on both items together. The grooves between the squares were cut post-firing, through the pale cream surface slip. This slip is also present on the plain underside. A small area of the larger piece has been made up in modern material. The two pieces are not joined but their relative positions can be inferred almost exactly from the scored lines on the upper surfaces and the circular traces on the undersides. The number and distribution of the squares suggest that the object was a board for the Egyptian senet game.

Larger piece, length: 26cm; width: 15.2cm; thickness: 2.1cm.
Smaller piece, length: 12.3cm; width: 8.9cm; thickness: 1.7cm.
Both fragments together, length: 34.5cm.
Context: 'Qasr', east annexe (C), chamber 9 (this number is scratched on the object).
Bibliography: Petrie 1888, 74 § 71: 'draught-board made of a rectangular slab of terra-cotta marked in 3x10 squares, found broken up, with some draughtmen made of rounded chips of pottery, in chamber 9'; see Journal, 123: 'a draught board of pottery, broken up, was also here, 3 x 10 squares'; ibid., 142: 'three draughtboards have been found; one of pottery made on purpose, one scratched in a big dish from, & one scratched on stone'; see also Pusch 1979, 370–1, § 78, no. 69a; Piccione 1990, 440, no. E035.
Parallels: from Tell Dafana, see EA 22323, 23803 below, and Boston, MFA RES 87.148 (deaccessioned). The draughtmen are very probably EA 23835, 23836, 23837 and 23838 below.

EA 22323   1887,0101.1261

A circular pottery platter, reconstructed from four fragments with two small parts missing. The central part of the upper surface is scored with lines in a grid-pattern of 10 x 3 squares, for use as a gaming-board. The pattern was incised after firing. The platter is made from a low-fired red siltware fabric containing sand and grit temper. The surface was covered by a pale cream slip, which has worn off in places. The edge of the platter is rounded and the underside is uneven. The number and distribution of the squares suggest that the board was for the traditional Egyptian senet game.
Diameter: 31.5cm; thickness: 1.7cm.
Bibliography: Petrie 1888, 74 § 71: 'large plate scored up into 3 x 10 squares very roughly'; see also Journal, 142: 'three draughtboards have been found; one of pottery made on purpose, one scratched in a big dish from, & one scratched on stone'; Pusch 1979, 370–1, § 78, no. 69b; Piccione 1990, 440, no. E030.
Parallels: same as for EA 23802.

EA 23803   1887,0101.846

Part of a redware pottery dish or platter with a rim, covered by a white slip into which grid and other motifs have been roughly scored on the upper surface to use as a gaming-board. Ten squares are preserved, distributed in at least three rows. Comparison with similar items of the same provenance suggests that a grid of probably 3 x 10 squares was scored in the middle of the platter. Each of the three squares on the right side shows a hieroglyphic sign: from top to bottom, 1) a hawk facing to the right, perhaps on a stand, 2) a sign formed by two horizontal lines crossed by an oblique one, and 3) a part of an

Figure 4 EA 23803 (1:4)

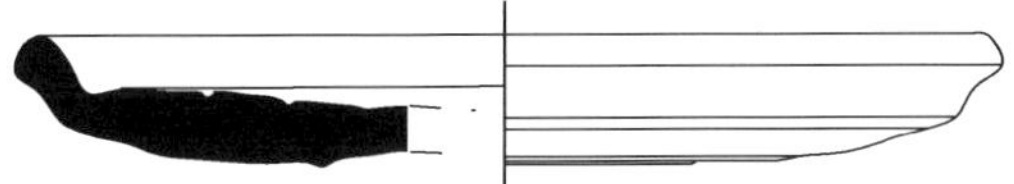

indeterminate sign with a vertical line on the left. The number and distribution of the squares and signs attest that the item is a gaming-board for the traditional Egyptian senet game.
Length: 13.7cm (max.); width: 11.6cm (max.); thickness: 3.1cm; diameter: 27cm (reconstructed).
Bibliography: Petrie 1888, 74 § 71: one of the 'pieces of plates scored up'; Journal, 142 (see EA 22323 above); Pusch 1979, 370–1, § 78, no. 69.c; Piccione 1990, 440, no. E040.

Gaming-pieces (Pl. 30)

EA 23835   1887,0101.873

Oval clay game-piece made from a recut sherd of pottery.
Length: 3.2cm; width 2.6cm; thickness: 1.2cm.
Context: 'Qasr', east annexe (C), chamber 9?
Bibliography: Petrie 1888, 74 § 71: very probably one of the 'draughtmen made of rounded chips of pottery in chamber 9', found with game-board EA 23802 above.

EA 23836   1887,0101.874

Oval clay game-piece made from a recut sherd of pottery
Length: 3.05cm; width: 2.3cm; thickness: 0.9cm.
Context: 'Qasr', east annexe (C), chamber 9?
Bibliography: same as for EA 23835 above.

EA 23837   1887,0101.875

Oval clay game-piece made from a recut sherd of pottery.
Length: 3.7cm; width 3.4cm; thickness: 1.7cm.
Context: 'Qasr', east annexe (C), chamber 9?
Bibliography: same as for EA 23835 above.

EA 23838   1887,0101.876

Oval clay game-piece made from a recut sherd of pottery
Length: 3cm; width: 2.2cm; thickness: 1.9cm.
Context: 'Qasr', east annexe (C), chamber 9?
Bibliography: same as for EA 23835 above.

EA 18463   1887,0101.712

Green glazed composition conical artefact, possibly a game-piece.
Height: 2.11cm, diameter: 1.17cm.
Context: provenance not specified in the Museum register, but possibly from Tell Dafana, as suggested by the context of the item in the list, if not from Tell Nebesha or any other eastern Delta site excavated by Petrie in 1886.
Bibliography: if from Tell Dafana, possibly the 'conoid draughtman' from Chamber 17, mentioned by in Petrie 1888, 74 § 72, if this is not EA 18453 (above, p. 53).

Die

GR 1911,0210.2

Ivory cubical die with dots carved in sunk relief.
Height: 1.18cm; length: 1.29cm; width: 1.27cm.
Context: 'Qasr', east annexe (C), chamber 27.
Bibliography: Petrie 1888, 75 § 72, pl. xl, 15: 'an ivory die found in chamber 27 (pl. xl. 15) and so carrying back such dice to the sixth century'.
Parallels: two other dice, made of limestone, come from Tell Dafana, probably from the Saite enclosure, see ibid., 73 § 70. London, PM UC 59225 and Boston, MFA 87.712); see also Petrie 1927, 57, pl. xlix; Laurent and Desti 1997, 302, no. 561.

15. Drill-cores, samples and slag

Drill-cores (Pl. 30)

EA 23833   1887,0101.884

Fragment of a calcite cylindrical drill-core, slightly tapering and broken at both ends, possibly a by-product of vessel manufacture.
Height: 3.2cm; diameter: 0.8cm.
Bibliography: Petrie 1888, 74 § 70: 'alabaster'.
Parallels: for this item and other drill-cores, see the other examples from the site in various collections; calcite: London, PM UC 72458 (4

items); Boston, MFA RES.87.116–117 (2 items); jasper: Boston, MFA RES 87.114- 115 (2 items); syenite: Boston, MFA 87.118.

EA 23832   1887,0101.690
Calcite drill-core, a by-product of vessel manufacture, cylinder-shaped with a kind of flange around one end, partly broken. The other end is flat and also partly broken.
Height: 1.3cm; diameter: 1cm.
Bibliography: Petrie 1888, 74 § 70: 'alabaster'.
Parallels: same as for EA 23833 above.

EA 18478   1887,0101.688
Fragment of a red jasper cylindrical artefact, broken at both ends, chipped on one side, possibly a drill-core, a by-product of bead or amulet manufacture.
Height: 1.1cm; diameter: 0.8cm.
Context: provenance not specified in the Museum register, but probably from Tell Dafana, as suggested by the context of the item in the list.
Bibliography: Petrie 1888, 74 § 70: 'jasper'.
Parallels: from Tell Dafana, Boston, MFA RES.87.114–115.

EA 18476   1887,0101.689
Basalt cylindrical artefact, with a flat base and slightly rounded top, possibly a drill-core or a weight.
Height: 1cm; diameter: 0.85cm.
Context: same as for EA 18478 above.
Bibliography: Petrie 1888, 74 § 70: 'basalt'.

EA 18480   1887,0101.693
Fragment of an obsidian cylindrical artefact, tapering towards one end on one side, and with uneven top surface; probably a drill-core, a by-product of vessel manufacture.
Context: same as for EA 18478 above.
Height: 2.2cm; diameter: 1.1cm.
Bibliography: Petrie 1888, 74 § 70: 'obsidian'.

EA 18477   1887,0101.691
Fragment of a cylindrical black and white granite artefact, broken at both ends, probably a drill-core, a by-product of bead or amulet manufacture.
Height: 1.2cm; diameter: 1.1cm.
Context: same as for EA 18478 above.
Bibliography: Petrie 1888, 74 § 70: 'syenite'.
Parallels: from Tell Dafana, Boston, MFA RES.87.118.

EA 18475   1887,0101.692
Fragment of a dark grey basalt cylindrical artefact, broken at both ends, probably a drill-core, or raw material for amulet manufacture.
Height: 0.8cm; diameter: 0.9cm.
Context: same as for EA 18478 above.
Bibliography: Petrie 1888, 74 § 70: 'basalt'.

Samples (Pl. 30)

EA 18501   1887,0101.694
Sample of lapis lazuli.
Length: 1.7cm; width: 1.5cm; thickness 0.4cm.
Context: provenance not specified in the Museum register, but possibly from Tell Dafana, as suggested by the context of the item in the list.
Bibliography: Petrie 1888, 74 § 70: possibly the ' piece of sliced lapis lazuli'.

EA 23839   1887,0101.760
Rectangular pumice-stone roughly squared off, with softly rounded edges.
Length: 5cm; width: 3.57cm; thickness: 2.82cm.
Context: 'Qasr', east annexe (C), chamber 19 (number written in black on the object).
Bibliography: Petrie 1888, 74 § 70: 'a piece of pumice was found in chamber 19'.

EA 23813   1887,0101.871
Fragment of an unidentified limestone artefact.
Length: 3.76cm (max.); width: 2.38cm (max.).

EA 23996   1887,0101.987
Sample of fossilized wood.
Length: 2.6cm; width: 1.5cm; thickness: 0.4cm.
Bibliography: recorded as a 'fragment of haematite' in the museum register, which would fit with Petrie 1888, 79 § 78: 'some very fine haematite'.

EA 23840   1887,0101.1416
A triangular block of sulphur.
Height: 1.8cm; length: 2.9cm; width: 2.8cm.
Context: 'Qasr', east annexe (C), chamber 17.
Bibliography: Petrie 1888, 75 § 72: 'native sulphur in chamber 17'.

EA 23860   1887,0101.813
Irregularly shaped sample of lead ore (galena).
Length: 3.3cm (max.); width: 2.7cm (max.); thickness: 1.1cm (max.).
Context: Saite enclosure (so-called 'Camp').
Bibliography: Petrie 1888, 74 § 70: 'some pieces of lead ore (galena) in the Camp'; ibid., 77 § 76: 'of lead a few pieces of ore (galena) were found'.
Parallels: Boston, MFA, RES.87.41-42 (deaccessioned); see also the samples of lead and copper ores in the foundation deposits of Psamtik I, EA 23556 (1887,0101.1364–1374) above.

EA 23860   1887,0101.814
Rectangular sample of galena with cut surfaces.
Length: 2.3cm (max.); width: 1.4cm (max.); thickness: 1.15cm (max.).
Context: Saite enclosure (so-called 'Camp').
Bibliography and parallels: same as for EA 23860 above.

EA 23860   1887,0101.815
Irregularly shaped sample of galena.
Length: 1.7cm (max.); Width: 1.2cm (max.).
Context: Saite enclosure (so-called 'Camp').
Bibliography and parallels: same as for EA 23860 above.

EA 23851   1887,0101.907-925
Nineteen chunks of base silver of various shapes and dimensions: three large, thick pieces of quadrangular shape with bevelled sides (1887,0101.907, .910 and .912); one quadrangular thin plaque (1887,0101.921), two small pebble-shaped pieces, flat and rounded (1887,0101.915 and .925); two made of irregular agglomerated chunks bonded by corrosion (1887,0101.911 and .913); and eleven of irregular polyhedral shape (1887,0101.908, .909, .914, .916 to 920; .922 to 924). A high copper content is indicated by the presence of green corrosion products.
Length: 2.7cm; width: 2.4cm; thickness: 1.27cm (1887,0101.907).
Length: 2.37cm; width: 1.26cm; thickness: 0.9cm (1887,0101.908).
Length: 1.8cm; width: 1.7cm; thickness: 1.3cm (1887,0101.909).
Length: 2.7cm; width: 2.34cm; thickness: 2.05cm (1887,0101.910).
Length: 3.4cm; width: 3.11cm; thickness: 2.46cm (1887,0101.911).
Length: 2.3cm; width: 1.87cm; thickness: 1.5cm (1887,0101.912).
Length: 2.6cm; width: 1.5cm; thickness: 1cm (1887,0101.913).
Length: 1.2cm; width: 1.04cm; thickness: 1.12cm (1887,0101.914).
Length: 1.3cm; width: 1.1cm; thickness: 0.68cm (1887,0101.915).
Length: 1.64cm; width: 1.05cm; thickness: 0.75cm (1887,0101.916).
Length: 1.08cm; width: 0.78cm; thickness: 0.61cm (1887,0101.917).
Length: 1.1cm; width: 1cm; thickness: 0.69cm (1887,0101.918).
Length: 0.91cm; width: 0.84cm; thickness: 0.56cm (1887,0101.919).
Length: 0.8cm; width: 0.76cm; thickness: 0.56cm (1887,0101.920).
Length: 1.5cm; width: 0.9cm; thickness: 0.24cm (1887,0101.921).
Length: 0.8cm; width: 0.68cm; thickness: 0.45cm (1887,0101.922).
Length: 0.57cm; width: 0.56cm; thickness: 0.57cm (1887,0101.923).
Length: 0.63cm; width: 0.55cm; thickness: 0.42cm (1887,0101.924).
Length: 0.6cm; width: 0.46cm; thickness: 0.4cm (1887,0101.925).
Bibliography: Petrie 1888, 76 § 75: part of the 'many pounds' weight of lumps of silver, melted and roughly cut up, besides large quantities of scrap silver in fragments of 20 to 200 grains found by the Bedawin'. These pieces are possibly the silver fragments described in Petrie's Journal, 152: 'I continually have to buy 5/- [shilling] to 10/- [shilling]

worth of silver scraps (cut up evidently for jeweller's use), from the
Bedawin. Of course they are worth nothing, but there is always the
chance of a coin or bit of jewellery among them; & if I do not buy, they
will take to Kantara & sell there, & then I may lo[o]se getting other
things that I do want. So I take everything that comes. It is lucky that
they did not find my big haul, almost as good a negative as the positive
that I did get it'.

GR 1890,0619.43

Irregular lump of blue frit, broken on two opposite sides, with a small
hollow on the top, probably from scraping pigment powder.
Length: 5.6cm; width: 3.2cm; thickness: 2.33cm.
Parallels: from Tell Dafana, Oxford, AM 1887.2510.

GR 1890,0619.44

Fragment of a round, flat lump of pale blue frit, with two chips missing
from the edge.
Length: 2.6cm; width: 2.4cm; thickness: 1.3cm.

Slag (Pl. 30)

EA 23991   1887,0101.778

Part of the side of a pottery crucible, the interior vitrified and coated in
places with green copper staining. A small part of the original rim
survives. The external pottery surface is very friable. Accompanied
under the same number by a small lump of copper slag.
Length (crucible): 12cm; width: 11.5cm; thickness: 5.2cm.
Length (slag): 3.92cm; width: 2.46cm; thickness: 1.39cm.
Context: Saite enclosure (so-called 'Camp').
Bibliography: Petrie 1888, 77 § 76: 'pieces of large crucibles covered
with copper slag are found'.

EA 23990   1887,0101.1010

Rough hemispherical hollow lump of iron slag with inclusions of
charcoal and ceramic chips, from the bottom of a hearth for iron
working; see the scientific report at Appendix 1, iii.
Length: 16.5cm; width: 14.4cm; thickness: 5.8cm.
Context: Findspot 52, iron working area in the south-east part of the
Saite enclosure (so-called 'Camp').
Bibliography: Petrie 1888, 59 § 57, p. 79 § 78: very probably the
'complete crucible bottom of slag mixed with charcoal'; Amborn 1976,
80.
Parallels: from Tell Dafana, see fragments GR 1888,0208.170 below,
Boston, MFA RES.87.84.

GR 1888,0208.170

Fragment of iron slag.
Length: 3cm (max.); width: 2.6cm; thickness: 2.2cm.
Context: Findspot 52, iron working area in the south-east part of the
Saite enclosure (so-called 'Camp').
Bibliography: Petrie 1888, 59 § 57, p. 79 § 78: on the large amount of
iron slag found, particularly 'all over the S.E. of the camp'.
Parallels: same as for EA 23990.

Chapter 4

Egyptian Pottery and Imported Transport Amphorae from Tell Dafana
Types and Distribution

Jeffrey Spencer

Introduction[1]

The Egyptian pottery found in the Egypt Exploration Fund excavations of 1886 at Tell Dafana[2] includes a range of vessel types and fabrics familiar from Late Period ceramics, but differs in some respects from the typical assemblages of the period found at most other excavated sites in the Delta, particularly in a more frequent use of marl clays. This characteristic, however, is shared with certain other sites in the local region, such as Tell el-Herr[3] and Migdol,[4] so the higher frequency of marlware may be connected with the desert locations of these places far from the alluvial flood-plain where the majority of Delta towns were situated. Another regular feature of the Tell Dafana pottery is the use of pale slips over red Nile silt fabric, probably intended as an economical imitation of the finer marl clay vessels. These slips vary in hue from green-grey to a pale yellow-cream and the marl vessels are of similar colours. The use of slips and of marl clay may have been further motivated by the presence at the site of imported Cypriote, Levantine and Greek products in foreign clays of similar shades. This hypothesis is supported by the use of marl fabrics to make low bowls with ring-bases which, although Egyptian products, owe much to foreign inspiration. The use of marl clays is, of course, much more common amongst the Late Dynastic pottery of Upper Egypt, predominantly for jars, and although marl jars are much rarer among the pottery of the Delta some very fine examples occur at Tell Dafana. The contrast between the pale grey-green marl wares of Upper Egypt and the overwhelmingly red hue of Delta silt ware pottery is one of the most noticeable differences between the Late Dynastic pottery of the south and the north. The finest of the marl clays used at Tell Dafana is superior to the usual Marl A2 of Upper Egypt (**Fig. 1**).[5] In addition to its use for bowls and fine jars mentioned above, marl clay was employed to make many of the jar lids and covers which were so very common at the site (**Fig. 2**). Petrie's explanation of the need for so many lids is almost certainly correct: that the remote desert

Figure 1 The finest marl fabric

Figure 2 Examples of lids

Figure 3 Platter, British Museum, EA 23687

location meant much carrying of liquids in vessels from a distance and lids were necessary to prevent contents being spilled or contaminated. They would certainly have been needed to exclude airborne dust, which on the exposed flat desert plain of Tell Dafana must have been (and still is) grim on any windy day. Some proof of this is offered by the relative scarcity of similar lids at Delta sites in the alluvial flood-plain, but their occurrence in some numbers at Tell el-Maskhuta in the Wadi Tumilat, another site in a sandy environment.[6] The influence of the local environment on pottery production may also explain the presence of large numbers of flat circular platters amongst the Tell Dafana pottery (**Fig. 3**). These would have been useful as surfaces on which food could be placed away from the grit. They are quite well made, mostly in silt clay but with a pale slip over all surfaces. Although platters do occur at other Delta sites, they are mostly coarse silt clay products made entirely by hand, usually with a raised edge, and were probably used for laying out bread.[7] This type of coarse platter is known also from more southerly sites such as El-Ashmunein[8] and Ehnasya[9]; its absence from the published ceramics of Qurna, Kafr Ammar and Lahun[10] may be due to selective recording. Another effect of the desert environment at Tell Dafana shows up in the presence of a large number of inclusions of quartz grains and other pieces of grit in the fabric, most particularly of the silt ware products (**Fig. 4**). This suggests local manufacture on the desert plain. The poor quality of many of the silt clay vessels may also be evidence for the lack of a skilled pottery industry at the site. The shapes of many of the jars have been distorted in manufacture to such an extent that some would probably have been rejected as wasters at a location with a more sophisticated pottery workshop. The fact that these inferior vessels were used emphasizes the rather remote setting of Tell Dafana, where bringing in better goods from outside would have placed heavy demands on time and resources. The finest of the marl clay vessels were much better produced and may indeed have been traded in from

Figure 4 Silt fabric of EA 23666 (British Museum), showing grit inclusions

other centres, as smaller quantities would have been involved. On the other hand, some of the more common marlware shapes, particularly the lids, are so simple that the local potters may have been able to produce reasonable versions. It is worth noting that some of the cylindrical cups exhibit distortion, being not truly circular in plan view, so some of these may also have been local. The proportion of marlwares in the assemblage was probably even higher than at first apparent because of the fragility of the finest of the marl vessels. As Petrie remarked:

> Beside the pottery here illustrated, the finest of all, the beautiful drab ware, remains; but that is so generally broken up that its forms can hardly be ascertained.[11]

From this we may assume that, although this ware was common, very little was brought away by Petrie. He also talks about 'dozens' of marl cups but very few intact ones, so this type must also be under represented in the museum examples:

> The cups 75, 76, 78, 79 are difficult to get perfect. Dozens of broken ones were found; but the only perfect examples of the thin drab cups, 76, were taken out of the insides of large amphoras, which were cracked, but not crushed in by the earth.[12]

Some examples of the best of the marl products from Tell Dafana were re-discovered in 2010 among a group of unidentified pottery in the British Museum. The discovery began when a mass of unregistered sherds from Tell Dafana, kept for a long time in the Department of Greece and Rome, was brought to the attention of this project.[13] These fragments were all of marl clay of varying degrees of fineness, and it proved possible to find some joins among the sherds and to make partial reconstructions of a few vessels, such as the bowl in **Figure 5**.[14] A search for parallels for these ceramics, and for the marlware generally, led to a small group of seven vessels stored in the Department of Ancient Egypt and Sudan. These had been part of a large transfer of ceramics from the Greek and Roman Department in 1912, but they lacked any acquisition details or provenance. All but two of the vessels consisted of the characteristic marl fabric of Petrie's 'drab ware' from Tell Dafana, the exceptions being a red-slipped Saite situla-shaped jar and a Phoenician-style amphora. On close examination, some of the jars were found to bear incised Tell Dafana Findspot numbers of the kind used by Petrie, thereby confirming the provenance. It is suspected that the marl jars in this group may have been reconstructed long ago from the sherd collection mentioned above. The seven

Figure 5 Bowl of fine marl clay, British Museum, EA 79644

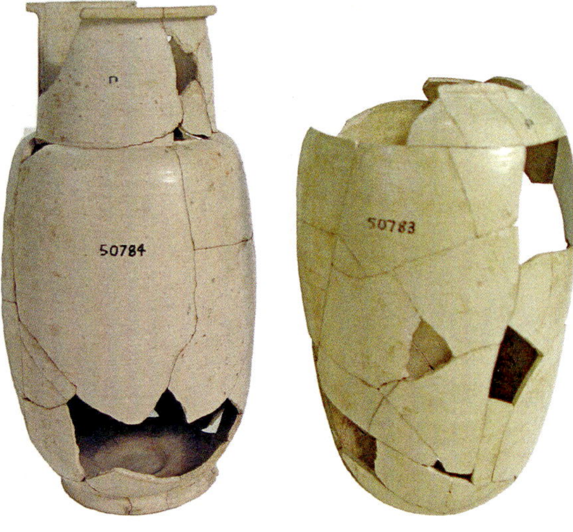

Figure 6 Fine marl jars, British Museum, EA 50783, 50784

Figure 7 Marl dish, British Museum, EA 23690

Figure 8 Mortarium, British Museum, EA 23685

vessels are included in the catalogue under numbers EA 50781 to 50786, and 50788. The best of this group are particularly fine, especially the jars EA 50783 and 50784, which are made in a mix of the marl clay which is compact, free of inclusions and worked to remarkable thinness (**Fig. 6**). Some other examples of similar quality fabric occur amongst the sherd collection, whilst other pieces consist of the more usual coarser marl clay.

Summary of the types represented

This description is intended to provide an overview of the principal types of vessel present among the ceramics from Petrie's work. The repertoire of sites at which similar pottery has been found, mentioned here, will be familiar to anyone who has worked on Late Dynastic ceramics. Some references to parallels for whole classes of vessels are cited in this discussion, but specific parallels for individual vessels are given in the catalogue (Chapter 5).

A most valuable resource for Late Period pottery is David and Barbara Aston's *Late Period Pottery from the New Kingdom Necropolis at Saqqara. Egypt Exploration Society – National Museum of Antiquities, Leiden, Excavations 1975–1995* (London/Leiden 2010). This not only contains many good parallels to the pottery from Tell Dafana, but also includes an analysis of Late Dynastic ceramics in which several stages are identified.[15] The bulk of the Tell Dafana material belongs in Aston's Phase B1, dated to the 7th to 6th centuries BC, with some vessels of the succeeding Phase B2.[16] A few pieces among the pottery found by Petrie date from the Ptolemaic Period, and came perhaps from the Hellenistic settlement mound at the north-west of the site, or from Ptolemaic pits cut within the Saite enclosure.

1. Flat platters (Pl. 31)

Circular, flat platters were fairly common products at Tell Dafana, although such simple products exhibit little variety of styles. They usually possess a very low ring- or disc-foot and some have a slightly concave upper surface (EA 23686). The finding of several below the floor of chamber 19 in the eastern annexes (Findspot 32) indicates that they date back to the early part of the 26th dynasty. They possess a green-grey surface slip over a coarse red silt fabric, the slip

probably being intended as an economical imitation of the appearance of marlware products. At most other Delta sites, uncoated red silt platters are more usual.

2. Dishes, basins and mortaria (Pl. 31)

Like the platters, the low dishes also occur in cream-slipped red siltware,[17] but there are some examples made entirely from marl clay of a pale green/cream colour. These may have been intended to imitate the appearance of imported ceramics in clays of similar colours, such as mortaria from Cyprus. The style of some of the low dishes with ring-feet (EA 23692–3, 79641, 23690) may also suggest inspiration by Greek products (**Fig. 7**). The fine marl plates do not seem to be a regular feature of many other Delta sites, but they are noted from Tell el-Maskhuta.[18] They also occur at Tell el-Herr, but mostly in later contexts of the Persian Period.[19] The large-diameter shallow basin of coarse red siltware (EA 22369) is a typical Late Period product known from a wide range of sites, including Tell Kedwa, Tanis, Tell el-Balamun and Saqqara. The two items EA 23685 and 23708 are examples of mortaria.[20] The former may be a local copy, made of a gritty, pink clay with a pale green-yellow surface slip. This was intended to imitate the appearance of imported mortaria from Cyprus, of which EA 23708 is an example. That these vessels were actually used is shown by the fact that EA 23685 has been worn through by grinding material in it (**Fig. 8**).

3. Bowls (Pls 31–2)

The range of bowls includes open bowls not dissimilar from the ceramic tradition of the Third Intermediate Period (EA

Figure 9 Bowl, British Museum, EA 23695

Figure 10 Imitation rivets on EA 23658 (British Museum)

23752); small flared dishes (EA 23665), convex sided bowls, some of which may well be Ptolemaic products, and finally, carinated bowls and dishes. The unusual vessels GR 1888,0208.62 and 63 at the foot of **Plate 31** were inspired by Achaemenid bowls, but with the addition of ring-feet. The bowls EA 23683 and 23682 are of a style known also from Tell el-Balamun, Mendes and Naukratis and references are cited in the catalogue. They are made in red silt pottery. The smaller bowls EA 79642 and 79643 are made in marl clay. EA 23688 is a specialized vessel of uncertain use with a central perforation in the base. The bowls EA 23724 and 23695 are finer products in compact, greenish marl clay (**Fig. 9**). Parallels for these are hard to find, but there is one from Saqqara.[21] EA 23679 is a utilitarian basin, of which only a large sherd survives. The excavations of 2009 at Tell Dafana produced a few more bowls (**Pl. 77**, nos 2.1–5.3).

4. Dishes, miniature vessels and cooking pots (Pl. 33)

The small vessels drawn at the top of **Plate 33** are all shown at half-scale (instead of the usual 1:4). They comprise dishes and cups, mostly in silt fabrics, only EA 23698 and 23699 being marl clay products. The object EA 22306, however, may well have been a cover because it bears a scar at the centre of the convex base (or top) where a handle may once have been attached. Some of the items shown here are sufficiently small to be considered as models (EA 23701–3, 23651–2) and it is noteworthy that a large quantity of model vessels was found in the excavations of 2009 at the site, from the temple area in the great enclosure (**Pls 79–81**). The closest parallels, however, are the model vases from the foundation deposits of Amasis in the temple at Mendes.[22] Another example of a flared cup similar in shape to EA 23699, but with a line of demotic text on the side, was found in 2009 (**Pl. 77**, no. 6.2). The vessels at the bottom of **Plate 33** (at 1:4 scale) are all utilitarian products in coarse silt clay, sometimes with a bright red surface slip, although much of this has been lost. The casserole EA 23658 was modelled on a metal form and has imitation rivets around the handles (**Fig. 10**). Another example like EA 23657 was found in 2009 (**Pl. 77**, no. 7.3).

5. Cups and neckless jars (Pl. 34)

The handled vessel EA 23718 is made in marl clay and is represented only by a fragment, so it is not certain whether there was a second handle on the opposite side. The cylindrical cups, drawn at the top of **Plate 34**, were sometimes made in red-slipped silt clay (EA 23654, 23704, 23653), but finer examples in green-grey marl clay are also common (EA 23696, 23697, 79645). Although better

manufactured than most of the ceramics from Tell Dafana, some of them still show irregularities in shape, such as being not truly circular in plan view. Other sites where this type has been recorded include Kafr Ammar, Tell el-Balamun and Saqqara. The slightly different examples EA 50786 and 79646 were better made in very compact green-grey marl clay, with fine rims and, in the case of 79646, multiple carinations at the base.

The jars on the rest of **Plate 34** are familiar siltware products of the Late Period. Most were red-slipped originally. The plain rimmed jars with pointed bases (EA 22342, 22328, and 22321) represent the continuation of traditional types from the Third Intermediate Period. EA 22325 is similar, but with a slightly more elaborate rim, and EA 22281 is a shouldered form. Additional examples of such jars were found in the excavations of 2009 at Tell Dafana (**Pl. 77**, nos 9.3, 9.5). The small vessels EA 22305 and 27430 are actually miniature versions of the type represented by EA 22324, 23707 and 22292, but without the handles. Petrie records finding the large jars of this type both with and without handles.

6. Tall jars (Pls 35, 59)

The range of silt jars on **Plate 35** is very characteristic of the 26th dynasty. It is interesting to note that almost every one of these jars has some defect in manufacture, usually manifested in some distortion of the shape. But the large amount of grit in the fabric, composed chiefly of fine quartz grains (basically, sand), suggests local manufacture in the

Figure 11 Marl cup, British Museum, EA 23697

Figure 12 Jar, British Museum, EA 22336

Figure 13 Jar, British Museum, EA 22301

desert at Tell Dafana, reinforcing the conclusion expressed above that there was a lack of skilled potters at the site. Presumably these utilitarian jars were not considered sufficiently important to merit their import from other centres with better production. Siltware jars of these forms were usually finished with a polished red slip, but the high salt concentration in the ground at Tell Dafana has destroyed all but traces of this on many of the vessels. Only two of the British Museum jars retain the original red coating (EA 22301, shown here in **Figure 13**, and EA 50782). The short-necked jars at the top of **Plate 35** (EA 23649, 22287, 22331) have affinities with Third Intermediate Period ceramics so are probably of the early 26th dynasty. The provenance of EA 22331, at Findspot 30 below the foundation of Casemate Building A, supports such a date. The jars with cylindrical shaped necks (EA 22336, 22341, 22335, 22301 and 50782) are common Saite products in red-polished silt fabric. Several fresh examples of the type with the narrow neck, like EA 22336, 22301 and 50782, were found in the 2009 excavations (**Pl. 78**, nos 10.1 to 10.9). The style with the small loop-handles was also made in metal during Saite times, and in fact, the pottery jars were probably modelled on metal originals. Jars with flared necks are shown at the bottom of **Plate 35**; an additional jar of this class was found in 2009 (**Pl. 78**, no. 11.1). The tall jar EA 22329 with a ring-foot and single handle is a Phoenician style.[23]

7. Jars and sink (Pl. 36)

The continuation of the series of jars at the top of **Plate 36** includes some fragmentary bases in Nile silt. The three vessels EA 50784, 50783 and 50785 are examples of the finest products in marl clay from the Tell Dafana pottery. Lacking any of the common faults observed in many pots from the site, they are expertly produced, with wall thicknesses of between 0.3 and 0.4cm. The fabric is the best of the marl clay and the exteriors of the jars were all polished horizontally (**Fig. 6**). The remaining jars on **Plate 36** include some rudimentary Bes jars in red siltware. A larger and finer Bes jar is shown in the photograph in **Figure 14**. The small pointed jar EA 22326 possessed a curious manufactured perforation and Petrie suggested it may have served as a baby-feeding vessel.

A second example from Tell Dafana of the same form as the handled vessel EA 23650 is now in the Department of Greece and Rome at the British Museum, under number GR 1888,0208.140. It is filled with a residue which has been identified as pistachio gum or mastic (see Appendix 1, ii). The uncontexted vessel EA 23709 may be Ptolemaic. The large vessel EA 22347 may have been used as a sink, as suggested by Petrie, having been manufactured with an opening in the base for drainage. An example with an open base is recorded from Saqqara[24] and many fragments from vessels with similar rim profiles are known from Delta sites, particularly Tell el-Balamun, Kom Firin and Mendes, but as most specimens are incomplete the presence of the open base cannot be established with certainty. In any case, there were variants with closed bases for other purposes,[25] which seem to have been in use from early Saite times down to the mid-5th century BC. Pieces of the characteristic moulded rim from this kind of vessel are the most common items to occur amongst the surface sherds on the dynastic settlement mound at Tell el-Balamun.

8. Jugs (Pl. 37)

The jug EA 23710 is of Levantine origin and is an example of the so-called Judaean juglet,[26] which was imported into Egypt and also produced as copies in local clays.[27] This type of jug has been found at many Egyptian sites, including Kafr

Figure 14 Bes jar, British Museum, EA 22312

Ammar, Saqqara, Tell Tebilla, Tell Kedwa and Tell Fara'on (Petrie's Tell Nebesha). The vessel EA 50788, with the miniature version EA 23711, are both copies of this type made in Egypt. Another example was found in the 2009 excavations (**Pl. 82**, top). The fragmentary vessel EA 23799 also appears to have been an import, and EA 23716 has been suggested by Maeir to be Palestinian.[28] Examples of the latter shape found by Petrie had either single or paired handles. Two imported Greek aryballoi (**Fig. 15**) have been included in the catalogue, since although not Egyptian neither are they part of the primary collection of painted Greek fineware from Tell Dafana discussed in Chapter 6.

9. Closed vases (Pl. 38)
These forms are less common than the tall jars. EA 22320 is probably a model (cf. the examples from the 2009 excavations, **Pls 80–1**). The style of EA 23715 with the stirrup handles is reminiscent of much earlier ceramic traditions from the New Kingdom. The form of EA 22310 is attested at Saqqara, Tell el-Balamun, Tell Fara'on and Tell el-Retaba (parallels are given in the catalogue). The round flask (EA 22340) is a common style for the 26th dynasty but is surprisingly rare in the Tell Dafana corpus.

10. Lids, jar-covers and stands (Pls 39–40)
Plate 39 is devoted to various forms of lids and jar-covers, many of marl fabric. The series of lids continues on the upper part of **Plate 40**, but the lower portion of this plate shows potstands[29] and a few specialist products. Many more lids were found in the excavations of 2009 (**Pls 82–3**), although most were of poorer quality than those of the Petrie material. Among the specialized items, the large cover EA 23725 seems to have been intended to cover food rather than to seal a vessel. At the base of **Plate 40** is a fragmentary object of curious design, with a central spout at the top surrounded by a flared rim, like a collar (EA 79650). The function of this piece is unclear, unless it was also a food-cover with the perforated top allowing steam to escape, as Petrie suggested.[30]

11. Amphorae (Pls 41–6)
Transport amphorae are a regular feature in the pottery from Late-Dynastic sites all over Egypt, the relics of trade for the goods they contained. They are common at Delta sites because of proximity to the Mediterranean and the Levant, and also doubtless because the Delta was the political centre of the age. Phoenician amphorae, as shown on **Plate 41**, are found at sites throughout Egypt and genuine imports may be accompanied by locally made copies. Their presence at Tell Dafana is to be expected.[31] The large store jars in the upper part of **Plate 42** are purely Egyptian products, EA 22351 being made of the fine pale grey marl fabric mentioned at the end of the Introduction. The amphora neck EA 23775 is probably from Rhodes and Hellenistic in date; it is a type which occurs frequently at other sites in the Delta. Earlier imports from East Greece were common at Tell Dafana, including amphorae from Samos, Chios and Lesbos (**Pls 43–6**).[32] Part of a Chian amphora with seals of Amasis is preserved (see above, pp. 68–9 and **Pl. 64**). The Tell Dafana pottery in the British

Figure 15 Imported aryballoi, British Museum, EA 23712, 23714

Museum includes one Klazomenian amphora (EA 22343, **Pl. 44**), another example of which was found in 2009 in the new excavations at the site (**Pl. 85**). Some of the Greek imports were copied in local clay, an example being the vase EA 22333 in the form of a Samian amphora but made from coarse Nile silt. One amphora has a more western origin; analysis of the fabric of the neck EA 23776 indicates a source somewhere in the Ionian or Adriatic sea region (see below Appendix 1, ii). Another style of amphora among the assemblage is the Cypriot basket-handled jar,[33] a tall transport-vessel with a pair of handles looped above the mouth. These occur widely in the Levant and appear as imports in Egypt, again with some local copies.[34] They were very common at Tell Dafana[35] but only a single example came to the British Museum; another is kept in the Egyptian Museum at Cairo (**Fig. 16**).

The Findspots of the pottery
Petrie's Findspot numbers for the different areas of the site are not only noted alongside his pottery drawings in the site publication, but in many cases they are also incised into the surface of the pots themselves. This may seem a rather brutal way to treat the finds, but these numbers have proved more permanent than many of the Museum numbers painted onto the vessels and have in many cases permitted the rediscovery of the provenance. Examination of the different types of ceramics recorded from each findspot shows a few points of interest despite the incomplete nature of the site documentation. Not all of the pottery was given a findspot, Petrie clearly found many

Figure 16 Basket-handled jar from Tell Dafana in Cairo (drawing: F. Leclère)

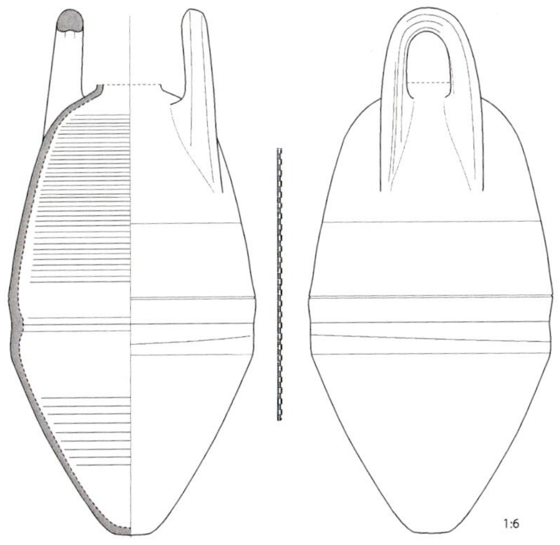

duplicates which he does not always mention, and locations with only a few recorded finds cannot be used. The presence of similar types of vessels in different contexts indicates that the phases of construction noted by Petrie do not differ that greatly in time. His determination of the building sequence was made by standard observation of the constructional details: which walls were built against others, which were cut by others and which overlaid older ones. But he noted that even the latest of his sequence of phases A to G were 'of Psamtik I, probably'. It should be remembered that a wall built against a pre-existing one may have been built only a very short time afterwards, and in fact may have been just a stage in a continuous programme of building. The pottery from the Casemate Buildings (Petrie's 'fort'), and from the adjacent annexes on the eastern side, supports a short date range for these buildings in the early part of the 26th dynasty. Some of the findspots refer to individual chambers in a single building and they may be considered as groups, whilst noting any particular differences which appear between separate chambers. An analysis of the findspots with reference to the pottery follows. For the position of the findspots, see the list on page 29 and the plan on **Plate 5**.

The foundation of Casemate Building A, Findspots 30, 35–40

This structure is securely dated to Psamtik I by foundation deposits. But it is only the foundation for the building and none of the occupied rooms above were preserved. The chambers in the platform are only structural voids, filled up with dirt originally, so any pottery would be random examples of vessels thrown in with the filling. This is borne out by the limited quantity of finds: only a jar from Findspot 30 and another jar, with a platter and a bowl, from 35. No pottery is recorded from the remaining chambers. The few vessels are typical Saite products; the chambers of this casemate do not seem to have been re-used by squatters at a later period, as happened in the casemate platform at Tell el-Balamun.

Figure 17 Basket-handled amphorae in Room 9 (EES Lucy Gura archive)

The Eastern Annexe of the casemate building, north half, Findspots 2, 3, 4, 9, 10, 11, 17 and 22 (Pls 48–9)

These are all individual rooms in the eastern annexe, which Petrie placed in his period C. Room 2 was just the entryway into the building so is unlikely to have had any other specific purpose. From it came a local jar, a bowl and several imported vessels: a Phoenician amphora, a Chian amphora and a basket-handled jar. These large vessels were probably deliveries dumped in the corners of the room. The remaining Findspots, apart from 10, apply to proper rooms which, unlike the casemate buildings, were preserved above floor level. Room 3 contained bowls, plates and lids, with a few small jars. One of the latter was a characteristic Saite situla with loop-handles at the sides of the neck. The next most productive room of this set was 11, again with silt bowls, a platter, simple jars and lids, but also a Phoenician imported jar with an inscription mentioning a regnal year 4 of an unknown king. There were also two fragments of Greek fineware dating from the late 6th century BC. A limited variety of pottery is recorded from Rooms 4, 9 and 17 but there were silt bowls and small jars, and numerous lids in 17. This room also yielded two fine Greek situlae and a fragment of a third. Room 9, apart from a couple of bowls, contained many examples of the Cypriot basket-handled jar, but only a single one was intact (**Fig. 17**). Finally, it should be noted that Findspot 10 was just a structural void. It contained only a typical Saite situla-type jar. Taken as a group, this set of rooms shows some clear similarities in the ceramic contents, with similar bowls in several of them and basket-handled jars in both 2 and 9. Findspot 22 is not a chamber but just a space behind the west wall of the annexe; it contained a silt jar and a lid.

The Eastern Annexe of the casemate building, south half, Findspots 19, 27 and 32 (Pls 50–1)

These locations are the continuation of the chambers in the eastern annexe building, so the division from the previous group is arbitrary. Findspot 27 had a limited range of ceramics, comprising some transport amphorae, two from East Greece and one Egyptian, a Phoenician jar, two very coarse bowls, a lid and a cover. There was one fine Greek fragment and the sherd EA 23770, perhaps from a basket-handled amphora. The greatest concentration of finds in the east annexe was in Rooms 19 A-C, here treated as a unit. Many lids were found, including the narrow types with cylindrical undersides (as EA 23738, 23739) which are not recorded from other locations. There were the common platters and silt bowls, but also some fine marlware plates and cups. Only one of the tall silt jar-types is noted, as EA 22336, but there were some large imported jars, comprising Phoenician and Chian amphorae. Some of the sink-type vessels with open base (as EA 22347) were present in 19A and 19C, the one in the latter room being found in a wall recess and full of organic debris and fish bones. A unique example of a large jar in fine Egyptian marlware was also found (EA 22351). The lack of this type elsewhere may be due to the fragility of the fabric, perhaps other examples did survive but were too broken to remove. Both the imported Judaean juglet and the siltware brazier are otherwise only recorded from the iron-working area at Findspot 52. The heavy marl clay sherd

EA 23810 came from Findspot 19, as did the nondescript sherd EA 23764 and a keg like EA 22357. A local copy of a Samian amphora was also present in large quantities. In addition to this assemblage, eight examples of Greek fineware were documented from Findspot 19. The greater range of ceramics at this location means that it contains some types not represented elsewhere, but it also includes others which are part of what appears to have been a fairly standard repertoire, common to various findspots. This suggests that the chambers 19 A–C were of some significance in terms of use, probably as a storage repository, and that is why the additional products are present, rather than there being a chronological distinction. This would also account for the presence of the Greek fineware.

Petrie allocated Findspot number 32 to the lower level in Room 19, under the floor. The pottery from this context is characterized by platters, dishes, bowls and the ubiquitous lids, but there was a lack of any large jars or transport amphorae, apart from just one small sherd which may have come from a basket-handled amphora (EA 23678). It is interesting that Findspot 28, which denotes a lower level in Chamber 18 in the Phase G structures south-east of the casemates, also lacks any large jars. Possibly these older layers represent a time before the flow of trade into Tell Dafana had been fully established.

The chambers to the south-east of the casemate buildings, Findspots 18, 28, 29 and 25 (Pls 52–3)

The structures to the south-east of the casemate buildings comprised a few chambers, allocated by Petrie to his construction Phase G. The repertoire of ceramics in chambers 18 and 29 were quite similar to each other, with platters, lids, small jars and transport amphorae. The latter included Chian and Phoenician jars, with (in 29) an amphora from Lesbos and a fragment from a similar vessel in 18 (EA 23772). These were accompanied in Room 18 by an Egyptian two-handled jar of large size. Curiously, there are no bowls, normally the most common of types, and only a single cup (in 18). The small jar with handles, as EA 23650, occurred in both locations, but was noted by Petrie as being common in chamber 18. Another feature shared by both these chambers was the presence of many pieces of Greek fineware, more than in any other location, even chamber 19. The limited distribution of the fine Greek wares at the site suggests that these may have arrived as gifts to the Egyptian temple, later broken and discarded, rather than for any widespread use. Such a conclusion would fit with the overwhelmingly Egyptian character of the site as evidenced by the objects and architecture. Among the Greek pieces from Findspot 18 was a painted neck-amphora which was manufactured in Naukratis (see Chapter 6, **Fig. 15**).[36] The finest of the Greek situlae, GR 1888,0208.1, came from Room 29 (see Chapter 6, **Fig. 12a**). Some items from Room 18 bore inscriptions: seals of Amasis (some of them on the Chian amphora EA 22356), seals of Psamtik II and a stamp of Nekau II (EA 23790). There were also seals of Amasis in Room 29. Five ostraca were found in Room 18, but none bear sufficient text to provide any useful information.

The lower level in Room 18 was designated Findspot 28. It has already been mentioned above for its lack of large jars.

Instead, it contained mostly bowls, cups and lids, together with a cooking pot and a silt jar in the form of EA 23707. Some of the bowls were fine marlware products, also noted in the iron-working area at Findspot 52 but nowhere else. Findspot 25 was actually outside the buildings of Phase G, to the south of Room 18. It contained examples of platters, bowls, lids and two types of silt jar, an assemblage with similarities to that from the early context at Findspot 32. This again suggests not too long an interval between Petrie's phases.

Findspots 21, 31, 54 and 55 (Pls 54, 57)

The first three of these locations were all described by Petrie as dry wells in the plain around the fort, the kind of feature regularly used for disposal of rubbish and an open context. His description of them being full of broken pottery shows that they were in fact soak-away drains, similar to examples found in the excavations of 2009. Despite the large number of smashed jars used in the drains, very little pottery was noted or brought back from these contexts, presumably just a few intact vessels being selected. This means that there is insufficient pottery to draw any conclusions. The vessels from these findspots were of similar types to those noted at several other locations, with Findspot 21 containing numerous transport amphorae of Greek or Phoenician origin. Such large vessels would have been useful in creating a soak-away drain, but only a few small vessels are recorded from the other two dry wells. Findspot 55 lay beside the great wall south of the casemates, which probably means somewhere in the vicinity of the southern wall of the great enclosure. This location produced a Samian amphora, an imported mortarium, together with some silt jars and lids. There were also small dishes like EA 23699 and 23670, as noted at Findspot 52.

The iron-working area in the south-eastern part of the enclosure, Findspot 52 (including 52W) (Pl. 56)

Although this Findspot appears frequently as a provenance with the pottery drawings in Petrie's publication, there is no mention of it whatsoever in the text. Its location is, however, recorded in Petrie's site Notebooks as 'iron works S. of the *Kasr*'. These are indicated on his published site-plan, but the number 52 has been omitted. Some finds are marked '52W', assumed to be the western part of the same area. Findspot 52 was deficient in transport amphorae with only two types recorded and lacked large jars in general, apart from a vessel of the type shown as Petrie's no. 5 on his plate xxxiii. The focus instead was on tableware, including platters, bowls and dishes, cups in silt and marl fabrics, cooking pots and small siltware jars. Some of the small dishes were of flared shapes like EA 23694, 23698 and 23699, recorded elsewhere only out on the desert at Findspots 54 and 55. The common situla-shape of Saite jar is entirely absent. There were, of course, some coarse siltware potstands and lids. Some of the smaller jars are of less common types, such as a Judaean juglet (as EA 23710) and a small simplified Bes jar (as EA 22304). One or two pieces from this context appear to be intrusive Ptolemaic products, presumably dumped in pits cut into the earlier levels. The presence of some later products of the Persian and Ptolemaic Periods among those which are classic 26th dynasty, as found elsewhere in the site, shows that this was an open context in which later material accumulated above, or was cut into the initial deposits. Some of this disturbance was doubtless the result of looting of the industrial area for useful metal.

The settlement area east of the enclosure, Findspots 50, 51 (Pls 54–5)

Petrie dug this one area of settlement outside the great enclosure, in a location which has now been taken for agriculture. A considerable amount of pottery was recovered here, including some of the earliest Greek pieces. The bulk of the ceramics came from the general area of the buildings designated Findspot 51. This was rich in amphorae, with examples from Chios, Lesbos and other East Greek sources, together with another local copy of a Samian amphora. There were also imported Phoenician amphorae from the Levant and fragments from basket-handled jars. The local Egyptian vessels tended to be utilitarian rather than fine: platters, cooking vessels, silt jars and cups, with some potstands and an example of the 'sink' vessel like EA 22347. The heavy platter with the form of EA 22369, although it may sometimes occur in funerary contexts, was mainly produced for domestic purposes so it is understandable that it is noted only from here.[37] The two bowls GR 1888,0208.62-63 were considered by Petrie to be early prototypes for fine Greek bowls, but they seem to be based on the shapes of Achaemenid bowls with the addition of a ring-foot.[38] There were also five examples of Greek decorated fineware at Findspot 51.

Findspot 50 was simply a soak-away drain cut down beside a wall in the settlement area and lined with recycled East Greek transport amphorae (one of them a local copy). An Egyptian siltware jar and dish were also found here.

Pottery from 'The Camp'

Petrie refers to numerous finds as coming from the Camp, that is, the great Saite enclosure, so as a provenance it is very imprecise. Examples of many types of pottery are mentioned as having being found here, but it is probable that some of these references may be duplicates of those to more specific findspots within the enclosure. Either way, the pottery from the Camp consists of a similar range of types to those found in other areas, with local silt bowls and jars, numerous lids, a few platters and marl plates, together with imported Greek and Phoenician amphorae. No particular class predominates, however, but an infrequency of Egyptian situla-shape jars is interesting in view of these being found in some quantity in the excavations of 2009 within the enclosure.

Notes

1. For the fine Greek painted pottery from Tell Dafana, see Chapter 6 of this volume, by Sabine Weber. An exhaustive publication of these ceramics by the same author is available (Weber 2012b).
2. This discussion is based on a combination of Petrie's published account in *Tanis II, Nebesheh and Defenneh* (London 1888), study of the Tell Dafana pottery in the British Museum and general consideration of the material in other collections, particularly the Petrie Museum at University College, London, Bristol City Museum, Bolton Museum, Kelvingrove Museum, Glasgow, The McLean Museum, Greenock, The McManus Galleries, Dundee, the Museum of Fine Arts, Boston, and Penn Museum, Philadelphia.
3. Defernez 1997; Defernez 2001.
4. Oren 1984.
5. Upper Egyptian Marl A2 is equated by Aston and Aston 2010, 5, with their Marl Fabric K2.
6. Paice 1987, 102, fig. 8.
7. Spencer 1996, pl. 61, A.1.18–32; Hamza 1997, pl. vii, nos 1–2; Bourriau and Aston 1985, pl. 37, no. 102; Brissaud 1991, pl. xi, nos 153–6; Hummel and Schubert 2004, pl. M, no. 11; Aston and Aston 2010, pl. 2, nos 31–4.
8. Spencer 1993, pl. 74, M68–M74 inclusive.
9. Lopez-Grande 1995, pl. xxxvi, f–h, j–l.
10. Petrie 1909a, 1915, 1923.
11. Petrie 1888, 66.
12. Petrie 1888, 65.
13. Thanks to Donald Bailey for drawing attention to this material.
14. These are included in the catalogue under British Museum numbers EA 79641 to 79651. The remainder of the sherd collection is numbered EA 79652.
15. Aston and Aston 2010, 167ff. gives a more detailed discussion of Late Dynastic pottery than the brief account in French 2004.
16. Aston and Aston 2010, 171–9.
17. Also noted at Migdol in Sinai, see Oren 1984, 16, fig. 20, no. 15.
18. Holladay 1982, pl. 6, no. 1; Paice 1987, 99, fig. 3, no. 1; other plates at Tell el-Maskhuta were of silt fabrics, ibid., fig. 3, nos 2–5, 10–11.
19. Defernez 2001, vol.1, 96, vol. 2, 422 and pl. xiii. The shallow vessel Type 31 is closest to the Tell Dafana versions; the later examples show increasing depth.
20. Villing and Schlotzhauer 2006, 37, 42 and figs 19–20.
21. Aston and Aston 2010, 155 and pl. 45, type 414. The bowl from Tell el-Maskhuta cited by Aston is considerably different.
22. Hansen 1967, pl. x, fig. 11.
23. Sagona 1982, 86–8 with fig. 3.
24. Aston and Aston 2010, pl. 3, no. 38; pl. 22, no. 181. Aston considers the type to be a funnel.
25. Wilson 1982, pl. xvii, no. 6.
26. See discussion of the type in Holladay 2004, 405–38 with figs 1–3.
27. Petrie 1915, pl. xxxiii, no. 60; Mostafa 1986, 10, no. 3; Aston and Aston 2010, pl. 46, no. 439; Hamza 1997, pl. ii, no. 6.
28. Maeir 2002, 239 and fig. 1, no. 5.
29. See Aston and Aston 2010, pl. 3, nos 46–50.
30. Petrie 1888, 65.
31. See Sagona 1982; Paice 1997, 98, figs 1–2; Hamza 1997, pls x–xii; Gratien 1997, pl. i, fig. 1, nos 8.425, 8.407 and 8.406; Hummel and Schubert 2004, 139 and pl. H; Aston and Aston 2010, pls 34–5.
32. East Greek amphorae are commonly found in Egyptian sites, in the Delta and elsewhere. Examples have been found recently at Kom el-Nugus (Plinthine), see Dhennin and Redon 2013. For the circulation of these and other Greek products in Egypt, see Villing 2013. On the shapes of Samian amphorae, see Grace 1971, 68–73; Cook and Dupont 1998 (reprinted 2001), 164–9.
33. See Oren 1984, 17–18, fig. 21, no. 11; De Rodrigo 2004; Sagona 1982, 88–91, fig. 4, no. 2.
34. Spencer 2008, 93–4, fig. 9.12; 96, fig. 9.17.
35. Petrie 1888, 63 § 59, p. 64 § 61.
36. Villing and Schlotzhauer 2006, 62–3 with fig. 39; Mommsen 2006.
37. Spencer 1996, pl. 61, nos A.1.14, A.1.20, A.1.27, A.1.32; Hamza 1997, pl. vii, nos 1–2; Bourriau and Aston 1985, pl. 37, no. 102; Brissaud 1991, pl. xi, nos 153–6; Hummel and Schubert 2004, pl. M, no. 11; Aston and Aston 2010, pl. 2, nos 31–4.
38. Petrie 1888, 61; see the parallels cited in the catalogue entry for GR 1888,0208.62.

Chapter 5
Catalogue of Egyptian Pottery, Transport Amphorae and Ostraca from Tell Dafana in the British Museum

Jeffrey Spencer

The order of this catalogue follows the sequence of vessels shown in the drawings on **Plates 31–47**. The scales of these drawings are indicated on the plates. Some items are illustrated alternatively or additionally in the photographs on **Plates 58–70**.

The primary reference for items in the Department of Ancient Egypt and Sudan (prefix EA), is by their Inventory Numbers (also known as Big Numbers), with the Registration Numbers following. The Department of Greece and Rome (prefix GR), uses only Registration Numbers, so these form the identifiers for pottery from that Department. As with the catalogue of objects in Chapter 3, where the context line is absent from an entry, no specific findspot at the site was recorded.

EA 23687   1887,0101.1260   **(Pl. 31)**

A circular platter of medium coarse red siltware pottery, all surfaces covered with a greenish-cream slip, worn and chipped away in parts. At the edge are three ridges running around the perimeter and in the centre of the underside is a very low ring-foot.
Diameter: 25.8cm; thickness: 1.95cm.
Context: 'Qasr', east annexe (C), chamber 11.

EA 23688   1887,0101.1256   **(Pl. 31)**

A circular platter of coarse red siltware pottery. The surfaces are covered by a pale cream slip, parts of which have eroded away. The underside exhibits concentric rings from rotary manufacture and has a very slight disk-base in the centre. A small part of the rim has been broken off and re-attached, with a small piece still missing.
Diameter: 19.cm; thickness: 1.4cm.
Context: 'Qasr', east annexe (C), Findspot 32, under the floor of chamber 19 A.
Parallels: compare the platters from Tell Dafana in Boston (MFA 87.645, 87.646).

EA 23686   1887,0101.1259   **(Pl. 31)**

A circular platter of coarse red siltware pottery, with a slightly concave upper surface and a low ring-foot. The surfaces are covered with a cream slip, parts of which have disappeared. There is a shallow groove around the perimeter on the upper surface. The fabric contains inclusions of sand and grit. The object has been repaired from three fragments. A small piece is missing from the rim.
Diameter: 31.4cm; thickness: 2.3cm.
Context: 'Qasr', east annexe (C), Findspot 32, under the floor of chamber 19 A.
Bibliography: Petrie 1888, 65 § 61, pl. xxxiv, 35.
Parallels: a similar platter from Findspot 52 at Tell Dafana is in Bristol, CMAG H.1995, and another in Boston, MFA 87.646, but without the groove around the edge.

EA 23691   1887,0101.1116   **(Pl. 31)**

A circular dish of green-grey marlware pottery, with a flat base and slightly everted rim. The exterior (now very worn) is covered with remains of a cream-coloured slip.
Height: 3.4cm; diameter: 33cm.
Context: 'Qasr', east annexe (C), Findspot 32, under the floor of chamber 19 A.
Bibliography: Petrie 1888, pl. xxxiv, 36.

EA 22370   1887,0101.1128   **(Pl. 31)**

Red pottery dish, repaired from three pieces, with remains of a yellow-cream slip on all surfaces. The edge curves upwards to an angular rim. The height is slightly irregular. The coarse red siltware fabric contains many inclusions of grit.
Height: 4cm; diameter: 28.cm.
Context: if this style of dish and EA 23692 below belonged to the vague type described by Petrie as 'between 31 and 35', or 'between 34 and 36', then they would have had a wide distribution in Findspots 2, 3, 4, 9, 19, 25, 27, 32, 35, 50 and 51.

Bibliography: Petrie 1888, 66.
Parallels: Paice 1987, 99, fig. 3, no. 10; simpler form in Oren 1984, 16, fig. 20 no. 15.

EA 23692   **1887,0101.1213**   **(Pls 31, 58)**
A pottery dish with carinated sides, a broad rim and a ring-foot. The dish is made of a pale pink-grey marl fabric and the surfaces are covered by a pale cream-yellow slip, parts of which have flaked off. Part of the rim is missing. The vessel shows clear signs of fast wheel production.
Height: 2.7cm; diameter: 19.2cm.
Bibliography: Petrie 1888, pl. xxxv, 70.
Parallels: Oren 1984, 20, fig. 23, no. 3; Defernez 1997, pl. i, fig. 3, no. 17.

EA 23693   **1887,0101.1263**   **(Pl. 31)**
Two fragments from a pottery dish of the same carinated form as number 23692. The vessel was made of a micaceous pink marl clay with a cream-yellow surface slip. The two pieces come from the rim and base, and will join, although they have not been reunited.
Length: 11.7cm; width: 7.5cm (base piece).
Length: 11.7cm; width: 5.2cm (rim piece).
Height of complete vessel: 2.6cm; diameter: 19cm.
Context: 'Qasr', east annexe (C), chamber 19.
Bibliography: cf. Petrie 1888, pl. xxxv, 70.
Parallels: a similar dish from Findspot 52 at Tell Dafana is in Boston (MFA 87.641).

EA 79641   **2010,1002.1**   **(Pl. 31)**
Part of a low dish similar to 23692 above, but smaller in diameter and with a narrower rim. The sides exhibit a series of sharp carinations. The surviving part comprises two joined fragments, making up just over half of the original vessel. It is made in compact marl clay with smooth surfaces.
Height: 2.2cm; diameter: 13.5cm.
Context: Findspot 52, iron-working area in the south-east part of the Saite enclosure (so-called 'Camp').

EA 23690   **1887,0101.1300**   **(Pl. 31)**
A low dish of pale red pottery, with a projecting external rim and a low ring-foot. The surface is covered by a pale cream slip.
Height: 3.6cm; diameter: 21.7cm.
Context: 'Qasr', east annexe (C), chamber 3.
Parallels: Paice 1987, 99, fig. 3 no. 2.

EA 22369   **1887,0101.1129**   **(Pl. 31)**
A heavy platter of coarse red siltware pottery, with a rough, flat base and flared sides. The object was manufactured by hand on the ground surface, so the underside is a rough imprint of the ground. A small red-slipped pottery sherd is embedded in the base. There are traces of a red slip on the interior and exterior.
Height: 7.7cm; diameter: 40cm.
Context: probably from Findspot 51, domestic buildings in the urban area to the east of the Saite enclosure (so-called 'Camp').
Bibliography: Petrie 1888, 66 § 61, pl. xxxiv, 38.
Parallels: Spencer 1996, pl. 61, nos A.1.14, A.1.20, A.1.27, A.1.32; Hamza 1997, pl. vii, nos 1–2; Bourriau and Aston 1985, pl. 37, no. 102; Brissaud 1991, pl. xi, nos 153–6; Hummel and Schubert 2004, pl. M, no. 11; Aston and Aston 2010, pl. 2, nos 31–4.

EA 23685   **1887,0101.1258**   **(Pl. 31)**
A mortarium with a flat base and flaring sides. The fabric in the core is very coarse red-brown Nile silt, but the surface is coated with a slip of yellow-green clay. This was probably intended to imitate the appearance of imported mortaria. A hole has been worn through the base by use and the rim is much chipped.
Height: 5.3cm (max.); diameter: 23.8cm (max.).
Bibliography: Villing 2006, 37, 42 and fig. 19; id. 2013, 83, fig. 9.
Parallels: see under EA 23708 below.

EA 23708   **1887,0101.1215**   **(Pl. 31)**
A mortarium of rough grey-green marlware pottery, probably an import from the Levant. The vessel has a flat base and an external rim. Part of one side is missing.

Height: 9cm; diameter: 27.8cm.
Context: Findspot 55, by the great wall south of the 'Qasr'.
Bibliography: Villing 2006, 37, 42 (with erroneous number 23703) and fig. 20.
Parallels: Petrie 1915, pl. xi, no. 2; Holladay 1982, 109, pl. 16, nos 7, 9; Oren 1984, 18, fig. 21, nos 9–10; Spencer 1996, pl. 62, no. 55; pl. 86, no. 15; Defernez 1997, pl. ii, fig. 5, nos 23–4; Aston 1999, 238, pl. 75, no. 2082; Hummel and Schubert 2004, 172, pl. J, nos 2 and 5; Aston and Aston 2010, pl. 49, no. 464. For a similar Levantine example, see Lehmann 1998, 22, fig. 8, no. 8. For mortaria from Tell Tebilla, see http//:www.deltasinai.com/delta-10.htm.

GR 1888,0208.62   **(Pl. 31)**
A carinated pottery bowl. The mouth is broad with an everted rim at the top of a tall neck. The lower body has a rounded shoulder and a low ring base. The vessel has been repaired from two pieces and a part of the rim is missing. The red siltware fabric retains a dark grey core and is covered with a red-brown matt slip, which was wet-smoothed using a knife or spatula. The clay contains some fine mica, frequent medium-coarse grits and quartz grains. The shape is based on that of Achaemenid bowls, which occur in various materials, especially metal. Pottery examples were made from the 5th to the 3rd centuries BC. The ring-foot is a local Egyptian variation.
Height: 9.3cm; diameter: 16cm.
Context: Findspot 51, domestic buildings in the urban area to the east of the Saite enclosure (so-called 'Camp').
Parallels: from Tell Dafana, see GR 1888,0208.63 below. Grataloup 2010, 154 and fig. 12.5.5; Defernez 2001, 330, pl. lxxii, 208; see also the discussion of the bowls from Sardis in Dusinberre 2003, 176–95; the closest parallels would seem to be among the bowls from Deposit 4, in fig. 66 on p. 182, especially no. 14.

GR 1888,0208.63   **(Pl. 31)**
A carinated pottery bowl similar to the previous item, with a broad mouth and small everted rim. The body of the vessel has a rounded shoulder and broad ring-foot. The red siltware fabric has a dark core and the surfaces are covered by a matt red slip, which has worn off in places. The clay contains fine mica, medium-coarse grit and quartz grains. The vessel has been reconstructed from six sherds with about a quarter of the rim reconstructed in plaster. Although rather different from the previous item, the shape is still based on the Achaemenid bowl, but the neck rises more vertically in this example.
Height: 9.1cm; diameter: 14.5cm.
Context: Findspot 51, domestic buildings in the urban area to the east of the Saite enclosure (so-called 'Camp').
Parallels: same as for GR 1888,0208.62 above.

EA 23752   **1887,0101.856**   **(Pl. 32)**
Six joined fragments of a red-brown pottery dish with a rounded base and flaring sides. The uncoated siltware fabric is relatively coarse and grey-black in section. Two small pieces are missing: one from the rim and one from the base. On the rim is an area of grey encrustation, a mixture of gypsum crystals and quartz grains.
Height: 4.1cm; diameter: 21.4cm.
Context: 'Qasr', east annexe (C), chamber 3.

EA 23664   **1887,0101.1126**   **(Pls 32, 58)**
Red siltware pottery bowl with flat base, flaring sides and rounded lip, the whole is covered with a burnished red slip, worn in parts. On the interior, this slip was decorated with polishing in a spiral design. This fashion occurs in the Third Intermediate Period and persists into the Late Period. The fabric contains sand, grit and a small quantity of chaff. The rim is damaged and there has been exfoliation of the exterior surface, probably due to salt action.
Height: 4.5cm; diameter: 13.5cm.
Parallels: Hummel and Schubert 2004, pl. K, no. 30.

EA 23665   **1887,0101.1211**   **(Pl. 32)**
A flared dish (more probably than a jar-cover) of coarse red siltware pottery, the whole is covered with a red slip. The flat base was string-cut from the wheel. The fabric contains many inclusions of grit and sand. The object is irregular in shape and was probably a waster.
Height: 3.75cm; diameter: 14cm.

Context: 'Qasr', east annexe (C), Findspot 32, under the floor of chamber 19 A.
Parallels: Spencer 1996, pl. 61, A.2.12; Spencer 1993, pl. 44, A.1.7–14; Aston 1999, 208, pl. 64, no. 1886, p. 216, pl. 65, no. 1928.

EA 23706   **1887,0101.1396**   **(Pl. 32)**
Base-sherd from a pottery bowl, made in coarse red-brown silt clay. The sides are thick and the flat base was string-cut.
Height: 2.2cm; width: 5.7cm.

EA 23663   **1887,0101.1122**   **(Pl. 32)**
An open bowl of red siltware pottery, finished with a red slip on the interior and exterior. The slip has been enhanced with a pebble-burnished spiral stripe. The bowl has a low ring-base and a plain, rounded rim, below which there is a groove on the exterior. There is a crack in each side.
Height: 6.8cm; diameter: 21.4cm.
Context: 'Qasr', east annexe (C), chamber 11.
Bibliography: Petrie 1888, pl. xxxiv, 31.

EA 23660   **1887,0101.1214**   **(Pl. 32)**
A bowl of coarse red siltware pottery, with a poorly made ring-foot. The convex sides turn inwards at the top to an angled rim with an internal, flattened edge. Part of the rim is missing. The uncoated silt fabric has been fired sufficiently to produce red surfaces but the core remains grey. The fabric contains many particles of grit. The bowl is irregular and the level of the rim varies. This is a poor-quality version of the ubiquitous footed bowls with incurved rims known from Ptolemaic contexts. Most examples possess a red-polished surface slip. The poor manufacture of this bowl suggests that it was a product of the local inferior pottery industry of Tell Dafana. Compare 23705 below.
Height: 10.7cm; diameter: 20.3cm (max.).
Context: Findspot 52, iron-working area in the south-east part of the Saite enclosure (so-called 'Camp'), according to the Museum Register.
Bibliography: Petrie 1888, pl. xxxv, 72. A similar bowl from Tell Dafana is in Boston (MFA 87.635).
Parallels: Spencer 1996, pl. 51, nos 27–30; pl. 53, no. 8.

EA 23659   **1887,0101.1235**   **(Pl. 32)**
An open bowl of uncoated red siltware pottery, with a string-cut flat base and plain, rounded rim. The interior shows lines of rotary production, but the vessel is not regular; the diameter at the rim varies between 14.20 and 15cm.
Height: 7.8cm; diameter: 14.8cm (median).
Bibliography: Petrie 1888, pl. xxxv, 52.
Parallels: Spencer 1993, pl. 50, A.3.93.

EA 23705   **1887,0101.1280**   **(Pl. 32)**
A bowl of red siltware pottery, with a circular ring-foot and convex sides, which converge to a plain rim. The micaceous fabric was covered on the interior and exterior by a red slip, although not all of this has survived. A large section of the body is missing. Probably Ptolemaic.
Height: 6.7cm; diameter: 11.2cm.
Parallels: see under EA 23660 above. A similar Ptolemaic bowl from Tell Dafana is in Boston (MFA 87.635).

EA 23661   **1887,0101.1145**   **(Pl. 32)**
Open bowl of coarse red siltware pottery, with flared sides and a roughly shaped foot. The latter consists of a solid lump of fired clay of circular but rather irregular shape, carelessly string-cut from the potter's wheel. The vessel is poorly manufactured with thick sides and an irregular diameter. The coarse fabric contains inclusions of grit and a few marks of burnt-out chaff. The rim is chipped.
Height: 9.8cm; diameter: 18.6cm (max.).
Context: 'Qasr', east annexe (G), Findspot 25, south of chamber 18.
Bibliography: Petrie 1888, pl. xxxiv, 14.
Parallels: Petrie 1909, pl. xlix, nos 765–6.

EA 23662   **1887,0101.1209**   **(Pl. 32)**
Dish of coarse red siltware pottery, with a small foot, flaring sides and an angled rim. The rim is chipped in two places. The surfaces bear scanty traces of a red slip, which on the interior appears to have been pebble-burnished in a spiral pattern. The coarse fabric was incompletely fired (showing black in the core) and contains a considerable amount of grit, but shows only a few voids from burnt-out chaff. The vessel is irregular and the level of the rim is uneven.
Height: 11.2cm (max.); diameter: 30cm (max.).
Context: 'Qasr', east annexe (C), chamber 3.
Parallels: Hummel and Schubert 2004, pl. N, no. 14. A smaller parallel is in Boston (MFA 87.638).
Bibliography: Petrie 1888, pl. xxxiv, 17.

EA 23683   **1887,0101.1123**   **(Pl. 32)**
Open bowl of coarse red siltware pottery, with a rounded base, flaring sides and wide collared rim. The base has been roughly trimmed by hand. The fabric contains many inclusions of grit, chiefly small grains of quartz and flint. The vessel is irregular in shape and may have been a waster.
Height: 6.5cm (max.); diameter: 18.6cm (max.).
Context: 'Qasr', east annexe (C), chamber 9.
Bibliography: Petrie 1888, pl. xxxiv, 30.
Parallels: Spencer 1993, pl. 47, A.3.14; Defernez 1997, pl. i, fig. 2, no. 14; Aston 1999, 219, pl. 66, no. 1948.

EA 23682   **1887,0101.1265**   **(Pl. 32)**
Red-brown pottery bowl, made in a coarse silt fabric, grey-black in the centre of the section due to a low firing temperature. Partially reconstructed from fragments (incorporating 1887,0101.868) with some pieces missing from the rim. The sides are vertical and the base slightly convex. The surface has flaked off owing to erosion or salt action, but some traces of a yellow colour on the sides might indicate that there was originally a cream-yellow slip.
Height: 5.4cm; diameter: 26.8cm.
Context: 'Qasr', east annexe (C), chamber 3.
Bibliography: Petrie 1888, pl. xxxiv, 34.
Parallels: Spencer 1996, pl. 61, A.3.2, A.3.3; Defernez 2001, pl. ix; Aston 1999, 208, pl. 64, no. 1888.

EA 79642   **2010,1002.2**   **(Pl. 32)**
Part of an open bowl of red siltware pottery, with a cream surface slip. The flattened base is very slightly convex and the rim is plain. About half of the vessel survives.
Height: 3.6cm; length of fragment: 14cm; estimate of original diameter of vessel: 15.2cm.
Context: 'Qasr', east annexe (G), Findspot 28, below chamber 18.
Parallels: Oren 1984, 16, fig. 20, no. 13. Fragments of two similar vessels are among the sherd collection from Tell Dafana in the Department of Ancient Egypt and Sudan, British Museum.

EA 79643   **2010,1002.3**   **(Pl. 32)**
Part of small dish of pale red siltware pottery, with a cream surface slip. About half of the vessel survives. It has a slightly convex base and near vertical sides. The plain rim is chipped in places.
Height: 3cm; diameter: 7.2cm.
Context: the Findspot number 52 may have been lightly scratched into the base of the object, but is now very faint.
Bibliography: a similar vessel type from Findspots 52 and 55 is shown in Petrie 1888, pl. xxxv, no. 62.
Parallels: fragments of two similar vessels are among the sherd collection from Tell Dafana in the Department of Ancient Egypt and Sudan, British Museum.

EA 23668   **1887,0101.1124**   **(Pl. 32)**
Redware pottery object in form of dish with a central round hole; repaired from fragments (one lost). The red siltware fabric has inclusions of sand and grit, especially small quartz grains, and the core is a blue-grey colour. The surfaces were covered by a bright red slip, much of which still remains in place. The central hole was made pre-firing from the exterior of the base; creating it caused a slight ridge of clay to form around its perimeter on the interior.
Height: 2.7cm; diameter: 15.3cm.
Context: western part of Findspot 52, iron-working area in the south-east quarter of the Saite enclosure (so-called 'Camp').
Bibliography: Petrie 1888, pl. xxxv, 71.

EA 79644 2010,1002.4 **(Pl. 32)**
Part of a convex-sided bowl of fine marlware pottery. There is a slight ridge below the plain rim. The object has been reconstructed from several sherds with one piece separate, but undoubtedly belonging to the vessel. This fragment bears Petrie's Findspot number 28.
Height: 5.6cm (incomplete); diameter: 16cm.
Context: 'Qasr', east annexe (G), Findspot 28, below chamber 18.
Parallels: see EA 23724 below.

EA 23724 1887,0101.1271 **(Pl. 32)**
Grey pottery bowl with rounded base, slightly flaring sides and everted ledge rim. The dull grey marl fabric is relatively fine and covered by a grey-green slip, the whole is reconstructed from fragments and significant areas of the vessel have been reconstructed in modern material.
Height: 6.1cm; diameter: 17.3cm.
Bibliography: Petrie 1888, pl. xxxv, 53.
Parallels: numerous fragments from the rims of two more bowls of this type are among the sherd collection from Tell Dafana kept in the Department of Ancient Egypt and Sudan.

EA 23695 1887,0101.1278 **(Pl. 32)**
A convex sided bowl with a ring-foot and an everted, flat-topped rim. A slight ridge runs around the perimeter below the rim. A small part of the rim has been damaged. The core fabric of the vessel consists of pale green-grey marlware but all surfaces still retain some small areas of an original smooth pale green slip.
Height: 5.3cm; diameter: 15.2cm.
Context: Findspot 52, iron-working area in the south-east part of the Saite enclosure (so-called 'Camp').
Bibliography: Petrie 1888, pl. xxxiv, 15.
Parallels: Aston and Aston 2010, pl. 45, no. 414.

EA 23679 1887,0101.1218 **(Pl. 32)**
Part of the side and base of a pottery bowl including part of the flared rim, below which were two grooves. The exterior bears remains of a red slip which was originally burnished in horizontal stripes; on the inside there is a thin, streaky, pale cream slip. The piece consists of three joined fragments. The pink-red fabric contains many pores and inclusions of grit. The original vessel was a flared bowl with a rim diameter of around 32cm.
Height: 17cm; length of fragment: 21cm.
Bibliography: Petrie 1888, pl. xxxiv, 18.

EA 22306 1887,0101.1208 **(Pl. 33)**
A bowl or cover of straw-tempered red siltware pottery, of deep, rounded shape with a flaring lip. The edge of the lip has a rounded rim. The interior and exterior were red-slipped, and on the former the slip has been enhanced with spiral burnishing. On the outside some of the slip has disappeared and parts of the surface have laminated. There are cracks in the sides of the bowl and chips missing from the rim. A circular scar, where some additional feature has been broken off, marks the centre of the base on the exterior. If a projecting handle had originally been attached at this position, then the object would more probably have been a lid or cover.
Height: 10.2cm; diameter: 16.3cm.

EA 23656 1887,0101.1299 **(Pl. 33)**
Bowl with a rounded base, flared sides and an everted rim. The compact red siltware fabric is covered on the interior and exterior by a pale pink slip. One point on the rim is chipped.
Height: 5.1cm; diameter: 10.2cm (max.).
Context: Findspot 52, iron-working area in the south-east part of the Saite enclosure (so-called 'Camp').
Bibliography: Petrie 1888, 65 § 61, pl. xxxv, 51.

EA 22316 1887,0101.1241 **(Pl. 33)**
A cup of micaceous, red siltware pottery with a shallow pointed base and flared rim. The exterior was covered with a red slip, now worn away in places; this slip was carried over onto the interior of the rim.
Height: 4.57cm; diameter: 6.8cm.
Context: probably from the 'Qasr', east annexe (G), chamber 18.
Bibliography: Petrie 1888, 65 § 61, pl. xxxv, 47.

Parallels: Brissaud 1991, pl. ix, no. 100; cf. the foundation deposit pots in Hansen 1967, pl. x, fig. 11 (lower centre).

EA 23698 1887,0101.1275 **(Pls 33, 58)**
Miniature cup of pale cream-green marlware pottery, with a slightly convex base and straight sides, which rise to a plain rim. The surface was smoothed by the application of a thin slip of clay of similar colour to the core fabric. The latter has been exposed on the interior of the vessel by the loss of much of the original surface coating.
Height: 3.1cm; diameter: 6cm.
Context: Findspot 52, iron-working area in the south-east part of the Saite enclosure (so-called 'Camp').

EA 23699 1887,0101.1276 **(Pls 33, 58)**
Miniature cup of pale pink marlware pottery, with a shallow, pointed base, straight sides and a plain rim. Parts of the rim are chipped. The surfaces are covered by a thin pale cream-green slip.
Height: 2.4cm; diameter: 5.5cm.
Context: Findspot 52, iron-working area in the south-east part of the Saite enclosure (so-called 'Camp'), or Findspot 55, by the great wall south of the 'Qasr'.
Bibliography: Petrie 1888, pl. xxxv, 62.

EA 23700 1887,0101.1274 **(Pls 33, 58)**
Miniature cup of coarse red siltware pottery with remains of a pale cream slip on the interior and exterior. The base is convex and the sides almost straight. The plain rim is slightly chipped.
Height: 2.8cm; diameter: 4.4cm.
Context: Findspot 55, by the great wall south of the 'Qasr'.

EA 23694 1887,0101.1216 **(Pl. 33)**
A low dish of coarse red siltware pottery. The interior and exterior surfaces are covered by a cream slip, which has worn off in places. Sand, mica and grit inclusions are present in the fabric. The shape is slightly irregular, particularly the base.
Height: 5.1cm; diameter: 13.7cm.
Context: Findspot 52, iron-working area in the south-east part of the Saite enclosure (so-called 'Camp').
Parallels: Brissaud 1991, pl. vii, no. 51. A similar vessel from Tell Dafana is in Boston (MFA 87.640).

EA 23702 1887,0101.1394 **(Pl. 33)**
A miniature dish of uncoated, coarse red siltware pottery. The vessel has a flat, string-cut base and a flared rim. Part of the rim is chipped.
Height: 1.64cm; diameter: 4.6cm.

EA 23703 1887,0101.1395 **(Pl. 33)**
A miniature dish of uncoated coarse red siltware pottery. The base is flat, possibly string-cut, and the rim is flared.
Height: 1.3cm; diameter: 4.5cm.

EA 23701 1887,0101.1287 **(Pl. 33)**
A miniature cup of uncoated coarse red siltware pottery. Irregularly produced, with a rough string-cut base.
Height: 2.85cm; diameter: 4.5cm.
Context: 'Qasr', east annexe (G), chamber 4.

EA 23651 1887,0101.1290 **(Pl. 33)**
A miniature jar of uncoated coarse red siltware pottery, with an irregular, string-cut base, convex sides and rounded rim. The fabric contains grit inclusions and exhibits voids from burnt-out chaff.
Height: 5.4cm; diameter: 5.5cm.
Context: western part of Findspot 52, iron-working area in the south-east quarter of the Saite enclosure (so-called 'Camp').
Bibliography: Petrie 1888, pl. xxxv, 56.

EA 23652 1887,0101.1283 **(Pl. 33)**
A miniature jar of uncoated coarse red siltware pottery, with a rough base and convex sides. At the top there is a rounded rim with a slight groove below. The surface has been wet-smoothed, not very well, by hand.
Height: 4.7cm; diameter: 5.2cm.

EA 23680 **1887,0101.1300** **(Pl. 33)**

A small pottery bowl of uncoated, pale red siltware, with flared sides and a roughly flat, string-cut base.
Height: 4.2cm; diameter: 8.8cm.
Context: 'Qasr', east annexe (G), Findspot 28, below chamber 18.
Bibliography: Petrie 1888, pl. xxxv, 58.

EA 23681 **1887,0101.1267** **(Pl. 33)**

A small pottery beaker of coarse siltware. The surface is discoloured, possibly by burning. Part of the rim is missing. There is a roughly flat string-cut base.
Height: 5.8cm; diameter: 6cm.
Context: Findspot 54, dry well south of the 'Qasr'.
Bibliography: Petrie 1888, pl. xxxv, 60.

EA 23720 **1887,0101.1319** **(Pl. 33)**

A very rough bowl of coarse red siltware pottery, with a flattened base and convex sides, which turn inwards at the top to a contracted mouth. This is finished with a rounded rim, part of which is broken. The sides have been damaged near the top and the broken surfaces show a black core below the red surface, an indication of low-temperature firing. The fabric was made of Nile silt with the addition of chopped straw, but very few other inclusions. The lack of any sand or similar temper has resulted in the clay cracking during firing. The whole object was very crudely manufactured by hand and the shape is irregular. On the interior there is an applied boss of clay projecting from one side for a length of about 5cm. Petrie says of this object that it was 'exactly like what was found at Naukratis'.
Height: 13.7cm; diameter: 23.1cm (max.).
Context: 'Qasr', east annexe (C), chamber 27.
Bibliography: Petrie 1888, 65 § 61, pl. xxxiv, 26.
Parallels: a parallel from Petrie's Findspot 19 at Tell Dafana is in Boston (MFA 87.637) and another, from Naukratis, is in the Department of Greece and Rome at the British Museum (GR 1974,1119.1); see also Petrie 1915, pl. xi, no. 5; Hogarth 1905, 125, fig.5, no. 5.

EA 23657 **1887,0101.1227** **(Pls 33, 58)**

A bowl of coarse red siltware pottery with a slightly rounded base, sides drawn in towards a rounded rim and two pierced lug-handles; the whole is covered with a red slip.
Height: 6cm (max.); diameter: 13.6cm (at rim).
Context: Findspot 52, iron-working area in the south-east part of the Saite enclosure (so-called 'Camp').
Bibliography: Petrie 1888, pl. xxxv, 54.

EA 22302 **1887,0101.1225** **(Pl. 33)**

Rounded bowl of coarse red siltware pottery, much of the surface eroded through salt action. There is a small rounded rim. The sides expand to the point of maximum diameter, and then turn quite sharply inwards to the rounded base. The interior shows clear signs of rotary manufacture, although the shape is actually irregular. Each side near the top bears two small scars which would seem to be the result of loop-handles having been broken or sheared off.
Height: 7cm; diameter: 12.2cm.
Parallels: A similar vessel from Tell Dafana is in Boston (MFA 87.631).

EA 23658 **1887,0101.1226** **(Pls 33, 58)**

A cooking pot of coarse red siltware pottery, with remains of a bright red exterior slip. The micaceous fabric contains inclusions of grit. The surface has been affected by salts and much has flaked off. The vessel has a rounded base, convex sides and an open mouth with a plain rim. A small loop handle is attached at either side. Around the better preserved handle are four applied blobs of clay, two set in line with the top of the handle and the other two at the base, intended as imitations of rivets on a metal vessel. The bad condition of the other side makes it impossible to say whether this feature was matched at that location. Repaired from three fragments with part of the rim and side missing.
Height: 14cm; diameter at rim: 21cm; max. width: 24.8cm.
Context: Findspot 52, iron-working area in the south-east part of the Saite enclosure (so-called 'Camp').
Bibliography: Petrie 1888, pl. xxxiv, 16.
Parallels: cf. Defernez 2001, pl. viii, no. 23; Brissaud 1991, pl. x, no. 125. A similar vessel from Findspot 28 at Tell Dafana is in Boston (MFA 87.631).

EA 23718 **1887,0101.1247** **(Pl. 34)**

Part of a pink marlware pottery cup with a flattened base and vertical sides. There are three light grooves below the rim and a deeper groove around the edge of the base. One handle survives at the side; the evidence of parallels from Migdol shows that there was no corresponding handle on the other broken side. The fragment comprises just over half of the original object. The surface is covered by a cream-yellow slip.
Height: 7.8cm; length: 13.2cm; width: 11.2cm.
Context: 'Qasr', east annexe (G), Findspot 28, below chamber 18.
Bibliography: Petrie 1888, pl. xxxv, 50.
Parallels: Oren 1984, 16, fig. 20, nos 18, 22.

EA 23654 **1887,0101.1253** **(Pl. 34)**

A cup of coarse red siltware pottery with a slightly convex base, sides widening slightly to the rim. The exterior had a red slip, now partly lost, which appears to have been polished in horizontal bands. The fabric contains sand and grit. Repaired from four fragments.
Height: 10.5cm; diameter: 13.9cm.
Context: Findspot 52, iron-working area in the south-east part of the Saite enclosure (so-called 'Camp').
Bibliography: Petrie 1888, 65 § 61, pl. xxxv, 79.

EA 23704 **1887,0101.1143** **(Pl. 34)**

A deep cup of coarse red siltware pottery, the exterior covered by remains of a red slip. The base is flattened but remains convex. The vertical sides are slightly convex and there are three grooves around the vessel beneath the rim. The interior shows marks of rotary manufacture. All the upper part of one side is missing.
Height: 14.5cm; diameter: 10.8cm.
Context: Findspot 51, domestic buildings in the urban area to the east of the Saite enclosure (so-called 'Camp').
Bibliography: Petrie 1888, 65 § 61, pl. xxxv, 75.
Parallels: see Petrie 1915, pl. xxxiii, nos 9–13 and id. 1906, pl. xxxix F, nos 136–9; Spencer 1996, pl. 63, B.2.5; Bourriau and Aston 1985, pl. 37, no. 105; id. 1997, pl. i, nos 33–4; Aston and Aston 2010, pl. 12, nos 86–7.

EA 23696 **1887,0101.1302** **(Pl. 34)**

A cup of pale cream-green marlware pottery, with slightly convex base and convex sides. The rim is plain with a thin edge, chipped in places. There is a groove around the vessel just above the base. The interior of the sides exhibits clear rilling-lines. The pale greenish fabric contains some grit inclusions.
Height: 8.5cm; diameter: 9cm.
Context: 'Qasr', east annexe (C), chamber 19 A.
Bibliography: Petrie 1888, 65 § 61, pl. xxxv, 76.
Parallels: Oren 1984, 15, fig. 18; 16, fig. 20, nos 17, 21; Aston and Aston 2010, pl. 18, no. 150. A similar cup from Tell Dafana is in Boston (MFA 87.642).

EA 23697 **1887,0101.1270** **(Pls 34, 58)**

A cup of pale cream-grey marlware pottery. The sides rise almost vertically from the flattened base to a plain rim. There is a slight groove around the exterior at the base of the sides. This appears to be the result of manufacturing the base as a separate piece which was then attached, the groove marking the join. Viewed from above, the diameter can be seen to be slightly irregular.
Height: 6.2cm; diameter: 7.2cm.
Context: Findspot 52, iron-working area in the south-east part of the Saite enclosure (so-called 'Camp').
Parallels: Aston and Aston 2010, pl. 17 no. 126. A similar cup from Tell Dafana is in Boston (MFA 87.643).

EA 23653 **1887,0101.1244** **(Pl. 34)**

A tall cup of coarse pale red siltware pottery, with a slightly pointed base and straight sides. The plain rim is damaged with a small part missing. The exterior bears extensive remains of a bright red slip. The micaceous fabric contains many inclusions of grit and sand. The interior shows clear marks of rotary manufacture and hand-smoothing, but the shape is not entirely regular.
Height: 10.3cm; diameter: 8.8cm.
Context: Findspot 51, domestic buildings in the urban area to the east of the Saite enclosure (so-called 'Camp').

Bibliography: Petrie 1888, 65 § 61, pl. xxxv, 78.
Parallels: Bourriau and Aston, pl. 37, no. 122.

EA 79645   **2010,1002.5**   **(Pl. 34)**

A cup of fine marlware pottery, repaired from fragments. Most of the base is missing. The shape is rather distorted, the vessel being not truly circular in plan view.
Height: 5.3cm; diameter: 8.2cm.
Context: 'Qasr', east annexe (G), Findspot 28, below chamber 18.
Parallels: see EA 23697 above. Fragments of four similar vessels are among the sherd collection from Dafana in the Department of Ancient Egypt and Sudan, British Museum.

EA 50786   **1912,0217.6**   **(Pls 34, 59)**

A cylindrical cup of grey-green marlware pottery, with a flat base (restored). The sides are very slightly convex and rise to a flat-topped, projecting rim. Below the rim is a narrow ridge running around the vessel. The exterior is covered by a thin grey-green slip, which has been polished in horizontal stripes. The cup has been re-assembled from fragments with some parts restored in modern material.
Height: 7.9cm; diameter: 10.2cm.

EA 79646   **2010,1002.6**   **(Pl. 34)**

Two fragments from a cup of fine marlware pottery, comprising the base and part of one side. There is a thin projecting rim with a slight ridge below. The wall of the cup is very thin (3mm) and the fabric is a hard grey clay with minimal inclusions (see **Fig. 1** in Chapter 4).
Height: 11cm; diameter: 9.2cm (estimates from fragments).
Parallels: fragments of four similar vessels are among the sherd collection from Tell Dafana in the Department of Ancient Egypt and Sudan, British Museum.

EA 22342   **1887,0101.1134**   **(Pl. 34)**

Jar of red siltware pottery, with a shallow pointed base. The sides converge to a narrow mouth with a plain rounded rim. Re-assembled from fragments (three still separate), with some parts of the base missing. The fabric was incompletely fired and has a grey core; it also contains many inclusions of grit, mainly small chert and limestone fragments. Parts of the exterior still show a thin red slip, but much of this has been lost through exfoliation. The side of the vessel shows cracking from faulty manufacture.
Height: 20.9cm; diameter: 13.2cm.
Context: Findspot 51, domestic buildings in the urban area to the east of the Saite enclosure (so-called 'Camp').
Bibliography: Petrie 1888, pl. xxxv, 63.

EA 22321   **1887,0101.1301**   **(Pl. 34)**

Narrow, red siltware pottery jar with a narrow mouth; the sides expand from the mouth to a maximum width and then converge to a pointed base. The uncoated fabric contains inclusions of sand and grit. Parts of the exterior surface have flaked off, probably the result of salt crystallization. One side is cracked.
Height: 11.4cm; diameter: 6.2cm.
Context: 'Qasr', east annexe (C), chamber 11.
Bibliography: similar to the form shown in Petrie 1888, pl. xxxv, 61. Perhaps the same vessel or a similar generic type.
Parallels: Spencer 1996, pl. 70, D.4.20. A similar but not identical jar from Tell Dafana is in Bristol, CMAG H2245.

EA 22328   **1887,0101.1147**   **(Pl. 34)**

Jar of coarse red siltware pottery, with a pointed base and plain rim. The convex sides converge to the mouth. The surface is now very eroded, but there are a few traces of an external red slip. The sides have some deep cracks.
Height: 15.4cm; diameter: 11.7cm.
Context: Findspot 55, by the great wall south of the 'Qasr'.

EA 22305   **1887,0101.1220**   **(Pl. 34)**

A closed jar of pale red-brown siltware pottery, with a slightly pointed base. The exterior is covered by a bright red slip, parts of which have eroded away. The narrow mouth is surrounded by a plain rounded rim, below which is a carinated ridge. Rilling-lines of rotary

manufacture show on the interior. The fabric contains mica, sand and small grits.
Height: 8.61cm; diameter: 7.27cm.
Context: Findspot 52, iron-working area in the south-east part of the Saite enclosure (so-called 'Camp').

EA 27430   **1887,0101.1266**   **(Pl. 34)**

A jar of pale brown siltware pottery, with a rounded base. The sides narrow to the rim, below which there is a raised ridge. Much of the surface has flaked off through salt action, but traces on the base suggest that the original surface may have been cream in colour. The edges of the rim are damaged.
Height: 8.6cm; diameter: 7.6cm.
Bibliography: Petrie 1888, pl. xxxvi, 96.
Parallels: a similar jar from Tell Dafana is Philadelphia E165. Another, but with less rounded sides, is in Bristol, CMAG H2254.

EA 22325   **1887,0101.1150**   **(Pl. 34)**

Pottery jar of coarse red-brown siltware, with a shallow pointed base and convex sides narrowing to the (chipped) rim, below which are a double ridge and incised grooves. The exterior is covered with a pale red slip. The shape of the body is slightly irregular.
Height: 17.4cm; diameter: 11.7cm (max.).
Context: 'Qasr', east annexe (C), chamber 11.

EA 22281   **1887,0101.1121**   **(Pl. 34)**

Pottery jar of uncoated red siltware with a narrow mouth, low rim and convex shoulder. The sides descend almost straight from the point of maximum diameter to the pointed base, the end of which is missing. The core of the fabric is dull grey and the surface red. Part of the rim is missing.
Height: 17cm; diameter: 9.4cm.
Context: 'Qasr', east annexe (C), Findspot 7.
Bibliography: Petrie 1888, pl. xxxv, 59.

EA 22324   **1887,0101.1132**   **(Pl. 34)**

Jar of red siltware pottery, with a pointed base, convex sides, and narrowed mouth. Below the plain rim there is a sharp carination in the side of the vessel, where the profile steps out some 4mm. Below this step are two very shallow grooves. The surface around the rim and down one side is pitted from salt action, and there is a hole broken through the side, from which a crack extends to the rim. The exterior was originally red-slipped, but the slip only survives on one side where the surface has not exfoliated. A scar shows where a loop-handle has been sheared off from the side just below the carination; a similar handle was also cut from the opposite side, but here the scar is barely visible owing to deterioration of the surface.
Height: 22.2cm; diameter: 16.6cm.
Context: Findspot 52, iron-working area in the south-east part of the Saite enclosure (so-called 'Camp').
Bibliography: Petrie 1888, pl. xxxiv, 28 (type).
Parallels: see the similar jars in Spencer 1993, pl. 63, D.1.70, D.1.74; Petrie 1909, pl. xlix, nos 777–8; Lopez-Grande 1995, pl. xlvi.e. A similar vessel from Tell Dafana, but without handles, is in Boston (MFA 87.634).

EA 23707   **1887,0101.849, 851, 854-5**   **(Pls 34, 58)**

A red siltware pottery jar restored from several pieces. The jar had convex sides with a red-slipped surface. The base is rounded with a slight central point and the sides converge to a wide mouth with a plain rim. Below the rim is a projecting carination, and slightly lower at either side is a small loop-handle. An incised groove runs around the vessel through the handles.
Height: 19.7cm; diameter: 15.8cm.
Context: Findspot 55, by great wall south of the 'Qasr'.
Bibliography: Petrie 1888, pl. xxxiv, 28 (type).
Parallels: see above, under EA 22324. Also Aston and Aston 2010, pl. 12, no. 85. A similar vessel from Tell Dafana is in Boston (BMFA 87.632).

EA 22292   **1887,0101.1113**   **(Pl. 34)**

An ovoid jar of coarse red siltware pottery, with a shallow pointed base, convex ribbed sides and two small handles near the rim. A few cracks extend down from the rim. The micaceous fabric contains inclusions of grit, sand and small limestone chips. There are a few

remaining patches of a red slip on the exterior, but most of this has disappeared owing to salt erosion.
Height: 18.5cm; diameter: 17.2cm.
Context: Findspot 52, iron-working area in the south-east part of the Saite enclosure (so-called 'Camp').
Parallels: Myśliwiec 1987, pl. xi, no. 3.

EA 23649   1887,0101.1133   (Pl. 35)

Jar of coarse red siltware pottery, with a flat base and convex sides. The sides widen to the shoulder and are finished with an everted rim. The exterior is covered by a red slip, which extends over the inside of the rim.
Height: 25cm; diameter: 19.2cm.
Context: 'Qasr', east annexe (C), chamber 2.
Bibliography: Petrie 1888, pl. xxxiii, 11.

EA 22287   1887,0101.1313   (Pls 35, 59)

A tall, narrow jar of coarse red siltware pottery, with a pointed base. The sides rise almost vertically, with a slight narrowing at the mid-point, to a rounded shoulder. From this they converge to a narrow mouth, which is surrounded by a low, external rim. The exterior of the jar bears remains of a polished red slip. The fabric contains a fair amount of grit and shows marks of burnt-out straw temper.
Height: 24cm; diameter: 11cm.
Context: 'Qasr', east annexe (D), chamber 22.
Bibliography: Petrie 1888, 65 § 61, pl. xxxiv, 24.
Parallels: Petrie 1906, pl. xxxix F, no. 157; Paice 1987, fig. 7, no. 2.

EA 22331   1887,0101.1117   (Pl. 35)

A tall jar of coarse red siltware pottery, with a rounded base, convex shoulder and a short neck. The shape of the body of the jar is distorted, with an uneven profile to the sides. The exterior is covered by a red slip. Both the core fabric and the slip contain many inclusions of fine grit, probably from sand. The irregularity of the body of the vessel and the variance in the rim diameter indicate carelessness in manufacture.
Height: 34.5cm; diameter: 14.1cm (max.).
Context: 'Qasr', casemate building A, cell 30. This jar was found with others of the same type in this location.
Bibliography: Petrie 1888, 54 § 53, p. 65 § 61, pl xxxiv, 23.

EA 22336   1887,0101.1148   (Pl. 35)

Jar of coarse red siltware pottery, with a rounded base, slightly convex sides and a neck that narrows to the rim and is decorated with a medial ridge. The fabric contains inclusions of grit and there is a large limestone fragment embedded in the interior wall. The vessel is rather irregular and has the appearance of having been made using slow rotation. There is an incised scratch on the shoulder, made post-firing and perhaps one of Petrie's marks, but it is illegible.
Height: 24.7cm; diameter: 9.7cm (max.).
Context: None recorded, but examples of this type of jar were found at Findspots 19, 25, 35 and 51.
Bibliography: Petrie 1888, 65 § 61, pl. xxxiv, 19.
Parallels: similar jars from Tell Dafana are in Boston (MFA 87.628) and Philadelphia (Penn Museum E158). The latter is marked with Petrie's Findspot number 55.

EA 22341   1887,0101.1118   (Pl. 35)

A tall jar of red siltware pottery, with a blunt, pointed base, rounded shoulder and short, cylindrical neck. The shape of the body is slightly irregular, with a degree of distortion in the diameter and a depression in the lower part of the side. The sides were worked quite thin, so much so that they became fragile and there is a hole broken through at one side. The compact red silt fabric contains particles of grit and is covered on the exterior by a smooth red slip, parts of which have been lost, especially on the shoulder.
Height: 34.1cm; diameter: 13.2cm.
Context: 'Qasr', east annexe (C), chamber 3.
Bibliography: Villing 2013, 91, fig. 17.

EA 22335   1887,0101.1131   (Pls 35, 59)

A tall, situla-shaped jar made of coarse red-brown siltware pottery. The exterior was covered by a red slip, but most of this has flaked off. At the top there is a cylindrical neck with a plain rim. The vessel has a slight shoulder, near vertical sides and a rounded base. The micaceous fabric contains many inclusions of grit, mostly small pieces of limestone or chert.
Height: 26.4cm; diameter: 10.7cm.
Context: Findspot 50, a 'dry well' in the urban area to the east of the Saite enclosure (so-called 'Camp').
Bibliography: Petrie 1888, 65 § 61, pl. xxxiv, 21.
Parallels: Paice 1987, fig. 7, no. 1; Bourriau and Aston, pl. 37, no. 111; Aston 1999, 224, pl. 69, no. 1996; Aston and Aston 2010, pl. 13, no. 96. A similar jar from Tell Dafana is in the Petrie Museum (UC 19251).

EA 22301   1887,0101.1130   (Pl. 35)

A red siltware pottery jar of tall, narrow shape, modelled on the form of a metal situla, with a rounded base and a cylindrical neck. The top of the neck is missing. On opposite sides of the neck were two small pierced handles, near the top, but only one remains. The exterior is covered with a hard, polished red slip. On the inside clear marks of rotary production are visible.
Height: 24.5cm; diameter: 9cm.
Context: 'Qasr', east annexe (C), chamber 3.
Bibliography: Petrie 1888, 65 § 61, pl. xxxiv, 20.
Parallels: see the reference under EA 50782 below.

EA 50782   1912,0217.2   (Pl. 35)

A tall situla-shaped jar of red siltware pottery, with a cylindrical neck and tubular body. Repaired from many fragments with missing parts replaced by modern material. On either side of the neck was a small loop-handle, one of which is preserved, the other reconstructed. The base is rounded. The exterior bears a polished, bright red slip.
Height: 27.4cm; diameter: 10.2cm.
Context: 'Qasr', east annexe (C), chamber 10.
Parallels: See the similar vessel in Aston and Aston 2010, pl. 16, no. 112.

EA 22339   1887,0101.1157   (Pls 35, 59)

A tall jar of coarse red siltware pottery, with a pointed base, ovoid body and flared neck. The vessel became distorted in manufacture and the diameter at the rim varies from 10.6 to 11.5cm. The uncoated fabric contains much grit. Clear marks of rotary manufacture are visible on the interior. A few fragments from the rim have been broken and repaired.
Height: 25.3cm; diameter: 12cm.

EA 23722   1887,0101.850   (Pl. 35)

A tall, narrow jar of coarse red siltware pottery, with a pointed base and flared neck. The vessel has been re-assembled from fragments, but a large section of one side is missing. The silt fabric shows no signs of ever having been slipped (although the surface is eroded so evidence may have been lost). The fabric contains a considerable quantity of small limestone chips together with grit.
Height: 34cm; diameter: 13.6cm.

EA 22338   1887,0101.1153   (Pl. 35)

A tall jar of pale red-brown siltware pottery, with a cylindrical neck, convex sides and a shallow, pointed base. There are some remains on the exterior of the neck and shoulder of a red slip, but if it was ever polished, all the polish has now disappeared. The coarse fabric is very sandy and contains many inclusions of grit. The interior shows clear rilling-marks from rotary manufacture.
Height: 30.4cm; diameter: 12.6cm (max.).
Context: Findspot 8, west of the 'Qasr'.
Parallels: Similar, Aston and Aston 2010, pl. 27, no. 234.

EA 22329   1887,0101.1140   (Pl. 35)

A tall, shouldered jar of coarse red siltware pottery, with vertical sides and a small ring-foot. The top of the vessel has been broken and the neck and rim are missing. There are remains of a single handle, which was attached below the rim, but only a small part has survived. The silt fabric contains sand, a small quantity of grit but no straw temper. The surfaces have been eroded, probably by salt action, but there are still one or two small traces of a red slip. The vessel was not well manufactured: the ring-foot is very rough and the shape of the whole jar is not completely regular, so the diameter varies between 13.6 and 14.1cm.

Height: 40.5cm (max.); diameter: 14.1cm (max.).
Context: 'Qasr', east annexe (C), chamber 27.
Parallels: Gratien 1997, pl. i, fig. 1, no. 89.77; the wide distribution of
this type of vessel has been noted, and they seem to have been used
over a long period, see Sagona 1982, 86–8 with fig. 3; see also Lehman
1998, 25, fig. 10, no. 2. The British Museum jar resembles Palestinian
examples, although with a ring-foot instead of a pointed base.

EA 22286   1887,0101.1127   (Pl. 36)

Pottery jar of pale red-brown uncoated siltware with a shallow pointed
base, convex sides widening to the shoulder and a straight-sided neck
expanding to the (damaged) rim. The fabric has inclusions of grit and
voids from burnt-out straw.
Height: 18.8cm; diameter: 9.8cm (max.).
Context: Findspot 52, iron-working area in the south-east part of the
Saite enclosure (so-called 'Camp').
Bibliography: Petrie 1888, 65 § 61, pl. xxxiv, 25.

EA 23800   1887,0101.1407   (Pl. 36)

A coarse red siltware pottery jar with a blunt, pointed base and
rounded shoulder; neck and rim lost; incompletely re-assembled from
fragments. The upper part bears traces of burning. This form of vessel
was common in the Third Intermediate Period so this example may
represent a continuation of the type or could be residual.
Height: 21.2cm; diameter: 17.2cm.
Parallels: Petrie 1923, pl. lx, type 60 G; Mostafa 1986, 10, no. 1;
Hummel and Schubert 2004, pl. L, no. 10.

EA 23848   1887,0101.1421   (Pl. 36)

Part of the conical lower body of a pottery jar, re-assembled from
fragments. Made of low-fired brown silt clay with a chaff temper.
Height: 18cm (max.); diameter: 12.7cm (max.).

EA 23801   1887,0101.1408   (Pl. 36)

Part of the base of a coarse red-brown pottery vessel, slightly rounded
with flaring sides. The fabric is greyish in section; the exterior is
covered with a dark-brown slip. Reconstructed from fragments.
Height: 7.1cm (max.); diameter: 10.3cm (max.).

EA 50784   1912,0217.4   (Pls 36, 59)

A jar of fine grey-green marlware pottery. The vessel has a low
ring-foot, convex sides with a rounded shoulder, and a cylindrical
neck. The top of the neck is finished with a flat-topped, projecting rim.
Repaired from many fragments with some pieces missing. The
exterior is covered by a smooth pale grey-green slip, which has been
polished horizontally, producing a faint striped effect. The underside
of the foot was left unpolished.
Height: 22.1cm; diameter: 11.8cm (max.).

EA 50785   1912,0217.5   (Pls 36, 59)

A jar of dull grey-green marlware pottery, with a small ring-foot,
ovular body and cylindrical neck. The top of the neck is finished with
a flat-topped, projecting rim. Repaired from many fragments and
restored in places with modern materials. The exterior was covered by
a thin and smooth greenish slip, which shows signs of horizontal
polishing on the surviving parts. The side bears traces of a demotic
docket (kindly read by Brian Muhs), giving a measure of the original
contents: 2+ 1/3 +? *hin*.
Height: 18.6cm; diameter: 13.4cm.

EA 50783   1912,0217.3   (Pls 36, 59)

Polished grey marlware pottery jar, restored from many fragments
with numerous areas missing and two portions of modern plaster
restoration. This is a very thin-walled vessel with a convex shoulder
and slightly pointed base. The exterior is covered by a thin greenish
slip, which has been polished in horizontal stripes. The original neck is
totally missing. It was formerly restored with fragments from a similar
vessel, but these have now been removed and are stored with the jar
although not attached to it. The fabric of the separate neck differs from
that of the vessel, being a slightly darker shade of grey and unpolished.
Height: 18.8cm; diameter: 12cm (vessel).
Height: 4.8cm; diameter: 8.7cm (neck).
Parallels: Aston and Aston 2010, pl. 18, no. 140.

EA 22312   1887,0101.1304   (Pl. 60)

Pottery jar with a blunt pointed base and convex sides, which converge
slightly to a small, rounded shoulder, above which is a slightly flared
neck with an everted rim. One side of the body is indented and
decorated with applied and incised features in the form of the god Bes.
The headdress of the representation forms one side of the neck of the
vessel, decorated with a buff-coloured slip.
Height: 20.2cm; diameter: 11.2cm (max.).
Context: 'Qasr', east annexe (C), chamber 9.
Bibliography: Petrie 1888, 65 § 61, pl. xxxv, 65.

EA 22304   1887,0101.1246   (Pls 36, 60)

A small Bes jar of coarse red siltware pottery, with a blunt pointed base
and convex sides. The narrow mouth is surrounded by a short,
cylindrical neck, which was finished with a slightly flared rim. The rim
has been broken and the top edge is missing. The coarse fabric shows
voids from burnt-out straw. On the exterior is a red slip, worn off in
places. The side of the vase is decorated with a much abbreviated Bes
face, formed of applied blobs of clay for the ears and eyes, the latter set
in a slight depression.
Height: 10.8cm (max.); diameter: 7.1cm.
Context: Findspot 52 W, iron-working area in the south-east part of
the Saite enclosure (so-called 'Camp').
Bibliography: Petrie 1888, 65 § 61, pl. xxxv, 64.

EA 22297   1887,0101.1286   (Pls 36, 60)

Small Bes jar, made of coarse red siltware pottery, with a drop-shaped
body, flaring rim and lug-handles on either side of body. On the side,
three small spots of clay have been applied to represent the nose and
eyes of the Bes image. The rim is damaged. The fabric contains
inclusions of stone, mostly limestone and chert grains.
Height: 6.1cm; diameter: 4cm.
Bibliography: Petrie 1888, 65 § 61, pl. xxxv, 66.
Parallels: Petrie 1915, pl. xxxiii, no. 47; id.1909, pl. liv, nos 826–8;
Spencer 1993, pl. 67, G.1.10; Aston and Aston 2010, pl. 26, no. 228.

EA 22326   1887,0101.1243   (Pl. 36)

A red siltware pottery vase with a pointed base, convex shoulder and
narrow neck. The top of the neck is broken and all the surface of the
vessel has decayed due to salt action. A spout has been broken from the
lower part of the side and is not present; a scar and a hole through the
vessel mark its former location.
Height: 15.7cm; diameter: 9cm.
Context: 'Qasr', east annexe (C), chamber 4.
Bibliography: Petrie 1888, 65 § 61, pl. xxxv, 57.

GR 1888,0208.164   (Pl. 60)

A miniature Egyptian copy of a Levantine basket-handled jar, with a
low-placed carination and pointed but rounded base, narrow flat
shoulder and raised rim; two lugs are placed on each side of the
shoulder, in imitation of the paired opposed ring-handles on the
full-sized jars. Made of red Nile silt clay.
Height: 3.91cm; diameter: 2.76cm.
Bibliography: Bailey 2008, 169, no. 3668, pl. 119; mentioned in Weber
2012b, 244, n. 328.
Parallels: a considerably larger version from Hawara is shown in Petrie
1889, pl. xiv, no. 6.

GR 1888,0208.165   (Pl. 60)

A miniature copy of an East Greek pottery amphora, made in compact
pink clay with traces of a white deposit in places. The neck is missing.
Before firing, a bird facing to the left, with a tripartite tail, was carved
on one side between the shoulder and the base.
Height: 2.2cm; diameter: 2.5cm.

EA 23650   1887,0101.1254   (Pls 36, 60)

Jar of coarse red siltware pottery, with a ring-foot and two small
handles beneath an everted rim. The level of the rim is not regular, but
lies at a slight slope. The shape is based on a situla. The exterior
surface bears remains of a polished red slip. In the red fabric are
inclusions of grit, particularly limestone and chert grains. Re-
assembled from fragments.
Height: 11.7cm (max.); width: 9cm (at handles); diameter: 8cm.
Context: 'Qasr', east annexe (G), chamber 18.

Bibliography: Petrie 1888, 65 § 61, pl. xxxv, 55. This type of jar was said by Petrie to be 'rather common in chamber 18'. Mentioned in Weber 2012b, 237, n. 273.
Parallels: see GR 1888,0208.140 below. There is another example in Liverpool, WM 47.56.11.

GR 1888,0208.140   (Pls 36, 60)

A pottery jar with two small handles, made from hard pink clay with abundant gritty inclusions. The shape of the vessel is slightly irregular. A few traces of a thick matt red slip remain on the exterior. The rim is chipped. Inside the jar is a lump of hardened resinous substance. This was analysed in 1889 by E.M. Holmes and found to be Chian turpentine from *Pistacia sp.* (see the reference below). A new analysis in 2008 confirmed this identification (see Appendix 1, i).
Height: 11.5cm; diameter at rim: 9cm.
Context: 'Qasr', east annexe (C), chamber 3.
Bibliography: Petrie 1888, 65 § 61, pl. xxxv, 55; Holmes, 1889, 387–9; Weber 2012b, 237, n. 273 and pl. 51j–k.
Parallels: see EA 23650 above.

EA 23709   1887,0101.1139 (Pl. 36)

A jar of coarse red siltware pottery, with a short flared foot, bulbous body and short, cylindrical neck. There are two small handles, one at either side of the neck. An incised groove runs around the vessel at the level of the base of the handles. The rim is damaged. The fabric contains inclusions of grit and small chips of limestone. There are voids left from burnt-out chaff. Poorly produced and irregular in shape, with one side curved more than the other.
Height: 25.8cm; diameter: 16.6cm (max.).
Bibliography: Petrie 1888, pl. xxxiv, 27 (not a very accurate drawing).

EA 22347   1887,0101.1231 (Pls 36, 61)

An open vessel of coarse red siltware pottery, with a rounded base and near vertical sides. The rounded rim has a moulded external profile. There is a shallow groove around the vessel some 3cm below the bottom of the rim moulding. The base is perforated by a small hole, apparently part of the original design, since a low rim surrounds the opening. The vessel exhibits irregularities: the level of the rim varies and the profiles of the sides are not regular. The exterior bears substantial remains of a slip, which varies in colour from pink to pale cream. Petrie considered this vessel to have been a kind of sink while Aston interprets it as a funnel, but the purpose in either case would have been to channel liquid. The existence of similar vessels with similar rim profiles but closed bases has been noted in Chapter 4. Examples occur in contexts from the 7th to the 5th centuries BC with many slight variations in rim profile.
Height: 30cm (max.); diameter: 25.7cm (max.).
Context: Findspot 51, domestic buildings in the urban area to the east of the Saite enclosure (so-called 'Camp').
Bibliography: Petrie 1888, pl. xxxiv, 37.
Parallels: Spencer 1996, pl. 65, C.4.18, C.4.23, C.4.44–48, pl. 85, no. 17; Wilson 1982, pl. xvii, no. 6; Hummel and Schubert 2004, pl. M, no. 8; Aston and Aston 2010, pl. 3, no. 38; pl. 22, no. 181.

EA 23810   1887,0101.1327 (Pl. 61)

A piece from the rim and side of a marl clay pottery vessel. The shape of the surviving piece suggests that it came from a large open vessel like a basin. The rim has an external lip and below it is a ridge.
Length: 38cm; width: 24cm.
Context: 'Qasr', east annexe (C), chamber 19 A.

EA 23710   1887,0101.1205 (Pls 37, 61)

A complete jar of pale brown marlware pottery, with an external pale green slip. The slip is continued a short distance into the interior of the neck. The vessel has a flat base, rounded sides narrowing to an angular shoulder and then converging to a narrow neck. At one side of the neck is a single handle running between the neck and the shoulder. The top of the neck is finished with an external rim. The form is that of a Judaean juglet, see EA 50788 below.
Height: 14.2cm; diameter: 9.6cm.
Context: Findspot 52, iron-working area in the south-east part of the Saite enclosure (so-called 'Camp').
Bibliography: Petrie 1888, pl. xxxv, 44; Maeir 2002, 238, fig.1, no. 1.

Parallels: a larger example in Petrie 1915, pl. xxxiii, no. 60; Mostafa 1986, 10, no. 3; Aston and Aston 2010, pl. 46, no. 439.

EA 23711   1887,0101.1284 (Pls 37, 61)

Marlware pottery juglet with a low ring-base, bulbous body with shoulder and a single handle at the base of the neck. Re-assembled from fragments; much of the body is missing. This is another example of the Judaean juglet, but as a miniature vessel.
Height: 5.35cm; diameter: 4cm.
Parallels: Hamza 1997, pl. ii, no. 6.

EA 50788   1912,0217.8 (Pls 37, 61)

A fine example of a Judaean juglet, made from a pale green-cream clay, with a slightly convex base and convex sides. There is a distinct shoulder, from which the sides converge to a narrow neck, at one side of which is a loop-handle. The top of the neck is finished with a flared rim, which is slightly damaged. Reconstructed from fragments with some pieces missing. The exterior (and perhaps interior) is covered by a thin pale greenish slip. This type of vessel was produced in Judea and imports into Egypt are recorded from other sites, including Kafr Ammar, Saqqara, Tell Tebilla, Tell Kedwa and Tell Fara'on (Petrie's Tell Nebesha). Local copies were also made, of which the preceding vessels EA 23710 and 23711 are examples from Tell Dafana.
Height: 22cm; diameter: 13.2cm (max.).
Context: 'Qasr', east annexe (C), chamber 19 A.
Parallels: Petrie 1915, pl. xxxiii, no. 60; Mostafa 1986, 10, no. 3; Aston and Aston 2010, pl. 46, no. 439; Hamza 1997, pl. ii, no. 6; Mumford *et al.* 2009, http://www.deltasinai.com/delta-09.htm.

EA 23799   1887,0101.1406 (Pl. 37)

Jug of dull grey marlware pottery with a small, flat foot, bulbous body and one surviving handle. Re-assembled from fragments; much of the body and the entire rim lost. Possibly a copy of a Greek style oinochoe jug like examples from Naukratis referenced below.
Height: 14.9cm; diameter: 10.2cm.
Parallels: GR 1910,0222.232b; see also GR 1886,0401.1380.

GR 1906,0301.9   (Pl. 62)

Fragment (neck) of small pottery flask with trefoil mouth and an annular ridge around the middle of the neck, two added clay buttons on either side of the spout, suggesting eyes, as well as two patches of clay under the spout and at the base of the front part of the neck. The intention seems to have been to reproduce the appearance of a bird. Broken remains of a loop-handle are preserved behind the neck. The rear part of the rim is broken and missing. The fabric is compact pale green-cream marl clay, possibly of Egyptian origin, which would imply that the vessel was a local copy of a foreign product. The form of the piece is, however, East Greek, as noted by Petrie (see below).
Height: 2.43cm; width: 2.03cm; diameter of neck: 0.97cm (min.).
Bibliography: Petrie 1888, 74 § 71, pl. xl, 3: 'a curious little neck of a vase of drab pottery is distinctly Greek and not Egyptian'.

EA 22293   1887,0101.1295 (Pl. 37)

A pottery jar of pale red-brown siltware, the exterior covered by remains of a pale cream wash, streaks of which have run down into the interior. There is a single handle from the rim to the shoulder. The sides are convex and the base pointed. The rim, a small part of which is missing, was slightly flared.
Height: 10cm; diameter: 8.6cm.
Bibliography: Petrie 1888, pl. xxxv, 41.
Parallels: Petrie 1915, pl. xxxiii, no. 36.

EA 23716   1887,0101.1135 (Pl. 37)

A single-handled wheel-made jug of micaceous red siltware pottery, with a squat rounded body, rounded base and tapering cylindrical neck. There is a flared rim at the top and a handle runs from the rim to the body. The rim is slightly chipped. The exterior bears traces of a red-brown slip. The underside is partly blackened from use as a cooking vessel.
Height: 10cm; diameter: 12cm.
Context: a two-handled variant was found at Findspot 52.
Bibliography: Petrie 1888, pl. xxxv, 43 (variants with one or two handles were found); see also Maeir 2002, 239, fig. 1, no. 3.

EA 23712   1887,0101.1292   (Pl. 37)

Imported pottery aryballos made of pale cream fabric, decorated on the exterior with two horizontal stripes of red paint. The same colour also occurs on the rim. There is a small pierced handle beneath the rim. The base is flat. The exterior bears patches of incrustation, probably gypsum.
Height: 6.3cm; diameter: 5.2cm.
Bibliography: Petrie 1888, pl. xxxv, 49; Weber 2012b, 373, no. TD 289.
Parallels: from an Egyptian context, part of a similar juglet was found at Migdol, see Oren 1984, fig. 25, no. 2.

EA 23714   1887,0101.1291   (Pl. 37)

An imported creamware pottery aryballos, with a small, flat base and convex sides. The body surface and ledge-rim have been damaged and one part of the rim is missing. There was a small loop-handle below the rim on one side; this also has been broken. Around the body are faint remains of bands of reddish-coloured paint, one at the point of greatest diameter and the other at the top of the body.
Height: 6.99cm; diameter: 5.42cm.

EA 22319   1887,0101.1297   (Pl. 37)

A small pottery vase of fine pale red ware, with a rounded base, convex sides and short neck.
Height: 4cm; diameter: 4.5cm.
Context: Findspot 52, iron-working area in the south-east part of the Saite enclosure (so-called 'Camp').
Bibliography: Petrie 1888, pl. xxxv, 74.
Parallels: Lopez Grande 1995, pl. xlix, g.

EA 23719   1887,0101.1242   (Pl. 38)

Pottery jar of dull grey coarse siltware. The dark colour is probably the result of low temperature firing. The vessel is irregular in shape, with a roughly flat base; convex sides and a low vertical rim around the mouth. The rim is damaged in places.
Height: 8.8cm; diameter: 10.8cm.
Context: 'Qasr', east annexe (C), chamber 2.

EA 22283   1887,0101.1151   (Pl. 38)

A rounded jar of coarse red uncoated siltware pottery, with a slightly pointed base and convex sides. The rim is slightly flared with a rounded edge. Many inclusions occur in the fabric, comprising grit, grog and voids from burnt-out straw. Repaired from fragments with some pieces missing. The shape of the vessel is rather irregular.
Height: 11.5cm; diameter: 12.8cm.
Context: 'Qasr', east annexe (C), chamber 27.
Parallels: Aston and Aston 2010, pl. 26, no. 223.

EA 23655   1887,0101.1149   (Pl. 38)

Squat red siltware pottery jar, with a flat base; convex sides, narrow neck and a flared rim. Complete except for a few small pieces missing from the rim. The exterior was covered by a polished red slip, part of which remains, one side has been blackened by burning.
Height: 10.7cm; diameter: 13cm.
Context: Findspot 52, iron-working area in the south-east part of the Saite enclosure (so-called 'Camp').
Bibliography: Petrie 1888, pl. xxxv, 69.

EA 22291   1887,0101.1223   (Pl. 38)

A globular vase of coarse red-brown siltware pottery, with a narrow mouth surrounded by an external, flat-topped rim. Parts of the rim are missing. The soft-fired fabric contains sand and grit inclusions. All the exterior surface was originally covered by a red slip, but much of this has been lost owing to salt crystallization. This salt damage has also eroded some of the underlying core fabric. There is a long horizontal crack in the side of the vase.
Height: 7.2cm; diameter: 8cm.
Bibliography: Petrie 1888, pl. xxxv, 68.

EA 22315   1887,0101.1289   (Pl. 38)

A round-bodied vase of pale pink marlware pottery. The vessel has a narrow mouth and small, flat base. The exterior may have had a pale pink-cream slip. The edges of the rim are chipped and there is a gash in one side of the vase. The surface bears patches of white incrustation.
Height: 6.4cm; diameter: 6.3cm.

EA 22320   1887,0101.1285   (Pl. 38)

A model jar of coarse red-brown siltware pottery, with a pointed base and rounded shoulder. The narrow mouth is surrounded by a low rim, set flat against the top of the body. The exterior surface bears remains of cream colour, possibly salt induced. The vessel is irregular in shape, there are cracks in one side, and some of the surface has flaked off.
Height: 6.67cm; diameter: 5.14cm.
Bibliography: Petrie 1888, pl. xxxv, 73.

EA 22314   1887,0101.1291   (Pl. 38)

A rounded red siltware pottery bowl, repaired from six fragments. Two pierced lug handles are placed below the rim, on opposite sides of the vessel. The rounded base is slightly pointed with the lowest point a little off-centre. Small grits (including very small flints and bits of quartz) are present in the fabric, with a few voids from burnt-out straw. On the exterior are remains of a red slip.
Height: 5.1cm; width: 7.95cm (at handles).
Context: 'Qasr', east annexe (G), Findspot 28, below chamber 18.

EA 23715   1887,0101.1281   (Pl. 38)

A small jar of pink marlware pottery with a surface cream-grey slip. The vessel has a small ring-foot, convex sides and a stirrup handle attached at each side. The everted rim has a flat top. The edges of the rim have been chipped and some of the slip lost from the top.
Height: 6.7cm; width: 9cm (at handles); diameter: 7.6cm.
Context: Findspot 52, iron-working area in the south-east part of the Saite enclosure (so-called 'Camp').
Bibliography: Petrie 1888, pl. xxxv, 48.

EA 23717   1887,0101.1234   (Pls 38, 62)

Miniature double-vase of rough red siltware pottery, consisting of two linked vases with flat bases and concave sides expanding to the shoulders, and then closing to narrow mouths with everted rims. Both rims are partly broken. The two vases were made separately and then joined by applying a bridge of clay between them at the level of the shoulders.
Height: 10.7cm; width: 9.5cm; depth: 4.6cm.
Context: Findspot 52, iron-working area in the south-east part of the Saite enclosure (so-called 'Camp').
Bibliography: Petrie 1888, pl. xxxv, 42.

EA 22310   1887,0101.1130   (Pl. 38)

An alabastron-shaped vase with a narrow neck and rounded base, made in red siltware pottery. The flat rim is chipped. The exterior bears traces of a red slip, polished in stripes around the vessel.
Height: 13cm; diameter: 6.2cm.
Parallels: Petrie 1906, pl. xxxix F, no. 203; Mostafa 1988, 15, fig. 2; Spencer 1996, pl. 84, no. 29; Aston and Aston 2010, pl. 45, no. 407.

EA 22340   1887,0101.1144   (Pls 38, 62)

A pink pottery flask of circular shape with a biconvex body, decorated on each side with concentric grooves. A narrow neck is inserted at the top and is flanked at its base by two small handles, one at either side. These handles are degenerate versions and non-functional. The top of the neck is finished with a projecting rim. As usual for this type of vessel, the flask was made in two halves, joined around the perimeter. There are a few traces of an external red slip.
Height: 15.7cm; diameter: 12.3cm.
Bibliography: Petrie 1888, 65 § 61, pl. xxxv, 67.
Parallels: for similar flasks, see Spencer 1993, pl. 72, K.1.27, K.1.29; Holladay 1982, pl. 6, no. 4; Aston and Aston 2010, pl. 17, no. 124.

EA 23748   1887,0101.1107   (Pl. 39)

A circular lid of pink pottery with a slightly domed upper surface and hollowed underside. The edges are chipped. Traces of a greyish deposit may be remains of a slip, or simply the consequence of salt action. The pink fabric may have been imported.
Height: 0.9cm; diameter: 3.62cm.
Bibliography: Petrie 1888, pl. xxxvi, 87.

EA 23746   1887,0101.1112   (Pl. 39)

Lid from a vessel, made of hard, green-grey marlware pottery. Circular in shape with a slightly domed upper surface. The underside

is hollowed in the middle with a projecting rim and a flat flange around the perimeter.
Height: 1.4cm; diameter: 8.27cm.
Context: 'Qasr', east annexe (C), Findspot 32, under the floor of chamber 19 A.
Bibliography: Petrie 1888, pl. xxxvi, 90 (type).

EA 23760   1887,0101.1224   (Pl. 39)

Lid from a vessel, made of hard, green-grey marlware pottery. Circular in shape with a domed upper surface. The underside has a hollowed centre with a surrounding rim; outside of which is a flange extending to the perimeter of the object.
Height: 1.8cm; diameter: 9.8cm.
Context: 'Qasr', east annexe (G), Findspot 25, south of chamber 18.
Bibliography: Petrie 1888, pl. xxxvi, 92 (type).

EA 23747   1887,0101.1114   (Pl. 39)

A circular jar lid of hard, grey marl pottery. The surface is covered by remains of a pale cream-green slip. The top is plain, smooth and convex. On the underside there is a central hollow surrounded by a slight ridge, with a flat surface around the perimeter.
Height: 0.9cm; diameter: 5.6cm.
Context: Findspot 8, west of the 'Qasr', or 25, 'Qasr', east annexe (G), south of chamber 18.
Bibliography: Petrie 1888, pl. xxxvi, 88 (type).
Parallels: Hummel and Schubert 2004, pl. T, 23.

EA 79647   2010,1002.7   (Pl. 39)

A small, circular lid of pale green marlware pottery. The upper surface is convex and the underside has a projecting ring to fit a vessel. No slip is now evident, but one may have been lost.
Height: 0.9cm; diameter: 6.5cm.

EA 23743   1887,0101.1109   (Pl. 39)

Circular pottery jar-cover of coarse red siltware pottery. The surface bears remains of some kind of incrustation, perhaps caused by burning. The top is slightly convex and the underside has a raised rim to fit a vessel.
Height: 1.6cm; diameter: 10.2cm.
Context: 'Qasr', east annexe (G), Findspot 28, below chamber 18.
Bibliography: similar to Petrie 1888, pl. xxxvi, 91, but this is not recorded from Findspot 28. Petrie's type 90 is noted from this Findspot, but that shape is rather different.
Parallels: a similar lid is in Philadelphia (Penn Museum E163), also from Findspot 8.

EA 23744   1887,0101.1206   (Pl. 39)

A circular jar lid of pale grey-green marl ware pottery, with a convex top. The underside has a projecting rim to fit the neck of a vessel, with a flat flange all round the perimeter. Part of the rim is broken. A reddish incrustation stains the concave centre of the underside.
Height: 2cm; diameter: 12.8cm.
Context: Findspot 52, iron-working area in the south-east part of the Saite enclosure (so-called 'Camp').
Bibliography: Petrie 1888, pl. xxxvi, 91.

EA 23745   1887,0101.1105   (Pl. 39)

A circular lid of pale green marlware pottery. The top is smooth and convex, and shows concentric lines of pebble-burnishing. The underside has a raised ridge surrounding a concave centre, but is flat around the perimeter. Rilling-lines from fast wheel production are evident on the underside.
Height: 1.5cm; diameter: 10.6cm.
Context: 'Qasr', east annexe (G), Findspot 28, below chamber 18.
Bibliography: the most similar lid in Petrie 1888 is that on pl. xxxvi, 91, but this is not recorded from Findspot 28. Petrie's type 90 is noted from this Findspot, but that shape is rather different.

EA 23667   1887,0101.1106   (Pl. 39)

A circular jar-cover of red siltware pottery, the surface covered with remains of a pale cream slip. The level of the convex top is irregular. The red fabric has inclusions of grit, chert and quartz.
Height: 1.8cm; diameter: 11cm.

EA 23689   1887,0101.1108   (Pl. 39)

Red siltware pottery jar-cover of circular shape, with remains of a pale cream slip on all surfaces. The slip is better preserved on the underside. Mica and grit inclusions are visible in the fabric.
Height: 1.5cm; diameter: 13.5cm.
Context: 'Qasr', east annexe (C), chamber 19 A.

EA 23666   1887,0101.1269   (Pl. 39)

A pottery cover (or possibly a dish?) made of coarse red-brown siltware with a red surface slip. The slip has been polished by pebble-burnishing, and on the exterior this has been executed in concentric stripes. Much of the slip has been lost through flaking of the surface. The fabric contains many inclusions of grit, particularly quartz grains from coarse sand.
Height: 1.9cm; diameter: 14.4cm.
Context: 'Qasr', east annexe (C), Findspot 32, under the floor of chamber 19 A.
Parallels: a similar item from Tell Dafana is in Boston (MFA 87.639).

EA 23742   1887,0101.1312   (Pl. 39)

Red-brown siltware pottery jar-cover with flattened conical top, edge chipped. The hollowed underside is surrounded by a raised rim, intended to fit a vessel.
Height: 2.1cm; diameter: 7.5cm.
Context: Findspot 8, west of the 'Qasr'.
Parallels: a similar lid from Tell Dafana is in Boston (MFA 87.648).

EA 23741   1887,0101.1125   (Pl. 39)

Domed pottery jar lid, made in a pale red silt fabric. The underside is hollow with a circular rim to fit a vessel. The surface has been eroded.
Height: 5.1cm; diameter: 11.3cm.
Context: Findspot 52, iron-working area in the south-east part of the Saite enclosure (so-called 'Camp').
Bibliography: Petrie 1888, pl. xxxvi, 93.

EA 23730   1887,0101.1252   (Pl. 39)

A circular jar lid of coarse red siltware pottery. The clay in the centre has been drawn up to form a rough handle. The surfaces have been damaged by salt action and the top of the handle is broken. The object has been repaired from three fragments. The underside is slightly concave, with a central hollow below the handle, where the clay was pushed up. The micaceous fabric contains grit and sand, and exhibits voids from burnt-out straw.
Height: 2.7cm; diameter: 6cm.
Context: 'Qasr', east annexe (C), chamber 17.
Bibliography: Petrie 1888, pl. xxxvi, 80.
Parallels: Hummel and Schubert 2004, pl. T, no. 27.

EA 22317   1887,0101.1217   (Pl. 39)

Pottery jar-cover (or cup?) made from coarse red siltware; convex sides curve in to the rim; pointed base (or top if a lid). Some traces of a red exterior slip remain, but most of surface has decayed through salt action.
Height: 5.8cm; diameter: 9.2cm.
Context: 'Qasr', east annexe (C), Findspot 31, a 'dry well' east of chamber 19.
Bibliography: Petrie 1888, 65 § 61, pl. xxxv, 46 (drawn as a vessel).

EA 79648   2010,1002.8   (Pl. 39)

A red siltware pottery lid with a central handle. The upper surface originally had a bright red slip, of which very slight traces remain. The rim is slightly chipped.
Height: 3.3cm; diameter: 5.6cm.

EA 23740   1887,0101.872   (Pl. 39)

A circular lid of pale green-grey marl clay pottery. Around the perimeter is a vertical flange, part of which has been broken away. In the centre of the underside is a cylindrical projection to fit the neck of a vessel. A handle was attached in the centre of the slightly domed top, but this has been broken off leaving a hole in its former location.
Height: 1.06cm; diameter: 3.2cm.

EA 23733   1887,0101.1251   (Pl. 39)

A circular jar-cover made of pale grey marlware pottery, with a

conical top and central knob-handle. Handle and rim are chipped.
Height: 2.6cm; diameter: 6.5cm.
Context: 'Qasr', east annexe (C), chamber 17.
Bibliography: Petrie 1888, pl. xxxvi, 82.

EA 23732   **1887,0101.1104**   **(Pl. 39)**
Pottery jar lid, re-assembled from fragments with a small part missing
from the edge. In the centre of the convex top there is a projecting
knob-handle. The underside is concave, with a sharp-edged rim
around the perimeter. Made in a hard green marl fabric, with spiral
pattern pebble burnishing of the top surface.
Height: 2.6cm; diameter: 7.4cm.
Context: 'Qasr', east annexe (C), chamber 19 A.

EA 79649   **2010,1002.9**   **(Pl. 39)**
Fragment from a lid of red silt pottery, the surfaces covered by a cream
slip. The piece constitutes about half of the original object. At the top
there is a slight trace of the beginning of a central handle.
Height: 3.4cm; length of fragment: 11.8cm; estimated full original
diameter: 12cm.
Context: Findspot 52, iron-working area in the south-east part of the
Saite enclosure (so-called 'Camp').

EA 23806   **1887,0101.1272**   **(Pl. 39)**
A pottery vessel cover of coarse red siltware, with a central knob-
handle on top. The handle has a depression in the centre. Much of one
edge is missing and the surface of the object is eroded and flaking. The
clay was fired only to a low temperature and most of the core has
remained black.
Height: 5.6cm; width: 18.7cm; original full diameter: 21.6cm.
Parallels: Brissaud 1991, pl. xi, no. 150; Aston and Aston 2010, pl. 3, no.
43.

EA 23731   **1887,0101.1250**   **(Pl. 39)**
A circular jar lid of pale red siltware pottery, with a knob-handle at the
centre of the convex top. The surface is pale pink-cream, probably
salt-induced rather than slipped. The fabric contains mica and grit.
The concave underside has a rim all round the edge.
Height: 3.7cm; diameter: 10.2cm.
Context: Findspot 52, iron-working area in the south-east part of the
Saite enclosure (so-called 'Camp').

EA 23728   **1887,0101.1219**   **(Pl. 39)**
Circular pottery vessel cover of coarse red siltware pottery, with a
central knob-handle and flaring sides. There are traces of a red slip on
the underside; this probably once covered all surfaces but it has been
lost owing to exfoliation of the surfaces. The exterior is considerably
pitted from this decay.
Height: 4.3cm; diameter: 14.2cm.
Context: 'Qasr', east annexe (C), Findspot 32, under the floor of
chamber 19 A.
Parallels: Aston and Aston 2010, pl. 22, no. 184.

EA 23727   **1887,0101.852**   **(Pl. 39)**
Coarse red siltware pottery jar lid, circular, with a central knob-
handle on top. Some areas of red slip survive, especially underneath.
Re-assembled from four fragments with part of one side missing. Mica,
sand and grit occur as inclusions in the fabric.
Height: 4.9cm; diameter: 13cm.

EA 23726   **1887,0101.1264**   **(Pl. 40)**
Circular lid of pale beige pottery with a pale yellowish-green slip
inside and out. Broken and repaired from two fragments, with part of
the side missing. A peg-handle is attached in the top centre, but the top
of the handle is broken. The fabric is pale sandy marl clay with a
tendency to laminate.
Height: 6cm; diameter: 14.3cm.

EA 23729   **1887,0101.1249**   **(Pl. 40)**
A circular jar lid of red siltware pottery, with a domed shape and a
knob-handle attached to the centre of the top. The pale red-brown
fabric contains sand and mica. All surfaces are covered by a bright red
slip, worn off in places, especially from the handle.

Height: 4.6cm; diameter: 9.5cm.
Context: 'Qasr', east annexe (C), chamber 3.
Bibliography: Petrie 1888, pl. xxxvi, 99.

EA 23737   **1887,0101.1103**   **(Pl. 40)**
A circular jar lid of pale pink marlware pottery, with a central
projecting handle on the top. The underside is hollowed and stained
with a green gritty substance. The edge is slightly chipped.
Height: 3.95cm; diameter: 5.8cm.
Bibliography: Petrie 1888, pl. xxxvi, 95.
Parallels: Bourriau and Aston, pl. 37, no. 116. A similar lid from Tell
Dafana is in the Petrie Museum (UC19353) and another with a more
tapered handle in Bolton (H1997), from Petrie's Findspot 28.

EA 23734   **1887,0101.1314**   **(Pl. 40)**
A circular jar-cover of micaceous, red siltware pottery. The lid has a
domed top with a knob-handle in the centre. There is a carination part
way up the height of the sides where the angle changes from near
vertical to a more gradual slope. Edges chipped.
Height: 5.7cm; diameter: 9.6cm.
Context: 'Qasr', east annexe (C), chamber 3.
Bibliography: Petrie 1888, pl. xxxvi, 100.

EA 23739   **1887,0101.1111**   **(Pl. 40)**
A small jar-stopper of grey marlware pottery. The lower part consists
of a hollow cylinder, topped by a broad flange with a flat underside and
convex top. Attached to the top of this, in the centre, is a projecting
handle of flared shape.
Height: 5.1cm; diameter: 5.6cm.
Context: 'Qasr', east annexe (C), chamber 19 A.
Bibliography: Petrie 1888, pl. xxxvi, 94.

EA 23738   **1887,0101.1110**   **(Pl. 40)**
A jar-stopper of pale grey marlware pottery, consisting of a hollow,
cylindrical lower section topped by a broad flange with a flat underside
and convex top. Attached to the centre of the flange is a projecting
handle with flared sides.
Height: 5.2cm; diameter: 4.8cm.
Context: 'Qasr', east annexe (C), chamber 19A.
Bibliography: Petrie 1888, pl. xxxvi, 81.

EA 23736   **1887,0101.1288**   **(Pl. 40)**
A circular jar-cover of grey marlware pottery, with a deep hollow on
the underside and a tall, central knob-handle on the top. The pottery
fabric displays traces of pink in the core. The edge is chipped in places
and one side of the top of the handle has been broken off.
Height: 7cm; diameter: 6cm.
Context: none recorded, but similar objects were found at Findspots 18
and 52.
Bibliography: Petrie 1888, pl. xxxvi, 97.
Parallels: a slightly wider example is in Boston (MFA 87.649).

EA 23749   **1887,0101.769**   **(Pl. 65)**
A heavy jar-stopper made of red siltware pottery. The fabric contains
grit and voids from burnt-out chaff. The top is convex and has been
roughly smoothed. On the underside there is an integral projecting
boss of hemispherical shape to fit the mouth of a vessel. All the lower
part was made as a unit, expanding from the boss to a wide flange with
an incurved edge. The hollow interior was sealed by adding more clay
to bridge the top. The seam of this closure lies about 2cm from the
perimeter of the object. The incised mark on the side is Petrie's
Findspot number.
Height: 10.2cm; diameter: 18.2cm (max.).
Context: 'Qasr', east annexe (C), chamber 3.
Bibliography: Petrie 1888, 66 § 61, p. 72 § 69, pl. xxxvi, 84.

EA 23750   **1887,0101.772**   **(Pl. 65)**
A jar-stopper of marlware pottery. The dull beige fabric contains
much sand and coarse grit. The lower part consists of a deep, rounded
boss to fit a vessel. At the top the sides widen to a projecting flange and
the convex top is marked with two recessed bands which cross at the
centre. This object probably dates from the Ptolemaic Period.
Height: 7.4cm; diameter: 10.2cm.

Context: Findspot 60, on the north-west Ptolemaic mound.
Bibliography: Petrie 1888, 66 § 61, pl. xxxvi, 85, 85a.
Parallels: Bolton H.1998, also from Tell Dafana.

EA 23725   **1887,0101.1268+1273**   **(Pls 10, 62)**

Part of a pottery cover with an open base and sides which converge to meet at a domed top, to which a circular handle is attached. Repaired from fragments with a number of pieces missing from the sides. Made from micaceous green marl clay. The interior and exterior were covered by a smooth slip, the colour of which varies from pale green to cream. This was probably burnished originally, as traces of spiral-pattern burnishing on the handle suggest.
Height: 18cm; diameter: 16.2cm.
Context: None recorded, but other examples were recovered from the 'Qasr', east annexe (C), Findspots 19A and 27.
Bibliography: Petrie 1888, 65 § 61, pl. xxxiv, 13.

EA 23672   **1887,0101.1245**   **(Pl. 40)**

Circular potstand of coarse red siltware pottery. The fabric contains grit and sand. The surface of the object has been eroded.
Height: 6.2cm; diameter: 16.2cm.
Context: Findspot 52, iron-working area in the south-east part of the Saite enclosure (so-called 'Camp').
Bibliography: Petrie 1888, pl. xxxiv, 33.
Parallels: from Tell Dafana, see EA 23673, 23674, 23675 below. Hamza 1997, pl. i. nos 14–17.

EA 23673   **1887,0101.1207**   **(Pl. 40)**

Circular potstand of coarse red siltware pottery. The uncoated fabric contains many inclusions of fine grit. The object is slightly irregular in shape.
Height: 7.2cm; diameter: 16.8cm.
Context: Findspot 52, iron-working area in the south-east part of the Saite enclosure (so-called 'Camp').
Parallels: same as for EA 23672 above.

EA 23675   **1887,0101.1203**   **(Pl. 40)**

A cylindrical potstand of coarse red siltware pottery. The uncoated fabric has a grey core from incomplete firing and contains inclusions of grit. Part of the lower rim has been broken and a small area is missing. The object is slightly irregular in shape.
Height: 7.4cm; diameter: 14.2cm.
Parallels: same as for EA 23672 above.

EA 23674   **1887,0101.1202**   **(Pl. 40)**

Coarse red siltware pottery vessel stand, cylindrical shape with flared top and base. The rounded rim at the top is chipped. The micaceous fabric has a black core and red surfaces, and contains a quantity of grit.
Height: 7.8cm; diameter: 15.6cm.
Parallels: same as for EA 23672 above.

EA 23676   **1887,0101.1293**   **(Pl. 40)**

Vessel-stand of coarse siltware pottery. Irregular in shape, the lower edge of the rim is not horizontal. The micaceous orange-red fabric is covered by a dull red slip.
Height: 4.92cm; diameter: 9.55cm.

EA 23670   **1887,0101.1142**   **(Pl. 40)**

Red siltware pottery stand of cylindrical shape, flared at the foot. Part of the rim and side are missing, as is a portion of the foot. One piece of the foot has been detached and rejoined. Exterior is a brighter red than interior. There is a small hole through each side. The coarse fabric was fired at a low temperature and has remained grey in the core. It contains many voids from burnt-out chaff, a small amount of grit and some grog temper.
Height: 19.5cm; diameter: 25.7cm (max.).
Bibliography: Petrie 1888, 65 § 61, pl. xxxiii, 8.

EA 23671   **1887,0101.1296**   **(Pl. 62)**

Red pottery tripod stand with a very rough underside, through which a hole has been broken. Repaired from three pieces. One of the three projections is broken off and missing.

Height: 19.5cm (max.); length: 23cm (max.); width: 21cm.
Context: Findspot 51, domestic buildings in the urban area to the east of the Saite enclosure (so-called 'Camp').
Bibliography: Petrie 1888, 65 § 61, pl. xxxiii, 9. Petrie notes these stands were found 'all over the plain at Defenneh'.
Parallels: part of a similar object from Tell Dafana is in Boston (BMFA 87.627); see also Oren 1984, 21, fig. 24, no. 5; Aston 1999, 209, pl. 65, no. 1895; Aston and Aston 2010, pl. 42, nos 364–5.

EA 23677   **1887,0101.1221**   **(Pls 10, 62)**

A cylindrical brazier of coarse red siltware pottery, with a flared foot and a wide flange around the perimeter just below the mid-point of the height. The upper part, above this ridge, is perforated by ten small holes, made from the exterior while the clay was soft. At the top the object is finished with a small roll-rim, parts of which have been chipped. The interior is closed just below the level of the flange. The exterior bears traces of a bright red slip. About half the edge of the foot is missing.
Height: 10.7cm; diameter: 14.9cm (at central flange); full original diameter 16.3cm.
Context: Findspot 52, iron-working area in the south-east part of the Saite enclosure (so-called 'Camp').
Bibliography: Petrie 1888, 65 § 61, pl. xxxv, 77.
Parallels: examples from Tell Dafana are in Boston (MFA 87.651) and in the Petrie Museum (UC19256); see also Wilson 1982, pl. xx, no. 9; Leonard 1997, 295, fig. 7.8; Hamza 1997, pl. i, no. 19.

EA 23669   **1887,0101.1311**   **(Pls 40, 63)**

Part of a narrow conical redware pottery object, perhaps a conduit for the transmission of air into a furnace, although there is no sign of burning on the object. The wider end is broken off and an unknown amount is missing. The narrow end has a short section of reduced diameter, finished with a rounded rim, part of which is missing. The exterior has remains of a red slip.
Length: 25.7cm; diameter: 6.8cm (max.).

EA 79650   **2010,1002.10**   **(Pls 40, 62)**

The upper part of an object of fine marlware pottery, reconstructed from fragments. It consists of a cylindrical spout at the top, surrounded by a flared collar, with the convex sided body of the vessel below. Parts of the rim around the collar are missing. The function is unclear, but it may be the object interpreted by Petrie as a food-cover with an open spout to allow steam to escape. Petrie mentions a similar object, kept in Cairo, which incorporated a perforated cylindrical tube.
Height: 10.2cm (incomplete); diameter: 14cm.
Context: 'Qasr', east annexe (G), Findspot 28, below chamber 18.
Bibliography: see comments in Petrie 1888, 65 § 61.
Parallels: part of a second object of the same type is kept among the sherd collection from Tell Dafana at the British Museum.

EA 79651   **2010,1002.11**   **(Pl. 62)**

An unusual object of pale red siltware pottery, with a pale cream-grey surface slip. The item consists of a hollow stem with a rounded element at one end and decorative ridges around the perimeter. There are three raised ridges, each of which is double, with thinner incised lines in between. Possibly part of the stem from a lamp similar to one found at Mendes (see Wilson reference below). If this suggestion is correct, the sides near the base would have continued their expansion to create a stable foot, whilst above the round element at the top a dish for the actual lamp would have existed.
Height: 12.3cm; diameter: 5.6cm.
Parallels: see Wilson 1982, pl. xx, no. 8; Hamza 1997, pl. i, no. 32; Mostafa 1988, 17, no. 12.

EA 22332   **1887,0101.1230**   **(Pl. 41)**

A Phoenician amphora of compact pink pottery, with a small foot, pointed base, convex sides and a sharply angled shoulder, from which the sides converge to a raised rim. The exterior is covered by a cream-coloured slip, parts of which have flaked off. One side of the jar has been damaged above the shoulder and also about half-way up the body. A handle is attached at either side at the level of the shoulder carination, but through a manufacturing error these are not set accurately at opposite ends of the maximum diameter, but are offset to one side.

Height: 41.7cm; width: 31.2cm (across handles); diameter: 26.4cm.
Context: Findspot 51, domestic buildings in the urban area to the east of the Saite enclosure (so-called 'Camp').
Parallels: Sagona 1982, 81, fig. 2, no. 6 (without peg-foot); Paice 1987, 98 and fig. 1; Hamza 1997, pl. x, nos 1–2, 4–5; Aston 1999, 232, pl. 72, no. 2045. For Phoenician amphora found at Tell Tebilla, see http://www.deltasinai.com/delta-10.htm.

EA 50781 1912,0217.1 **(Pl. 41)**

A local copy of a Phoenician-style amphora of red siltware, with a pointed base and swelling sides. A low rim surrounds the narrow mouth, below which is a sloping flange to a sharp carination. At this point a loop-handle is attached on either side. The exterior exhibits remains of a pale cream-white slip, probably intended to reproduce the appearance of true imports. The red fabric contains voids from burnt-out chaff with inclusions of grit and limestone.
Height: 36.3cm; diameter: 18.4cm (max.).
Parallels: Sagona 1982, 81, fig. 2, no. 3.

EA 22346 1887,0101.1222 **(Pls 41, 63)**

A Phoenician amphora of red siltware pottery, with a pointed base, convex sides, and sharp shoulder carination. Above the latter the sides converge to a contracted mouth, surrounded by a low, rounded rim. There is a loop-handle on either side at the shoulder. The exterior bears remains of a pale pink slip.
Height: 39cm; width: 29cm (across handles); diameter: 21.5cm.
Context: 'Qasr', east annexe (C), chamber 2.
Bibliography: Petrie 1888, pl. xxxiii, 4.
Parallels: Petrie 1915, pl. xi, no. 34; Sagona 1982, 81, fig. 2, no. 7; Paice 1987, 98 and fig. 1; Myśliwiec 1987, pl. xii, nos 3–5.

EA 22350 1887,0101.1141 **(Pl. 41)**

An amphora of Phoenician style, but made in local coarse red-brown siltware with a surface red slip. Much of the slip has been lost. The vessel has a shallow pointed base, a bulbous body, a sharp carination at the shoulder and a short, cylindrical neck. Part of the neck is missing. A loop-handle is attached at either side at the level of the shoulder. The fabric contains sand and shows many voids from burnt-out chaff, but is almost free of grit.
Height: 42.7cm; width: 34cm (across handles); diameter: 28.6cm.
Parallels: see the similar, but not identical vessel in Sagona 1982, 81, fig. 2, no. 10.

EA 22344 1887,0101.1137 **(Pls 41, 63)**

A Phoenician amphora of compact pale pink marlware pottery, with a rounded base and bulbous body. Two handles are attached near the top, at the level of the angular shoulder. There was a short cylindrical neck, but most of this has been broken off and is missing. The exterior is covered by a pale cream-yellow slip, most of which still remains although there has been some loss. The fabric contains small chips of limestone. The jar is inscribed on one side with three lines of early demotic text in black paint.
Inscription details (kindly provided by Rob Demaree and Brian Muhs): the upper two lines were written in the same hand and contain a text reading [1] 'Year 4, fourth month of winter, day 9. [2] Harvest of Year 3 of the storeroom' (followed by a personal name?). The lower third line of text was written separately in larger script and begins with the words *tp-nfrw*, probably 'finest' in reference to quality. The rest of this line may contain a title. It is likely that this third line of text was the first to be written on the jar; the quality designation probably referring to the original contents of this Phoenician amphora, perhaps wine. The second inscription above would have been added when the empty jar was re-used for the storage of grain in Year 4 of an unnamed king.
Height: 44cm; diameter: 21.3cm (max.).
Context: 'Qasr', east annexe (C), chamber 11.

EA 22351 1887,0101.1152 **(Pl. 42)**

A tall jar of pale green marlware pottery, with a shallow pointed base and convex sides. The neck is missing, but must have been quite narrow. The exterior is covered with a polished pale green slip to give an eggshell-like appearance. The vessel has been reconstructed from fragments and some areas of the sides have been damaged, resulting in loss of the surface. The marl fabric is very homogenous.

Height: 46.6cm; diameter: 30.2cm.
Context: 'Qasr', east annexe (C), chamber 19 A.
Parallels: Similar shape in silt clay, Aston and Aston 2010, pl. 28, no. 246.

EA 18672 1887,0101.1237 **(Pl. 42)**

A complete amphora of coarse red siltware pottery, with a rounded base, convex ribbed sides and a carinated shoulder. The sides converge from the shoulder to a short cylindrical neck, which is finished with an external roll rim. A loop-handle is attached at either side at the level of the shoulder carination. The rim has been slightly chipped. The micaceous fabric exhibits voids from burnt-out chaff temper, but contains very little grit.
Height: 49.8cm; diameter: 29.4cm.
Context: 'Qasr', east annexe (C), chamber 27.
Bibliography: Petrie 1888, pl. xxxiii, 3; see Maeir 2002, 239, fig. 1, no. 7.
Parallels: Aston 1999, 186, pl. 56, no. 1698; Aston and Aston 2010, pl. 5, no. 60.

EA 23775 1887,0101.247 **(Pl. 42)**

Neck and shoulder section of a pottery amphora with a handle attached at either side of the neck. It is probably an Egyptian copy of a Rhodian amphora dating from the Ptolemaic Period. The vessel was made of coarse red-brown silt fabric and the exterior was covered by a red slip, much of which has flaked off. The slip was extended into the interior of the neck. The fabric contains mica but few other inclusions and the firing has left a grey core. The Museum Register refers to the presence of a Greek and demotic inscription on this vessel, but this has disappeared apart from very minor traces of black paint near the lower edge of the object.
Height: 31.3cm (max.); width: 28.6cm (at top of handles).

EA 18674 1887,0101.1236 **(Pl. 43)**

Chian amphora of pale brown pottery, with a peg-foot and two handles. Surface almost completely lost through salt crystallization and the fabric extremely weak. A small area of slipped surface remains at the top of the neck and is a dull cream colour. The fabric is pink with a few inclusions of grit and chips of limestone. The loss of the slip has revealed a join at the base of the neck, showing that it was manufactured separately and then united with the body.
Height: 81.5cm; diameter: 27.4cm (max.).
Context: 'Qasr', east annexe (C), chamber 19.
Bibliography: Petrie 1888, 64 § 61, pl. xxxiii, 2 (type).
Parallels: for jars from Egyptian contexts see the example from Naukratis in Petrie 1886c, pl. xvi, 4; also from Sais, Wilson 2007; Chian amphorae were also found at Migdol, Oren 1984, 24–5, fig. 22, no. 1. Aston suggests that local copies may have been made at Naukratis, see Aston and Aston 2010, 8, under Fabric P21.

EA 18677 1887,0101.1238 **(Pl. 43)**

A Chian amphora of pale pink pottery, the exterior discoloured to patches of grey and white by salt action. The tall cylindrical neck is flanked by a pair of handles. The swelling body tapers to a peg-foot. The vessel is damaged, with a hole in the upper body.
Height: 87cm; diameter: 30.1cm (max.).
Bibliography: Petrie 1888, 64 § 61, pl. xxxiii, 2 (type).
Parallels: see EA 18674; also Aston and Aston 2010, pl. 47, no. 447.

EA 22356 1887,0101.770 **(Pl. 64)**

Upper part of a Chian amphora, similar in form to the preceding two examples. One of the handles between the neck and shoulder is complete but the other one is broken off short at the bottom. The exterior bears an incised five-pointed star at the top of the shoulder (see Chapter 7, p. 128). A broken piece of the jar has been re-attached with a modern copper staple. The mouth is closed with plaster bearing multiple seals of Amasis. Details are given with the other plaster sealings in the catalogue of objects, Chapter 3, pp. 68–9.

EA 22343 1887,0101.1200 **(Pl. 44)**

Klazomenian amphora of pale cream pottery. The vessel has a handle on either side of the cylindrical neck. The exterior is finished with a cream slip on which are painted dark red bands of decoration. These

consist of two close-set horizontal bands at the shoulder and another lower on the body, with two bands which begin at the rim and run down the outside of each handle, then down the body as far as the lower horizontal band. The side of the jar is perforated by ten drill-holes, made post-production, at the level of the shoulder.
Height: 75cm; diameter: 36.9 (max.).
Bibliography: Johnston 2006, 26, fig. 16; 28, Table 1, no. 4; Weber 2012b, 375, no. TD 300.
Parallels: another Klazomenian amphora was found at Tell Dafana in the 2009 excavations by M. Abd el-Maksoud, see **Pl. 85**.

EA 18676   1887,0101.1228   (Pl. 44)
An amphora of pale red-brown pottery, with a pale cream slip on the exterior. Two loop-handles are attached to the upper part of the sides and they rise up above the top of the vessel. This is an example of the so-called 'Basket-handled Jar', well known from Cyprus and the Levant. The mouth is quite narrow and is finished with an external rim. The ovoid body of the jar has a slight ridge at the point of maximum width, with a few light lines running around the diameter.
Height: 102cm (including handles); diameter: 40.5cm (max.).
Context: 'Qasr', east annexe (C), chamber 9. Petrie notes many examples of these jars in this chamber, but mostly broken up.
Bibliography: Petrie 1888, 63 § 59, p. 64 § 61, pl. xxxiii, 6.
Parallels: Sagona 1982, 89, fig. 4, no. 2; Oren 1984, 18, fig. 21, no. 11; Gratien 1997, pl. i, fig. 1, no. 5.70; see also Introduction, p. 98, n. 26. Another vessel of this type from Tell Dafana is in the Egyptian Museum in Cairo; see the drawing by François Leclère on p. 95, **Fig. 16**.

EA 23776   1887,0101.738   (Pl. 45)
Neck from an amphora of pale brown pottery, with a pale cream slip on the interior and exterior. The fabric contains many inclusions of white limestone chips, flint and other bits of grit. It has a tendency to laminate, possible as a consequence of salt action, with the result that the object is cracked in numerous places. At each side of the neck is a scar marking where a handle has been broken away. A handle fragment 1887,0101.870, which, according to the register, joined this neck, is not present. A red-painted *alpha* (now very faint) is on the exterior. There is also an incised mark, but this is most probably a rough attempt to write Petrie's Findspot number 19. The precise origin of this amphora remains uncertain but scientific analysis by Michela Spataro (see Appendix 1, ii) suggests a source in the Ionian or Adriatic region (see also Chapter 7, p. 128).
Height: 10.6cm; diameter: 15cm.
Context: 'Qasr', east annexe (C), chamber 19.
Bibliography: Weber 2012b, 376, no. TD 305.

EA 22333   1887,0101.1330   (Pls 45, 65)
A copy of a fractional Samian amphora, made in Egyptian coarse red silt clay. The vessel has a small foot from which the sides widen to an angular shoulder before converging to a narrow, cylindrical neck. There is a handle at either side of the neck, running between the neck and the shoulder. At the top of the neck is an external roll rim, which is slightly chipped. The exterior of the vase bears remains of a pale greenish-cream slip. The micaceous fabric contains many voids from burnt-out chaff, but hardly any grit. There is a deep crack in one side and a fragment has been replaced. The incised mark on the shoulder is the excavator's number, 19A.
Height: 34cm; diameter: 22.6cm (max.).
Context: 'Qasr', east annexe (C), chamber 19 A.
Bibliography: Petrie 1888, 65 § 61, pl. xxxiv, 39 (type); cf. Johnston 2006, 28, Table 1, no. 3; Weber 2012b, 377, no. TD 306; Villing 2013, 82, fig. 7.
Parallels: Petrie remarks on there having been 'dozens of others' in this chamber; Smolárikova 2002, 37–8, 116, pl. i, no. 1.

EA 22330   1887,0101.1146   (Pls 45, 65)
A Samian pottery amphora made in a compact, micaceous red fabric, with a small foot from which the concave sides widen to a rounded shoulder before converging to a cylindrical neck. On either side of the neck a loop-handle extends to the shoulder. The top of the neck is finished with an external rim. About one-third of the circumference of the rim and top of the neck are missing, part of the foot is broken and there are two deep chips in the side of the jar. The top of one of the

handles is also damaged. The exterior is covered by a cream-yellow slip. On top of the shoulder is a mark consisting of three incised lines, executed pre-firing (see Chapter 7, p. 128).
Height: 42.2cm; diameter: 26.2cm (max.).
Bibliography: Petrie 1888, pl. xxxiii, no. 10b ('rounder, unpainted vases'); Johnston 2006, 28, Table 1, no. 14; Weber 2012b, 376, no. TD 302.
Parallels: a very similar vessel with an ancient potmark on the shoulder, also from Petrie's excavations at Tell Dafana (Findspot 50), is in Boston, MFA 87.626; see also Oren 1984, 26–7 with fig. 22, no. 6; Hamza 1997, pl. xiii, no. 1; see more generally, Smolárikova 2002, 37.

EA 18673   1887,0101.1239   (Pl. 45)
A complete East Greek pottery amphora, possibly Klazomenian, with a small foot and rounded shoulder. The sides expand from the foot to the shoulder and then converge to a narrow, cylindrical neck, which is finished with a rounded, external rim. At either side of the neck is a loop-handle, extending from the neck to the shoulder. The red silt fabric contains grit, especially small particles of quartz and limestone. There are remains of a pale cream-yellow slip on the body, especially on the lower part. No doubt it once covered the whole vessel, but much has been lost due to flaking of the surface, which shows visible evidence of lamination.
Height: 45.5cm; diameter 29.2cm.
Context: Findspot 50, a 'dry well' in the settlement area.
Parallels: Hamza 1997, pl. xv, no. 1.

GR 1888,0208.140a   (Pl. 45)
A Samian pottery amphora made in a compact, micaceous red-brown fabric. The jar has a small foot, concave sides, rounded shoulder and a short, cylindrical neck. On either side of the neck a loop-handle extends to the shoulder. There are two incised marks on the shoulder: one made pre-firing beside the base of one handle; the other incised post-firing near the neck (**Pl. 65**); see Chapter 7, p. 128. The surface is damaged in places, especially towards the foot.
Height: 42.cm; diameter: 28.cm.
Context: Findspot 55, by the great wall south of the 'Qasr'.
Parallels: see EA 18673 above.

EA 23772   1887,0101.774   (Pl. 65)
Shoulder-sherd of a greyware pottery amphora from Lesbos, including the base of the neck and root of one handle. On the exterior of the shoulder is part of an incised mark: the letter N (see Chapter 7).
Length: 21.8cm; width: 16.8cm; depth: 5.8cm.
Context: 'Qasr', east annexe (G), chamber 18.
Bibliography: Petrie 1888, pl. xxxiii, 12 (type); Johnston 2006, 28, Table 1, no. 5.
Parallels: London, PM UC19247.

EA 18675   1887,0101.1102   (Pl. 46)
Pottery amphora from Lesbos with a handle on either side of the narrow neck, a pronounced shoulder and wide body which tapers to a narrow, flat base. At the top of the neck is an external rim, the level of which is irregular and part of which is missing. The foot has been broken off and repaired. The fabric exhibits a black core and grey surface and contains inclusions of limestone and mica.
Height: 54.4cm; diameter: 36cm (max.).
Context: Findspot 50, a 'dry well' in the urban area to the east of the Saite enclosure (so-called 'Camp').
Parallels: Petrie 1909, pl. liv, nos 854, 856; id. 1915, pl. xi, no. 43; Oren 1984, 20, fig. 23, no. 6; Hamza 1997, pl. xvii, no. 2; Smolárikova 2002, 39–40, pl. ii, no. 1 and lower photo on p. 120.

EA 22345   1887,0101.1240   (Pl. 46)
An East Greek pottery amphora with a small flared foot, convex sides widening to the shoulder, two handles and a cylindrical neck, finished with an external rim. The exterior was covered by a pale slip, which varies from cream to pink in colour in different areas, but much of this slip has disappeared owing to exfoliation of the surface. The core fabric is compact and dull brown in colour; it contains sand and small flecks of limestone. In applying the handles to the neck too much pressure was exerted, with the result that the neck was deformed to an elliptical shape instead of a circle.

Height: 42cm; diameter: 28cm (max.).
Context: Findspot 51, domestic buildings in the urban area to the east
of the Saite enclosure (so-called 'Camp').
Bibliography: Weber 2012b, 376, no. TD 304.

EA 22349   1887,0101.1101   (Pl. 46)
Redware pottery amphora from northern Greece, repaired from
fragments. The vessel has a narrow neck flanked by two handles, a
wide swelling body and pointed base, which is broken. The exterior is
covered by a smooth red slip over the compact pink core fabric. The
mark on the shoulder is the excavator's Findspot number, quite clearly
52 on this vessel. (Petrie noted others from Findspot 51).
Height: 57cm; diameter: 40cm.
Context: Findspot 52, iron-working area in the south-east part of the
Saite enclosure (so-called 'Camp').
Bibliography: Petrie 1888, pl. xxxiii, 1.
Parallels: Petrie 1909, pl. liv, no. 850.

EA 22357   1887,0101.1232   (Pl. 47)
A keg of coarse red siltware pottery, with a roughly globular body and
an applied cylindrical neck, finished with an external rim. At the base
of the neck are two small handles. The vessel has been poorly made
and is quite irregular, the body apparently made as two separate ends
and then joined. The irregularities suggest hand manufacture on a
turntable with a slow rotary speed. The fabric contains many small
pieces of grit, mostly chips of limestone. The underside has
deteriorated considerably through salt action, which has caused the
fabric to laminate.
Height: 30.3cm; length: 25.8cm (max.); width: 23cm.
Context: none recorded, but perhaps 'Qasr', east annexe (C), chamber
19, as noted beside Petrie's drawing.
Bibliography: Petrie 1888, 65 § 61, pl. xxxiv, 29.
Parallels: Aston 1999, 186–7, pl. 56, no. 1701.

EA 22367   1887,0101.1310   (Pls 47, 61)
A bellows made from coarse red siltware pottery, in the form of a
cylindrical chamber with a flat base and oblique rim, and a long
straight pipe of semi-circular cross section, branching off from near
the base of the chamber on one side. The underside of the whole object
is rough, showing it was manufactured on the ground surface, but the
other surfaces have been smoothed by hand. In the base are two small
round holes linked by a recessed groove. One of the holes, in the
projecting tubular portion, penetrates just 9mm into the object and
then ends. The other, in the bottom of the cylindrical part, passes right
through to the interior to emerge close to the outlet for the pipe. These
holes and the connecting groove are evidence for an ancient repair of
the object after the projecting pipe had been broken from the cylinder.
A staple, probably of copper, would have been inserted in each hole
and along the groove to bind together the two parts. The object was
fired at a low temperature and retains a black core; see further
Appendix 1, iii.
Height: 19.2cm; length: 54cm.
Context: Findspot 52, iron-working area in the south-east part of the
Saite enclosure (so-called 'Camp').
Bibliography: Petrie 1888, 64 § 61, pl. xxxiii, 7; Coutts 1988, 94–5 [79].

EA 27719   1887,0101.1165   (Pl. 47)
Part of the upper section of a pottery vessel conserved from four joined
fragments, with one small piece loose. Handmade from coarse silt clay
with much chaff temper. The fabric is red in section but the surfaces
are brown. A part of the mouth is preserved on the piece, surrounded
by a raised rim.
Length: 42.8cm (max.); width: 29cm (max.).

Sherd collections
In addition to the individual registered sherds catalogued below, a
large group of fragments, mostly of marlware, is kept under number
EA 79652.

EA 23790   1887,0101.842   (Pl. 65)
Fragment of a marlware pottery jar handle bearing an impressed
cartouche of a king Nekau.
Length: 3.55cm; width: 3.12cm; thickness: 2.17cm.

Context: 'Qasr', east annexe (G), chamber 18.
Bibliography: Petrie 1888, 59 § 57, p. 72 § 69.

EA 23678   1887,0101.1255   (Pl. 66)
Irregularly shaped sherd from a large pale-pink vessel, the exterior
covered with a pale green slip. The sherd has been perforated after
production with five round drill-holes and the beginning of a further
one. The minimum diameter of the vessel (between 40 and 45cm),
thickness (up to 1.6cm) and slightly concave outside profile suggest that
the container was an amphora, probably of the Cypriot basket-
handled type; cf. GR 2010,5002.19 below.
Height: 9.5cm; width: 12.6cm.
Context: 'Qasr', east annexe (C), Findspot 32, under the floor of
chamber 19 A.

EA 23754   1887,0101.1303   (Pl. 66)
Fragment from the top of the round and domed lid of a vessel, made of
a pale pink ware covered with a pale beige slip, surmounted with a
small U-shaped handle.
Length: 5.88cm.
Bibliography: Petrie 1888, pl. xxxvi, 86.

EA 23758   1887,0101.1402   (Pl. 66)
A pottery rim-sherd with an external decorative design consisting of
four or five loops of black paint with remains of blue infill on a light
yellow background. A faded blue line runs parallel to the rim, and
there is a slightly thicker one on the interior. Probably Ptolemaic.
Height: 2.1cm; width: 1.6cm; thickness: 0.3cm.
Context: Probably from the north-west Ptolemaic mound.

EA 23759   1887,0101.883   (Pl. 66)
Painted red ware pottery rim-sherd from a small bowl with an
asymmetric handle attached. Probably from Crete. The exterior was
black glazed and the interior, red.
Height: 2.7cm; width: 3.9cm; thickness: 0.4cm.

EA 23761   1887,0101.832   (Pl. 66)
A sherd of red pottery with a cream slip on the exterior surface. The
fabric appears to be Cypriot and the fragment may have come from a
basket-handled amphora. On the exterior is a scratched hieroglyphic
text reading /// *m-ȝḥt*.
Height: 9.2cm; width: 8.8cm.
Bibliography: Petrie 1888, 74 § 71; Weber 2012b, 375, no. TD 297.

EA 23762   1887,0101.824   (Pl. 66)
A curved sherd of pale pink pottery with a dull cream slip on the
exterior surface. The fabric appears to be of Cypriot origin, and the
fragment may have come from a basket-handled amphora. There is an
incised emblem on the exterior, cut post-production in an unusual
fashion almost as though it had been chiselled. This was probably
done with a flint point. The mark has been interpreted as the
hieroglyph for the name of the goddess Neith, but this interpretation is
far from certain.
Length: 15cm; width: 6.2cm.
Bibliography: Petrie 1888, 74 § 71; Weber 2012b, 375, no. TD 298.

EA 23763   1887,0101.822   (Pl. 66)
A sherd of micaceous red pottery, probably from some kind of
transport amphora. The fabric is compact micaceous clay of pale red
colour, and the exterior bears a dull grey-green slip. On the outside are
some incised marks, made post-production, consisting of two long
scratched lines with associated smaller marks. Perhaps from the same
vessel as EA 23764 and GR 2010,5002.28 and 29; see Chapter 7, p. 129.
Length: 20.4cm; width: 12.2cm.

EA 23764   1887,0101.836   (Pl. 66)
A sherd of micaceous red pottery with pale beige surfaces, probably
some kind of transport amphora. There are incised lines on the
exterior surface, made post-production. Perhaps from the same vessel
as EA 23763 and GR 2010,5002.28 and 29; see Chapter 7, p. 129.
Length: 11.8cm; width: 9.2cm; thickness: 1.2cm.
Context: 'Qasr', east annexe (C), chamber 19.

EA 23765   **1887,0101.823**   **(Pl. 66)**

A pottery sherd of Egyptian marl clay with scratched post-firing marks on the exterior surface; see Chapter 7, p. 129.
Length: 10cm; width: 8cm.
Context: 'Qasr', east annexe (C), chamber 27.

EA 23766   **1887,0101.825**   **(Pl. 66)**

A sherd of Egyptian red siltware pottery from the wall of a large vessel. Both surfaces are red-slipped with horizontal stripes from pebble-burnishing. The body fabric is dull red with a grey core. The original exterior surface bears an incised mark, made post-firing, consisting of a straight line with two other lines diverging from it at an angle of about 45 degrees; see Chapter 7, p. 129.
Length: 8.2cm; width: 4.5cm.
Context: Findspot 8, west of the 'Qasr'.

EA 23767   **1887,0101.837**   **(Pl. 66)**

A sherd of red pottery, from the top of a Samian amphora. The exterior bears part of incised mark, made pre-firing.
Length: 6.6cm; width: 3.7cm; thickness: 1cm.
Context: Findspot 21, a 'dry well' south-west to the 'Qasr'.
Bibliography: Petrie 1888, pl. xxxiii, 10, second mark below the note: 'on rounder, unpainted vases'; Johnston 2006, 28, Table 1, no. 10.

EA 23768   **1887,0101.838**   **(Pl. 66)**

A sherd of red pottery, perhaps from the same amphora as 23767. Part of the base of the neck is preserved on the fragment. The exterior bears part of an incised single letter, made pre-firing; see Chapter 7, p. 128.
Length: 7.6cm; width: 4.6cm.
Context: Findspot 21, a 'dry well' south-west to the 'Qasr'.
Bibliography: Petrie 1888, pl. xxxiii, 10, first mark below the note: 'on rounder, unpainted vases'; Johnston 2006, 28, Table 1, no. 11.

EA 23769   **1887,0101.773**   **(Pl. 67)**

Greyware pottery sherd from a Lesbian amphora, with an incised triangular mark on the exterior surface (see Chapter 7, p. 128). The mark was made before firing. The micaceous fabric is black in the core but grey on the surface.
Length: 18cm; width: 8.3cm; thickness: 0.9cm.
Context: Findspot 51, domestic buildings in the urban area to the east of the Saite enclosure (so-called 'Camp').
Bibliography: Petrie 1888, 65 § 61, pl. xxxiii, 12; Johnston 2006, 28, Table 1, no. 6; Weber 2012b, 374, no. TD 295.
Parallels: see EA 23772, London, PM UC19247 (complete) and maybe Cairo, EM JE 27388 (deaccessioned).

EA 23770   **1887,0101.821**   **(Pl. 67)**

A thick, curved sherd of cream-grey pottery with an incised triangular mark on the exterior surface, see Chapter 7. The mark was made post-production. The fabric exhibits many pores in the section and contains inclusions of limestone, and possibly shell. The fragment probably came from a basket-handled amphora.
Length: 15.8cm; width: 10.6cm.
Context: 'Qasr', east annexe (C), chamber 27.
Bibliography: see Petrie 1888, pl. xxxiii, 6 (piece from Findspot 27).

EA 23771   **1887,0101.1403**   **(Pl. 67**

A sherd from the shoulder of an amphora with a mark (Archaic Greek *epsilon*) on the exterior (see Johnston, Chapter 7). The mark was made pre-firing. The pottery fabric is highly micaceous red clay with inclusions of limestone grit. The exterior is a pale red-brown.
Length: 9.4cm; width: 3.9cm.
Context: 'Qasr', east annexe (C), chamber 27.
Bibliography: See Petrie 1888, pl. xxxiii, 1 (fragment from Findspot 27); Johnston 2006, 28, Table 1, no. 7.

EA 23778   **1887,0101.834**   **(Pl. 67)**

A sherd of brown-grey pottery with part of a thick red-brown motif painted on the external cream slip. The motif comprises a vertical line crossed by a U-shaped one. It clearly comes from underneath one of the handles of a transport amphora imported from Chios.
Length: 9.4cm; width: 8.3cm.

GR 2010,5002.9   **(Pl. 67)**

A sherd of dull grey pottery with an external pale yellow-cream slip, over which are painted black lines. There are two straight lines, which cross at a right-angle, and a curved line. The dense marl fabric contains inclusions of a white material, possibly limestone, but no mica. Probably from Chios.
Length: 8.3cm; width: 8cm.
Bibliography: Weber 2012b, 379, no. TD 323.

GR 2010,5002.12   **(Pl. 67)**

A small fragment of red-brown pottery, with a beige slip on the exterior. Over this are painted bands of red paint, one horizontal and one vertical. The micaceous fabric contains inclusions of white grit and some large brown grains, possibly chert. The fragment comes from a transport amphora.
Length: 6.5cm; width: 4.3cm.
Bibliography: Weber 2012b, 380, no. TD 326.
Parallels: Weber 2012b, 297, no. KB14, pl. 42m.

GR 2010,5002.19   **(Pl. 67)**

A fragment from the rim and shoulder of an amphora, probably of the basket-handled type. It consists of compact pale red clay with few inclusions, just a little sand. The interior surface varies in colour from pale red to cream, an effect of firing. The exterior is covered by a pale cream slip. Most of the rim survives at the top of the fragment. Four holes have been drilled through the fragment post-firing: two near the base and two in the left-hand side.
Height: 9.3cm; width: 8cm.
Bibliography: Weber 2012b, 382, no. TD 333.

GR 2010,5002.28   **(Pl. 67)**

A small sherd from an amphora, broken on all edges. The micaceous fabric is compact red clay with a tendency to laminate. Inclusions of sand, grit and some larger quartz grains are visible. The exterior is covered by a pale green-cream slip. A triangular mark was incised on the exterior before firing (see Chapter 7, p. 128). Perhaps from the same vessel as EA 23763 and 23764.
Length: 8.1cm; width: 4cm.
Bibliography: Weber 2012b, 383, no. TD 342.

GR 2010,5002.29   **(Pl. 67)**

Part of the shoulder of a transport amphora, made up from four joined sherds. The exterior bears a cream slip and an incised mark, made after firing, possibly a sequence of Greek letters, the final one being *omega* (see Chapter 7). Perhaps from the same vessel as EA 23763 and 23764.
Height: 20cm; width: 21cm.
Bibliography: Weber 2012b, 384, TD 343.

EA 23812   **1887,0101.775**   **(Pl. 69)**

A fragment of the side and base of a vessel. The marl fabric contains a large amount of grit, chiefly quartz grains. The base was flat and the side almost vertical. The interior and, to a lesser extent, the base are coated with a layer of blue frit and it is likely that the fragment comes from a vessel used for the preparation of this material.
Height: 8.6cm; width: 8.5cm; depth: 3.7cm.
Context: Saite enclosure (so-called 'Camp').
Bibliography: Petrie 1888, 75 § 72.

GR 1890,0619.39   **(Pl. 69)**

A fragment from the side of a vessel of large diameter made of very coarse pale beige clay. There was a flat-topped rim. Traces of light blue-green pigment remain on top of the rim and on the inner face. The bottom of the object is a finished edge, also with traces of blue colour. This implies that the base of the vessel must have joined the side just above this level, although a clear fracture line is not apparent. The fragment comes probably from a container for the preparation of coloured frit, like EA 23812 above.
Height: 9.5cm; width: 7.1cm; thickness: 1.7cm.
Bibliography: Petrie 1888, 75 § 72, comments about EA 23812: 'a piece of a pot of refractory material, in which blue frit has been prepared in the furnace.'
Parallels: in addition to EA 23812 above, see Boston, MFA 87.152 (deaccessioned), also from Tell Dafana.

EA 23777　　　　**1887,0101.861**　　　　**(Pl. 69)**

Fragment of the rim and carinated side of a pottery vessel, with a cream slip and black-painted zig-zag marks on the exterior surface. The coarse red silt fabric contains white inclusions, probably limestone. This stray Ramesside fragment among the later pottery of Tell Dafana came from a deep level, see below.

Height: 8.6cm; width: 7.4cm; thickness: 1.5cm.

Context: probably from the 'Qasr', casemate building A, in a lower square chamber at the base of the southern part of the central cell.

Bibliography: Petrie 1888, 54 § 53 states: 'in the lower square chamber within the southern large chamber were some fragments of similarly rough pottery; and a piece with a rude wavy brown on a white facing, which might at first be almost mistaken for the roughest Roman painting, but which from its position must be the latest degradation of the fine colouring of the eighteenth dynasty, which fell off even in the Ramesside times'; see also ibid., 54 § 52, about the same findspot: 'yet the base of this lower room was just about the base level of the corners of the fort, and some pieces of pottery which cannot be referred to Ramesside but rather to Psametic times, were found at the bottom of it'.

EA 23779　　　　**1887,0101.817**　　　　**(Pl. 69)**

A sherd of Egyptian grey-green marlware from the shoulder of a jar. There is a ridge on the exterior surface, a smooth grey-green slip and part of a black line rectilinear motif.

Length: 11.2cm; width: 10cm.

Unmarked sherds (not illustrated)

None of these pottery fragments have any recorded contexts.

EA 23806　　　　**1887,0101.1335**

A fragment of pale beige marl pottery, broken on all the edges, with the inner surface coated with patches of blue frit. The fabric is friable and exhibits numerous pores.

Length: 8.2cm; width: 5.4cm; thickness: 1.1cm.

EA 23806　　　　**1887,0101.860**

A fragment from the rounded rim of a red siltware pottery plate.

Length: 6.6cm; width: 5.8cm.

EA 23806　　　　**1887,0101.857**

A small sherd of red siltware pottery, broken on all edges. The exterior is red-slipped.

Length: 4.6cm; width: 4.5cm.

EA 23806　　　　**1887,0101.858**

A small piece from the rim of a platter of large diameter. Made from coarse red siltware.

Length: 9cm; width: 6cm; thickness: 1.4cm.

EA 23806　　　　**1887,0101.859**

A small rim-sherd from a red siltware pottery dish.

Length: 6.5cm; width: 3.8cm.

EA 23806　　　　**1887,0101.843**

Part of the side of a red siltware pottery vessel, perhaps a cooking pot. A damaged portion of the rim survives, to which a small loop-handle is attached. Probably Ptolemaic.

Height: 12.7cm; width: 6cm.

EA 23806　　　　**1887,0101.866**

Part of the side of a grey marl jar, with a loop-handle attached.

Height: 8cm; width: 6.1cm.

EA 23806　　　　**1887,0101.867**

Part of the side of a jar, with an attached loop-handle. The marl fabric is pale pink in section, with a cream slip on the exterior and handle. The interior surface has fired to beige.

Height 11cm; width: 9.2cm.

EA 23806　　　　**1887,0101.830**

A body-sherd from a large marlware jar, broken on all the edges.

Height: 12.20; width: 16.2cm.

EA 23806　　　　**1887,0101.869**

A small piece from the rim of a vessel. The fabric is unusual green marl clay, full of inclusions of pale calcareous grit.

Length: 5.5cm; width: 2.2cm; thickness: 1.5cm.

EA 23806　　　　**1887,0101.804**

Fragment of pottery or stone from a crucible.

Length: 2.3cm; width: 1.7cm.

Ceramics not located

Some pottery recorded in the original 1887 registration of the material from Tell Dafana is no longer retrievable. Certain items are known to have decayed through salt action to a point where they disintegrated or were so damaged that they were removed from the collection. Although a few objects noted in the register as suffering from flaking are not actually recorded as having been disposed of, it is likely that these also have disintegrated completely. The descriptions below are taken from the written register. Some items were never assigned inventory numbers and are listed here only by their AES registration numbers, which all begin 1887,0101. The lack of inventory numbers suggests they may have decayed soon after arrival in the Museum.

EA 22348

Redware pottery amphora; light brown slip; much flaking.

Height: 37cm.

EA 23751

Imported East Greek amphora.

Context: 'Qasr', Findspot 12, to the south of casemate building A.

Bibliography: Petrie 1888, pl. xxxiii, 10; cf. Weber 2012b, 375, no. TD 299.

EA 22334

'Rough red vase or jar 16 inches high'.

EA 23721

'Rough red ware, drab face. Fragment of stand with handle 7 inches long'.

1887,0101.1212 'Cover fragment, 8 inches'.

1887,0101.1277 'jar cover, disintegrating'.

1887,0101.1279 [no description].

1887,0101.1294 'Red ware jar 2.75 inches'.

Items removed from the collection

EA 22280　　　　**1887,0101.1120**

Rough redware pottery jar, disintegrated and destroyed by 1953, according to a note in the Register.

Height: 12.7cm (max.); diameter: 8.8cm.

EA 22327　　　　**1887,0101.1136**

Redware pottery vase, rounded body. Disintegrated and destroyed by 1953, according to a note in the Register.

Height: 11.7cm.

Context: Findspot 52, iron-working area in the south-east part of the Saite enclosure (so-called 'Camp').

Bibliography: Petrie 1888, pl. xxxv, 45.

EA 23684　　　　**1887,0101.1248**

Circular lid or dish of red pottery. Disposed of.

Diameter: 15.2cm.

Ostraca

Petrie recovered a few ostraca at Tell Dafana, but they are not figured in his publication, which contains only a brief reference to 'about a dozen fragments of demotic inscriptions on pieces of jars and cups' (Petrie, 1888, 74 § 71). Few of these pieces bear any extensive text, the majority having just fragments of signs in hieratic, demotic or Greek. There is also a demotic inscription on the complete pottery jar EA 22344, described above with the rest of the pottery. Thanks are due to Robert Demarée and Brian Muhs for kindly providing readings of the inscriptions in those cases where sufficient survives to attempt any interpretation.

EA 23786   **1887,0101.816**   **(Pl. 70)**

A red pottery ostracon, exterior covered with a buff-coloured slip, with traces of a few black-painted demotic signs, apparently part of a docket. The ostracon has been repaired from two fragments.
Length: 8.2cm; width: 12cm.
Context: 'Qasr', east annexe (G), chamber 18.
Bibliography: Petrie 1888, 74 § 71.

EA 29484   **1887,0101.818**   **(Pl. 70)**

A light-brown pottery ostracon from the body of a vessel, interior slightly grooved and exterior polished, with remains of one line of black-painted early demotic text on the exterior. Perhaps part of the same vessel as EA 23780, 23781 and 29485 below.
Height: 5.6cm width: 5.9cm.
Bibliography: Petrie 1888, 74 § 71.

EA 23787   **1887,0101.819**   **(Pl. 70)**

A red pottery ostracon, fragment from the body of a vessel, with faint traces of one line of hieratic text.
Length: 5.8cm; width: 5.9cm.
Context: 'Qasr', east annexe (G), chamber 18.
Bibliography: Petrie 1888, 74 § 71.

EA 23782   **1887,0101.826**   **(Pl. 69)**

A cream-coloured pottery ostracon, consisting of a fragment from the side and base of a marlware cup. The junction between the side and base is grooved. A few signs from the end of a black-painted line of hieratic text, of which only the word *nht* 'sycamore' is visible, have been painted on the lower part of the side of the vessel.
Length: 3.4cm; width: 5.4cm; diameter: 11cm (when intact).
Bibliography: Petrie 1888, 74 § 71.

EA 29485   **1887,0101.827**   **(Pl. 70)**

A light-brown pottery ostracon from the body of a vessel, interior slightly grooved and exterior polished, with remains of one line of black-painted text on the exterior, probably hieratic. Perhaps part of the same vessel as EA 29484 above, 23780 and 23781 below.
Height: 4.3cm; width: 3.2cm.
Bibliography: Petrie 1888, 74 § 71.

EA 23781   **1887,0101.828**   **(Pl. 69)**

A cream-coloured pottery ostracon, from the body of a vessel, with traces of one large black-painted sign, probably hieratic. Similar to, and perhaps from the same vessel as EA 29484 and 29485 above, 23780 below.
Length: 5.5cm; width: 2.8cm.
Bibliography: Petrie 1888, 74 § 71.

EA 23783   **1887,0101.829**   **Pl. 69**

A cream-coloured pottery ostracon, on a marlware sherd from the body of a vessel, with traces of one black-painted demotic sign.
Length: 4.6cm; width: 3.5cm.
Context: 'Qasr', east annexe (G), chamber 18.
Bibliography: Petrie 1888, 74 § 71.

EA 23784   **1887,0101.831**   **(Pl. 69)**

A cream-coloured pottery ostracon, fragment of the body of a vessel, with traces of black-painted demotic or hieratic (?) signs.
Length: 3.2cm; width: 1.6cm.
Context: 'Qasr', east annexe (G), chamber 18.
Bibliography: Petrie 1888, 74 § 71.

EA 23785   **1887,0101.833**   **(Pl. 69)**

A red pottery ostracon, exterior ribbed and covered with a buff-coloured slip, with traces of black-painted demotic signs.
Length: 5.9cm; width: 4.3cm.
Context: 'Qasr', east annexe (G), chamber 18.
Bibliography: Petrie 1888, 74 § 71.

EA 23780   **1887,0101.835**   **(Pl. 69)**

A cream-coloured pottery ostracon from the rim of a vessel, with traces of one line of black-painted hieratic or early demotic text.
Length: 6.2cm; width: 7.4cm.
Bibliography: Petrie 1888, 74 § 71.
Perhaps part of same vessel as EA 23781, 29484 and 29485.

EA 23788   **1887,0101.1404**   **(Pl. 70)**

A red pottery ostracon, currently in two sections, repaired from six fragments from the shoulder of a large vessel, probably an amphora, with traces of one line of black-painted demotic text on the exterior, another one above, shorter, slightly oblique and partly faded. A group of two other signs, maybe Greek, is painted above them, on the right side, with traces of another inscription on the left side.
Brian Muhs proposed the following reading:
Nekht-… (personal name) <empty space> 9 aroura(?) of Nau(?)-nes-… (personal name).
Both names included the name of a god of uncertain identity.
Height: 15cm; width: 34.5cm.
Bibliography: Petrie 1888, 74 § 71.

EA 23789   **1887,0101.1405**   **(Pl. 70)**

A red pottery ostracon, fragment from a vessel, with parts of three black-painted Greek (?) letters, perhaps from a Coptic text.
Length: 1.4cm; width: 2.2cm.
Bibliography: Petrie 1888, 74 § 71.
It cannot be confirmed, from the Museum register, that this item comes from Tell Dafana.

Chapter 6

The Greek Painted Pottery from Tell Dafana

Sabine Weber

Introduction[*]

While the spectrum of finds recovered at Tell Dafana by Petrie consists mainly of Egyptian objects, a substantial quantity of Greek painted pottery and Greek trade amphorae[1] (see also Chapters 4, 5 and 7) was also found, which to this day remains the largest find complex of Archaic Greek vases to be discovered in Egypt besides those of Naukratis. It is this pottery that has particularly occupied the minds of scholars ever since and led to the assumption that Greek mercenaries lived at Tell Dafana and that the site might be identified with one of the *Stratopeda* mentioned by Herodotus (2.154) – erroneously as we now know (see Chapter 1).

Most of the Greek painted pottery was found – with fragments sticking out of the ground 'first picked up by children in the dinner hour'[2] – together with Egyptian material in the area of chambers 18, 19A and 29 in the annexe buildings south-east of Petrie's so-called *Kasr*, details of which have been given by François Leclère in Chapter 1.[3]

Production centres

The Greek vases found at Tell Dafana were manufactured in various Greek production centres. Vases are recorded from the Greek mainland (Corinth and Athens), Eastern Greece (North Ionia, South Ionia and probably Aeolis and Eastern Doris) and Egypt (very probably Naukratis) itself. Hardly any complete vessels were found, but many vases could be restored from the numerous joining fragments that had been excavated.

It is very probable that some individual sherds in fact belong to the reconstructed vessels, but were omitted from the reconstructions which took place (probably at the British Museum) very soon after their discovery. The overall number of Greek vases found in Tell Dafana is therefore probably smaller than the recorded approximate 344 fragments appear to suggest.[4]

The whole assemblage of Greek fragments – today distributed amongst many collections worldwide – has been published and discussed more fully elsewhere,[5] so it will suffice to give only a brief summary below.

Corinth

Although Petrie did not recognize any Corinthian pottery among his finds, there are in fact at least two sherds which were manufactured in Corinthian workshops:[6] a body sherd of a Late Proto-Corinthian or Early Corinthian closed vessel, probably an oinochoe, and an Early Corinthian rounded aryballos from the late 7th/early 6th century BC. Numerous aryballoi of this kind are housed in European museums with the recorded provenance 'Egypt', but without further details as to the exact findspot.[7] Therefore, it is clear that there were imports of this kind of pottery to Egypt, but apparently not to the site of Tell Dafana in any quantity.

Athens

Attic black figure pottery vessels are more numerous (97 fragments).[8] They date from the beginning to the end of the third quarter of the 6th century BC. Among the earliest fragments are the so-called horse-head amphorae (**Fig. 1**), which were also found in Naukratis.[9] Another group of amphora sherds is close to vases of the group of the Tyrrhenian amphorae.[10] Fragments from a large amphora feature two registers, one depicting the Calydonian boar hunt and the other funeral games (boxing and wrestling in front of a referee) with large tripods as prizes (**Fig. 2**). In contrast to Naukratis, where vases for example by the Gorgo Painter, Lydos and the Amasis Painter were found,[11] the Attic pottery found in Tell Dafana was not painted by first-rank vase painters. Two fragments are stylistically near the Princeton Painter, a painter who worked during the second quarter of the 6th century BC, but the vases from Tell Dafana might be a little later. Among the latest vases is a so-called Kassel cup (**Fig. 3**).[12] In terms of shapes, the bulk of the Attic pottery belongs to amphorae, mainly neck amphorae, but there are also drinking vessels: a skyphos (**Fig. 4**), five cups and a lidded cup.

Petrie found no Attic red figure pottery at Tell Dafana. The Attic imports generally seem to come to an end around the beginning of the last quarter of the 6th century BC. Only two fragments that may come from Tell Dafana are later: a fragment of an Attic black-figure cup with leaf decoration to be dated to the end of the 6th century BC[13] and a fragment of a small, open black-glazed vessel with stamped palmetto decoration, probably a kantharos, belonging to the 4th century BC.[14] This latter fragment may well come from the Ptolemaic settlement which was situated north-west of the Saite enclosure or not from Tell Dafana at all (having been put incorrectly in a box with material from Tell Dafana). Attic transport amphorae – *à la brosse* and SOS amphorae – have also been found at Tell Dafana.[15]

Aeolis (?)

Fragments from a large lid and a bowl in a grey ware fabric, often termed 'Lesbian *bucchero*', were probably manufactured in the region of Aeolis.[16] Two of the three sherds emerged as chemical twins in Neutron Activation (NA) analyses, but their provenance could not be determined.[17] Besides these fragments, Lesbian/Aeolian grey ware transport amphorae have also been found at Tell Dafana.[18]

North Ionia

Pottery from North Ionia is among the most numerous of the Greek finds from Tell Dafana (99 fragments and partly restored vases).[19] There are a few sherds painted in the animal style (R.M. Cook's Late Wild Goat (LWG); NiA I in the terminology of M. Kerschner and U. Schlotzhauer)[20] with animal frieze or patterned decoration. Most of the finds belong to amphorae and hydriai painted in a North Ionian black-figure style (identified as Klazomenian black figure by Cook; NiA II) which can be dated to the period from around the middle to the end of the 6th century BC. The earliest examples belong to the so-called Tübingen Group (**Fig. 5**).[21] Vases of this group have also been found in Mendes and Benha in Egypt.[22]

At Tell Dafana these vases were found for the first time in such a quantity that a painter was even named after the site's excavator, the Petrie Painter (**Figs 6–7**). Vases by the Petrie Painter and by the Petrie Group date from the third quarter of the 6th century BC. Three sherds were analysed with NA and two of them could be added to a chemical group labelled group E (**Fig. 6**).[23] The topographic localization of group E, which is also attested in samples from other studies by M. Kerschner and H. Mommsen, is North Ionia, more precisely very possibly the area of Klazomenai.[24] Besides the Petrie Painter/Group, only a few other painters and groups are represented, including vases by the so-called Urla Group (**Fig. 8**),[25] which are almost contemporary with the vases by the Petrie Painter.[26] Vases by these painters and groups have also been found at Naukratis but in fewer numbers.[27] The latest North Ionian black figure vases belong to the so-called Knipovitch class and are also amphorae.[28] Most of the vases in this group have been found in the Greek colonies of the Black Sea area. It is very probable that these painters were active in the last quarter of the 6th century BC.

Fineware pottery imports from Chios were frequent at Naukratis,[29] but are absent in Tell Dafana with the sole exception of a Chian chalice.[30] There is, however, a transport amphora that bears seals of the pharaoh Amasis on the plaster stopping (EA 22356, see Chapters 3, pp. 68–9, and 5, p. 112), thus giving the pot a *terminus ante quem*.[31]

South Ionia

South Ionian pottery is also commonly found at Tell Dafana (45 partly restored vases and fragments).[32] Of its earlier phase (Late South Ionian Archaic I (SiA I) or Middle Wild Goat style in Cook's terminology) only a single sherd of a closed shape, very probably of a oinochoe (**Fig. 9**),[33] could be determined. This was found in chamber 1 of Petrie's *Kasr*, the western part of the casemate structure, and therefore somewhat apart from the other Greek pottery, which came mostly from chambers 18, 19A and 29 in the eastern annexes of the main complex.

By contrast, numerous sherds of the later phase of South Ionian Fikellura style pottery (SiA II) were found in Tell Dafana (**Fig. 10**).[34] The chronology of these vases has recently been a matter of some debate. Traditionally, the beginning of the Fikellura style has been dated to the late second quarter of the 6th century BC (about 560 BC), its end to around 500 BC (or more precisely 494 BC, the date of the destruction of Miletus by the Persians).[35] More recently, however, U. Schlotzhauer put forward new evidence suggesting that the beginning of this style of vase painting might have been somewhat earlier. His argument rests primarily on the fact that both the South Ionian animal style (SiA I) and the 'black figure' Fikellura style (SiA II) are sometimes found on the same pot. The styles therefore must be contemporary at least for a short time. The end of the South Ionian animal style (SiA I) is usually dated to around 600/590 BC, so either the vases in this style were produced for longer, or the production of vases in the Fikellura/SiA II style began earlier.

The place of production of Fikellura/SiA II style pottery was almost certainly Miletus and its territory.[36] One amphora from Tell Dafana was analysed by NA and fitted into chemical group D, which can be associated with the city of Miletus (**Fig. 10**).[37] At Tell Dafana only a few painters or groups who worked in this style are represented: the Altenburg Painter and Altenburg Group, Lion Group, Volute-zone Group, Mykonos Group and New York Group; there are also a number of fragments that cannot be

Figure 1 Attic black figure horse head amphora, British Museum, GR 1888,0208.92a

Figure 2 Attic black figure amphora with representations of the Calydonian boar hunt and funeral game, British Museum, GR 1888,0208.102

Figure 3 Fragment of Attic black figure Kassel cup, British Museum, GR 1888,0208.138

Figure 4 Fragment of Attic black figure skyphos, British Museum, GR 1888,0208.137

Figure 5 North Ionian black figure amphora, Tübingen Painter, British Museum, GR 1888,0208.66

Figure 6 North Ionian black figure hydria or amphora, Petrie Painter, British Museum, GR 1888,0208.171

Figure 7 North Ionian black figure amphora, Petrie Painter, British Museum, GR 1888,0208.71a

Figure 8 North Ionian black figure amphora, Urla Group, British Museum, GR 1888,0208.101

Figure 9 South Ionian fragment of an oinochoe with animal frieze decoration, SiA I, British Museum, GR 1888,0208.58

Figure 10 South Ionian amphora, Fikellura style, MileA II, British Museum, GR 1888,0208.46a

Figure 11 South Ionian fragment, Fikellura style, SiA II, British Museum, GR 1888,0208.56

attributed to a specific painter or group. The vases by the Altenburg Painter belong to the earliest phase of the style, while fragments with simple chevron pattern probably date to its final phases (**Fig. 11**). The whole period from the beginning to the end of production thus appears to be represented at the site.

The shapes of Fikellura/SiA II pottery essentially correspond to those found among the North Ionian vases: mainly table amphorae and just one cup. The preservation of the cup fragment does not allow a precise identification of its shape; it might be a cup with everted rim or another type.[38] In Naukratis, by contrast, Ionian cups with everted rims are among the most numerous finds of South Ionian pottery.[39] Many of them bear dedicatory inscriptions to Apollo, a few also to Aphrodite or to the Dioskuroi.

Painted pottery from Samos could not be identified at Tell Dafana, but transport amphorae from the island are attested.[40] In Naukratis, Samian painted pottery appears not to have been particularly common, either, but a number of ritual vessels with dipinti, manufactured on Samos, were used in the Samian filial cult of Hera at Naukratis.

East Doris (?)

The so-called 'situlae' (**Figs 12–14**), large open containers, are the most prominent Greek vases from Tell Dafana.[41] They are also highly distinctive for this site: even though examples have been found elsewhere in Egypt (Memphis[42] and possibly Naukratis[43]) as well as on Rhodes and Samos, Tell Dafana remains by far the most important findspot for this group of vases.

Petrie called the vases 'situlae' because they reminded him of the Egyptian bronze situlae with bail handle,[44] but in fact the Greek vases are much higher and have two small vertical handles below the mouth. Mouth and neck are very

wide and the vessels have a small ring-foot. They are clearly storage vessels (an example from Rhodes preserves a lid) and could not have been used in the same manner as the Egyptian bronze situlae.[45] The shape of the long ovoid body is common in Egyptian pottery used for storage and may have played a role in designing the Greek 'situla',[46] but with the difference that the Greeks added the foot and the painted decoration.

Cook distinguished three different groups of Greek 'situlae' according to shape and decoration. The decorative scheme of each of these is distinctive. Group A, which is apparently not represented at Tell Dafana, has horizontal stripes around the body and a wavy-line decoration. Vases of this group have been found at Vroulia on Rhodes. Group B features a central figural scene flanked by ornamental decoration in the handle zone, while the rest of the vase is painted in black glaze with thin horizontal lines, either reserved or painted in added purple. To this group belongs the most prominent example of the 'situlae' from Tell Dafana, the so-called Typhon 'situla' (**Fig. 12a–b**), as well as the vase from Memphis.[47] Group C includes most of the Greek 'situlae' from Tell Dafana (**Figs 13–14**).[48] These vases have a large figural scene in the handle zone, while the rest of the vase is decorated with zones of palmettes and lotus flowers, their outlines incised into the black glaze and highlighted with added purple. The shape of group C vases is more slender than that of group B. There are also a number of fragments from stamnoi in a similar fabric and with similar decoration, as well as a fragment of what may have been an amphora.[49]

Three 'situlae', two stamnoi and the amphora were analysed with NA and showed a distinctive resemblance in their chemical composition so as to form a single chemical group, christened TD, short for its find-place Tell Dafana[50]. This group stands out distinctly from other groups, but so far has not been definitely located. Analyses by P. Dupont on a 'situla' fragment with a recorded Egyptian provenance showed a chemical resemblance to samples from two Vroulian cups, widely regarded as Rhodian products, thus raising the possibility that Rhodes – or at least the East Dorian region – was also the place of manufacture of the 'situlae'.[51]

Other East Greek pottery sherds

A number of sherds could not be identified with certainty, as a result of their state of preservation, limited information

Figure 12a–b East Dorian (?) Typhon-'situla', British Museum, GR 1888,0208.1

Figure 13a East Dorian (?) 'situla', stick-fighting, British Museum, GR 1888,0208.5, 1888, 0208.6

Figure 13b Detail of the scene on the vessel in Fig. 13a (drawing: K. Morton)

Figure 14a–b: East Dorian (?) 'situla', falcon on *nb*-basket, British Museum, GR 1888,0208.3 (drawing: K. Morton)

being given in their publication, or because no close parallels appear to be known.[52] For most of them, however, their style and shape makes it likely that they were manufactured in North Ionia.

Local Egyptian manufacture (so-called Naukratis workshop)

One neck amphora (**Fig. 15**),[53] decorated with a band of opposed triangles on the neck, a cable motif on the shoulder and roughly sketched scales on the belly, was regarded as unusual by Cook, who suggested that it 'was made in the locality of Tell Defenneh'.[54] The vase is completely covered by a yellow-pinkish slip, even the underside of the foot, which hides the actual reddish colour of the rough clay. The decoration can be compared with East Greek pottery of the 6th century BC but has no exact parallels. Analysis by NA showed that the vessel was made with Egyptian (Nile silt) clay and therefore manufactured in Egypt, but shaped and painted in an East Greek manner. It thus closely matches a range of vessels found at Naukratis dating from the 6th century BC that are similarly made in a hybrid East Greek style, but of local manufacture, as the analysis of several examples from Naukratis has shown. It is very probable that the amphora from Tell Dafana comes from the same workshop, which was probably located in Naukratis and run by one or several Greek potters.[55] Although this is the only such example of painted pottery from Tell Dafana, a local imitation of a Samian transport amphora – although far less routinely made and in coarser fabric, hence probably not the work of a Greek potter – has also been found at the site.[56] Beyond Naukratis and Tell Dafana, locally produced Greek-style pottery – an Ionian cup with everted rim – was identified by E. Oren at Tell Kedwa on the eastern fringe of the Delta.[57]

Shapes

The repertoire of shapes of the Greek painted pottery found by Petrie at Tell Dafana is remarkable. The chart in **Fig. 16** shows the overall number and percentages of fragments that can be attributed to a certain shape.[58] The vessels from Tell Dafana are almost exclusively storage vessels, such as amphorae (211),[59] hydriai (9)[60] and fragments of large closed vessels (27, which may be either amphorae, hydriai or stamnoi),[61] 'situlae' (41)[62] and stamnoi (9).[63] By contrast, there are only a few large open vessels such as kraters or large bowls (2),[64] only one fragment that belongs to a jug (oinochoe),[65] a few cups,[66] one skyphos,[67] one kantharos[68] and three plates.[69] Unguent containers such as Corinthian aryballoi are also rare.[70] A lid[71] and fragments of unidentifiable shape,[72] some of them featuring handles, complete the repertoire of shapes. The fact that this picture contrasts strongly with the pottery assemblage from Naukratis was already noted by Petrie[73] and further confirmed in the studies by M. Venit,[74] K. Smolárikova,[75] U. Schlotzhauer[76] and most recently the British Museum's Naukratis Project.[77] The most striking difference is the number of storage vessels (amphorae, hydriai and 'situlae') at Tell Dafana in relation to the few drinking vessels, which make up the most part of the pottery material found at Naukratis. In addition to this, amidst the thousands of fragments of Greek pottery at Naukratis only a single possible 'situla' shaped vase could be identified.[78] At Tell

Dafana, however, there are 41 within a total preserved assemblage of less than 400. This suggests that the Greek pottery at Tell Dafana must have had a different function to that found at Naukratis, where the vast majority was clearly associated with ritual praxis in the Greek sanctuaries of the site.[79]

Iconography

The iconography of the Greek vases found in Tell Dafana shows a very limited, but in parts highly interesting repertoire. Attic vases are decorated with animals, warrior/battle scenes, and very seldom with mythical scenes. Among these, scenes of the Calydonian boar hunt (**Fig. 2**), a mythical athletic competition in honour of a deceased person (possibly Pelias or Patroklos) and one of the deeds of Herakles (possibly his struggle with Triton) are the most remarkable.

North Ionian vases show processions of dancing women, satyrs, the goddess Athena on a chariot,[80] Oedipus and the sphinx (**Fig. 8**), Odysseus and Kirke,[81] and some unusual scenes that as yet cannot be fully explained, such as a naked man with his hands tied behind him.[82]

The vases painted in the South Ionian animal style (WG style/SiA I) feature rows of animals, geese, wild goats and hounds chasing hares. The South Ionian vases in the Fikellura style (SiA II) bear representations of animals (e.g. hounds and hares), as well as rare Dionysiac themes, such as dancing komasts, satyrs and maenads.

For the most part, the iconography of the Greek pottery from Tell Dafana is thus fairly standard for the types and styles of vessels represented and no particular local pattern seems discernible. This also seems to be true for the majority of the images on the special group of East Dorian 'situlae', which mostly feature hybrid creatures such as sirens and sphinxes, or animals such as lions, panthers, bulls, horses and birds.[83] Mythological scenes, such as Bellerophon and the chimaera, are rare.[84]

However, three of the 'situlae' are different, since they are decorated with subjects that clearly reflect Egyptian

Figure 15 Greek style amphora made from Egyptian Nile silt clay, British Museum, GR 1888,0208.57

iconography:[85] two men fencing with clubs (**Fig. 13**) – a sport common in Egypt but not then known in Greece[86] – in addition to a falcon on a *neb*-basket clearly imitating an Egyptian hieroglyph (**Fig. 14**), probably signifying 'lord', 'lord of …' or perhaps originally (as the scene is only partly preserved on this fragment) 'the two lords of Upper and Lower Egypt'. The third vase, an almost completely preserved 'situla', features the depiction of a winged, serpent-tailed and snake-strangling 'Typhon' (**Fig. 12a**), one of the most monstrous figures in Greek mythology. The daemon is confronted on the other side of the vessel by a youthful winged 'hunter', perhaps a representation of the wind god Boreas (**Fig. 12b**). This unusual iconography might well represent a particular reference to the area of the Nile Delta in general and Tell Dafana in particular. 'Typhon' is probably to be seen in connection with the Egyptian myth of Horus and Seth.[87] The mighty Egyptian god of chaos, Seth, worshipped as the desert god of Lower Egypt, was equated by Herodotus with Greek Typhon,[88] who was represented –

Figure 16 Distribution of shapes in the Greek painted pottery of Tell Dafana

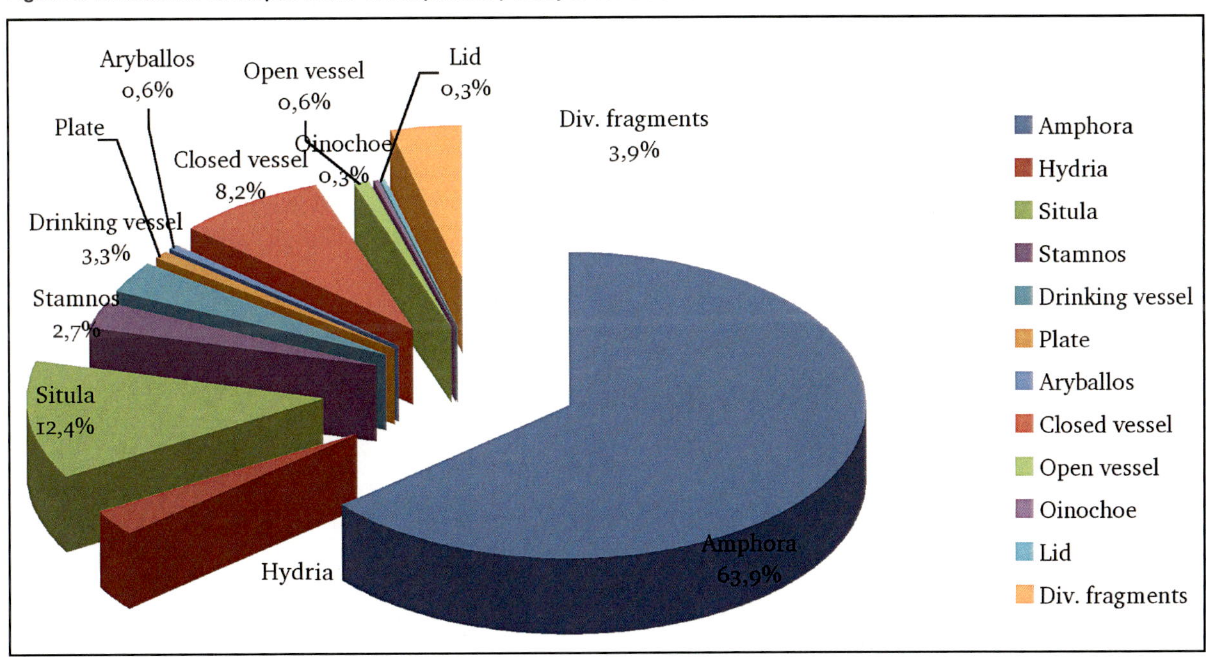

albeit rarely – from the 7th century BC on Peloponnesian shield bands and Corinthian pottery as a male bearded creature with snake legs, just like on the 'situla' from Tell Dafana, even if here, uniquely, he is shown grasping snakes. Seth struggled with his nephew Horus, the god of Upper Egypt, for power over the united country but was overpowered and, according to legend, banished and buried at Lake Serbonis (Lake Bardawil) on the Mediterranean coast of northern Sinai – that is, East of Pelusium and of Tell Dafana.[89] In the Egyptian tradition, however, Seth was not depicted as a snake but as the Seth animal, an animal close to a donkey with big ears.

Such images were not just placed on the vases by chance; they are each unique in the repertoire of Greek vase iconography and were clearly created with Egypt in mind. The same phenomenon of Greek storage vessels specially painted with Egyptian themes is also attested elsewhere in Egypt, at Memphis, Karnak and Thebes.[90]

Conclusion

Greek painted pottery appears to have reached Tell Dafana from about 600 BC and continued to arrive until the end of the 6th century BC,[91] with clear peaks in the second and third quarters of the 6th century BC, within the reign of Amasis. Attic red-figure pottery is lacking and the East Greek pottery also does not seem to go beyond the 6th century BC – in fact, imports had largely ceased already by or during the final quarter of the 6th century. This contrasts strongly with other places in Egypt, where a steady flow of Attic red figure pottery imports continues throughout the 5th century BC, for example at Naukratis, Kom el-Bakar and Memphis, even if on a reduced scale compared to the Archaic Period.[92] Perhaps the end of the Greek imports to Tell Dafana needs to be seen in relation to the Persian invasion of Egypt in 526/5 BC. For this reason, the Greek pottery assemblage from Tell Dafana has sometimes been taken by scholars as a chronological reference point particularly for North and South Ionian pottery.[93] However, the link with a historical date is merely a supposition, and except for the *terminus ante quem* provided by the sealings of Amasis on a Chian transport amphora there are no precise chronological indicators within the assemblage, and the vases from Tell Dafana cannot be considered a means for dating, but have to be dated themselves.

Compared with other provenances of Greek pottery of this period in Egypt, the Tell Dafana finds are unique. In the city and trading port of Naukratis, the broad range of different shapes is indicative of a different kind of use, first and foremost as votive offerings and symposion crockery in the Greek temples. At other find places in Egypt, at Sais[94] and perhaps also at Elephantine,[95] it is not impossible that Greek pottery played a role within an Egyptian temple, as at Tell Dafana, but the shape range differs from that at Tell Dafana. In the necropoleis of Abusir,[96] Saqqara and Thebes-West, Greek pottery was found in Egyptian funerary contexts (used as burial offerings or as containers for embalming material) either in the tomb shafts or the vicinity of the tomb.[97]

Following the identification by F. Leclère of the casemate buildings of Tell Dafana on the basis of their architectural design as storage facilities (see Chapter 1) set within a large Egyptian temple complex, the finds (both Egyptian and Greek) from this distinctive area must be interpreted within the particular context of preparing and storing offerings, or other goods, in an Egyptian temple. The shapes of most of the Greek vases lead to the conclusion that they probably served as luxurious storage containers. The finding of an amphora of likely Naukratite manufacture as well as imports of Attic black-figure, North and South Ionian pottery (also present at Naukratis even if other vase shapes were preferred there), suggests that at least some, if not all, of the Greek vases were transported to Tell Dafana via Naukratis. The pots may have been sent to Tell Dafana by Greeks who were familiar with or even involved in the Egyptian rituals at Tell Dafana.[98]

The Greek painted pottery found at Tell Dafana (in addition to finds of iron weapons and armour) has been the reason why many archaeologists suspected that Greeks lived at the site, attributing the use of these vessels to Greek mercenaries stationed there. The acceptance of the fact that the site is an Egyptian temple town does not, however, necessarily exclude a Greek presence, because the location of Tell Dafana at the Eastern border of ancient Egypt was of strategic interest and Greek mercenaries may well have been stationed there together with Egyptian soldiers and mercenaries of other ethnic backgrounds.

Notes

* I am very grateful to the staff of the Department of Ancient Egypt and Sudan at the British Museum, especially Jeffrey Spencer and François Leclère, the Department of Greece and Rome, especially Alexandra Villing with the Naukratis team and Dyfri Williams, for constant support. Last but not least I wish to thank Ursula Höckmann and Udo Schlotzhauer for many discussions on this subject.
1 Weber 2012b, 242–4, nos TD 291–305, 323, 326. Trade amphorae are included in the catalogue of pottery (Chapter 5).
2 Petrie 1888, 58.
3 Cf. ibid.; Weber 2012b, 221–31. It is not possible to locate the precise findspot of all Greek fragments, but for some of them Petrie 1888 gives the chamber number in his publication, others have either a scratched or a pencilled number that indicates the chamber or location where they were found. Underneath the floor of chambers 18 and 19A, Petrie found two further 'chambers' or deposits that held only Egyptian pottery. Therefore, the Greek pottery provides a useful *terminus ante quem*.
4 Weber 2012b, 309–88, nos TD 1–362; among these catalogue entries are also Egyptian, Cypriote and other fabrics which are omitted here from the discussion on the Greek painted pottery: nos TD 307–13, 317, 319, 322, 331, 333, 335, 337, 338, 342, 348.
5 Weber 2012b, 216–44, 275–80, 309–88.
6 Aryballos: Brussels, MRAH, E4437 (Weber 2012b, 231, no. TD 1, pl. 44a; Oinochoe: Philadelphia, E147.22, Schaus and Benson 1995, pl. 44.6 (Weber, op. cit., 231, no. TD 2).
7 Weber 2012b, 263, 420–6, no. Äg 1–7. 10–30.
8 Cook 1954, 40–4 pls GB607–9; Venit 1982, 121–482; Weber 2012b, 231–2, nos TD 3–90 (delete nos 60 and 61), 321, 315, 321, 336, 346, 349 (?), 352, 355 (?), 356–8.
9 Picozzi 1970/71, 36; Birchall 1972, 47; Venit 1982, 200–3; Möller 2000, 230; Weber 2012b, 231, nos TD 3–7; for the distribution and use of the horse-head amphorae in general, see Kreuzer 1998, 95–114; Mommsen 2000, 703; Schäfer 2002, 58–9.
10 Weber 2012b, 232, 314–15, nos TD 25–8.
11 Venit 1982, 148–70.
12 Cook 1954, pl. G.B. 608, 33; Weber 2012b, 232, 325, no. TD 90.
13 Ibid., 232, 378, no. TD 315.
14 Ibid., 232, 386, no. TD 352.

15 Ibid., nos TD 291, 292; see also Chapters 5 and 7 of this volume.
16 Ibid., 232–3, 325–6, nos TD 91–3, pl. 45a–b.
17 All NA analyses mentioned in this chapter were carried out by H. Mommsen and A. Schwedt, Helmholtz-Institut für Strahlen- und Kernphysik, Bonn. The results of the analyses are published in Villing and Schlotzhauer 2006, 53–68 and 69–76; Mommsen *et al.* 2012, 434–51.
18 Weber 2012b, 374, nos TD 294, 295.
19 Ibid., 233–5, 326–48, nos TD 94–188, pp. 378–81, nos TD 316, 326, 327 (?), 328, 330. There are also two Klazomenian transport amphorae and a fragment of a third: nos TD 299, 300, 326, see also Chapters 5 and 7 of this volume.
20 Boardman 1998, 148–9; Cook in Cook and Dupont 1998, 95–107; Kerschner and Schlotzhauer 2005, 1–54.
21 Weber 2012b, 234, 328, nos TD 100–1.
22 Ibid., 213, no. Men 7, p. 215, no. Benha 1.
23 Ibid., 330, no. TD 108, pl. 46b (British Museum GR 1888,0208.77a) = chemical single; 332, no. TD 116, pl. 46e (British Museum GR 1888,0208.171) = group E; 339, no. TD 147, pl. 46g (British Museum GR 1888,0208.117) = group E.
24 Villing and Schlotzhauer 2006, 57–8; Weber 2012b, 234, nos TD 102–39. On Klazomenian black figure pottery in general see Özer 2004, 199–219.
25 Weber 2012b, nos TD 139–75.
26 On the Urla Group see Özer 2009, 255–60.
27 Schlotzhauer 2012, 39.
28 Weber 2012b, 234, 346, nos TD 178–9, pl. 46f.
29 Chian pottery at Naukratis was used especially as dedication to Aphrodite: Lemos 1991, 191–4; Williams 2006, 126–32.
30 Petrie 1888, 62; Weber 2012b, 233, no. TD 94, which is probably the fragment in Philadelphia, E147.33.
31 See Weber 2012b, 374–5, no. TD 296; Villing 2013, 76, fig. 2.
32 Weber 2012b, 235–6, nos TD 189–229bis, 285(?), 340, 351?).
33 Aytaçlar 2006, 58 no. 36; Weber 2012b, 235, 282, 349, no. TD 190, fig. 47a.
34 Weber 2012b, 235–6, nos TD 189–229bis, 340.
35 Cook in Cook and Dupont 1998, 89; Wascheck 2008, 47–87.
36 Schlotzhauer 2007, 265–9; Schlotzhauer 2012, 123–4.
37 Villing and Schlotzhauer 2006, 59–60; Schlotzhauer 2012, 125–6.
38 Weber 2012b, 372, no. TD 285, p. 381, no. TD 329, pl. 65 g i.
39 Schlotzhauer 2012, 45–55.
40 Weber 2012b, 376, nos TD 301, 302 (?), 303; see Chapter 7.
41 Weber 2006, 145–54; Weber 2012b, 236–40; Villing 2013, 91–3.
42 Philadelphia, 29-71-189. Weber 2012b, 280–1, 399, no. M 25, pl. 57a-b.
43 London, British Museum, GR 1886,0401.1311; Schlotzhauer 2012, 160, no. Nau 133, pl. 29a-b.
44 Petrie 1888, 62.
45 Bommas 2005, 252–72.
46 Villing 2013, 91–2, figs 19–20.
47 At least three vases belong to group B, perhaps three more: fragments of feet and rim recall morphologically the so-called Typhon 'situla', cf. Weber 2012b, 239, nos TD 332, 347, 360.
48 Of an overall assemblage of 41 'situlae', 36 belong to group C: see Weber 2012b, 362–9, nos TD 241–73 (quater).
49 On the chemical analysis see Weber 2006, 149–51; Weber 2012b, 240; Mommsen *et al.* 2012, 441, 443.
50 Mommsen *et al.*, 2012, 441.
51 Dupont and Thomas 2006, 79, fig. 6, sample no. DEF 1 and p. 80.
52 Weber 2012b, 359–60, nos TD 230–7, pp. 372–3, nos TD 284–9, p. 379, no. TD 322, pp. 380–1, nos TD 327, 328, 329, 331, p. 388, no. TD 362.
53 GR 1888,0208.57; Villing and Schlotzhauer 2006, 63, fig. 39; Weber 2007, 306–7, fig. 32; Weber 2012b, 241–2, no. TD 290, pl. 52 c-d; Villing 2013, 87–8, fig. 13.
54 Cook 1954, 38–9, pl. GB606.3.
55 Schlotzhauer 2012, 62–5.
56 EA 1887,0101.1330; Johnston 2006, 28 no. 3; Weber 2012b, 243, 377, no. TD 306, pl. 53g; Villing 2013, 82, fig. 7.
57 Oren 1984, 20; Weber 2012b, 244, 388, no. TQ 1.
58 The chart is based on the catalogued material published by Weber 2012b, 309–88. From these catalogue entries the Greek transport amphorae have been excluded (nos TD 291–305, 323, 326, 343), as

has the material that is not Greek (Weber 2012b, nos TD 306, 307–14, 317, 319, 333, 337, 338, 342, 348).
59 Of the overall 211 amphora fragments, 125 are from neck amphorae (Weber 2012b, nos TD 10–14, 16–41, 43, 45, 48, 50–1, 56–9, 64–5, 67, 73–6, 78, 81, 98–103, 105–8, 110, 115–19, 121–2, 124–5, 134–6, 148, 151–4, 156, 163, 165, 167, 170, 174, 176, 186, 191–211, 214–28, 290, 340, 344), 15 from belly amphorae (nos TD 3–9, 55, 66, 69–70, 80, 284, 321, 341). The rest could not be distinguished definitely (nos TD 15, 44, 46–7, 49, 52–4, 63, 68, 71–2, 77, 79, 82, 104, 109, 111–12, 120, 123, 126–33, 137–8, 149–50, 155, 157–62, 164, 166, 168–9, 171–2, 173, 175, 177–83, 187–8, 233–4, 235, 335, 336, 345, 350–1, 354–8, 361).
60 Ibid., nos TD 139–40, 142–4, 146–7, 189, 359.
61 Ibid., nos TD 62, 83, 95, 97, 113–14, 141, 145, 184–5, 212–13, 229–229bis, 230, 232, 282–3, 286–7, 316, 325, 327, 330, 332, 349, 353.
62 Ibid., nos TD 238–73 (quater), 347, 360.
63 Ibid., nos TD 92, 274–81.
64 Ibid., nos TD 91, 236.
65 Ibid., no. TD 190.
66 Ibid., nos TD 86–90, 285, 315, 329.
67 Ibid., no. TD 85.
68 Ibid., no. TD 352.
69 Ibid., nos TD 96, 231, 328.
70 Ibid., nos TD 1, 289.
71 Ibid., no. TD 320.
72 Ibid., nos TD 2, 42, 84, 93, 237, 288, 318, 322, 324, 331, 334, 339, 346.
73 Petrie 1888, 61–2.
74 Venit 1982, 567–70.
75 Smoláriková 2002, 27–8, 96–8.
76 Schlotzhauer 2012, 23–194.
77 Forthcoming.
78 Schlotzhauer 2012, 160, no. Nau 133, pl. 29a–b.
79 Cf. the dedicatory inscriptions to the Greek gods of Naukratis such as Apollo, Aphrodite, Hera etc., as well as the sanctuary crockery that was transferred from the Samian sanctuary of Hera to that of Naukratis to serve the same function there as in Samos. Ibid., 56–7, 65–7.
80 Weber 2012b, no. TD 142.
81 Ibid., no. TD 164.
82 Klazomenian amphora attributed to the Urla Group, British Museum GR 1952,0505.13; ibid., no. TD 169. Cook (1954, 25, no. 17) suggested an identification as Prometheus. The whole preserved scene is not clear as the man holds something painted in white in his hand.
83 Images of rams, of course, might potentially have a special significance in an Egyptian context, being sacred to the Egyptian god Amun: see Weber 2012b, 267–8, 270–1.
84 Ibid., no. TD 241.
85 Weber in Schlotzhauer and Weber 2005, 86–93; Weber 2006, 148; Weber 2012b, 269–81.
86 Egyptian depictions of fencing show that this sport could be performed either in Egyptian cult practices, for example in honour of Osiris, at international competitions in the presence of the pharaoh or as military training. In Greece stick fighting was not common during the 6th and 5th centuries BC but there is literary evidence that fencing was a popular training exercise within the Macedonian military in the 4th century BC: Plutarch, *Alexander*, 4.6; cf. Weber 2012b, 277–9.
87 Carrez-Maratray 1999, 284–6; Höpflinger 2010, 95, 98–9, 166; Weber 2012b, 279–80.
88 Pherekydes 3 F 4 DK.
89 Herodotus 3.5.
90 The phenomenon of a link between the depiction on a vase and the location where it was found is well attested for vases from Greek sanctuaries and has been termed by F. Brommer (1984, 178–84) 'Themenwahl aus örtlichen Gründen'. It may very well apply also to a few Greek vases found in Egypt; see Bailey 2006, 155–7; Weber 2012b, 270–81. Four vases in particular stand out. From Memphis comes a Greek 'situla' that shows on one side a striding male figure with a long staff, an unusual picture in the Greek repertoire, and on the other two confronted bulls. At Memphis, the Apis bull was

worshipped and it is very likely that the vase was intentionally made for this site (Philadelphia 29-71-189; ibid., 280–1, 399, no. M 25). From Karnak comes a North Ionian black-figure vase with a picture of a ram (Berlin, Staatliche Museen zu Berlin, inv. V.I.5844, ibid., 270–1, 410, no. K 5), which fits in well with the cult of the Egyptian god Amun, whose zoomorphic appearance was that of a ram. Also at Karnak a large closed vessel painted in a North Ionian black-figure style was found, which depicts a boat procession, a ritual common at Karnak (Oxford, AM 1924.264; ibid., 410, no. K 6). Last but not least a North Ionian neck amphora, probably made at Teos, with painted cartouches of the pharaoh Apries was found at Thebes (Basel, Sammlung H.A. Cahn HC1175 and London, PM UC30035a-b; ibid., 273–4, 415, no. Th 1).

91 The earliest pieces are Late Protocorinthian/Early Corinthian (Weber 2012b, no. TD 2) and South Ionian animal style (SiA I) vase fragments (ibid., no. TD 190). The sherds are small and do not have significant features, which enable us to date them early or late within the distinctive phase. Since the chronology of these styles varies between the last decade of the 7th and the first two decades of the 6th century BC it is not clear at which stage within this period the vases were produced; on the chronology of the South Ionian animal style (SiA I) see Schlotzhauer 2012, 120.

92 Venit 1982; Weber 2012a, 304–5.

93 Bäbler 2004, 69–70.

94 Weber 2012b, 209–12, 301–4, nos Sa 1–13 (only selected fragments mentioned there, more to be published). The shapes range from Early Corinthian unguentaria (2), an Early Corinthian oinochoe (?), a large Attic red-figure open vessel, fragments of Chian chalices (3, probably belonging to the same pot but not joining), a large North Ionian bowl and a plate and a cup (NiA I and I/II) to South Ionian cups with everted rim (2) and a neck amphora (SiA II) and there are fragments from rim and foot of table amphorae (both Attic and Ionian) and transport amphorae from Lesbos, Chios, Klazomenai and Samos.

95 Greek transport amphorae (from Attica [1], Lesbos [1], Chios [3] and Samos[1]) have been found in the waste deposit of a store room of the temple of Khnum, ibid., 262, 419, no. E 5–10. A fragment of an Attic black-figure amphora, a North Ionian closed vessel and two Attic *à la brosse* amphorae were found in Elephantine, but without any particular indication of their findspot.

96 Smolárikóva 2002, 71–82; Smolárikóva 2009, 79–88.

97 Weber 2012b, 250–6, 261–2. On the complexity of the consumption of Greek pottery in Egypt, see Villing 2013, 73–101.

98 There is evidence that Greeks living in or visiting Egypt honoured Egyptian gods as early as the 6th century BC, making dedications to Neith of Sais and Apis of Memphis: see Weber 2012b, 212, 281. During the 5th century BC under the reign of Darius I a Greek was even involved in the cult of Thoth at Hermopolis: ibid., 257.

Chapter 7
Graffiti and Dipinti on Greek Pottery from Tell Dafana

Alan Johnston

Greek epigraphic evidence at Tell Dafana is confined to marks on vases. The pots with such markings fall mainly into two categories, transport amphorae and decorated closed vases; there is a small residue of 'others'. There are in addition marks that can be characterized as Egyptian or 'pan-Mediterranean'. The discussion below is based on these criteria. It will be noted that the texts are neither dedicatory nor do they specifically refer to ownership.

Decorated pots

The pieces in this category are all feet of large closed vases, with the exception of one lid and one foot with some of the decorated body preserved; the shape of all of these objects points inevitably to decorated pots. The decorated piece (GR 1949,0516.7 and several joining fragments) was until recently the only example known, but the discovery of the rest in the British Museum has produced a larger and interesting group. The marks had already been drawn by the excavator and published in the site report[1] and they can be identified with the pieces now located, with the exception of the fifth piece in Petrie's left column, which unfortunately remains lost.

All the marks are red dipinti, which could have been applied before or after firing. Before the re-discovery such marks were unknown on larger closed vases of the Archaic period from Egypt and rarely found in any case on such vases made in East Greece, GR 1949,0516.7 being something of an exception. Some red marks were known from sites such as Tocra and Naukratis, but few compared with the number of graffiti.[2] The Tell Dafana pieces are then indicative of some particular biography in the material concerned.

Two of the marked feet are clearly East Greek, GR 1949,0516.7 by decoration, GR 2010,5002.41+49 by shape (see **Pl. 68**). Others are almost certainly the feet of Attic black-figure amphorae or, just possibly, hydrias, though uncertainty remains concerning two or three, because of the fabric which is fine and with an amount of mica which is high for Attica and low for East Greece.

The marks themselves do not speak loud. Several belong to the truly 'pan-Mediterranean' range, the X and at least one 'arrow'; we cannot be sure whether they are used here as simple signs or Greek alphabetic letters. However, the mark on GR 2010,5002.17 is painted under the lid of what was presumably an amphora, and its purpose was probably to ensure the fitting of a lid to an amphora after the pieces were retrieved from the kiln (**Pl. 68**). However, if we are tempted to interpret all these marks in the same way, it should be noted that such marks appear at roughly the same mid-6th century period, even if rarely, on hydrias and kraters which would not have been lidded. There is one more non-alphabetic mark in the group which also points away from such a conclusion, the 'anchor' sign on the Attic foot, GR 2010,5002.43 (**Pl. 68**). Similar marks are found on a range of Attic and East Greek pot shapes of the 6th century; in addition, the type of mark would seem to reflect transportation by ship, therefore in some sense a trader's, not potter's, mark.[3]

The Greek alphabetic marks are largely mundane. Three need some comment: GR 2010,5002.22 has a ligature of *alpha* and *nu*, with no close parallel, but not an unexpected mark at this time, as it applies to the *eta-rho* ligature on GR 1949,0516.7; GR 2010,5002.37 might appear to have a *digamma* (**Pl. 68**), not in use in the alphabets of Athens or Ionia at this period (except in the latter case as a numeral), but the mark may well have been an *epsilon* extending further upwards beyond the preserved fragment; and a Corinthian form of *beta* on the still missing Petrie 1888, pl. xxxii, 5. The shape of this mark is highly distinctive and must surely represent this letter, used in Corinth and Megara, and their colonies; one 'rogue' usage is on an Attic transport amphora from Histria[4] of a date *c.* 590–80 BC; it is perhaps Megarian in view of the relative proximity of Byzantion. Whether the Tell Dafana foot is Attic, East Greek or Corinthian cannot be said, though Corinthian pottery is rare at Tell Dafana. On the other hand we do find the letter on some Corinthian pots found elsewhere, including Rhodes.[5] There is no comment from Petrie about the clay of the piece, which he describes as 'buff' for the whole group; one may ponder whether he would have noted the much lighter colour of a Corinthian piece. On balance one might take it as non-Corinthian, and an apparently isolated example of a user of that alphabet putting a form of commercial mark on an Attic or East Greek pot.

In sum, these marks expand the horizons of such markings, highlighting the sporadic nature of our previous corpus, and hinting at a much wider range of trading 'patterns' than might otherwise have been assumed.

Transport amphorae

It is not always possible to confirm the identity of smaller sherds as coming from transport amphorae, and I reserve comment on a very few such pieces for a 'miscellaneous' section below.

One may state at the outset that the range of both amphorae and marks is wide. Weber 2012b, 373–7 catalogues a fully representative selection, from Athens, Lesbos, Chios, Samos, Klazomenai and Cyprus, to which one West Greek piece is added below. The marks typologically fall into three categories: dipinto, pre-firing graffito and post-firing graffito, and can be alphabetic or otherwise. One piece has two marks and a second may have. Points of interest are very varied, although in certain cases they concern the creation of groups of marks, or types of mark. Here can be mentioned GR 1888,0208.60, whose graffito ∏ET finds a precise (unpublished) parallel on a closely similar Attic jar from

Figure 1 Samian amphora, Museum of Fine Arts, Boston, 87.626: arrow mark on the shoulder (courtesy Museum of Fine Arts)

Cerveteri; not only does this relieve one from thinking that PET(rie) had been scratching again, but also removes any thought that we have an Egyptian name rendered in Greek lettering (**Pl. 68**). In fact together they constitute an extremely rare example of more than one transport amphora of our broad period having the same mark of more than one letter or sign.[6]

More common are pre-firing marks on Samian amphorae; three are on jars from Tell Dafana, EA 22330 (1887,0101.1146), 23771 (1887,0101.1403) and GR 1888,0208.140a, form a set with *delta*,[7] *epsilon* and probably *digamma* respectively (**Pls 65, 67, 45**). That last letter is presumably a numeral, since these Samian marks clearly are numerical, in the Ionian system, and refer to some form of seriation in the production or firing process.[8] Two others, possibly from the same amphora, are less clearly so: EA 23768 (1887.0101,838) with a *tau* preserved, perhaps from the same vase as EA 23767 (1887,0101.837) with only part of what may have been a non-alphabetic mark (**Pl. 66**).

There are other certain or possible pre-firing marks in our corpus: perhaps A on GR 2010,5002.28 (which may be from the same jar as other sherds with a post-firing text; see below), seemingly *nu* (at least) on the Lesbian amphora, EA 23772 (1887,0101.774) (**Pl. 65**) and another Lesbian shoulder fragment has a *delta* inscribed before firing, EA 23769 (1887,0101.773) (**Pl. 67**).

HI, the post-firing graffito on GR 1888,0208.140a (once re-numbered, erroneously, as GR 1977,1011.2) does raise questions; read left to right it could join many other abbreviations for 'hieron', 'sacred', were it not for the fact that a) no Greek sanctuary is known at Tell Dafana and b) on Samos, the place of manufacture, the aspirate was not used (**Pl. 65**). It is possible that the piece could have been dedicated in the Egyptian sanctuary by a non-Ionian, or that a non-Ionian, for example Hierokles, cut the mark or had it cut for an Ionian Ierokles; or perhaps more likely we should read it retrograde as a numeral, 18, perhaps indicating the capacity of the jar in Ionian *kotylai* or *arysteres*.[9]

Two further Samian amphorae with pre-firing graffiti may be mentioned briefly: Boston MFA 87.626 with an arrow mark (Petrie 1888, pl. 34, 10 'on 50', see **Fig. 1**) and an unregistered jar with an anchor mark in the Department of Greece and Rome, probably from Tell Dafana, but with no accredited provenance.[10]

EA 23776 (1887,0101.738) is of greater interest as an amphora, a rare West Greek import of the period (**Pl. 45**), rather than for its single-letter dipinto, *alpha*; the type is found in a broad range of sites from Corcyra to Himera and the lower Adriatic and this is reflected in the analysis of the clay to be found in Appendix 1, ii. EA 22356 (1887,0101.770) too is more significant for its cartouche of Amasis impressed on the plaster capping on its mouth rather than the 'pan-Mediterranean' pentalpha graffito (**Pl. 64**).

GR 2010,5002.29, probably made on Samos according to Neutron Activation (NA) analysis of the fabric, could well be from the same amphora as 28, noted above for its pre-firing mark.[11] Two large graffito letters are partly preserved, cut after firing, an *omega* preceded by either a *zeta* or more probably *xi*, since there appears to be a trace of the central horizontal of a *xi* preserved (**Pl. 67**). The interpretation is not easy; the collocation of letters is not very common, but nothing apt comes to mind. It is possible that two further sherds, EA 23764 (1887,0101.836) and EA 23763 (1887,0101.822) may come from the same vessel; each presents part-preserved signs or letters (**Pl. 66**).

EA 23770 (1887,0101.821) is perhaps a Cypriot jar with a mark that would seem to be a 'lunate' *delta* (**Pl. 67**); the form is not used on Cyprus with its syllabic script, nor by any of the regular Greek visitors to Egypt. The geographically closest user is Side in Pamphylia.[12] Two further jar fragments of probable Cypriot origin have Egyptian graffiti, EA 23761 and 23762; these are included in Chapter 5 and have been published in Weber 2012b, 375, nos TD 297–8, pl. 53b–c.

Other

Two sherds of Egyptian jars with graffiti may be noted. One (EA 23766 [1887,0101.825]) has a mark of generic 'arrow' shape, though its form is closer to a Greek *psi* or *chi*. It constitutes perhaps the best candidate in our set for a graffito cut at Tell Dafana itself, and it is regrettable that it is so fragmentary (**Pl. 66**). EA 23765 (1887,0101.823) is also only part-preserved; if we have the right half of a symmetrical mark however, it would be peculiarly close to an enigmatic trademark appearing on late 6th-century Attic black-figured vases from Etruria (**Pl. 66**).[13]

The foot of an Attic black-glazed kantharos of the 4th century (GR 2010,5002.38) stands far apart from the rest of the material, and its underfoot graffito is inscrutable.

One further piece to be noted is EA 23822, a small rectangular stone implement, dubbed by Petrie a 'whetstone', with enigmatic but seemingly deliberate signs on two opposed sides. One of them is possibly in Cypro-Syllabic script but the reading is extremely difficult because of wear and surface scratching.

Concordance of BM registration numbers and entries (TD) in Weber 2012b

GR 1949,0516.7	207
GR 1888,0208.60	291
EA 22356	296
EA 22343	300
Boston MFA 87.626	301
GR 1888.0802.140a	303 (alt. inv. 1977,1011.2)
EA 23776	305
EA 22333	306
not identified	314
GR 2010,5002.17	331
20	334
22	336
27	341
28	342
29	343
37	351
38	352 kantharos
41+49	354
42	355
43	356
45	358

Notes

1 Petrie 1888, pls xxviii, xxxii.
2 There is a maximum of 20 underfoot marks on larger vessels among the roughly 230 underfoot marks listed in Johnston 2006a, 170–5 (excluding banded amphorae). Unless otherwise stated, all pieces are in the British Museum.
3 For such anchor marks see Johnston 1979, 192–3 and 236.
4 Bîrzescu 2012, 344, no. 1360, with earlier bibliography.
5 Johnston 1979, 170, nos 27 and 28.
6 Johnston, 2000. The graffito on an SOS amphora from Cerveteri, published in Weber 2012b, 374 as no. TD 292r, 'Sostratos eimi', is a phantom; the full text 'Thorakos eimi' has still to be published.
7 The letter would be of the 'arrow' shape occasionally attested from the later Archaic period.
8 Johnston 2006b, 27.
9 Johnston 1979, 223–4.
10 Johnston 1987, 129 fig. 1a–b; the piece does not have a room number inscribed on it, as do most jars from Tell Dafana; an alternative provenance would be the Fikellura cemetery at Kamiros.
11 Prof. Hans Mommsen, Helmholtz-Institut für Strahlen- und Kernphysik, University of Bonn, places the sherd firmly in his Samian group (H. Mommsen, pers. comm.; details of the analysis will be published in due course). Typologically a white slip is unusual for Samian production.
12 See Destrooper-Georgiades 1995 for an earlier 5th century coin using the form in its Greek legend. I am grateful to Andrew Meadows for bibliographical help and for the advice that a second such coin appeared on the market in January 2013.
13 Johnston 1979, 122–3, type 9D.

Chapter 8
The Excavations of 2009 at Tell Dafana

Mohamed Abd el-Maksoud,
Aiman Ashmawy Ali, Al-Sayed Abd
el-Aleem, Hisham Hussein and
Mustafa Nur el-Din

Introduction

Owing to the risks surrounding the area of Tell Dafana, (new irrigation and drainage canals, expanding cultivated land and a high water table) a team from the Supreme Council for Antiquities (SCA), led by Dr Mohamed Abd el-Maksoud, initiated a programme of rescue excavation at the site.[1] The aim was to shed fresh light on one of the most important sites in the eastern Delta. The work was carried out in April and May 2009 and was an important factor in reconfirming the significance of Tell Dafana as a rich archaeological site which deserves study and protection. Excavations were continued in 2010 in the northern part of the site, and these will be published in due course. Here we give a preliminary account of the work of the first season, during which the walls of various structures apparent from surface traces were cleaned to gain a better understanding of their layout.

In this season the SCA mission concentrated its work in the area to the south and south-west of the mound where Petrie excavated the casemate building in 1886; it is a region of low, flat ground approximately 2.5m lower than the mound to the north. The goal of the excavation was to trace the enclosure wall and to define the architectural elements inside. Excavation was limited to defining the wall faces by the removal of the surface dust, without going deep except for a few individual probes to check the depth of the surviving brickwork and the relationships between the walls.

The enclosure wall

The great enclosure wall of what Petrie referred to as the 'Camp'[2] was traced on the surface in several parts of the site during his excavations but was never fully excavated, so he drew the walls as simple outlines, without any detail. In 2009 the SCA team cleaned the southern part of the eastern wall for some 225m of its length towards the north, and found its thickness to be 14m (**Pl. 71a**). However, the face of the wall was found not to run straight as drawn by Petrie, but to possess projecting buttresses at intervals. These buttresses projected from the wall face by 60cm, so the thickness of the wall between them was reduced to 13.4m (**Fig. 2**). A trench was cut beside the southern part of the wall to determine its depth and it was found, at least in this part, to be preserved to just four courses of bricks down to its foundation level (**Pl. 73a**). These courses were stepped brick footing courses built on the sand, each course of brick being set back by 10cm.

We also cleaned the southern wall of the enclosure, which is 380m long and 14.5m wide (**Pl. 71b–c**). Remains of towers were discovered at the south-east and south-west corners, with dimensions of 27 x 27m. A test trench cut beside the south wall showed at this point that just seven courses of bricks were preserved down to its foundation level, these courses being stepped like those in the eastern wall, mentioned above (**Pl. 71b**). In the middle of this wall there is an entrance or gate 10m wide, which was excavated by Petrie[3] and re-cleaned by us (**Pl. 71d**). This southern gate gave access to the enclosure and the temple area, most probably from the land route or caravan route to the south of the site.

The temple

After cleaning the southern wall, we started excavating to the north of the central gate, an excavation that led to the discovery of a large temple built of mudbrick (**Fig. 1, Pl. 8**). Only the foundations of this temple are preserved; it consists of three successive halls or courts arranged around a central axis (**Pl. 72a**).[4] The first court is 64m long and 64m wide internally with an eastern wall 6.5m in width. The wall on the western side is 6.1m wide while the northern wall, which fulfilled the role of a pylon, is 8.75m wide. A gate in the middle of the latter wall led to the second court, which is 44m long and 54m wide, with walls to the east and west which are each 6m in width (**Pl. 72b–d**). The northern wall of this court acted as the second pylon of the temple and was 8.5m wide, with a central gate leading to the third court. Like the second court, this also measures 44 x 54m and both the eastern and western walls are 6m wide. This configuration of three successive courts from the southern gate, arranged on an axial plan, is typical of Egyptian temple design, but at the northern limit of the third court, where some kind of shrine or sanctuary might have been expected, we found instead a very substantial mudbrick wall with buttresses, running across the axis of the temple and founded at a greater depth than the other walls noted above (**Pls 74b–c, 75a**). The location of the buttresses appears to have been irregular, but there is certainly a clear recess in the south face, not far from the north-east corner of the court. At the western end of this recess, the bricks of the adjacent projecting section are slightly inclined (**Pl. 75b**).[5] The nominal width of the wall is 13.6m and there is still 1.6m depth of brickwork preserved. A trench was cut in the north-east corner of the third court to determine the relationship between the eastern and northern walls of the

Figure 1 The temple and magazines (Google Earth)

court, and the surviving depth of the brickwork. Here, only two courses of bricks remained above the foundation level in the eastern wall of the temple; in the north wall there were up to 14 courses, slightly inclined. This massive northern wall is older than the other temple walls, and it has evidently been re-used as the north wall of the great temple of Tell Dafana. In this case, it is possible that the sanctuary could have consisted of a stone naos situated on the axis a short distance in front of it. This would conform to standard Late Period temple design, as seen at Mendes, Tell Fara'on and Tell el-Balamun.[6] It is worth mentioning that some other temple foundations re-used older walls as the limit of their foundation trenches.[7] Traces of round pits lined with bricks

Figure 2 Plan showing the excavated features

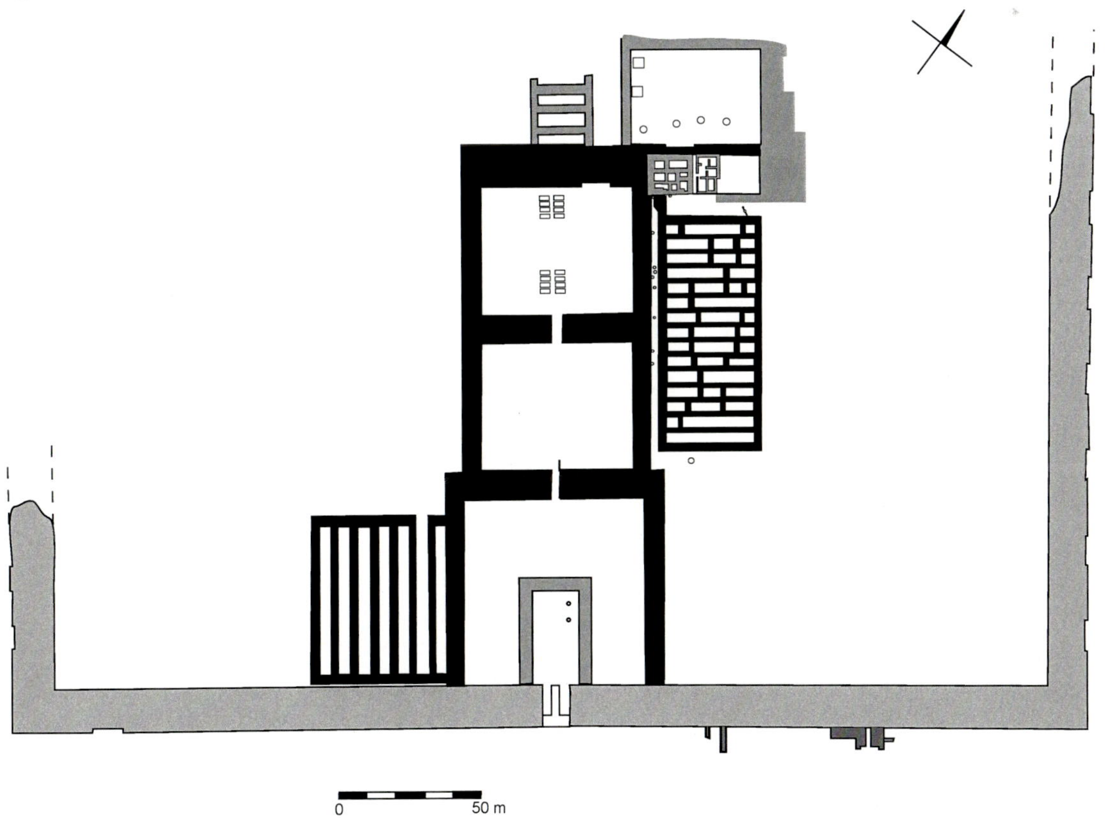

in the first and second courts may indicate the positions of column bases in these halls, unless they mark tree pits.

Magazines

East and south-west of the temple area we excavated two massive complexes of mudbrick magazines, the first located to the east of the second and third courtyard of the temple. They consist of 15 long units, each one 35m long and 3.5m wide internally (**Figs 2–3, Pls 73c, 74a**). The fact that no doors or entrances were found shows once more that the preserved remains consist only of foundations. The western limit of this set of magazines consists of a 1.2m wide wall, parallel to the east wall of the temple. The magazines were separated from the temple by a narrow street (**Pl. 73c**).

To the north of the magazines there was a rectangular hall full of refuse pits. An elaborate drainage system made of pottery was discovered in the hall, with a ceramic pipe leading to a massive soak-away drain (**Pl. 75d–e**). The water was conducted to a deep pit in which empty Chian amphorae with their bases broken off had been stacked one on top of another, and surrounded by similar old amphorae and other broken pottery. This type of feature is similar to the 'dry wells', noted by Petrie.[8] The fact that Petrie found several such 'dry-wells' shows that numerous soak-aways must have been constructed. The large size of the soak-away pit indicates that it was expected to deal with a considerable inflow of water, the source of which is much more likely to have been rainfall rather than any temple-related activity.[9] Torrential downpours with associated thunderstorms are not uncommon in winter and spring in the Nile Delta. Parts of a similar drain were discovered in the street between the magazines and the temple.

Excavations in the south-west corner of the enclosure led to the discovery of the foundations of another set of magazines connected to the temple, west of the first courtyard. These magazines were built of mudbrick and consist of at least seven long rows of units, each one 57m long and 4.5m wide, with the entrance placed at the north (**Fig. 2**). The design is similar to the magazines at the Ramesseum and Medinet Habu in Thebes.[10]

Figure 3 The magazines east of the temple (Google Earth)

A casemate building and a house

The remains of a small casemate building were discovered directly on top of the large wall with buttresses that runs from west to east across the northern part of the temple; it is situated on the eastern part of the wall to the north-east of the third court (**Pl. 76a–b**). This rectangular casemate building is 14m × 15m in size, built of mudbrick. Only the foundations are preserved; the fact that no doors or entrances were found shows the remaining brickwork must be below the original floor level. The building contains eight rooms, one of which, situated on the western side, was filled with pure sand. Traces of a house were discovered to the east of this casemate building, but it was not fully excavated. It was built directly on top of the large wall with buttresses, situated on the eastern part of the wall to the north-east of the third court of the temple. This rectangular building measures 14m × 8m and is built of mudbrick. The entrance was located to the west. The location above the cut-down remains of the large mudbrick wall shows that these structures belong to a period some time later than the wall itself.

Small finds

Many objects were discovered or picked up from the surface during this season, including grinding stones of sandstone, stone-footed platters of black granite or basalt, and a fecundity figure of sandstone. In addition, many bronze arrowheads were found, similar to the hundreds of arrowheads discovered by Petrie, which may reflect some military activity at the site, although this is by no means certain. Some curious carved stone objects with depictions of rough figures in incised relief were also discovered (**Fig. 4**), at least one of which may be a crude attempt to represent a foreign soldier with a shield.[11]

A more conventional figure in limestone was also discovered, showing a seated individual holding some item, although damage makes an identification uncertain (**Fig. 5**). This object resembles seated figures holding pottery vessels, as known from Naukratis.[12]

The pottery discovered in 2009

The ceramics include both local and imported pottery, and are mostly similar to the types discovered and published by

Figure 4 Two stone plaques with roughly carved figures

Petrie (see the catalogue in Chapter 5, and Petrie 1888, pls xxxiii–xxxvi), although there are some additional types not represented among his finds.

The first noticeable characteristic of the pottery found in this work is the rarity of marl fabrics, which contrasts with their more common occurrence among the ceramics from Petrie's excavation. This difference must be related to the location of the work; the temple area, not dug by Petrie, clearly contains a different set of pottery from that found in some of the other areas he excavated, such as the casemate building and the adjacent chambers. The pieces of siltware pottery from the temple are additional examples of types known from Petrie's finds, with the singular addition of a large quantity of miniature vessels or models. The types recovered in the excavation of 2009 are described below, following the sequence of the drawings by Emam Salah on **Plates 77–83**.

Plate 77 (all drawn at 1:4)

Nos 1.1 and 1.5
Two examples of siltware platters, one with a low ring-base. Both of these have dished tops and plain round rims. Thin slips of a pale cream colour cover the surfaces, like examples found by Petrie.

Nos 2.1–2.8
Siltware dishes with flat bases, flared sides and rounded rims. Compare BM EA 23665 from the Petrie material (**Pl. 32**); also Petrie 1923, pl. lix, nos 5D–5G.

No. 3.2
Flat-based siltware dish with concave, flared sides and plain, rounded rim.

No. 4.2
Silt bowl with a flattened base, convex sides and rounded rim.

Nos 5.1, 5.3
Flat-based bowls with convex sides and incurved rims. Compare BM EA 23659 from the Petrie material (**Pl. 32**).

No. 6.2
A dish of pale red siltware pottery, with a pale cream surface slip. The base is slightly pointed and the straight sides are flared. The shape is close to that of BM EA 23698 and EA 23699 (**Pl. 33**). The exterior bears a horizontal line of inscription in demotic, painted in black. Cary Martin has kindly considered the inscription from photographs and made the following comments: after the opening sign, a clear early demotic *p3*, the next sign looks like *m r*, which could be 'overseer', followed perhaps by *p r*, 'domain, house', and then a short divine name (possibly Amun). Alternatively, we could have the personal name, *P3-m r-iḥ*[13] were it not for the fact that there appear to be too many signs. But the next sign appears to be *s3*, 'son of', so a personal name does seem more likely. The next group could be *Nḫt-*, just possibly the personal name *Nḫt=w* or *Nḫt=w-s*.[14]

No. 7.3
An open casserole of red siltware, with a loop-handle at

Figure 5 Limestone seated figure

either side. This is paralleled by BM EA 23657 from the Petrie material (**Pl. 33**).

No. 8.2
A cylindrical cup of pale grey-green marlware. Compare BM EA 23697 from the Petrie material (**Pl. 34**); also Wilson 1982, pl. xiv, no. 11.

Nos 8.6, 8.8
Silt jars with pointed bases, convex sides and plain rims.

No. 9.0
This may be a siltware jar with a pointed base, or perhaps only the lower half of a tall jar. The broken upper edge makes a definite conclusion problematic.

Nos 9.3, 9.5
Silt jars with pointed bases, convex sides, contracted mouth and plain rims. Compare BM EA 22342 and EA 22328 from the Petrie material (**Pl. 34**).

Plate 78 (all drawn at 1:4)

Nos 10.1 to 10.9
These are all varieties of tall, situla-shaped jars typical of the 26th dynasty. The shape is that of a tall jar with a blunt pointed or rounded base, vertical sides, distinct shoulder and cylindrical neck, sometimes with handles, like number 10.9. They are made in red siltware clay with an external red slip. Number 10.5 is like BM EA 22336 and the handled jar (number 10.9) resembles BM EA 22301 and EA 50782 (**Pl. 35**); see also Aston and Aston 2010, pl. 16, no. 112.

No. 11.1
Tall siltware jar with a pointed base, tapered body and cylindrical neck. The closest parallel from the Petrie material is BM EA 22286 (**Pl. 36**), although the proportions are rather different; cf. Aston and Aston 2010, pl. 14, no. 99.

No. 11.5
Tall siltware jar, originally with a pointed base, now missing. The jar had a rounded shoulder, cylindrical neck and external rim.
The tall jars from the 2009 excavations are all long-necked examples; the short-necked versions found by Petrie, such as

EA 22287 and 22331 (**Pl. 35**), are not represented in the new material.

Nos 12.1, 12.3, 12.5

Three examples of the necks of trade-amphorae. Probably Samian, or local copies. Some more complete examples of amphorae were found but not drawn. They are shown in the photographs on **Plate 85**. One is Samian and the other, larger example is Klazomenian, both types found also by Petrie. The third amphora, with the thick handles, is Corinthian A, variant 4A.[15]

Plates 79–81 (scale 1:2)

All the items drawn on these plates are miniature or model vessels and they are all made in silt fabrics. Although many of these were found in 2009, they are rare among Petrie's material from Tell Dafana. These vessels resemble very closely those from 26th dynasty foundation deposits, particularly the Amasis deposits from the temple of Mendes.[16] It seems possible that they may have come from a disturbed foundation deposit in the recently identified temple at Tell Dafana. This view is supported by additional parallels among the foundation deposits from the pyramid-tombs of Nuri in Sudan.[17] The varieties of these model vessels from the 2009 excavations at Tell Dafana are:

- Small, simple dishes with carinated sides (**Pl. 79**, top row).
- Small, open miniature bowls with flared concave sides and projecting, rounded rims (over 20 examples on **Pl. 79**). Compare BM EA 23680 from the Petrie material (**Pl. 33**).
- Slightly taller cup-shaped miniatures with flat bases and fairly straight sides expanding to plain rims (15 examples on **Pl. 80**). The only comparable item from the Petrie material is BM EA 23681 (**Pl. 33**).
- Models of shouldered jars, with roughly pointed or peg-bases (4 examples at base of **Pl. 80**). Compare the similar vessels BM EA 23652 and 22320 from the Petrie material (**Pls 35, 38**).
- Shouldered types with blunt, flat bases (9 examples on **Pl. 81**). This form is not very different from the previous one, but the base is slightly wider.
- Miscellaneous forms (5 examples at base of **Pl. 81**). One of these is like BM EA 22305 (**Pl. 34**) and may be a miniature jar rather than a model. Two at the base of **Plate 81** possess collared necks.

Plate 82 (scale 1:2)

Two complete examples of siltware braziers or incense burners were found, shown on the left of the plate. There were also three fragments from the bases of additional examples. One similar piece was found in the EEF excavations (Petrie 1888, pl. xxxv, 40); other parallels are published in Petrie 1923, pl. lix, nos 13B–13K and Wilson

1982, pl. xv, nos 3–4. Three similar objects from Naukratis are in the British Museum (GR 1888,0601.733, 1888,0601.732 and 1888,0601.734).

There was an example of an imported Judaean juglet, with globular body, narrow neck and handle from neck to shoulder. This is like BM EA 23710 and 50788 from Tell Dafana (**Pl. 37**). The remainder of **Plate 82** and the following **Plate 83** are devoted to the series of lids and jar-covers. The discovery of many lids in the excavations of 2009 corresponds well with their regular presence in Petrie's material, although there are very few marl clay lids from the 2009 finds. The varieties found in 2009 include:

- Small rough simple lids (9 examples on **Pl. 82**). The closest parallel in the Petrie material is BM EA 23730.
- Larger lids with convex sides, although some of these may be dishes. Ten examples were recorded, the first three, shown on **Plate 82**, are quite small. The only example like these from the Petrie material is BM EA 22317 (**Pl. 39**).[18] The larger versions follow at the top of **Plate 83**. Parallels are known from Saqqara but have been interpreted as dishes; see Aston and Aston 2010, pl. 20, nos 161–3.
- Domed lids without handles (5 examples on **Pl. 83**). Only one of these is of a form exactly paralleled in the Petrie material, and it consists of pale grey marl clay. The others are thicker and heavier types in siltware.
- Lids with handles (13 examples on **Pl. 83**). These include domed shapes with a fairly roughly made central handle, as well as finer lids with carinated sides and well-shaped handles. Both forms are represented among the Petrie material (see **Pls 39–40**).

Notes

1. The excavation team comprised Hesham Hussein, Mustafa Nur el-Din, Hisham Abd el-Moemen, Tarek Harash, Mahmud Galal, Aiman Ashmawy Ali and Nasef Abd el-Wahed.
2. Petrie 1888, 52–3, pl. xliii.
3. Petrie 1888, 59–60.
4. Cf. Leclère 2007a, 14–17.
5. Perhaps the buttressed effect is an example of a wall built in separate blocks of brickwork, like many Late-Dynastic temple walls.
6. Wilson 1982, pl. 1; Petrie 1886, 13–4; Spencer 1994, 37, pls 8b, 9.
7. Brissaud and Zivie-Coche 1998, 63, pl. ivb; 102, pl.i; Spencer 1996, 37.
8. Petrie 1888, 60.
9. Petrie op. cit., described a large example: 'one SW of the *Kasr* being about 10 feet in depth to the sand, all filled with shards'.
10. Hölscher 1941, 78–82, pl. 10, 64–5.
11. Cf. the earlier representations on the 'Warrior Jar' in the National Museum of Athens.
12. For example, BM GR 1888,0601.46.
13. Lüddeckens 2014, 188–90.
14. Lüddeckens 2014, 647.
15. See Sourisseau 2006, 138–9, fig. 5.
16. Hansen 1967, pl. x, fig. 11.
17. Dunham 1955, pls 134–5.
18. See also Aston and Aston 2010, pl. 22, nos 185–7.

Commentary

Jeffrey Spencer

The architecture and material culture of Tell Dafana studied during this project point to it having been the location of an Egyptian Late Dynastic town with limited cross-cultural connections. The purpose of the great enclosure has been revealed by the discovery of the Egyptian temple it contained, placing it amongst the range of Late Period temples with encircling walls which are such a well-attested feature of Egyptian towns. The ancillary structures inside the enclosure belong to a repertoire of standard components of such temple-complexes, especially the casemate buildings, paralleled at numerous other sites and most closely in the temple-enclosures of Naukratis and Tell el-Balamun. The excavations in 2009 confirmed the existence of storage magazines flanking the temple in a manner already present in Egyptian architecture from the New Kingdom. Like all the other examples of Late Period temple enclosures, that of Tell Dafana was never a fortification or military camp, but a definition of the sacred space around the temple. Outside the enclosure, the architecture visible from satellite imagery again shows an Egyptian character, with evidence for many houses built on small casemate foundations.

The Egyptian nature of the site is reinforced by the nature of the antiquities recovered by excavation, which are overwhelmingly of native design and manufacture. They are typical of the kinds of objects found at many sites of the period, especially in the Delta.

As with the objects, the pottery is again primarily Egyptian. The types of pottery vessels found by Petrie, with more of a similar kind from the excavations of 2009, are a good assemblage of Late Period products, from platters and bowls to jars and lids, which find parallels among Egyptian ceramics from locations across the Delta and into Upper Egypt. In fact, the Tell Dafana material found and published by Petrie is so characteristic of Late Period Egyptian pottery that it has become one of the main reference collections for this period. Of course, the complete assemblage includes numerous imported vessels of foreign manufacture, mostly transport amphorae, but these are by no means unusual finds at other sites in Egypt and do not imply any special foreign connection to Tell Dafana. The location of the town, on the eastern fringe of the Nile Delta, was particularly convenient for imports from the Levant or across the Mediterranean, but similar imports found their way much deeper into Egypt.

Consequently, Petrie's interpretation of the site as a camp for Greek troops, based on the account of Herodotus, is now seen to be unsupported by other evidence, with the only remaining distinctive link between Tell Dafana and Archaic Greece being the presence of a large quantity of painted Greek pottery, discussed by Sabine Weber in Chapter 6. The amount is more than that found at any other Egyptian site except Naukratis, and has been the basis for inferring a special relationship between the town and the Greeks. As it is well known that mercenaries from the Greek world served in the army under Psamtik I and his successors, it is only logical to assume that some of these troops would at some time have been present – probably on a temporary basis as required, like all military gatherings – at Tell Dafana. The site was close to the frontier and was probably the starting point for expeditions into Sinai, as suggested by the stela of

Apries recently discovered near the site, which talks of just such a campaign. Therefore, there would certainly have been Greeks at Tell Dafana, but certainly not as a settled community like that at Naukratis, otherwise we would expect to find much more Greek pottery, inscriptions and other objects of Greek manufacture. The fine Greek pottery found by Petrie was not widely distributed across the site, but concentrated in just a few findspots in the annexes to the casemate buildings, principally Findspots 18, 19A and 29, where it had been discarded together with Egyptian pottery. The fact that some of the finest vessels possessed decoration which appears to have been devised specifically for Egypt suggests that these containers may originally have been sent as gifts to the Egyptian temple of the site, as suggested by Sabine Weber. As such, it would have gone into store with other temple-related material, probably in the building on the casemate foundation 'A', until it was broken and dumped outside.

The identification of Tell Dafana as an Egyptian temple town not only disposes of all the theories based on Petrie's interpretation that it was a military camp, but also serves to reinforce the special nature of the other site noted for Greek connections in the Nile Delta, Naukratis, which appears even more unique.

Appendix 1
Scientific Analyses

i. Identification of the contents of a 6th-century BC pot from Tell Dafana

Satoko Tanimoto and Rebecca Stacey

The small pottery jar GR 1888,0208.140 was found in the excavations by Petrie at Tell Dafana for the Egypt Exploration Fund in 1886. The form of this red siltware jar was reported by Petrie to be common, but only a few complete examples were brought away from the site. Two jars are in the British Museum: the one mentioned above in the Department of Greece and Rome and another in the Department of Ancient Egypt and Sudan, EA 23650 (**Pls 36, 60**). The first example is particularly interesting in that it is half-filled with a yellow resin-like material, the initial investigation of which by E.M. Holmes in 1889[1] suggested might be Chios turpentine. A second analysis carried out sometime prior to 1954 identified the contents as mastic (from *Pistacia sp.*), although the original report cannot be located. Re-analysis of the material by gas chromatography – mass spectrometry (GC-MS) was requested from the Department of Conservation, Documentation and Science at the British Museum to test this interpretation.[2] The new analysis, details of which are given below, confirmed the material to be Pistacia resin. There is however, a problem in describing the material as mastic, as strictly speaking this term is specific to resin from *Pistacia lentiscus*, not other resin-producing species of Pistacia, but the results of the analysis did not permit species differentiation[3] (see further the discussion below).

Sample preparation and analysis

A small sample (*c.* 1 mm^3) was removed from a cracked area on the surface of the yellow material in the jar from Tell Dafana. This sample was given the reference M1a. It was extracted with 1ml dichloromethane (DCM) and 50µl aliquots were removed and dried under nitrogen. Prior to analysis these were derivatized with bis(trimethylsilyl) trifluoroacetamide (BSTFA) + 1% trimethylchlorosilane (TMCS) to form trimethylsilyl (TMS) derivatives.

The analysis was performed on an Agilent 6890N gas chromatograph (GC) coupled to an Agilent 5973N mass spectrometer (MS). Injection was in splitless mode at 250°C and 11.59 psi, with a purge time of 0.8 min. An Agilent HP5-MS column (30m x 0.25mm, 0.25µm film thickness) fitted with 1m x 0.32mm retention gap was used. The carrier gas was helium in constant flow mode at 1.5 ml/min. After a 1 min isothermal hold at 50°C the oven was temperature programmed to 200°C at 12°C/min, then to 300°C at 5°C/min, then to 325°C at 10°C/min with the final temperature held for 5 min. The MS interface temperature was 280°C. Acquisition was in scan mode (50–600 amu/sec) after a solvent delay of 7.5 min. G1701DA Chemstation (G1701DA) software was used for system control and data collection/manipulation. Mass spectral data were interpreted manually with the aid of the NIST/EPA/NIH Mass Spectral Library version 2.0 and comparison with published data.[4]

Peak	Compound	MW	Principal (most abundant) fragment ions [% abundance]
1	Nor-β-amyrone (3-oxo-28-nor-olean-12-ene)	410	204[100]; 189[42]; 205[22]; 175[22]; 119[19]; 191[16]; 410[9]; 395[3];
2	Moronic acid TMS (3-oxo-olean-18-en-28-oic acid TMS)	526	73[100]; 189[82]; 187[37]; 203[28]; 190[24]; 409[14]; 307[11]; 526[11]; 320[3]; 511[3];
3	Oleanoic acid TMS (3-oxo-olean-12-en-28-oic acid TMS)	526	73[100]; 203[92]; 143[65]; 408[58]; 189[56]; 202[50]; 526[13]; 511[11]; 320[10]; 307[8]; 393[6];
4	Oxidized oleanane type component TMS	526	73[100]; 189[56]; 95 [44]; 135 [38]; 105 [34]; 119 [33]; 218 [33]; 121 [30]; 190 [22]; 295 [16]; 409 [15]; 444 [9]; 307 [8]; 424 [7]; 205 [7]; 511 [6] 526[5];
5	(Iso)masticadienonic acid TMS (3-oxo-13α,14β,17βH, 20αH-lanosta-8,24-dien-26-oic acid TMS or 3-oxo-13α, 14β,17βH,20αH-lanosta-7,24-dien-26-oic acid TMS)	526	95[100]; 73[96]; 511[82]; 169[51]; 421[45]; 257[37]; 393[15]; 526[7]; 435[6];

Table 1 Triterpenoid compounds identified in the yellow resinous sample from Tell Dafana jar (with details of principal mass spectral fragment ions). Peak numbers correspond with the peak labels on the chromatograms in Figure 1 (MW= molecular weight, TMS=trimethylsilyl derivative)

Results and interpretation

Note: numbers in brackets [n] refer to peak numbers on the chromatograms and in **Table 1**.

The sample from the Tell Dafana jar contained significant amounts of stable triterpenoids, such as moronic acid (TMS) [2], oleanonic acid [3] and oxidised oleanane type components [4], which are characteristic of archaeological Pistacia resin, although compounds such as 18α-oleanonate, 3α-acetoxy-iso masticadienolate which are typically seen in unaged Pistacia resin were not detected (see **Fig. 1** and **Table 1**). This composition is consistent with the observations of the earlier analysis and confirms the Pistacia origin of the resin.

Commentary[5]

Analysis of the contents of the Tell Dafana jar by GC-MS has confirmed the previous identification of Pistacia resin, possibly mastic. As mentioned above, the source of mastic is *Pistacia lentiscus*, widespread in the Mediterranean and important in the economy of Chios. However, since the analytical results do not permit a certain identification of the species from which the Tell Dafana resin was derived, it could be terebinth (turpentine), which was the conclusion reached by Holmes. Studies have shown that resins from Pistacia trees were traded into Egypt in antiquity, but, as in the present case, it has not often been possible to determine

Figure 1 Partial GC-MS chromatogram (25–40 mins) of the yellow resinous sample from Tell Dafana jar. Peak labels on chromatogram correspond with the peak numbers in Table 1

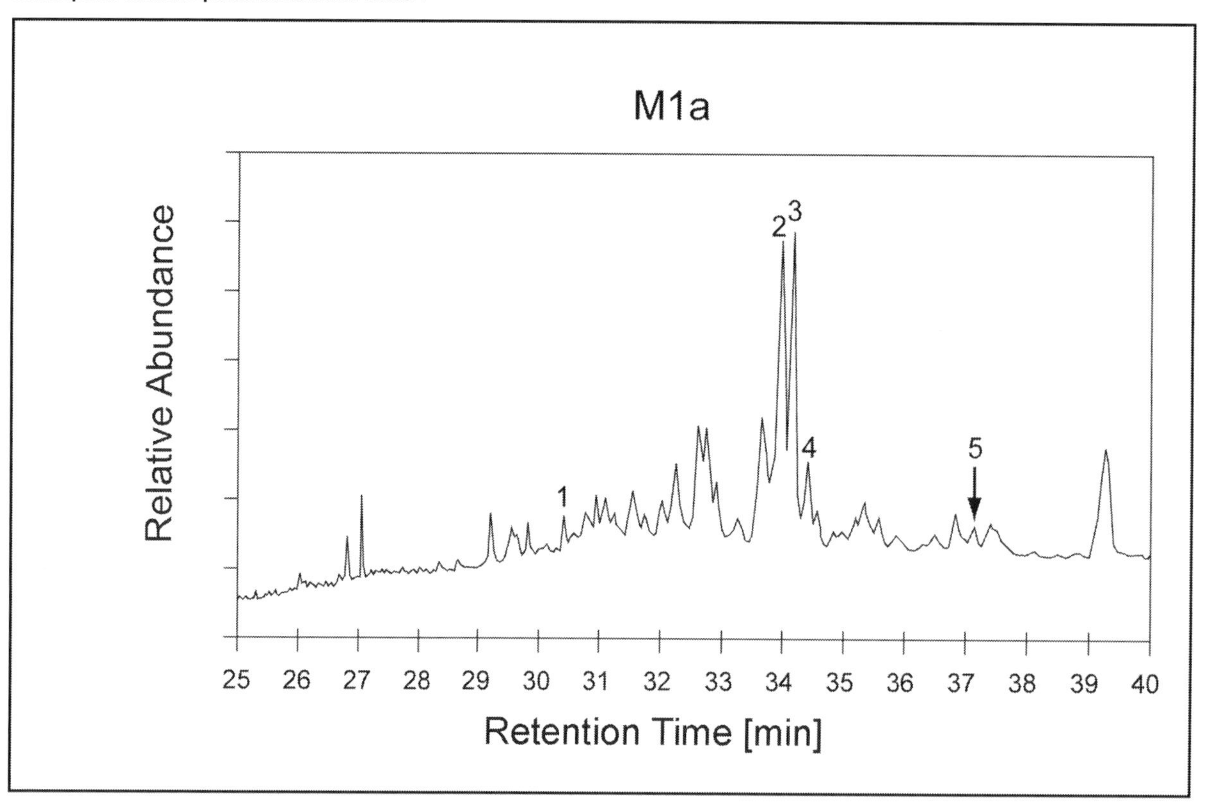

the species of Pistacia involved. In addition to *P. lentiscus*, the species *P. terebinthus*, a source of turpentine, the related *P. atlantica* and also *P. palaestina* occur in the Mediterranean and Levant. Resin from all of these species appears to have been traded, with different applications.[6]

The resin traded in Canaanite jars during the Late Bronze Age was most probably terebinth.[7] Study of these transport-jars and residues on them has proved the import of Pistacia resin into Egypt at this period.[8] Canaanite amphorae (produced in the region between Tel Aviv and Haifa) from El-Amarna and Memphis contained Pistacia resin. Some jars were marked with the Egyptian word for incense, *sntr*. Chemical analysis of a select number of samples using GC-MS established that every sample, including those from Canaanite amphorae inscribed *sntr*, consisted of resin of the genus *Pistacia*.[9] Resin from El-Amarna has been claimed to be terebinth,[10] but other sources state that species identification was not achieved.[11] The Egyptian term *sntr* was, however, also applied to resins of different types from African sources, so would seem to have been a generic term for any material that could be burnt as incense.

About a ton of Pistacia resin was found in Canaanite jars from the Late Bronze Age shipwreck discovered off the coast of southwest Turkey at Uluburun.[12] It has been suggested that the jars contained wine flavoured with resin, but additional analysis showed that it was Pistacia resin itself that was being shipped.[13] According to C. Haldane the material was terebinth resin.[14] The use of Canaanite amphorae to transport resin shows an efficient use of large containers in the Late Bronze Age, and there is no reason to suppose that jars of equivalent or larger size would not have been used in the Late Period with a range of Egyptian, Levantine and Greek amphorae available. The resin in the jar from Tell Dafana must have been repackaged into this small vessel, suggesting a high value on the product in Egypt.

Notes

1 Holmes 1888, 387–9.
2 CDS Analytical request no. AR2007/95.
3 On another unsuccessful attempt to distinguish Pistacia to species level, see Stern *et al.* 2008, 351–70.
4 Stern *et al.* 2003, 457–69.
5 With additional material by A.J. Spencer.
6 For a good summary of the different *Pistacia* species, see Serpico and White 2000b, 434–6.
7 van Alfen 2002.
8 Serpico *et al.* 2003, 365–75.
9 Serpico and White 2000a, 884–97.
10 Serpico, cited in Haldane 1993, 353.
11 Serpico and White 2000, 459.
12 Mills and White 1989, 37–44; Bass 1987, 726–7; Pulak 1998, 188–224; Haldane 1993, 348–60.
13 Stern *et al.* 2008, 2188–2203.
14 Haldane, op. cit., 352–3. The identification was based on analyses by Mills and White 1989, and Hairfield and Hairfield 1990. White suggested the source might have been *Pistacia atlantica*.

ii. Petrographic and SEM-EDX analyses of an amphora from Tell Dafana

Michela Spataro

Abstract

A small fragment from the neck of an amphora from Tell Dafana in Egypt (EA 23776) was sent for scientific analysis[1] to characterize its fabric and suggest a provenance on the basis of parallels with published material from the Mediterranean basin. Initially attributed to Corinth or Miletos, recent work by A. Villing (British Museum, Department of Greece and Rome) and A. Johnston (University College London) has excluded a Milesian or Corinthian provenance and suggested that the fragment might come from a region to the west or north-west of Greece, including Kerkyra/Corfu and southern Italy. Thin section analysis and scanning electron microscopy with energy dispersive X-ray analysis were carried out to characterize the amphora fabric and the results were compared to published research; they suggest a possible provenance from the Ionian and Adriatic Sea regions.

Introduction

The neck of a fragmented pale brown amphora (EA 23776; **Fig. 1** below and **Pl. 45**) found at Tell Dafana, in the Nile Delta in Lower Egypt, was submitted for analysis. The amphora has a pale slip on both the interior and exterior surface and its fabric is laminated.

Archaeologists had suggested that this fragment comes from an Archaic Greek transport amphora and suggested a provenance of either Corinth on the Greek mainland or Miletos on the west coast of modern Turkey. However, visual examination of the piece by Johnston and Villing established that though the amphora was clearly Greek, neither Corinth nor Miletos was likely to have been the place of production, either in terms of typology or in terms of fabric (as far as could be determined by macroscopic examination). Alan Johnston suggested that from his experience the closest typological parallels could be found to the west or north-west of Greece, broadly in the region between Kerkyra/Corfu and Southern Italy. Since very few objects (and in particular no other trade amphora) from this part of the world are known from Egypt in this early period, a further

Figure 1 The neck of the amphora (British Museum, EA 23776) discussed in this report

	1st b 100x	2nd b area (rich in microfossils)	3rd b 100x	4th b 100x	5th b 100x	Average	s.d.
Na$_2$O	1.95	1.55	1.55	1.28	1.62	1.6	0.2
MgO	4.71	5.58	4.89	4.6	5.05	5.0	0.4
Al$_2$O$_3$	15.72	15.76	14.95	14.61	15.02	15.2	0.5
SiO$_2$	55.78	53.47	56.66	60.19	55.25	56.3	2.5
K$_2$O	2.28	2.08	2.19	1.88	2.14	2.1	0.1
CaO	13.71	14.86	13.67	11.73	14.68	13.7	1.2
TiO$_2$	0.63	0.64	0.58	0.47	0.63	0.6	0.1
MnO	0	0.09	0.08	0.09	0.14	0.1	0.1
FeO	5.21	5.97	5.43	5.14	5.46	5.4	0.3

Table 1 Tell Dafana, sample EA 23776: SEM-EDX compositional results of five bulk analyses at 100x, with average and standard deviation. Results are reported as normalized % oxides

investigation of this hypothesis was essential for the understanding of Egyptian relations with the Greek world, the subject of the Tell Dafana Project published in this volume.

Sampling and method

Scientific analysis of the fabric was requested to characterize the paste of the amphora and identify similarities and differences with the published literature for comparative material analysed in thin section.[2]

A sample from the core of the neck (which did not include the slip) was carefully collected using clippers and prepared as a polished thin section. The polished thin section was examined using a polarising microscope (Leica DMRX) and by scanning electron microscopy-energy dispersive X-ray analysis (SEM-EDX).

Multiple SEM-EDX analyses were carried out on the sample (**Tables 1 –2**). The Hitachi S-3700N SEM was used at a pressure of 30Pa with a 20kV accelerating voltage; the sample was analysed uncoated. The following elements were calibrated using a mixture of glass and mineral standards: Na, Mg, Al, Si and K. The other elements (Fe, Mn, Ti and Ca) were calibrated using default calibrations generated by the Oxford Instruments EDX INCA Analyser software. The quantitative results for the nine elements were converted into oxide percentages. These percentages were normalized (oxygen by stoichiometry), to take into account the fact that oxygen and carbon are not measured, and are semi-quantitative.

Results

Optical microscopy analysis

The amphora has a light brown, calcareous, micaceous and slightly fossiliferous fabric (**Fig. 2**), with some well-sorted fine quartz (15%; typical size 0.03 x 0.03mm; a few inclusions are coarser), some fine muscovite mica (>2%), very occasional fine fragments of serpentine, occasional plagioclase, rare sub-angular felsic rock fragments, rare stretched metamorphic polycrystalline quartz, some coarse flint inclusions, rounded calcareous fragments, some red clay fragments, some microfossils (Globorotalid (?), Foraminifera; micritic filling of cells), some iron oxides and opaques.

Table 2 Tell Dafana, sample EA 23776: SEM-EDX compositional results of individual minerals particularly rich in sodium, iron and magnesium oxides. Results are reported as normalized % oxides

	23776 200x bulk on a large mineral sp1	23776 200x bulk on the same large mineral sp2	23776 200x bulk on a second mineral sp3	23776 200x spot an on mineral Fe rich	23776 200x spot an on mineral Mg rich	23776 mineral in the 1st b 100x
Na$_2$O	6.96	5.01	6.45	0.48	1.79	7.96
MgO	0.52	2.76	1.15	1.52	21.74	0.87
Al$_2$O$_3$	23.11	24.68	24.59	3.39	18.51	21.53
SiO$_2$	58.42	56.71	58.99	9.62	35.77	61.76
K$_2$O	2.47	6.4	5.22	0.29	2.87	3.02
CaO	5.78	1.19	1.7	3.89	2.46	2.92
TiO$_2$	0.07	0.09	0.11	0.14	0.08	0.08
MnO	0.12	0	0	0.17	0.35	0
FeO	2.56	3.15	1.79	80.51	16.42	1.85

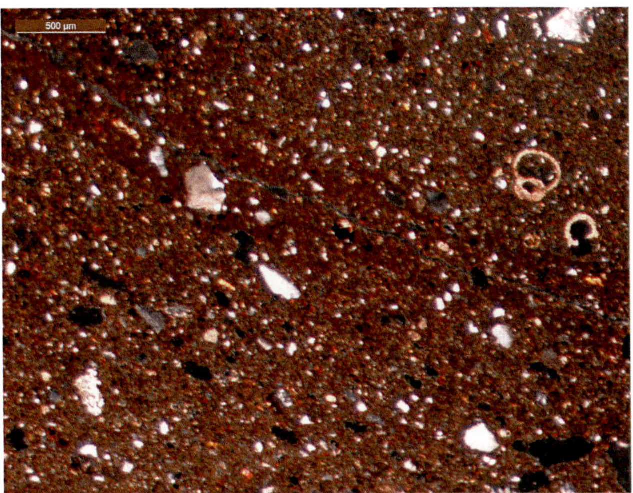

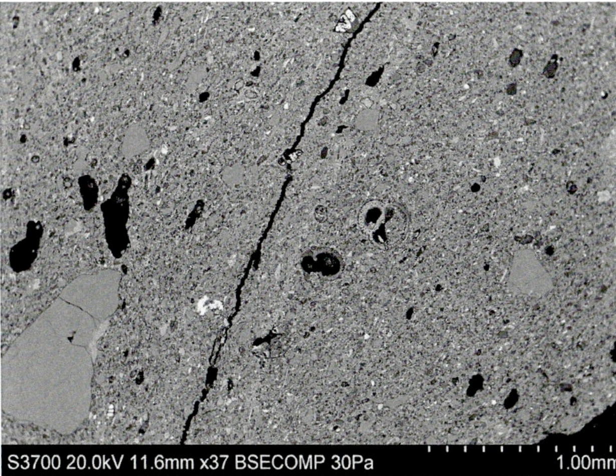

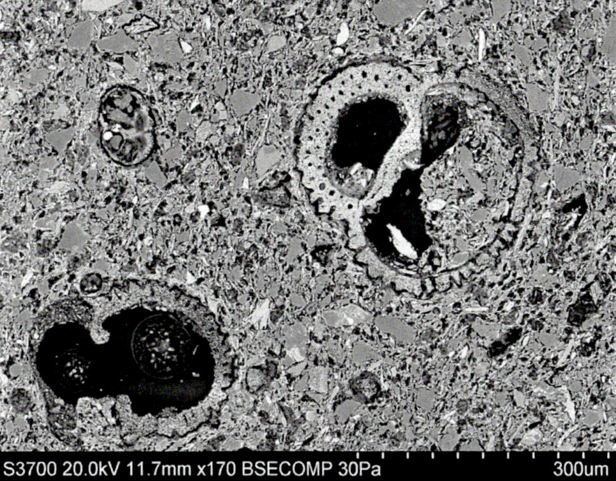

Figure 2 Photomicrograph of the fabric of amphora EA 23776, showing a micritic, micaceous and fossiliferous fabric (cross-polarized light [XPL], field of view 1.74mm)

Figure 3 Backscattered SEM images of the fabric of the amphora EA 23776: (top) at low magnification showing a fine fabric with mostly well-sorted inclusions, and (bottom) at high magnification showing the microfossils (Globorotalid?, Foraminifera)

SEM-EDX analysis

Five bulk analyses were carried out at 100x (each covering an area of about 1.5 x 1mm) on the paste of the amphora (**Table 1**, **Figs 2–3**). The paste is homogeneous (**Fig. 4**), with high content of silica, calcium and iron oxides. The high calcium content is also due to the micritic infilling of the voids and microfossil chambers. The high silica content is mainly due to the quartz sand, which includes some coarse grains of polycrystalline quartz and flint. Magnesium oxide is relatively high (**Table 1**), mainly due to specific minerals, as shown by the spot analysis in **Table 2**, probably related to serpentine.

Discussion and conclusions

Unfortunately the minerals identified in the fabric analysis of the Tell Dafana amphora sample are geologically widespread. Nevertheless, a few suggestions about its possible provenance can be made on the basis of the published work on amphorae.[3] Inclusions such as serpentine and chert are typical of Rhodian amphorae, as pointed out by Peacock and Williams.[4] In thin sections these amphorae contain red, brown and yellow serpentine, a sparse scatter of fine quartz, occasional olivine and clinopyroxene and pieces of chert and cryptocrystalline limestone. Peacock suggested a Rhodian source on the basis of fabric similarities with Greek amphorae bearing Rhodian stamps.[5]

I. Whitbread (pers. comm. 2011) defines the Tell Dafana fabric as an imitation of Corinthian A amphora, but says

Figure 4 Line chart of the SEM-EDX compositional results of the five bulk analyses from Table 1, showing the homogeneity of the amphora fabric throughout the potsherd

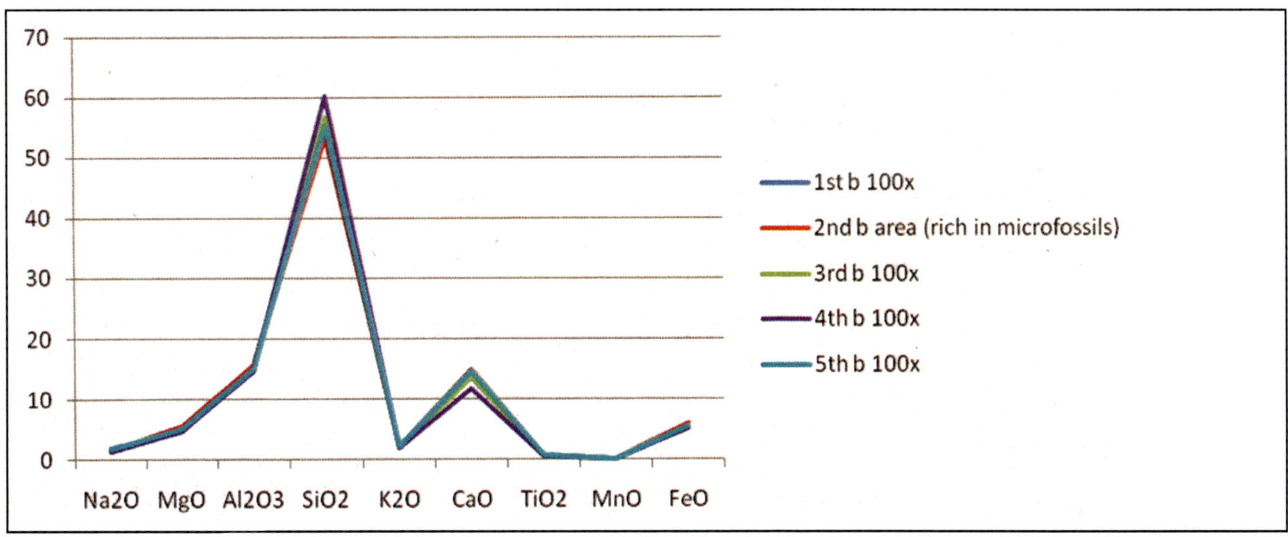

that there is no information on its provenance. There are no identical fabrics described in his book.[6] The geologist R. Sauer (V. Gassner, pers. comm. 2011) suggests that, on the basis of the presence of chert, serpentine and microfossils, the amphora might have been manufactured along the eastern or western coastlines of the Adriatic Sea or along the coast of the Ionian Sea. Finally, the scientific analysis of middle and late Neolithic *figulina* pottery (very fine pottery with few inclusions used as prestige item), which was manufactured in different specialized regional workshops along both the Adriatic coastlines, shows very similar micritic fabrics to the Tell Dafana amphora with chert, microfossils, calcareous pellets and muscovite, but not serpentine inclusions.[7]

In conclusion, the thin section optical microscopy and SEM-EDX analyses allowed characterization of the amphora fabric; the minerals identified are geologically widespread and therefore more than one possible provenance could be suggested on the basis of published work, among them the Ionian and Adriatic regions.

Acknowledgements

We would like to thank Alan Johnston (UCL, Institute of Archaeology), Alexandra Villing (British Museum, Department of Greece and Rome), Catherine Higgitt and Roberta Tomber (British Museum, Department of Conservation and Scientific Research) and Ian Whitbread (University of Leicester) for their comments. Special thanks are due to Prof. Verena Gassner and Dr Roman Sauer (Institut für Klassische Archäologie, Universität Wien).

Notes

1   CSR Analytical Request No. AR2011/27.
2   E.g. Gassner 2003; Peacock and Williams 1986; Whitbread 1985.
3   Gassner 2003; Peacock and Williams 1986; Whitbread 1985.
4   Peacock and Williams 1986; Class 9.
5   Archaeology Data Service.
6   Whitbread 1995.
7   Spataro 2002, 179–91; Spataro 2009.

iii. Report on metalworking items from Tell Dafana

Paul Craddock

Hearth bottom, EA 23990 (Fig. 1, Pl. 30)

This is a roughly hemispherical piece of slag with a pronounced depression in the centre of the flat face. Its measures 16.5 x 14.4cm with a thickness of 5.8cm. Such pieces are frequently found on sites where iron has been hammered at red heat (*smithed*).[1] The iron has to be frequently annealed by heating to around 1000° C in a hearth. In the smithing process some of the iron oxidises and during the annealing some of this oxide reacts with any clay or sandy material to form a slag. At the necessary annealing temperatures this will be semi-molten and will pick up pieces of charcoal, clay lining and so forth, and sink to the bottom of the hearth forming the somewhat heterogeneous lump exemplified by the present piece. The blast from the bellows would be directed down into the centre of the hearth creating the observed depression in the semi-molten mass.

In the solid state traditional iron smelting process, smithing of the iron has to be carried out at two quite separate stages.[2] The initial product of the smelt was a lump of iron (*bloom*), which had to be consolidated, and have most of the smelting slag squeezed out by hammering at white

Figure 1 Mass of iron slag, British Museum, EA 23990

Figure 2 Pot bellows, British Museum, EA 22347

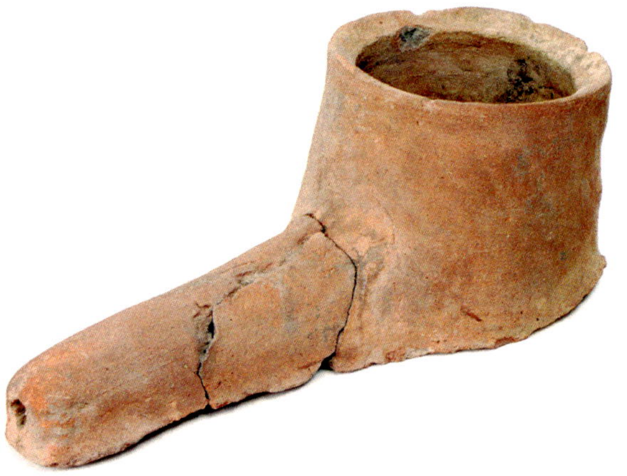

heat (*bloom smithing*) to form a billet or bar. In the second stage, the iron will have been fabricated into artefacts by hammering (*forging*) at red heat. It is impossible to be sure which operation is represented here, but the smelting stage produces large quantities of slag. There is now no surviving evidence for smelting slag, but one would have expected Petrie, who was interested in technical matters, to have at least have mentioned it if it had been present.

The pot bellows, EA 22347 (Fig. 2, Pls 47, 61)

This a complete example of a ceramic pot bellows incorporating both the bellows chamber and a short bellows pipe in one unit. The pipe probably fed directly into a separate clay nozzle (tuyère) which would have penetrated deep into the hearth. If the pipe itself had acted as the tuyère then one would have expected evidence of burning on the end and also the bellows unit would then have been uncomfortably close to the fire. The pot bellows illustrated in the very naturalistic and detailed wall paintings on the tomb of Rekhmira, and also those on the tomb of Puyemra, painted a thousand years earlier, seem to have a reed acting as the bellows pipe leading into a completely separate tuyère at its other end.[3] To have the bellows pipe integral with the bellows chamber seems inherently unsatisfactory as movement whilst being operated could lead to the pipe breaking off, as has in fact occurred. However, the ceramic pot bellows from Tell Edh-Dhiba'i, Baghdad, dated to the third millennium BC, also seems to have had an integral bellows pipe, which had broken off about 2cm along its length.[4]

The profile of the bellows tube is curved, but with a flattened bottom showing it sat directly onto the ground. This is quite typical for bellows and tuyère units feeding smithing hearths rather than smelting furnaces, where the tuyère entered the furnace above ground level and the pipes are completely circular in section.[5]

Therefore, both the hearth bottom and the bellows unit seem to provide evidence for metalworking with a hearth rather than primary smelting.

Notes

1. Tylecote 1987, 317–19.
2. Tylecote 1987, 151–62.
3. Scheel 1989, 24–5.
4. Davey 1979.
5. Tylecote 1981.

Appendix 2
Collections Holding Material from Tell Dafana

United Kingdom
Aberystwyth, University College of Wales*
Birmingham, Museum and Art Gallery
Bolton City Museum
Brighton, Museum and Art Gallery
Bristol, Museum and Art Gallery (including items previously in Bath, Literary and Scientific Institution)
Cambridge, Fitzwilliam Museum
Dundee, The McManus Art Gallery and Museum
Edinburgh, National Museum of Scotland
Glasgow, Kelvingrove Art Gallery and Museum
Greenock, McLean Museum and Art Gallery
Liverpool, World Museum
London, British Museum (Department of Ancient Egypt and Sudan; Department of Greece and Rome)
London, Harrow School Old Speech Room Gallery and Museum
London, Petrie Museum of Egyptian Archaeology
Oxford, Ashmolean Museum
Reading, Ure Museum*
Sheffield Weston Park Museum
St Helens, World of Glass Museum
Swansea, Wellcome Collection of Egyptian Antiquities
Warrington, Museum and Art Gallery
York, Yorkshire Museum
[Godalming, Charterhouse School (material sold in 2002)]
[London, Royal College of Surgeons (material destroyed during WWII)]
[London, Pharmaceutical Museum (?)]
[London, Biblical Museum (?)]
[Rochdale Touchstones Heritage Centre (?), possibly with items previously in Manchester Heywood Free Library]
[St Albans Museum (?)]

Outside the United Kingdom, in Europe
Belgium
Brussels, Musées royaux d'Art et d'Histoire

Germany
Heidelberg, Antikenmuseum der Universität*
[Berlin, Ägyptisches Museum (objects destroyed during WWII)]

Greece
Athens, British School at Athens*

Ireland
Dublin, University College, The Classical Museum*
Mullingar, St Finian's College*

Netherlands
Amsterdam, Allard Pierson Museum* [ex- New York, Metropolitan Museum and Philadelphia, Penn Museum]

Outside Europe
Australia
Sydney, Macquarie University
Sydney, Nicholson Museum

Canada
Toronto, Royal Ontario Museum
[Montreal (?)]

Egypt
Cairo, Egyptian Museum
Alexandria, Bibliotheca Alexandrina*

Japan
Kyoto, University Museum*

United States of America
Boston, Museum of Fine Arts
Chicago, Oriental Institute Museum
New York, Metropolitan Museum* [from Philadelphia, Penn Museum]
Philadelphia, Penn Museum

[Chautauqua, Archaeological Museum (torn down in 1929 and
    collection dispersed)]
[Brooklyn Museum (?)]
[Rochester Museum (?)]
[San Francisco, Leland Stanford University (?)]
[Wellesley College (?)]
[Colorado (?)]

* only Greek sherds
[x] collections sold, destroyed, unclear or untraceable.

Abbreviations for museums cited frequently in the text

(BM) EA, British Museum, London, UK, Department of
    Ancient Egypt and Sudan
(BM) GR, British Museum, London, UK, Department of
    Greece and Rome
(BM) ME, British Museum, London, Department of the
    Middle East
Baltimore, WAG, Walters Art Gallery, Baltimore, MD, USA
Bolton, Bolton City Museum, Bolton, UK
Boston, MFA, Boston Museum of Fine Arts, Boston, Mass., USA
Bristol, CMAG, Bristol City Museum and Art Gallery, Bristol, UK
Cambridge, FM, Fitzwilliam Museum, Cambridge, UK
Cairo, EM, Egyptian Museum, Cairo, Egypt
Edinburgh, NMS, National Museums of Scotland, Edinburgh, UK
Liverpool, WM, World Museum, Liverpool, UK
London, PM, Petrie Museum, University College London, UK
Oxford, AM, Ashmolean Museum, Oxford, UK
Philadelphia, Penn Museum, Philadelphia, Penn., USA
Sydney, MAC, Macquarie University, Sydney, Australia
Sydney, NM, Nicholson Museum, Sydney, Australia
Toronto, ROM, Royal Ontario Museum, Toronto, Canada

Bibliography

For the abbreviations of periodicals and series titles used here, see
http://www.ifao.egnet.net/uploads/publications/enligne/
Abreviations.pdf

Abd el-Aziz, E. 2007, 'A New Year's flask', in El-Sharkawy, B.S. (ed),
The Horizon. Studies in Egyptology in Honour of M.A. Nur el-Din (10–12
April 2007), Cairo, 23–6.

Abd el-Maksoud, M. 1998, *Tell Heboua (1981–1991). Enquête archéologique
sur la Deuxième Période Intermédiaire et le Nouvel Empire à l'extrémité
orientale du Delta*, Paris.

Abd el-Maksoud, M. and Valbelle, D. 2013, 'Une stèle de l'an 7
d'Apriès, découverte sur le site de Tell Défenneh', *RdE* 64, 1–12.

Adriaen, M. 1963, *S. Hieronymi presbyteri opera* I, *Opera exegetica* 2.
Commentariorum in Esaiam Libri I-XI, CCSL 73.

Adriaen, M. 1985, *S. Gregorii Magni Opera. Moralia in Iob Libri XXIII-
XXXV*, CCSL 143B.

Agut, D. 2011, *Le sage et l'insensé. La composition et la transmission des sagesses
démotiques*, BEHE (Sciences historiques et philologiques) 347.

Aimé-Giron, N. 1941, 'Adversaria Semitica (III). VII. Báal Ṣaphon et
les dieux de Taḥpanḥès dans un nouveau papyrus phénicien', *ASAE*
40/2, 433–60.

Albright, W.F. 1950, 'Die Festung des (Generals) Pinehas, Baal
Zephon', in Baumgartner, W., Eissfeldt, O., Elliger, K. and Rost, L.
(eds), *Festschrift A. Bertholet zum 80. Geburtstag gewidmet von Kollegen und
Freunden*, Tübingen, 1–14.

Alt, A. 1943, 'Taphnaein und Taphnas', *ZDPV* 66, 64–8.

Amborn, H. 1976, *Die Bedeutung der Kulturen des Niltals für die
Eisenproduktion im subsaharischen Afrika*, Studien zur Kulturkunde 39,
Wiesbaden.

Amin, N. (ed.) 2005, *The Historical Sites of Egypt. A Comprehensive
Atlas-EBook by the Egyptian Antiquities Information System. of the SCA)* I.
Ash-Sharqiyyah Governorate. Cahiers of Historical Sites, Cairo.

Amyx, D.A. 1988, *Corinthian Vase-painting of the Archaic Period* II,
Berkeley.

Andrews, C.A.R. 1981, *Catalogue of Egyptian Antiquities in the British
Museum*, III. *Jewellery* I, London.

Andrews, C.A.R. 1990, *Ancient Egyptian Jewellery*, London.

Andrews, C.A.R. 1994, *Amulets of Ancient Egypt*, London.

Angerstorfer, A. 2007, 'Hofni und Pinhas', in Bauks, M. and Koenen,
K. (eds), *Das wissenschaftlichen Bibellexikon im Internet (WiBiLex),
Alttestamentlicher Teil* [http://www.wibilex.de], 1–4.

[Anon.] 1882a, *Lower Egypt in 4 sheets* [Great Britain] Intelligence
Branch War Office, 1/200,000.

[Anon.] 1882b, *Carte de la Basse-Égypte dressée d'après les travaux de
l'expédition française de Linant Pasha et de Mahmud Bey pour le service de
l'administration des domaines affectés en garantie de l'emprunt contracté le 31
octobre 1878*, 1/400,000, Cairo.

[Anon.] 1886a (18 June), 'Pharaoh's house in Tahpanhes', *The London
Times*, London, 13.

[Anon.] 1886b (28 June), 'Mr. Petrie's discovery. A pharaoh's house
found in a corner of the Delta. The kitchen of the palace, the
butler's pantry, and the scullery – how the discovery came to be
made', *New York Times*, New York.

[Anon.] 1886c (3 July), 'Pharaoh's house in Tahpanhes', *The Evening
Post: New York*, New York, 3.

[Anon.] 1886d (10 July), 'A Pharaoh's house found in a corner of the
Delta', *The American Architect and Building News* 20/550, Boston, 22–3.

[Anon.] 1886e (August), 'The antiquary's note-book. Ancient Egypt
– remarkable discovery', *The Antiquary. A Magazine devoted to the Study
of the Past* 14, London, 81–3.

[Anon.] 1886f (7 August), 'Recent Egyptian research', *Saturday Review of
Politics, Literature, Science and Art* 62/1606, London, 189–90.

[Anon.] 1886g (11 August), 'Remarkable archaeological discovery', *The
Border Watch* 24/2373, Mount Gambier, 4.

[Anon.] 1886h (13 August), 'Pharaoh's house in Tahpanhes', *The Burra
Record. A Paper for the North and North-East*, Burra, 3.

[Anon.] 1886i (13 August), 'Great discoveries in Egypt', *The Northern
Argus* 18/1557, Clare, 4.

[Anon.] 1886j (14 August), 'Interesting archaeological discovery',
Launceston Examiner: Commercial and Agricultural Advertiser 46/193,
Launceston, 6.

[Anon.] 1886k (21 August), 'Pharaoh's house in Tahpanhes. The Egypt
Exploration Fund', *The South Australian Register* 51/12409, Adelaide,
4–6.

[Anon.] 1886gl (24 August), 'Pharaoh's house in Tahpanhes', *The Sydney Morning Herald* 15,105, Sydney, 3.

[Anon.] 1886m (27 August), 'Interesting items. Pharaoh's house', *The Mercury and Weekly Courier* 599, Collingwood and Fitzroy, 3.

[Anon.] 1886n (28 August), 'Notes on art and archaeology', *The Academy* 747, 142.

[Anon.] 1886o (1 September), 'Egyptian antiquities at Oxford Mansion', *The London Times*, London, 13.

[Anon.] 1886p (3 September), 'Recent discoveries in Egypt a witness to the truth of the Bible history', *The Kiama Independent and Shoalhaven Advertiser* 24/2484, Kiama, 3.

[Anon.] 1886q (4 September), 'The Egypt Exploration Fund. Annual exhibition of antiquities from sites in the Delta', *The Academy* 748, 158–9.

[Anon.] 1886r (4 September), *The Capricornian*, Rockhampton, 11.

[Anon.] 1886s (4 September), 'Recent notes from the land of Egypt', *Chambers's Journal of Popular Literature, Science and Arts* 140/3, London, Edinburgh, 564–7.

[Anon.] 1886t (4 September), 'Mr Petrie's collection', *Saturday Review of Politics, Literature, Science and Art* 62/1610, London, 329.

[Anon.] 1886u (8 September), 'Recent Egyptian research', *The Colonist* 28/4524, Nelson, 3–4.

[Anon.] 1886v (8 September), 'Pharaoh's house in Tahpanhes', *The Auckland Star* 17/211, Auckland, 3.

[Anon.] 1886w (18 September), 'Le château de Tahpanhès', *L'univers illustré* 29/1643, Paris, 602–6.

[Anon.] 1886x (27 September), 'Pharaoh's house', *Evening News*, Sydney, 3.

[Anon.] 1886y (29 September), 'Pharaoh's house', *The Budget* 1/39, Milburn, 3.

[Anon.] 1886z (4 October), 'Pharaoh's house. Ruins of a palace referred to by the prophet Jeremiah', *Aurora Daily Express* 1276, Aurora, 3.

[Anon.] 1886aa (9 October), 'Pharaoh's house in Tahpanhes', *The South Australian Weekly Chronicle* 29/1468, Adelaide, 16.

[Anon.] 1886bb (23 October), 'Pharaoh's house in Tahpanhes', *The Warwick Examiner and Times* 20/1314, Warwick, 5.

[Anon.] 1886cc (30 October), 'Recent notes from the land of Egypt', *Chambers's Journal of Popular Literature, Science and Arts* 140/3, London, Edinburgh, 703–4.

[Anon.] 1886dd (October), 'Notes of the quarter. V. Excerpta orientalia', *JRAS* 18/4, 550–68.

[Anon.] 1886ee (October), 'Notes on travels and exploration. Biblical remains in Egypt', *Dublin Review* 16/2, Dublin, 460–1.

[Anon.] 1886ff (20 November), 'Meeting of societies. Archaeological Institute (Thursday, Nov. 4)', *The Academy* 759, 350.

[Anon.] 1886gg (9 December), 'The Egypt Exploration Fund', *The London Times*, London, 7.

[Anon.] 1886hh (25 December), 'Egypt Exploration Fund', *The Academy* 764, 433–5.

[Anon.] 1887a (January), 'Meeting of antiquarian societies. Archaeological Institute', *The Antiquary. A Magazine Devoted to the Study of the Past* 15, London, 36.

[Anon.] 1887b (6 December), 'A Relic of antiquity', *The Kapunda Herald* 23/2024, Kapunda, 3.

[Anon.] 1887c (9 December), 'Miscellaneous', *The Northern Argus* 23/2024, Clare, 3.

[Anon.] 1888 (17 November), 'Tanis', *Saturday Review of Politics, Literature, Science and Art* 66/1725, London, 590–1.

[Anon.] 1894 (30 March), 'Kasr Bint el-Yehudi. The palace of the Jew's daughter', *Launceston Examiner: Commercial and Agricultural Advertiser* 54/76, Launceston, 3.

[Anon.] 1898, 'Extrait de l'inventaire du Musée de Ghizeh comprenant les objets entrés dans les collections du 1er janvier au 31 décembre 1897', *BIE* (3e série) 8, 279–306.

[Anon.] 1951, *Carte de l'isthme de Suez avant le percement du canal maritime*, 1/500,000, Société d'Études Historiques et Géographiques de l'Isthme de Suez.

Archaeology Data Service, http://archaeologydataservice.ac.uk/ archives/view/amphora_ahrb_2005/petrology.cfm?id=74&CFID =1640&CFTOKEN=F9E49875-0934-443A-BD86FA54DE245015 consulted 3 June 2011.

Arnaudiès, A. 2005, 'Transcription ou translittération? Propositions d'écriture des noms arabes égyptiens en archéologie', *Le Muséon* 118 3/4, 241–68.

Aston, D.A. 1999, *Pottery from the Late New Kingdom to the Early Ptolemaic period, Elephantine* 19, Mainz.

Aston, D.A. and Aston, B.G. 2010, *Late Period Pottery from the New Kingdom Necropolis at Saqqara. Egypt Exploration Society – National Museum of Antiquities, Leiden, Excavations 1975–1995*, London.

Audebeau, C. et al. 1897, *Carte de la Basse-Égypte et de la province du Fayoum*, 1/200,000, Cairo.

Audebeau Bey, Ch. 1919, 'Note sur l'affaissement du nord du Delta égyptien depuis l'empire romain', *BIE* 1 (Session 1918–1919), 117–34.

Austin, M.M. 1970, *Greece and Egypt in the Archaic Age*, *PCPS* 51, Suppl. 2.

Aytaçlar, M.N. 2006, 'South Ionian orientalizing style squat oinochoai', *Arkeoloji Dergisi* 7, Izmir, 51–68.

B., O. 1892 (November), 'Ten years digging' [Review of Petrie, W.M.F. 1892, *Ten Years Digging*, London], *Wesleyan-Methodist Magazine*, London, 829–35.

Bäbler, B. 2004, *Archäologie und Chronologie. Eine Einführung*, Darmstadt.

Badger, G.P. 1862, *A Visit to the Isthmus of Suez Canal Works, Foreign and Commonwealth Office Collection*, London.

Baedeker, K. (ed.) 1885, *Egypt. Handbook for Travellers* I. *Lower Egypt, with the Fayûm and the Peninsula of Sinai*, Leipzig and London.

Baedeker, K. (ed.) 1928, *Ägypten und der Sudan. Handbuch für Reisende* (8th edn), Leipzig.

Baer, C. (ed.) 2007, *Thomas Aquinas. Commentaries on St. Paul's Epistles to Timothy, Titus, and Philemon*, South Bend.

Bailey, D. 2006, 'The Apries amphora – another cartouche', in Villing and Schlotzhauer 2006, 155–7.

Bailey, D.M., 2008, *Catalogue of Terracottas in the British Museum* IV. *Ptolemaic and Roman Terracottas from Egypt*, London.

Bakr, M.I. and Kalloniatis, F.H. 2010, *Egyptian Antiquities from Kufur Nigm and Bubastis*, Berlin.

Ball, Rev. C.J. 1889 (7 May), 'Inscriptions of Nebuchadrezzar the Great. XI. The Nin-Mag cylinders', *PSBA* 11, 248–53.

Ball, J. 1942, *Egypt in the Classical Geographers*, Cairo.

Barbara, S. 2012, 'Armées en marche et découvertes herpétologiques dans l'Antiquité', *Anthropozoologica* 47/1, Paris, 15–50.

Bass, G. F., 1987, 'Oldest known shipwreck reveals splendors of the Bronze Age', *National Geographic* 172, 693–734.

Baud, M. 2010, 'La maison du roi: le palais', in Baud, M. (ed.), *Méroé. Un empire sur le Nil*, Paris, 241–5.

Baud, M. 2011, 'Premières données sur le palais royal de Mouweis', in Rondot, V., Alpi, F. and Villeneuve, F. (eds), *La pioche et la plume. Autour du Soudan, du Liban et de la Jordanie. Hommages archéologiques à Patrice Lenoble*, Paris, 339–57.

Baurain, C. 1997, *Les Grecs et la Méditerranée orientale. Des 'siècles obscurs' à la fin de l'époque archaïque*, Paris.

Béal, J.C. 1983, *Catalogue des objets de tabletterie de la civilisation gallo-romaine de Lyon, Centre d'études romaines et gallo-romaines de l'université Jean Moulin Lyon III*, N.S. 1, Lyon.

Béal, J.C. 1984, 'Les objets de tabletterie antique du Musée archéologique de Nîmes', *Cahier des musées et monuments de Nîmes* 2, Nîmes, 89–90.

Beecher, W.J. 1889 (July), 'The postexilic history of Israel. I.', *The Old and New Testament Student* 9/1, New York, 29–36.

Berchère, N. 1863, *Le désert de Suez: cinq mois dans l'isthme*, Paris.

Bernand, A. 2000, 'Map 74 Delta', in Talbert, R.J.A. (ed.), *Barrington Atlas of the Greek and Roman World. Map by-Map Directory* 2, Princeton and Oxford, 1117–24.

Besques, S. 1986, *Catalogue raisonné des figurines et reliefs en terre-cuite grecs, étrusques et romains* 4/1. *Époques hellénistique et romaine. Italie méridionale – Sicile – Sardaigne*, Paris.

Betro, M.C., Belli, G., Costa, B. and Giaconi, M. 1982, 'Mito e propaganda in età tolemaica', *EVO* 5, 35–9.

Bettalli, M. 1995, *I mercenari nel mondo Greco* I. *Dalle origine alla fine del V. siecolo aC, Studi e testi di storia antica* 5, Pise.

Biberstein Kazimirski, (de) A. 1860, *Dictionnaire arabe-français contenant toutes les racines de la langue arabe* I, Paris.

Bierbrier, M.L. 2012, *Who Was Who in Egyptology* (4th edn), London.

Bietak, M. 1975, *Tell el-Dab'a* II. *Der Fundort im Rahmen einer archäologisch-geographischen Untersuchung über das ägyptische Ostdelta*, DÖAWW 4.

Bietak, M. (ed.) 2003, *The Synchronisation of Civilisations in the Eastern Mediterranean in the Second Millennium BC* II. *Proceedings of the SCIEM 2000 Euro-Conference, Haindorf, 2nd–7th May 2001. CCEM* 4, DÖAWW 29.

Bietak, M. 2005, 'Neue Paläste aus der 18. Dynastie', in Jánosi, P. (ed.), *Structure and Significance. Thoughts on Ancient Egyptian Architecture*, DÖAAW 33, 131–68.

Bietak, M. 2007, 'Où est le palais des Hyksôs? À propos des fouilles à Tell el-Dabʿa et Ezbet Helmi', *CRAIBL*, 749–80.

Bietak, M. 2010, 'Houses, palaces and development of social structure in Avaris', in Bietak, Czerny and Forster-Müller 2010, 11–68.

Bietak, M., Czerny, E. and Forster-Müller, I. (eds), *Cities and Urbanism in Ancient Egypt, Papers from a Workshop in November 2006 at the Austrian Academy of Sciences*, UZK 35, DÖAWW 60.

Bietak, M. and Forstner-Müller, I. 2003, 'Ausgrabung im Palastbezirk von Avaris. Vorbericht Tell el-Dabʿa/ʿEzbet Helmi Frühjahr 2003', *ÄL* 13, 39–50.

Bietak, M. and Forstner-Müller, I. 2005, 'Ausgrabung eines Palastbezirkes der Tuthmosidenzeit bei ʿEzbet Helmi/Tell el-Dabʿa, Vorbericht für Herbst 2004 und Frühjahr 2005', *ÄL* 15, 65–100.

Bietak, M. and Forstner-Müller, I. 2007, 'Ausgrabung eines Palastbezirkes der Tuthmosidenzeit bei ʿEzbet Helmi/Tell el-Dabʿa, Vorbericht für das Frühjahr 2007', *ÄL* 17, 33–58.

Billerbeck, M. and Zubler, C. (eds), *Stephani Byzantii Ethnica* II. *Corpus Fontium Historiae Byzantinae* 43/2, Berlin and New York.

Birchall, A. 1972, 'Attic horse-head amphorae', *JHS* 92, 46–63.

Bîrzescu, J. 2012, *Histria* XV. *Die archaischen und frühklassischen Transportamphoren*, Bucarest.

Bissing (von), F.W. 1901, *Nos 3426–3587. Metalgefässe*, CGC, Vienna.

Bissing (von), F.W. 1902, *Nos 3618–4000, 18001–18037, 18600, 18603. Fayencegefässe*, CGC, Vienna.

Bissing (von), F.W. 1903, 'Die griechisch-römischen Altertümer im Museum zu Kairo', *AA*, 145–51.

Bissing (von), F.W. 1923–4, 'Untersuchungen über die "phoinikischen" Metallschälen', *JDAI* 38–9, 180–241.

Bissing (von), F.W. 1949 (January), 'Forschungen zur Geschichte und kulturellen Bedeutung der griechischen Kolonie Naukratis in Agypten', *FuF* 25/1, 1–2.

Bissing (von), F.W. 1951, 'Naukratis', *BSRAA* 39, 33–82.

Björkman, G. 1971, *A Selection of the Objects in the Smith Collection of Egyptian Antiquities at the Linköping Museum, Sweden*, Stockholm.

Blanchard, H. 1909, *Handbook of the Egyptian Gods and Mummy Amulets*, Cairo.

Blanquet, C.H. 1992, 'Typologie de la bouteille de Nouvel An', in Obsomer, C. and Oosthoek, A.L. (eds), *Amosiadès. Mélanges offerts au Professeur Claude Vandersleyen par ses anciens étudiants*, Louvain, 49–54.

Boardman, J. 1998, *Early Greek Vase Painting*, London.

Boardman, J. 1999, *Greeks Overseas. Their Early Colonies and Trade* (4th edn), London.

Boardman, J. 2003, *Classical Phoenician Scarabs. A Catalogue and Study*, BAR-IS 1190.

Böhm, S. 1990, *Die 'Nackte Göttin'. Zur Ikonographie und Deutung unbekleideter weiblicher Figuren in der frühgriechischen Kunst*, Mainz.

Bommas, M. 2005, 'Situlae and the offering of water in the divine funerary cult: A new approach to the ritual of Djeme', in Amenta, A., Luiselli, M.M. and Novella Sordi, M. (eds), 'L'acqua nell'antico Egitto. Vita, Rigenerazione, incantesimo, medicamento', *Proceedings of the First International Conference for Young Egyptologists, Italy, Chianciano Therme, 15–18 October 2003*, Rome, 257–72.

Bonnet, C. 1987, 'Typhon et Baal Saphon', in Lipiński, E. (ed.), *Studia Phoenica V. Phoenicia and the East Mediterranean in the First Millenium B.C.*, OLA 22, 101–43.

Bonwetsch, G.N. and Richard, M. (eds) 2000, *Hippolyt, Werke* I.1. *Kommentar zu Daniel*, GCS Neue Folge 7.

Borchardt, L. 1930, *Nos 1–1294. Statuen und Statuetten von Königen und Privatleuten* III, CGC, Cairo.

Borghouts, J. 1986, *Nieuwjaar in het oude Egypte*, Leiden.

Bourguignon d'Anville, J.-B. 1766, *Mémoires sur l'Égypte ancienne et moderne, suivis d'une description du Golfe Arabique ou de la Mer Rouge*, Paris.

Bourriau J. and Aston, D.A. 1985, 'The pottery', in Martin, G.T., *The Tomb-Chapels of Paser and Raia at Saqqara*, London, 32–55.

Bouteron, E. and Chekib Pasha, S.E. 1888, *Carte de la Basse-Égypte*, 1/200,000, Cairo; ibid., 1/400,000, Cairo.

Bowers Peterson, S. 2006, *The Cult of Dushara and the Roman Annexation of Nabataea*, PhD thesis, McMaster University, Hamilton.

Brady, M. 2005, 'Biblical interpretation in the pseudo-Ezekiel fragments (4Q383-391)', in Henze, M. (ed.), *Biblical Interpertation at Qumran, Studies in the Dead Sea Scrolls and Related Literature*, Grand Rapids, 88–109.

Brandl, B. 1984, 'The engraved tridacna-shell discs', *AnatStud* 34, 15–41.

Braude, W.G. (ed.) 1968, *Pesikta Rabbati. Discourses for Feasts, Fasts, and Special Sabbaths* I, Yale Judaica Series 18, New Haven and London.

Braun, T.F.R.G. 1982, 'The expansion of the Greek world. VIIIth to VIth Century BC', *CAH* III/3, 32–56.

Braun T., 2004, 'Spines of winged snakes', in Karageorghis, V. and Taifacos, I. (eds), *The World of Herodotus. Proceedings of an International Conference held at the Foundation Anastasios G. Leventis, Nicosia, September 18–21 2003*, Nicosia, 265–85.

Brissaud, P. 1991, 'Répertoire préliminaire de la poterie trouvée a Sân el-Hagar (1ère partie)', *CCE* 1, 77–80.

Brissaud, P. and Zivie-Coche, C. (eds) 1998, *Tanis. Travaux récents sur le Tell Sân el-Hagar. MFFT 1987–1997*, Paris.

Brommer, F. 1984, 'Themenwahl aus örtlichen Gründen', in Brijder, H.A.G. (ed.), *Ancient Greek and Related Pottery. Proceedings of the International Vase Symposium in Amsterdam, 12–15 April 1984*, Amsterdam, 178–84.

Brooks, W.A. 1860 (1 July), 'The isthmus of Suez navigation project, considered in reference to the physical impediments to its realization', *The Civil Engineer and Architect's Journal* 23, London, 197–200.

Brown, F. 1886 (October–December), 'Notes on biblical archaeology', *AJA* 2/4, 428–32.

Brown, F. 1887, 'Recent explorations in Egypt', *Journal of the American Geographical Society of New York* 19, New York, 164–93.

Brownlee, A.B. 1989, 'A black-figure parody of the ransom of Hector', *RevArch* 3–21.

Brugsch, H. 1879, *Dictionnaire géographique de l'ancienne Égypte* I, Leipzig.

Brunner-Traut, E. 1981, *Die Ägyptische Sammlung der Universität Tübingen*, Mainz.

Brunner-Traut, E. and Brunner, H. 1984, *Osiris, Kreuz und Halbmond. Die drei Religionen Ägyptens*, Mainz.

Budge, E.A.W. 1920, *An Egyptian Dictionary* II, London.

Bürchner L. 1903, 'Daphne', *RealEnc Suppl.* I, 338.

Calderini, A. 1966, *Dizionario dei nomi geografici e topografici dell'Egitto greco-romano* I/2, Madrid.

Calderini, A. [Daris, S.] 1973, *Dizionario dei nomi geografici e topografici dell'Egitto greco-romano* II/2, Milan.

Calmet, A. 1714, *Commentaire littéral sur tous les livres de l'Ancien et du Nouveau Testament. Jérémie et Baruch*, Paris.

Calmet, A. 1715, *Commentaire littéral sur tous les livres de l'Ancien et du Nouveau Testament. Ézéchiel et Daniel*, Paris.

Calmet, A., 1722, *Dictionnaire historique, critique, chronologique, géographique et littéral de la Bible* II, Paris.

Caminos, R.A. 1954, *Late-Egyptian Miscellanies*, London.

Canby, J.V. 1979, 'The jewelry of ancient Egypt', in Garside, A. (ed.), *Jewelry: Ancient to Modern. A Studio Book*, New York, 20–51.

Capel, A.K. and Markoe, G.E. (eds) 1996, *Mistress of the House, Mistress of Heaven, Women in Ancient Egypt*, Cincinatti.

Carrez-Maratray, J.Y. 1999, *Péluse et l'angle oriental du delta égyptien aux époques grecque, romaine et byzantine*, BdE 124.

Carrez-Maratray, J.Y. 2000, 'Le "monopole de Naucratis" et la "bataille de Péluse": ruptures ou continuités de la présence grecque en Égypte des Saïtes aux Perses', *Transeuphratène* 19, 159–72.

Carrez-Maratray, J.Y. 2005–6, 'L'archéologie du Delta oriental. Bilans et persepctives', *BSAC* 38, 194–204.

Carrez-Maratray, J.Y. and Defernez, C. 2012, 'L'angle oriental du Delta: les Grecs avant Alexandre', in Ballet, P. (ed.), *Grecs et Romains en Égypte. Territoires, espaces de la vie et de la mort, objets de prestige et du quotidien*, BdE 157, 31–46.

Caubet, A. and Pierrat-Bonnefois, G. (eds) 2005, *Faïences de l'Antiquité. De l'Égypte à l'Iran, Catalogue de l'exposition du Musée du Louvre 10 juin–12 septembre 2005*, Paris.

Cenival (de), F. and Yoyotte, J.† 2012, 'Le papyrus démotique CG 31169 du Musée du Caire', in Zivie-Coche, C. and Guermeur, I. (eds), 'Parcourir l'éternité'. Hommages à Jean Yoyotte, BEHE (Sciences religieuses) 156/1, Turnhout, 239–79.

Champollion, J.-F. 1814, *L'Égypte sous les pharaons ou recherches sur la géographie, la religion, la langue, les Écritures et l'Histoire de l'Égypte avant l'invasion de Cambyse* II, Paris, 1814.

Chaparro Gomez, C. (ed.) 1985, *Isidorus Hispalensis. De ortu et obitu Patrum*, Paris.

Chappaz, J.L. 1982, 'Une stèle de donation de l'an 21 de Ioupout II au Musée d'Art et d'Histoire', *Genava* 30, 71–81.

Charles, R.H. 1916, *The Chronicle of John (c. 690 A.D.), Coptic Bishop of Nikiu*, London.

Charvet, P. and Yoyotte, J. (eds) 1997, *Strabon. Le voyage en Égypte. Un regard romain*, Paris.

Chauveau, M. 2011, 'Le saut dans le temps d'un document historique: des Ptolémées aux Saïtes', in Devauchelle 2011, 39–46.

Chester, G.J. 1880 (July), 'A journey to the biblical sites in Lower Egypt – From Sân to El Arîsh', *PEFQS*, 144–58.

Christies 2012, *Antiquities Auction 2605 – 5th December 2012*, New York.

Chuvin, P. and Yoyotte, J. 1986, 'Documents relatifs au culte pélusien de Zeus Casios', *RevArch*, 41–63.

Clédat, J. 1909, 'Notes sur l'isthme de Suez, I – Kantarah', *RT* 31, 113–20.

Clédat, J. 1923, 'Notes sur l'isthme de Suez (suite)', *BIFAO* 21, 55–106.

Clédat, J. 1924, 'Notes sur l'isthme de Suez (suite)', *BIFAO* 23, 27–84.

Colin, G. 1995, 'L'Égypte pharaonique dans la Chronique de Jean, évêque de Nikiou', *RdE* 46, 43–54.

Colin, F. 2011, 'Le 'Domaine d'Amon' à Bahariya de la XVIIIe à la XXVIᵉ dynastie: l'apport des fouilles de Qasr 'Allam', in Devauchelle 2011, 47–84.

Contardi, F. 2009, 'Tachpanhes', in Bauks, M. and Koenen, K. (eds), *Das wissenschaftliche Bibellexikon im Internet (WiBiLex), Alttestamentlicher Teil* (http://www.wibilex.de), 1–4.

Cook, R.M. 1933–4, 'Fikellura Pottery', *ABSA* 34, 1–91.

Cook, R.M. 1937, 'Amasis and the Greeks in Egypt', *JHS* 57, 227–37.

Cook, R.M. 1954, *CVA. Great Britain 13, British Museum 8*, Oxford.

Cook, R.M. and Dupont, P. 1998, *East Greek Pottery*, London.

Cooney, J. 1976., *Catalogue of Egyptian Antiquities in the British Museum IV. Glass*, London.

Corteggiani, J.-P. 1973, 'Documents divers. I-VI, *BIFAO* 73, 143–53.

Coulson, W.D.E. and Leonard, A. 1982, *Cities of the Delta I. Naukratis*, ARCER.

Cour-Marty, M.A. 1989, *Les poids dans l'Égypte ancienne*, PhD, Uni. of Paris IV (unpublished).

Coutellier, V. and Stanley, D.J. 1987, 'Late Quaternary stratigraphy and paleogeography of the eastern Nile delta, Egypt', *Marine Geology* 77, 257–75.

Coutts, H. 1988, *Gold of the Pharaohs*, Edinburgh.

Crum, W.E. 1917, 'The Chronicle of John, bishop of Nikiu, Translated from Zotenberg's Ethiopic text by R.H. Charles', *JEA* 4, 207–9.

Daressy, G. 1890, 'Notes et remarques. LXXXVI', *RT* 14, 185.

Daressy, G. 1906, *Nos 38001–39384. Statues de Divinités*, CGC, Cairo.

Daressy, G. 1910–11, 'La liste géographique du papyrus no. 31169 du Caire', *Sphinx* 14, 155–71.

Daressy, G. 1915, 'L'eau dans l'Égypte antique', *MIE* 8, 201–14.

Daressy, G. 1928 (December), 'Les branches du Nil sous la XVIIIᵉ dynastie', *BSRGE* 16/3, 225–54.

Daressy, G. 1929 (June), 'Les branches du Nil sous la XVIIIᵉ dynastie', *BSRGE* 16/4, 293–329.

Daressy, G. 1930 (May), 'Les branches du Nil sous la XVIIIᵉ dynastie', *BSRGE* 17/2, 81–115.

Daressy, G. 1931 (March), 'Les branches du Nil sous la XVIIIᵉ dynastie', *BSRGE* 17/3, 189–223.

Daressy, G. 1933 (July), 'Les branches du Nil sous la XVIIIᵉ dynastie', *BSRGE* 18/2, 169–202.

Daris, S. 1996, *Dizionario dei nomi geografici e topografici dell'Egitto greco-romano, Suppl. 2 (1987–93)*, Pisa, Rome.

Daris, S. 2007, *Dizionario dei nomi geografici e topografici dell'Egitto greco-romano, Suppl. 4 (2002–5)*, Pisa, Rome.

Dasen, V. 2000, 'Squatting komasts and scarab-beetles' in Tsetskhladze, G.R., Prag, A.N.J.W. and Snodgrass, A.M. (eds), *Periplous, Papers on Classical Art and Archaeology Presented to Sir John Boardman*, London, 89–97.

Davey, C.J. 1979, 'Some ancient Near-Eastern pot bellows', *Levant* 11, 101–11.

Davidson, P.F. and Andrew, O. 1984, *Ancient Greek and Roman Gold Jewelry in the Brooklyn Museum*, Brooklyn.

Defernez, C. 1997, 'La céramique préptolémaïque de Tell el-Herr', in *CRIPEL* 5, 57–70.

Defernez, C. 2001, *La céramique d'époque perse à Tell el-Herr: étude chrono-typologique et comparative, CRIPEL Suppl. 5/1–2*.

Delange, E. 2007, 'The complexity of alloys: new discoveries about certain bronzes in the Louvre', in Hill and Schorsch 2007, 39–49.

Delange, É. (ed.) 2012, *Les fouilles françaises d'Éléphantine (Assouan), 1906–1911. Les archives Clermont-Ganneau et Clédat*, Paris.

Demaria, S. 2006, 'Der koptische Kambyses Roman', in Panaino, A. and Piras, A. (eds), *Proceedings of the 5th conference of the Societas Iranologica Europæa held in Ravenna, 5–11th October 2003 I. Ancient and Middle Iranian Studies*, Milan, 65–74.

De Meulenaere, H. 1951, *Herodotos over de 26ste dynastie (II, 147-III, 15). Bijdrage tot het historisch-kritisch onderzoek van Herodotos' gegevens in het licht van de Egyptische en andere contemporaire bronnen, BiMus 27*.

De Meulenaere, H. 1964, Trois empreintes de sceaux', *CdE* 39, 25–30.

De Meulenaere, H. 1975, 'Daphne', *LÄ*, I, 990.

Den Brinker, A.A., Muhs, B.P. and Vleeming, S.P. (eds) 2005, *A Berichtigungsliste of Demotic Documents, StudDem 7*.

De Rodrigo, A.D. 2004, 'Basket-handled jars: their origin and function,' in Redford 2004, 211–20.

Desplaces, E. 1861a (June), 'Les travaux du canal de Suez à vol d'oiseau', *L'isthme de Suez. Journal de l'union des deux mers* 119, Paris, 190–2.

Desplaces, E. 1861b (July), 'Chronique de l'isthme', *L'isthme de Suez. Journal de l'union des deux mers* 121, Paris, 211–13.

Desplaces, E. 1861c (December), 'Lettres sur les travaux de l'isthme', *L'isthme de Suez. Journal de l'union des deux mers* 132, Paris, 395–400.

Desplaces, E. 1866 (15–18 June), 'Les antiquités de l'Égypte', *L'isthme de Suez. Journal de l'union des deux mers* 239, Paris, 183–7.

Destrooper-Georgiades, A. 1995, 'An unusual coin from Side', *Νομισματικα Χρονικα* 14, 13–20.

Devauchelle, D. 2005, 'Tahpanhès', *SDB* 13/75, 875–80.

Devauchelle, D. (ed.), 2001, *La XXVIe dynastie. Continuités et ruptures. Promenade saïte avec Jean Yoyotte*, Paris.

Dhennin, S. and Redon, B. 2013 (Autumn), 'Plinthine on Lake Mareotis', *EgArch* 43, 36–8.

Di Berardino, A. (ed.) 1988, *Dizionario patristico e di antichità cristiane 3. Atlante patristico. Indici*, Genova.

Dickerman, L. 1890 (May), 'Mr Petrie's discoveries at the biblical Tahpanes', *The Old and New Testament Student* 10/5, Chicago, 279–81.

Diderot, D. 1765, *Encyclopédie ou dictionnaire raisonné des sciences, des arts et des métiers* 15, Paris.

Dillery, J. 2005 (December), 'Cambyses and the Egyptian Chaosbeschreibung tradition', *ClassQuart* 55/2, 387–406.

Dimant, D. 1994, 'An apocryphon of Jeremiah from Cave 4 (4Q385B –4Q385 16)', in Brooke, G.J. (ed.), *New Qumran Texts and Studies, Proceedings of the First Meeting of the International Organization for Qumran Studies, Paris 1992*, Studies on the Texts of the Desert of Judah 15, Leiden, 11–30.

Dimant, D. 2001, *Qumran Cave 4. XXI. Parabiblical Texts 4. Pseudo-Prophetic Texts*, Discoveries in the Judaean Desert 30, Oxford.

Döpp, S. 2003, 'Kambyses' Feldzug gegen Ägypten: Der sogenannte Kambyses-Roman und sein Verhältnis zu griechischer Literatur', *Göttinger Forum für Altertumswissenschaft* 6, Göttingen, 1–17 (http://www.gfa.d-r.de/603/doepp.pdf).

Donner, H. 1979, *Pilgerfahrt ins Heilige Land, Die ältesten Berichte christlicher Palästinapilger (4.-7. Jahrhundert)*, Stuttgart.

Donner, H. 1983, 'Das Nildelta auf der Mosaikkarte von Madeba', in Görg, M. (ed.), *Fontes atque pontes: Eine Festgabe für Hellmut Brunner*, ÄAT 5, 75–89.

Donner, H. 1992, *The Mosaic Map of Madaba*, Palestina Antiqua 7, Kampen.

Donner, H. and Röllig, W. 1966, *Kanaanäische und aramäische Inschriften I. Texte*, (2nd edn), Wiesbaden.

Donner, H. and Röllig, W. 1968, *Kanaanäische und aramäische Inschriften II. Kommentar* (2nd edn), Wiesbaden.

Doxiadis, E. 1995, *The Mysterious Fayum Portraits, Faces from Ancient Egypt*, London.

Dozy, R. and de Goeje, M.J. (eds) 1886, *Muhammad al-Idrisi, Description de l'Afrique et de l'Espagne*, Leiden.

Droste zu Hülshoff (von), V., Hofmann, E., Schlick-Nolte, B. and Seidlmayer, S. 1991, *Statuetten, Gefässe und Geräte. Liebighaus – Museum alter Plastik. Ägyptische Bildwerke 2*, Melsungen.

Drower, M.S. 1995, *Flinders Petrie: A Life in Archaeology* (2nd edn), London.

Drower, M.S. (ed.) 2004, *Letters from the Desert. The Correspondence of Flinders and Hilda Petrie*, Oxford.

Dubois, J. (ed.) 1965, *Le Martyrologe d'Usuard. Texte et commentaire*, Subsidia Hagiographica 40, Brussels.

Ducat, J. 1963, 'Les vases plastiques corinthiens', *BCH* 87/2, 431–58.

Dümichen, J. 1894, *Zur Geographie des alten Ägyptens*, Lepizig.

Dümmler, F. 1895, 'Zu den griechischen Vasen von Tell Defenneh', *JDAI* 10, 35–46.

Dunham, D. 1955, *Royal Cemeteries of Kush* II: *Nuri*. Boston.

Dunham, D. 1963, *Royal Cemeteries of Kush* V: *The West and South Cemeteries at Meroe*. Boston.

Dupont, P. and Thomas, A. 2006, 'Naukratis: Les importations grecques orientales archaïques. Classification et détermination d'origine en laboratoire', in Villing and Schlotzhauer 2006, 77–84.

Dusinberre, E.R.M. 2003, *Aspects of Empire in Achaemenid Sardis*, Cambridge.

Edgar, M.C.C. 1904a, *Nos 27631–28000 et 32368–32376. Greek Bronzes*, CGC, Cairo.

Edgar, M.C.C. 1904b, *Nos 27425–27630. Greek Sculpture*, CGC, Cairo.

Edgar, M.C.C. 1906, *Nos 33301–33506. Sculptor's Studies and Unfinished Works*, CGC, Cairo.

Edgerton, W.F., 1937, *Medinet Habu Graffiti Facsimiles*, OIP 36.

Edwards, I.E.S. and James, T.G.H. 1984, 'Egypt', in Boardman, J. (ed.), *CAH. Plates to Volume III* (2nd edn), Cambridge.

Embabi, N.S. 2004, *The Geomorphology of Egypt. Landforms and Evolution* I. *The Nile Valley and the Western Desert*, Cairo.

Empereur, J.Y. 2002, 'Les Grecs en Égypte', in Karageorghis, V. (ed.), *The Greeks beyond the Aegean: from Marseilles to Bactria: Papers Presented at an International Symposium Held at the Onassis Cultural Center, New York, 12th October 2002*, New York, 23–42.

Engelbach, R. 1931, *Index of Egyptian and Sudanese Sites from which the Cairo Museum Contains Antiquities*, Cairo.

Erichsen, W. 1956, *Eine neue demotische Erzählung*, AAW Mainz 2.

Erman, A. 1890 (19 July), 'Der Egypt Exploration Fund und seine Arbeiten. Tell Defenneh', *BPW* 29/30, 959–60.

Fantalkin, A. 2001, 'Meẓad Ḥashavyahu: its material culture and historical background', *Tel Aviv* 28/1.

Favard-Meeks, C. 1998, 'Mise à jour des ouvrages de Flinders Petrie sur les fouilles de Tanis', in Brissaud and Zivie-Coche 1998, 101–78.

Fay, B. 1990, *Ancient Egyptian Jewelry in the Collection of the Verein zur Förderung des Ägyptisches Museums in Berlin-Charlottenburg e.V.*, Mainz.

Fazzini, R. 2001, 'Four unpublished ancient Egyptian objects in faience in the Brooklyn Museum of Art', *JSSEA* 28, 55–66.

Felder, E.C. 1988a, *Die ägyptischen Pilger- und Neujahrsflaschen und ihre Sonderformen. Inaugural-Dissertation zur Erlangung des Doktorgrades der Philosophie an den Freien Universität Berlin*, Berlin.

Felder, E.C. 1988b, *Die ägyptischen Pilger- und Neujahrsflaschen und ihre Sonderformen, Katalog II. Neujahrflaschen und Amulette*, unpublished PhD, Freien Universität Berlin.

Fiema, Z.T. and Jones, R.N. 1990, 'The Nabatean king-list revised: further observations on the second Nabataean inscription from Tell esh-Shuqafiyah, Egypt', *ADAJ* 34, 239–48.

Figueras, P. 2000, *From Gaza to Pelusium. Materials for the Historical Geography of North Sinai and Southwestern Palestine (332 BCE–640 CE)*, Beer-Sheva Studies by the Department of Bible and Ancient Near East 14, Beer-Sheva.

Fontaine, A.L. 1948, 'Daphnæ', *BSEHGIS* 1 (1947), 41–57.

Fontaine, A.L. 1955, *Monographie cartographique de l'isthme de Suez, de la péninsule du Sinaï, du nord de la chaîne arabique, suivie d'un catalogue raisonné sur les cartes de ces régions*, MSES 2.

Forstner-Müller, I. 2010, 'Settlement patterns at Avaris, a study on two cases', in Bietak, Czerny and Forstner-Müller 2010, 103–24.

Fortia d'Urban, A.J. 1845, *Recueil des itinéraires anciens*, Paris.

Foucart, G. 1901, 'Extraits des rapports adressés pendant une inspection de la Basse-Égypte en 1893–1894', *ASAE* 2, 44–83.

Frankfort, H. and Pendlebury, J.D.S. 1933, *The City of Akhenaten* II. *The North Suburb and the Desert Altars*, London.

Freeman-Grenville, G.S.P., Chapman III, R.L. and Taylor, J. (eds) 2003, *Palestine in the Fourth Century A.D. The Onomasticon by Eusebius of Cesarea*, Jerusalem.

French, P. 2004, 'Distinctive pottery from the second half of the sixth century BC', *CCE* 7, 91–8.

Friedman, F. 1998, *Gifts of the Nile: Ancient Egyptian Faience*, London.

Frothingham Jr, A.L. 1886 (October–December), 'Archaeological news. Summary of recent discoveries and investigations', *The American Journal of Archaeology and of the History of the Fine Arts* 2/4, Baltimore, 460–506.

Frothingham Jr, A.L. 1889 (March), [Review of W.M.F. Petrie, *Tanis II – Nebesheh (Am) and Defenneh (Tahpanhes)*, London, 1888], *The American Journal of Archaeology and of the History of the Fine Arts* 5/1, 51–4.

Fry, C. (ed.) 2010, *Lettres croisées de Jérôme et Augustin*, Paris.

Fürst, A. (ed.) 2002, *Augustinus – Hieronymus. Epistulae mutuae. Briefwechsel. Lateinisch Deutsch*, Fontes Christiani 41, Turnhout.

Furtwängler, A. 1890 (19 July), [Review of 'W.Fl. Petrie, *Tanis* II - *Nebesheh (Am) and Defenneh (Tahpanhes)*, London, 1888]', *BPW* 29/30, 917–21.

Furtwängler, A.E., 2011, 'Tridacna – Warum auch nicht mal griechisch?', in Pilz, O. and Vonderstein, M. (eds) *Keraunia. Beiträge zu Mythos, Kult und Heiligtum in der Antike*, Beiträge zur Altertumskunde 298, Berlin, Boston and Göttingen, 47–51.

Gardiner, A.H. 1937, *Late-Egyptian Miscellanies*, Brussels.

Gardiner, A.H. 1941, 'Ramesside texts relating to the taxation and transport of corn', *JEA* 27, 19–73.

Gardiner, A.H. 1948, *The Wilbour Papyrus* III, London.

Gardner, E.A. 1888, *Naukratis* II, London.

Gardner, E.A. 1889, 'Early Greek vases and African colonies', *JHS* 10, 126–33.

Garstang, J. 1911, *Meroe, The City of the Ethiopians*, Oxford.

Gascoigne, A.L. 2007, 'The water supply of Tinnis. Public amenities and private investments', in Gascoigne, A.L. and Bennison, A.K., *Cities in the Pre-Modern Islamic World. The Urban Impact of Religion, State and Society*, Abingdon, 161–76.

Gassner, V. 2003, *Materielle Kultur and Kulturelle Identität Eleas in spätarchaisch-frühklassischer Zeit. Untersuchungen zur Gefäss-und Baukeramik aus der Unterstadt (Grabungen 1987–1993)*, Archäologische Forschungen 8, Velia-Studien II, Vienna.

Gaster, M. (ed.) 1899, *The Chronicles of Jerahmeel*, London.

Gauthier, H. 1925a, *Dictionnaire des noms géographiques contenus dans les textes hiéroglyphiques* 1, Cairo.

Gauthier, H. 1925b, *Dictionnaire des noms géographiques contenus dans les textes hiéroglyphiques* 2, Cairo.

Gauthier, H. 1926, *Dictionnaire des noms géographiques contenus dans les textes hiéroglyphiques* 3, Cairo.

Gauthier, H. 1927, *Dictionnaire des noms géographiques contenus dans les textes hiéroglyphiques* 4, Cairo.

Gauthier, H. 1929, *Dictionnaire des noms géographiques contenus dans les textes hiéroglyphiques* 6, Cairo.

Gilmore, G. and Ray, J. 2006, 'A fixed point in Coptic chronology: the solar eclipse of 10 March, 601', *ZPE* 158, 190–2.

Gingras, G.E. 1970, *Egeria: Diary of a Pilgrimage*, Ancient Christian Writers 38, New York.

Giveon, R. 1985, *Egyptian Scarabs from Western Asia from the Collections of the British Museum*, OBO series archeologica 3.

Glanville, S.R.K. 1955, *The Instructions of 'Onchscheschonqy (British Museum Papyrus 10508). Catalogue of Demotic Papyri in the British Museum*, London.

Glorie, F. 1964, *S. Hieronymi Presbyteri Opera* I. *Opera Exegetica* 4. *Commentariorum in Hiezechielem Libri XIV*, CCSL 75.

Godley, A.D. (ed.) 1920, *Herodotus The Persian Wars. Book 1–2*, LCL 117.

Golb, N. 1965, 'Topography of the Jews of Medieval Egypt: inductive studies based primarily upon documents from the Cairo Genizah', *JNES* 24, 251–70.

Görg, M. 1999, 'Tachpanhes – eine prominente judäische Adresse in Ägypten', *BiblNot* 97, 24–30.

Görg, M. 2001, 'Pinhas', in Görg, M. and Lang, B. (eds), *Neues Bibellexikon* 3, 151.

Górka, K. and Rzepka, S. 2011, 'Infant burials or infant sacrifices. New discoveries from Tell el-Retaba', *MDAIK* 67, 93–100.

Grace, V.R. 1971, 'Samian amphoras', *Hesperia* 40, 52–95.

Grataloup, C. 2010, 'Occupation and trade at Heracleion-Thonis', in Robinson, D. and Wilson, A. (eds), *Alexandria and the North-western Delta. Joint Conference Proceedings of Alexandria: City and Harbour (Oxford 2004) and The Trade and Topography of Egypt's North-West Delta (Berlin 2006)*, Oxford Centre for Maritime Archaeology Monograph 5, Oxford, 151–9.

Gratien, B. 1997, 'Tell el-Herr: sondage stratigraphique', *CCE* 5, 71–80.

Grene, D. (ed.) 1987, *Herodotus. The History*, Chicago, London.

Gressmann, H. 1927, *Altorientalische Bilder zum Alten Testament*, Berlin.

Griffith, F.Ll. 1886, 'Report on Tell Nebesheh and Tell Gemayemi', *Egypt Exploration Fund. Report of the Fourth Annual General Meeting and Balance Sheet 1885–86*, London, 9–14.

Griffith, F.L. 1888 (12 May), 'Egypt Exploration Fund. A visit to El Ârish', *The Academy* 836, 331–2.

Griffith, F.L. 1923, 'Oxford Excavations in Nubia', *AAALiv* 10, 73–171.

Griffith, F.L. 1931, 'Une ancienne colonie grecque en Haute-Égypte', *REgA* 3, 74–7.

Grimal, N. 1999, 'Travaux de l'IFAO en 1998–1999. Personnels et laboratoires', *BIFAO* 99, 531–56.

Gryson, R. and Somers, V. (eds) 1996, *Commentaires de Jérôme sur le prophète Isaïe. Livres VIII–XI*, Vetus Latina 30, Freiburg.

Gubel, E. and Cauet, S. 1987, 'Un nouveau type de coupe phénicienne', *Syria* 64, 193–204.

Guermeur, I. 2005, *Les cultes d'Amon hors de Thèbes. Recherche de géographie religieuse*, BEHE (Sciences religieuses) 118.

Guermeur, I. and Thiers, C. 2001, 'Un éloge xoïte de Ptolémée Philadelphe. La stèle BM EA 616', *BIFAO* 101, 197–219.

Guichard, S. and Pierrat Bonnefois, G. 2005, 'À la XXVIᵉ dynastie égyptienne: le mystère des gourdes du Nouvel An', *DossArch* 304, 46–51.

Haider, P.W. 1988, *Griechenland - Nordafrika. Ihre Beziehungen zwischen 1500 u. 600 v. Chr.*, Impulse der Forschung 53, Darmstadt.

Haider, P.W. 1996, 'Griechen im Vorderen Orient und in Ägypten bis ca. 590 v. Chr.', in Ulf, C. (ed.), *Wege zur Genese griechischer Identität: Die Bedeutung der früharchaischen Zeit*, Berlin, 50–115.

Haider, P.W. 2001, 'Epigraphische Quellen zur Integration von Griechen in die ägyptische Gesellschaft der Saitenzeit', in Höckmann and Kreikenbom 2001, 197–215.

Haigh, D.H. 1868, 'To the editor. Assyro-aegyptisches', *ZÄS* 6, 80–3.

Hairfield, H.H., Jr and Hairfield, E.M., 1990. 'Identification of a Late Bronze Age resin', *Analytical Chemistry* 62/1, Washington, 41a–45.

Haldane, C., 1993, 'Evidence for organic cargoes in the Late Bronze Age', *WorldArch* 24/3, 348–60.

Hall, H.R. 1913, *Catalogue of Egyptian Scarabs, etc., in the British Museum* I. *Royal Scarabs*, London.

Hamilton, J. and Lizars, D. 1831, *The Edinburgh Geographical and Historical Atlas*, Edinburgh.

Hamza, O. 1997, 'Qedwa', *CCE* 5, 81–102.

Hansen, D.P. 1967, 'Mendes 1965 and 1966: The Excavations at Tell el Ruba', *JARCE* 6, 5–16.

Hartung, U. *et al.* 2007, 'Tell el-Fara'in – Buto, 9. Vorbericht', *MDAIK* 63, 69–165.

Hartung, U. *et al.* 2009, 'Tell el-Fara'in – Buto, 10. Vorbericht', *MDAIK* 65, 83–190.

Hartung, U. and Ballet P. 2010, 'Report on the work of the German Archaeological Institute at Tell el-Fara'in/Buto in 2007', *ASAE* 84, 165–202.

Haupt, L. 2012, 'Identifikation einer Sandsteinstatuette aus Gala Abu Ahmed', *MittSAG* 23, 71–5.

Heath, D.B. and Corbaux F. 1855, *The Exodus Papyri*, London.

Heidorn, L.A. 1999, 'Dorginarti', in Bard, K. (ed.), *Encyclopedia of the Archaeology of Ancient Egypt*, London, 307–10.

Heidorn, L.A. 2013, 'Dorginarti: fortress at the mouth of the rapids', in Jesse, F., Vogel, C. (eds), *The Power of Walls – Fortifications in Ancient Northeastern Africa. Proceedings of the International Workshop held at the University of Cologne 4th–7th August 2011*, Colloquium Africanum 5, Cologne, 293–307.

Herdejürgen, H. 1978, *Götter, Menschen und Dämonen: Terrakotten aus Unteritalien*, Basel.

Herrmann, C. 1985, *Formen für ägyptische Fayencen: Katalog der Sammlung des Biblischen Instituts der Universität Freiburg Schweiz und einer Privatsammlung*, OBO series archeologica 60.

Herrmann, C. 1994. *Ägyptische Amulette aus Palästina/Israel: mit einem Ausblick auf ihre Rezeption durch das Alte Testament*, OBO series archeologica 138.

Herrmann, C. 2003. *Die ägyptischen Amulette der Sammlungen Bibel+Orient der Universität Freiburg, Schweiz: anthropomorphe Gestalten und Tiere*, OBO series archeologica 22.

Herrmann, C. 2006, *Ägyptische Amulette aus Palästina/Israel* III, OBO series archeologica 24.

Herrmann, C. and Staubli T. 2010, *1001 Amulett. Altägyptischer Zauber, monotheisierte Talismane, säkulare Magie*, Stuttgart.

Higgins, R.A. 1954, *Catalogue of the Terracottas in the Department of Greek and Roman Antiquities British Museum* I. *Greek: 730–330 B.C.*, London.

Hill, M. 2004, *Royal Bronze Statuary from Ancient Egypt. With Special Attention to the Kneeling Pose*, Egyptological Memoirs 3, Leiden.

Hill, M. and Schorsch, D. (eds) 2007, *Gifts for the Gods, Images from Egyptian Temples*, New Haven.

Hinkel, F.W. and Sieverstsen, U. (eds) 2002, *The Archaeological Map of the Sudan, Suppl.* IV. *Die Royal City von Meroe und die repräsentative Profanarchitektur in Kusch*, Berlin.

Hölbl, G. 1979a, *Beziehungen der ägyptischen Kultur zu Italien* I. *Textteil*, Leiden.

Hölbl, G. 1979b, *Beziehungen der ägyptischen Kultur zu Italien* II. *Katalog*, Leiden.

Höckmann, U. 2001, 'Bilinguen: Zu Ikonographie und Stil der karisch-ägyptischen Grabstelen des 6. Jhs. v. Chr. Methodischen Überlegung zur griechischen Kunst der archaischen Zeit in Ägypten', in Höckmann and Kreikenbom 2001, 217–32.

Höckmann, U. (ed.) 2012, *Griechische Keramik des 7. und 6. Jahrhunderts. v. Chr. aus Naukratis und anderen Orten in Ägypten*, Archäologische Studien zu Naukratis III, Worms.

Höckmann, U. and Kreikenbom, D. (eds) 2001, *Naukratis. Die Beziehungen zu Ostgriechenland, Ägypten und Zypern in archaischer Zeit. Akten der Table Ronde in Mainz, 25–27 November 1999*, Mainz.

Hodjash, S. 1999, *Ancient Egyptian Scarabs. A Catalogue of Seals and Scarabs from Museums in Russia, Ukraine, the Caucasus and the Baltic States*, Moscow.

Hoffmann, F. 1992–3, 'Einige Bemerkungen zur Geschichte von König Amasis und dem Schiffer', *Enchoria* 19–20, 15–21.

Hoffmann, F. and Quack, J.F. 2007, *Anthologie der demotischen Literatur*, EQTÄ 4.

Hogarth, D.G., Edgar, C.C. and Gutsch, C. 1898–9, 'Excavations at Naukratis', *ABSA* 5, 22–97.

Hogarth, D.G., Lorimer, H.L. and Edgar, C.C., 1905, 'Naukratis 1903', *JHS* 25, 105–36.

Holladay, J.S. 1982, *Cities of the Delta* III. *Tell el-Maskhuta*, Malibu.

Holmes, E.M. 1889, 'Note on two resins used by the ancient Egyptians', *The Pharmaceutical Journal and Transactions*, November 17, London, 387–9.

Hölscher, U. 1941, *The Excavation of Medinet Habu* III, OIP 54.

Homès-Fredericq, D. 1982, 'Un goulot de bouteille de Nouvel An, trouvé à Lehun (Jordanie)', in Quaegebeur, J. (ed.) *Studia Paulo Naster oblata* II. *Orientalia antiqua*, OLA 13, 79–91.

Hope, C. 1988, *Gold of the Pharaohs*, Sydney.

Hopflinger, A.K. 2010, *Schlangenkampf. Ein Vergleich von ausgewählten Bild- und Textquellen aus dem griechisch-römischen und dem altorientalischen Kulturraum*, Zurich.

Hornung, D. 1965, 'Die Sonnenfinsternis nach dem Tode Psammetichs I', *ZÄS* 92, 38–9.

Hornung, E. and Staehelin, E. 1976, *Skarabäen und andere Siegelamulette aus Basler Sammlungen*, Mainz.

Hostens-Deleu, R. 1979, 'Beeldhouwersmodellen in de egyptische afdeling van de koninklijke musea voor kunst en geschiedenis', *BMRAH* 49, 5–65.

How, W.W. and Wells, J. 1912, *A Commentary on Herodotus with Introduction and Appendixes* I. *Books I-IV*, Oxford.

Hummel, R. and Schubert, S.B. 2004, 'Ceramic analysis', in Redford 2004, 135–84.

Hussein, H.M. and Abd el-Aleem, S. 2013, 'Tell el-Kedwa (Qedua): Saite fortresses on Egypt's eastern frontier. The 2007 season of SCA fieldwork', in *MSA/EES Delta Survey Workshop 22–23 March 2013, British Council, Cairo* (http://www.ees.ac.uk/userfiles/file/DW13 Hussein_Abd el-Aleem.pdf).

Hüttner, M. 1995, *Mumienamulette im Totenbrauchtum der Spätzeit. Eine Untersuchung an Objekten in der Sammlung des Kunsthistorischen Museums*, BeitrÄg 12.

Jacotin, P. 1826a, *Carte géographique de l'Égypte et des pays environnans réduite d'après la Carte topographique levée pendant l'expédition de l'Armée francaise... (1818)*, in *Description de l'Égypte ou recueil des observations et des recherches qui ont été faites en Égypte pendant l'expédition de l'armée française. Atlas géographique* (2nd edn, C.L.F. Pancoucke), Paris.

Jacotin, P. 1826b, *Carte topographique de l'Égypte et de plusieurs pays limitrophes levée pendant l'expédition de l'armée française...(1826)*, in *Description de l'Égypte ou recueil des observations et des recherches qui ont été faites en Égypte pendant l'expédition de l'armée française, Atlas géographique* (2nd edn, C.L.F. Pancoucke), Paris.

Jacotin, P. and Jomard, E. 1818a, *Carte ancienne et comparée de l'Égypte d'après la grande carte topographique levée pendant l'expédition de l'armée française (1/1,500,000)*, in *Description de l'Égypte ou Recueil des observations* qui ont été faites en Égypte pendant l'expédition de l'armée française. Antiquités, Mémoires II (1st edn), Paris (see also Jomard 1830, ibid., XVIII/3. État moderne, 2nd edn, C.L.F. Pancoucke], after p. 266).

Jacotin, P. and Jomard, E. 1818b, Carte ancienne et comparée de la Basse-Égypte d'après la grande carte topographique levée pendant l'expédition de l'armée française (1/500,000), in Description de l'Égypte ou Recueil des observations qui ont été faites en Égypte pendant l'expédition de l'armée française. Antiquités, Mémoires II (1st edn), Paris (see also Jomard 1830, ibid., XVIII/3. État moderne, 2nd edn, C.L.F. Pancoucke], after p. 266 and first map).

Jacotin, P. and le Père, G. 1809, Carte hydrographique de la Basse-Égypte, in Description de l'Égypte ou Recueil des observations qui ont été faites en Égypte pendant l'expédition de l'armée française. État moderne, Planches I, Paris (see also ibid. 1822, 2nd edn, C.L.F. Pancoucke).

Jaeger, B. 1982, Essai de classification et datation des scarabées de Menkhéperrê, OBO series archaeologica 2.

James, P. 2003, 'Naukratis revisited', Hyperboreus. Studia Classica 9/2, St Petersburg, 25–264.

Jansen, H.L. 1950, The Coptic Story of Cambyses' Invasion of Egypt. A Critical Analysis of its Literary Form and its Historical Purpose, Oslo.

Jansen-Winkeln, K. 2004, 'Daphnae', in Cancik, H. and Schneider, H. (eds), Brill's Encyclopaedia of the Ancient World New Pauly. Antiquity 4, Leiden and Boston, 80.

Jassen, A.P. 2007, Mediating the Divine. Prohecy and Revelation in the Dead Sea Scrolls and Second Temple Judaism, Leiden.

Jeffery L.H. 1990, The Local Scripts of Archaic Greece: a Study of the Origin of the Greek Alphabet and its Development from the Eighth to the Fifth centuries B.C., Revised Edition with Supplement by A.W. Johnston, Oxford.

Johnson, J.H. 2004 (19 July), 'N', The Demotic Dictionary of the Oriental Institute of the University of Chicago, Chicago (http://oi.uchicago.edu/pdf/CDD_N.pdf).

Johnson, J.H. 2012 (14 July), 'T', The Demotic Dictionary of the Oriental Institute of the University of Chicago, Chicago (http://oi.uchicago.edu/pdf/CDD_T.pdf).

Johnston, A.K. 1861, The Royal Atlas of Modern Geography, Edinburgh, London.

Johnston, A.W. 1979, Trademarks on Greek Vases, Warminster.

Johnston, A.W. 1987, 'Amasis and the vase trade', in True, M. (ed.), Papers on the Amasis Painter and his World, Malibu, 125–40.

Johnston, A.W. 2000, 'ΠΕΤ; food for thought', ZPE 133, 236.

Johnston, A.W. 2006a, Trademarks on Greek Vases, Addenda, Oxford.

Johnston, A.W. 2006b 'The Delta: from gamma to zeta', in Villing and Schlotzhauer 2006, 23–30.

Jomard, E.F., 1822, 'Index géographique ou liste générale des noms de lieux de l'Égypte', Description de l'Égypte ou recueil des observations et des recherches qui ont été faites en Égypte pendant l'expédition de l'armée française, État Moderne. II/2, Paris, 787–848.

Jomard, E.F., 1830, 'Index géographique ou liste générale des noms de lieux de l'Égypte', Description de l'Égypte ou recueil des observations et des recherches qui ont été faites en Égypte pendant l'expédition de l'armée française XVIII/3. État moderne (2nd edn, C.L.F. Pancoucke), Paris, 35–266.

Jones H.L. (ed.) 1932, Strabo, Geography VIII, Book 17. General Index, LCL 267.

Jones, R.N. and Fiema, Z.T. 1992, 'Tahpanhes', in Freedman, D.N. (ed.), Anchor Bible Dictionary 6, New York, 308–9.

Jones, R.N., Hammond, P.C., Johnson, D.J. and Fiema, Z.T. 1988 (February), 'A second Nabataean inscription from Tell esh-Shuqafiya, Egypt', BASOR 269, 47–57.

El-Kadi, G. and Bonnamy A. 2007, Architecture for the Dead. Cairo's Medieval Necropolis, Cairo.

Kahn, D. 2008, 'Some remarks on the foreign policy of Psammetichus II in the Levant (595–589 B.C.)', JEH 1/1, 139–157.

Kammerzell, F. 1993, Studien zu Sprache und Geschichte der Karer in Ägypten, GOF (IV. Reihe Ägypten) 27.

Karageorghis, V. 1995, The Coroplastic Art of Ancient Cyprus IV. The Cypro-Archaic Period. Small Male Figurines, Nicosia.

Karageorghis, J. 1999, The Coroplastic Art of Ancient Cyprus V. The Cypro-Archaic Period. Small Female figurines B. Figurines moulées, Nicosia.

Keel, O. 1995, Corpus der Stempelsiegel-Amulette aus Palästina/Israel von den Anfängen bis zur Perserzeit. Einleitung, OBO series archeologica 10.

Keel, O. 1997, Corpus der Stempelsiegel-Amulette aus Palästina/Israel von den Anfängen bis zur Perserzeit I. Von Tell Abu Farag bis 'Atlit, OBO series archeologica 13.

Keel, O. 2010a, Corpus der Stempelsiegel-Amulette aus Palästina/Israel von den Anfängen bis zur Perserzeit II. Von Bahan bis Tel Eton, OBO series archeologica 29.

Keel, O. 2010b, Corpus der Stempelsiegel-Amulette aus Palästina/Israel von den Anfängen bis zur Perserzeit III. Von Tell el-Far'a Nord bis Tell el-Fir, OBO series archeologica 31.

Keel, O. and Uehlinger, C. 1990, Studien zu den Stempelsiegeln Palestina/Israel III. Die Frühe Eisenzeit, OBO series archeologica 100.

Keimer, L. 1952, 'Une statue de prisonnier remontant au Nouvel Empire', ASAE 49, 37–9.

Kemp, B.J. 1977a, 'A Building of Amenophis III at Kôm el-'Abd', JEA 63, 71–82.

Kemp, B.J. 1977b, 'The Palace of Apries at Memphis', MDAIK 33, 101–8.

Kerschner, M. and Schlotzhauer, U. 2005, 'A new classification system for East Greek pottery'. Ancient West & East 4/1, 1–56.

Kiepert, H. 1860, Neuer Handatlas. Alle Theile der Erde, Berlin.

Kischkewitz, H. 1970, 'Zum Lotos- und Affenmotiv der altägyptischen Neujahrsflaschen', FuB 12, 141–6.

Klostermann, E. (ed.) 1966, Eusebius. Das Onomastikon der biblische Ortsnamen, Hildesheim (reprint of Klostermann, E. (ed.) 1904, Die griechischen Christlichen Schriftsteller der ersten drei Jahrhunderte, Eusebius Werke III, Leipzig).

Knoop, R.R. 1987, Antefixa Satricana. Sixth-Century Architectural Terracottas from the Sanctuary of Mater Matuta at Satricum (Le Ferriere), Assen/Maastricht, Wolfeboro.

Koehler, L. and Baumgartner, W. 1990, Hebräisches und aramäisches Lexikon zum Alten Testament 4 (3rd edn, J.J. Stamm), Leiden, New York, Copenhagen and Cologne.

Koenig, Y. 2007, 'The image of the foreigner in the magical texts of ancient Egypt', in Kousoulis, P. and Magliveras, K. (eds), Moving across the Borders, Foreign Relations, Religion and Cultural Interactions in the Ancient Mediterranean, OLA 159.

Kopeliovich, D.D. 2012, 'Was Jeremiah the Prophet murdered? A comparison between the Jewish and Christian traditions', Hebrew Higher Education. A Journal for Methodology and Pedagogy in the University Teaching of Hebrew Language and Literature 14, 7–15.

Kreuzer, B. 1998, 'Untersuchungen zu den attischen Pferdekopfamphoren', BABesch 73, 95–114.

Lacerenza, G. 1996, 'Nabateo e origini della scritura araba. A proposito di una recente pubblicazione', Studi epigrafici e linguistici sul Vicino Oriente 13, Verona, 109–20.

Lacovara, P. 1990, Deir el-Ballas: Preliminary Report on the Deir el-Ballas Expedition 1980–1986, Winona Lake.

Lacovara, P. 2006, 'Deir el Ballas and the development of the early New Kingdom royal palace', in Czerny, E., Hein, I., Hunger, H., Melman, D. and Schwab, A. (eds), Timelines: Sudies in Honour of Manfred Bietak, OLA 149/1, 187–96.

Ладынин, И.А. 2004, 'Дафны в библейской и египетско-христианской традиции о финале царствования Априя (кон. 570-нач. 560-х гг до Н.Э.)' [= Ladynin, I.A. 2004, 'Daphnae in the biblical and christian egyptian tradition about the last years of the reign of Apries (end of the 570s – beg. of the 650s B.C.)'], VDI 2004/3, 3–13.

Ladynin, I.A. 2007, 'Iw ("Island") and ^{URU}Pūṭū-Yaman ("The city of Greek Buto"): Two toponymes in the sources on the Babylonian invasion into Egypt in 567 B.C.', in Goyon, J.C. and Cardin, C. (eds), Proceedings of the Ninth International Congress of Egyptologists, Grenoble, 6–12th September, OLA 150/2, 1071–6.

Lagarce, E. and Leclant, J. 1976, 'II. Vase plastique en faïence Kit. 1747: Une fiole pour eau de jouvence', in Clerc, G., Karageorghis, V., Lagarce, E. and Leclant, J. (eds), Fouilles de Kition II. Objets égyptiens et égyptisants: scarabées, amulettes et figurines en pâte de verre et en faïence, vase plastique en faïence. Sites I et II, 1959–1975, Nicosia, 183–290.

Lagarde (de), P. (ed.) 1959, S. Hieronymi presbyteri opera Pars I. Opera exegetica 1, CCSL 72.

Lambdin, T.O. 1962, 'Tahpanhes', The Interpreter's Dictionary of the Bible 4, Nashville and New York, 510.

Lammert, F. 1931, 'Stratopeda', RealEnc IV A 1, 329.

Larcher, P.H. 1844, Historical and Critical Comments on the History of Herodotus I, London.

Laurent, V. and Desti, M. 1997, Antiquités égyptiennes. Inventaire des collections du MBA de Dijon, Besançon.

Leclère, F. 2007a (Spring), 'An Egyptian temple at Tell Dafana?', EgArch. 30, 14–17.

Leclère, F. 2007b, 'Un "sanctuaire" d'époque hellénistique à Tell el-Herr', in Valbelle, D. (ed.), *Tell el-Herr* II. *Les niveaux hellénistiques et du Haut-Empire*, Paris.

Leclère, F. 2008, *Les villes de Basse Égypte au Ier millénaire av. J.C.: Analyse archéologique et historique de la topographie urbaine*, BdE 144.

Lehmann, G. 1998, 'Trends in the local pottery development of the Late Iron Age and Persian Period in Syria and Lebanon ca. 700 to 300 BC', *BASOR* 311, 7–38.

Lehmann, M. 2011, 'Vorbericht über die Grabungstätigkeiten der Herbstkampagne 2009 im Areal A/II von Tell el-Dab'a', *ÄL* 21, 47–65.

Lehmann, M. 2012 (Spring), 'The City of Avaris after the New Kingdom', *EgArch* 40, 29–31.

Lehmann, M. 2013, 'Skylines, bridges and mud in the Delta and elsewhere. A comparison of Egyptian and Yemeni tower houses', in *MSA/EES Delta Survey Workshop 22–23 March 2013, British Council, Cairo* (http://www.ees.ac.uk/userfiles/file/DW13 Lehmann.pdf).

Leitz, C. (ed.) 2002a, *Lexikon der ägyptischen Götter und Götterbezichnungen* 4. *nbt –h*, OLA 113.

Leitz, C. (ed.) 2002b, *Lexikon der ägyptischen Götter und Götterbezichnungen* 5. *h̠ - ḥ̠*, OLA 114.

Leitz, C. (ed.) 2003, *Lexikon der ägyptischen Götter und Götterbezichnungen* 8. *Register*, OLA 129.

Lemm (von), O. 1900, 'Kleine koptischen Studien XVIII. Bemerkungen zum koptischen Kambyses-Roman', *Bulletin de l'Académie Impériale des Sciences de St-Petersbourg* 13/1, St Petersburg, 64–115.

Lemos, A.A. 1991, *Archaic Pottery from Chios. The Decorated Styles*, Oxford.

Lenoble, P. and Rondot, V. 2003, 'À la redécouverte d'El-Hassa. Temple à Amon, palais royal et ville de l'Empire méroïtique', *CRIPEL* 23, 101–15.

Leonard, A. 1997, *Ancient Naukratis: Excavations at a Greek Emporium in Egypt*, Part I: *The Excavations at Kom Geif*, Cambridge, MA.

Leospo, E. 1986, *Museo archeologico di Asti. La collezione egizia*, Turin.

Letellier, B. and Ziegler, C. 1978, *Le Louvre présente au Muséum de Lyon les animaux dans l'Égypte ancienne: [exposition] du 6 novembre 1977 au 31 janvier 1978*, Lyon.

Lichtheim, M. 1980, *Ancient Egyptian Literature. A Book of Readings* III. *The Late Period*, Berkeley, Los Angeles and London.

Liepsner, T.F. 1980, 'Modelle', *LÄ* 4, 169–80.

Linant de Bellefonds, L.M.A., 1855, *Carte hydrographique de la Basse Égypte et d'une partie de l'isthme de Suez*, 1/250,000; ibid., 1882 (version revised and completed 'pour les Chemins de fer et le canal de Suez').

Linant de Bellefonds bey, L.M.A. 1872–3, *Mémoires sur les principaux travaux d'utilité publique exécutés en Égypte depuis la plus haute Antiquité jusqu'à nos jours*, Paris.

Lindenberger, J.M. 2003, *Ancient Aramaic and Hebrew Letters*, Society of Biblical Literature – Writings from the Ancient World 4, Leiden and Boston.

Lipińska, J. 1964, 'The Expression ⏑—⦙⦙⦙', *RO* 26/2, 143–4.

Lipiński, E. 1995, *Dieux et déesses de l'univers phénicien et punique*, StudPhoen 14, OLA 64.

Lloyd, A.B. 1975, *Herodotus. Book II* I. *Introduction*, Leiden.

Lloyd, A.B. 1976, *Herodotus. Book II* II. *Commentary 1–98*, Leiden.

Lloyd, A.B. 1988a, *Herodotus. Book II* III. *Commentary 99–182*, Leiden

Lloyd, A.B. 1988b, 'Herodotus' account of pharaonic history', *Historia* (W) 37/1, 22–53.

Lopez-Grande, M.J., Quesada Sanz, F. and Molinero Polo, M.A. 1995, *Excavaciones en Ehnasya el Medina (Heracleopolis Magna)* II, Madrid.

Loprieno, A. 1998, '*Nḥsj* "der Südländer"?', in Guksch, H. and Polz, D. (eds), *Stationen. Beiträge zur Kulturgeschichte Ägyptens. R. Stadelmann gewidmet*, Mainz, 211–17.

Lull, J. 2007, 'Sobre el eclipse solar del papiro demótico Berlín 13588 y el "eclipse lunar" de la Crónica del príncipe Osorkón', *BAEO* 43, 255–66.

Macaulay, G.C. (ed.) 1890, *The History of Herodotus Translated into English*, London and New York.

MacCoull, L.S.B. 1986, 'An isopsephistic Encomium on Saint Senas by Dioscorus of Aphrodito', *ZPE* 62, 51–3.

Maeir, A.M. 2002, 'The relations between Egypt and the Southern Levant during the Late Iron Age: the material evidence from Egypt', *ÄL* 12, 236–46.

Magnanini, P. 1973, *Le Iscrizioni fenicie dell'Oriente: testi, traduzioni, glossari*, Rome.

Magnarini, F. 2004, *Catalogo ragionato di una collezione di Scarabei-Sigillo Egizi*, BAR-IS 1241.

Mahmud bey [el-Falaki] 1872 (1289 A.H.), [*Map of Lower Egypt* (Arabic)], 1/100,000, Leipzig.

Maier, M.P. 2002, *Ägypten – Israels Herkunft und Geschick. Studie über einen theo-politischen Zentralbegriff im hebräischen Jeremiabuch*, Frankfurt.

Maillot, M. 2013 (July–August), 'Les palais de Méroé, relais du pouvoir', in *L'Égypte à la croisée des mondes, Dossier pour la Sciences* 80, Paris, 66–71.

Maillot, M. forthcoming 1, 'The palace of Muweis in the Shendi Reach: a comparative approach', *Proceedings of the 12th International Conference of Nubian Studies*, London.

Maillot, M. forthcoming 2, 'The palace of Muweis in the Shendi Reach: a case study', *Actes du colloque Les maisons-tours en Égypte Durant la Basse Époque et les périodes ptolémaique et romaine, 29–30 Novembre 2012*, Paris.

Makkay, J. 1989, *The Tiszaszölös Treasure*, Budapest.

Malaise, M. 1991 [Review of 'Obsomer, C. 1989, *Les campagnes de Sésostris dans Hérodote. Essai d'interprétation du texte grec à la lumière des réalités égyptienne*, Brussels], *RBPH* 69, 198–202.

Mallet, D. 1893, *Les premiers établissements des Grecs en Égypte (vii⁰ et vi⁰ siècles)*, MMAF 12.

Maraval, P. (ed.) 1982, Égérie, *Journal de voyage (Itinéraire)*, SourcChr 296, Paris.

Marcolongo, B. 1992, 'Évolution du paléo-environement dans la partie orientale du Delta du Nil depuis la transgression flandrienne (8000 B.P.) par rapport aux modèles de peuplement ancien', *CRIPEL* 14, 23–31.

Markoe, G. 2000, *Phoenicians*, London.

Marouard, G. 2010, *Archéologie, architecture et images de la maison urbaine d'époque hellénistique et romaine dans la chôra égyptienne*, PhD University of Poitiers (unpublished).

Marouard, G. 2012, 'Les quartiers d'habitat dans les fondations et refondations lagides de la chôra égyptienne. Une révision archéologique', in Ballet, P. (ed), *Grecs et Romains en Égypte. Territoires, espaces de la vie et de la mort, objets de prestige et du quotidien*, BdE 157, 121–40.

Martin, G.T. 1981, *The Sacred Animal Necropolis at North Saqqara. The Southern Dependencies of the Main Temple Complex*, London.

Martinière (de la), A.A.B. 1738, *Le grand dictionnaire géographique et critique* 8, La Haye, Amsterdam and Rotterdam.

Martinière (de la), A.A.B. 1768, *Le grand dictionnaire géographique et critique* 2, Paris.

Martinière (de la), A.A.B. 1776, *Le grand dictionnaire géographique et critique* 3, La Haye and Amsterdam.

Maspero, G. 1883, *Guide du visiteur du musée de Boulaq*, Cairo.

Maspero, G. 1894, *Notice des principaux monuments exposés au musée de Gizeh*, Cairo.

Maspero, G. 1902, *Guide du visiteur au Musée du Caire*, Cairo.

Maspero, G. 1903, *Guide to the Cairo Museum*, Cairo.

Maspero, G. 1915, *Guide du visiteur du musée du Caire*, 1915 (4th edn), Cairo.

Masson, A. 2007, 'Le quartier des prêtres du temple de Karnak: rapport préliminaire de la fouille de la maison VII, 2001–2003', *CahKarnak* 12, 593–655.

Mathieu, B. 2000, 'Travaux de l'IFAO en 1999–2000. C. Personnels et laboratoires', *BIFAO* 100, 539–58.

Mathieu, B. 2001, 'Travaux de l'IFAO en 2000–2001. C. Personnels et laboratoires', *BIFAO* 101, 572–91.

Matouk, F.S. 1971, *Corpus du scarabée égyptien* I. *Les scarabées royaux*. Beirut.

Matouk, F.S. 1977, *Corpus du scarabée égyptien* II. *Analyse thématique*, Beirut.

Mauch, T.M. 1962, 'Phinehas', *The Interpreter's Dictionary of the Bible* 3, Nashville and New York, 799–800.

Muchiki, Y. 1999, *Egyptian Proper Names and Loanwords in North-West Semitic*, Atlanta.

Meeks, D. 2002, 'Coptos et les chemins de Pount', *Topoi* (L)-*Suppl.* 3, 267–335.

Meeks, D. 2003, 'Locating Punt', in O'Connor, D. and Quirke, S. (eds), *Encounters with Ancient Egypt* VII. *Mysterious Lands*, London, 53–80.

Miles, R.H. 1866a (1 June), 'Voyage d'une mer à l'autre à travers l'isthme de Suez', *L'isthme de Suez. Journal de l'union des deux mers* 238, Paris, 170–3.

Miles, R.H. 1866b (March), 'Egypt: and a voyage from sea to sea through the isthmus of Suez', *The New Monthly Magazine* 136/543, London, 354–69.

Miller, W. H. 1886 (September), 'Pharaoh's house in Tahpanhes', *The Leisure Hour*, London, 636–7.

Miller, M.C. 1997, *Athens and Persia in the Fifth Century BC: A Study in Cultural Receptivity*, Cambridge.

Millie, J. 1869 (Octobre), *Isthme et canal de Suez. Son passé, son présent et son avenir*, Milan.

Mills, J. and White, R. 1989, 'The identity of the resins from the Late Bronze Age shipwreck at Ulu Burun(Kas)', *Archaeometry*, 31/1, 37–44.

[Ministry of Finance, Egypt] 1914, 'Index' in *Atlas of Egypt Compiled at the Offices of the Survey Department, Scale 1/50,000. I. Lower Egypt Comprising Maps of the Cultivated Area between Mediterranean Sea and Cairo*, Cairo.

[Ministry of Finance, Egypt] 1928, *Index to Place Names Appearing on the 1:500,000 Scale Map of Egypt*, Cairo.

Möller, A. 2000, *Naukratis. Trade in Archaic Greece*, Oxford.

Möller, G. 1904, *Ägyptische Urkunden aus den Königlichen Museen zu Berlin. Koptische Urkunden* I, Berlin.

Mommsen, H. 2000. 'Pferdekopfamphoren', in Cancik, H., Schneider, H. and Landfester, M. (eds), *Der Neue Pauly Enzyclopadie der Antike* IX. *Das classische Alterum und seine Rezeption*, Stuttgart, 703.

Mommsen, H. 2006, 'Neutron Activation Analysis of pottery from Naukratis and other related sites', in Villing and Schlotzhauer 2006, 69–76.

Mommsen, H., Schlotzhauer, U., Villing, A. and Weber, S. 2012, 'Herkunftsbestimmung von archaischen Scherben aus Naukratis und Tell Defenneh durch Neutronenaktivierungsanalyse', in Höckmann 2012, 433–55.

Monnier, F. 2010, *Les forteresses égyptiennes. Du Prédynastique au Nouvel Empire, Connaissance de l'Égypte ancienne* 11, Brussels.

Montet, P. 1957, *Géographie de l'Égypte ancienne* I, Paris.

Mostafa, I.A. 1986, 'Tell Fara'on-Imet', *BCE* 11, 8–12

Mostafa, I.A. 1988, 'Tell Fara'on-Imet', *BCE* 13, 14–22.

Moyer, I.S. 2011, *Egypt and the Limits of Hellenism*, Cambridge.

Muhs, B. 1994, 'The Great Temenos of Naukratis', *JARCE* 31, 99–113.

Müller, K. (ed.) 1861, *Geographi graeci minores* 2, Paris.

Müller W.M. 1903, 'Tahpanhes', 'Tahpenes', in Cheyne, T.K. and Black, J.S. (eds), *Encyclopaedia Biblica: a Critical Dictionary of the Literary, Political and Religion History, the Archeology, Geography and Natural History of the Bible* 4, London, 4887–8.

Müller, W.M. 1906 (June), 'The local Semitic god of the biblical Tahpanhes', in *Egyptological Researches. Results of a Journey in 1904*, Washington, 30–1.

Müller, W. 1911, 'Das Land Gosen nach einem demotischen Schulbuch', *OLZ* 14, 195–8.

Müller, H.W. 1964, *Ägyptische Kunstwerke, Kleinfunde und Glas in der Sammlung E. und M. Kofler-Truninger*, Lüzern.

Müller, H.W. and Thiem 1998, *Die Schätzen der Pharaonen*, Augsburg.

Müller, H.P. 2000, 'Daphnis – ein Doppelgänger des Gottes Adonis', *ZDPV* 116, 26–41.

Müller-Winkler, C. 1987, *Die ägyptischen Objekt-Amulette*, OBO series archaeologica 5.

Mumford, G.D. 1998, *International Relations Between Egypt, Sinai, and Syria-Palestine during the Late Bronze Age to Early Persian Period (Dynasties 18–26: c.1550–525 BC)*, PhD, University of Toronto.

Murray, A.S. 1892, *Handbook of Greek Archaeology*, London.

Myśliwiec, K. 1987, *Keramik und Kleinfunde aus der Grabung im Tempel Sethos I in Gurna*, Mainz.

Naso, A. 2006, 'Etruscan and Italic finds in north Africa; 7th–2nd century BC', in Villing and Schlotzhauer 2006, 187–98.

Naville, E. 1890, *The Mound of the Jew and the City of Onias*, London.

Neubauer, A. 1868, *La géographie du Talmud*, Paris.

Newberry, P.E. 1907, *Scarab-Shaped Seals*, London.

Newberry, P.E. 1908, *Scarabs. An Introduction to the Study of Egyptian Seals and Signet Rings*, London.

Niemeier, W.D. 2001, 'Archaic Greeks in the orient. Textual and archaeological evidence', *BASOR* 322, 11–32.

Notley, R.S. and Safrai, Z. (eds) 2005, *Eusebius, Onomasticon. The Place Names of Divine Scripture Including the Latin Edition of Jerome*, Jewish and Christian Perspectives Series 9, Boston and Leiden.

Obsomer, C. 1989, *Les campagnes de Sésostris dans Hérodote. Essai d'interprétation du texte grec à la lumière des réalités égyptienne*, Brussels.

Oldfather, C.H. (ed.) 1933, Diodorus Sicilus, *Library of History. Book I–II.34*, LCL 279.

Oren, E.D. 1979, 'L'ishtme entre l'Asie et l'Afrique. Archéologie du Sinaï septentrional jusqu'à l'époque classique', in Rothenberg, B. (ed.), *Le Sinai: pharaons, mineurs, pélerins et soldats*, Paris, 181–92.

Oren, E.D. 1984, 'Migdol: a new fortress on the edge of the eastern Nile Delta', *BASOR* 256, 7–44.

Orlandi, T. (ed.) 1968, *Testi copti*, Milan.

Otto, E. 1958, *Ägypten. Der Weg des Pharaonenreiches* (3rd edn), Stuttgart.

Özer, B. 2004, 'Clazomenian and related black-figured pottery from Klazomenai: Preliminary observations', in Moustaka, A., Skarlatidou, E., Tzannes, M.C. and Ersoy, Y. (eds), *Klazomenai, Teos and Abdera: Metropoleis and Colony. Proceedings of the International Symposium Held at the Archaeological Museum of Abdera, 20–21 October 2001*, Thessaloniki, 199–219.

Özer, B. 2009, 'A painter from Urla Workshop', in Einicke, R. (ed.), *Zurück zum Gegenstand. Festschrift für Andreas E. Furtwängler*, Zentrum für Archäologie und Kulturgeschichte des Schwarzmeerraumes e. V. 16, Langenweißbach, 255–60.

Page-Gasser, M. and Wiese, A. 1997, *Ägypten: Augenblicke der Ewigkeit. Unbekannte Schätze aus schweizer Privatbesitz*, Mainz.

Pagliari, G. 2010, 'The Egyptian royal palaces in the first millennium BCE. An example of cultural continuity from the Middle Kingdom to the Late Period', in Bareš, L., Coppens, F. and Smoláriková, K. (eds), *Egypt in Transition: Social and Religious Development of Egypt in the First Millennium BCE. Proceedings of an International Conference, Prague, September 1–4, 2009*, Prague, 333–42.

Paice, P. 1987, 'A preliminary analysis of some elements of the Saite and Persian period pottery of Tell el-Maskhuta', *BES* 8, 95–107.

Paponot, F. 1884, *L'Égypte. Son avenir agricole et financier*, Paris.

Pardee, D. 1982, *Handbook of Ancient Hebrew Letters. A Study Edition*, Society of Biblical Literature Sources for Biblical Studies 15, Chico.

Parthey, G. and Pinder, M. (ed.) 1848, *Itinerarium Antonini Augusti et Hierosolymitanum*, Berlin.

Pasek, S. 2011, *Griechenland und Ägypten im Kontext der vorderorientalischen Großmächte: Die Kontakte zwischen dem Pharaonenreich und der Ägäis vom 7. bis zum 4. Jahrhundert vor Christus*, Munich.

Payne, G. and Mackworth-Young, G. 1936, *Archaic Marble Sculpture from the Acropolis*, London.

Peacock, D.P.S. and Williams, D.F. 1986, *Amphorae and the Roman Economy*, London.

Perdrizet, P. and Lefebvre, G. 1919, *Les grafittes grecs du Memnonion d'Abydos*, Nancy.

Perdu, O. 2002, *Recueil des inscriptions royales saïtes* I. *Psammétique Ier, EdE* 1.

Pernigotti, S. 1985, 'I più antichi rapporti tra l'Egitto e i Greci (secoli VII-IV A.C.)', in *Egitto e società antica, Atti del convegno Torino 8/9 VI –23/24 XI 1984*, Milan, 75–91.

Perreault, J. 1986, 'Céramique et échanges: les importations attiques du Proche-Orient du VIe au milieu du Ve siècle av. J.-C. Les données archéologiques', *BCH* 110, 145–75.

Petrie, W.M.F. 1885, 'The discovery of Naukratis', *JHS* 6, 1885, 202–6.

Petrie, W.M.F. 1886a (26 June), 'Egypt Exploration Fund. Tell Defenneh', *The Academy* 738, 458–9.

Petrie, W.M.F. 1886b, 'Mr. W.M. Flinders Petrie's Report', *Egypt Exploration Fund. Report of the Fourth Annual General Meeting and Balance Sheet 1885–86*, London, 14–19.

Petrie, W.M.F. 1886c, *Naukratis* I, *1884–5*, London.

Petrie, W.M.F. 1887, 'The finding of Daphnae', *ArchJourn* 44, London, 30–42.

Petrie, W.M.F. 1888, *Tanis* II – *Nebesheh (Am) and Defenneh (Tahpanhes)*, London.

Petrie, W.M.F. 1889a, *Hawara, Biahmu and Arsinoe*, London.

Petrie, W.M.F. 1889b, *Historical Scarabs: A Series of Drawings from the Principal Collections*, London.

Petrie, W.M.F. 1890, 'The Egyptian bases of Greek History', *JHS* 11, 271–7.

Petrie, W.M.F. 1892, *Ten Years' Digging in Egypt, 1881–1891*, London.

Petrie, W.M.F. 1905, *History of Egypt* III. *From the XIXth to the XXXth Dynasties*, London.

Petrie, W.M.F. 1906, *Hyksos and Israelite Cities*, London.

Petrie, W.M.F. 1909a, *Qurneh*, London.

Petrie, W.M.F. 1909b, *Memphis* I, London.

Petrie, W.M.F. 1909c, *The Palace of Apries (Memphis* II), London.

Petrie, W.M.F. 1910, *Meydum and Memphis* III, London.

Petrie, W.M.F 1911a, *Egypt and Israel*, London.

Petrie, W.M.F. 1911b, *Roman Portraits and Memphis* IV, London.

Petrie, W M F. 1914, *Amulets*, London.

Petrie, W.M.F. 1915, *Heliopolis, Kafr Ammar and Shurafa*, London.

Petrie, W.M.F. 1917a, *Tools and Weapons*, London.

Petrie, W.M.F. 1917b, *Scarabs and Cylinders with Names*, London.

Petrie, W.M.F. 1925, *Buttons and Design Scarabs*, London.

Petrie, W.M.F. 1926, *Ancient Weights and Measures*, London.

Petrie, W.M.F. 1927, *Objects of Daily Use*, London.

Petrie, W.M.F. 1931, *Seventy Years in Archaeology*, London.

Petrie, W.M.F. 1934, *Ancient Gaza* IV. *Tell el-Ajjul*, London.

Petrie, W.M.F. 1937, *Funeral Furniture, Stone and Metal Vases*, London.

Petric, W.M.F., Brunton, G. and Murray, M.A. 1923, *Lahun* II, London.

Piccione, P.A. 1990, *The Historical Development of the Game of Senet and its Significance for Egyptian Religion*, Disseration, Chicago, UMI Diss. Services, Ann Arbor.

Piccirilo, M. and Alliata, E. (eds) 1999, *The Madaba Map Centenary 1897–1997. Travelling through the Byzantine Umayyad Period. Proceedings of the International Conference Held in Amman, 7–9 April 1997*, Jerusalem.

Picozzi, M.G. 1970/71, 'Anfore Attiche a protome equine', *StudMisc* 18, 5–64.

Pococke R. 1743, *A Description of the East, and Some Other Countries* I. *Observations on Egypt*, London.

Polus (Poole), M. 1685, *Synopsis criticorum aliorumque Sacrae Scripturae interpretum et commentatorum* 3 (Leusden, J. ed.), London.

Pommerening, T. 2005, *Die altägyptische Hohlmaße*, SAK 10.

Porten, B. and Yardeni, A. 1989, *Textbook of Aramaic Documents from Ancient Egypt* II. *Contracts*, Jerusalem.

Porter, B. and Moss, R.L.B. 1934, *Topographical Bibliography of Ancient Egyptian Hieroglyphic Texts, Reliefs, and Paintings* IV. *Lower and Middle Egypt*, Oxford.

Porter, B. and Moss, R.L.B. 1952, *Topographical Bibliography of Ancient Egyptian Hieroglyphic Texts, Reliefs, and Paintings* VII. *Nubia, The Deserts, and Outside Egypt*, Oxford.

Posener, G. 1940, *Princes et Pays d'Asie et de Nubie. Textes hieratiques sur des figuirines d'envoutement du Moyen Empire*, Brussels.

Posener, G. 1987, *Cinq figurines d'envoutement*, BdE 101.

Pottier, E. 1933, *CVA, France* 12, *Musée du Louvre* viii, Paris.

Prisse d'Avennes, É. and Hamon, P.N. 1848, *L'univers pittoresque: Histoire et description de tous les peuples, Égypte Moderne* III, Paris.

Pulak, C. A., 1998, 'The Uluburun shipwreck: an overview', *IJNA* 27/3, 188–224.

Pusch, E. 1979, *Das Senet-Brettspiel im alten Ägypten*, MÄS 38.

Quack, J.F. 2000 [Review of Muchiki, Y., *Egyptian Proper Names and Loanwords in North-West Semitic*, Atlanta 1999], *Review of Biblical Literature* (http://www.bookreview.org), 1–4.

Quack, J.F. 2009, *Einführung in die altägyptische Literaturgeschichte* III. *Die demotische und gräko-ägyptische Literatur*, EQTÄ III.

Quack, J.F. 2013, 'Quelques apports récents des études démotiques à la compréhension du Livre II d'Hérodote', in L. Coulon *et al.* (eds), *Hérodote et l'Égypte. Regards croisés sur le Livre II de l'Enquête d'Hérodote*, CMO 51, 63–88.

Quaegebeur, J. 1990, 'Les rois saïtes amateurs de vin', *AncSoc* 21, 241–71.

Quaegebeur, J. 1995, 'À propos de l'identification de la "Kadytis" d'Hérodote avec la ville de Gaza', in van Lerberghe, K. and Schoors A. (eds), *Immigration and Emigration within the Ancient Near East. Festschrift E. Lipiński*, OLA 65, 245–70.

Quatremère, E. 1811, *Mémoires géographiques et historiques sur l'Égypte et sur quelques contrées voisines* I, Paris.

Quibell, J.E. 1898, *The Ramesseum*, London.

Quibell, J.E. 1900, *Hierakonpolis* I, London.

Radner, K. 2007, 'The winged snakes of Arabia and the fossil site of Makhtesh Ramon in the Negev', in Köhbach, M., Procházka, St., Selz, G.J. and Rüdiger Lohlker, R. (eds) 2007, *Festschrift für H. Hunger zum 65. Geburtstag*, WZKM 97, 353–65.

Radner, K. 2008, 'Esarhaddon's expedition from Palestine to Egypt in 671 BCE: a trek through Negev and Sinai', in Bonatz, B., Czichon, R.M. and Kreppner, F.J. (eds), *Fundstellen: Gesammelte Schriften zur Archäologie und Geschichte Altvorderasiens ad honorem H. Kühne*, Wiesbaden, 306–14.

Ramzī, M. 1953–4, *Al-qamûs al-gyûgrâfi lil bilâd al-misriyya min 'ahd qudamâ' al-misryîn ilâ sana 1945* [Geographical Dictionary of Egyptian Localities From Ancient Egypt to 1945] I, Cairo (in Arabic).

Ranke, H. 1935, *Die ägyptische Personennamen* I, Glückstadt.

Ranke, H. 1952, *Die ägyptische Personennamen* II, Glückstadt, Hamburg and New York.

Ray, J.D. 1976, *The Archive of Hor*, London.

Redford, D.B. 1994, *The Akhenaten Temple Project* III. *The Excavation of Kom el-Ahmar and Environs*, Toronto.

Redford, D.B. 1998, 'Report on the 1993 and 1997 seasons at Tell Kedwa', *JARCE* 35, 45–60.

Redford, D.B., 2004, *Excavations at Mendes* I. *The Royal Necropolis*, Leiden and Boston.

Reese, D.S. 1988, 'A new engraved Tridacna shell from Kish', *JNES* 47/1, 35–41.

Reese, B. and Sease, C. 2004, 'Additional unpublished engraved Tridacna and Anadara shells', *JNES* 63/1, 29–41.

Reiter, S. 1960, S. *Hieronymi presbyteri opera* I. *Opera exegetica* 3. *In Hieremiam Libri* VI, CCSL 74.

Richards, F.V. 2001, *The Anra Scarab. An Archaeological and Historical Approach*, BAR-IS 919.

Ritner, R.K. 1993, *The Mechanics of Ancient Egyptian Magical Practice*, SAOC 54.

Ritner, R.K. 2009, *The Libyan Anarchy: Inscriptions from Egypt's Third Intermediate Period*, Atlanta.

Robins, G. 1994, *Proportion and Style in Ancient Egyptian Art*, London.

Roebuck, C. 1951 (October), 'The organization of Naukratis', *ClassPhil* 46/4, 212–20.

Roeder, G. 1956, *Ägyptische Bronzefiguren*, Berlin.

Rollinger, R. 2004, 'Herodot (II 75f, III 107–109), Asarhaddon, Jesaja und die fliegenden Schlangen Arabiens', in Heftner, H. and Tomaschitz K. (eds), *Ad Fontes! Festschrift für Gerhard Dobesch zum fünfundsechzigsten Geburtstag am 15 September 2004*, Vienna, 927–44.

Rollinger, R. and Lang, M. 2005, 'Die fliegenden Schlangen Arabiens: Transfer und Wandlung eines literarischen Motivs in der antiken Überlieferung – Ein Florilegium', in Beutler, F. and Hameter, W. (eds), *'Eine ganz normale Inschrift'... und ähnliches zum Geburtstag von E. Weber. Festschrift zum 30 April 2005*, Althistorisch-Epigraphische Studien 5, Vienna, 101–9.

Rowe, A. 1936, *A Catalogue of Egyptian Scarabs, Scaraboids, Seals and Amulets in the Palestine Archaeological Museum*, Cairo.

Ruge, W., Benzinger, I., Oberhummer, E. *et al.* 1901, 'Daphne', *RealEnc* IV, 2136–8.

Rumpf, A. 1925 [Review of Pfuhl, E., *Malerei und Zeichnung der Griechen*, Munich, 1923], *Gnomon* 1, 323–40.

Rumpf, A. 1927, *Chalkidische Vasen*, Berlin, Leipzig.

Rumpf, A. 1933, 'Zu den Klazomenischen Denkmälern', *JDAI* 48, 55–83.

Ryholt K. 2013, 'A demotic narrative in Berlin and Brooklyn concerning the Assyrian invasion of Egypt (Pap. Berlin P. 15682 + Pap. Brooklyn 47.28.21-B)', in Lepper, V. (ed.), *Forschungen in der Papyrussammlung. Eine Festgabe für das Neue Museum, Ägyptische und Orientalische Papyri und Handschriften des Ägyptischen Museums und Papyrussammlung Berlin* I, Berlin, 337–53.

Rzepka, S. *et al.* 2009, 'Tell el-Retaba 2007–2008', *ÄL* 19, 241–80.

Rzepka, S. *et al.* 2011, 'New Kingdom and the Third Intermediate Period in Tell el-Retaba', *ÄL* 21, 139–84.

Rzepka, S. *et al.* 2012, 'Tell el-Retaba Season 2009', *PAM* 21 (Research 2009), 107–23.

Sagona, A.G. 1982, 'Levantine storage jars of the 13th to 14th century B.C.,' *OpAth* 14, 73–110.

Said, R. 1992, 'The geological history of the Nile delta', in Van den Brink, E.C.M. (ed.), *The Nile Delta in Transition: 4th–3rd Millennium BC. Proceedings of the Seminar held in Cairo, 21–24 October 1990, at the Netherlands Institute of Archaeology and Arabic Studies*, Tel Aviv, 259–67.

Said, R. 1993, *The River Nile. Geology, Hydrology and Utilization*, Oxford.

Salmon P., 1981 (2nd edn), *La politique égyptienne d'Athènes*, Brussels.

Sauer, R. and Gassner, V. 2008, 'Thin section and heavy mineral analyses of Western Greek amphorae samples', in Nieto, X. and Santos, M. (eds), *El vaixell Grec Arcaic de Cala Sant Vicenç*, Monografies del Casc 7, Museu d'Arqueologia de Catalunya Centre d'Arcqueologia Subaquàtica de Catalunya, Girona, 355–71.

Sayce, A.H. 1884 (19 January), 'Letter from Egypt. Abydos: Dec. 27, 1884', *The Academy* 611, 51.

Sayce, A.H. 1886a (1 May), 'Letter from Egypt. Cairo: April 10, 1886', *The Academy* 730, 310–11.

Sayce, A.H. 1886b (July), 'Contemporary records. II. Oriental history', *Contemporary Review* 50, London, 144–7.

Sayce, A.H. 1889a (July), 'Blessed be Abram of the most high God', *Hebraica* 6/4, 312–14.

Sayce, A.H. 1889b (July–December), 'Les tablettes cuneiforms de Tel el-Amarna', *RevArch* (3rd S.) 14, 342–62.

Sayce, A.H. 1890, 'The Cuneiform inscriptions of Tel el-Amarna', *Journal of the Transactions of the Victoria Institute or Philosophical Society of Great Britain* 24, London, 12–27.

Sayce, A.H. 1923, *Reminiscences*, London.

Scandone Matthiae, G. 1975, *Scarabei e scaraboidi egiziani ed egittizzanti del Museo nazionale di Cagliari*, Collezione di studi fenici 7, Rome.

Schäfer, H. 1910, *Ägyptische Goldschmiedarbeiten*. Berlin.

Schäfer, H., 1937, 'Eine nordsyrische Kultsitte?', *ZÄS* 73, 54–6, pl. 7.

Schäfer, M. 2002, *Zwischen Adelsethos und Demokratie. Archäologische Quellen zu den Hippeis im archaischen und klassischen Athen*, Munich.

Schaus, G.P. and Benson, J.L. 1995, *CVA Philadelphia, University Museum* 2, Philadelphia.

Scheel, B. 1989 *Egyptian Metalwork and Tools*, Aylesbury.

Schipper, B.U. 1999, *Israel und Ägypten in der Königszeit*, OBO series archeologica 170.

Schleiden, M.J. 1858, *Die Landenge von Suês zur Beurteilung des Canalprojects und des Auszugs der Israeliten aus Aegypten nach den aeltern und neuren Quellen dargestellt*, Leipzig.

Schlotzhauer, U. 2007, 'Zum Verhältnis zwischen sog. Tierfries- und Fikellurastil in Milet', in Cobet, J., Niemeyer, W.D. and Zimmermann, K. (eds), *Frühes Ionien. Eine Bestandsaufnahme. Akten des Symposions Panionion (Güzelçamlı), 26. September bis 1. Oktober 1999*. Milesische Forschungen 5, Mainz, 263–93.

Schlotzhauer, U. 2012, 'Untersuchungen zur archaischen griechischen Keramik aus Naukratis', in Höckmann, U. (ed.), 2012, 23–194.

Schlotzhauer, U. and Villing, A. 2006, 'East Greek pottery from Naukratis: the current state of research', in Villing and Schlotzhauer 2006, 53–68.

Schlotzhauer, U. and Weber, S. 2005, 'Verschiedene Aspekte griechischer Keramik des 6. Jahrhunderts v.Chr. aus Ägypten', in Bisang, W., Bierschenk, T., and Verhoeven, U. (eds), *Prozesse des Wandels in historischen Spannungsfeldern Nordostafrikas/Westasiens. Akten zum 2. Symposium des SFB 295, Mainz, 15–17 Oktober 2001, Kulturelle und sprachliche Kontakte* 2, Wurzburg, 69–114.

Schoske, S. and Wildung, D. 1985, *Entdeckungen. Ägyptische Kunst in Süddeutschland*, Mainz.

Schulz, R. 2003, 'Löwenkopf Usech mit Menit', in Hasitzka, M., Diethart, J. and Dembski, G. (eds), *Das Alte Ägypten und seine Nachbarn, Festschrift zum 65 Geburtstag von Helmut Satzinger*, Krems.

Schulz, R. and Seidel, M. 2009, *Egyptian Art. The Walters Art Museum*, Baltimore.

Schwartz, J. 1949, 'Les conquérants perses et la littérature égyptienne', *BIFAO* 48, 65–80.

Schwemer, A.M. 1995, *Studien zu den frühjüdischen Prophetenlegenden Vitae Prophetarum I. Die Viten der großen Propheten Jesaja, Jeremia, Ezechiel und Daniel*, TSAJ 49.

Schwemer, A.M. (ed.) 1997, *Vitae Prophetarum, Jüdische Schriften aus hellenistisch-römischer Zeit* I/7, Gütersloh.

Segall, B. 1956 (June), 'Notes on the iconography of cosmic kingship', *The Art Bulletin* 38/2, 75–80.

Sélincourt (de), A. (ed.) 1954, *Herodotus, The Histories*, Harmondsworth.

Serpico, M. and White, R., 2000a, 'The botanical identity and transport of incense during the Egyptian New Kingdom', *Antiquity* 74, 884–97.

Serpico, M. and White, R., 2000b, 'Resins, amber and bitumen', in Nicholson, P.T. and Shaw, I. (eds), *Ancient Egyptian Materials and Technology*, Cambridge, 430–74.

Serpico, M., Bourriau, J., Smith, L., Goren, Y., Stern, B. and Heron, C. 2003, 'Commodities and containers: a project to study Canaanite amphorae imported into Egypt during the New Kingdom', in Bietak 2003, 365–75.

Servin, A. 1948, 'Kantarah. Aperçus historiques', *BSEHGIS* 1 (1947), 59–68.

Settgast, J. 1978, *Von Troja bis Amarna. The Norbert Schimmel Collection, New York*, Mainz.

Seyrig, H. 1944, 'Antiquités syriennes. Heracles-Nergal', *Syria* 24, 62–80.

Sharon, I. and Zarzecki-Peleg, A. 2006, 'Podiums structures with lateral access: Authority ploys in royal architecture in the Iron Age Levant', in Gitin, S., Wright, J.E. and Dessel, J.P. (eds), *Confronting the Past. Archaeological and Historical Essays on Ancient Israel in Honor of W.G. Dever*, Winona Lake, 145–67.

Silverman, D.P. 1997, *Searching for Ancient Egypt: Art, Architecture, and Artifacts from the University of Pennsylvania Museum of Archaeology and Anthropology*, Dallas.

Simons, J.J. 1959, 'Taḥpanhes', *The Geographical and Topographical Texts of the Old Testament. Studia Francisci Scholten Memoriae Dicta* 2, Leiden, 443, § 1319.

Sionita, G. and Hesronita, J. (eds) 1619, Al-Edrisi, *Geographia nubiensis* (latin edition), Paris.

Smith, C. 1886 (11 September), 'Pharaoh's palace of Daphnae (Tahpanhes), in Egypt', *The Illustrated London News*, 293–6.

Smith, H. 1968, 'A note on amnesty', *JEA* 54, 209–14.

Smith, H. and Hughes, G. 1980, 'The story of Onchscheshonqy', *Serapis* 6, Studies in Honour of C.F. Nims, 133–56.

Smith, H.S., Davies, S. and Frazer, K.J. 2006, *The Sacred Animal Necropolis at North Saqqara. The Main Temple Complex. The Archaeological Report*, London.

Smith, M. 1991, 'Did Psammetichus I die abroad?', *OLP* 22, 101–9.

Smith, M. 1989 [Review of Thissen, H.J. 1984, *Die Lehre des Anchcheschonqi (P. BM 10508)*, PTA 32], *JNES* 48/1, 51–4.

Smith, M.S. 1995, '384. 4Qpap Apocryphon of Jeremiah B?', in Broshi, M. *et al.* (eds), *Qumran Cave 4 XIV. Parabiblical Texts 2. Pseudo-prophetic Texts*, Discoveries in the Judaean Desert 19, Oxford, 137–52.

Smith, W.S. 1998, *The Art and Architecture of Ancient Egypt* (revised ed. with additions by W.K. Simpson), New Haven and London.

Smolárikova, K. 2002, *Abusir VII. Greek Imports in Egypt: Graeco-Egyptian Relations during the First Millennium BC*, Prague.

Smoláriková, K. 2006, 'The mercenary troops – an essential element of the Late Period's military power', in Daoud, K. and Abd el-Fatah, S. (eds), *The World of Ancient Egypt. Essays in Honor of A. Abd el-Qader el-Sawi*, CASAE 35, 245–8.

Smoláriková, K. 2008, *Saite Forts in Egypt. Political-Military History of the Saite Dynasty*, Prague.

Smoláriková, K. 2009, 'Embalmer's deposits of the Saite tombs at Abusir', *GM* 223, 79–88.

Snodgrass, A. 1964, *Early Greek Armour and Weapons from the End of the Bronze Age to 600 B.C.*, Edinburgh.

Snodgrass, A.M. 2006, *Archaeology and the Emergence of Greece*, Ithaca, New York.

Socin, A. 1881, 'Bericht über neue Erscheinungen au dem Gebiete der Palästinaliteratur', *ZDPV* 4, 127–56.

Sørensen, L.W. 2001, 'Archaic Greek painted pottery from Cyprus, Naukratis and Tell Defenneh', in Höckmann and Kreikenbom 2001, 151–61.

Sotheby's 1993, *Antiquities: Property from the Collections of the Museum of Fine Arts, Boston, Occidental College, and from Various Sources, Monday June 14 1993*, New York.

Sourdille, C. 1910, *La durée et l'étendue du voyage d'Hérodote en Égypte*, Paris.

Sourisseau, J.C. 2006, 'Les amphores commerciales de la nécropole de Rifrisolaro à Cammarine. Remarques préliminaires sur le productions Corinthiennes de Type A', in Pelagatti, P., Di Stefano, G. and De Lachenal, L. (eds), *Camarina: 2600 anni dopo la fondazione. Nuovi studi sulla citta e sul territorio. Atti de Convegno Internazionale Ragusa 7 dicembre 2002/7–9 aprile 2003*, Rome.

Spalinger, A. 1977, 'Egypt and Babylonia: a survey (*c.* 620 BC–550 BC)', *SAK* 5, 221–44.

Spalinger, A.J. 1978, 'Psammetichus, king of Egypt: II', *JARCE* 15, 49–57.

Spataro, M. 2002, *The First Farming Communities of the Adriatic: Pottery Production and Circulation in the Early and Middle Neolithic*, Quaderni della Società per la Preistoria e Protostoria della Regione Friuli-Venezia Giulia, Quaderno 9, Trieste.

Spataro, M. 2009, 'The first specialised potters of the Adriatic region: the makers of Neolithic figulina ware', in Forenbaher, S. (ed.), *A Connecting Sea: Maritime Interaction in Adriatic Prehistory*, 59–72. BAR-IS 2037.

Spencer, A.J. 1979, *Brick Architecture in Ancient Egypt*, Warminster.

Spencer, A.J. 1993, *Excavations at El-Ashmunein* III. *The Town*, London.

Spencer, A.J. 1996, *Excavations at Tell el-Balamun 1991–1994*, London.

Spencer, A.J. 1999, 'Casemate foundations once again', in Leahy, A. and Tait, J. (eds), *Studies on Ancient Egypt in Honour of H.S. Smith*, London, 295–300.

Spencer, A.J. 2001, 'Fieldwork, 2000–01. The Delta survey', *JEA* 87, 9–11.

Spencer, A.J. 2009, *Excavations at Tell el-Balamun 2003–2008* (http://www.britishmuseum.org/research/research_projects/excavation_in_egypt/reports_in_detail.aspx).

Spencer, A.J. 2011, 'The Egyptian temple and settlement at Naukratis', *BMSEA* 17, 31–49 (britishmuseum.org/PDF/Spencer2011.pdf).

Spencer, A.J. and Spencer, P.A. 2000 (Spring), 'The EES Delta survey', *EgArch* 16, 25–7.

Spencer, J.R. 1992, 'Phinehas', in Freedman, D.N. (ed.), *Anchor Bible Dictionary* 5, New York, 346–7.

Spencer, N. 2008, *The British Museum Expedition to Kom Firin, Report on the 2008 season*, London (britishmuseum.org/pdf/Kom%20Firin%202008a.pdf).

Spencer, N. 2009, *The British Museum Expedition to Kom Firin, Report on the 2009 season*, London (britishmuseum.org/pdf/KomFirin%202009%20low-res.pdf).

Spencer, N. 2011, 'The British Museum expedition to Kom Firin 2007', *ASAE* 85, 553–606.

Spencer, N. 2014, *Kom Firin II. The Urban Fabric and Landscape*, British Museum Research Publication 192, London.

Spencer, P.A. (ed.) 2007, *The Egypt Exploration Society – the Early Years*, London.

Spiegelberg, W. 1904, 'X. Thachpanches = Daphnæ', *Ägyptologische Randglossen zum Alten Testament*, Strasburg, 38–43.

Spiegelberg, W. 1906–8, *Nos 30601–31270, 50001–50022. Die demotischen Denkmäler. Die demotischen Papyrus*, II, CGC, Strasbourg.

Spiegelberg, W. 1909, *Ausgewählte Kunst-Denkmäler der aegyptischen Sammlung der Kaiser Wilhelms-Universität Strassburg*, Strasburg.

Spiegelberg, W. 1914, *Die sogennante demotische Chronik des pap. 215 der BN zu Paris*, DemStud 7.

Spiegelberg, W. 1930, 'Zu dem alttestamentlichen Namen der Stadt Daphnae', *ZÄS* 65, 59–60.

Spratt (Captain), T.A.B. 1860a, 'Extracts from a dissertation on the true position of Pelusium and Farama', *House of Commons Parliamentary Papers (Accounts and Papers)* 42, London, 451–5 [13–17].

Spratt (Captain), T.A.B. 1860b, 'Account of researches in the bay of Pelusium relative to the identity of the situations of Pelusium and Farama', in Spratt 1860a 455–67 [17–26].

Stanley, J.D. and Toscano, M.A. 2009 (January), 'Ancient archaeological sites buried and submerged along Egypt's Nile Delta coast: gauges of Holocene Delta margin subsidence', *Journal of Coastal Research* 25/1, West Palm Beach, 158–70.

Steingass, F. 2005, *Arabic-English Dictionary*, New Delhi.

Stern, B. Heron, C., Corr, L., Serpico, M. and Bourriau, J. 2003, 'Compositional variations in aged and heated Pistacia resin found in Late Bronze Age Canaanite amphorae and bowls from Amarna, Egypt', *Archaeometry* 45/3, 457–69.

Stern, B., Heron, C., Tellefsen, T. and Serpico M. 2008, 'New investigations into the Uluburun resin cargo', *JAS* 35, 2188–203.

Stern, B., Lampert Moore, C. D., Heron, C. and Pollard, A. M. 2008, 'Bulk stable light isotopic ratios in recent and archaeological resins: towards detecting the transport of resins in antiquity', *Archaeometry* 50/2, 351–70.

Stricker, B.H. 1958, 'De wijsheid van Anchsjesjonq', *OMRO* 39, 56–79.

Stucky, R.A. 1974, 'The engraved Tridacna shells', *Dédalo* 19, São Paulo.

Stucky, R. 2007, 'Les Tridacnes à décor gravé', in Fontan, E. and Le Meaux, H. (eds), *La Méditerranée des Phéniciens. De Tyr à Carthage*, Paris, 219–23.

Szafranski, Z.E. 2003, 'The impact of very high floods on platform constructions in the Nile basin of the mid second millennium BC', in Bietak 2003, 205–18.

Tallon, F. 1995, *Les pierres précieuses de l'Orient ancien des Sumériens aux Sassanides*, Paris.

Thissen, H.J. 1984, *Die Lehre des Anchscheschonqi (P. BM 10508)*, PTA 32.

Thissen, H.J. 1989, *Die demotischen Graffiti von Medinet Habu. Zeugnisse zu Tempel und kult im ptolemäischen Ägypten. Transkription, Übersetzung und Kommentar*, DemStud 10.

Thissen, H.J. 1991, 'Die Lehre des Anchcheschonqi', in *Weisheitstexte, Mythen und Epen*, TUAT III/2, 251–77.

Thon, J. 2007, 'Pinhas, Sohn Eleasars', in Bauks, M. and Koenen, K. (eds), *Das wissenschaftlichen Bibellexikon im Internet (WiBiLex), Alttestamentlicher Teil* (http://www.wibilex.de), 1–4.

Timm, S. 1984, 'Aphnaion', *Das christlich-koptische Ägypten in arabischer Zeit*, TAVO 41/1, 137–9; 'Daphnai', ibid., TAVO 41/2, 551–5.

Timm, S. 1992, 'Taphnas', ibid., TAVO 41/6, 2510–14.

Tomkins, H.G. 1886 (11 September), 'Takhpankhes', *The Academy* 30/749, 172.

Tomkins, H.G. 1888 (24 March), 'The route from Syria to Egypt', *The Academy* 829, 206–7.

Tomoum, S.M. 2005, *The Sculptors' Models of the Late and Ptolemaic Periods: A Study of the Type and Function of a Group of Ancient Egyptian Artefacts*, Cairo.

Toussoun, O. 1922, *Mémoire sur les anciennes branches du Nil (époque arabe)*, MIE 4.

Tov, E. 1992, 'Three fragments of Jeremiah from Qumran Cave 4', *RevQum* 15/60, 531–41.

Tov, E. 1997, '72a. 4Q Jerd', in Ulrich, E. *et al.* (eds), *Qumran Cave 4. X. The Prophets*, Discoveries in the Judaean Desert 15, Oxford, 203–5.

Traunecker, C. 1987, 'Les "temples hauts" de Basse Époque: un aspect du fonctionnement économique des temples', *RdE* 38, 147–62.

Tresson, P. 1935–8, 'L'inscription de Chéchanq Ier au musée du Caire: un frappant exemple d'impôt progressif en matière religieuse', in *Mélanges Maspero* I.*Orient ancien*, MIFAO 66/2, 818–40.

Trindade Lopes, H.M. 2012, 'The Portuguese archaeological project at Memphis: The Apries Palace Project in Kôm Tumân (Memphis)', *Hathor* (N.S.) 1, 137–52.

Tronchère, H. 2010, *Approche paléoenvironnementale de deux sites archéologiques dans le Delta du Nil. Avaris et la branche Pélusiaque. Taposiris et le lac Mariout*, PhD, Lyon 2, September 2010 (unpublished).

Tylecote, R.F. 1981, 'From pot bellows to tuyères', *Levant* 13, 107–18.

Tylecote, R.F. 1987, *The Early History of Metallurgy in Europe*, London.

Valbelle, D. 2011, 'Mission archéologique franco-égyptienne de Tell el-Herr', *ASAE* 85, 639–49.

Valbelle, D., Nogara, G. and Defernez, C. 2011, 'Une construction hypogée de la première moitié du Vᶜ siècle av. J.-C. à Tell el Herr. Rapport préliminaire', *ASAE* 85, 627–38.

van Alfen, P.G., 2002. *Pant'agatha. Commodities In Levantine-Aegean Trade During The Persian Period, 6–4th c. B.C.*, PhD diss. University of Texas at Austin.

van der Doelen, G.A. *et al.* 1998, 'Comparative chromatographic and mass-spectrometric studies of triterpenoid varnishes: fresh material and aged samples from paintings', *Studies in Conservation* 43, 249–64.

Vandier, J. 1958, *Manuel d'archéologie égyptienne* III. *Les Grandes Époques, La statuaire égyptienne*, Paris.

Vandier, J. 1964, 'Iousâas et (Hathor)-Nébet-Hétépet', *RdE* 16, 55–146.

Vandier d'Abbadie 1937, 'À propos d'une chauve-souris sur un ostracon du Musée du Caire', *BIFAO* 36, 117–23.

Vandorpe, K. 1991, 'Les villages des Ibis dans la toponymie tardive', *Enchoria* 18, 115–22.

Vassilika, E. 1992, 'Museum acquisitions,1990. Egyptian antiquities accessioned in 1990 by museums in the United Kingdom', *JEA* 78, 267–72.

Vaujany (de), H. 1885, *Alexandrie et la Basse-Égypte*, Paris.

Venit, M.S. 1984, *Painted Pottery from the Greek Mainland Found in Egypt 650–450 B.C.*, PhD, New York 1982, Ann Arbor.

Vercoutter, J. 1945, *Les objéts égyptiens et égyptisants du mobilier funéraire carthaginois*, Paris.

Vernier, E. 1927, *Nos 52001–53855. Bijoux et orfèvrerie*, CGC, Cairo.

Verreth, H., 1999 (April–June), 'The Egyptian eastern border region in Assyrian sources', *JAOS* 119/2, 234–47.

Verreth, H., 2003, 'Sin, Senou, Senos and Pelousion', *CRIPEL* 23, 51–71.

Verreth, H., 2006, *The Northern Sinai from the 7th century BC to the 7th century AD: a Guide to the Sources*, Leuven (www.trismegistos.org/sinai/index.html).

Verreth, H., 2011, *Toponyms in Demotic and Abnormal Hieratic texts from the 8th century BC till the 5th century AD. Version 1.0*, Trismegistos online Publications 5, August 2011, Leuven (www.trismegistos.org/downloads/process.php?file=TOP_5.pdf).

Vigouroux, F. 1912a, 'Phinée Phinées', *Dictionnaire de la Bible* 5, Paris, 319–20.

Vigouroux, F. 1912b, 'Taphnès, Taphnis', *Dictionnaire de la Bible* 5, Paris, 1191–4.

Villing, A. 2006, 'Drab bowls for Apollo: the mortaria of Naukratis and exchange in the Archaic eastern Mediterranean,' in Villing and Schlotzhauer, 2006, 31–46.

Villing, A. 2013, 'Egypt as a "market" for Greek pottery. Some thoughts on production, consumption and distribution in an intercultural environment', in Tsingarida, A. and Viviers, D. (eds), *Pottery Markets in the Ancient Greek World (8th–1st Centuries B.C.), Proceedings of the International Symposium held at the Université Libre de Bruxelles 19–21 June 2008*, Brussels, 73–101.

Villing, A. and Schlotzhauer, U. (eds) 2006, *Naukratis: Greek Diversity in Egypt, Studies on East Greek Pottery and Exchange in the Eastern Mediterranean*, British Museum Research Publication 162, London.

Vittmann, G. 2003, *Ägypten und die Fremden im ersten vorchristlichen Jahrtausend*, Mainz.

Vodoz, I. 1979, *Les scarabées gravés du Musée d'art et d'histoire de Genève*. AegHelv 6.

Vogel, C. 2004, *Ägyptische Festungen und Garnisonen bis zum Ende des Mittleren Reiches*, HÄB 46.

Vogel, C. 2010, *The Fortifications of Ancient Egypt, 3000–1780 BC*, Oxford.

Wallenstein, K. 1971, *Korinthische Plastik des 7. und 6. Jahrhunderts vor Christus*, Bonn.

Walters, H.B. 1926, *Catalogue of the Engraved Gems and Cameos, Greek, Etruscan and Roman, in the British Museum*, London.

Wascheck, F. 2008, 'Fikellura-Amphoren und – Amphoriskoi von Milet', *AA* 2008/2, 47–87.

Wasmuth, M. and Ögüt, B. 2010, 'A Syro-Hittite weather-god in Egypt?', in Matthiae, P., Pinnock, F., Nigro, L. and Marchetti, N. (eds), 2010, *Proceedings of the 6th International Congress on the Archaeology of the Ancient Near East, May, 5th–10th 2008, 'Sapienza' - Università di Roma* I. *Near Eastern Archaeology in the Past, Present and Future. Heritage and Identity – Ethnoarchaeological and Interdisciplinary Approach, Results and Perspectives – Visual Expression and Craft Production in the Definition of Social Relations and Status*, Wiesbaden, 567–8.

Wastlhuber, C. 2011, *Die Beziehungen zwischen Ägypten und der Levante während der 12. Dynastie. Ökonomie und Prestige in Außenpolitik und Handel, Inauguraldissertation zur Erlangung des Doktorgrades der Philosophie an der Ludwig Maximilians-Universität München* (hedoc.ub. uni-muenchen.de/12817/1/Wastlhuber_Christian.pdf).

Weber, S. 2001, 'Archaisch ostgriechische Keramik aus Ägypten außerhalb von Naukratis', in Höckmann and Kreikenbom 2001, 127–50.

Weber, S. 2006, 'East Greek 'Situlae' from Egypt', in Villing and Schlotzhauer 2006, 145–54.

Weber, S. 2007, 'Greek painted pottery in Egypt: evidence of contacts in the seventh and sixth centuries BC', in Kousoulis, P. and Magliaveras, K. (eds), *Moving Across Borders. Foreign Relations, Religion and Cultural Interactions in the Ancient Mediterranean*, OLA 159, 299–316.

Weber, S. 2012a, 'Egypt and North Africa', in Smith, T.J. and Plantzos, D. (eds), *A Companion to Greek Art* I, Oxford, 293–311.

Weber, S. 2012b, 'Untersuchungen zur archaischen griechischen Keramik aus anderen ägyptischen Fundorten', in Höckmann 2012, 196–432.

Wehr, H. 1979, *A Dictionary of Modern Written Arabic* (4th edn), Wiesbaden.

Weigall, A.E.P. 1908, *Nos 31271–31670. Weights and Balances*, CGC, Cairo.

Weiland, C.F. and Kiepert, H. 1855, *Allgemeiner Hand-Atlas der Erde und des Himmels nach den besten astronomischen Bestimmungen, neuesten Entdeckungen und kritischen Untersuchungen entworfen* (41st edn of the *Allgemeiner Hand-Atlas der ganzen Erde*), Geographisches Institut, Weimar.

Weinstein, J.M. 1973, *Foundation Deposits in Ancient Egypt*, Dissertation, Pennsylvania, UMI Diss. Services, Ann Arbor.

Wenzel, H. 1889, 'Notes of the quarter (July–September, 1889). IV. Notes and News', *JRAS* 21/4, 1129–33.

Whitbread, I.K. 1995, *Greek Transport Amphorae*, British School at Athens. Fitch Laboratory Occasional Paper 4, Exeter.

Wiese, A. 2001, *Antikenmuseum Basel und Sammlung Ludwig. Die ägyptische Abteilung*, Mainz.

Wilbour, C.E. 1936, *Travels in Egypt [December 1880 to May 1991]*, Brooklyn.

Wildung, D. 1984, *Sesostris und Amenemhet: Ägypten im Mittleren Reich*, Freiburg and Munich (French transl. id. 1984, *L'âge d'or de l'Égypte: Le Moyen Empire*, Paris).

Wilkinson, J. 1981, *Egeria's Travels to the Holy Land* (3rd edn), Warminster.

Wilkinson, J. 2002, *Egeria's Travels*, (3rd edn reprint), Warminster.

Wilkinson, J.G. 1842, 'A tour to Bubastis, Sebennytus and Menzaleh', *Miscellanea Aegyptiaca*, Alexandria.

Wilkinson, J.G. 1843, *Modern Egypt & Thebes* I, London.

Wilkinson, J.G. 1847, *Hand-book for Travellers in Egypt*, London.

Wilkinson, J.G. 1880, *J. Murray's Hand-book for Travellers in Egypt*, London.

Williams, D. 2006, 'The Chian pottery from Naukratis', in Villing and Schlotzhauer 2006, 127–32.

Wilson, E. 1891, *Guide to the Bristol Museum*, Bristol.

Wilson, K.L. 1982, *Cities of the Delta* II. *Mendes*, Malibu.

Wilson, P. 1997, *A Ptolemaic Lexikon. A Lexicographical Study of the Texts in the Temple of Edfu*, OLA 78.

Wilson, P. 2007, *Sais Report, 2007* (www.dur.ac.uk/penelope. wilson/302007.html).

Winnicki, J.K. 1991a, 'Kuschiten (Nubier) in Südsyrien und im Ostdelta', *Sixth International Congress of Egyptology. Turin, 1st–8th September 1991. Abstracts of Papers*, Turin, 418–19.

Winnicki, J.K. 1991b, 'Der zweite Syrische Krieg im Lichte des demotischen Karnak-Ostrakons und der griechichischen Papyri des Zenon-Archivs', *JJP* 21, 87–104.

Winnicki, J.K. 1998, 'Kuszyci (Nubijczycy) w Południowej Syrii', *Światowit. Roczniki instytutu archeologii uniwersytetu Warszawskiego* 41/A, Warsaw, 33–48.

Winnicki, J.K. 2000, 'Zustrom und Asiedlung der Nomaden vom Nordosten Ägyptens im Niltal in der griechisch-römischen Zeitperiode', *JJP* 30, 165–78.

Winter, F. 1903, *Die antiken Terrakotten* III/1. *Die Typen der figürlichen Terrakotten*, Berlin, Stuttgart.

Wiseman, D.J. 1966 (Autumn), 'Some Egyptians in Babylonia', *Iraq* 28/2, 154–8.

Woolley, C.L. 1921, *Carchemish: Report on the Excavations at Jerablus on Behalf of the British Museum* II. *The Town Defences*, London.

Wright, B. (ed.) 2010, Berchère, N., *Le désert de Suez: cinq mois dans l'isthme, Modern Humanities Research Association Critical Texts* 24, London.

Wuillemier, P. 1939, *Tarente des origines à la conquête romaine*, Paris.

Yeung, M.W. 2002, *Faith in Jesus and Paul: A Comparison with Special Reference to 'Faith That Can Remove Mountains' and 'Your Faith Has Healed/Saved You'*, WUNT 2/147.

Yoyotte, J. 1972, 'Pétoubastis III', *RdE* 24, 216–23.

Zauzich, K.T. 1984, 'Von Elephantine bis Sambehdet', *Enchoria* 12, 193–4.

Zauzich, K.T. 1985 'Ägyptologische Bemerkungen zu den neuen aramäische Papyri aus Saqqara', *Enchoria* 13, 115–18.

Zauzich, K.T. 1987, 'Das topographische Onomastikon im P. Kairo', *GM* 99, 83–91.

Zayadine, F. 1990, 'The pantheon of Nabatean inscriptions in Egypt and Sinai', *Aram* 2, Oxford, 151–74.

Zazoff, P. 1983, *Die Antiken Gemmen. Handbuch der Archäologie*, Munich.

Zedler, J.H. 1744, *Grosses vollständiges Universallexicon aller Wissenschafften und Künste* 41, Leipzig.

Zimmerli, W. 1983, *Ezekiel 2: a Commentary on the Book of the Prophet Ezekiel, Chapters 25–48*, Philadelphia.

Zotenberg, H. (ed.) 1883, *Chronique de Jean, évêque de Nikiou. Texte éthiopien*, Paris.

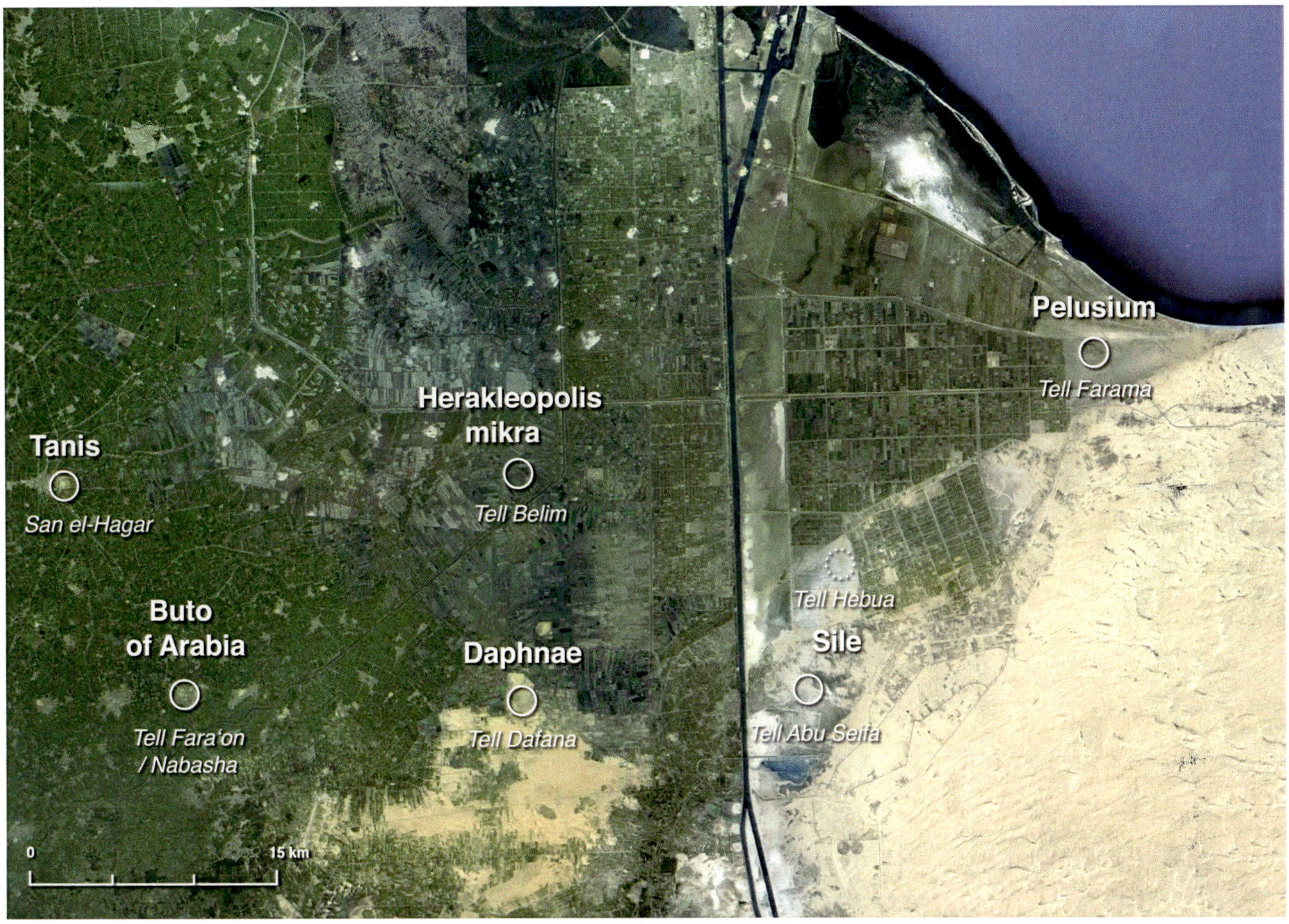

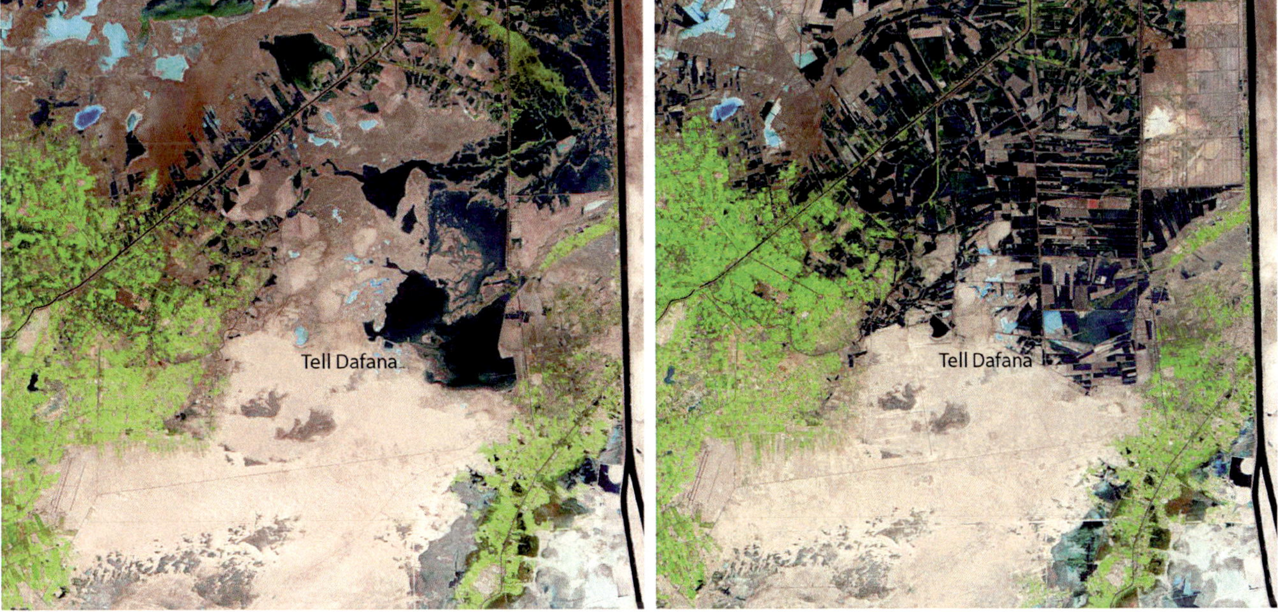

(a) Satellite image showing the location of Tell Dafana and its environs (Google Earth)

(b) Landsat images showing development around Tell Dafana between 1984 and 1990 (U.S. Geological Survey)

Plate 1

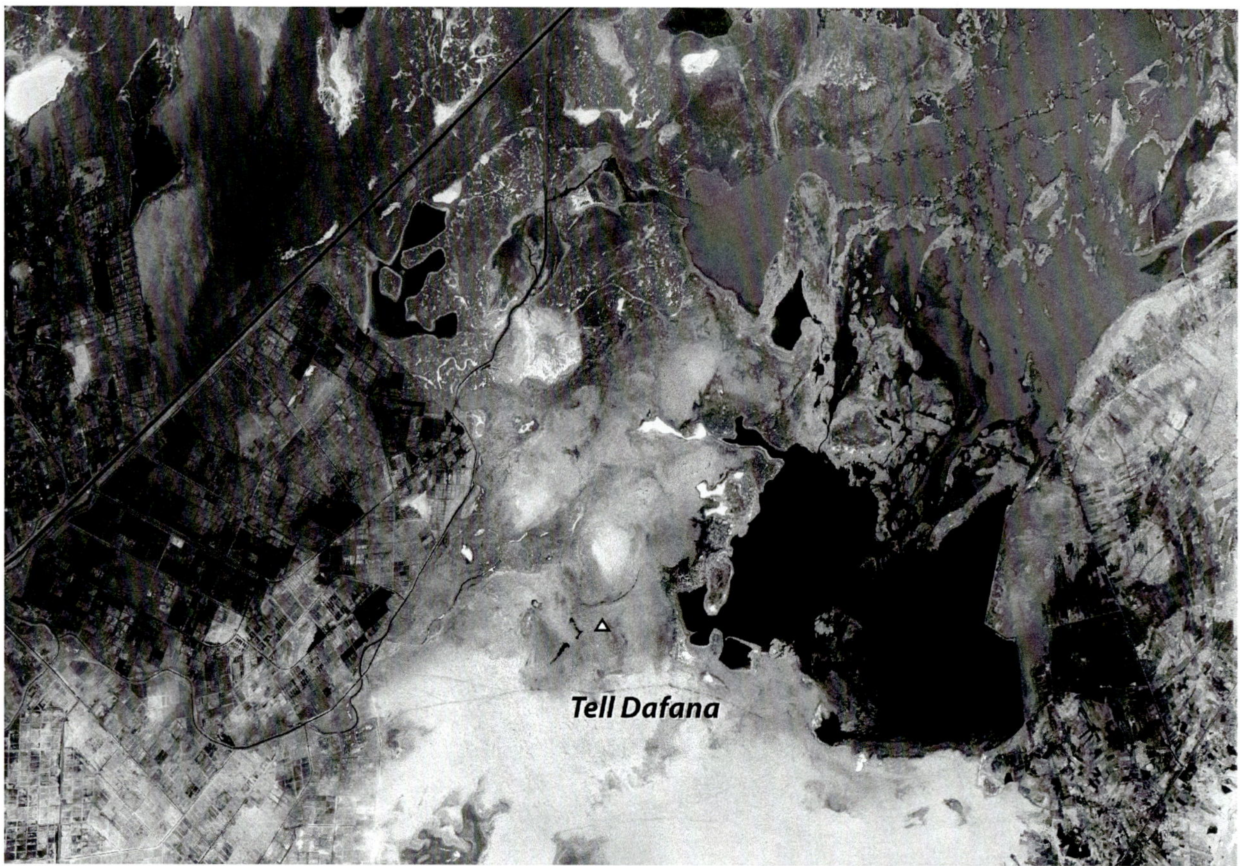

(a) Extract from CORONA image showing the region of Tell Dafana in June 1967 (U.S. Geological Survey)

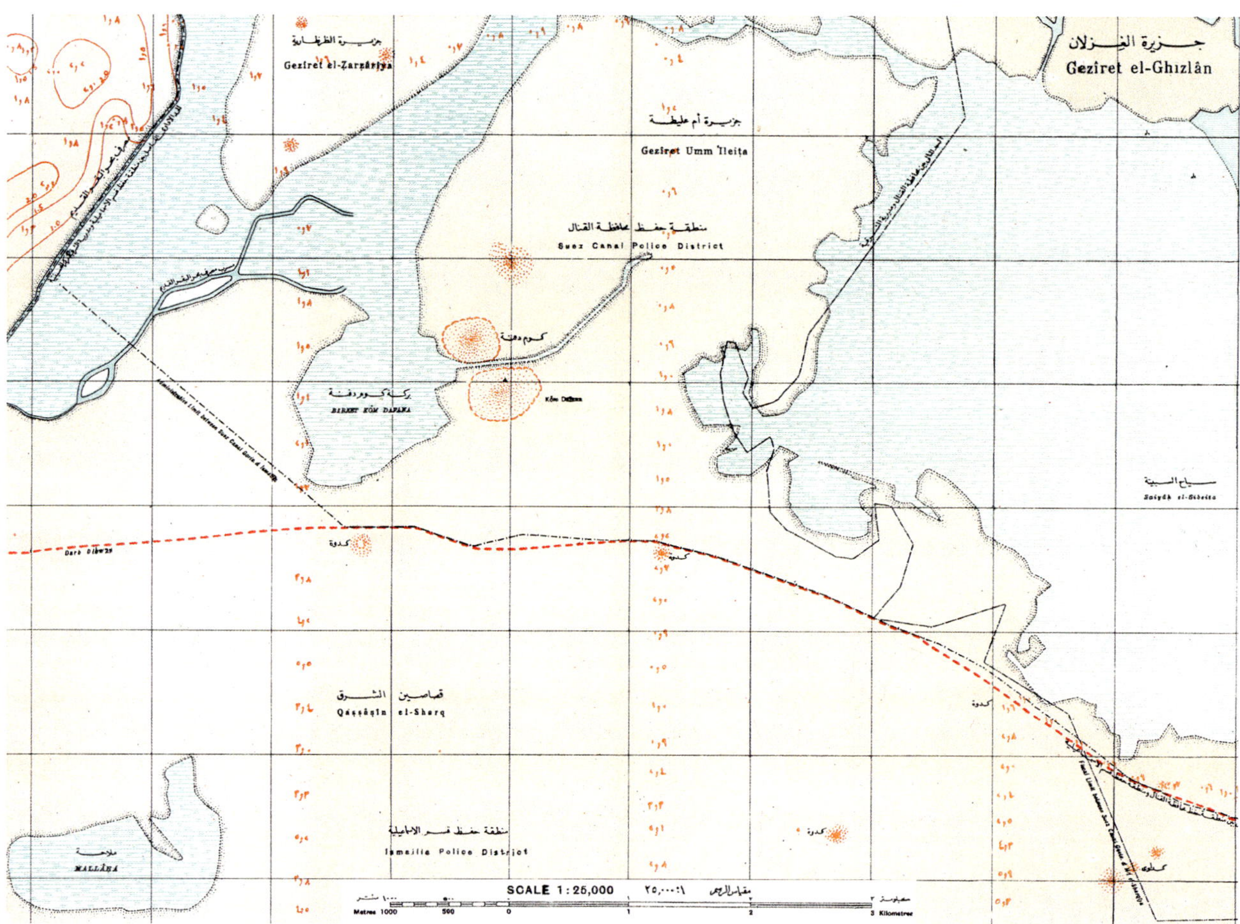

(b) Extract from the *Survey of Egypt* 1:25,000 map from 1949 (Geziret el-Ghizlan)

Plate 2

(a) Map from the *Description de l'Egypte* (after Jacotin 1826a, sheet 2)

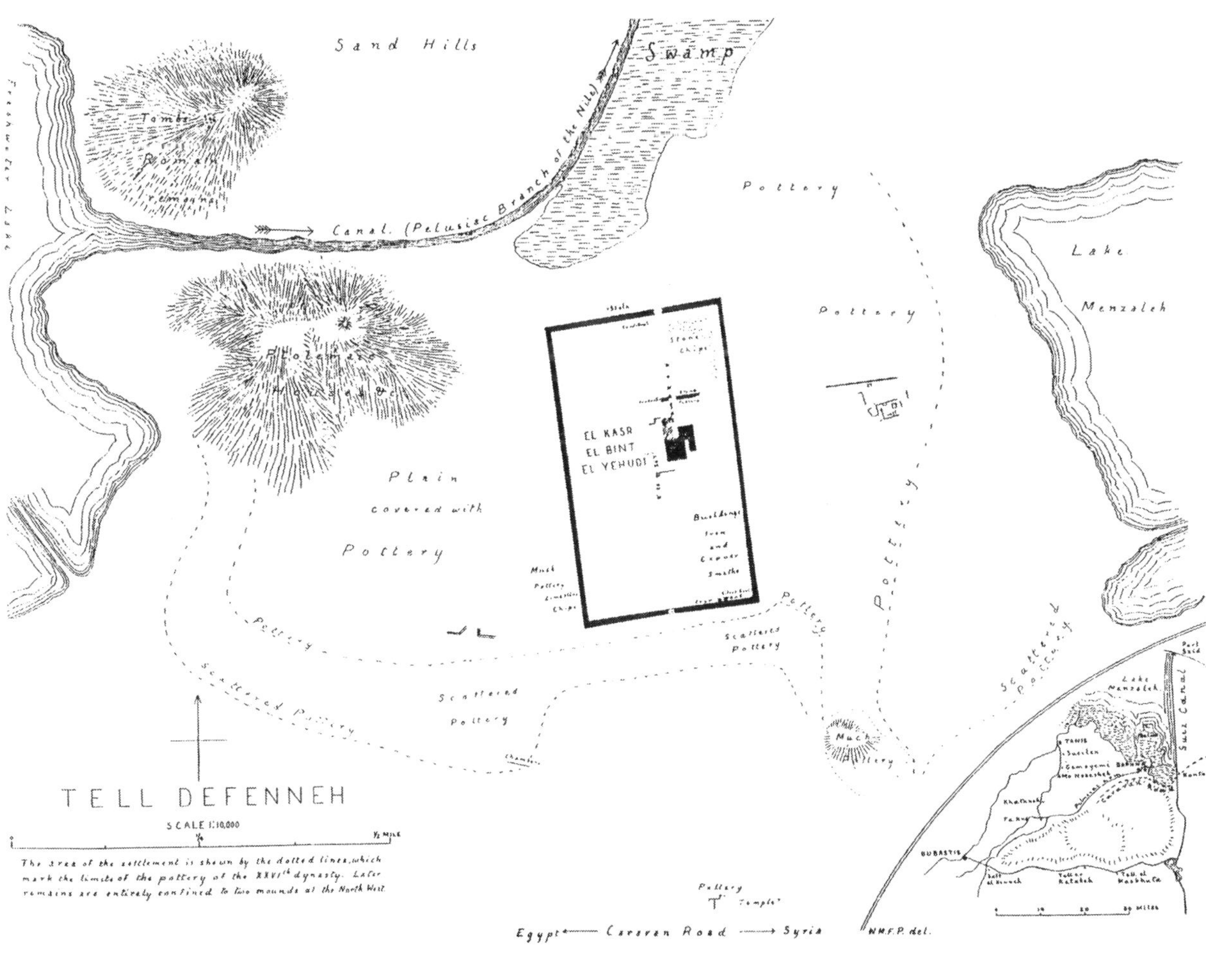

(b) Petrie's plan of the site (Petrie 1888, pl. lxiii)

Plate 3

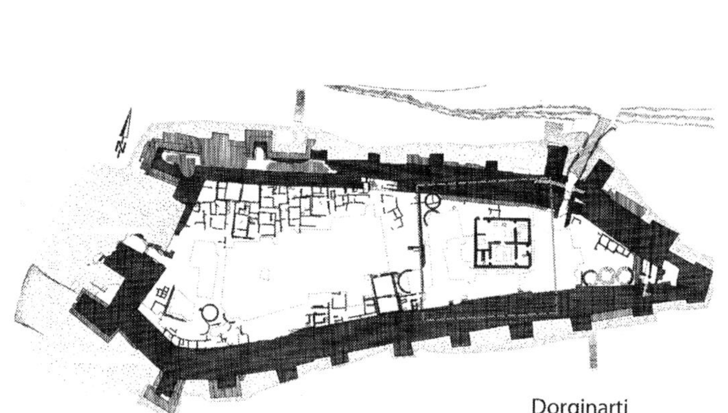

(a) The Saite fortress at Dorginarti (after Heidorn 2013, 298, fig. 4)

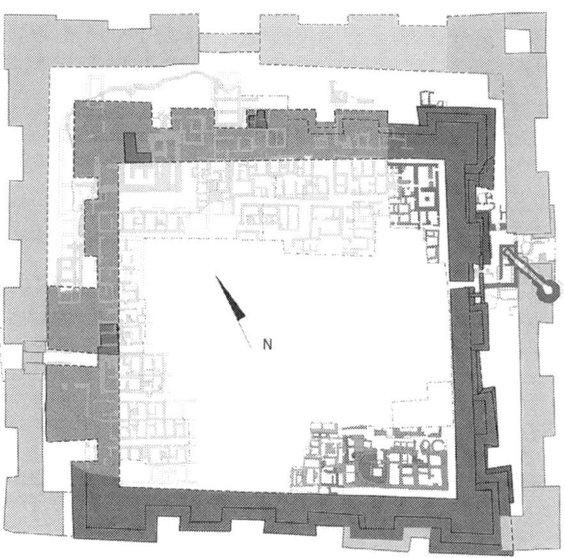

(b) The Saite and Persian fortresses of Tell el-Herr (after Valbelle *et al.* 2011, 635, plan 2)

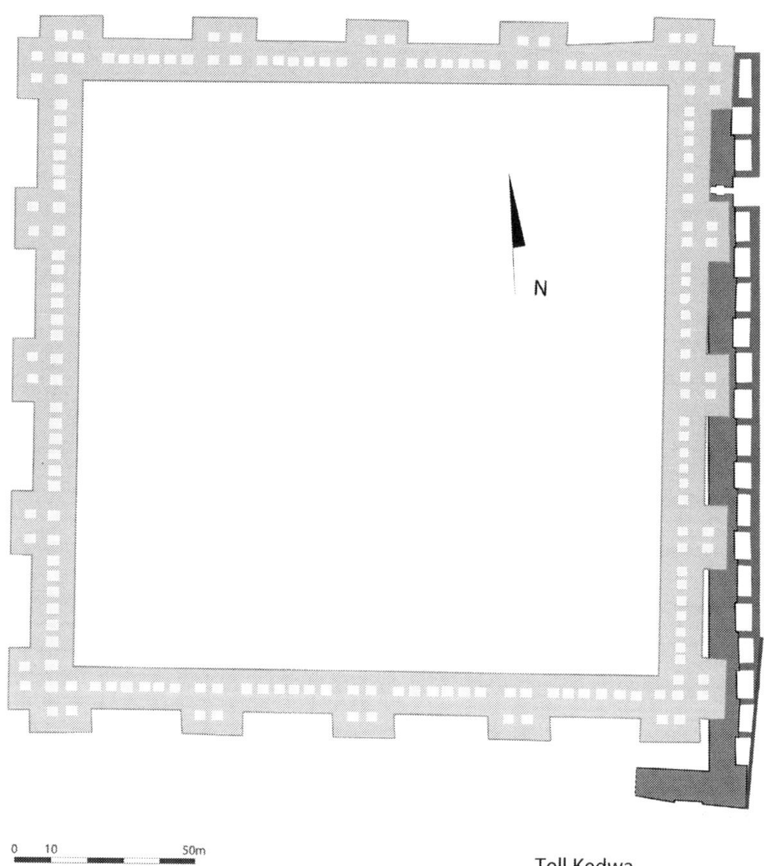

(c) Tell Kedwa (after Hussein 2013, 6, fig. 9)

Plate 4 Late Period fortifications at uniform scale

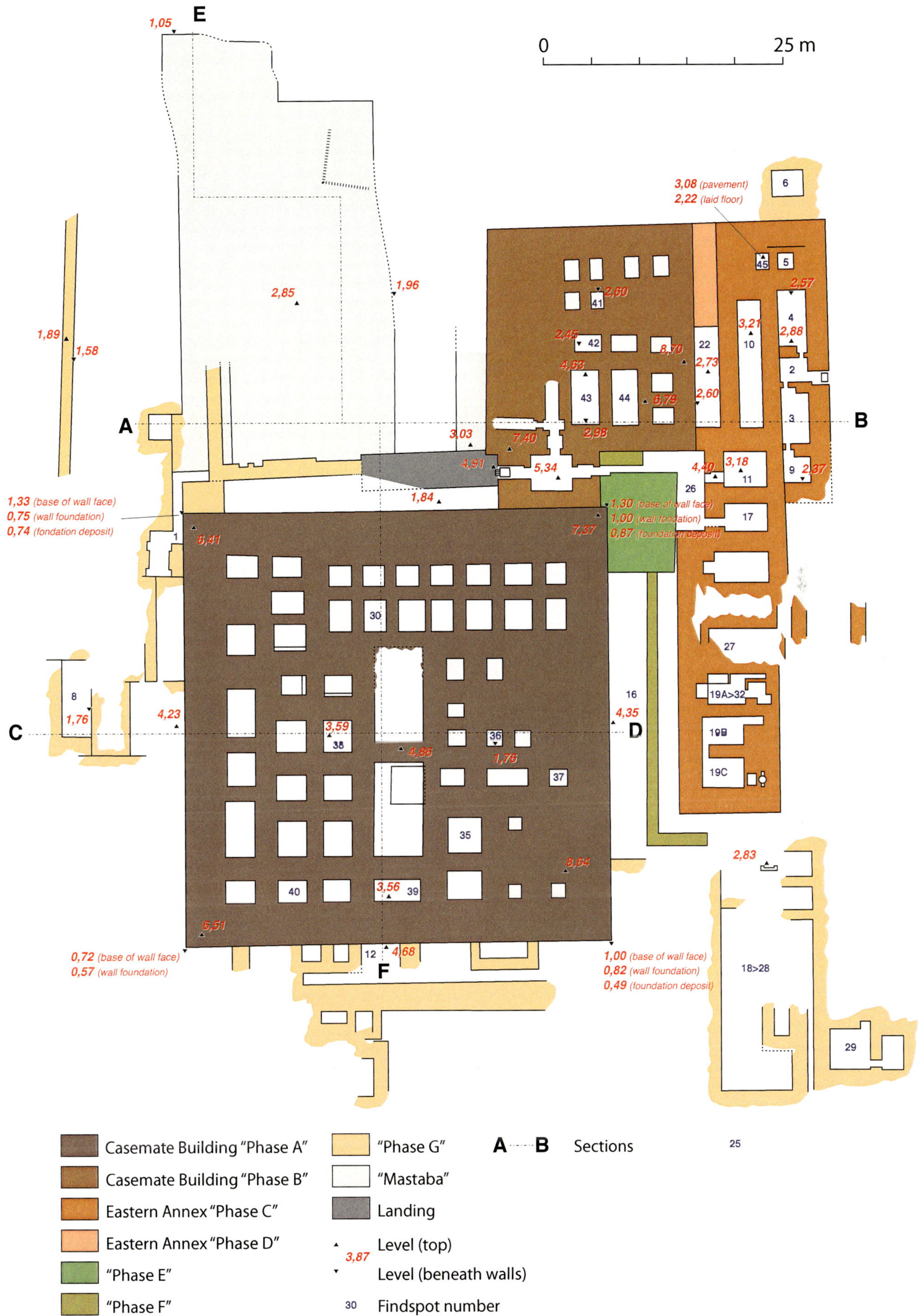

Plate 5 Plan of the casemate buildings and surrounding structures at Tell Dafana, with levels and findspots (F. Leclère, after Petrie 1888, pl.xliv)

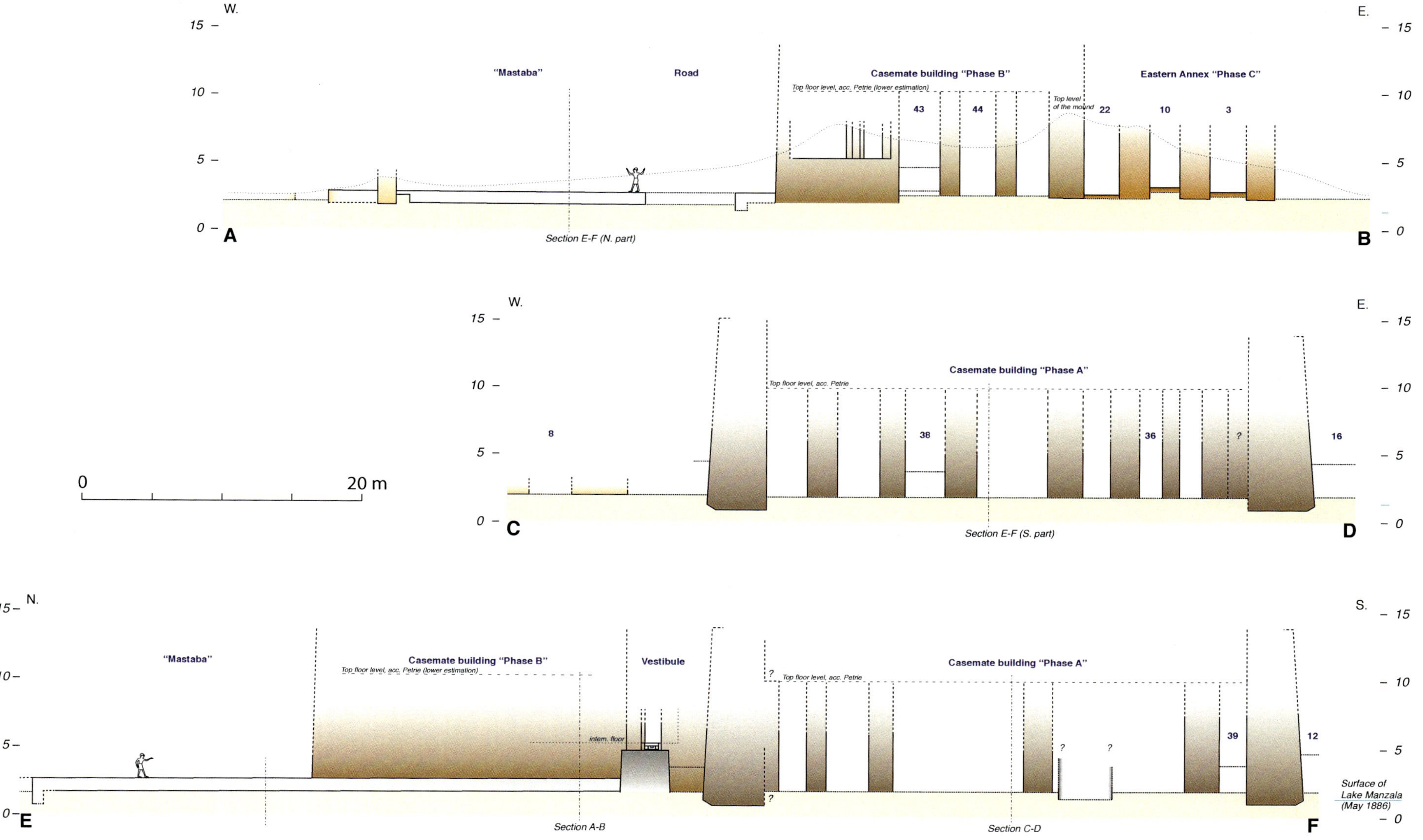

Plate 6 Reconstructed sections of the casemate buildings at Tell Dafana, with levels (F. Leclère)

Petrie Levels (inches)	Calculated levels* (meters)	Location and description
500	8,7000	*Kasr*, Building B, W. of Chamber 22, highest top level preserved.
		Kasr, supposed level of top of cell domes.
498	8,6492	*Kasr*, Building A, S.E. part, top level.
449	7,4046	*Kasr*, Building B, S.W. corner, N.W. of vestibule.
448	7,3792	*Kasr*, Building A, N.E. part, top level.
425	6,7950	*Kasr*, Building B, S.E. part, E. of Cell 44, top level.
414	6,5156	*Kasr*, Building A, S.W. corner, top level.
410	6,4140	*Kasr*, Building A, N.W. corner, top level (highest surface burnt).
368	5,3472	*Kasr*, Buildings A-B, mortared floor of vestibule between both buildings and passages in the S.W. quarter of B.
351	4,9154	*Kasr*, Buildings A-B, stone sill at W. entry of the vestibule.
349	4,8646	*Kasr*, Building A, central part, top level (possibly wrong ?)
342	4,6868	*Kasr*, Building A, general ground level along S. side.
340	4,6360	*Kasr*, Building B, Cell 43, surface of sand (highest level at N. end).
331	4,4074	*Kasr*, Eastern annexe C, Chamber 11, stone sill — and (base of)later plastering on walls.
329	4,3566	*Kasr*, Building A, general ground level along E. side.
324	4,2296	*Kasr*, Building A, W. part, general top level.
310	3,8740	*Kasr*, top of rubbish over "mastaba", S. end.
299	3,5946	*Kasr*, Building A, Cell 38, surface of sand filling.
298	3,5692	*Kasr*, Building A, Cell 39, mud base (i.e. surface of sand filling ?).
284	3,2136	*Kasr*, Eastern annexe C, Chamber 10, mortared floor..
283	3,1882	*Kasr*, Eastern annexe C, Chamber 11, floor.
279	3,0866	*Kasr*, Eastern annexe C, Chamber 45, upper pavement.
277	3,0358	*Kasr*, top of raised road along W. side of "palace" (= Building B) up to the entry, S. end.
275	2,9850	*Kasr*, Building B, Cell 43, surface of sand (lowest level at S.).
272	2,9088	*Kasr*, "mastaba" surface (highest level).
271	2,8834	*Kasr*, Eastern annexe C, Chamber 4, laid floor, and/or base of plastering on walls.
270	2,8580	*Kasr*, "mastaba" average surface from 4 different measurements (268 -272).
269	2,8326	*Kasr*, S.E. of the complex, Chamber 18, top of threshold in the N.
268	2,8072	*Kasr*, "mastaba" surface (lowest level), near S. end.
267	2,7818	*Kasr*, between "mastaba" and Building A, top of mud.
265	2,7310	*Kasr*, Eastern annexe C, Chamber 22, laid floor.
260	2,6040	*Kasr*, Building B, Cell 41, surface of sand.
		Kasr, Eastern annexe C, Chamber 22, surface of sand beneath walls.
259	2,5786	*Kasr*, Eastern annexe C, Chamber 4, surface of sand.
254	2,4516	*Kasr*, Building B, Cell 42, surface of sand.
251	2,3754	*Kasr*, Eastern annexe C, Chamber 9, surface of sand beneath walls.
245	2,2230	*Kasr*, Eastern annexe C, Chamber 45, base of clearing.
235	1,9690	*Kasr*, "mastaba", surface of sand beneath.
234	1,9436	*Kasr*, Building A, base of wall at gap on N. side of Building A [i.e. base of "causeway"?].
232	1,8928	*Kasr*, top of outlying wall to the W.
230	1,8420	*Kasr*, between "mastaba" and Building A, surface of sand.
227	1,7658	*Kasr*, Building A, Cell 36, surface of sand beneath walls.
		Kasr, Chamber 8 (west of Building A), surface of sand beneath walls.
		Surface of sandy plain.
		Sea level during High Nile.
222	1,6388	Plain, 200 yards (180 m) E. of *Kasr*, lowest surface.
220	1,5880	*Kasr*, base of outlying wall to the W.
212	1,3848	Sea level in May 1886 (Lake Manzala when low Nile).
		Kasr, Building A, south part of large central cell, sand beneath walls of the smaller and earlier square structure.
210	1,3340	*Kasr*, Building A, N.W. corner, base of wall face.
209	1,3086	*Kasr*, Building A, N.E. corner, base of wall face.
199	1,0546	*Kasr*, "mastaba", base of N. retaining wall.
197	1,0038	*Kasr*, Building A, N.E. corner, foundation.
		Kasr, Building A, S.E. corner, base of wall face.
192	0,8768	*Kasr*, Building A, N.E. corner, foundation deposit.
190	0,8260	*Kasr*, Building A, S.E. corner, foundation.
187	0,7498	*Kasr*, Building A, N.W. corner, foundation.
186	0,7244	*Kasr*, Building A, S.W. corner, base of wall face.
180	0,5720	*Kasr*, Building A, N.W. corner, foundation deposit.
		Kasr, Building A, S.W. corner, foundation.
177	0,4958	*Kasr*, Building A, S.E. corner, lowest level of foundation deposit.
162	0,1148	*Kasr*, Building A, S.E. corner, lowest level cleared under foundation deposit.
0	-4,0000	Petrie arbitrary datum (round 17 feet below sea level — Lake Manzala)

*: *The datum for the levels calculated in metres is arbitrarily set 4m above Petrie's arbitrary datum [calculation= (Petrie level x 0,0254) - 4]*

Plate 7 Petrie levels recalculated (after Petrie 1888, 94–5; see also p. 55 and pl. xxiii; Notebook 74f, 18–19, 33, 42–5)

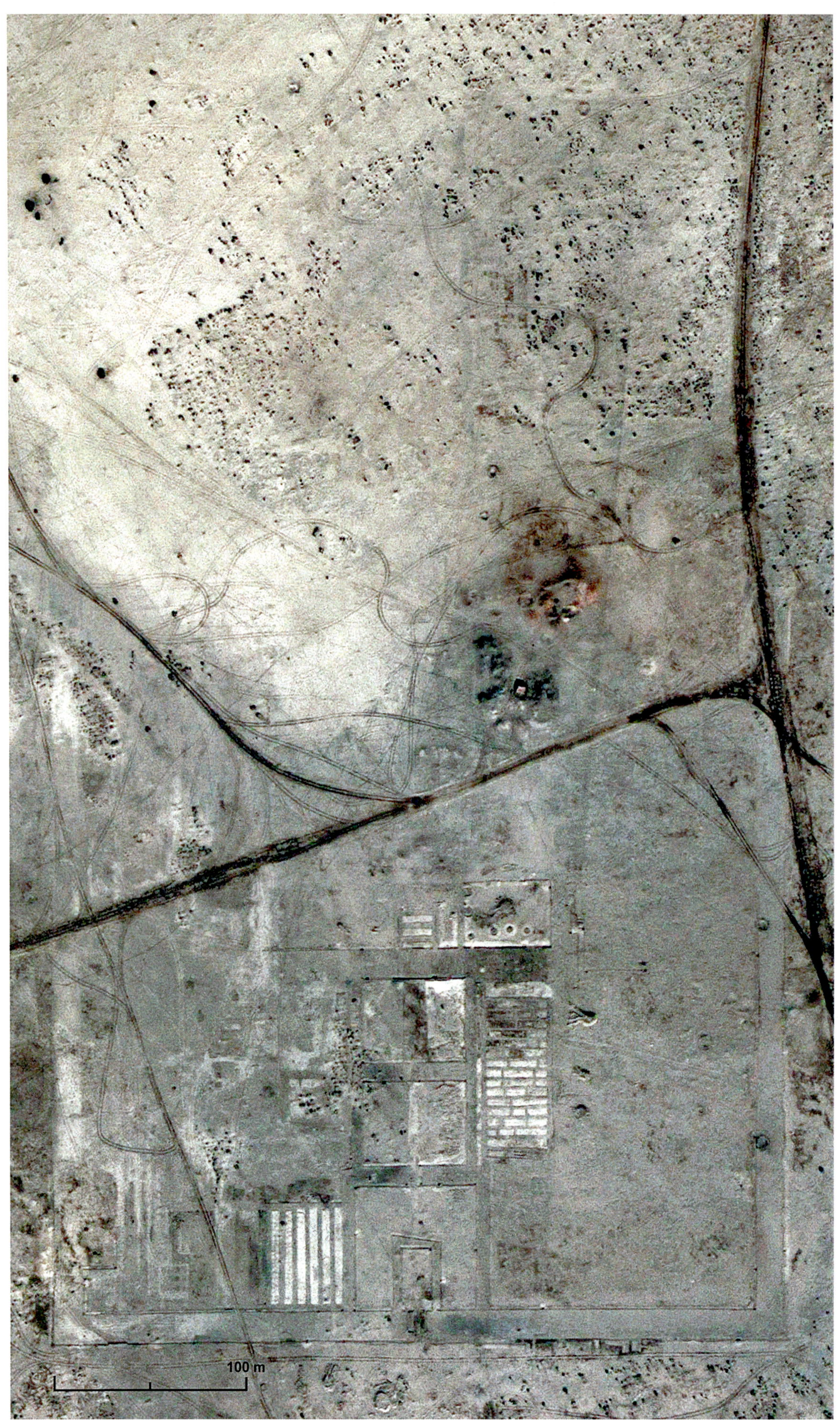

Plate 8 Satellite image of the enclosure and temple at Tell Dafana, after the excavations of 2009 (Google Earth)

Plate 9 Satellite image of the site of Tell Dafana and its surroundings in 2010 (Google Earth)

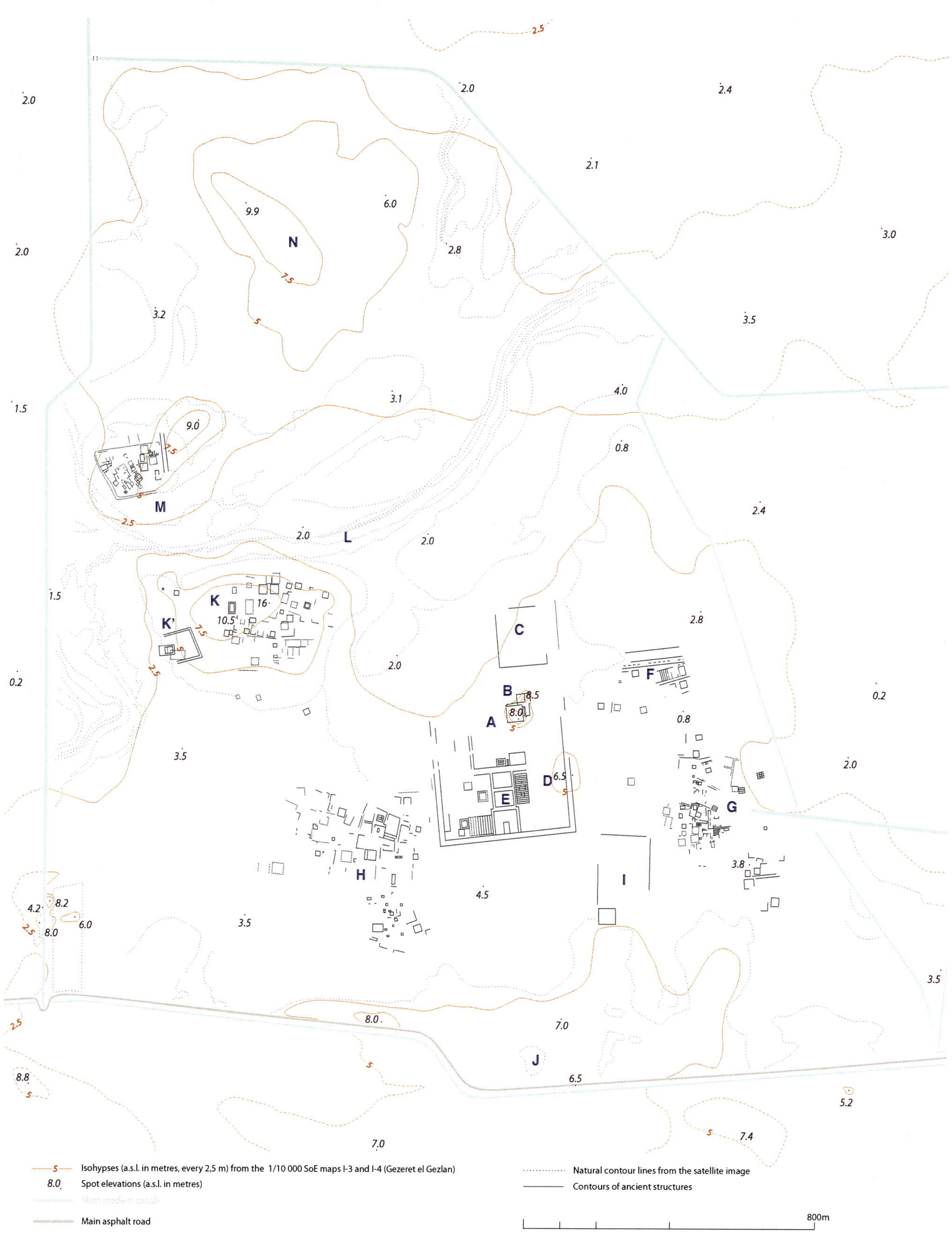

Plate 10 General sketch map of the site of Tell Dafana from the satellite image (F. Leclère)

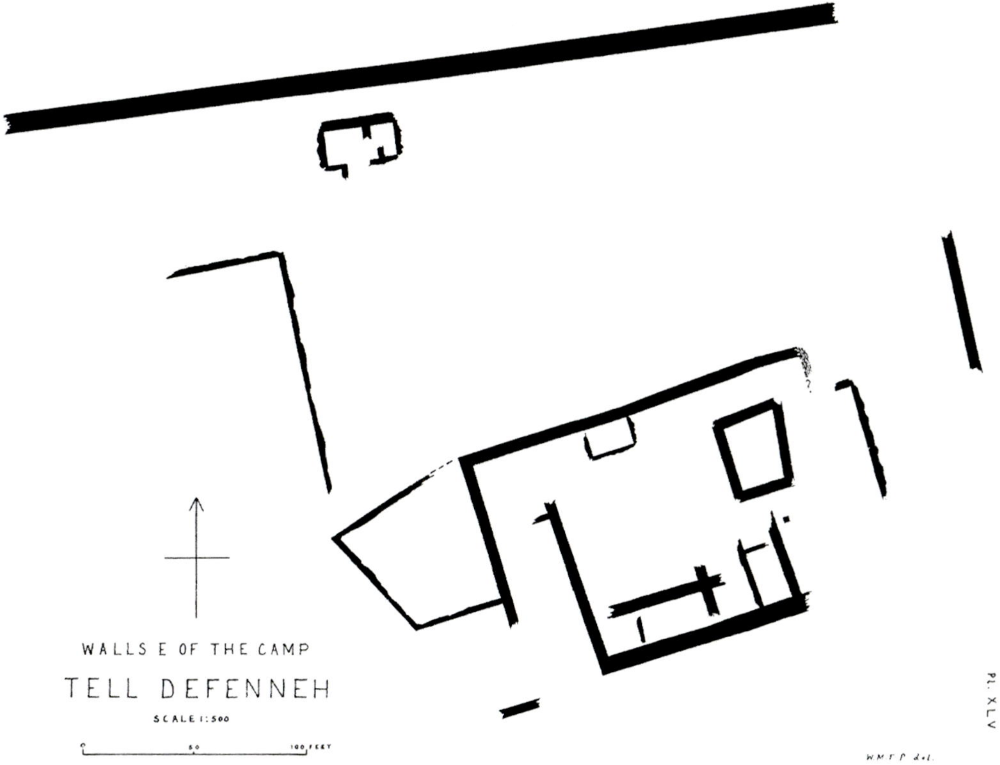

(a) Petrie's plan of the eastern quarter at Tell Dafana (Petrie 1888, pl. xlv)

(b) Satellite image, detail of the eastern quarter at Tell Dafana (Google Earth)

Plate 11

(a) Satellite image, detail of the south-eastern quarter at Tell Dafana (Google Earth)

(b) Satellite image, detail of the south-western quarter at Tell Dafana (Google Earth)

Plate 12

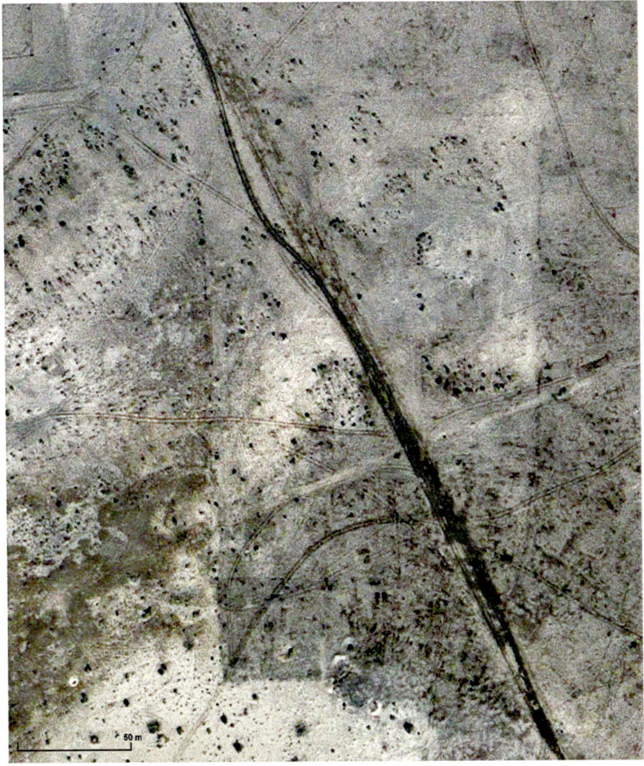

(a) Satellite image, detail of the area immediately south-east of the main enclosure at Tell Dafana (Google Earth)

(b) Satellite image, detail of the area near the road, at the southern edge of the site, in the axis of the enclosure at Tell Dafana (Google Earth)

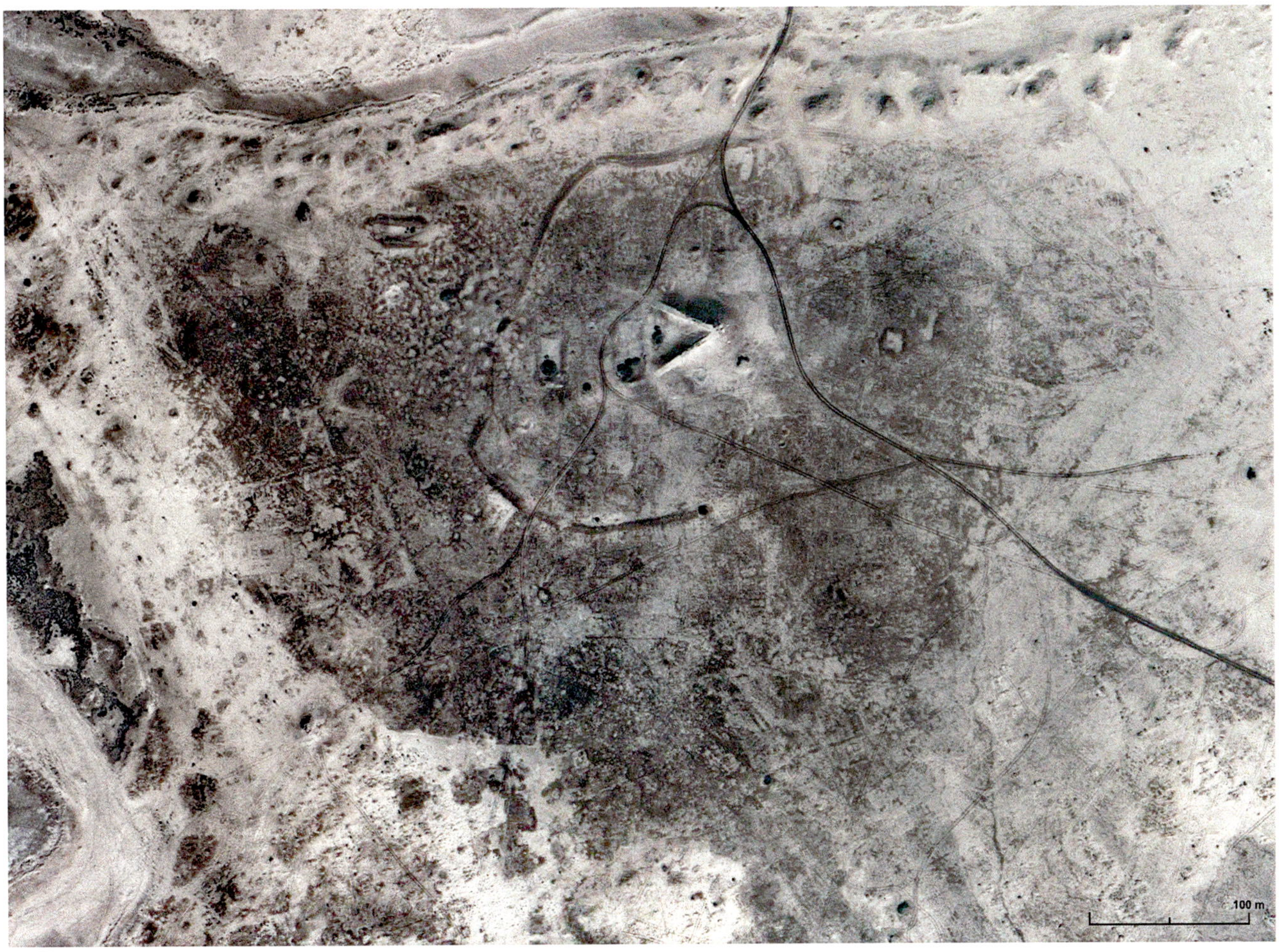

(c) Satellite image, detail of the north-west 'Ptolemaic' mound at Tell Dafana (Google Earth)

Plate 13

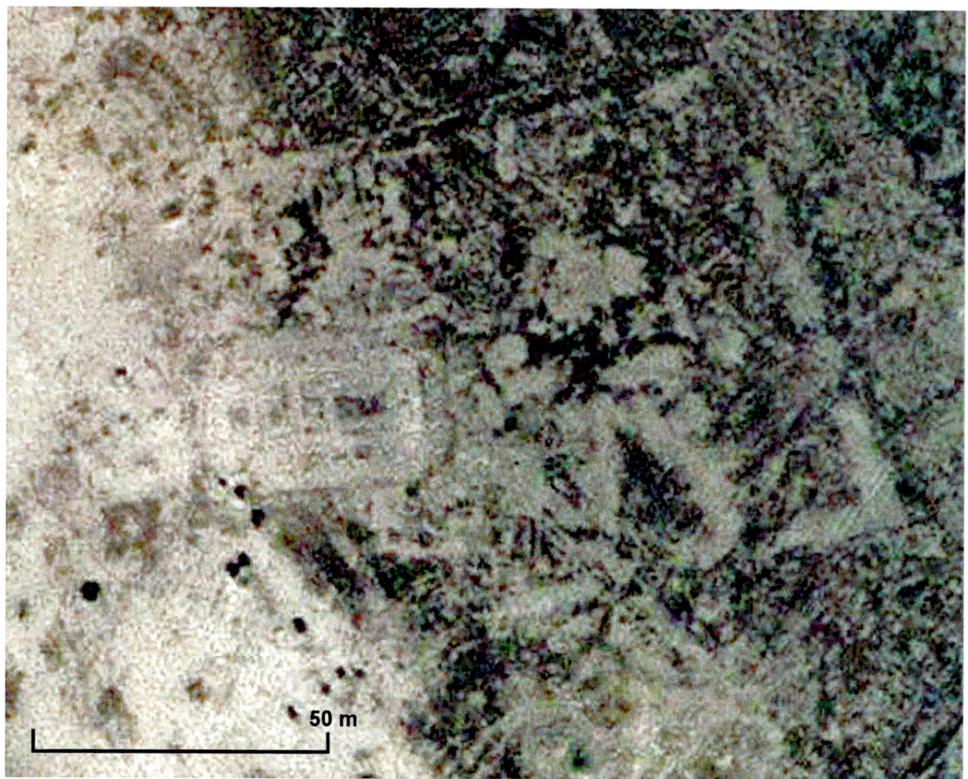

(a) Satellite image, detail of the enclosure at the western edge of the north-west 'Ptolemaic' mound at Tell Dafana (Google Earth)

(b) Satellite image, detail of the north-west 'Roman' mound at Tell Dafana (Google Earth)

Plate 14

Plate 15 Non-pottery vessels from Tell Dafana in the British Museum (not to scale)

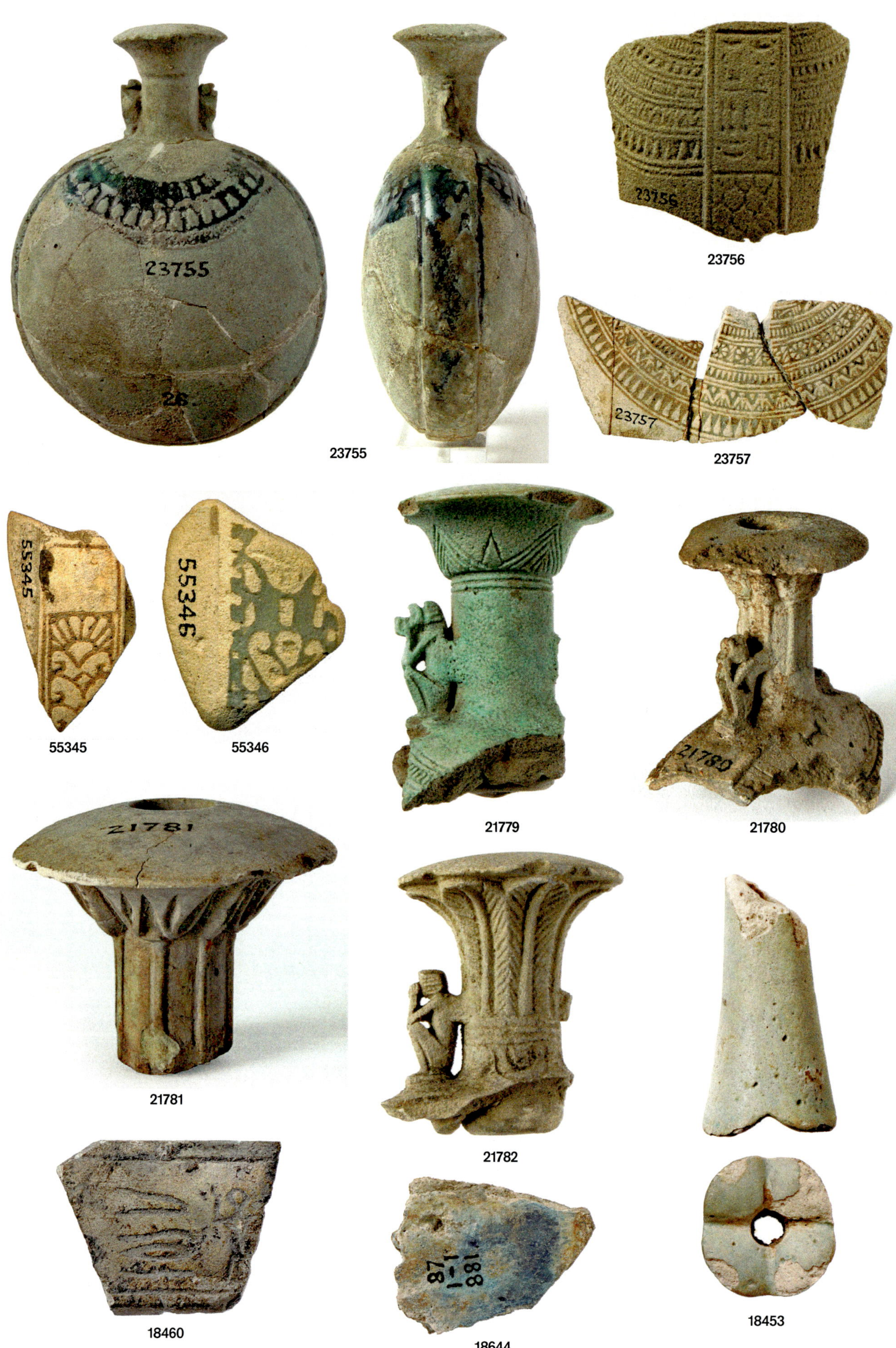

Plate 16 Non-pottery vessels from Tell Dafana in the British Museum (not to scale)

Plate 17 Foundation deposits of Psamtik I (23556 = 1887,0101.1354-74) and Apries (18562) from Tell Dafana in the British Museum (not to scale)

1887,0101.1376   1887,0101.1377   1887,0101.1378   1887,0101.1379   1887,0101.1380   23641

18486

23820

23646

1887,0101.771

1887,0101.1413

1887,0101.1414

1887,0101.1375+1381

1887,0101.1415

23992

23993

Plate 18 Foundation deposit of Psamtik I (EA 23557), other foundation deposits and other architectural elements from Tell Dafana in the British Museum (not to scale)

23431

23866

23868

23434

23436

23873

18493

1906,0301.2

1906,0301.4

1906,0301.5

Plate 19 Sculpture in bronze and pottery from Tell Dafana in the British Museum (not to scale)

Plate 20 Sculpture in pottery and stone from Tell Dafana in the British Museum (not to scale)

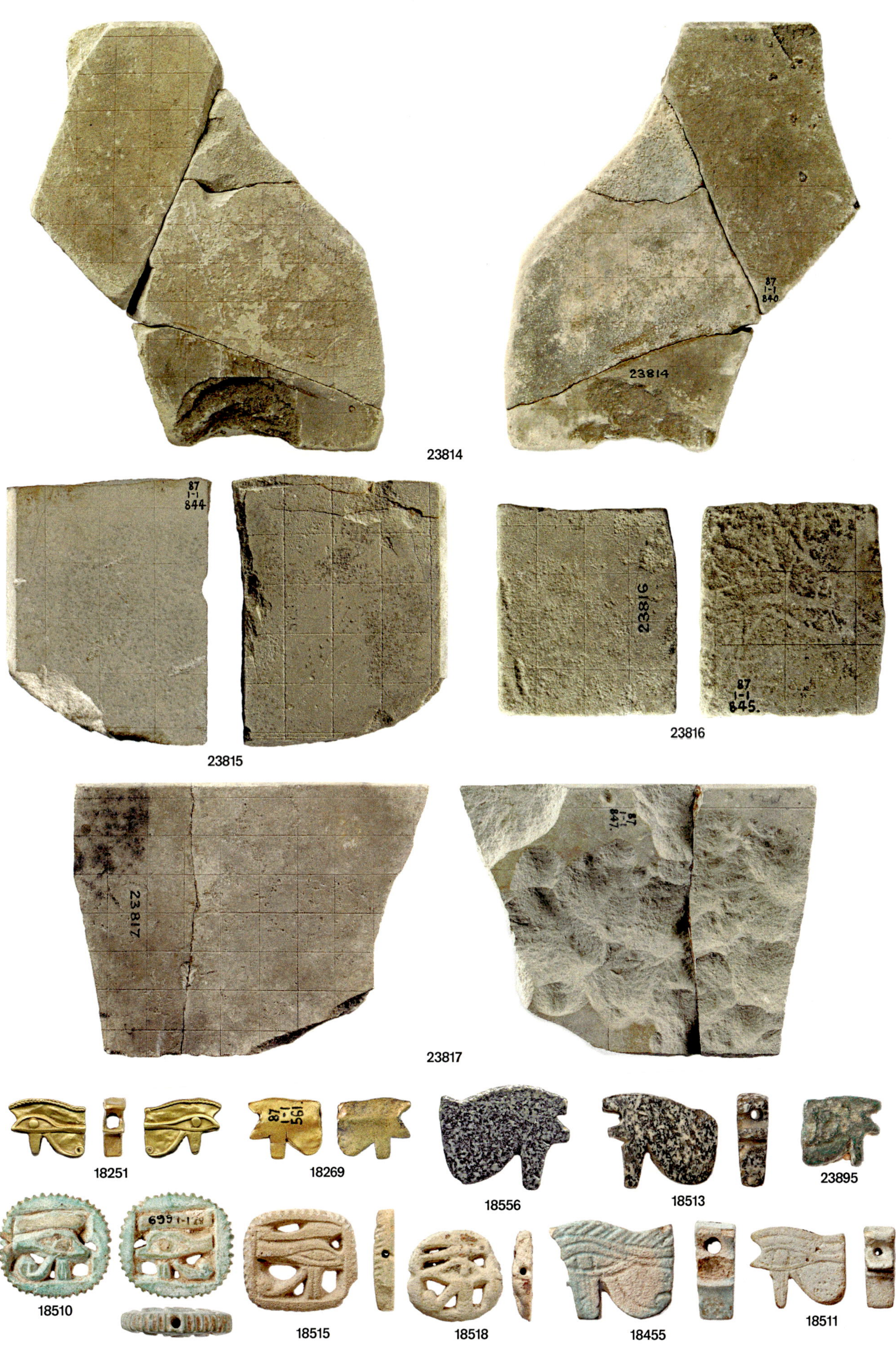

Plate 21 Trial-pieces and amulets from Tell Dafana in the British Museum (not to scale)

Plate 22 Amulets from Tell Dafana in the British Museum (not to scale)

Plate 23 Amulets and scarabs from Tell Dafana in the British Museum (not to scale)

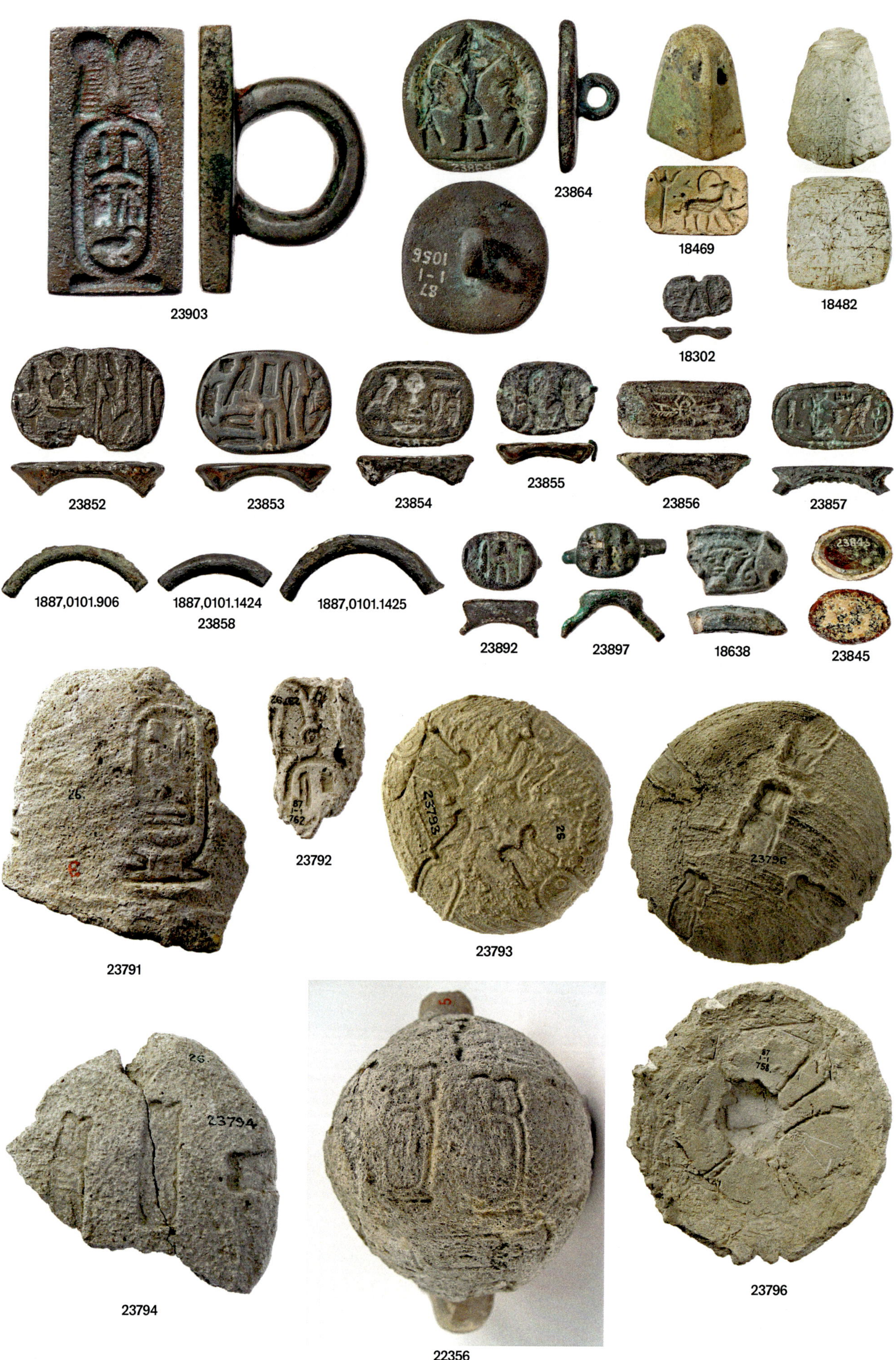

Plate 24 Seals, signet-rings and seal impressions from Tell Dafana in the British Museum (not to scale)

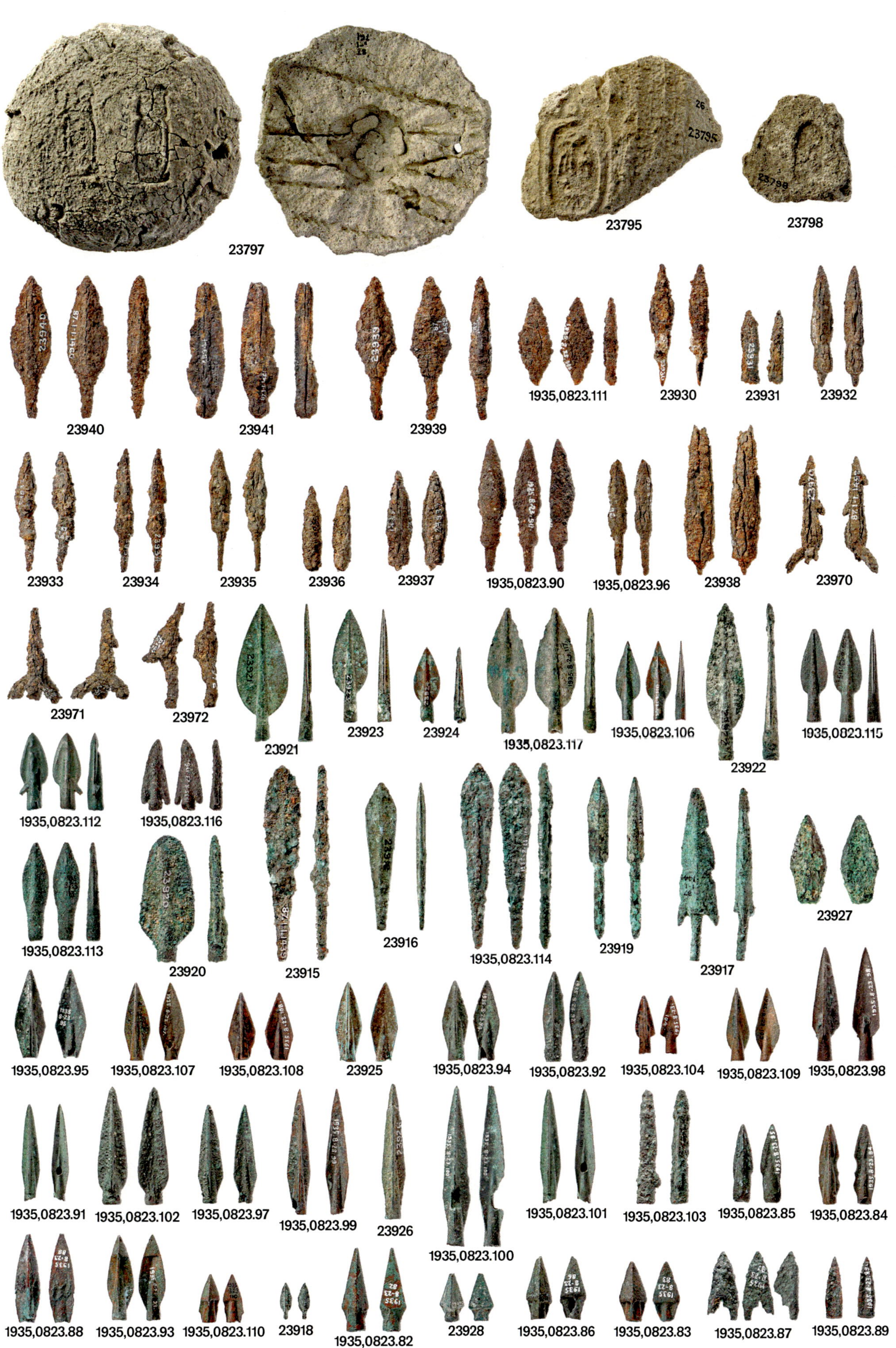

Plate 25 Seal impressions and weapons (arrowheads) from Tell Dafana in the British Museum (not to scale)

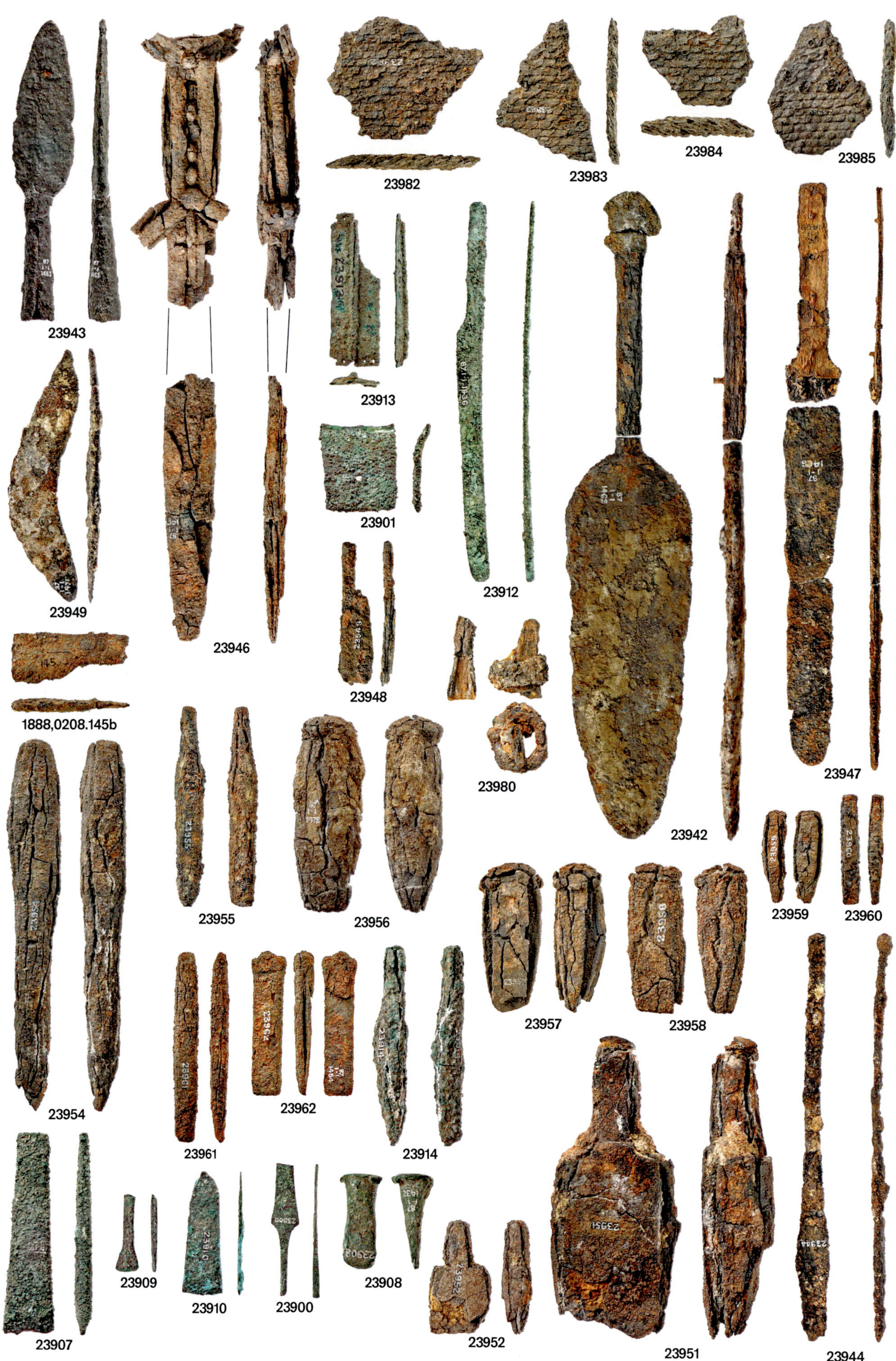

Plate 26 Metal weapons and tools from Tell Dafana in the British Museum. All items at 1:3 except 23909, 23900 and 1888,0208.145b at 1:2

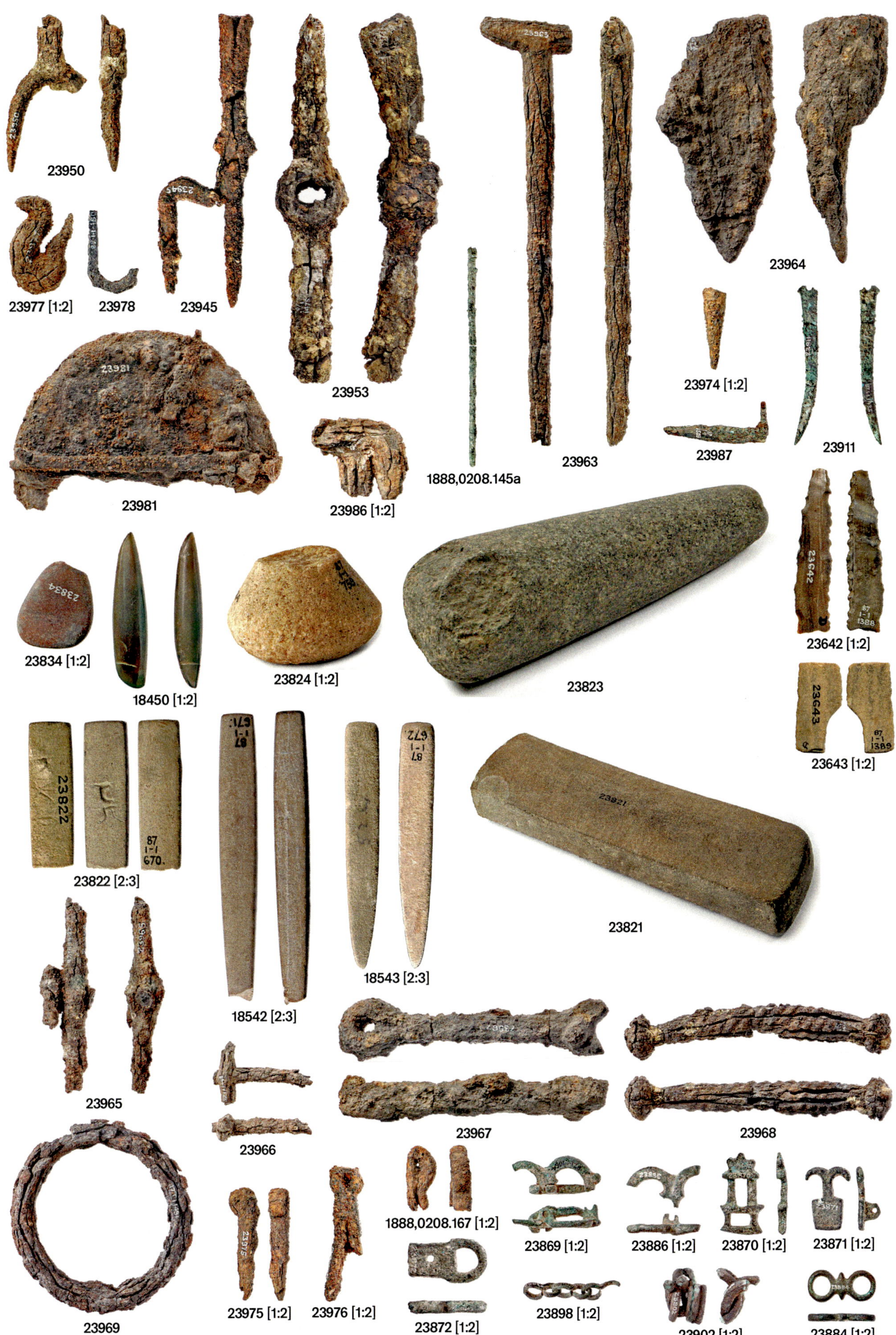

Plate 27 Metal and stone tools; metal fittings from Tell Dafana in the British Museum. Scale 1:3 except where otherwise indicated

Plate 28 Fittings and equipment; jewellery from Tell Dafana in the British Museum

Plate 29 Jewellery from Tell Dafana in the British Museum (not to scale unless otherwise indicated)

Plate 30 Games, drill-cores, samples and slag from Tell Dafana in the British Museum (not to scale unless otherwise indicated)

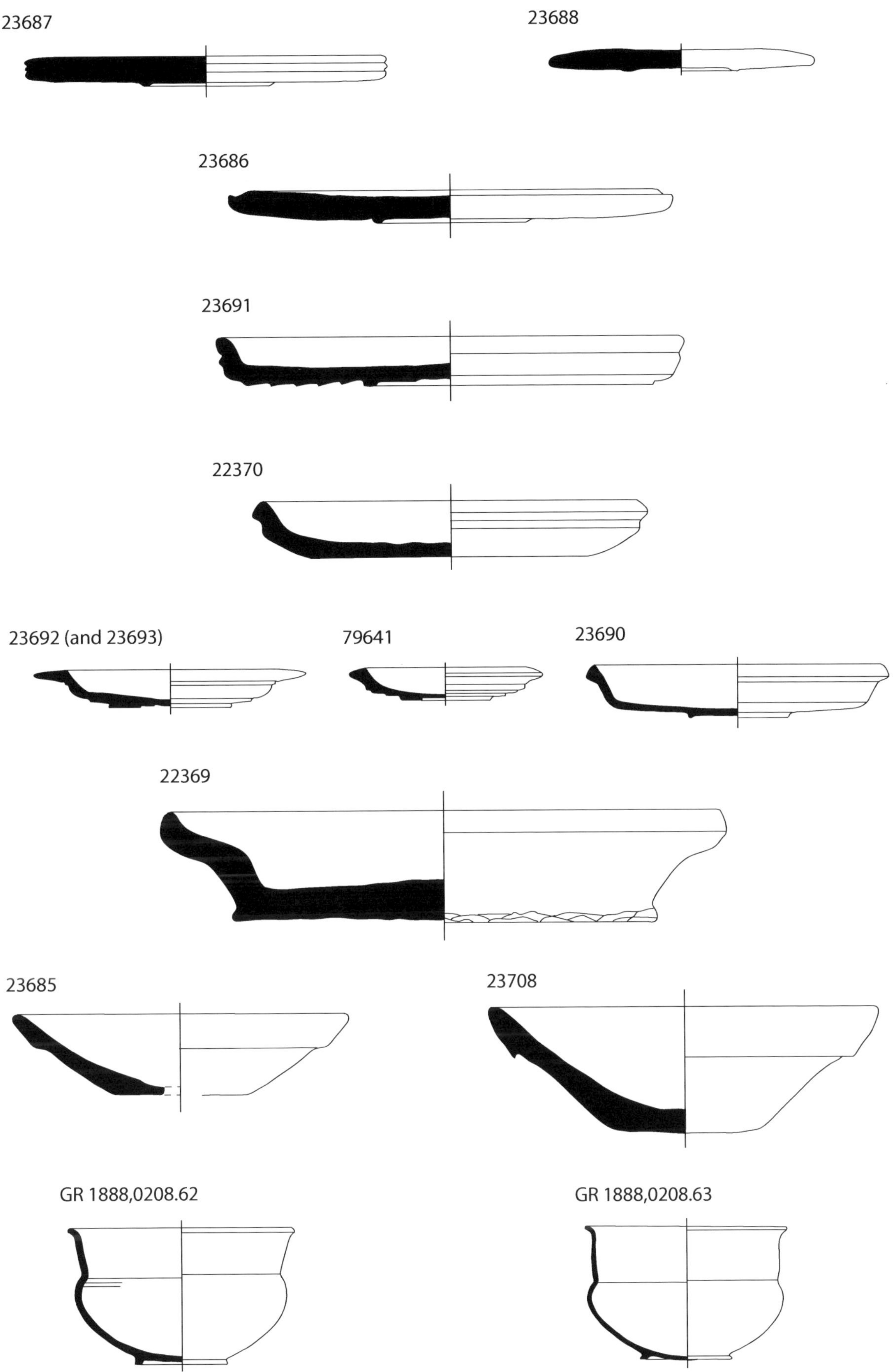

Plate 31 Pottery platters and mortaria from Tell Dafana in the British Museum (all 1:4)

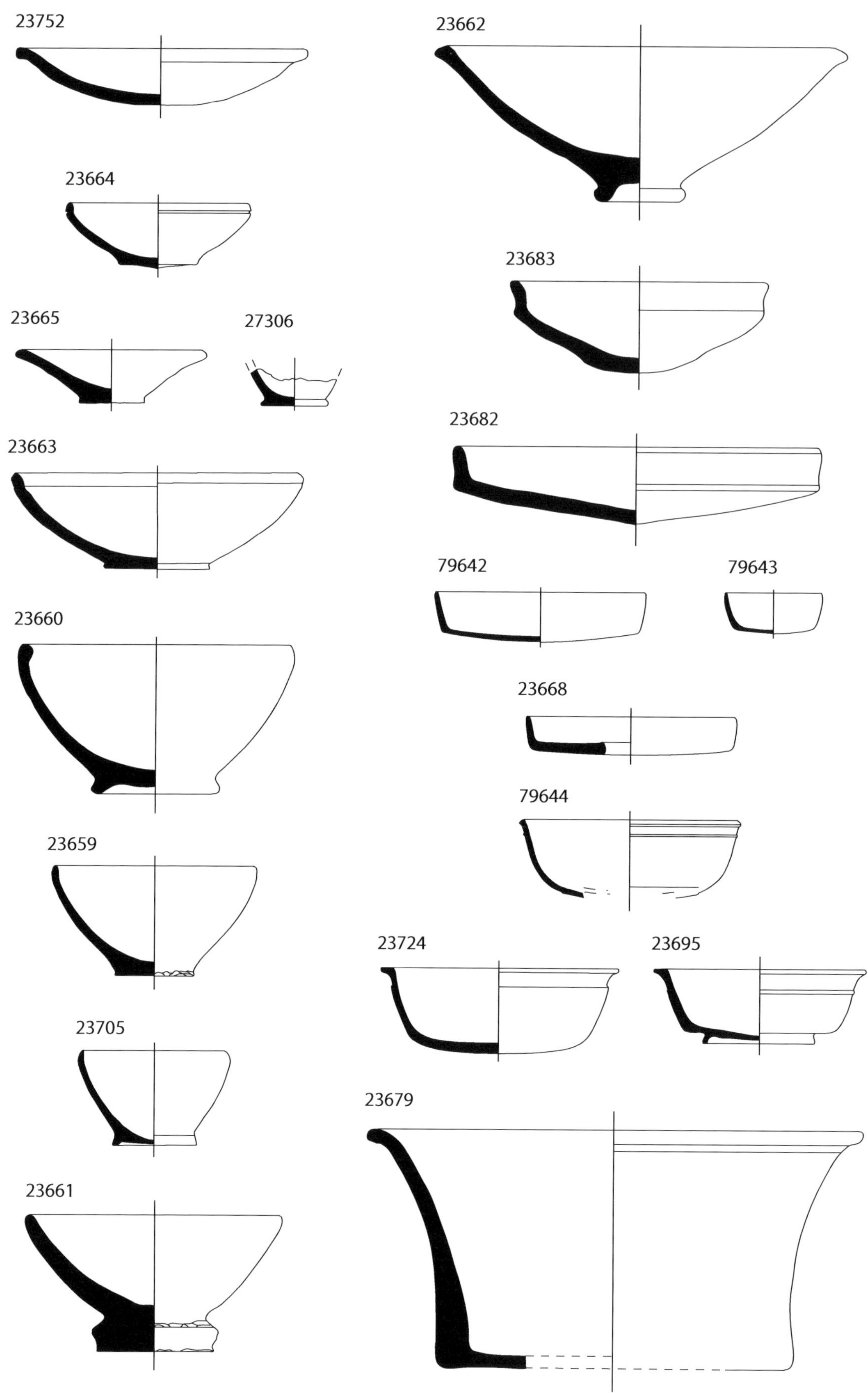

Plate 32 Pottery dishes and bowls from Tell Dafana in the British Museum (all 1:4)

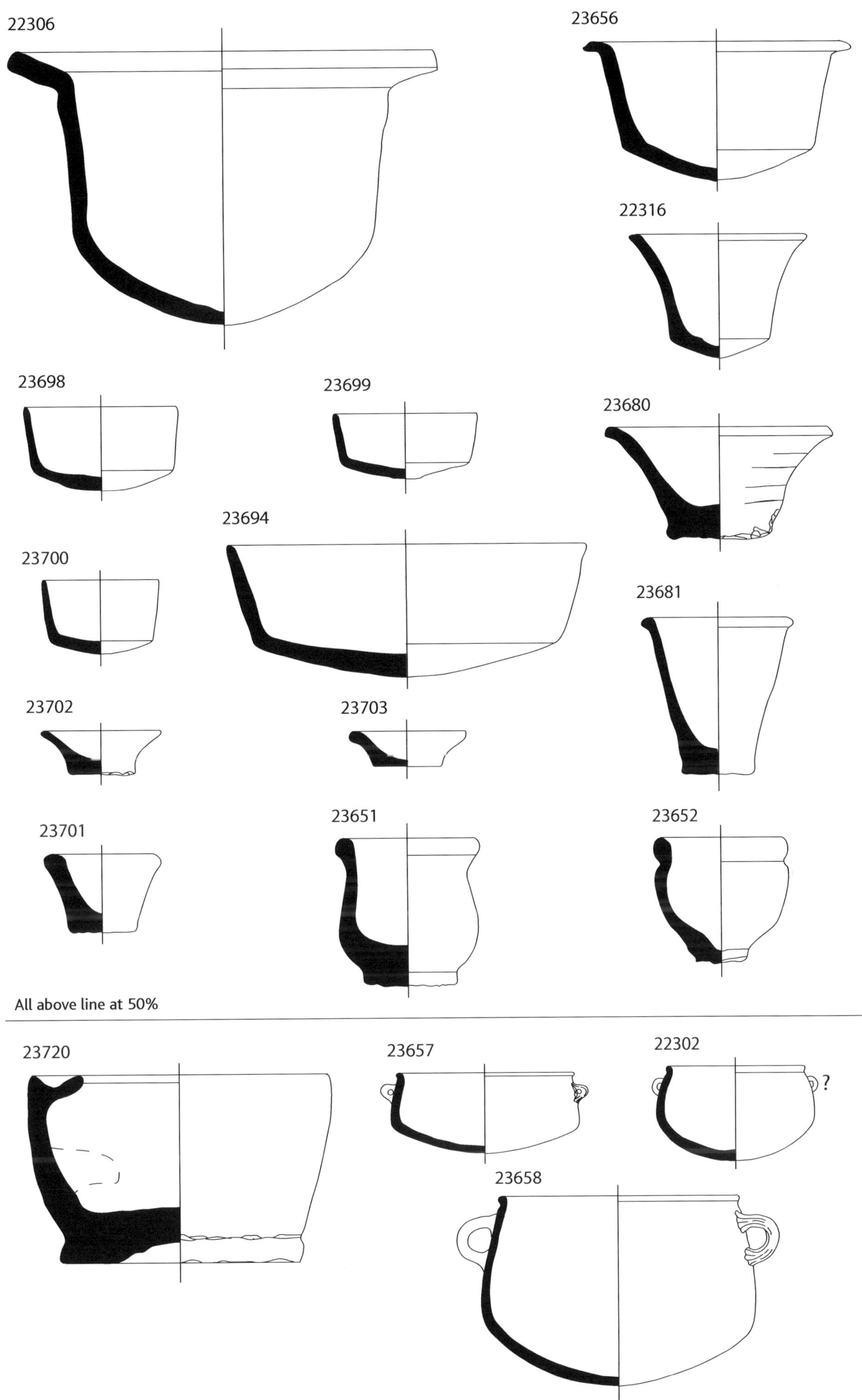

Plate 33 Pottery bowls and miniature vessels from Tell Dafana in the British Museum (1:2 and 1:4)

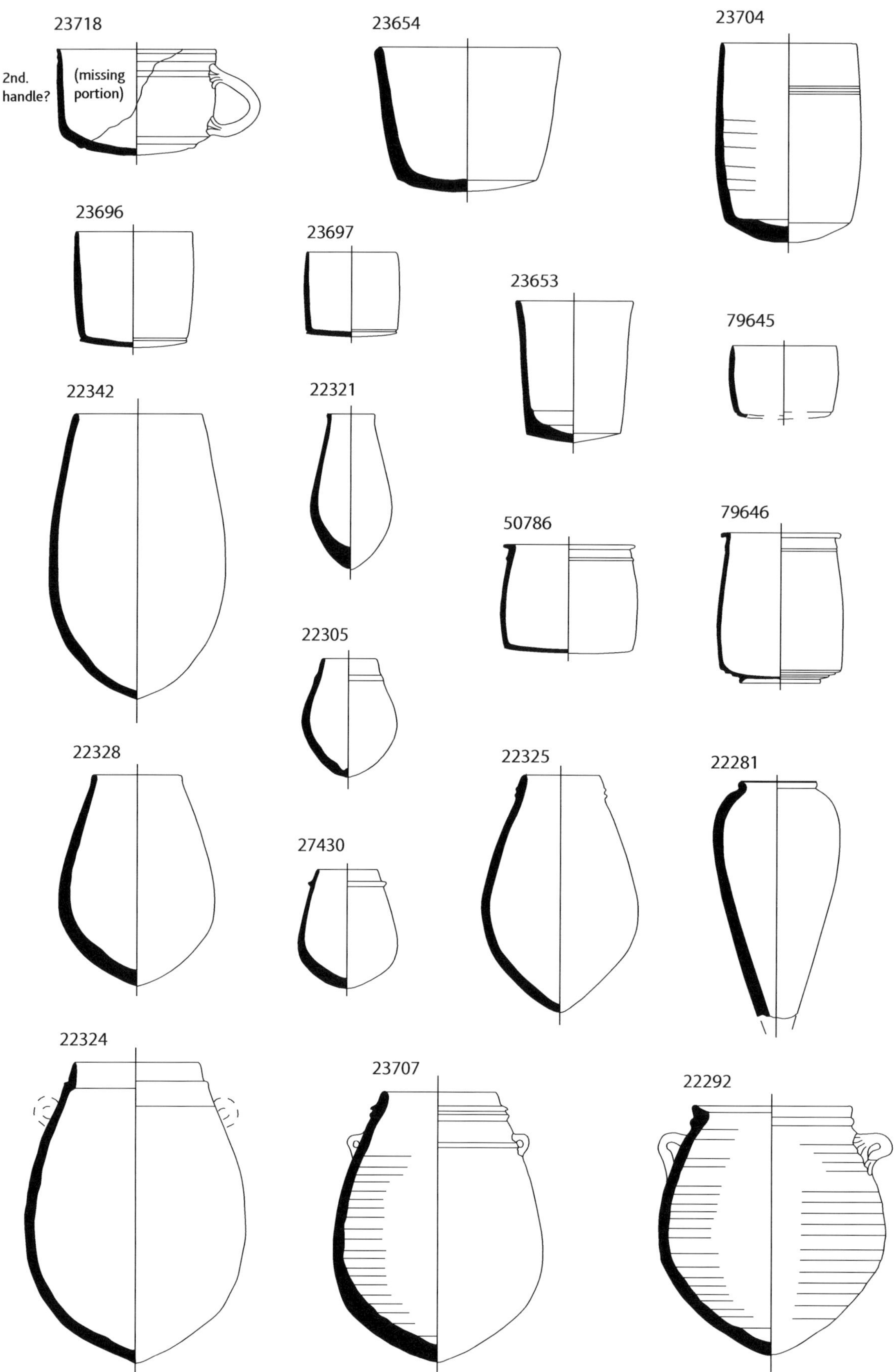

Plate 34 Pottery cups and jars from Tell Dafana in the British Museum (all 1:4)

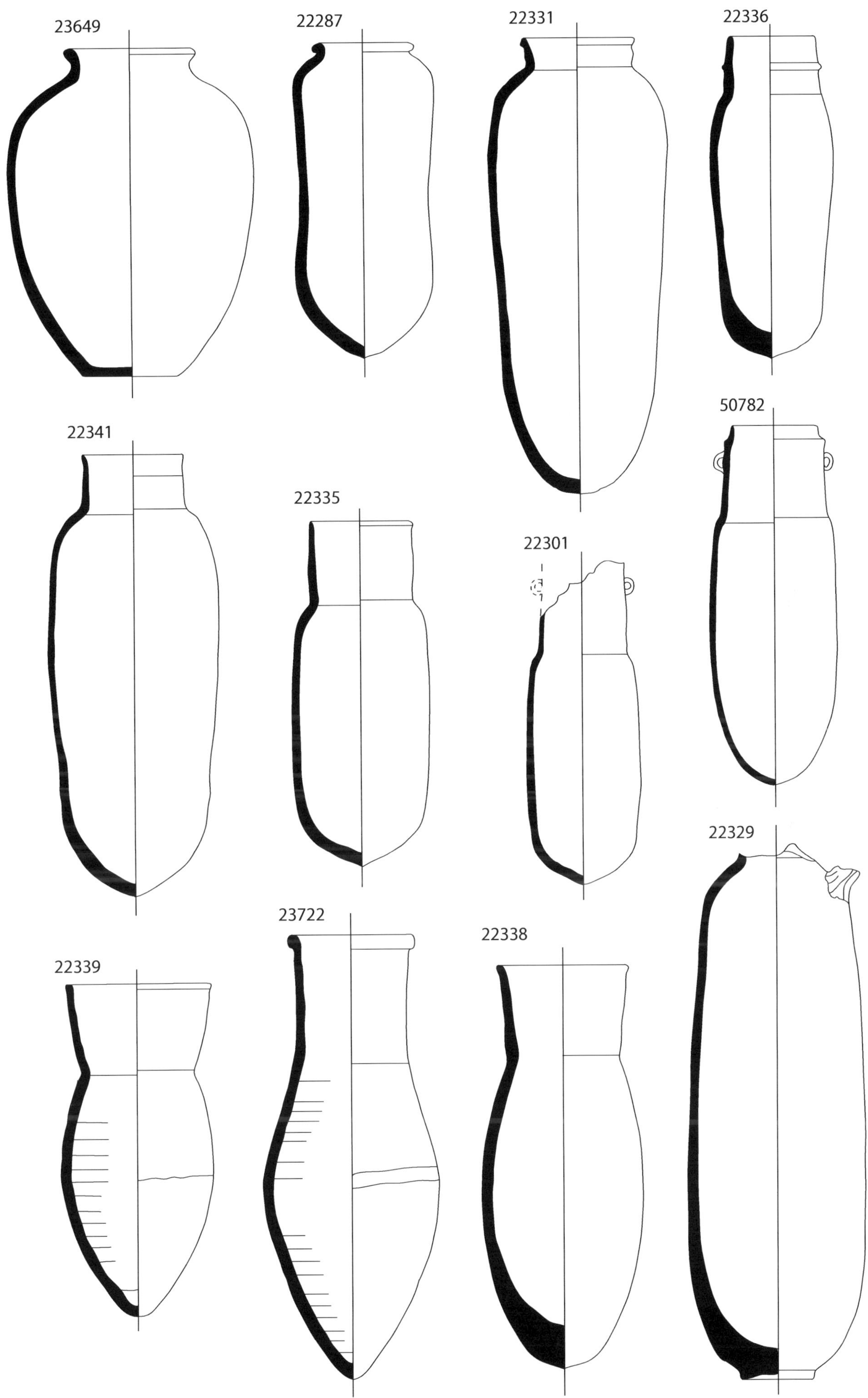

Plate 35 Pottery tall jars from Tell Dafana in the British Museum (all 1:4)

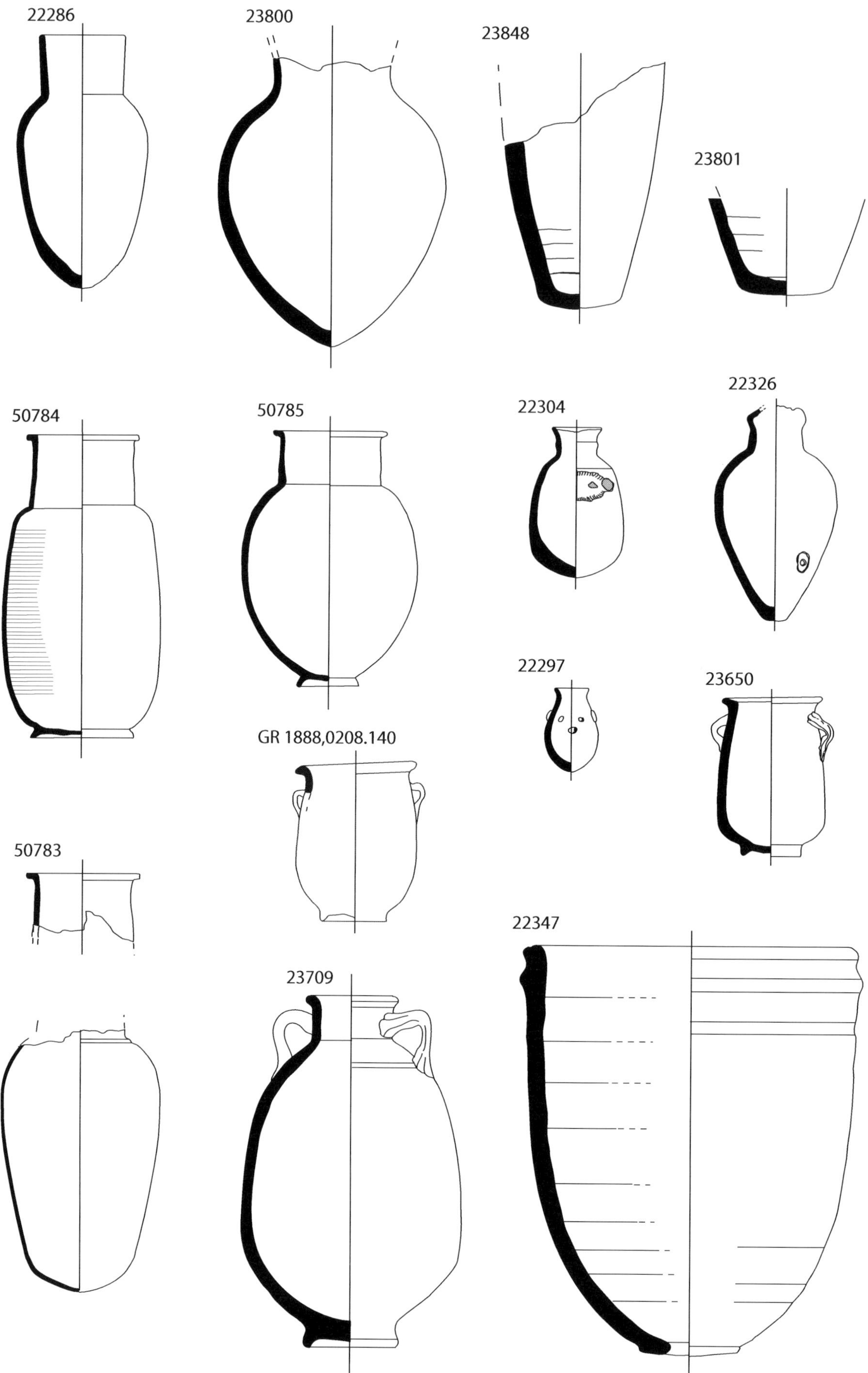

Plate 36 Pottery jars and sink from Tell Dafana in the British Museum (all 1:4)

Plate 37 Pottery jugs from Tell Dafana in the British Museum (all 1:2)

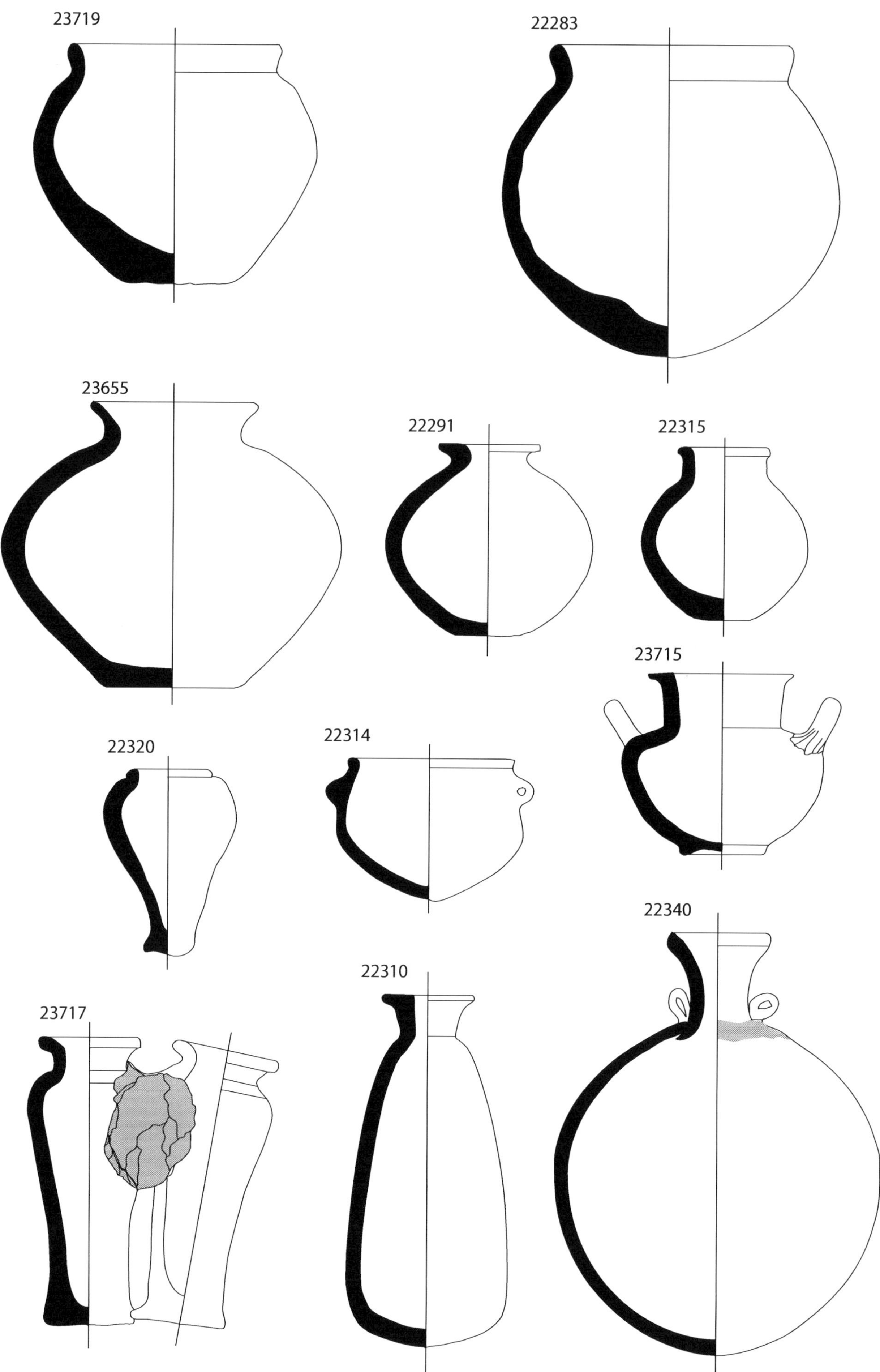

Plate 38 Pottery closed vases from Tell Dafana in the British Museum (all 1:2)

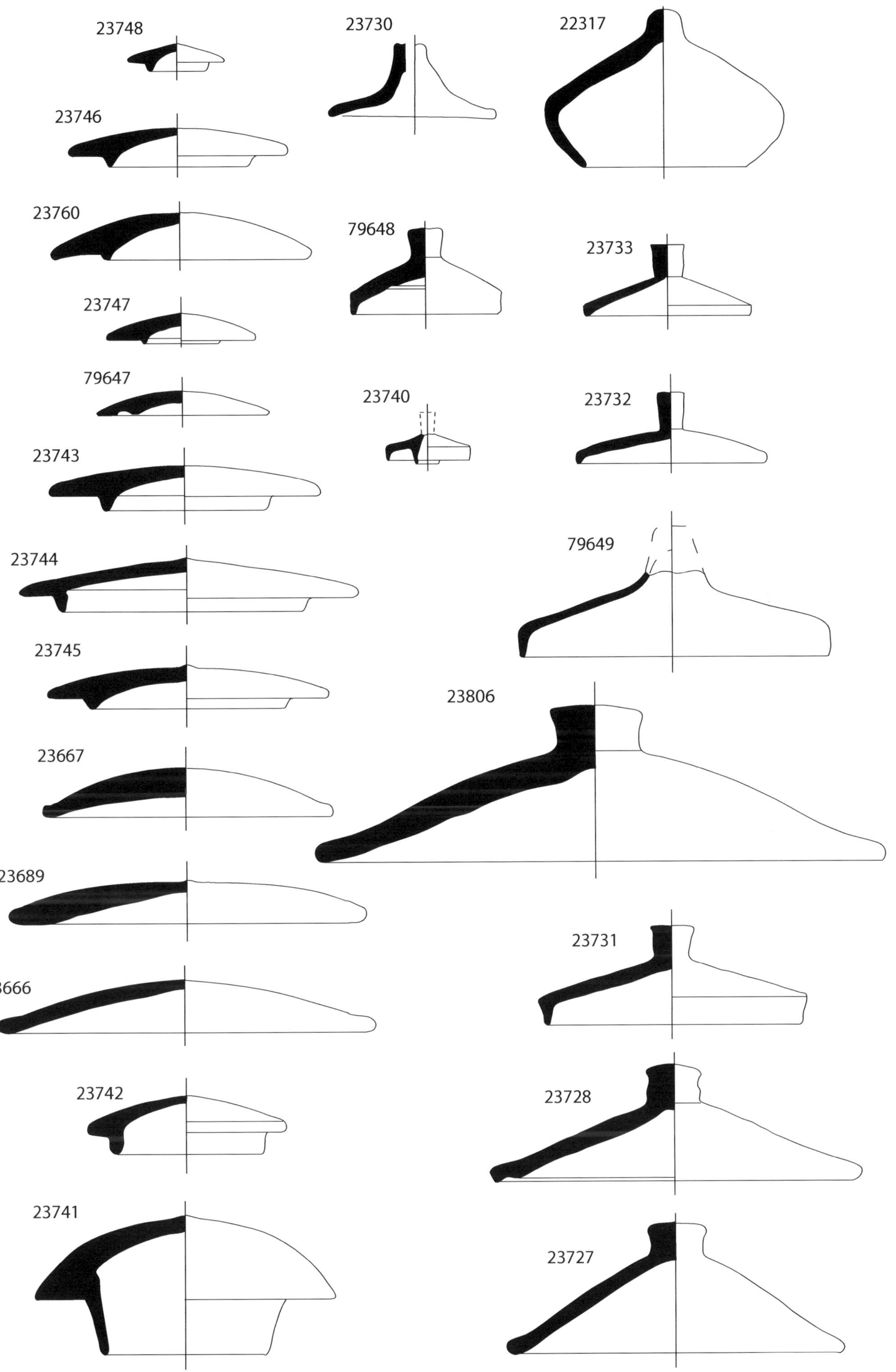

Plate 39 Pottery lids from Tell Dafana in the British Museum (all 1:2)

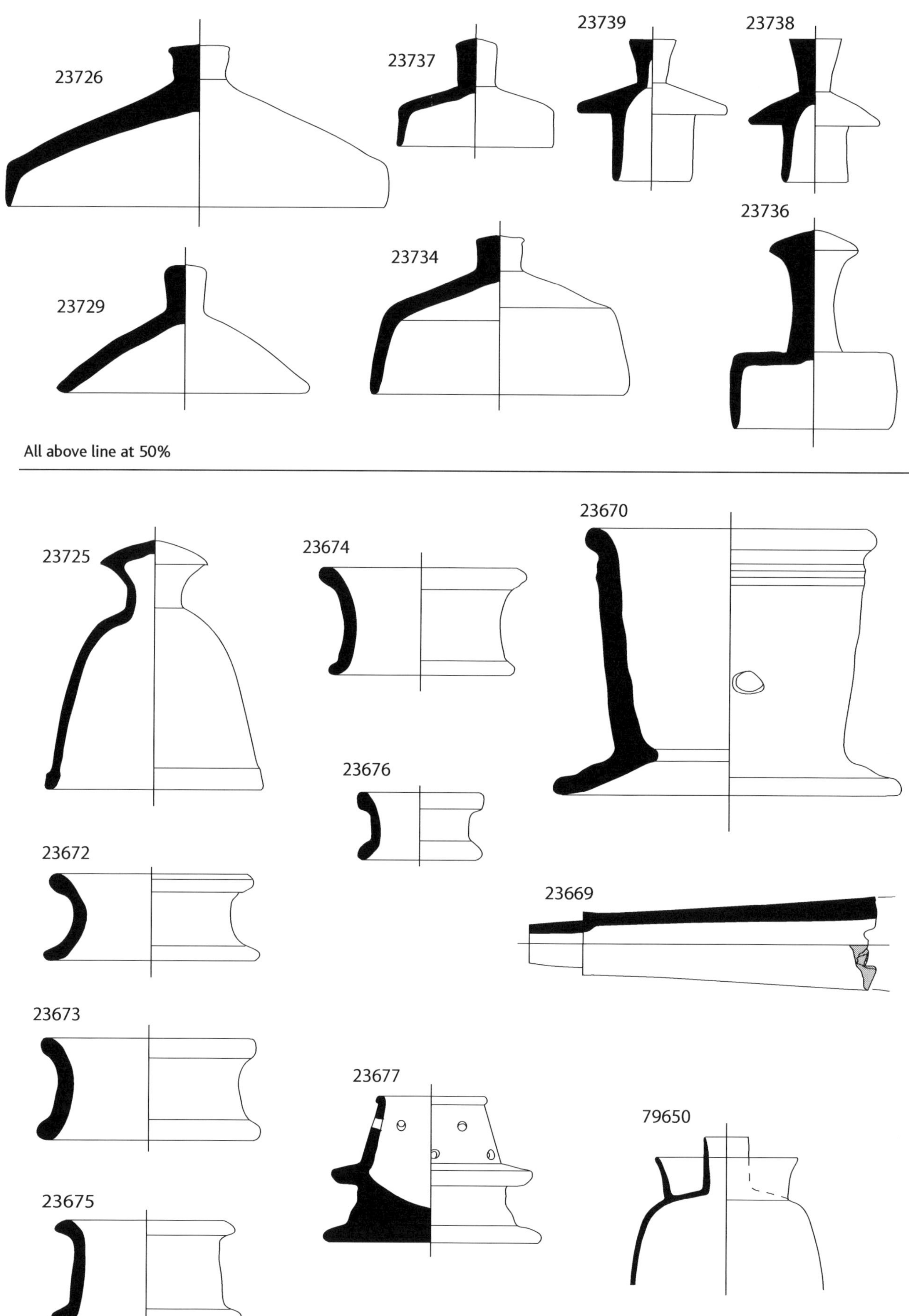

Plate 40 Pottery lids, covers, potstands and miscellaneous items from Tell Dafana in the British Museum (all 1:4)

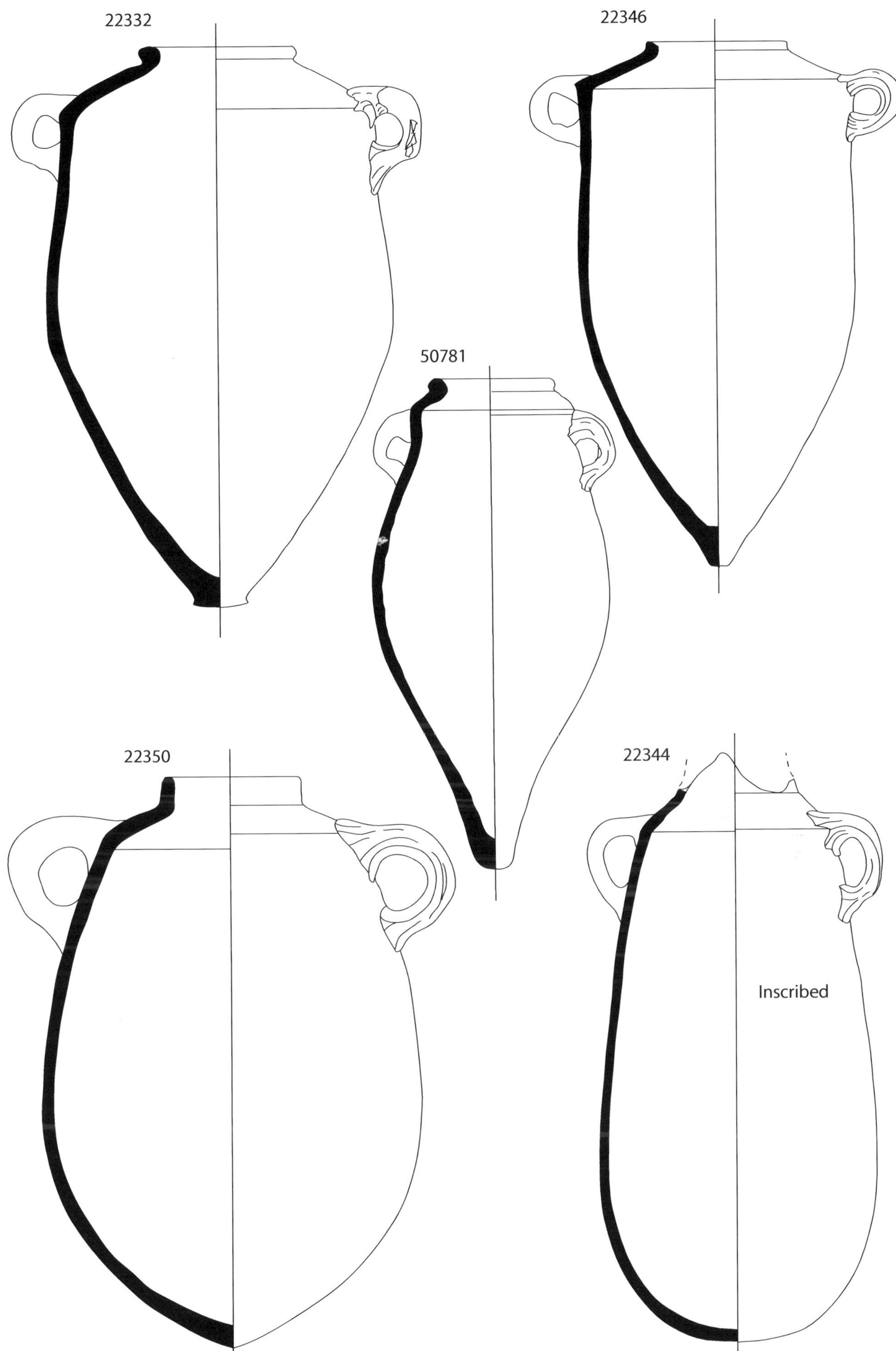

Plate 41 Pottery: Phoenician jars from Tell Dafana in the British Museum (all 1:4)

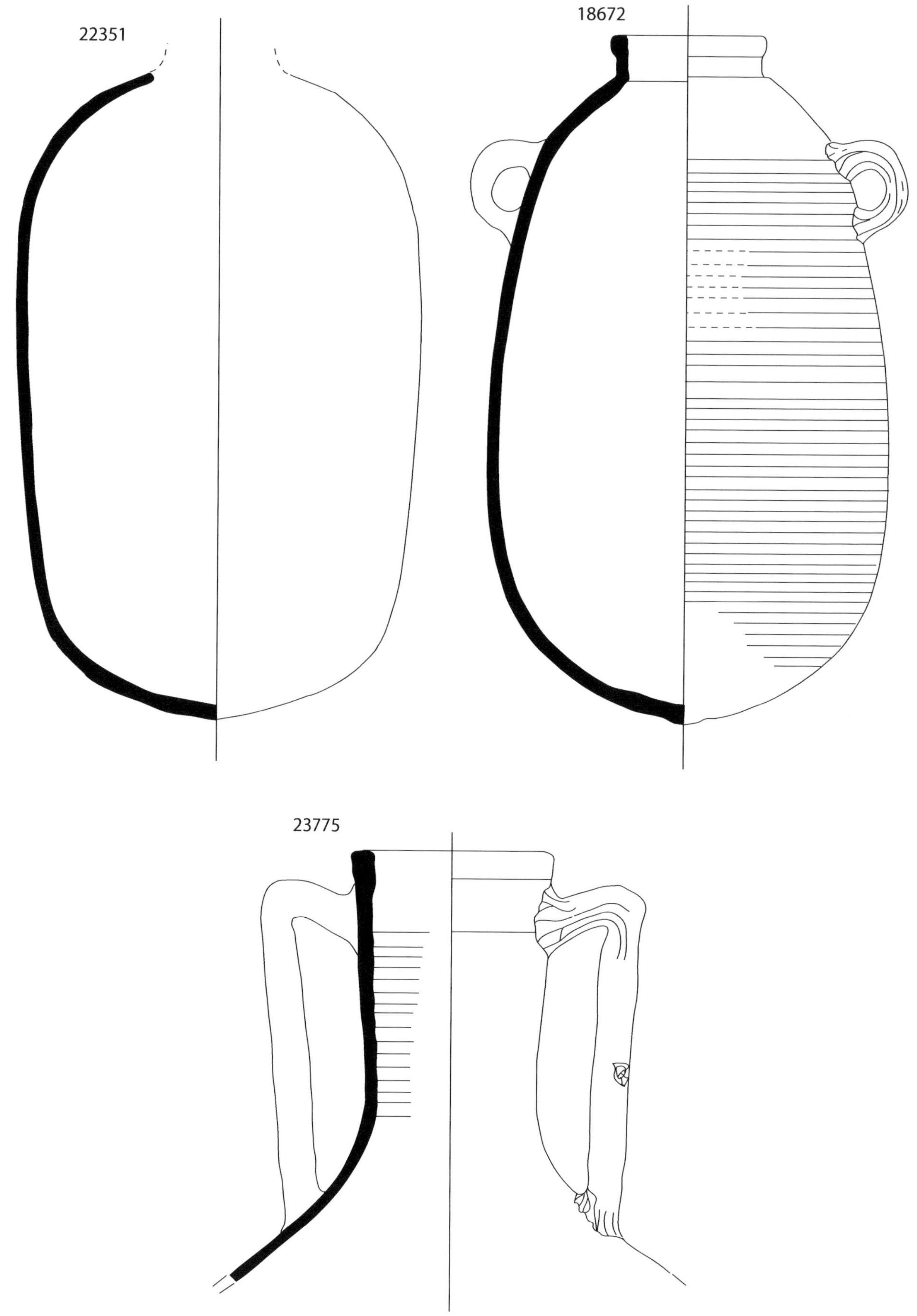

Plate 42 Pottery: large jars and amphora from Tell Dafana in the British Museum (all 1:4)

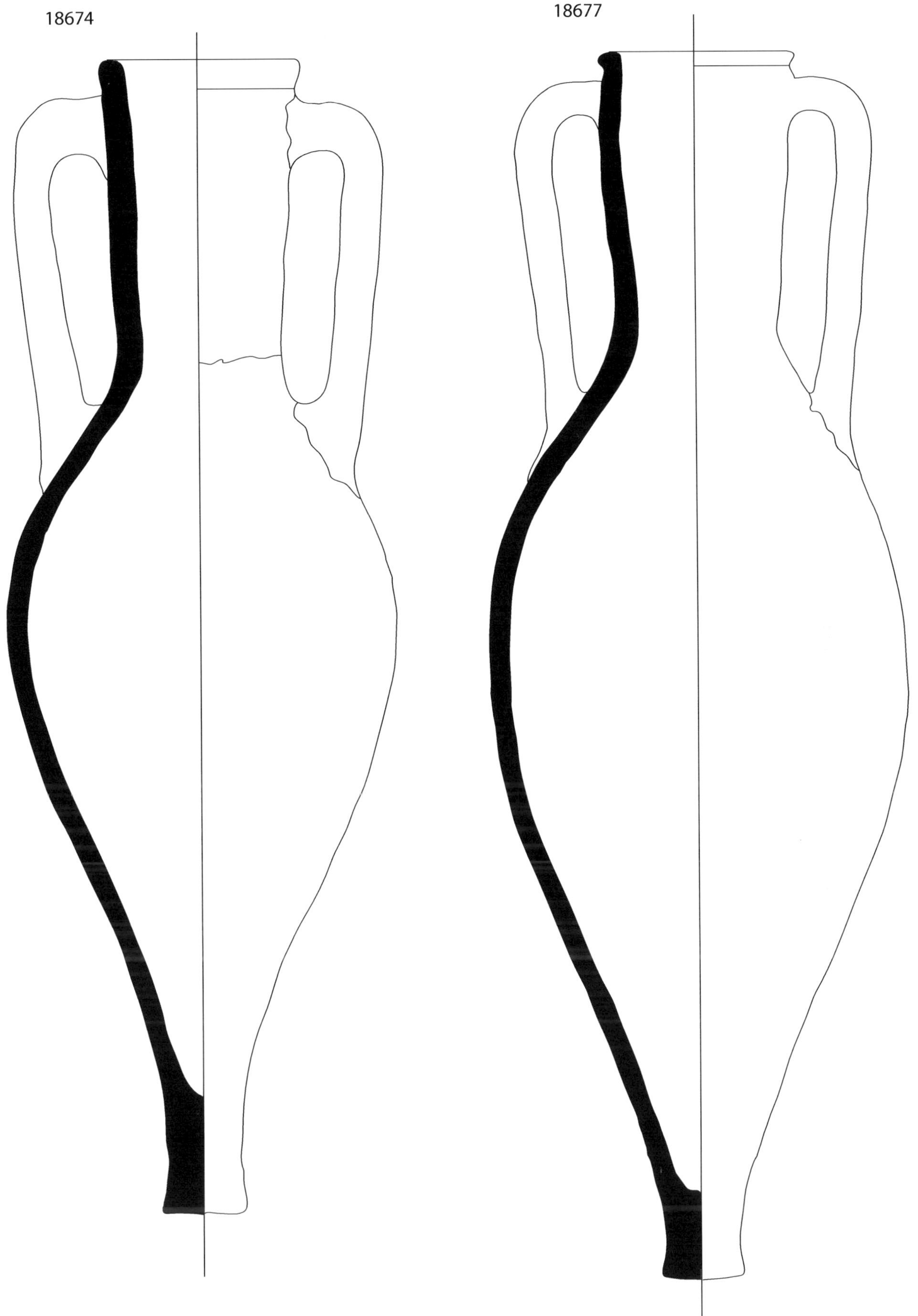

Plate 43 Pottery: Chian amphorae from Tell Dafana in the British Museum (all 1:4)

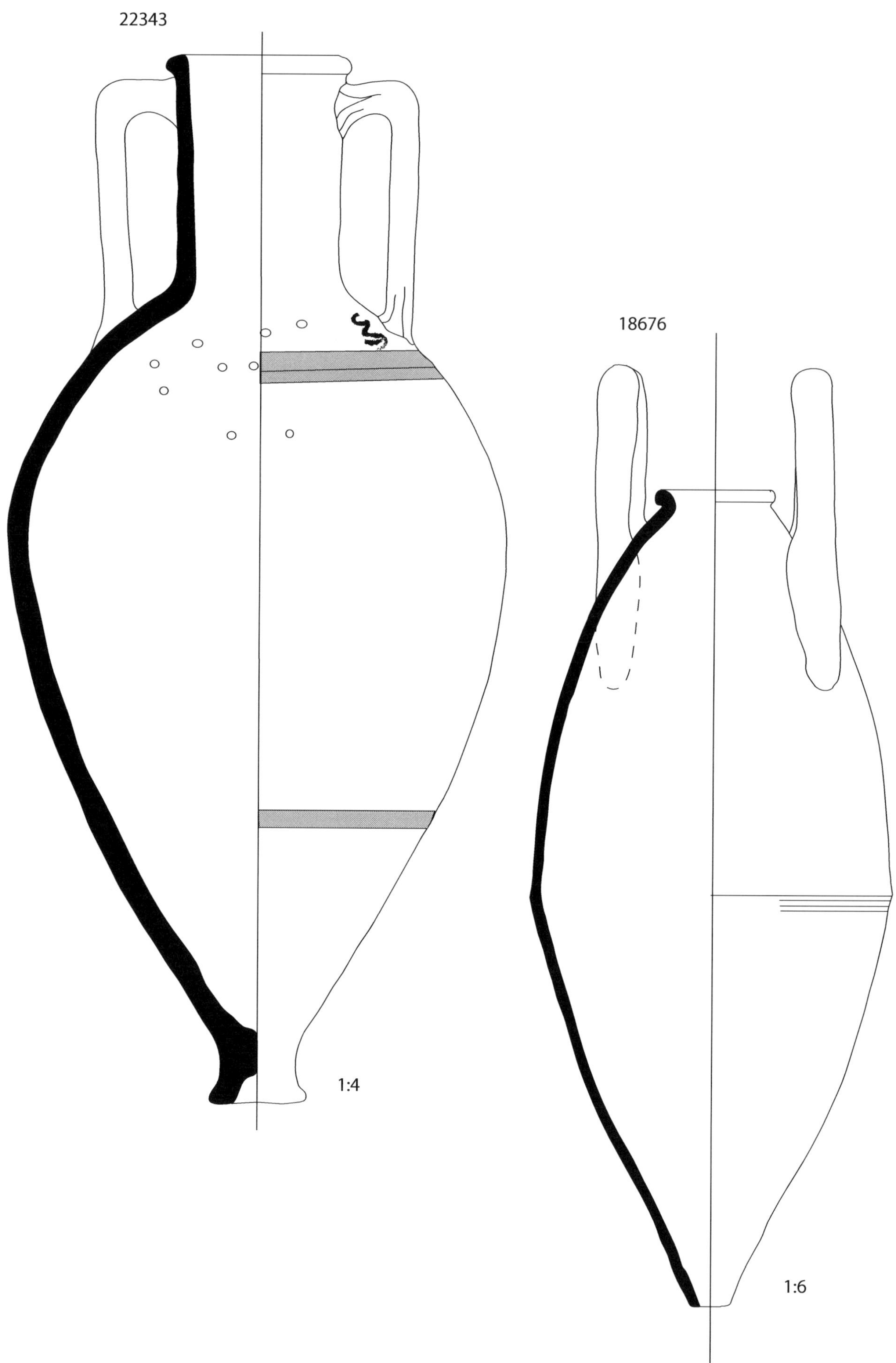

Plate 44 Pottery: Klazomenian amphora and basket-handled jar from Tell Dafana in the British Museum

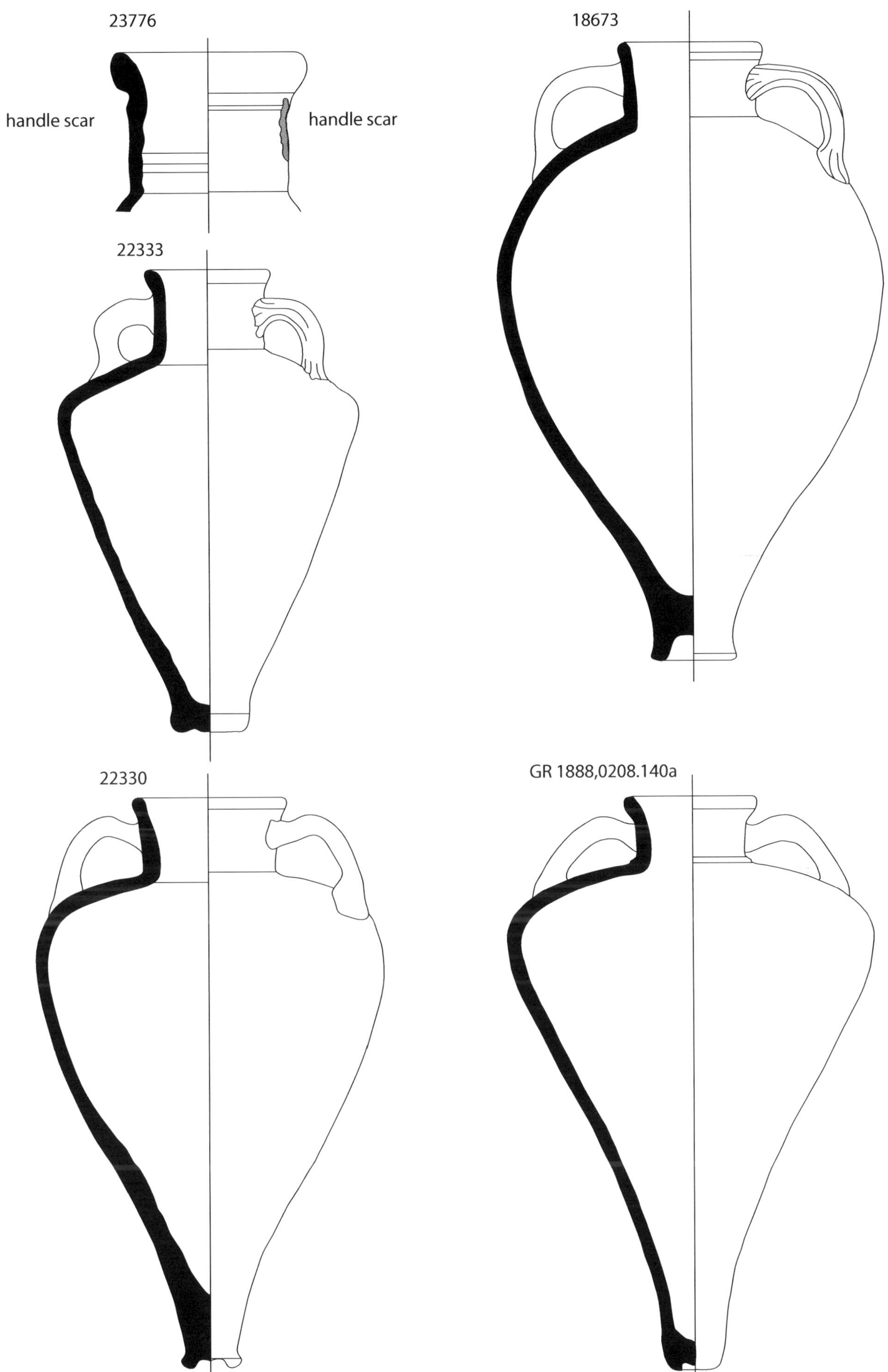

Plate 45 Pottery: Italian, Samian and other Greek amphorae from Tell Dafana in the British Museum (all 1:4)

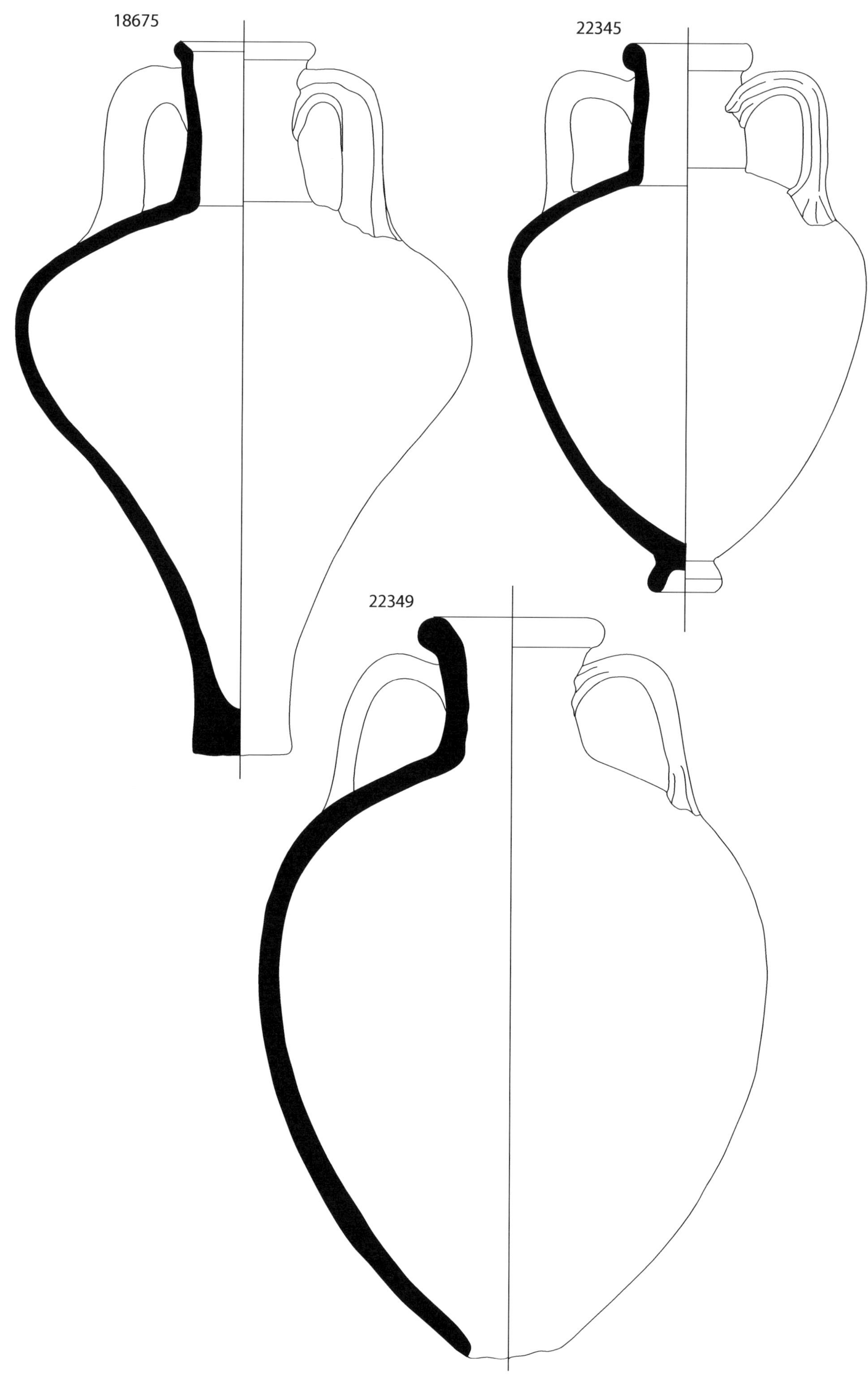

Plate 46 Pottery: Lesbian and other East Greek amphorae from Tell Dafana in the British Museum (all 1:4)

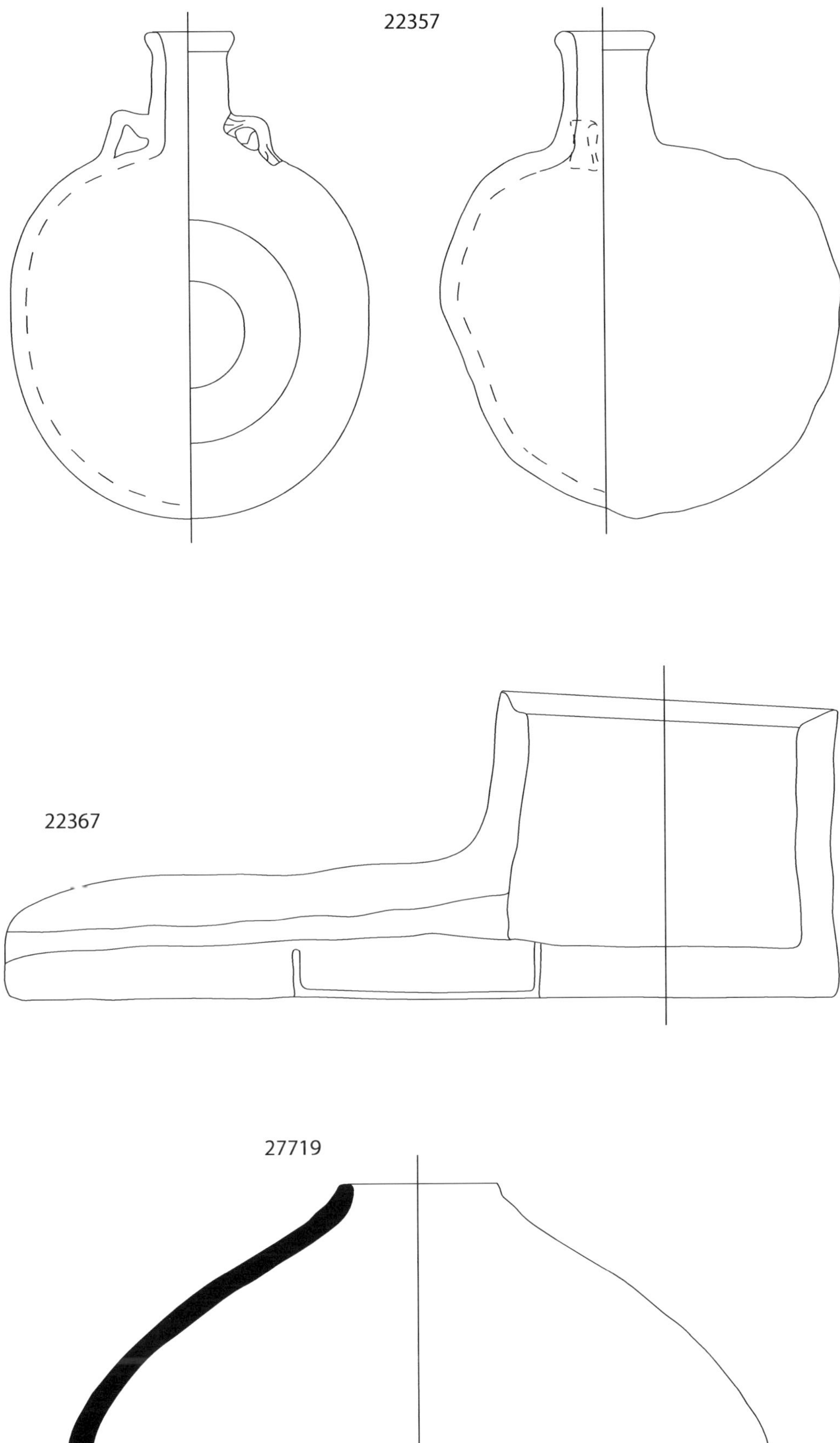

Plate 47 Pottery keg, bellows and vessel top from Tell Dafana in the British Museum (all 1:4)

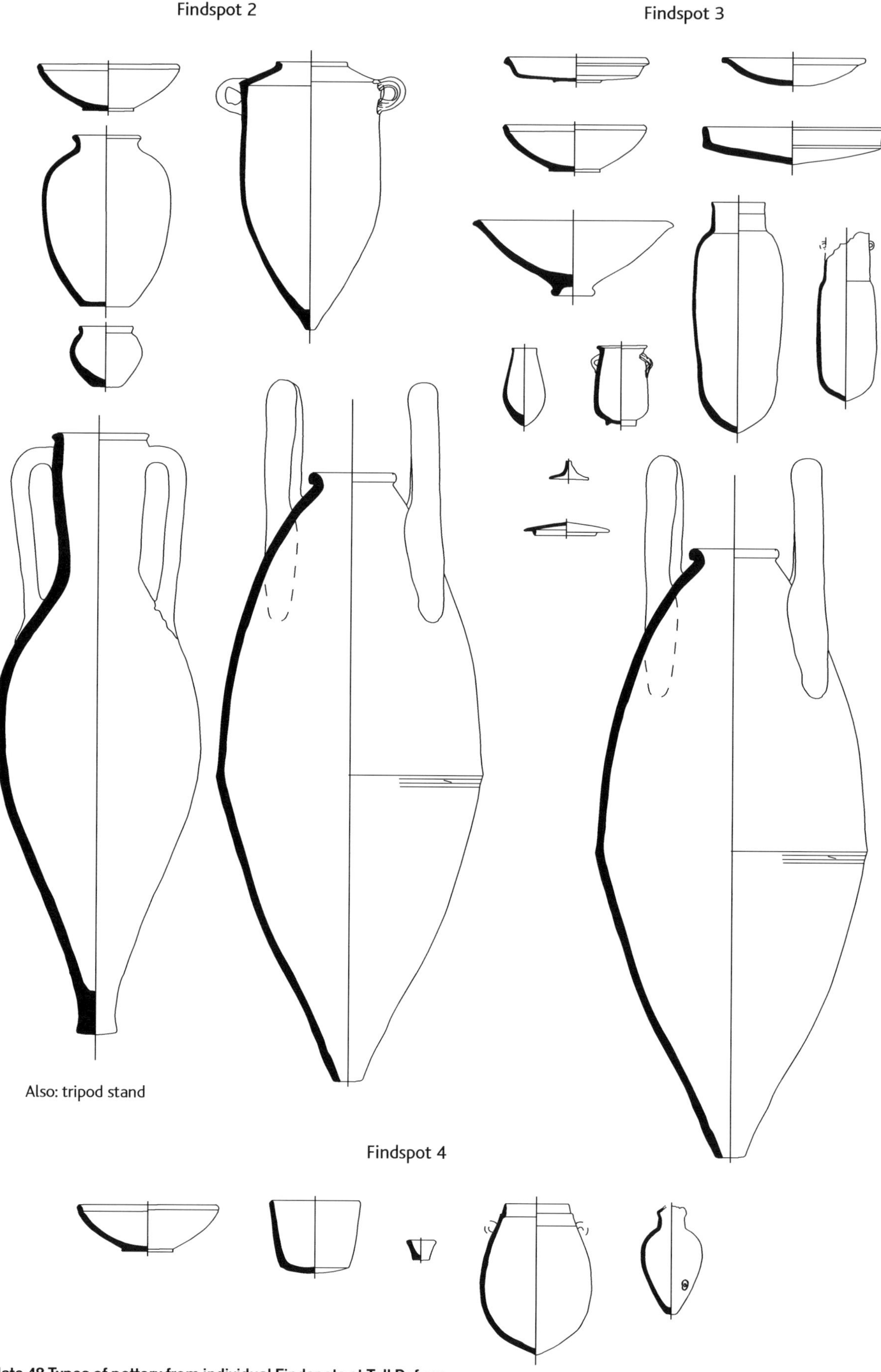

Plate 48 Types of pottery from individual Findspots at Tell Dafana

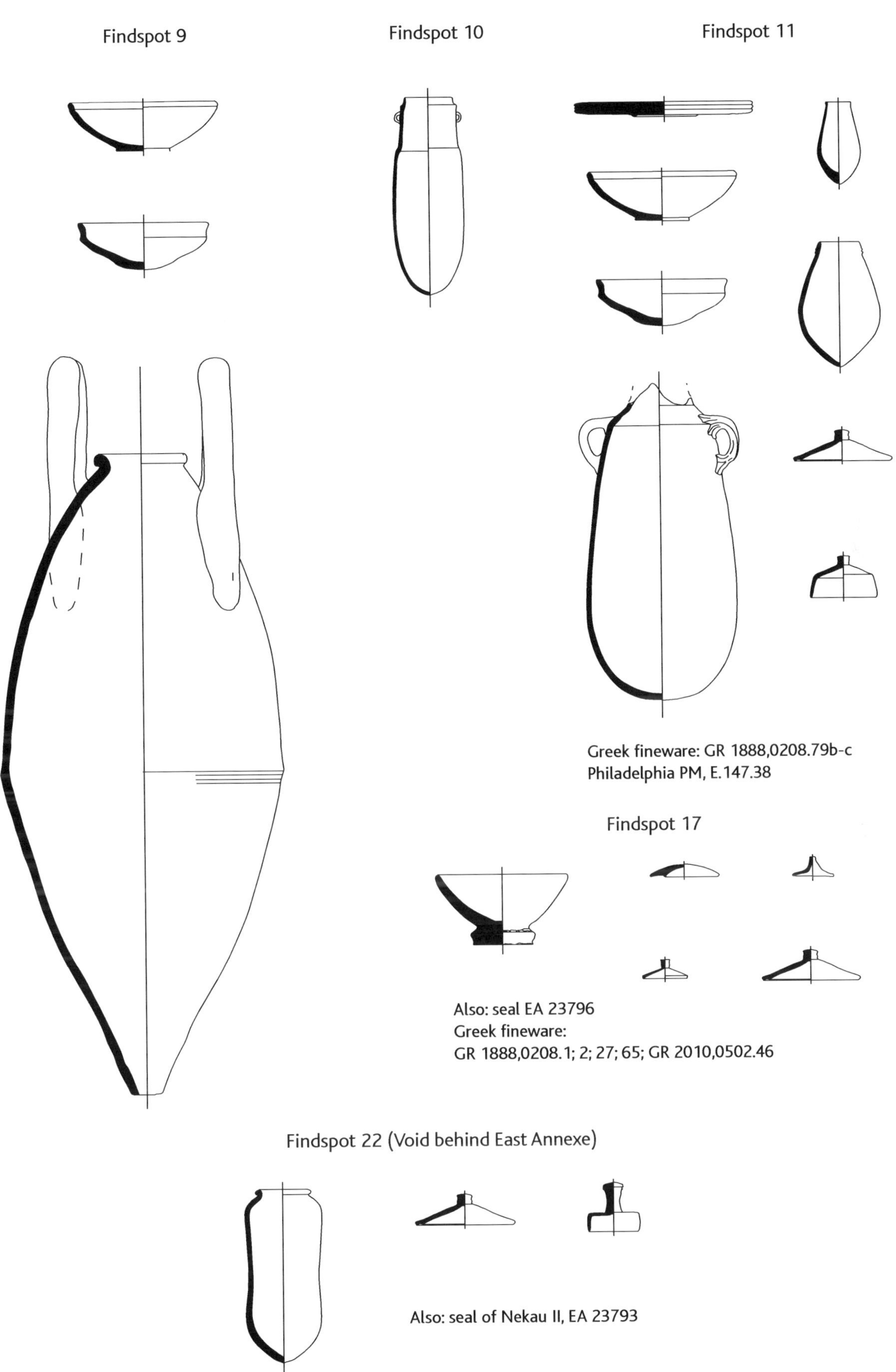

Plate 49 Types of pottery from individual Findspots at Tell Dafana

ANNEXE TO EAST OF CASEMATE BUILDING, SOUTH PART, PETRIE'S PHASE C

Findspot 19 (a-c)

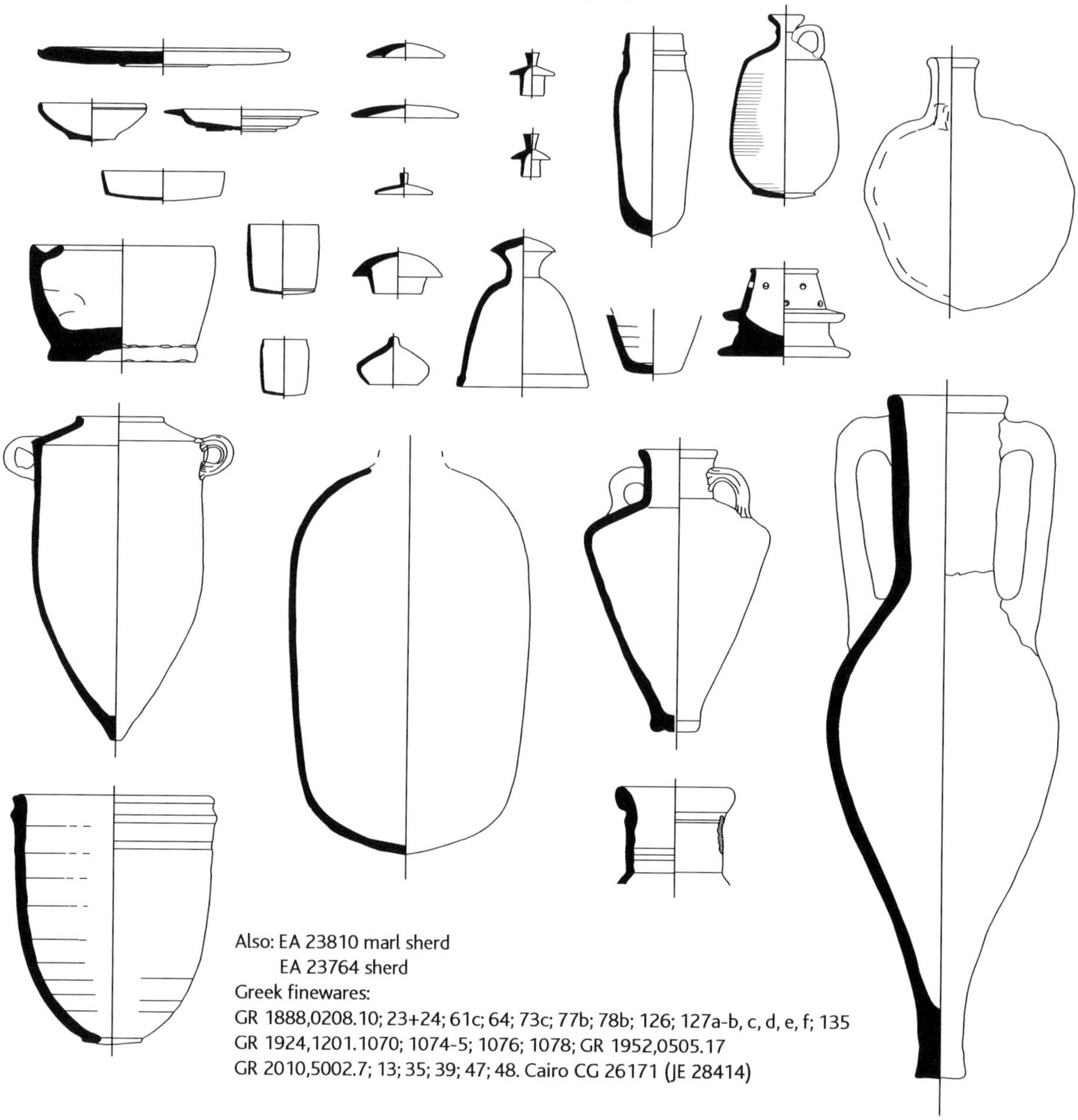

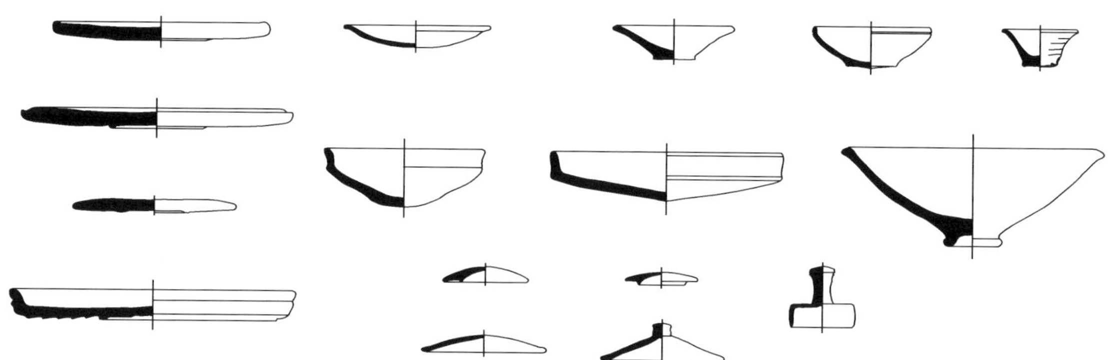

Also: EA 23810 marl sherd
EA 23764 sherd
Greek finewares:
GR 1888,0208.10; 23+24; 61c; 64; 73c; 77b; 78b; 126; 127a-b, c, d, e, f; 135
GR 1924,1201.1070; 1074-5; 1076; 1078; GR 1952,0505.17
GR 2010,5002.7; 13; 35; 39; 47; 48. Cairo CG 26171 (JE 28414)

Findspot 32 (= below floor in 19)

Also one sherd perhaps from a basket-handled amphora, EA 23678

Plate 50 Types of pottery from individual Findspots at Tell Dafana

Findspot 27

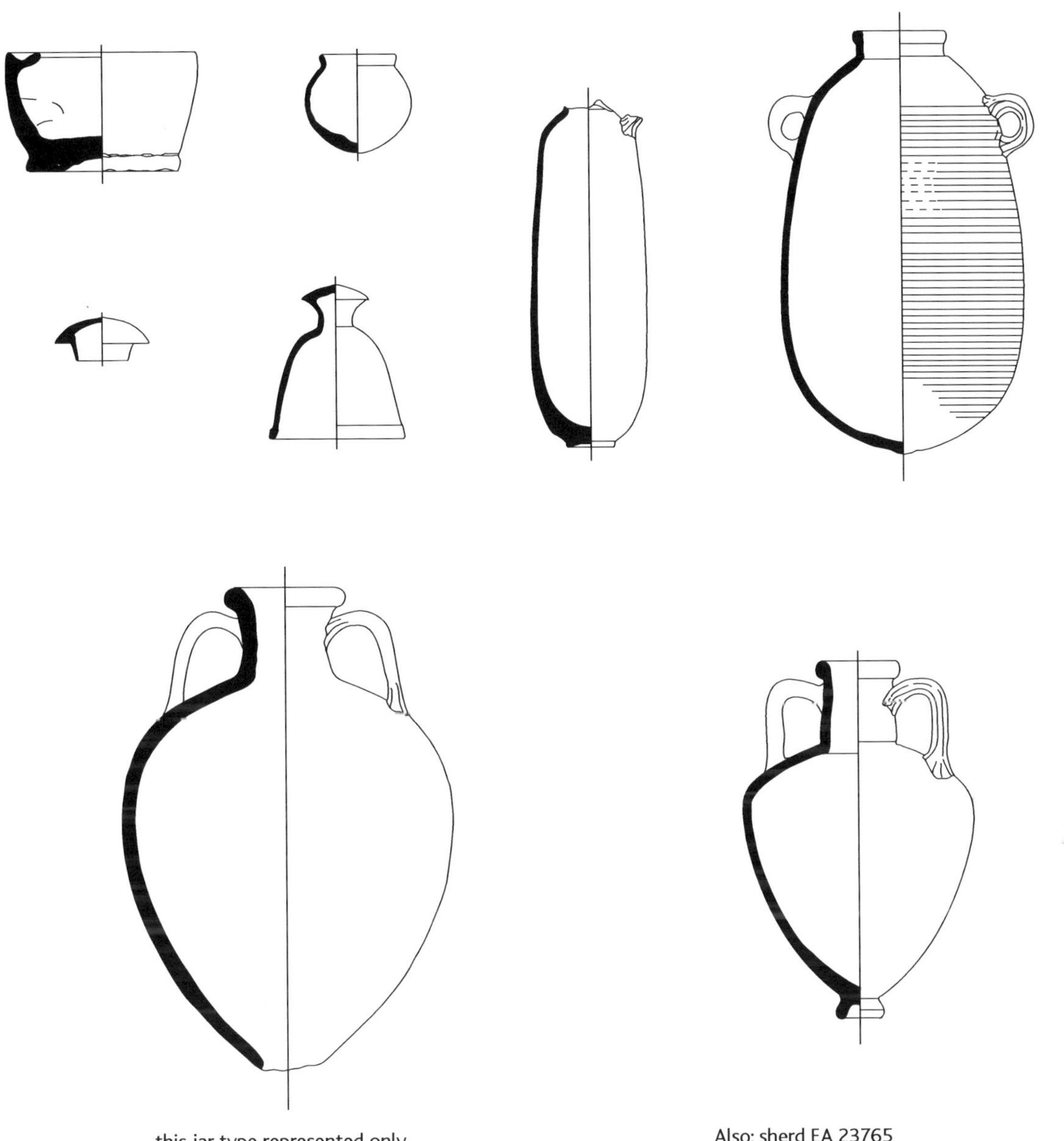

this jar type represented only
by sherd EA 23771

Also: sherd EA 23765
Greek amphora GR 1888,0208.52; 134a.

Plate 51 Types of pottery from individual Findspots at Tell Dafana

Findspot 18

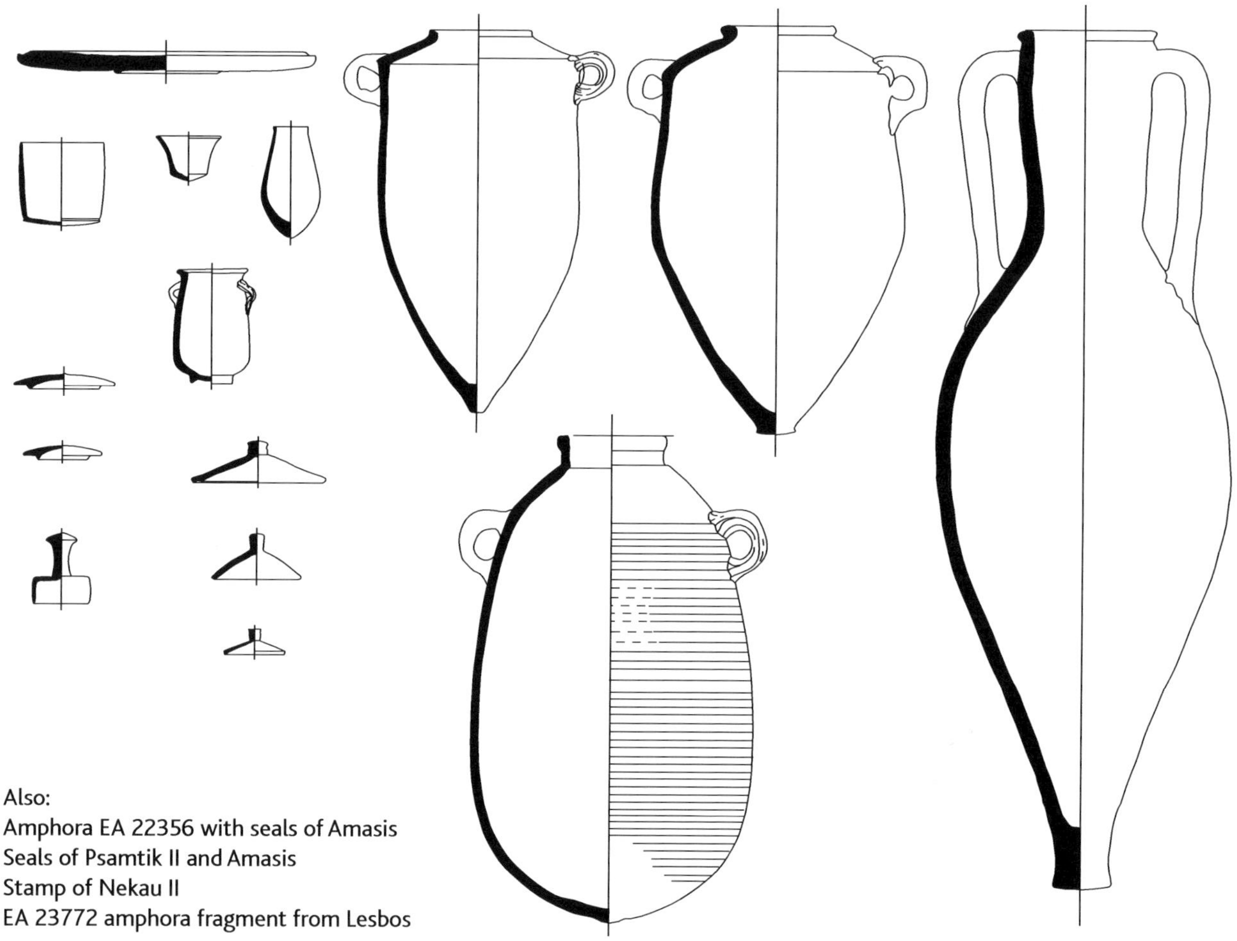

Also:
Amphora EA 22356 with seals of Amasis
Seals of Psamtik II and Amasis
Stamp of Nekau II
EA 23772 amphora fragment from Lesbos

Greek wares: GR 1888,0208.28; 55b; 56a-d; 56p; 56u.4; 56.u.6; 57; 68; 70e, f; 76d; 77b; 80a, b; 92a; 102; 106h; 117; 139a, b,c,d
1924,1201.1046; 1047; 1049; 1056; 1060; 1062; 1063; 1064; 1069; 1071-3; 1077, 1081; 1083; 1091; 1094; 1097
GR 2010,5002.2; 6; 16; 18; 22

Findspot 28 (lower level in 18)

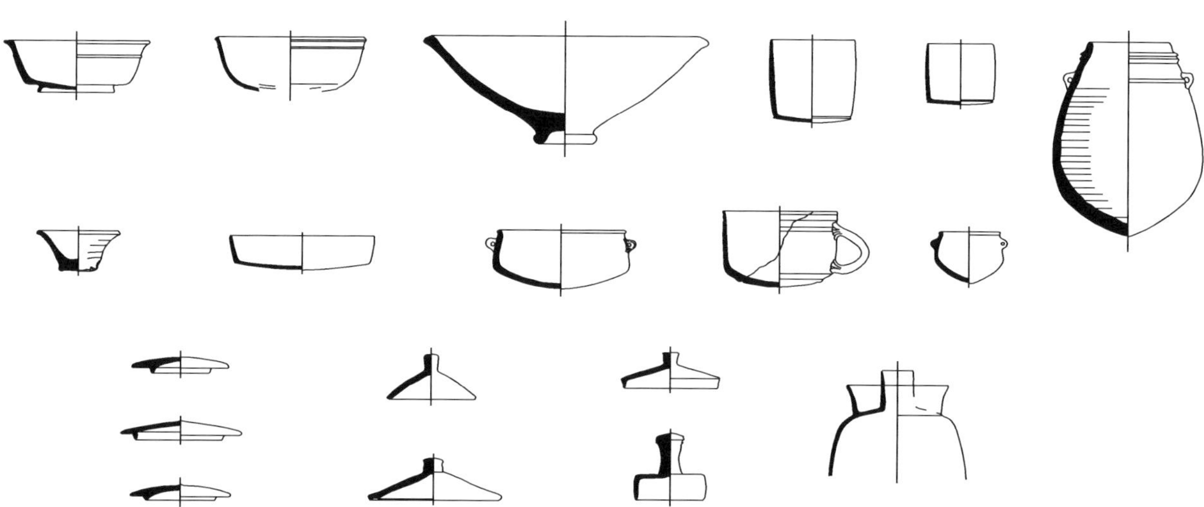

Plate 52 Types of pottery from individual Findspots at Tell Dafana

Findspot 29 (chamber South-East of casemate, Petrie's phase G)

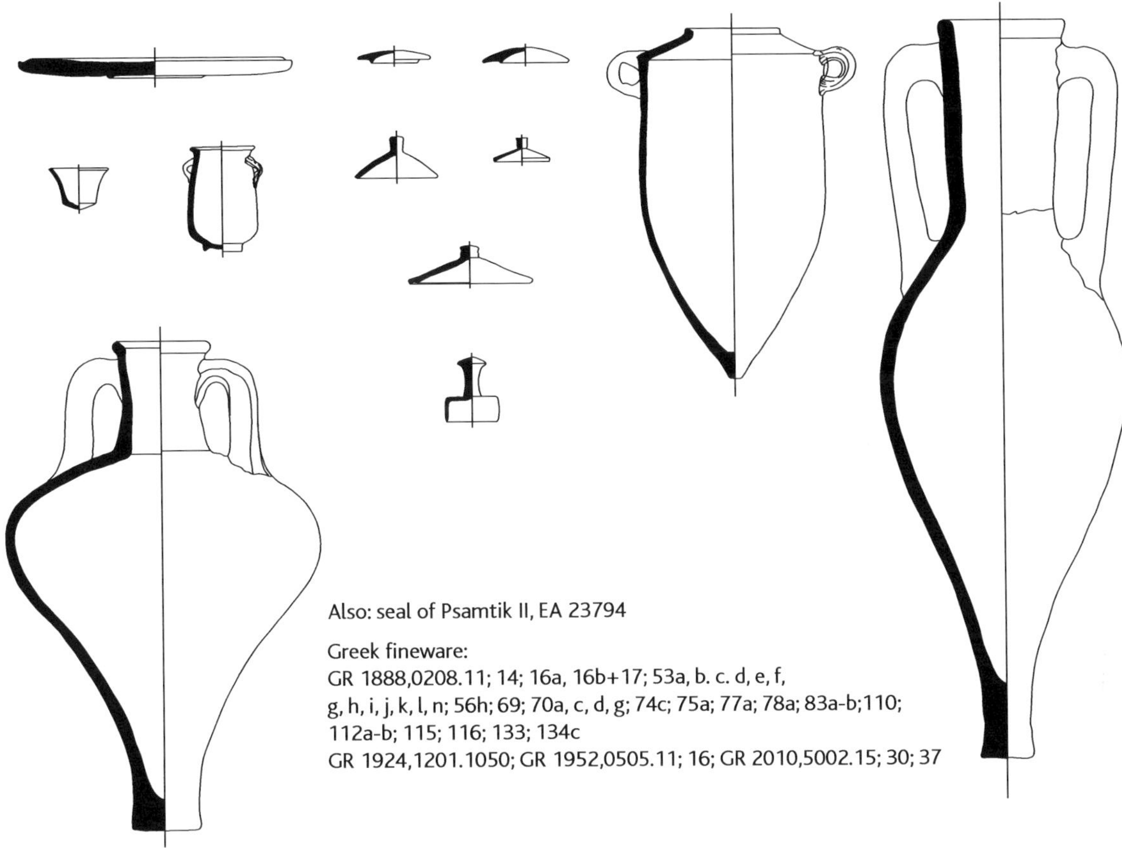

Findspot 25 (outside chambers South-East of casemate, Petrie's phase G)

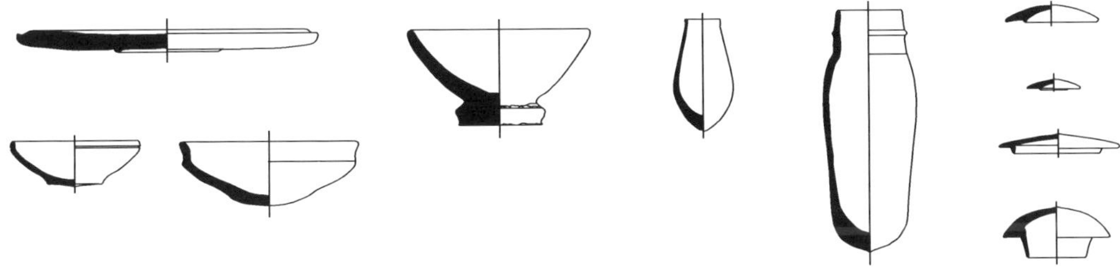

Plate 53 Types of pottery from individual Findspots at Tell Dafana

Findspot 50

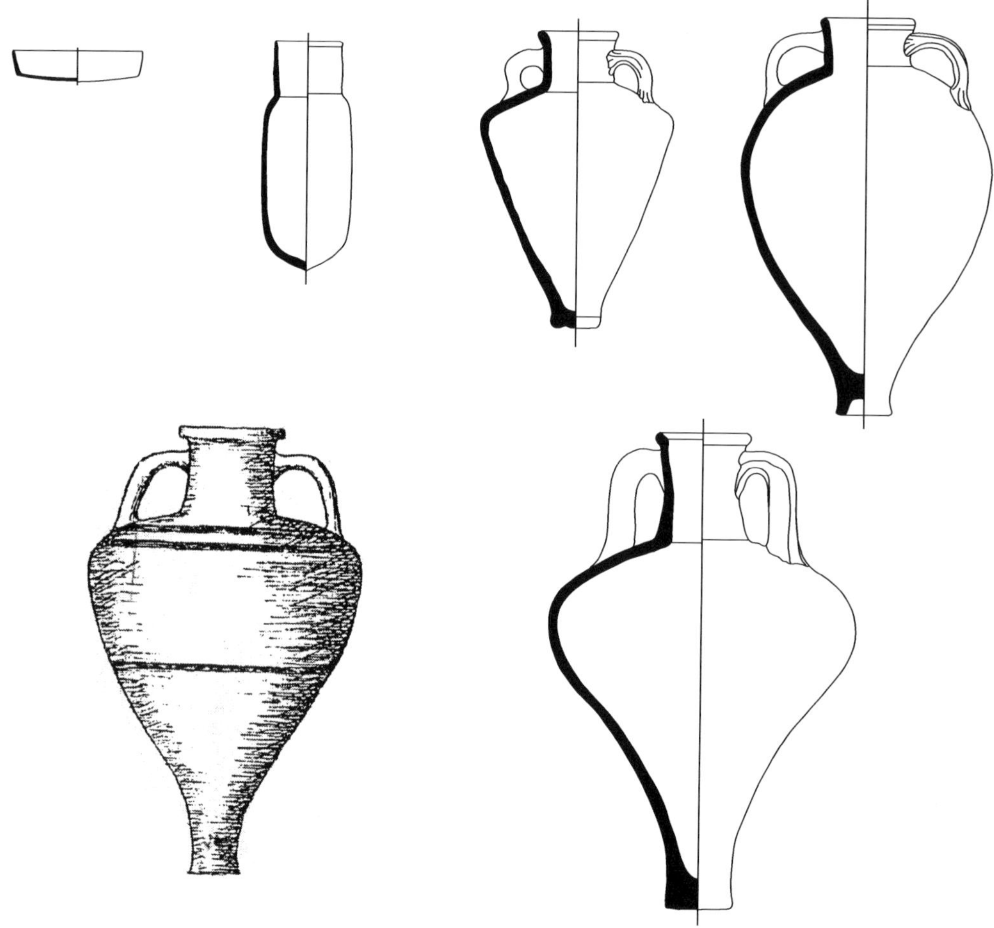

Findspot 55 (By the Great Wall South of the casemate building)

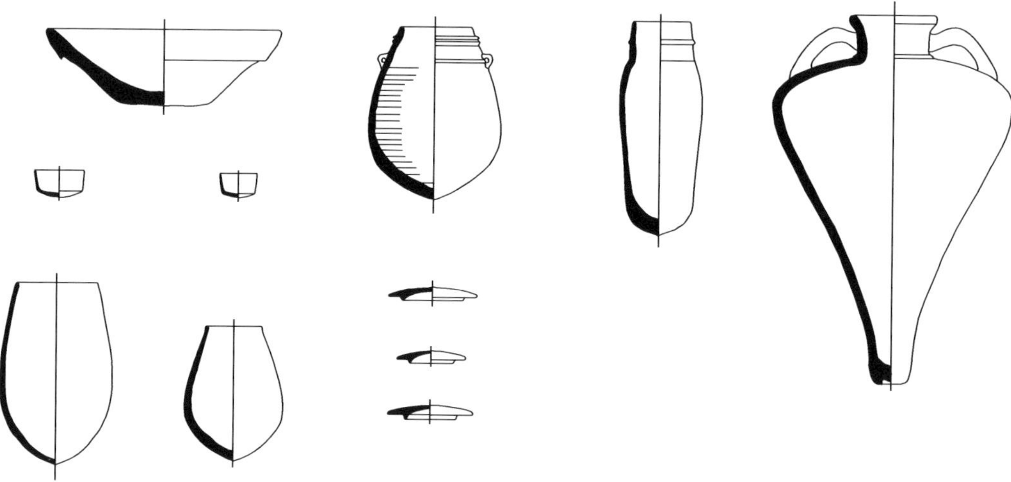

Plate 54 Types of pottery from individual Findspots at Tell Dafana

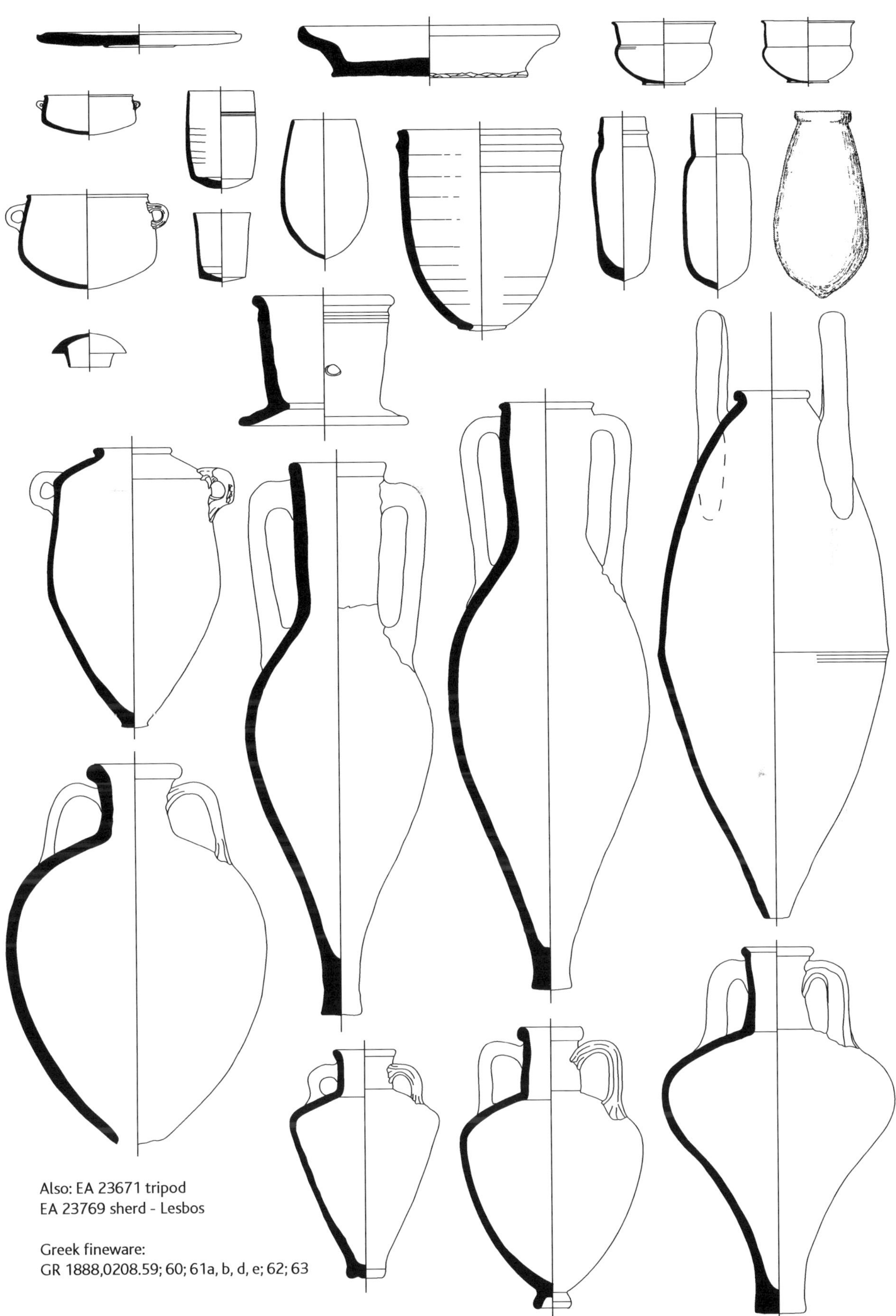

Also: EA 23671 tripod
EA 23769 sherd - Lesbos

Greek fineware:
GR 1888,0208.59; 60; 61a, b, d, e; 62; 63

Plate 55 Types of pottery from individual Findspots at Tell Dafana

Findspot 52

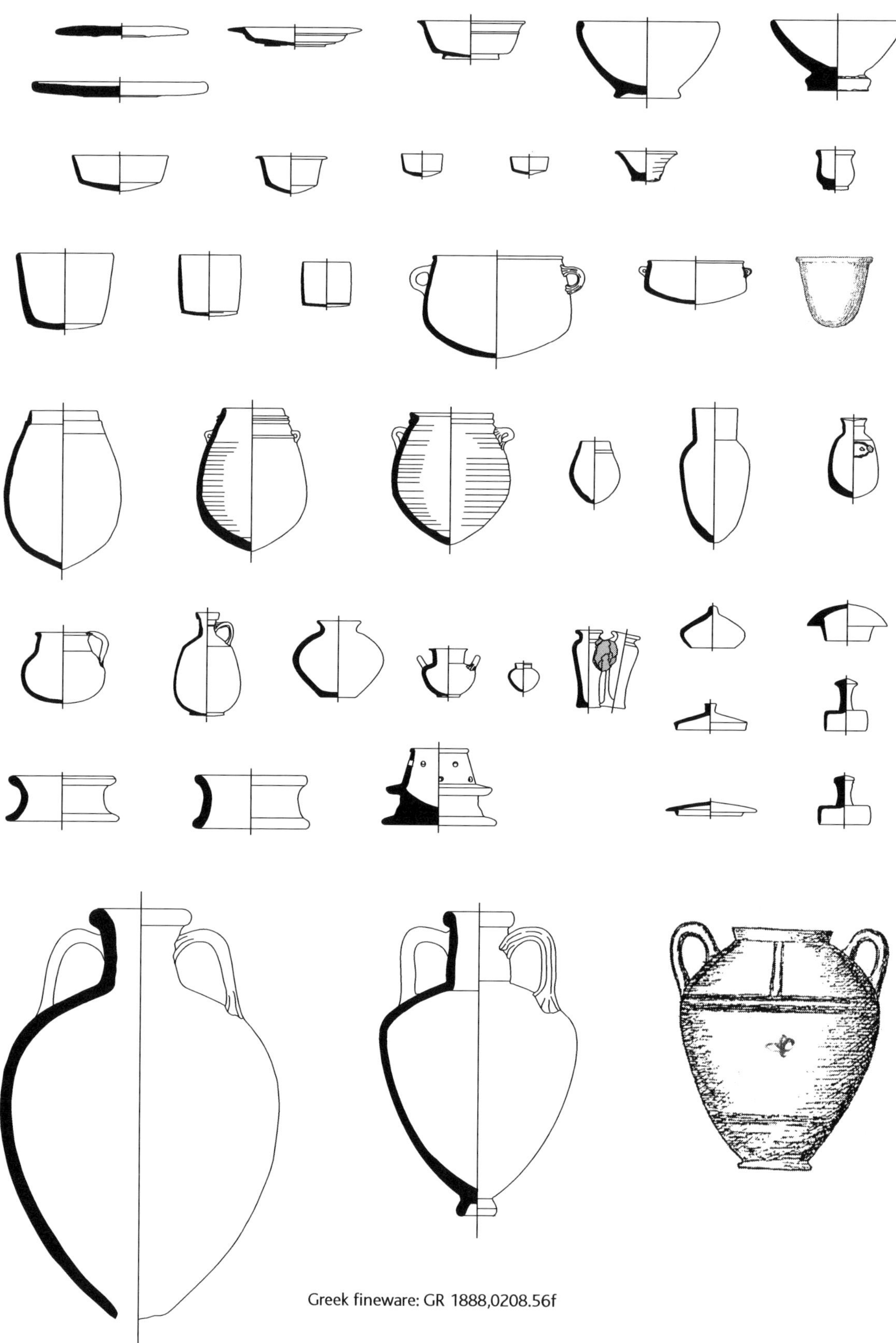

Plate 56 Types of pottery from individual Findspots at Tell Dafana

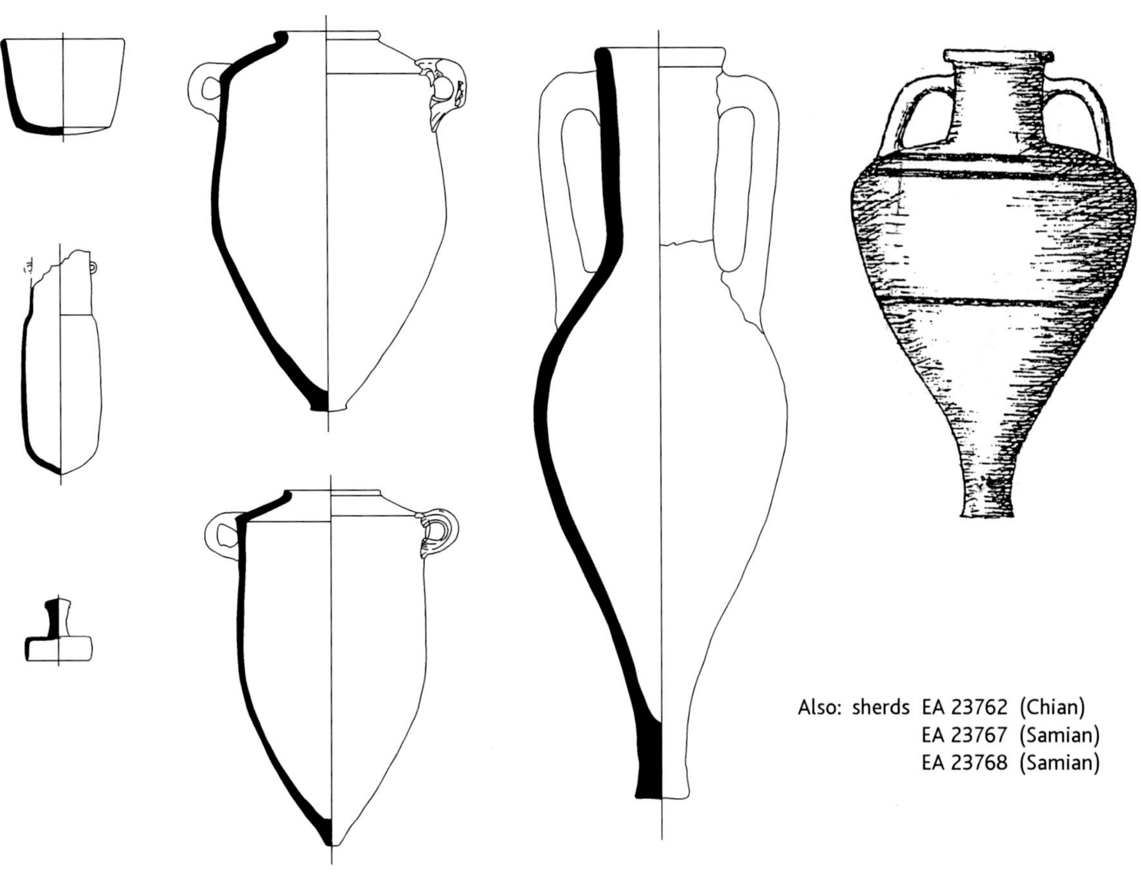

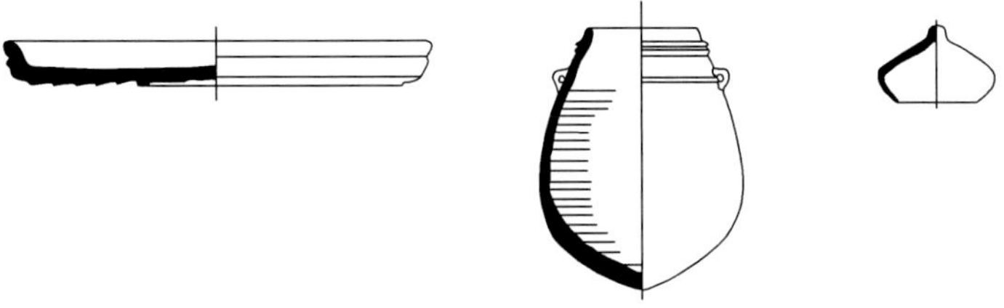

Plate 57 Types of pottery from individual Findspots at Tell Dafana

Silt platter 22370

Marl plate 23692

Silt bowl 23664

Marl and silt dishes 23698, 23699, 23700

Silt cooking pot 23657

Silt cooking pot 23658

Silt jar 23707

Marl cup 23697

Silt jar 22292

Plate 58 Pottery vessels from Tell Dafana in the British Museum

Siltware jars 22287, 22335, 22339

Fine marl jars 50783 to 50786, with detail of mark on 50785 (inset)

Plate 59 Pottery vessels from Tell Dafana in the British Museum

Abbreviated Bes jar 22304

Fine Bes jar 22312

Abbreviated Bes jar 22297

Model amphora
GR 1888,0208.164

Model amphora with incised
bird-mark GR 1888,0208.165

Silt jar 23650, with similar vessel containing pistachio gum GR 1888,0204.140

Plate 60 Pottery vessels from Tell Dafana in the British Museum

Plate 61 Pottery vessels and bellows from Tell Dafana in the British Museum

Plate 62 Pottery vessels from Tell Dafana in the British Museum

Tuyère 23669

Phoenician amphora 22346

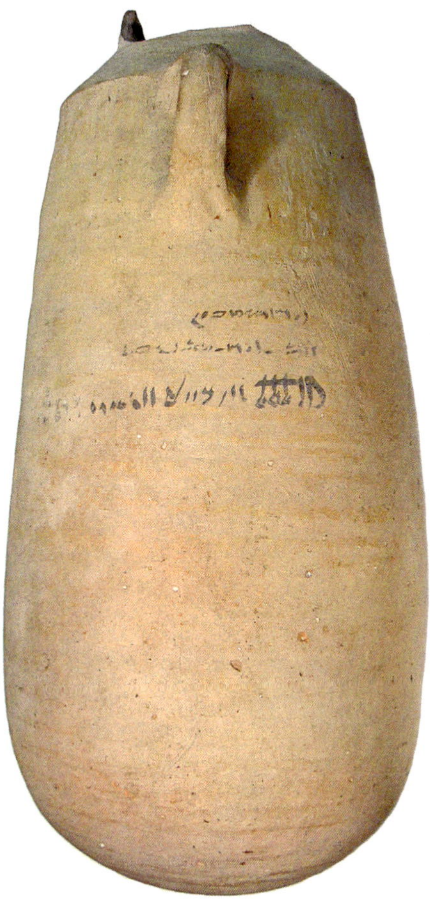

Inscribed Phoenician amphora 22344

Inscription on amphora 22344

Plate 63 Pottery stands, covers and miscellaneous items from Tell Dafana in the British Museum

Sealed amphora 22356, front with incised mark

Sealed amphora 22356, reverse

Sealed amphora 22356, detail

Sealed amphora 22356, side

Plate 64 Pottery vessels from Tell Dafana in the British Museum

Egyptian copy of a Samian amphora, 22333

Marks on Samian amphora GR 1888,0208.140a

Marked amphora fragment from Lesbos 23772

Samian amphora with mark, 22330

Jar-stopper 23749

Jar-stopper 23750

Stamped handle of Nekau II 23790

Plate 65 Pottery vessels, stoppers and stamp from Tell Dafana in the British Museum

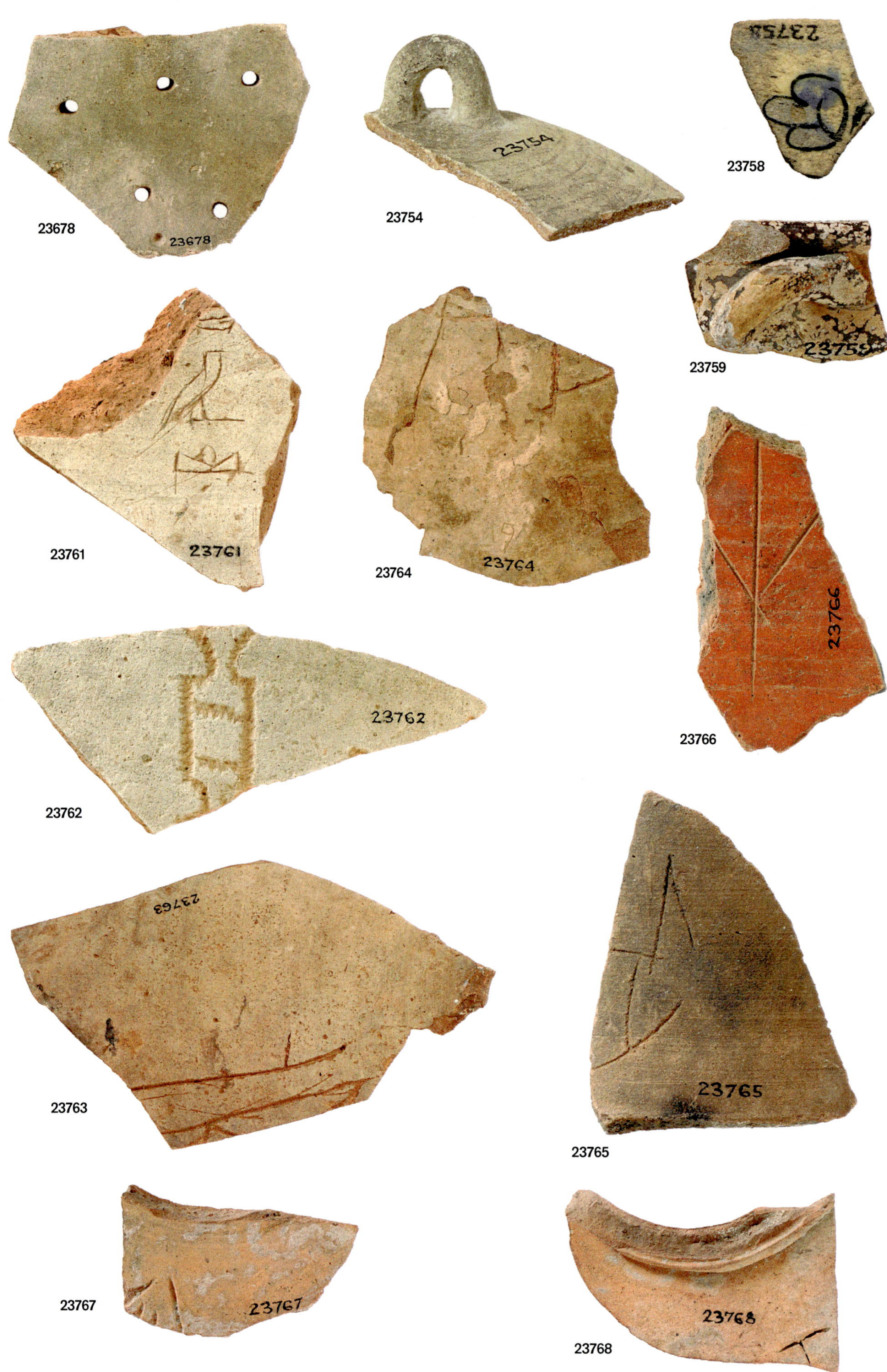

Plate 66 Pottery fragments from Tell Dafana in the British Museum

Plate 67 Pottery fragments from Tell Dafana in the British Museum

Plate 68 Pottery fragments from Tell Dafana in the British Museum

Plate 69 Pottery fragments and ostraca from Tell Dafana in the British Museum

23786

23787

29484

29485

23789

23788

Plate 70 Pottery ostraca from Tell Dafana in the British Museum

(a) The south-east corner of the enclosure wall, from the south (all images on this page SCA/M. Abd el-Maksoud)

(b) South side of the enclosure wall, testing for the depth

(c) South side of the enclosure wall, looking west from the central gate

(d) The central gate in the south side of the enclosure wall

Plate 71 Excavations in 2009 at Tell Dafana

(a) The axis of the temple from the first court, looking north, with the mound of the casemate buildings on the right

(b) Gate leading to the second court

(c) West wing of the 'pylon' at the gate leading to the second court

(d) East wing of the 'pylon' at the back of the first court

Plate 72 Excavations in 2009 at Tell Dafana

(a) Excavation of the east wall of the temple, with the passage outside it

(b) The depth of the brickwork of the eastern temple wall

(c) The east wall of the temple, with the passage and the magazines on the right, all after cleaning

Plate 73 Excavations in 2009 at Tell Dafana

(a) Looking east along the second pylon to the wall of the temple and the magazines beyond

(b) The large wall at the back of the temple, from the north-east corner

(c) The large wall at the back of the temple, with the recess. North-east corner in the foreground

Plate 74 Excavations in 2009 at Tell Dafana

(a) The large wall at the back of the temple, south face with recess

(b) One end of the recess in the wall at the back of the temple, showing inclined bricks

(c) Pottey jar for a drain embedded in the ground

(d) Drain-pit with a ceramic pipe entering from the left

(e) Centre of the drain-pit: an Egyptian siltware jar with the base broken out stands on another, with Chian amphorae lying horizontally at the sides and the ceramic pipe at the back

Plate 75 Excavations in 2009 at Tell Dafana

(a) The wall across the back of the temple at the north-east, overbuilt by the small casemate foundation

(b) Casemate foundation above the cut-down wall at the back of the temple, looking west

Plate 76 Excavations in 2009 at Tell Dafana

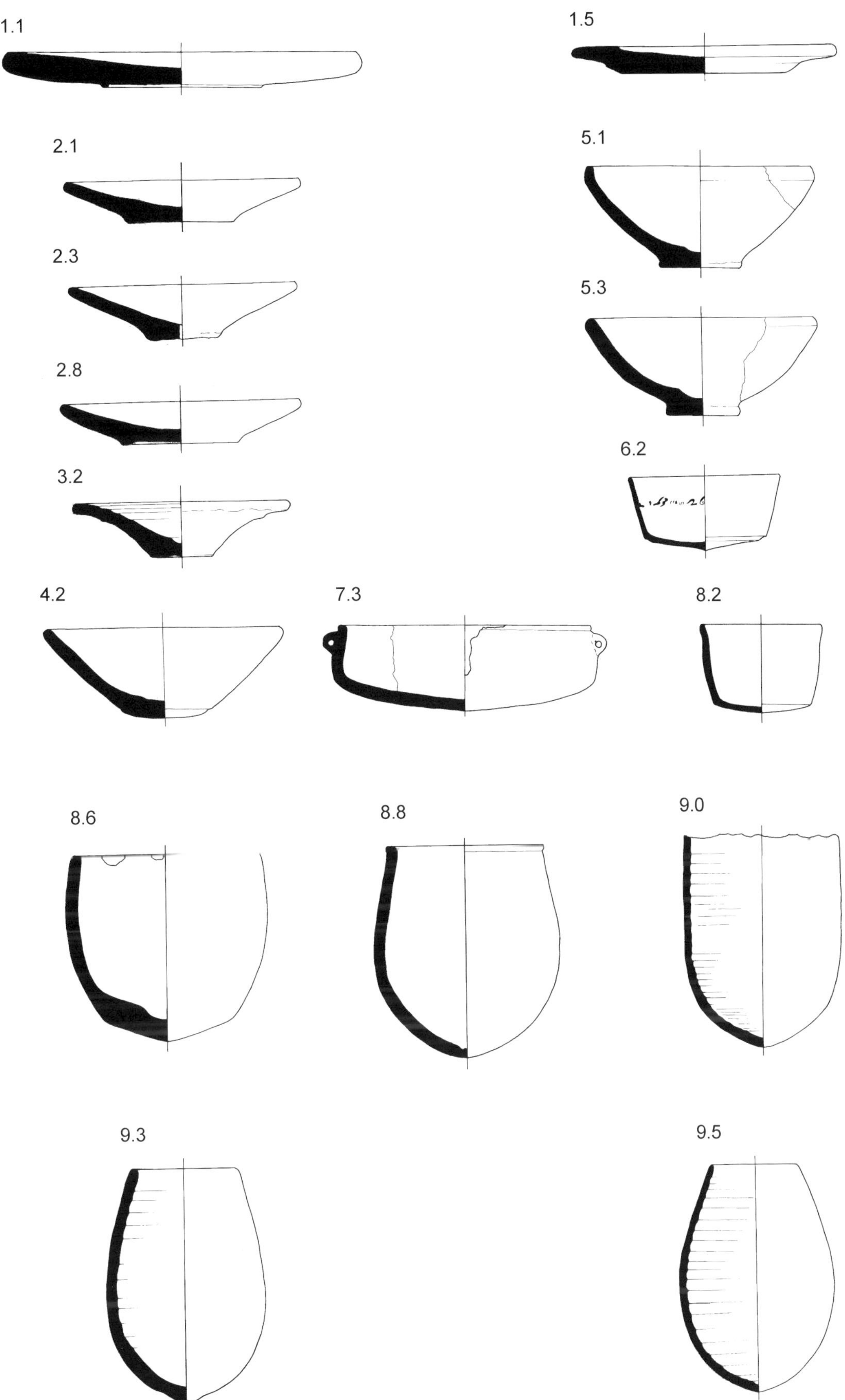

Plate 77 Pottery from the excavations of 2009 at Tell Dafana (all 1:4)

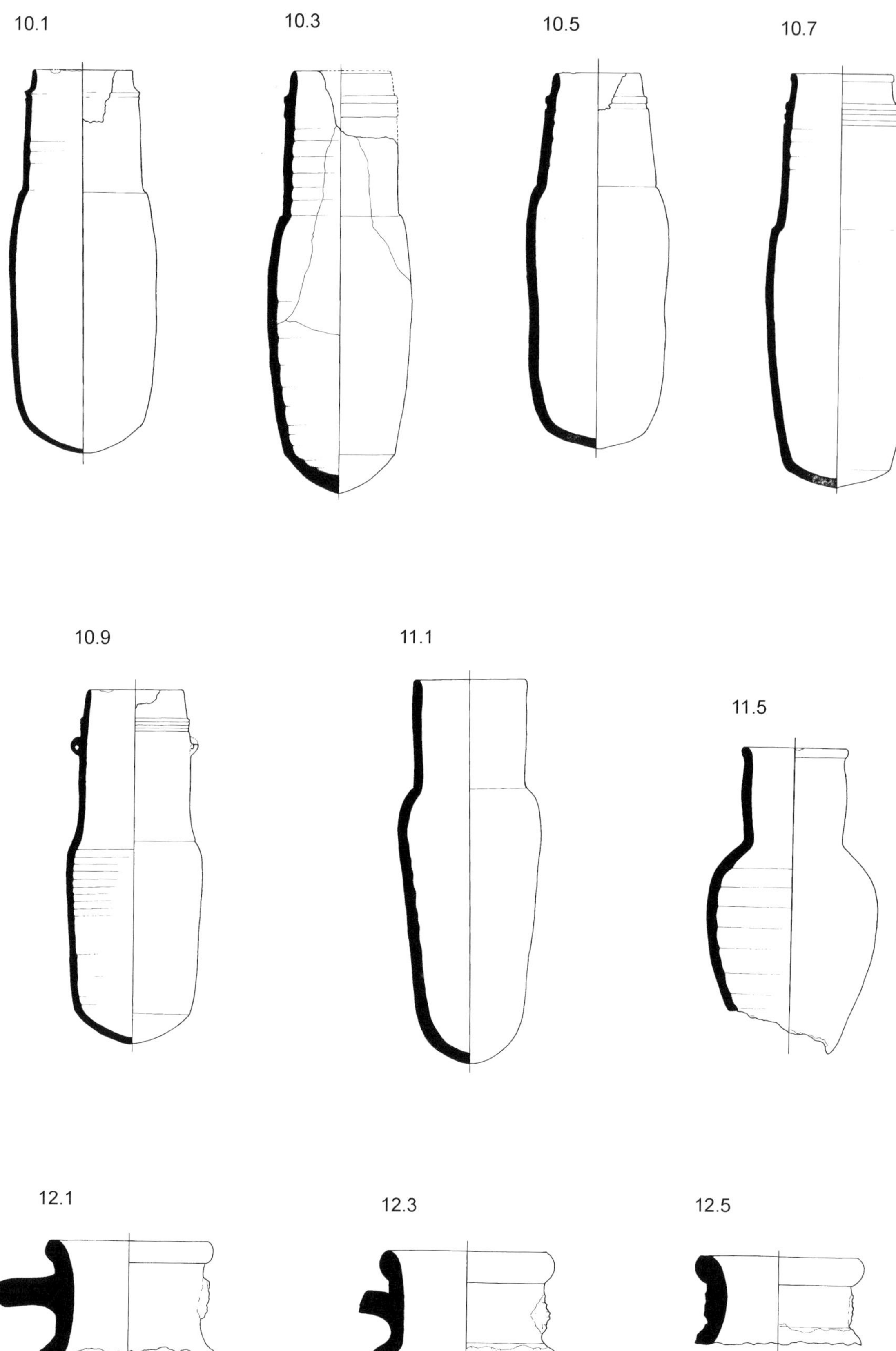

Plate 78 Pottery from the excavations of 2009 at Tell Dafana (all 1:4)

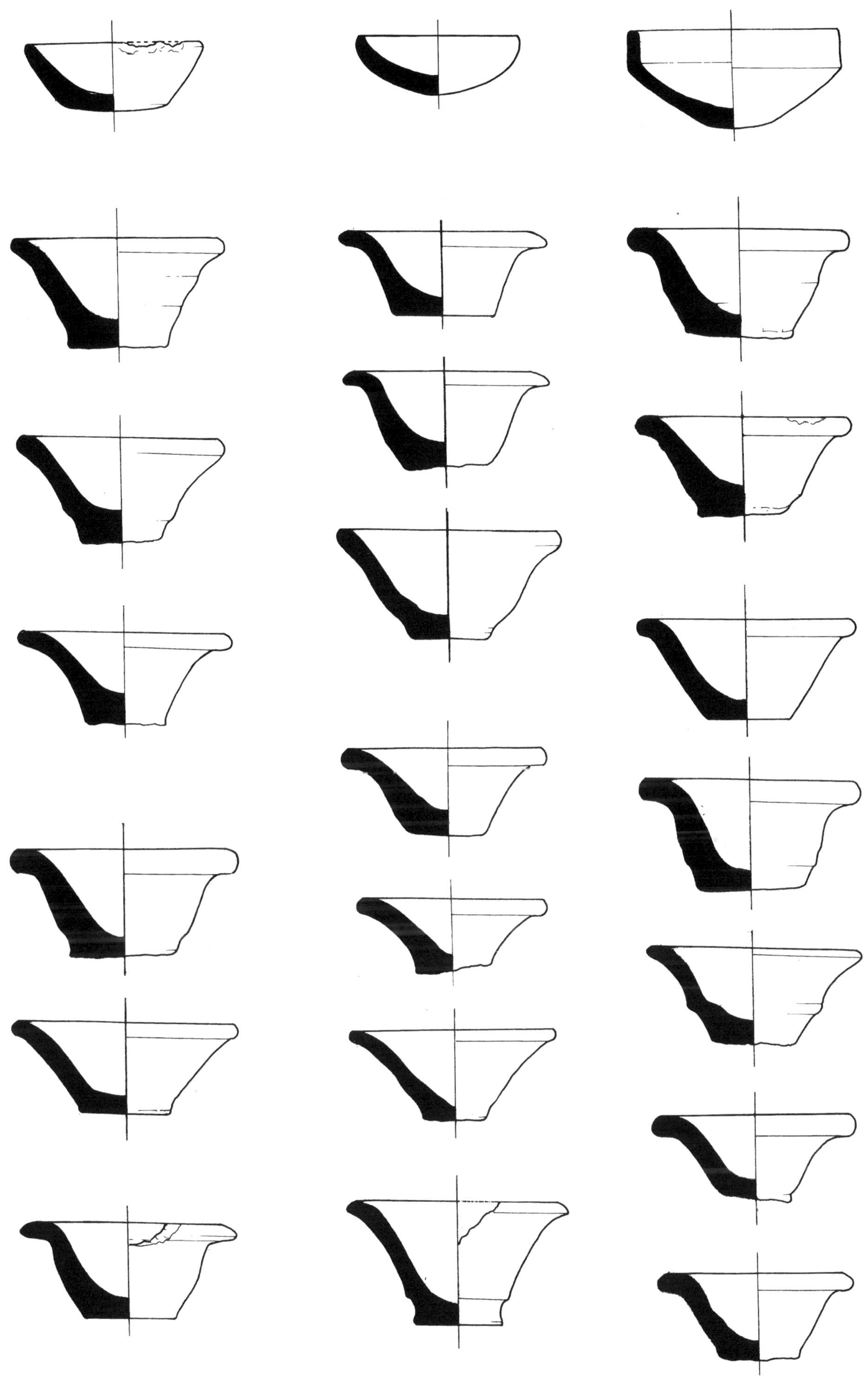

Plate 79 Pottery from the excavations of 2009 at Tell Dafana (all 1:2)

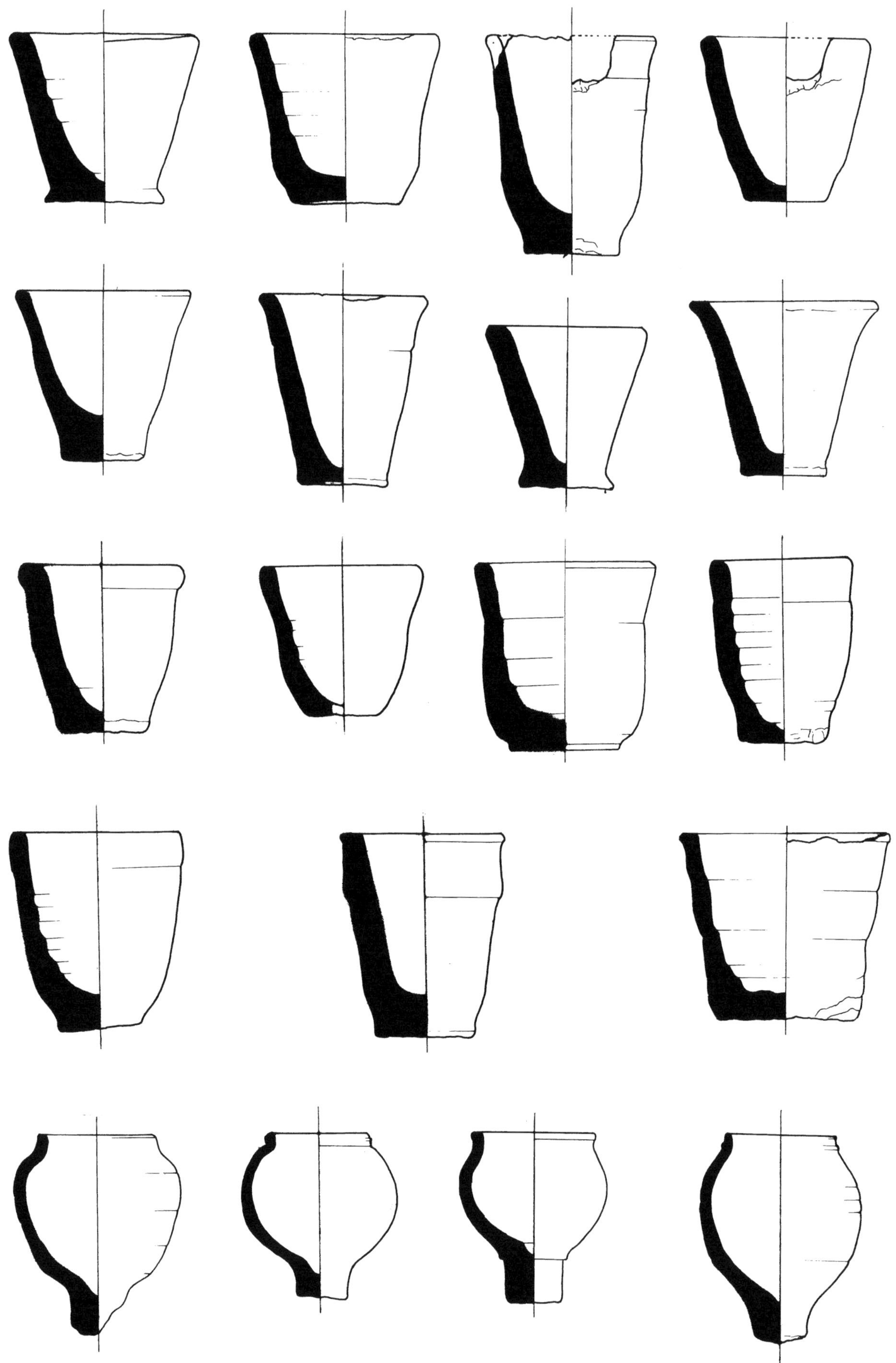

Plate 80 Pottery from the excavations of 2009 at Tell Dafana (all 1:2)

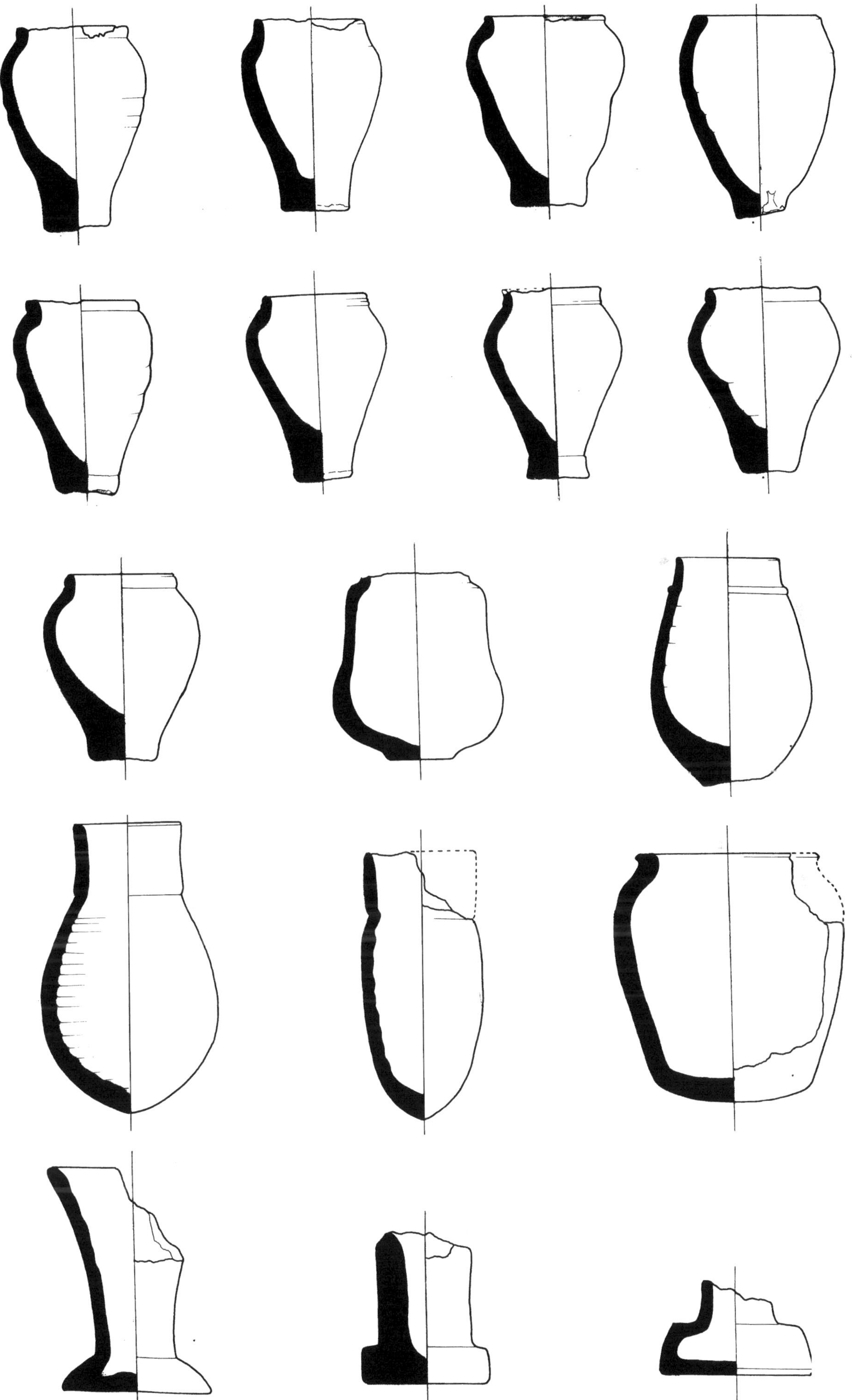

Plate 81 Pottery from the excavations of 2009 at Tell Dafana (all 1:2)

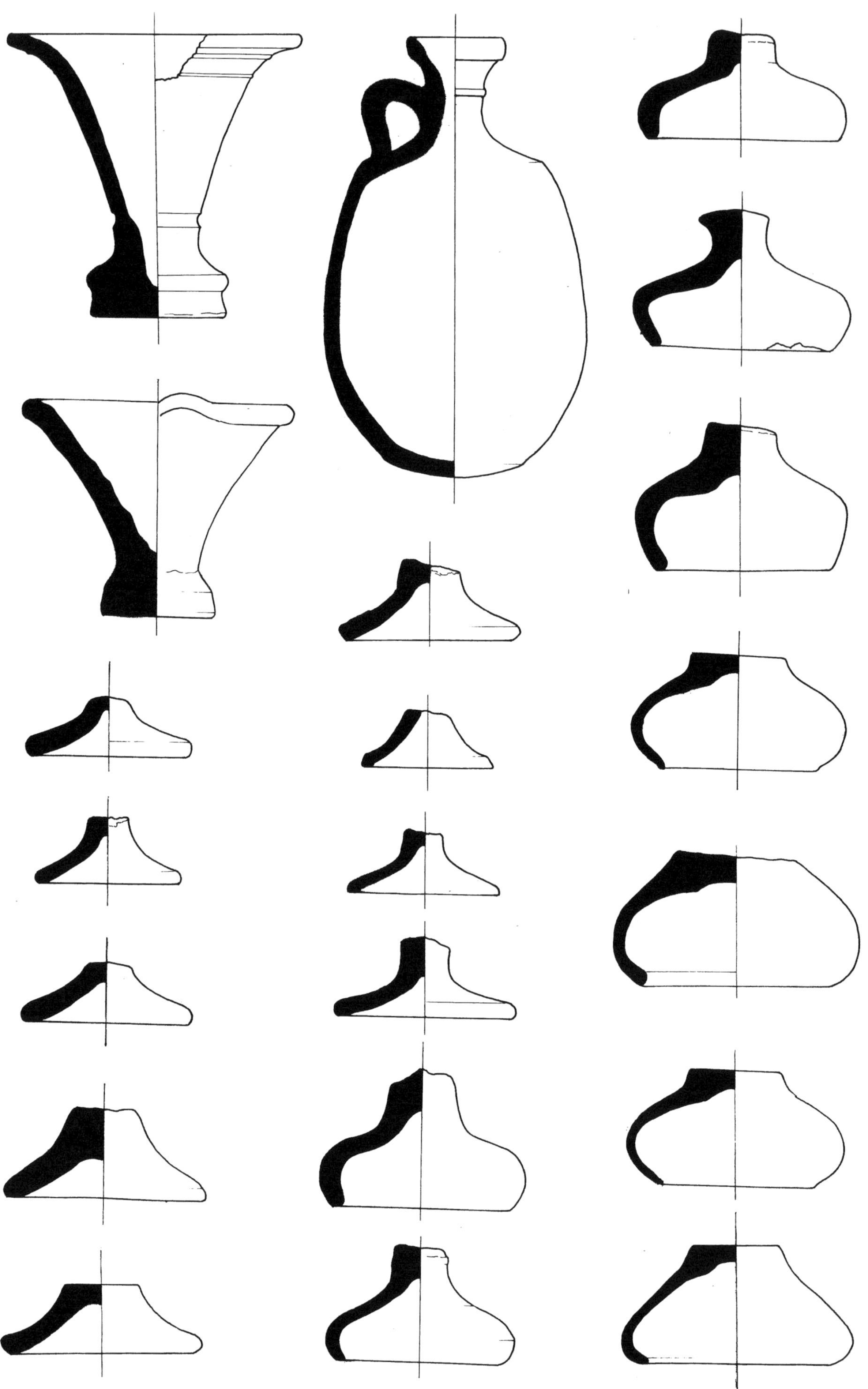

Plate 82 Pottery from the excavations of 2009 at Tell Dafana (all 1:2)

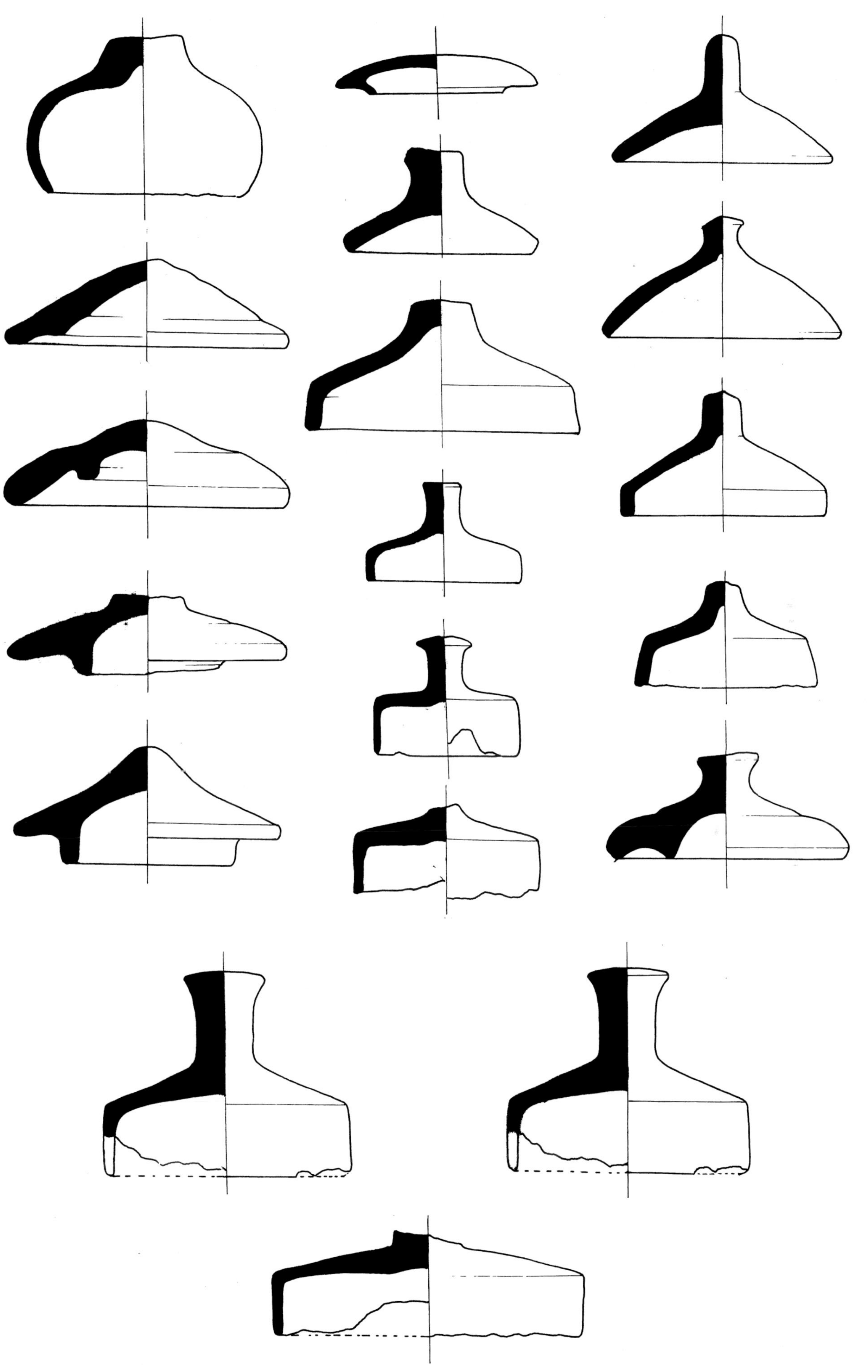

Plate 83 Pottery from the excavations of 2009 at Tell Dafana (all 1:2)

Plate 84 Pottery from the excavations of 2009 at Tell Dafana: examples of the types discovered

Plate 85 Pottery from the excavations of 2009 at Tell Dafana: Klazomenian, Samian and Corinthian amphorae

Units	SW corner	NW corner	SE corner	NE corner	Comments
2 gold plaques (inscr.)		1		1	BM, EA 23556 - 1887,0101.1355 and part of Cairo, EM, JE 27385
2 silver plaques (inscr.)		1		1	BM, EA 23556 - 1887,0101.1356 and part of Cairo, EM, JE 27385
3 lead (or tin?) plaques (inscr.)		1	1	1 (Boston, MFA 87.529)	the two others are BM, EA 23556 - 1887,0101.1358 (in fact made of tin) and part of Cairo, EM, JE 27385
4 copper plaques (inscr?)	1	1	1 (Boston, MFA 87.528)	1	the three others are BM, EA 23556 - 1887,0101.1357 and part of Cairo, EM, JE 27385; the fourth one is unlocated
1 carnelian plaque (inscr.)		1 (BM, EA 23556 - 1887,0101.1360)			
2 felspar plaques (inscr.)		1		1	one is part of Cairo JE 27385, the other is unlocated
3 lapis lazuli plaques (inscr.)		1	1 (Boston, MFA 87.720)	1	one other is part of Cairo JE 27385, the third one is unlocated
3 jasper plaques (inscr.)		1	1 (Boston, MFA 87.719)	1	the 2 others are BM, EA 23556 - 1887,0101.1359 and part of Cairo, EM, JE 27385
4 green glazed plaques (inscr.)	1	1 (Boston, MFA 87.653)	1	1 (BM, EA 23556 - 1887,0101.1354)	the 2 others are part of Cairo, EM, JE 27385 and Berlin, ÄM 100080 (destroyed)
2 mudbrick models			1	1	part of Cairo, EM, JE 27385 and BM, EA 23556 (1887,0101.1361); on plate xxiii of Petrie 1888, the plaque no. 2 should be read no. 12
1 calcite half-disc plaque			1		Unlocated
Galena samples			2 or 3? (BM, EA 23556 - 1887,0101.1364-1365)		2 fragments according to Petrie's publication (p. 55), 3 according to his Journal (p.158); the third one, if it exists, is unlocated, but 2 fragments of lead ore are also recorded in Boston, MFA, RES.87.41-42 (deacc.)
Copper ore samples			12? (BM, EA 23556 - 1887,0101.1362-1363, 1366-1374)		12 fragments according Petrie 1888, pl. xxii; 11 in the BM, the last one probably part of Cairo JE 27385
1 green glazed libation cup			1		Unlocated; crushed (Petrie, Journal, 158)
2 quartzite corn-rubbers			2		Unlocated; left at the site?
Head and two legs of an ox			Part of the leg bones and teeth are in the BM (EA 23557 - 1887,0101.1375-1381) and in Boston, MFA (RES.87.14-15), skull and part of the leg bones in the Cairo Museum, unregistered.		

Plate 86 Distribution of the foundation deposits from Tell Dafana